ITRAVELBOOKS HAWAII

Elissa Altman,
Contributing Editor

ibooks
new york
www.ibooks.net

Distributed by Simon & Schuster, Inc.

A Publication of ibooks, inc.

© 2002 Tembo LLC

Original Material © 2002 Tembo LLC
New Material © 2002 ibooks, inc.

All rights reserved, including the right to reproduce this book
or portions thereof in any form whatsoever.
Distributed by Simon & Schuster, Inc.
1230 Avenue of the Americas, New York, NY 10020

ibooks, inc.
24 West 25th Street
New York, NY 10010

The ibooks World Wide Web Site Address is:
http://www.ibooks.net

ISBN 0-7434-5279-8
First ibooks, inc. printing October 2002
10 9 8 7 6 5 4 3 2 1

Cover design by Mike Rivilis

HAWAII

Welcome to ITRAVELBOOKS

Congratulations! By choosing an *ITRAVELBOOK*, you have just selected the savviest, most reliable, up-to-date guidebook available today. In a world filled with travel guides of every shape and kind, why pick us?

The answer is simple: An *ITRAVELBOOK* does what no other guidebook does. It is dedicated to providing you with the *most affordable, authoritative, up-to-the-minute* information available. If you're planning a trip, why spend your vacation dollars on expensive guides that you'll only use once before the information becomes obsolete?

ITRAVELBOOKS gathers all the critical knowledge you'll need for an enjoyable, fun vacation at every price level, and packs it into an inexpensive, user-friendly paperback format that you can take anywhere. Need a quick tip on what to eat in a London pub? Check our *ITRAVELBOOK TIPS* for fast, at-your-fingertips information. Want to know the fabulous things you can do for free on every Hawaiian island? Go straight to *ITRAVELBOOK FREEBIES*. Or, simply download the entire guidebook for free—or any parts of it you wish—from our website, and take it with you on your laptop or your PDA. Our electronic version will contain the most current, up-to-the-minute travel advice and information, including real-time rate changes, great new restaurants for you to try at every price range, exciting new sights to see, location-finder maps, and much more.

The first truly interactive print/electronic guidebooks, *ITRAVELBOOKS* value the traveler's opinion over all others and puts you in the travel writer's seat; we want to hear about your experiences—what you liked, what you didn't like, new discoveries and finds you might have stumbled upon on your adventure—and we'll use your information in our next edition. Please join us at http://www.itravelbooks.net to become a part of the ITRAVELBOOKS team.

HOW TO USE YOUR ITRAVELBOOK

Our goal at *ITRAVELBOOKS* is to provide you with the most user-friendly companion for your trip available. Underline us; circle us; highlight us; write on us; download us; upload us into your PDA or your laptop. We're meant to be used.

Your *ITRAVELBOOK* is divided into three main sections:

orientation will give you all the basic information you'll need. Everything from area codes to currency values, money-saving ideas, tipping guides, free things to do, great ideas for kids, customs regulations, and whether it rains in Oahu in October is located here. **This section also contains extremely important travel information regarding airport security, and should be reviewed carefully.** (Regularly updated information will appear on the electronic version of the *ITRAVELBOOKS*.)

The second section of the book is devoted to the locales themselves. Here, you'll find some brief historical information, followed by important details about hotels, restaurants, museums, hikes, activities for every age group, and our recommended attractions and sights. You'll also find specific information for business travelers, singles, seniors, and adventure lovers.

Finally, the brief appendix will be devoted to local language and common expressions (so if you hear something you don't quite understand, you can look it up). In addition, you will find *ITRAVELBOOK TIPS* sprinkled throughout the book: these are quick and easy suggestions on everything from what to wear to what kind of bicycle to rent, and will help make your travel to paradise all the more wonderful.

Rating the Accommodations and Restaurants

ITRAVELBOOKS include accommodations, activities, and dining experiences of every type, and in all price ranges and levels of quality, which are subjective and therefore may not always be equal. The dollar signs speak for themselves; the stars, however, rate the subjective experience. (For example, a very expensive accommodation may be experientially only "good" and therefore receive only two stars.) Refer to the following accommodation price and quality chart when making your selection:

Hotels and other accommodations, double occupancy, per night

$$$$	Very Expensive ($200+)
$$$	Expensive ($150-$200)
$$	Reasonable ($100-$150)
$	Great Deal ($75 - $100)
★★★★	Extraordinary
★★★	Very good
★★	Good
★	Very basic, good value

Restaurants and Dining Experiences

Prices are based on an average dinner for two, and include appetizers. Alcoholic beverages, dessert, and coffee are not included.

$$$$	Very Expensive ($200-$300+)
$$$	Expensive ($100-$150)
$$	Reasonable ($50-$75)
$	Great Deal (under $25-$50)
★★★★	Extraordinary
★★★	Very Good
★★	Good
★	Very basic (i.e., a fruit stand on the beach)

HAWAII

TABLE OF CONTENTS

INTRODUCTION	9
WELCOME TO HAWAII	37
THE BIG ISLAND	43
OAHU	141
MAUI	264
KAUAI	396
MOLOKAI	481
LANAI	520
ITINERARIES	548
APPENDIX	554

INTRODUCTION

Every cliché and superlative you've heard applies to Hawaii, a spectacular chain of islands steeped with palms, balms, breezes, and leis, not to mention tourists. A modern, pulsating Paradise Lost where the raw, astonishing natural beauty of the place sits side-by-side with the high-rises of Honolulu; where Asian honeymooners, members of the U.S. military, well-to-do retirees, golf pros, tennis junkies, hikers, bikers, gourmets and gourmands, middle-class vacationers, surfers, and hippies rub shoulders. No longer purely a haven for the wealthy, Hawaii offers a lot for everyone at every level of income and interest: package deals oozing "authentic" luaus, tee times, and romance abound, but the inclined traveler can also find bliss independently.

Hawaii is where people–young, old, single, coupled, straight, gay, and every conceivable combination thereof–come to live out their ultimate tropical dreams. The perfect honeymoon, the perfect wave, the perfect sunset, the perfect home video—they can all be choreographed around a turquoise sea of bikini-clad beach bunnies, muscle-bound native boys, and dancing hula girls. The evening news may be worrisome, startling, and depressing, but Hawaii will whisk even the most dedicated news junkie away from the world's troubles: let the trade winds soothe your nerves, run your toes in the sand, sip a mai tai, and say goodbye–at least temporarily–to militant fundamentalists, the IRS, and even your mother-in-law.

This string of some of the planet's most extraordinarily beautiful and remote islands is, oddly enough, part of the United States; in short, you'll feel as though you've died and gone to heaven—but you didn't have to give up flush toilets or hamburgers to get there. (And you probably didn't even have to pray.)

What's your fancy? A hike down a remote canyon? Horseback riding through volcanic craters? Surfing 30-foot waves? Top-notch, ocean-side dining in shorts and flip-flops? Cycling, diving, playing a round of golf on a championship course? Or being pampered like Hawaiian royalty and feasting on some of the finest international cuisine while surrounded by hordes of celebrities and Beautiful People? ITravelbooks HAWAII will be an authoritative and invaluable essential on your trip to this spectacular, safe, and beautiful haven.

ORIENTATION

THE ISLANDS

The island chain that comprises Hawaii includes the southernmost island of Hawaii (often known as the Big Island, because it is); Maui; Lanai; Molokai; Oahu (home to Honolulu and Waikiki); Kaui; and the infrequently visited Niihau. Each island offers a unique experience, stunning scenery, activities for every age and price range, and is absolutely worth a visit if your schedule allows for it.

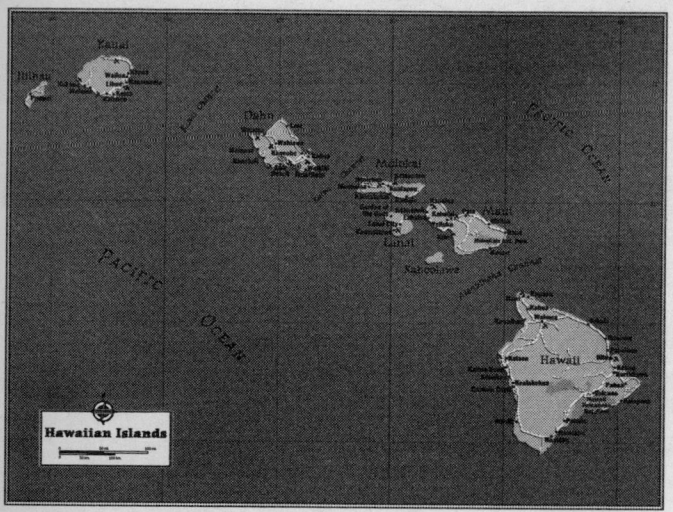

MOTHER NATURE AND THE HAWAIIAN CLIMATE

Travel to Hawaii whenever you like, whenever you can. The weather, while it might not be absolutely perfect, will always be close to it especially if you're escaping the evil winter doldrums. Much like a permanent massage, Hawaii is body-and-mind friendly. Everyone, from the most stressed-out, suit-wearing businessman, to moms with multitudes of toddlers, will be affected by Hawaii's laid-back climate. Days are sunny, humidity is low, pollution is practically non-existent and—even on the warmest days—blissful trade winds will gently caress you.

The coolest months are December through March, when daytime temps are in the mid-70s and the evenings can drop down into the 50s (and 30 degrees is not unheard of at the Mauna Kea Crater on the Big Island). August and September are usually the hottest months, with highs in the 90s during the day, as well as higher humidity. But on average, the air temperature is in the 80-85 degree range, and the water temperature is a blissful 75-80 degrees.

Rain

In the islands, rain usually occurs—if only a few drops—every day, with the northeast side of each island getting the most precipitation. The rainy season ordinarily occurs between December and March (prime tourist season), although showers are brief: rain rarely lasts all day and should not be a factor in planning your trip or other island outings. On the other hand, when the rare big storm does come in, it can be a whopper.

> **ITRAVELBOOK TIP:** Always tuck a lightweight, collapsible umbrella into your bag, whatever your destination.

The Hawaiian Winds

The Trade Winds are our friends; billowing throughout most of the summer and half of the winter, they're what keep Hawaii breezy and balmy instead of sticky and oppressive. The Kona Winds, however—much like the powerful coffee of the same name—are not quite as friendly. They tend to be more humid and cloying, and generally blow from October through April. Happily, the Konas are rare during the summer.

Volcanic Eruptions

Hawaii is a blissful paradise, even if the Big Island does have periodic volcanic eruptions. Contrary to popular belief, islanders don't exactly run from these events. And while they don't roast marshmallows over them either, they do like to see them. Bring a lawn chair, experience Mother Nature at her fieriest, and enjoy the post-eruption haze, better known to locals as vog.

GETTING THERE, GETTING HOME

Entry Requirements

Entry requirements for U.S. citizens are a joy—no passport or visa necessary, and no need to change money. Canadian citizens need proof of residence (passport, birth certificate, etc.) but don't require a visa.

Citizens of other countries must carry a valid passport, appropriate visa (check with your local embassy or consulate), and a return ticket out of town.

Customs Regulations must be taken seriously. Basic allowances are, per adult, one liter of alcohol, 200 cigarettes or 100 cigars or three pounds of smoking tobacco (the legal kind!) plus gifts totaling $100 or less. Visitors must spend at least 72 hours in the United States to qualify. Foreign visitors may also bring in or leave with $10,000 in United States or foreign currency without doing any paperwork. As for food, plants, and seeds—*forget it*.

Exiting Hawaii

When the dreaded time comes to leave this island paradise, your bags will go through **Agricultural Inspection**, where they will be examined for items forbidden from leaving Hawaii. These include fresh gardenias, live insects, sugarcane, soil, and some fruits (check with the FDA at your time of departure). You can, however, bring home pineapples, fresh leis, seashells, coconuts, and, of course, your tan.

> **ITRAVELBOOK TIP**: Despite the relaxed nature of the place, Hawaiian customs and immigration officers are extremely zealous about their jobs, and utterly humorless. Don't try anything funny.

Getting to Hawaii by Air

The majority of flights set down at **Honolulu International Airport** (**http://www.state.hi.us/dot/airports/index.htm**), connecting with various international, domestic, and inter-island carriers. Some flights head directly for Maui, or the Big Island, with non-stops from the mainland originating in Los Angeles, San Diego, San Francisco, St. Louis, Seattle, New York, Boston, and other cities.

HAWAII

International arrivals come in from Japan, Australia, New Zealand, Canada, the Philippines, and other locations in Asia and the South Pacific. Flights from the mainland's west coast take approximately five hours air time, with an extra 20 to 30 minutes to get from the airport to Waikiki hotels by taxi or airport bus.

> **ITRAVELBOOK TIP**: Since September 11, 2001, air travel safety has become, by necessity, of prime concern to carriers and travelers alike. Expect and prepare for potentially lengthy airport safety checks: show the required identification (usually a driver's license or a passport), open your bags when asked to, and bring a good book to keep busy if the line is long.

Airport Information

Mainland travelers flying to Honolulu International Airport should familiarize themselves with the following before embarking on their trip:

- Check with your airline on how early you should arrive. Usually it is 2-3 hours ahead of the departure time.

- When you arrive at the airport, go directly to the agriculture inspection station. All luggage going to the mainland must be checked and tagged before you go to the airline check in.

- Some airlines have worked out an agreement with the FAA for curbside check in. Ask your airline if they provide this service. If so, the porter will take your bag through agriculture inspection and you can proceed to the ticket counter or gate to check in. Some airlines will only permit persons with electronic tickets to use curbside check in. Ask in advance about this service.

- You will be asked for a state-or government-issued photo ID when you check in your bags, get your boarding pass, go through security, and before you can board your plane. Keep your ID handy.

- Check in as much of your luggage as possible. It will reduce the time you spend having your carry-ons searched at security check points, and will speed up boarding of the plane.

- Check with your airline about how many carry-on items you are allowed. Most airlines limit carry-ons to a personal item (purse, briefcase) and one other item, such as a backpack, computer, bag, etc.

- Say your goodbyes at home. Only ticketed passengers are permitted beyond the security check point. If you need assistance, let your airline know and they will arrange for whatever help you need.

- Unaccompanied minors may be escorted to a gate. Make arrangements with your airline.

- Check your pockets, key chains, and carry-ons for any sharp objects, including knives, letter openers, scissors, nail clippers, knitting needles, etc. These items are not permitted aboard the plane, but may be checked with luggage. These items will be confiscated at security checkpoints.

Inter-island travelers should review the following, which applies to all airports on all islands:

- Plan to arrive 90 minutes before your flight. Ask your airline if you should arrive earlier than that.

- Parking is limited in airport lots, so plan to have someone drop you off and pick you up. If you must park, allow time to walk from the overseas parking lot at Honolulu International or remote lots at Neighbor Island airports, if nearby parking lots are full.

- Be sure to say your goodbyes at home. Curbside access is allowed for active loading and unloading only. A driver may not wait at curbside for you, or leave their car unattended to help you with your bags.

- Check in as much of your luggage as possible. This will prevent delays while going through security check points and boarding the plane. Take only what you'll need during the flight on board with you.

- Don't tape or tie your boxes closed until after they have been inspected and are ready to be checked in at the ticket counter. Bring strapping tape with you to secure your boxes.

- Don't gift wrap any presents that you may be carrying onto the airplane. You may be asked to unwrap them at a security check point.

- Leave all sharp objects such as knives, scissors, fishing hooks, etc. at home, or pack them in your check-in bags. They are not allowed on board the plane and will be confiscated at security check points.

- If you are using flight coupons, fill out the coupon before you leave home. If you do not have baggage to check, you may proceed through the security check point and check in at the ticket counter and obtain a boarding pass (except Kona, where you must check in and receive a boarding pass before going through security).

- If your name is called for screening at the gate before you can board the plane, please cooperate with airline personnel. The FAA requires random screening, as well as screening of passengers who buy tickets at the last minute, have one-way tickets, or are not checking luggage.

- Remember, only passengers with tickets and boarding passes may go through security checkpoints.

- Wait for all arriving passengers in the baggage claim area. Do not send children to greet passengers at security checkpoints. They will add to the congestion and may delay travelers trying to catch a flight.

- Keep your state or government photo ID handy. You will be asked for it when you check in, when you go through the security checkpoint, and when you board the plane.

- Never make comments about bombs or other weapons to anyone in jest. All such comments are taken seriously and the person making the remark will be detained by security. It is a **federal offense** to make certain threats at an airport.

Domestic Carriers

American Airlines http://www.aa.com	(800) 433-7300
Continental Airlines http://www.continental.com	(800) 231-0856
Delta Airlines http://www.delta.com	(800) 221-1212
Hawaiian Airlines http://www.hawaiianair.com	(800) 367-5320
Northwest Airlines http://www.nwa.com	(800) 225-2525
United Airlines http://www.ual.com	(800) 225-5825

International Carriers

Air New Zealand (800) 262-1234
http://www.airnz.co/nz

Canadian Airlines (800) 426-7000
http://www.canadianairlines.ca

China Airlines (800) 227-5118
http://www.china-airlines.com

Garuda Indonesia (800) 826-2829
http://www.garuda-indonesia.com

Japan Airlines (800) 525-3663
http://www.jal.co.jp/

Korean Airlines (800) 421-8200
http://www.koreanair.com

Phillipine Airlines (800) 435-9725
http://www.phillipineair.com

Qantas (800) 227-4500
http://www.qantas.com.au

Getting to Hawaii by Sea

Despite the recent sharp cutbacks on the cruise-ship circuit, Hawaii remains a popular stop. If you opt for this method, keep in mind that your stay will most likely be a brief one- or two-day port of call on the way to or from Mexico, Asia, Australia, or other South Pacific islands.

Cruise lines to contact for more details of their Hawaiian expeditions include:

Cunard (800) 221-4770
http://www.cunardline.com

Holland America (800) 426-0327
http://www.hollandamerica.com

Princess Cruises (800) 421-0522
http://www.princesscruises.com

Royal Caribbean (800) 327-6700
http://www.royalcaribbean.com

Society Expeditions (800) 426-7794
http://www.societyexpeditions.com

For cruises around the Hawaiian islands, sign on for a three-, four-, or seven-day inter-island voyage with the very reasonable and well-regarded American Hawaii Cruises (**http://www.1cruise.com /hawaii/passport.htm** or (800) 765-7000.) Contact them for information about special offers and packages specifically designed for kids, golfers, honeymooners, and all couples in love.

Getting Around Hawaii

By Car

Driving is by far your best option for getting around. Oahu's bus system (http://www.thebus.org) is excellent, but it's an exception—most of the islands have little in the way of public transportation.

Major car rental companies are set up at all airports, and many have desks in the larger hotels and resorts. Your best bet is to reserve ahead, especially during the high season, when your choice of vehicle may be sharply limited. If you're booking a package, a car is often included in the deal. Visit each rental company's website: they may offer discounts to travelers who book on the web.

> **ITRAVELBOOK TIP:** Before you pick up your car, check with BOTH your personal auto insurance and credit card companies to see if you are covered for the collision damage waiver. Many credit card companies, such as American Express, offer free coverage when you book using their card, but consumers still regularly report being bullied into buying extra collision damage insurance at the time of the rental. If you know for sure that you're covered, simply waive the fee—which can run into hundreds of extra dollars. If you're not sure, it's always better to be safe than sorry.

If you are more of an adventurous type and would like to try your hand at the dangerous vehicular activity called *off-roading* (which is slang for taking four-wheel-drive vehicles—usually Jeeps hiked up on higher suspensions—on incredibly scenic but next-to-impassable roads), make sure that you rent an *off-roading* vehicle from a company that specializes in it. Otherwise, you'll destroy your rental car and possibly risk life and limb.

Hawaii's main highways and roads are paved and in good condition. The back roads, however, are another story—you may need to rent a four-wheel drive vehicle to get to some remote locations (check with your rental company for rules and regulations). (Be advised that this is not the same as the aforementioned off-roading. See above.) Before you rent, consider where you'll be driving.

Rental Car Directory

Alamo	(800) 327-9633
http://www.goalamo.com	
Avis	(800) 831-8000
http://www.avis.com	
Budget	(800) 527-0700
http://www.budget.com	
Dollar	(800) 367-7006
http://www.dollar.com	
Hertz	(800) 654-3011
http://www.hertz.com	
National	(800) 227-7368
http://www.nationalcar.com	

Hawaiian driving etiquette is very simple: Don't honk unless it's an emergency. Do not speed up to pass a car (Hawaiians do not like being passed), and SLOW DOWN when entering small towns and villages.

Bicycles, Mopeds, and Scooters

You can rent bicycles on all of the islands, but your cycling experience will depend on what island you're on, and where you want to go. Pedaling around Waikiki, while congested, is simple. Most of the coastal routes on all the islands are well-paved and provide stunning views (especially on Oahu). Heading into the backcountry, however, can be more challenging: many of the roads have narrow shoulders, some have no shoulders at all, and some of the roads appear to be only shoulders. If you're unsure, traveling with children, or just want a more relaxed ride, contact a local reputable rental location for tips on where—and where not—to go. (See island chapters for recommended rental agencies.) For an excellent map of Honolulu bicycle routes, contact the **Honolulu City and County Bike Coordinator** (808) 527-5044.

> **ITRAVELBOOK TIP**: Paradise will cease to be blissful if you can't sit down comfortably. We strongly recommend renting mountain bikes with soft seats and shock absorbers for ease of handling, rear comfort, and safe navigation on bumpy and rutted roads, instead of lighter-weight road bikes. Get to your bike rental agencies early in the morning, if possible. And if the nearest rental agent has no mountain bikes left, go somewhere else.

Mopeds and scooters offer a faster way to get around, providing you know how to ride them. They're a bit scarcer on the islands than bikes, but once found, they provide an inexpensive, sweat-free way to travel. Don't be a big shot: even if you think you're *Easy Rider* material, always wear a helmet, and ask the rental agent to give you a free lesson. Look for suggested rental agencies in the individual island chapters.

Taxis

Taxis are available on all islands, but they are not for those on a tight budget. Fares tend to be hefty—$1.50 for the flag fall—and $1.50 per mile, depending on where you are and where you're headed. (Drivers are also allowed to charge $.30 per suitcase.) You can often negotiate the price of long-distance trips, particularly between your hotel and the airport, which generally runs $20 plus tip to Waikiki from Honolulu International Airport (work this out in advance, however). It's very difficult to hail a taxi (Hawaiian taxis are supposed to be radio-dispatched only), but occasionally you'll luck out and grab the attention of a hungry renegade on their way somewhere. But to be on the safe side, call a cab from your hotel or restaurant—and remember, the cab will most likely arrive on "Hawaiian time" (late). If you need to be somewhere, or need to catch a plane, allow plenty of extra time, or ask your hotel if it provides airport shuttle service (most do). **Trans Hawaiian Services** (808) 566-7333 runs an airport shuttle service to Waikiki from Honolulu. Fare is $7 one-way, $13 round-trip.

Ferry

The only available ferry services running between the islands are **The Maui Princess** (http://www.mauiprincess.com/molokai.htm or (808) 661-8397) which travels between Lahiana (on Maui) and Molokai, while **Expeditions** (808) 661-3756 runs a Lahaina-Lanai shuttle.

By Air

Inter-island travel via airplane is by far the easiest and most practical way to move between islands. Major carriers are **Hawaiian Airlines** (http://www.hawaiianair.com/ or (800) 367-5320 or (808) 838-1555) and **Aloha Airlines** (http://www.alohaair.com/ or (800) 367-5250 or (808) 935-5771), both long-established companies with frequent daily service between all the islands. Check each of their websites to find special rates, package deals, promotions, coupon books, air passes, and more information. Fares change at a dizzying speed, so book well ahead of time. Island Air (800) 323-3345 or (800) 652-6541 and Mahalo Air (800) 462-6256 or (808) 833-5555, are two of the newer, smaller turbo-prop airlines, and offer better deals across the board.

Accomodations

Like any vacation spot, Hawaii offers accommodations that range from the exorbitantly expensive and ultra-luxurious to the elder-and-youth-hostel "bring your own sheets" variety of establishment, and everything in between. If you choose to visit the islands with a tour company, you will most likely have your choice of different levels of luxury (and you'll pay accordingly). However, if you are traveling independently, consider taking advantage of the multitudes of smaller guest houses, bed-and-breakfasts, and off-the-beaten path hotels and inns. Very often the prices will be lower, and the accommodations, especially in some of the more remote locations, lovely.

> **ITRAVELBOOK TIP**: When making your hotel reservations, consider the following: will you be traveling with children? Your significant other? Is it a romantic getaway? Will you be spending very little time in your room? Do you want the bustle and also the amenities that a larger hotel has to offer? Are you a business traveler with modem needs? Will you want to get the kind of "insider" information traditionally offered by bed-and-breakfast proprietors? Do you want other guests to know of your comings and goings? All of these issues—in addition to how much you want to spend—will help narrow down your choices.

Smaller and Alternative Accommodations

Even if you're generally inclined to stay in one of the super-luxe resorts or hotels that will spoil you rotten with room service, poolside bars, health clubs, and terrycloth robes, it's a good idea to be aware of all of your options. If you're traveling with a family group or with friends, renting a condo might be the way to go; likewise, if you're on your own, a hostel or bed-and-breakfast might be more appropriate. And if you really want to rough it, pack your sleeping bag and go camping.

Bed and Breakfasts

All Islands Bed and Breakfast
(800) 542-0344 or (808) 263-2342
http://home.hawaii.rr.com/allislands/
Offers reduced rates for interisland flights and car rentals

Bed and Breakfast Hawaii   (800) 733-1632
http://www.bandb-hawaii.com/

Bed and Breakfast Honolulu
(800) 262-9912 or (808) 885-4550
http://www.hawaiibnb.com/
Offers reduced rates for inter-island flights and car rentals

Hawaii's Best Bed and Breakfasts
(800) 262-9912 or (808) 885-4550
http://www.bestbnb.com/
Offers reduced rates for inter-island flights and car rentals

Pacific Hawaii Bed and Breakfast
(800) 999-6026 or (808) 487-1228

Condos, Apartments, Homes, and Villas

Aloha Condominiums
http://www.alohacondos.com/

CondoRentals Hawaii   (800) 367-5004
http://www.condorentalshawaii.com/

Villas of Hawaii   (800) 522-3030
http://www.villasofhawaii.com/

Hostels and YMCAs

Armed Services YMCA   (808) 524-5600

Honolulu International Youth Hostel (808) 946-0591
http://www.hiayh.org/reservations/reserve3.htm

YMCA Central Oahu   (808) 941-3344

YMCA Kauai   (808) 742-1182

YMCA Maui   (808) 244-3153

Camping

Many state-run campgrounds require reservations and camping permits, but most of the islands allow unreserved camping at beaches and parks. Contact the Division of State Parks offices listed below for more information. And if you do decide to camp, pack a strong mosquito repellent—the insect is relentless in Hawaii, especially at night.

Oahu

**Division of State Parks:
1151 Punchbowl Street, Honolulu 96813
(808) 548-7455**

City Park
in Waimanalo, on ocean side of SR 83

Keaiwa Heiau State Recreation Area
three miles northeast of SR 720, at the end of Aiea Heights Drive

Malaekahana State Recreation Area

one mile north of Laie, off SR 83

Sand Island State Recreation Area
off SR 92, at the end of Sand Island access road

Maui

**Division of State Parks:
54 High Street, Wailuku 96793
(808) 244-4354**

Haleakala National Park
27 miles southeast of Kahului,
accessed via SRs 36, 37, 377, and 378

Polipoli Spring State Recreation Area
about 10 miles from Kula on Waipoli Road, off SR 377

Waianapanapa State Park
2.5 miles northwest of Hana via SR 360, then north approximately one-half mile on Waianapanapa Road

Kauai
Division of State Parks:
State Building, 2060 Eiwa Street, Lihue 96766
(808) 254-4444

Kokee State Park
15 miles north of Kekaha on SR 550

Na Pali Coast State Park
get there by foot or boat through Haena

Polihale State Park
five miles north of Mana Village via a dirt road off SR 50

The Big Island
Division of State Parks:
75 Aupuni Street, Hilo 96720 (808) 961-7200

Hapuna Beach State Recreation Area
two miles south of Kawaihae on SR 19

Hawaii Volcanoes National Park, Kamoamo
62 miles south of Hilo, via SR 11

Hawaii Volcanoes National Park, Kipuka Nene
42 miles southwest of Hilo, via SR 11

Hawaii Volcanoes National Park, Namakani Paio
32 miles southwest of Hilo, on SR 11

Kalopa State Recreation Area
five miles southeast of Honokaa on SR 19

MacKenzie State Recreation Area
10 miles east of Pahoa on SR 137, then two miles south

Mauna Kea State Recreation Area
35 miles west of Hilo off SR 200

Molokai
Division of State Parks:
54 High Street, Wailuku 96793
(808) 244-4354

Palaau State Park
three miles north of Kualapuu, off SR 470

Inclusive Island Tours & Adventure Travel

Not everyone likes to travel alone, and not everyone likes to plan his or her own journey. Even some intrepid travelers we know might prefer to have an Experienced Other lead them by the hand for part or all of their Hawaiian odyssey. The following is a list of operators that conduct a broad range of island tours—everything from thrill-a-second kayaking and backpacking adventures to traditional luaus with stuffed pigs and similarly stuffed tourists:

- **AMERICAN WILDERNESS EXPERIENCE**: (800) 444-0099, http://www.gorp.com/awe/ Renowned adventure-tour operator with a variety of Hawaiian explorations available.

- **BACKROADS INTERNATIONAL**: (800) 462-2848, http://www.backroads.com, Environmentally-friendly cycling, hiking and camping tours. Highly regarded.

- **ELDERHOSTEL**: (617) 426-7788, http://www.elderhostels.org Inexpensive and interesting learning programs for ages 60+.

- **FAR HORIZONS**: (800) 552-4575, http://www.farhorizon.com Cultural and archaeological journeys, led by experts, to petroglyph fields, museums, and historic sites.

- **GLOBUS TOURS**: (800) 221-0900, http://www.globusandcosmos.com Top-class, all inclusive, every-second-planned motor coach tours.

- **GOLFTRIPS**: (800) 428-1940, http://www.golf-trips.com The golfer's best friend—resort-based packages complete with lessons, greens fees, and confirmed tee times.

- **HAWAII FOREST & TRAIL**: (808) 239-1993, http://www.hawaii-forest.com Narrated, naturalist-led day trips, via four-wheel drive, around the Big Island, including Hawaii Volcanoes National Park and the Hakalau Forest National Wildlife Refuge.

- **KAYAK KAUAI**: (800) 437-3507, http://planet-hawaii.com/outbound/ Challenging ocean kayak journeys along the Na Pali Coast and Kauai's south shore, plus backpacking tours and canoe, kayak, and mountain bike rentals.

HAWAII

- **KAUAI MOUNTAIN TOURS**: (808) 254-7224 http://www.hawaiiguide.com/tours/kauai/mountdes.htm Four-wheel-drive trips into Na Pali Kona Forest Reserve. Not for the faint of heart.

- **MAUPINTOUR:** (800) 255-4266, http://www.maupintour.com, Deluxe, fully-escorted, we'll-do-everything-for-you motor-coach tours.

- **NATURE EXPEDITIONS**: (800) 869-0639, http://www.naturexp.com Fifteen-day, four-island natural-history tours emphasizing geology, flora, and fauna.

- **OCEAN VOYAGES**: (415) 332-4681, http://www.ocean-voyages.com Seven-and-10-day yacht voyages throughout the islands, emphasizing the hidden nooks and crannies.

- **OUTFITTERS KAUAI**: (808) 742-9667, http://www.outfitterskauai.com

- Cycling and kayaking—escorted or self-guided—for a half-day or longer along Na Pali cliffs, backountry Kauai, and Hawaii's state parks.

- **PLEASANT HAWAIIAN HOLIDAYS**: (800) 242-9244, http://www.2Hawaii.com Been-around-forever, mainstream tour company packaging air, hotel, car, and a variety of traditional "Hawaiian vacation experiences."

- **SIERRA CLUB TRIPS**: (415) 776-2221, http://www.sierraclub.org The nature-lover's fraternity, offering hikes, kayaking, and camping trips to Kauai, Maui, and elsewhere.

- **TAUCK TOURS**: (800) 788-7885, http://www.tauck.com Highly-regarded, all-inclusive tour company for families, singles, and seniors. Top-notch accommodations, intelligent tour guides, often offers free air from west coast of mainland. Not to be missed if you're considering an all-inclusive tour. Expensive, and worth every penny.

- **TROPICAL ADVENTURES**: (800) 247-3483, http://www.divetropical.com. Organized dive extravaganzas from live-aboard boats.

- **WALKING THE WORLD**: (303) 225-0500, http://www.walkingtheworld.com Hiking and backpacking trips for the 50+ crowd.

What Will All This Fun Cost?

It doesn't have to cost a fortune. Really. You can do the whole luxury resort/trendy restaurant/fresh-lei-per-day sort of thing, or you can get by on an economical package deal that includes airfare, lodging, car rental, and a bunch of tours or attraction tickets. Or you can camp and cycle and feast on fruit for practically nothing. Here's a list of average prices for both high-end and low-end trips to paradise:

Luxury hotel room (double)	$200-$450+
Cheap hotel room (double)	$60-$75+
Dinner for two at expensive Honolulu Restaurant (without wine)	$65-$70 without tip
Lunch for two at a moderate Maui Restaurant (without wine)	$20-$30 without tip
Taxi ride from Honolulu International Airport to Waikiki	$20-$25 without tip
The Don Ho Cocktail Show	$30 without tip
Cup of Kona Coffee	$2.00
Local telephone call	$.25
Oahu Bus Fare	$1.00
Beginning Dive Course	$75
Sitting on the beach	Free
Half-day glass-bottom boat cruise	$50 per person, adult
Visit to USS Arizona Memorial	Free

ITRAVELBOOK'S MONEY-SAVING TIPS

• If you're a senior, child, student, or in the military, use it to your advantage and ask for applicable discounts on everything from airfare to museum admission.

• Take advantage of all the free stuff that mother nature has to offer: beaches, hikes, public gardens.

• If you're traveling with a group or the family, rent a condo and cook some of your own meals at home, and pack sandwiches for your day trips, sight-seeing, bike rides, hikes, etc. You'll save a bundle.

• Cheap food in Hawaii does NOT translate to a Big Mac and a bag of fries. You'll find a great assortment of fresh, ethnic foods on all the islands. (For a complete description of Hawaiian food delicacies, please see the appendix.)

• Keep a sharp eye peeled for airfare deals. If your schedule is flexible, you can fly more cheaply during mid-week than on weekends.

• Don't discard package deals. Many are an excellent, high-quality value, especially when a rental car is thrown in.

• Check the local newspapers, and attend local events: island-sponsored concerts, arts-and-crafts fairs, etc. They're a lot of fun, cheaper, and a lot more authentic than activities organized for the tourist trade.

• Early-bird dinners (or late lunches) can afford you a great meal in a top restaurant for substantially lower-than-prime-time prices.

• If you're a golfer, consider booking a tee time at one of the many municipal courses rather than the posh clubs. Greens fees are much cheaper. Ditto for the tennis set—most public courts are free, and in beautiful condition.

• Don't get married just for the hell of it (but if you're really serious about it, see our "Wedding Bliss" section, page 35).

ITRAVELBOOK'S FAVORITE FREEBIES

Like any good travel companion who knows their way around, we're not only here to provide you with information on where you can spend your hard-earned money: we also want to share the inside scoop on what Hawaii has to offer that's fabulous, fun—and FREE:

• Hike 760-foot Diamond Head for a 360-degree view of Waikiki, Honolulu, and the Pacific Ocean. Enter off Monsarrat Avenue and park inside the crater. Wear good shoes, take a camera, take a bottle of water, and take your time!

• Visit the USS Arizona Memorial, which has a visitor's center that chronicles the history of the attack on Pearl Harbor which killed more than 2,400 Americans and brought the United States into World War II. Open daily 8 a.m. to 5 p.m. Interpretive programs, including a documentary film about the attack and the boat trip to the USS Arizona Memorial, begin at 8:00 a.m. (7:45 a.m. in summer). The last program each day begins at 3:00 p.m. Closed Thanksgiving, Christmas, and New Years Day. **http://www.arizonamemorial.org/**

• A variety of musical performances are presented by the Royal Hawaiian Band at Kapiolani Park Bandstand (Sundays at 2 p.m.) and Iolani Place Bandstand (Fridays at 12:15 p.m.).

• Whale-watch in Maui on the coast between Lahaina and Maalaea, in season.

• Orchid-lovers shouldn't miss a visit to Hilo's Akatsuka Orchid Gardens (on the Big Island) with an enormous range of colors and varieties.

• Explore the petroglyph fields at the Mauna Lani Resort and royal Waikoloan Hotel on the Big Island.

• See daily demonstrations of quilt- and lei-making techniques at Kapaa's Marketplace at Coconut Plantation (Kauai).

• Take a walking tour of Honolulu's circa early-1800s Chinatown, a vibrant and colorful area that encompasses 15 blocks and is now the commercial home of a number of Asian ethnic groups.

• In Wailuku on Maui, stop by Kepaniwai Cultural Park, featuring pavilions, reconstructed houses, and gardens representing different ethnic groups in Hawaii. Very beautiful, very informative, very free.

- Visit Hilo Hattie, The Store of Hawaii, on Oahu, and enjoy free juice, entertainment, food samples, and craft demonstrations.

- Visit ILI'ILI'OPAE HEIAU on Molokai. One of Hawaii's largest heiau (ancient Hawaiian place of worship), it is on the National Register of Historic Places. Accessible by foot, off Highway 450, west of Ualapue.

- Nuts for Macadamia? Be sure to stop at PURDY'S NATURAL MACADAMIA NUT FARM, where Moloka'i native Tuddie Purdy and his wife Kammy have been kicking back on their five-acre farm with island visitors since 1980, talking story about all things nutty. Two miles west of Kualapu'u, on Lihi Pali Avenue, above the high school. Hours are from: 9:30 a.m.-3:30 p.m., Monday-Friday; 10 a.m.-2 p.m., Saturday; Sunday & holidays, by appointment. (808) 567-6601

Look for the best of the freebies in each section of this guide, separated by island.

Traveling with Children

Grab all the freebies and discounts you're entitled to, starting with the airlines: check special fares, meals, seats, and more. Contact your hotel prior to your arrival with the little ones, and inquire about hotel discounts for families traveling with children. Often, kids up to the age of 18 can stay free in their parents' rooms. If you're staying at a large resort complex, chances are good that there will be planned children's activities along with special pool and play facilities. Most hotels have a list of recommended babysitters, and it never hurts to ask for a few references.

> **ITRAVELBOOK TIP:** When traveling with children, check on age limitations BEFORE you book—you can save a bundle by switching to a hotel that will take your kids for free or at sharply discounted rates.

Once you're on the move, be sure to have whatever safety seats and seat belts are required for your child. Some car rental firms toss the safety seats in for free, and sometimes they're built into the vehicle, so there's no choice. Otherwise, you'll have to bring your own, or rent them at additional cost.

Almost every major attraction offers either reduced or free admission for children and students, and often there are "family fares" that allow the whole gang in for one price. If you're a member of anything (especially an automobile association), bring along your identification card and see if it will get you a discount. Be shameless. Kids of all ages will be knocked out by all of the free stuff that Mother Nature gave to Hawaii: volcanoes, waterfalls, canyons, pineapples, beaches, beaches, and more beaches.

ITRAVELBOOK TRAVELER'S DIRECTORY

Here is the information you'll need to comfortably get through a variety of day-to-day, where-is-it? how do I find it? help me! encounters. Please refer to the directories in the individual island chapters for even more specifics.

Area Code

808 is the area code for all of the Hawaiian islands.

Business, Postal, and Banking Hours

They vary. Hawaiians often begin their work day early (7-8 a.m.) and wrap things up by 3-4 p.m., so they can use the rest of the day to swim, fish, or hang out like the rest of the tourists. Postal hours are the same as in the rest of the States, and banks are usually open until 6 p.m. on Friday. ATMs are prevalent, as they are all over the mainland. Many shops and businesses in Waikiki and other high-profile tourist meccas stay open late all the time.

Disabled Travelers

Disabled travelers should contact the Commission on Persons with Disabilities, listed below, for accessibility and support services throughout the islands. Additionally, all hotel and restaurant listings in this guide are accessible, unless otherwise noted.

919 Ala Moana Boulevard, Room 101, Honolulu 96814
(808-586-8121)

54 High Street, Wailuku, Maui 96793
(808-243-5441)

1190 Waianenue Avenue, Box 1641, Hilo 96820

(808-933-4747)

3060 Eiwa Street, Room 207, Lihue, Kaui 96766
(808-241-3308)

For more general information, contact http://www.access-able.com/

Electrical Current

It's the usual mode, 110 volts, AC, 60 cycles, no adapter necessary.

Emergency

911

Fishing and Hunting Regulations

Obtain permits and other skin-and-gills info from the **Hawaii Department of Land and Natural Resources, Division of Conservation and Resources Management**, 1151 Punchbowl Street, Honolulu, 96813. (808-587-0077)

Gay and Lesbian Travelers

Hawaii is generally laid back enough to accept everyone, regardless of sexual orientation, which, like pretty much everything else, simply doesn't matter once you get to the islands. Gays and lesbians have been vacationing on these sandy shores for eons, and Hawaii remains one of the most gay-friendly places in the United States. Check in at the **Gay and Lesbian Community Center** in Honolulu, 1820 University Avenue, Suite 8, (808-951-7000) for up-to-the-minute information on local happenings. All of our listings are, at the very least, gay-friendly establishments. Please refer to the individual island chapters for more specific information.

Language

Hawaii is part of the United States, and situated where it is, is therefore as much—if not more—of a melting pot than the rest of the country. In fact, much of what you'll hear doesn't even sound American. You'll pick up some Hawaiian, and assorted bits of Chinese, Japanese, Portuguese, Korean, and Samoan, as well as a language known as "pidgin." Pidgin was born back in the plantation days when traders were trying to figure out a way to communicate with their laborers. Consequently, it's a blend of English, Hawaiian, Polynesian, Japanese, Filipino, Samoan, and a few other languages. Bear in mind that the islanders adore pidgin, and do not adore tourists who try to speak it. Check this guide's appendix for the English translation of common pidgin words and phrases, so that you can understand a bit of what you hear.

Liquor Laws

Legal drinking age in the land of exotic cocktails is 21. Oahu and Maui bars generally stay open until 2 a.m.; cabarets don't have to shut the doors until 4 a.m. Bars on the other islands are often locked up by 10 p.m. or 11 p.m. Alcohol—liquor, wine, and beer—can be purchased in supermarkets as well as liquor stores every day. Alcohol is off-limits in national and state parks.

Marijuana, a.k.a. PAKALOO

Yes, we know it's the state's biggest money-making crop. But—unlike pineapples and coffee beans—it's illegal to possess, use, grow, or sell. Penalties are harsh: arrest, court, high fines, property confiscation—AND jail. Ever see a narc wearing an aloha shirt and flip-flops? Just wait.

Money

Credit cards and traveler's checks are widely accepted, but some smaller establishments in more remote areas won't take anything other than greenbacks. ATM machines are ubiquitous.

Packing

If you're doing the whole stay-in-one-fancy-resort trip or a deluxe escorted tour (and someone else is carrying your bags), you can probably get away with packing anything you please. If, however, you're planning on traveling without a tour group, you'll end up—at some point—schlepping your gear along, and hating every minute of it. The rule of thumb is: PACK LIGHT. Bring the obvious necessities (this guidebook, a good sunblock, insect repellent, camera, toiletries, etc.). As for clothes, natural fibers are advised: synthetics (wrinkle-free though they might be) are hideously uncomfortable, and, like old fish, begin to smell after a few days in the heat. If you'll

HAWAII

be dining out occasionally, throw in some dressier gear for evenings out: a sport jacket for men (leave the tie at home) and an appropriately chic outfit for women are advised. If you're planning on doing some hiking, bring along a pair of hiking trousers (we love the kind that zip off to shorts), short hiking shoes, and a windbreaker.

Publications

Honolulu's two daily papers are the *Honolulu Advertiser* (morning) and the *Honolulu Star-Bulletin* (afternoon). *USA Today* and some mainland papers (usually a day or so behind) are also available. On the Big Island, there's the *Hawaii Tribune-Herald* and *West Hawaii Today*. On Kauai, you can pick up either the *Kauai Times* or the *Garden Island*; and on Maui, it's the *Maui News*. Local Hawaiian magazines include *Honolulu*, *Spirit of Aloha*, *Hawaii*, *Hawaii Business*, *Waikiki Beach Press*, and nearly a dozen others. Of course, on every island, you'll find local tourist magazines galore.

Shopping

Instead of hassling with packing those tricky coconuts and chocolate-covered macadamias, why not send them home without you? Many tourist shops and hotels will provide this service for you. Most fruit, however, won't be allowed out of the country via mail or packed luggage, the exception being the almighty pineapple. The easiest method to get it home, unfortunately, is to buy it at the airport. It'll be slightly more expensive, but pre-inspected, pre-boxed, and just waiting for you to take it home.

Smoking

Forbidden in all public buildings, movie theaters, and attractions. As for restaurants, smoking sections are becoming a rarity. Don't light up without asking first.

Taxes

Sales tax is only 4 percent, but hotel occupancy tax is now above 9 percent.

Telephones and Cell Phones

Pay phones—for those of you who still use them—are 25 cents for local calls (which include any place on an individual island), and more for inter-island chat. If you're calling from your hotel room, bear in mind that surcharges can be astronomical. Cell phones with mainland home numbers should get service on the islands. Check with your cellular carrier before leaving home to avoid surprises.

Time Zones

Time zones can be a bit confusing, as Hawaii does not conform to daylight-savings time. From the U.S. mainland, four time zones apply: Eastern Standard (five hours ahead of Hawaii), Central (four hours), Mountain (three hours), and Pacific (two hours). From April through October, take into account the daylight-savings factor on the Mainland.

Tipping

Tip 15-20 percent for restaurant servers, 15 percent for cabbies (plus a buck per bag). Tip $2-3 for bellhops and a couple of dollars per day for the hotel maid (more than that if you're in a posh resort). Tour guides should get an extra 15 percent tacked on. And, if you ask the concierge for a special favor or a maitre d' for a special table, tip accordingly.

Travel Insurance

Some companies to contact for insurance coverage (including health, baggage loss, and trip cancellation) are Access America ((800) 284-8300, **http://www.accessamerica.com/**), Travel Insured International ((800) 243-3274, **http://www.travelinsured.com/**) and Travel Guard International ((800) 826-1300, **http://www.travelguard.com/**).

Wedding Bliss

(Note, we said "wedding," not "wedded.") Hawaii is so hypnotically romantic that you might pop the question to a complete stranger. In fact, marriage and honeymoons are so popular here that the state even publishes a free information pamphlet (**http://www.gohawaii.com/hokeo/wedding/planner.html**). Hotels and resorts crowd each other in the quest to snatch your wedding and honeymoon business. Wedding coordinators do everything except say "I do" for you.

You can have anything your heart desires and your wallet can handle. Low budget? How about tying the knot in one of the national parks? Or on a secluded beach? For regulations and permits, contact the State Health Department, 1250 Punchbowl Street, Honolulu, 96813 (808) 548-5862.

BASIC WEDDING RULES

- Both partners must be at least 18 years old.
- You must have a valid license from the **State Department of Health, Marriage License Office** (see address, above).
- There is no waiting period.
- The license ($25, cash only) is valid for 30 days.
- Bring identification when applying for the license (a driver's license will do).
- Information about any previous marriages must be disclosed, as must names and birth places of each partner's parents.

ITRAVELBOOKS TIPS FOR SURVIVING IN PARADISE

OK: you've been lulled by the mesmerizing trade winds and hypnotic visions. You're wearing posies in your hair, and running barefoot through the sand. You're already planning to sell the farm and live here forever. It's time for the old reality check. Heed some simple basics, and then go back to dreaming:

- No matter how pretty those palms and flowers are, don't eat them. Some of the loveliest are also the most toxic.
- Never, EVER, discount the power of the ocean, no matter how calm or soothing it might appear to be. Regardless of how experienced a swimmer, surfer, or diver you are, always ask lifeguards or locals about conditions. Be especially wary of riptides and undertows, and don't turn your back on the water when rock-climbing or shell-collecting.
- Do not leave valuables in your car, whether it's locked or unlocked.
- No matter how fancy your digs are, never leave valuables in your hotel room. That's what the hotel safe is for. Ask about the coin-operated safes that many hotels now have in each room.

- If you happen to unwittingly stumble into someone's marijuana garden, do not feign ignorance and help yourself to that interesting-looking little weed. Leave instantly.

- Purses, wallets, cameras, and cell phones are on the theft hot list. Keep your eye and hands on both, especially in a crowded tourist area. Never leave a purse on the back of your chair, and always carry your wallet in your front pocket.

- Despite the bucolic nature of the place, use good common sense: stay in well-lighted areas at night, and do not hike, jog, or beach-walk alone in deserted or remote areas, at any hour.

WELCOME TO HAWAII!

The islands often seem like just one continual celebration, and in fact, whenever you choose to visit, chances are you'll be arriving in time for one celebration or another. Choose from luaus, ethnic festivals, sports events, and religious festivals. The following is a short list:

January

(Honolulu) First Night: The streets are jumping with New Year's revelry and top local bands.

(Oahu) Hula Bowl Game: Aloha Stadium hosts the annual college all-star football game.

(Molokai) Molokai Makahiki (Molokai): The last Saturday of the month launches the annual "time of peace" celebration with traditional games, native bands, a skin-diving tournament, and more.

(Oahu) Morey Boogie World Body Board Championships: Banzai Pipeline, on the North shore, draws body-boarders from around the world.

February

(Honolulu) Chinese New Year: Chinatown's the scene for all the hoopla (also known as the Narcissus Festival) including fireworks, lion dances, a queen pageant, and coronation ball.

(Oahu) Hawaiian Open Golf Tournament: Waialae Country Club is the scene for this must-do event that golfers of every rank and file won't want to miss.

(Oahu) Makaha World Surfing Championships: Head for Makaha Beach for this major long-board competition that draws surfers from all corners of the world. Buffalo's Annual Big Board Surfing Classic (using old wooden boards) is part of the event.

(Big Island) Mauna Kea Ski Meet: Watch (or join) this race down the volcano's slope (if there's snow).

(Oahu) NFL Pro Bowl: The annual pro football all-star game is held at Aloha Stadium.

(Honolulu) Punahou School Carnival: Lots of family fun at this yearly carnival, which features rides, local nibbles, arts-and-crafts booths and—at the end—a terrific White Elephant tent that dispenses the leftovers.

(Oahu) Sandcastle Building Contest: Hawaii's top architects vie with the University of Hawaii architecture students for best sand sculpture at Kailua Beach Park.

March

(Oahu) Polo: Opening Day for the March-through-August season of Sunday Polo Play.

(Statewide) Prince Kuhio Day: A day to honor Hawaii's first congressman (who probably would have rather been king). Ceremonies and events are held at various sites throughout the islands.

April

(Honolulu) Easter Sunrise Service: This veritable and venerable institution is held at the National Memorial Cemetery of the Pacific.

(Oahu) Honolulu International Bed Race: A charity fund-raiser (also known as the Carole Kai Bed Race) in which decorated beds on wheels are raced through the streets of Waikiki. Grab your jimmies and join the fun. A parade follows the race.

(Big Island) Merrie Monarch Festival: Modern and traditional hula feats are some of the islands' most popular events. The competition lasts a week and includes a parade, performances, workshops, and lots of hip movement. Tickets sell out about a year ahead and televised broadcasts of each day's events are followed more closely than *All My Children*.

May

(Statewide) Buddha Day: Celebrate the birth of the Serene One at various island temples.

(Honolulu) Hawaii State Fair: Two weekends' worth of state fair action over at Aloha Stadium: entertainment, exhibits, agricultural charms, and lots of local food to sample.

(Statewide) Lei Day: The great lei is celebrated with pageants and competitions, plus a Lei Day concert and crowning of the Lei Queen.

(Molokai) Molokai Ka Huia Piko: The birth of the hula is celebrated Molokai-style with music, dance, crafts, and local taste treats.

(Lanai) Pineapple Festival: The "Pineapple Island" hosts a full-on event with music, dancing, tournaments, demonstrations, contests, and arts and crafts.

(Maui) Seabury Hall Crafts Fair: The best prep school in town exhibits top artists in its annual fund-raising event.

June

(Big Island) Hilo Orchid Society Show: Orchid lovers descend upon Hilo's Civic Auditorium to catch whiffs and glances at hundreds of orchid varieties.

(Oahu) Japanese Festival: All kinds of Japanese cultural activities are held in Honolulu and Haleiwa, including dancing, candlelight ceremonies and a special Bon Odori tribute to the dearly departed.

(Statewide) King Kamehameha Day: This is a state holiday to honor Hawaii's first king who united all the islands. Festivities, parades, flowers are everywhere you look.

(Honolulu) Taste of Honolulu: Eat your way around City Hall for this three-day pigout that draws multitudes for tastings galore, plus cooking demonstrations and entertainment.

(Big Island) Waiki'I Music Festival: Head for the Polo Field at Waikii Ranch (with about 10,000 other fans) for this two-day Hawaiian "Woodstock" where the state's top performers take to the stage.

July

(Statewide) Fourth of July: Don't forget you're still in the United States! Celebrate Independence Day everywhere from rodeos on the Big Island to a parade of tall ships off the Oahu coast.

(Big Island) International Festival of the Pacific: Lots of Pacific and Asian food, music, floats, costumes, folk dancing, and sports competitions.

(Honolulu) Prince Lot Hula Festival: Much hula merriment, both ancient and modern, performed alfresco at Moanalua Gardens.

(Big Island) Volcano Wilderness Marathon: One-thousand-plus runners do a rigorous wilderness circuit in Hawaii Volcanoes National Park. Not recommended for the out of shape.

August

(Statewide) Admission Day: August 18th—the day the lucky United States officially claimed Hawaii as one of its own.

(Big Island) Establishment Day: A great, family-oriented event that celebrates Hawaiian heritage. Learn ancient arts, crafts, and traditional lore.

(Big Island) Hawaiian International Billfish Tournament: Head to Kona shore to ogle the big fishers of Hawaii and the world competing in marlin-snagging tournaments.

September

(Statewide) Aloha Week: It's an entire week of festivities to celebrate the "aloha spirit." Parades, luaus, pageants, and other entertainment galore.

(Waikiki) Outrigger Hotels Hawaiian Oceanfest: Ten days of ocean-oriented sports, including a biathlon, lifeguard challenge, and women-only windsurfing classic.

(Maui) Seiko Super Tennis Tournament: The leading pros compete at Wailea in this annual event.

Molokai-to-Oahu Canoe Race: A race using traditional outrigger canoes from remotest Molokai to Fort DeRussy in Honolulu. The women hit the Kaiwi channel in September; the men race in October.

October

(Big Island) Ironman World Triathlon: Fabulous event seducing thousands of I'm-faster-than-you-are athletes to the cycling/swimming/running race.

November

(Statewide) Hawaii International Film Festival: Free showings throughout the islands of Pacific Rim films.

(Oahu) Hawaii Pro-Surfing Championships: Big waves and big money draw the big names in surfing to the North Shore's Banzai Pipeline.

(Big Island) Kona Coffee Festival: Move over, Starbucks. Kona celebrates its coffee harvest with a week of tastings, bean-picking contests, parades, exhibits, and tours.

(Honolulu) Mission Houses Museum Christmas Fair: A popular event with do-your-Christmas-shopping, here arts, crafts, and specialty items.

December

(Statewide) Bodhi Day: Hang around one of the Buddhist temples to join in the pomp commemorating Buddha's enlightenment.

(Honolulu) Honolulu Marathon: International runners, televised coverage—what more could you ask of a running event?

HAWAII
THE BIG ISLAND

The Big Island is a compilation of "firsts," "mosts," and contrasts. It's the largest of the Hawaiian islands. It was the first Hawaiian island to be settled, and the most diverse. Its tip is the most-southern point of any other state, and it's geographically the youngest Hawaiian island. It supposedly has the tallest mountain in the world (Mauna Kea, when measured from the ocean floor) as well as the largest privately owned ranch (Parker Ranch) in the United States. It boasts the world's most powerful telescope (at Keck Observatory), along with Hawaii's most-tropical city (Hilo). Its two volcanoes are the largest in the world and the most active.

More like a miniature continent then a tropical isle, the Big Island presents dazzling contrasts within its borders. There are lava cliffs, jutting mountains, snowcapped peaks, sunbaked deserts, tropical forests, verdant valleys, crashing waterfalls, sleepy villages, tiny bed-and-breakfasts, fancy-schmancy resorts, and green-, black- and white-sand beaches. And, of course, there are volcanoes.

The island economy is based primarily on agriculture—responsible for more than half of Hawaii's vegetables, more than three-quarters of the fruit (particularly papayas), and almost all the macadamia nuts. The 250,000-acre Parker Ranch is thought to be the largest individually owned cattle ranch in the United States, and beef production at Parker and the 300-odd other Big Island ranches makes up about 65 percent of the state's total. The strong, rich coffee grown in the Kona region is the nation's only commercial coffee plantation. Other contributors to the economy are the military machine and tourism—and all help to support the island's 120,317 inhabitants.

The Big Island gets fewer tourists (slightly more than 1 million per year) than any other island, and most who do come hole up in one of the ritzy resorts along the Kona-Kohala coast. Many visitors think the island is boring, full of lava, beachless, and shopless. There are beaches—peopleless—enough shops, and plenty of vegetation (as well as lava). True, you won't find the hype-and-schlock scenes you might over on Maui or Oahu, but that's what is wonderful about the Big Island. You can come here, explore a microcosm of a mini-continent, not be bothered by anyone, and *really* feel as though you've gotten away from it all. In the 1960s, astronauts were sent over here to train on the moonscape of the Mauna Loa lava fields.

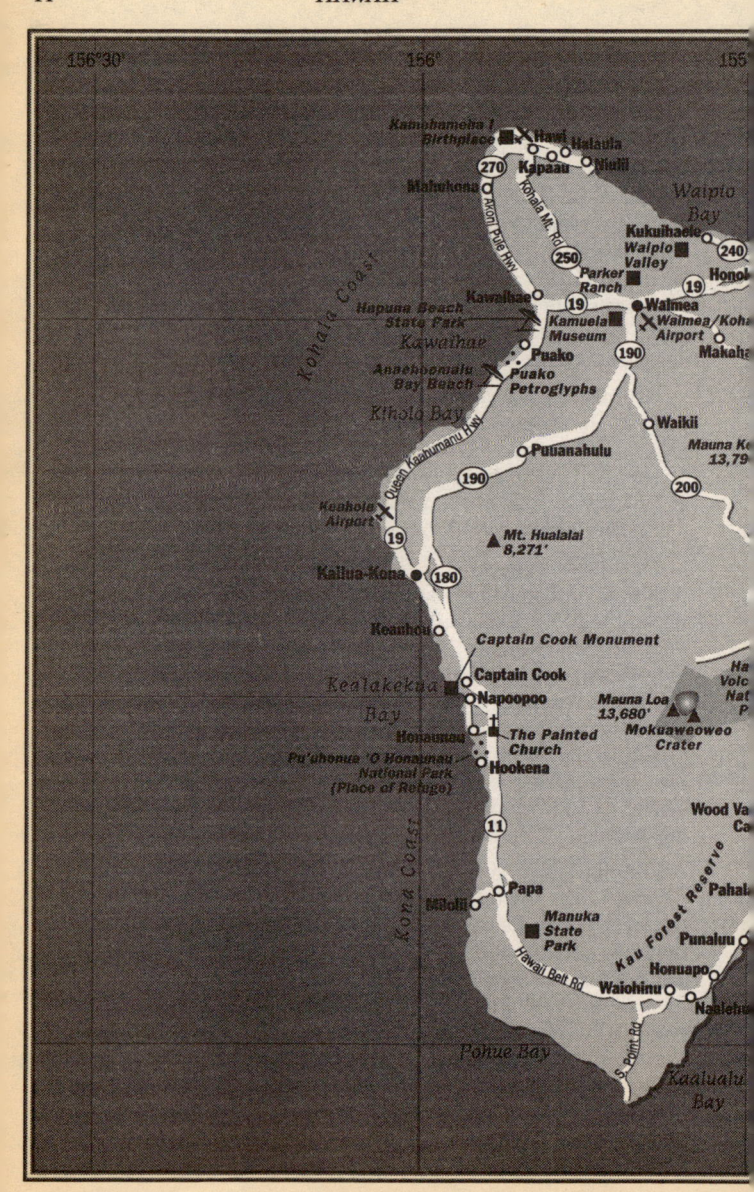

HAWAII

44

156°30'   156°   155°

- Kamehameha I Birthplace
- Hawi
- Halaula
- Kapaau
- Niulii
- Mahukona
- Kohala Mt. Rd.
- Akoni Pule Hwy
- (270)
- (250)
- Waipio Bay
- Kukuihaele
- Waipio Valley
- (240)
- Honok...
- Parker Ranch
- Kawaihae
- Kamuela Museum
- Walmea
- Waimea/Kohala Airport
- (19)
- Makaha
- Hapuna Beach State Park
- *Kawaihae*
- Puako
- Puako Petroglyphs
- Anaehoomalu Bay Beach
- *Kohala Coast*
- *Kiholo Bay*
- (190)
- Waikii
- Mauna Kea 13,79...
- Puuanahulu
- (200)
- Keahole Airport
- (19)
- Mt. Hualalai 8,271'
- Kailua-Kona
- (180)
- Keauhou
- Captain Cook Monument
- Captain Cook
- Napoopoo
- *Kealakekua Bay*
- Honaunau
- The Painted Church
- Pu'uhonua 'O Honaunau National Park (Place of Refuge)
- Hookena
- Mauna Loa 13,680'
- Mokuaweoweo Crater
- Hawaii Volcanoes National Park
- Wood Valley
- (11)
- Papa
- *Kona Coast*
- Naoli
- Manuka State Park
- Kau Forest Reserve
- Pahala
- Punaluu
- Honuapo
- Hawaii Belt Rd
- Waiohinu
- Naalehu
- S. Point Rd
- *Pohue Bay*
- *Kaalualu Bay*

HAWAII

Hawaii

0 — 10 mi. — 20 mi.
0 — 10 km. — 20 km. — 30 km.

PACIFIC OCEAN

Hamakua Coast

- Paauilo
- Ookala
- Laupahoehoe
- Papaaloa
- Maulua Bay
- Niroie
- Hakalau
- Akaka Falls
- Honomu
- Onomea
- Papaikou
- Hilo Bay
- ...na Kea ...te Park
- Boiling Pots
- Nanimau Gardens
- ...le Rd
- (200) Kaumana
- Hilo
- Hilo International Airport
- Panaewa Zoo, Equestrian Center
- Mauna Loa Macadamia Nut Factory
- (11) Keaau
- Kurtistown
- (130) (137) Nanawale
- Mountain View
- Pahoa
- (132) Kapoho
- Pohoiki
- Volcano House
- Glenwood
- Opihikao
- ...ter Rim ...ve
- Volcano
- Kilauea Volcano
- (130) (137)
- Kilauea Crater
- Kaimu
- Kehena Black Sand Beach
- (11) Hawaii Volcanoes National Park
- Kalapana
- Wahaula Heiau Ruins
- Lookout
- Wahaula
- Seabird Sanctuary

Big Island Facts

A.k.a.	The Big Island
Main city	Hilo
Flower	Red lehua
Color	Red
Area	4038 square miles
Length	93 miles
Width	76 miles
Population	120,317
Highest point	Mauna Kea (13,796 feet)

The Big Island Survival Guide

Getting There

You can fly into either Keahole-Kona International Airport or Hilo International Airport. **Keahole-Kona International Airport (www.hawaii.gov/dot/airports/hawaii/koa/)**, the choice of many visitors staying on the western side of the island, is about seven miles north of Kona and serves some 50-or-so mostly inter-island flights per week, plus United's San Francisco-to-Big Island run. You'll find basic airport amenities at the open-air terminal including snack shops, baggage lockers, concessions, visitor information, and a number of car rental desks. Airlines are:

UNITED	(800) 241-6522	HTTP://WWW.UAL.COM/
HAWAIIAN	(808) 326-5615	HTTP://WWW.HAWAIIANAIR.COM/
ALOHA	(808) 935-5771	HTTP://WWW.ALOHAAIR.COM/
ISLAND AIR	(808) 323-3345	
BIG ISLAND AIR	(808) 329-4868	

(Island Air and Big Island Air —for travel between Kona and Hilo.)

Car rental agencies are:

Alamo	(808) 329-8896	HTTP://WWW.GOALAMO.COM/
Avis	(808) 327-3000	HTTP://WWW.AVIS.COM/
Budget	(808) 329-8511	HTTP://WWW.BUDGET.COM/
Dollar	(808) 329-2744	HTTP://WWW.DOLLAR.COM/
Hertz	(808) 329-3566	HTTP://WWW.HERTZ.COM/
National	(808) 329-1675	HTTP://WWW.NATIONALCAR.COM/

Hilo International Airport is about two miles from the city's hotel district on Banyan Drive. The modern two-story terminal features a restaurant, a slew of concessions, baggage lockers, an information center, and car rental booths. Airlines are **Hawaiian, Aloha, Island Air, Big Island Air** (see numbers above), and **Mahalo Air** *(800) 277-8333*. Car rental agencies operating out of Hilo's airport are **Alamo** *(808) 961-3343*, **Avis** *(808) 935-1290*, **Budget** *(808) 935-6878*, **Dollar** *(808) 961-6059*, **Hertz** *(808) 935-2896* and **National** *(808) 935-0891*.

Waimea-Kohala Airport (known locally as Kamuela Airport), located outside Waimea, is served by **Trans Air** *(808) 934-5801*, out of Oahu, for inter-island commutes. Upolu Airport, a remote airstrip at Upolu Point at the island's northern tip, serves private planes and small charter operations.

Getting Around

You'll either need to rent a car or catch a taxi from Hilo International Airport—there is no public transportation and no shuttle service, either. The situation is the same at Keahole-Kona International Airport, except that some of the big Waikoloa resorts (Hilton Waikoloa Village, Royal Waikoloan, Mauna Kea, and Mauna Lani) offer shuttle service to guests.

Driving on the Big Island is relatively easy. One main thoroughfare, the Mamalahoa Highway, more or less circles the island, with Queen Kaahumanu hugging the Kona and Kohala coasts. Ali'i Drive is Kona's main tourist strip, while Hilo is an easy grid-designed town. Saddle Road, the byway that slices through the island, is usually verboten in the car rental contract.

In Hilo, you'll find **taxis** in front of baggage claim, otherwise call:

A-1 BOB'S	(808) 959-4800
ABC TAXI	(808) 935-0755
ACE ONE	(808) 935-8303
HAWAII TAXI OR HILO HARRY'S	(808) 959-6359, (808) 935-7091

For Kona-based taxis, call

ALOHA TAXI	(808) 325-5448
KONA AIRPORT TAXI OR MARINA TAXI	(808) 329-7779, (808) 329-2481

Don't forget to consider "Hawaiian time" when booking, especially for flights. Approximate fare between airports and town is $10, Hilo; $20, Kona; $45, Waikoloa.

The county-operated **bus service**, Hele-On Bus (**www.hawaii-county.com/mass transit/transit main.htm** or *(808) 961-6722* or *(808) 935-8241)*, provides transportation Mondays through Saturdays to a number of Big Island areas, including a run between Hilo and Kailua-Kona (about $8, one way). The Ali'i Shuttle goes the length of Kona's Ali'i Drive about every 45 minutes. **Chauffeured limo service** is provided by Robert's *(808) 329-1688, Kona, or (808) 935-2858, Hilo* and Luana's *(808) 326-5466*.

Narrow or nonexistent shoulders on the roads, combined with tour-bus traffic, make the Big Island unfavorable for **mopeds** and **bicycles**. If you have your heart set on cycling, opt for a mountain bike. Rent mopeds and bicycles from **DJ's Rentals** *(808) 329-1700, Kailua-Kona)*. Other outlets for bicycle rentals include **Dave's Bike and Triathlon Shop** *(808) 329-4522, Kona,* **Hawaiian Pedals Unlimited** *(808) 329-2294, Kona,* **Island Cycle Rentals** *(808) 329-7585,* **Pacific United Rental** *(808) 935-2974, Hilo* or **Teo's Safaris** *(808) 982-5221, Keaau, south of Hilo*. Many of the rental agencies also lead guided cycling tours.

Visitor Information

Both airports have visitor information booths with brochures and helpful attendants. Otherwise call in to one of the **Hawaii Visitor**

Bureau offices: *75-5719 Alii Drive, Kailua-Kona 96740* (<u>www.hvcb.org</u> *(808) 329-7787)*, in Kona; or *250 Keawe Street (808) 961-5797*, in Hilo. For information **before you arrive**, write or call: **Destination Kona Coast** (*Box 2850, Kailua-Kona 96745, (808) 329-6748)*; **Destination Hilo** (*Box 1391, Hilo 96721, (808) 935-5294)*; or **Big Island Group** (*HCO 2, Box 5900, Kamuela 96743, (808) 885-5900 or (800) 648-2444.*)

Bird's-Eye View

The state's southernmost island is a comparatively humongous 4038 square miles (93 miles long and 76 miles wide), which is about twice the size of all the other Hawaiian islands put together, and the only island with active volcanoes. The two most prominent volcanoes are Kilauea—erupting continually since 1983—and Mauna Loa, the world's largest active volcano (last eruption 1984). The two entry ports are Kailua-Kona on the west coast and Hilo on the east coast. The sunny, dry Kona district is where most of the condos and resorts (and tourists) are located, as well as the coffee plantations, the spot where Captain Cook was killed, and a string of beaches. Hapuna Beach and some famed resorts (including Laurence Rockefeller's Mauna Kea Resort) are north of Kailua-Kona (the center of Kona) in South Kohala. North Kohala—the peninsula at the northern tip of the island—is an area of isolated beach parks, ancient *heiau*, the almost has-been sugar plantation town of Hawi, cattle ranch land, rolling hills, the powerful Pololu Valley, and the birthplace of King Kamehameha. The Hamakua coast—on the island's northeast shores—offers sugarcane fields, the Waimea cowboy town (center of the Parker Ranch), lush valleys, ancient burial grounds, taro plantations, a couple of small towns, and Akaka Falls State Park, with its stupendous 442-foot waterfall. Hawaii's most tropical town, Hilo, is also the island's main city, a rural delight surrounded by rainforests, plant life, heaps of orchids, and other flowers. You can access Saddle Road either at Hilo or Kona to cut across the island right between Mauna Loa and Mauna Kea, the Big Island's highest point at 13,796 feet. The Puna district, southeast of Hilo, contains most of Hawaii Volcanoes National Park, some absolutely amazing lava fields, scads of hiking trails, small villages, and the Chain of Craters Road—passage to Mauna Loa. The southern point of the island is mostly made up of the eerie Kau Desert, along with some state parks and dramatic beaches. Ka Lae, at the very tip, marks the most southern land in the United States.

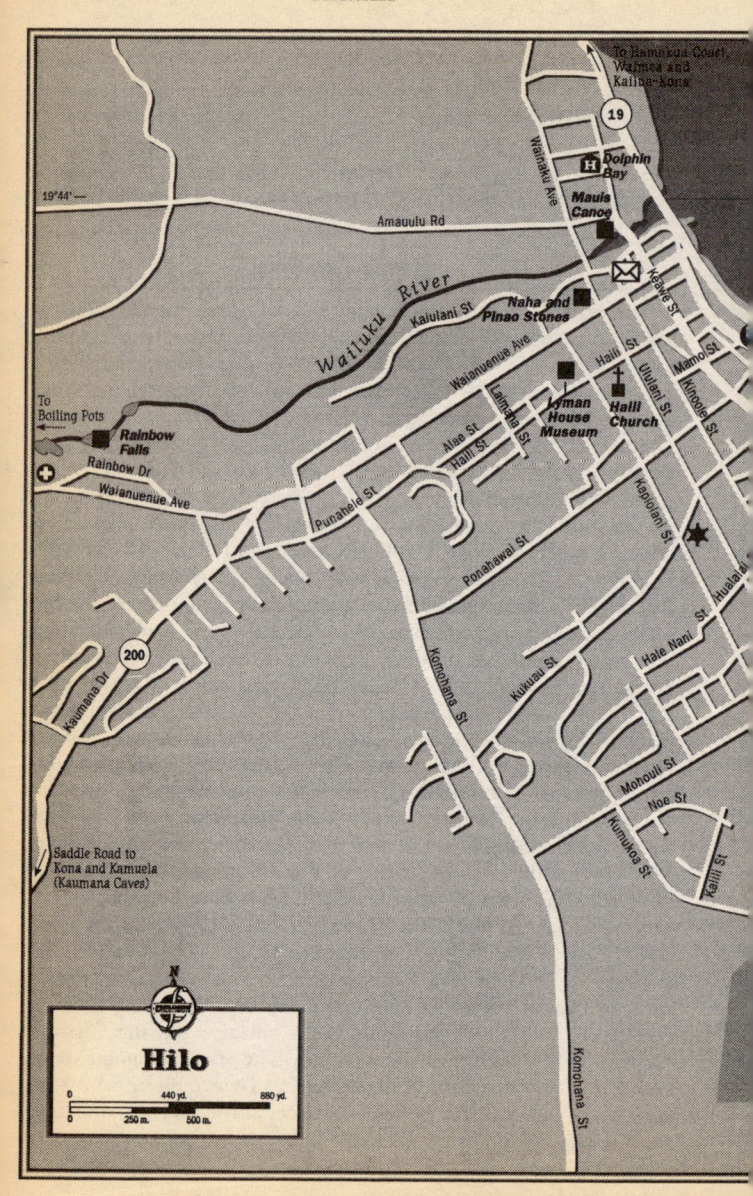

HAWAII

50

Hilo

- To Hamakua Court, Waimea and Kailua-kona
- 19
- Dolphin Bay
- Maui's Canoe
- Wainaku Ave
- 19°44'—
- Amauulu Rd
- Wailuku River
- Kaiulani St
- Naha and Pinao Stones
- Waianuenue Ave
- Keawe St
- Haili St
- Lyman House Museum
- Haili Church
- Ululani St
- Mamo St
- Kinoole St
- To Boiling Pots
- Rainbow Falls
- Rainbow Dr
- Waianuenue Ave
- Alae St
- Lanikaula St
- Punahele St
- Ponahawai St
- Kapiolani St
- Hualalai St
- Hale Nani St
- 200
- Kaumana Dr
- Komohana St
- Kukuau St
- Mohouli St
- Kumukoa St
- Noe St
- Kilili St
- Saddle Road to Kona and Kamuela (Kaumana Caves)
- Komohana St

N

0 440 yd. 880 yd.
0 250 m. 500 m.

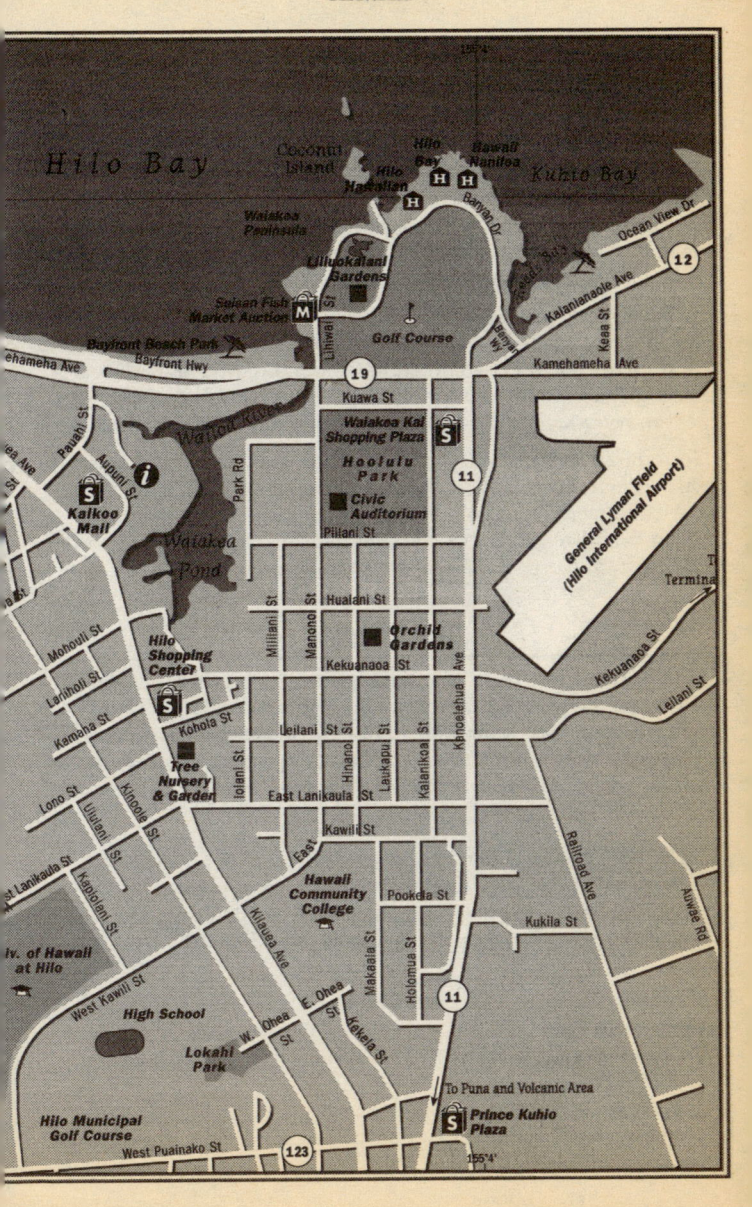

HAWAII

51

Nature Guide

Vast numbers of birds inhabit most areas of the Big Island. Commonly found forest birds include the *'oma'o* (Hawaiian thrush), *apapane, amakihi, akepa, palila, po'ouli and'i'iwi*. Endangered coastal birds are the *'a'o* (Newell shearwater) and *'ua'u* (Hawaiian petrel), both breeders on the higher elevations of the volcanoes. Other indigenous species that are growing scarce are the *nene* (the Hawaiian goose, and Hawaii's official state bird), *alala* (Hawaiian crow), and *'io* (Hawaiian hawk).

Lobelia and gesneriad species are prolific in the Big Island—both come in a vast array of sizes, shapes, and blossoms. *Panini* or prickly pear cactus is another common flora, found mostly in the North Kohala district. Many fern varieties as well as native koa and ohia trees can be sighted in the rainforests of Volcanoes National Park.

Introduced animals you might spot are feral cattle and sheep (both brought in by Captain Vancouver), feral donkeys, feral dogs, and Mediterranean mouflon sheep. Migrating humpback whales can be seen from late December through mid-March along the South Kona coast, in North Kohala, and off the Puna coast.

Beach Finder

Rumor has it that the Big Island is devoid of beaches. Not true. More to the point, the beaches (more than 80) are devoid of people. Take your pick from white-, black-, or green-sand stretches but—again—watch out for treacherous "rips," or riptides—ask locals for advice. The best beaches are up along the Kohala coast.

> **ITRAVELBOOK TIP:** The waters off Hawaii are stunning, but they are extremely dangerous: riptides abound. Ask for advice, look for lifeguarded beaches, and do NOT live dangerously: don't swim/surf/sail where you're told not to.

Kona Coast

Hookena Beach Park

About 25 miles south of Kailua-Kona, at the northern edge of Kauhako Bay.

Features dark gray sands and waters good for fishing, bodysurfing, and swimming. Picnic facilities, rest rooms, showers.

HAWAII

Honaunau Beach
Adjacent to the Puuhonau o Honaunau National Historical Park.
A top spot for scuba diving and snorkeling, as well as whale watching. Facilities are available at the park.

Napo'opo'o Beach Park
At Kealakekua Bay.
This was the last beach experience for Captain James Cook, who was slain here in 1779 (note the white obelisk memorial). The sand is black and the marine preserve is a great spot for scuba diving and snorkeling. Picnic facilities, basketball court, rest rooms, and showers.

Kahaluu Beach Park
Between Kailua-Kona and Keauhou.
Once frequented by King Kalakaua, this beach is popular with locals for swimming, snorkeling, and sunning. Watch the rips. Picnic area, showers, rest rooms, lifeguards, some parking.

White Sands Beach Park
In Kailua-Kona about a mile past the Kona Hilton.
A small area (often washed away in winter) with poor swimming and good board- and body-surfing. Lifeguards, showers, rest rooms.

Old Kona Airport State Park
At the end of Highway 11 north of Kailua-Kona.
Affords good surfing at the offshore break, tide pools for the kids, and swimming, snorkeling, and scuba diving for others. Rest rooms, showers.

Kona Coast Beach Park
Off Queen Ka'ahumanu Highway 19.
Where locals congregate for snorkeling, swimming, diving, and winter surfing. Picnic area, but no potable water or flush toilets.

Kohala Coast

Kiholo Bay
Along a four-wheel-drive track off Queen Ka'ahumanu Highway 19.

Draws nude sun-seekers to black-pebble beaches with fish ponds at either end. No facilities.

Anaehoomalu Beach

At the Royal Waikoloan Resort.
Ideal for most watersports, plus there are petroglyph fields and fish ponds nearby. Rest rooms, showers, equipment rental and instruction.

Holoholokai Beach Park

Off Queen Ka'ahumanu Highway 19, near the Ritz-Carlton.
A good surf and snorkel area with adjoining petroglyph park. No facilities.

Hapuna Beach

Off Queen Ka'ahumanu Highway 19, between the Mauna Lani and Mauna Kea Beach resorts.
Not only the best beach in Hawaii but—according to various esteemed sources—the best in the world. Sparkly white sands, shallow tidal pools, and steep cliffs, combined with ideal conditions (in summer) for swimming, surfing, snorkeling, etc., make it a top choice of both visitors and locals. Showers, rest rooms, snack bar, cabins for camping, parking lot, and crowds.

Kauna'oa Beach

At Mauna Kea Beach Resort.
Another beauty, but beware the high winter surf. Rest rooms, showers.

Samuel M. Spencer Beach Park

Near Kawaihae Harbor.
Offers family frolicking with its white sands and safe swimming. Showers, rest rooms, picnic and camping facilities, tennis courts.

Mahukona Beach Park

Near the Port of Mahukona.
Good for summer snorkeling and diving. Showers, rest rooms, camping area.

Hamakua Coast

Keokea Beach Park
Near the end of Highway 270 and Upolu Point.
Has a kid-friendly protected cove, green lawns, and black boulders, and very treacherous winter surf. Rest rooms, showers, picnic facilities, and a camping area.

Waipio Valley Beach
Off Highway 240, about eight miles from Honokaa.
Features nasty rips, but gorgeous viewing and picnicking. No facilities are available.

Hilo area

Reeds Bay Beach Park
Near central Hilo.
This is where the townsfolk head for calm waters and safe swimming. Showers, rest rooms.

Leleiwi Beach Park
South of downtown.
Good for a variety of watersports such as swimming, snorkeling, board- and bodysurfing, and net fishing. Picnic facilities, rest rooms, showers.

Onekahakaha Beach Park
A few miles south of Hilo.
Another safe spot with white sands and protected waters. Picnic facilities, lifeguards, showers, rest rooms.

Puna District

MacKenzie State Park
Off Highway 137.
A shady area with dangerous winter surf. Rest rooms, parking, camping area.

Puala' Park
Southeast of Pahoa.
Sports a newer beach with pond swimming. Picnic facilities, portable toilets.

Punaluu Beach Park

On Highway 11, about seven miles past Volcanoes National Park.
A lovely black-sand beach with nearby ancient ruins and fish ponds. Rest rooms.

Green Sand Beach (aka Papakolea Beach)

If you have a four-wheel-drive vehicle, head down to this beach and run your toes through green sand. No facilities, hazardous swimming, no protection from sun or wind. A good place for some peace and quiet, but no swimming?

Adventure Guide

Adventurers get to enjoy the true beauty of the Big Island's natural—and often otherwise inaccessible—attractions. **Hiking and camping** are especially superb, allowing close-up exploration of such sights as active volcanoes and Garden of Eden-like valleys.

In **Hawaii Volcanoes National Park**, the five-mile **Kilauea Iki Trail** leads you through the aftermath of volcanic eruption with not only views of the crater, but a cruise into the crater itself, past steam vents and through the **Thurston Lava Tube.** Other park trails take you to an astounding array of view points and—for those with health and stamina—up to the peak of 13,680-foot **Mauna Loa.**

> **TRAVELBOOK TIP:** Before embarking on any hike, check in at park headquarters to register your itinerary and inquire about conditions, a precaution that might very well save your life. Makes sure you are carrying sufficient water to prevent dehydration. Also, keep in mind your elevation level. If you experience any altitude problems, start descending at once. Altitude sickness manifests itself as: pounding headache, shortness of breath, dizziness, stomach upset, nervousness, or shakiness. For information and permits, contact Hawaii Volcanoes National Park (P.O. Box 52, Volcano 96718, (808) 967-7311).

An easy half-mile loop trail at **Akaka Falls State Park**, north of Hilo, lets you experience not only the 100-foot falls, but luscious rainforest and flora such as plumeria, ginger, and birds of paradise. Only diehards should attempt the **Muliwai Trail** into **Waimanu Valley**, about 10 hours **each way** into an almost-surreal beauty filled with exquisite valleys, waterfalls, views, and vegetation. Other trails will spirit you into the moonlike **Kau Desert**, or along remotest coastal regions.

The Big Island offers a huge range of **camping** opportunities. Choose everything from primitive sites to A-frame cabins, along the coast, or up a volcano. Campgrounds are administered by the national, state, and county parks, and require permits and reservations for overnight camping. For camping at Hawaii Volcanoes National Park, see address above. For information about state parks, contact the **Department of Land and Natural Resources** *(Division of State Parks, Box 936, Hilo 96720, (808) 961-7200);* for county parks, contact the **Department of Parks and Recreation** *(County of Hawaii, 25 Aupuni Street, Hilo 96720, (808) 961-8311).*

Superb visibility makes Big Island waters a joy for **scuba divers and snorkelers.** The Kona Coast affords calm waters, while advanced divers will probably want to drop down deep to explore some of the 60-plus miles of coral around the island. Top **dive sites** include **Red Hill**, south of the Kona Surf Hotel, with caverns, tubes, and lots of colorful tropical fish; **Plane Wreck Point**, off Keahole Point, which lets advanced divers get close to a wrecked Beechcraft covered with abundant dish such as fantails and damselfish; **Manta Ray Village**, off Kona Surf Hotel and Keauhou Bay, is your friendly manta-ray feeding ground; and **Aquarium**, in Kealakekua Bay, is a best bet for beginners who can explore in an underwater park filled with friendly fish.

Snorkeling is a year-round sport on the calm western shores with its abundance of marine life. Try **Hookena, Honaunau, Kealakekua, Kahaluu, White Sands, Old Airport, Hapuna** and **Spencer** beach parks and **Kona Coast State Park**. Various operators and dive shops will organize your scuba, snorkeling, and even "snuba" excursions, as well as provide equipment.

ITRAVELBOOK TIP: For those of you who'd like to try scuba diving but are leery of oxygen tanks, try SNUBA, which bridges the gap between scuba and snorkeling.

The Kona Coast is also ideal for year-round **ocean kayaking**. **Kailua** and **Kealakekua** bays are perfect for novices, though advanced types might want to try **Waipio Valley**. **Kailua Bay** is the departure point for soaring **parasailers** while **Anaehoomalu Bay** provides the setting for **wind surfers** with advanced wind surfers opting for **Puako** and **Hilo Bay**. Various **sailing excursions** depart from **Keauhou Bay, Honokohau Harbor, Waikoloa, Kawaihae Harbor,** and **Kailua Pier.**

The Big Island is not especially noteworthy for great **surfing**— the reefs can be dangerous and the surf uninspiring. Try **Wailua** and

Kealakekua bays, **Kahaluu, Lyman's,** and **Palm Trees** on the Kona Coast; **Hilo Bay Front Park, Keaukaha Beach Park,** and **Waipio Valley Beach** on the eastern shores.

What Else to See

The **Kona coast,** on the western side of the Big Island, is where most visitors congregate. Aside from the sunny skies and good beaches, the seaside town of **Kailua-Kona** offers requisite tourist delights such as restaurants, cocktail lounges, and a barrage of shops and boutiques—most of them centered along Alii Drive. Take a look inside **King Kamehameha's Kona Beach Hotel,** at Alii Drive and Palani Road. There's a shopping mall off the hotel lobby, as well as a small museum displaying Hawaiiana. You can take a tour of **Hulihee Palace** (behind the hotel), the restored 1838 home of Governor John Adams Kuakini and summer home of King David Kalakaua. Across from the palace, the 1836 **Mokualkaua Church** (also called the "Church of the Chimes") is Hawaii's oldest Christian church. **Kailua Pier,** across from the hotel, is the center of water activities and a great place to watch the returning fishing boats around sunset—or to sign up for an excursion on board the **Nautilus Semi-Submersible, Atlantis Submarine,** or one of the cruises. Pick up high-quality, local arts and crafts at **Kona Arts and Crafts Gallery,** across from the seawall. South of Hualalai Road, **Waterfront Row** houses various popular eateries, including the Chart House, Palm Café, and Under the Palm. Most afford spectacular views. **White Sands Beach,** off Alii Drive, is also known as "Disappearing Sands" beach, when late-autumn weather causes the sands to disappear. Nearby **Kahaluu Beach Park** stays put and offers protected swimming in its bay. **St. Peter's Catholic Church,** north of Kahaluu Beach, was built in 1889 and features a distinctive blue tin roof. Just north of Captain Cook, Napoopoo road leads to the **Captain Cook Monument,** where Cook was beaten to death in 1779. Continuing south, you'll reach **City of Refuge National Park,** near Honaunau, with ancient ruins and petroglyphs. At **Ka Lae,** down at the bottom of the island, you'll be positioned at the **southernmost point** in the United States.

Black lava marries glistening beaches up along the **Kohala Coast,** home to the island's very extravagant and expensive resorts. This is where you'll find—almost side by side—the one-more-fabulous-than-the-next mega-resorts such as Mauna Kea Beach Hotel, Ritz-Carlton Mauna Lani, Hilton Waikoloa Village, etc. You can take the inland route all the way up to **Hawi,** passing through some inspiring scenery that encompasses everything from lava fields to cattle ranches, or keep to the coastal (and resort) route. Stop for a tour of the **Natural Energy Lab of Hawaiian Authority,** near the Keahole-Kona Airport, or take a stroll at sunny **Wawaloli Beach Park.** Nearby **Kona Coast State Park** offers lava-field scenery, and **Anaehoomalu Bay** (near the royal Waikoloan) shelters ancient **royal fish ponds.** Near the Ritz-Carlton Mauna Lani, stop to explore the **Puako Petroglyph Archaeological Park** with its 400-year-old stone carvings. **Hapuna Beach State Park** is reputedly the most wonderful beach on the planet! In Mahukona, take a free tour of an ancient Hawaiian fishing village at **Lapakahi State Historical Park.** Rounding the Big Island's northern tip and heading down the **Hamakua Coast,** you'll find a statue of **Kamehameha the Great,** in front of the Kapauu Courthouse. At the end of Highway 270, in Makapala, don't miss the fabulous view from **Pololu Valley Lookout.** If you have the time, take the trail down to the black-sand beach.

In the ranching region of **Waimea,** you'll find "Parker Ranch" on just about every building. Find out all about these illustrious Parkers at the **Parker Ranch Visitor Center and Museum,** then do some shopping over at **Parker Square,** then visit the 1897 **Hale Kea,** home of a past Parker Ranch manager. Sick of the Parkers? The privately owned **Kamuela Museum** is filled with stimulating, offbeat memorabilia.

In **Hilo,** you'll find the tourist-oriented hotels over on **Banyan Drive,** planted with celebrity-planted banyan trees. Bask in garden glory at **Hilo Orchidarium,** on Manono Street, and **Liliuokalani Gardens,** at the end of Banyan Drive. More flowers, as well as fruit, produce, and locally made goods, are for sale at **Hilo Farmers Market,** at Kamehameha Avenue and Mamo Street. At **Wailuku River State Park,** catch the sunrise over **Rainbow Falls.** Or hit Saddle Road, and head up to **Mauna Kea.** Attractions south of town are **Nani Maui Gardens** and **Panaewa Rainforest Zoo.**

North of Hilo, the **Mamalahoa Highway** highlights local color as you cruise up the coast to sights such as **Hawaii Tropical Botanical Gardens, Akaka Falls State Park, Kolekole** and **Laupahoehoe** beach parks, **Macadamia Nut Plantation** and—finally—to **Waipio Valley,** just beyond Kukuihaele, where you can view exquisite natural beauty and ancient ruins.

Traveling down the island, south of Hilo, **Hawaii Volcanoes**

National Park—home of **Kilauea** (where the goddess Pele dwells) and **Mauna Loa** (the earth's largest mountain, when measured from the ocean floor)—will capture your attention. Continue south to run your toes in **Punaluu Black Sand Beach,** at Punaluu, and **Green Sand Beach,** on Mahana Bay. A few miles more and you're back at **Ka Lae,** that most southern point in the United States.

Hamakua Coast
Hiking and Camping

Kalopa State Recreation Area ★★★★
Five miles southeast of Honokaa, Hamakua Coast.
This recently renovated, scenic campground in a 100-acre native *ohia* forest preserve on the Hamakua Coast has reopened with improved camping and recreational facilities, more parking, handicapped-accessible pathways, and rest rooms. Three new campsites take up to four people each. Nature trails, including a circular trail through the koa and eucalyptus trees of Mauna Kea Forest, have been upgraded, and a new two-mile horseback-riding loop trail has been added. For camping permits, call the Division of State Parks at ☎ *(808) 933-4200.*

Honokaa
Beaches

Laupahoehoe Point Beach Park ★★★
Highway 19 on the Hamakua Coast, Honokaa.
The "point" here is a lava finger jutting out over a crashing sea with a designated county camping area that's wildly beautiful but windy. Laupahoehoe is perfect for fishing, picnicking, and woolgathering. Not so for swimming or snorkeling. A memorial at the ocean's edge was erected in memory of 20 children and their teachers killed in 1946 when a tsunami (tidal wave) destroyed their schoolhouse situated nearby. General admission: $1.

Horseback Riding Tours

Paniolo Riding Adventures ★★★
P.O. Box 363, Honokaa, 96727, ☎ *(808) 889-5354.*
www.hiohwy.com/p/panridad.htm
Paniolo Riding Adventures offers open range-riding on the 11,000-acre Ponoholo working cattle ranch in the Kohala Mountains. Depending on experience, riders can walk, trot, or

canter through lush pasturelands with breathtaking views. The company guarantees there will be "no mosquitoes." The 2.5-hour or four-hour rides include a 15-minute rest stop at the ruins of an ancient Hawaiian village or a native *ohia* grove. Bring your own snacks. Children must be eight years or older. Call for rates.

Waipi'o Na'alapa Trail Rides ★★★
P.O. Box 992, Honokaa, 96727, ☎ *(808) 775-0419.*
Experienced guides take riders on two-hour horseback rides through Waipio Valley, clip-clopping along waterfalls, jungle trails, taro patches, and historical, spiritual places. Trips at 9:30 a.m. and 1 p.m. Reservations must be made by 4:30 p.m. the day prior to trip. Cancellations can occur due to rain. No children under eight or riders over 250 pounds. General admission: $75.

Papaikou
Parks and Gardens

Hawaii Tropical Botanical Garden ★★★
Rural Route 143A, Papaikou, 96781, ☎ *(808) 964-5233.*
www.htbg.com.
The Hawaii Tropical Botanic Gardens is a 45-acre forest preserve at Onomea Bay, a former sugar port. Visitors walk on scenic paths marked by palms, heliconia, bromeliads, and fruit trees from around the world. A van shuttles visitors to the preserve every 20 minutes; purchase tickets at a converted yellow church seven miles north of Hilo. The coastal road to the church is well-marked.

Waipio Valley
Hiking

Waimanu Valley ★★★
Highway 19 from Honokaa to Route 240, Waipio Valley.
Rated as one of the three top hikes in Hawaii. Only for experienced hikers in good condition. Adjacent to Waipio Valley, it's a seven-hour hike (nine miles each way!) to this primeval valley. The trailhead starts from the Waipio Valley lookout pavilion and continues and continues and continues through lots of difficult switchbacks up 1200 feet to Waipio's northwest wall. The intrepid will be rewarded with the ultimate in seclusion.

Waipio Valley ★★★

10 miles north of Honokaa, on Highway 240, Waipio Valley.
Hiking, unofficial camping, and a broad, black-sand beach draw people to the historic, atmospheric Waipio Valley. The beach is the largest on the island, one mile wide and six miles long. Because of a stream entering the ocean here, you have a choice of fresh- or salt-water swimming. The beach has underwater boulders, and rip currents make ocean swimming dangerous, but fishing is great. The valley, reached by a narrow, steep, unpaved road, is subject to flooding and is accessible only to hikers or by those with four-wheel-drive vehicles. No facilities. Directions: Take Highway 19 north to Honokaa and pick up Route 240 to Waipio Valley State Park Lookout. If you don't want to drive or hike yourself, contact Waipio Valley Shuttle at ☎ *(808) 775-7121.*

Tours

Waipio Valley Wagon Tours ★★★

Waipio Valley Lookout, Highway 240, Waipio Valley,
☎ *(808) 775-9518.*
http://www.waipiovalleywagontours.com/
Tour Waipio Valley in a covered mule-drawn wagon. Your guide will inform you about the history of the area, where thousands of ancient Hawaiians lived, raising vast amounts of taro and other crops. This company claims that "cushioned seats, spring suspension designed by the Amish, combined with shock absorbers provided by GM, make for a fabulously smooth ride." Tours last 1.5 hours and leave at 9:30 and 11:30 a.m. and 1:30 and 3:30 p.m. daily. Meet at the Waipio Valley Lookout and be transported via four-wheel-drive vehicle to the valley. Reservations required. General admission: $40.

Hilo

Wailoa Center ★★

75 Aupuni Street, Hilo, 96720, ☎ *(808) 933-4360.*
Closed: Sunday.
Revolving exhibits of Big Island art are featured in the gallery of this state-run cultural center.

Beaches

Coconut Island Beach Park ★★

Hilo Bay, Hilo, 96720, ☎ *(808) 961-8311.*

HAWAII

Located over a bridge from Liliuokalani Gardens, Coconut Island Beach Park is a lovely setting for a family picnic or some low-key fishing. There's a diving tower and a naturally sheltered pool for kids. Parking lot and pavilion with rest rooms.

City Celebrations

Hilo Mardi Gras Festival ★★★★
c/o Main Street Program, 252 Kamehameha Avenue, Hilo, 96720, ☎ (808) 935-8850.

Hilo's Mardi Gras features a big parade with floats, crowning of a king and queen, music, bicycle and costume contests, ethnic food booths, and street fun held downtown every February. Each year a particular float stands out, such as one created by a local nursing home called "Heaven Can Wait." It all started as a neighborhood block party by New Orleans native Andre Oliver, the late owner of Roussel's restaurant, and local merchants. Unlike the Big Easy fete, this one is family-oriented, alcohol-free, and "generally" unrowdy.

Merrie Monarch Festival ★★★
Edith Kanakaole Auditorium, Hilo, ☎ (808) 935-9168.

An annual weeklong event, beginning on Easter Sunday, the festivities honor King David Kalakaua, a gifted musician who composed songs and created hulas. An impressive hula competition, which is the most prestigious in the state, is presented on the last three nights. Not surprisingly, the town is packed at this time. Call for prices and schedules of events.

ITRAVELBOOK FREEBIE

Suisan Fish Market and Auction ★★
85 Lihiwai Street, Hilo, 96720, ☎ (808) 935-9349.
Hours: 8 a.m.–early afternoon

Watch famous chefs and restaurant suppliers bid for the day's freshest catches, including marlin, tuna, and broadbill swordfish. Fishmarket for consumers next door.

Historical Sites

Palace Theater ★★★
Corner of Kamehameha Avenue and Haili Street, Hilo, ☎ (808) 935-8850.

This gracious art deco building, built in 1925, was the first deluxe playhouse on the Big Island. It was owned by Adam

Baker, son of the last royal governor of the island of Hawaii. The facade was restored in 1990, and at present work is continuing on the spacious interior, which includes an 800-seat auditorium. Ambitious plans are under way to use it as a movie theater and community performing arts center.

S. Hata Building ★★★
Furneaux Lane and Kamehameha Avenue, Hilo.
Now a shopping, office, and restaurant complex, this Renaissance revival building was constructed by the Hata family in 1912. Later confiscated by the U.S. government in World War II, it was returned to the family when one of the original owners' daughters bought it back from the government for $100,000 after the war.

Museums and Exhibits
Lyman Mission House and Museum ★★★
276 Haili Street, Hilo, 96720, ☎ *(808) 935-5021.*
<http://www.lymanmuseum.org>
Descendants of David and Sarah Lyman, Hilo's first Christian missionaries, converted this 1830s home into a museum. The handmade furniture, quilts, and other personal items evoke a sense of simplicity and self-sufficiency that is sorely lacking today. The house is on the National Register of Historic Places. Next door is a modern museum, opened in 1973, housing a valuable and extensive library of Hawaiiana and a worldwide collection of gems and minerals. General admission.

Parks and Gardens
Akaka Falls State Park ★★★
Highway 19, Hilo, 96720.
This well-maintained state park with a clearly marked trail encompasses 66 Eden-like acres, scented with wild ginger, tropical trees, plants, and flowers. The circular trail loops past two falls: Kahuna and Akaka. Akaka falls 420 feet into a mountain pool. It's an easy but sometimes slippery walk for the whole family. There's a paved parking lot and public rest rooms.

Nani Mau Gardens ★★
421 Makalika Street, one mile off Highway 11, Hilo, 96720,
☎ *(808) 959-3541.*
http://www.nanimau.com
This 20-acre botanical garden in the middle of a rainforest bursts with color and about 100 varieties of tropical fruit trees, and 2000 varieties of ginger, orchids, and anthuriums. A Hawaiian plant museum, ponds, and waterfalls can also be explored on self-guided tours, although guided tours are available by reservation. Restaurants, gift shops, and picnic pavilions. General admission.

Rainbow Falls and Boiling Pots ★★
Off Wainuenue Avenue on Rainbow Drive, outside Hilo.
The clearly marked trails to the falls are just a short distance out of Hilo. Best time for viewing the rainbows are on a clear morning when the sun shines on the water. If you turn left instead of right on the way to Rainbow Falls, drive to the lookout and see a remarkable series of pot-shaped depressions in the lava riverbed. When the river is high these "pots" seem to boil over with turbulent water. Absolutely no swimming.

The Shows

East Hawaii Cultural Center ★★★
141 Kalakaua Street, Hilo, 96721, ☎ *(808) 961-5711.*
Both an historical site and a cultural attraction, the East Hawaii Cultural Center, completed in 1932, is on the National Register of Historic Places. Resembling a Hawaiian *hale* (house) of the 1800s with a hipped roof, it served as headquarters for the Hilo County Police Department until 1975. Now home to Hilo Community Players, it's also an art gallery with regular exhibits by local and international artists. The Bard comes to Hilo in July when the HCP puts on "Shakespeare in the Park."

Tours

Mauna Loa Macadamia Nut Factory ★★★
Just outside Hilo off Highway 11, Hilo, 96720,
☎ *(808) 966-8612.*
http://www.hiohwy.com/m/malomnfa.htm
Learn how these delicious, fattening, and hard-to-crack nuts are grown, harvested, and processed. Best of all is the choco-

Ka'u

Naalehu
Beaches

Mahana Bay ★★
2.5 miles northeast of Kaulana Boat Ramp, Naalehu.
Three miles from the southernmost tip of the United States is this rare green-sand beach, made from crushed volcanic olivine crystals and lava. It's reached via a hot, three-mile hike from the nearest paved road. There's no fresh water or shade, and swimming can be treacherous because of a severe undertow. Yet it's a stunning, stark place to be alone. Directions: From Highway 11 (Hawaii Belt Road) take South Point Road. Near its end, take the left fork until the road becomes a rutted, dirt path. Use four-wheel-drive only, or walk 30–45 minutes.

Kona

Kailua-Kona
Beaches

Disappearing Sands Beach ★★★
Ali'i Drive, Kailua-Kona, 96740, ☎ (808) 961-8311.
So-called because the white-sand beach gets washed away in winter during periods of high surf, when all you will see is rocks. Good for swimming in summer months, intermediate bodysurfing. A lifeguard is on hand. Phones, showers, parking.

City Celebrations

Hawaiian International Billfish Tournament ★★★
Kailua-Kona, various locations, Kailua-Kona,
☎ (808) 329-6155.
http://www.konabillfish.com
Late July-early August. This is the world's premier international marlin fishing tournament. Expect plenty of revelry, back-slapping, and camera clicking as the big ones are weighed in direct from the boats.

Kona Coffee Cultural Festival ★★★★
Various locations, Kailua-Kona, ☎ (808) 326-7820.

This two-week fest honoring Kona and the Big Island's most popular crop runs from late October through early November. Events and happenings include agricultural exhibits, a recipe and coffee-picking contest, parade, food and craft booths, hula festival, and lively local entertainment.

ITRAVELBOOK FREEBIE
Hulihee Palace Concert Series ★★★
75-5718 Ali'i Drive, Kailua-Kona, 96720, ☎ *(808) 329-1877.*
Hawaiian music concerts are held on the grounds of the historic Hulihee Palace in Kailua-Kona every fourth Sunday of the month, except June and December. A favorite local event.

The Kona Brewing Company ★★
75-5629 Kuakini Highway, Kailua-Kona, 96740,
☎ *(808) 334-1133.*
Hours: 3–5 p.m.
Caffeine heads can chill out by taking a free 15-minute tour of the island's first microbrewery, located in the old West Hawaii Print Building. Afterward, purchase a six-pack or a case or more of the company's two handcrafted brewski varieties, Fire Rock Pale Ale or Pacific Golden Ale.

Historical Sites
Ahuena Heiau ★★★
At the end of Kailua Pier, Kailua-Kona.
This magnificently restored temple was the center of political power in the Hawaiian kingdom during Kamehameha the Great's heydey from 1812–1819. The king and his highest court advisers met here nightly; the monarch also died here on May 8, 1819. Shortly afterward, his son Liholiho (Kam II) abolished the ancient *kapu* system. The first Christian missionaries from New England were granted permission to come ashore here on April 4, 1820. Visitors are not permitted inside the temple.

Kaloko-Honokohau National Historic Park ★★★
73-4786 Kanalani Street, Building 14, Kailua-Kona, 96740,
☎ *(808) 329-6881.*
http://www.nps.gov/kaho/.
A settlement for Hawaiians until the 19th century, this 1300-acre park harbors more than 200 archaeological treasures,

including Hawaiian gravesites, fishing shrines, canoe landings, petroglyphs, *heiaus* (temples), and achiline ponds.

The Kona Inn Shopping Village ★★
75-5744 Ali'i Drive, Kailua-Kona, 96740.
http://www.hiohwy.com/k/koinshvi.htm
Once a low-key old Hawaiian-style resort, the Old Kona Inn was built in 1929 and has been gentrified into a shopping and restaurant complex. Aside from its preservation of the past, the hotel was built on the grounds of the personal *heiau* (temple) and living quarters of King Kam II. Some say the rocks of the *heiau* can be seen on the large oceanside lawn. The seawall here is one of the best picnic spots in town. Pop into the restaurant for fish displays that include mako shark and Pacific blue marlin.

Museums and Exhibits

Astronaut Ellison S. Onizuka Space Center ★★★
Keahole-Kona Airport, Kailua-Kona, 96745,
☎ *(808) 329-3441.*
http://www.planet-hawaii.com/astronautonizuka
Launch a 12-inch model of a space shuttle, fiddle with the interactive displays, or watch NASA space videos in this aerospace museum dedicated to Big Island native Ellison S. Onizuka, Hawaii's first astronaut, who died in the Challenger explosion. General admission.

Hulihee Palace ★★★
75-5718 Ali'i Drive, Kailua-Kona, 96740, ☎ *(808) 329-1874.*
http://www.daughtersofhawaii.org/hulihee/index.shtml
One of only three royal palaces in the United States, this two-story, modified Georgian style building was a vacation retreat for King Kalakaua and other royals until 1914 and is now a center of Hawaiian music, hula, and culture. Originally built for Gov. John Adams Kuakini in 1838, Hulihee Palace is constructed of native lava rock, coral, koa, and *ohia* timbers. It was restored in 1927 by the Daughters of Hawaii, who now operate it as a museum. An award-winning hula halau rehearses on the grounds many weekday afternoons. The Hulihee Palace Concert Series, a free outdoor Hawaiian music concert, is held on the fourth Sunday of the month (except June-December). General admission, with special rates for seniors and children.

Tours

Atlantis Submarines ★★★

Leaves from King Kamehameha's Kona Beach Hotel, Kailua-Kona, 96740, ☎ (808) 329-3175.
http://www.goatlantis.com/hawaii/default.htm

Explore Hawaii's thrilling underwater world without getting wet. This 80-ton sub is air-conditioned and features bench seating with 26-inch "viewports." The crew narrates the action during the 45-minute ride. Two expeditions are offered; the Expedition Adventure is a 100-foot dive with entertainment provided by a scuba team. This extended coastal cruise has views and narration of Kona's historic sites. A special, low-priced Discovery Adventure is of shorter duration, and seating is limited. Must be three feet tall to ride. General admission.

Benchmark Flight Center ★★★

Leaves from the Kona Airport, Kailua-Kona,
☎ *(808) 969-2000.*
http://planet-hawaii.com/above/bmoption.htm

If you always wanted to learn to fly but were too chicken or too cheap to get a license, try this "One Time" flight lesson offered by the Big Island's only FAA-certified flight school. The experienced pilots will run you through a preflight orientation in one of their four-passenger aircraft; once up in the air, you are handed the controls. The experience is guaranteed not to be boring: you'll be soaring above an active volcano, a pristine rainforest, or a plunging waterfall. At the conclusion, you get a flight logbook and a "Flight Adventure" certificate; time goes toward your private pilot's license. Your instructor will also critique your performance. Also offered are 45-minute to two-hour air tours from both Kona and Hilo. This company is permitted to fly at the lowest altitudes permitted by the FAA. The pilots claim a 100 percent accident-free record. General admission.

Classic Aviation Corporation Biplane Tours ★★★

P.O. Box 1899, Kailua-Kona, 96745, ☎ *(808) 329-8687.*
http://hoohana.aloha.net/biplane/

Go back to the golden era of aviation, dressed in a white-silk scarf and goggles while you take the stick for some light stunts (the pilot does the takeoffs and landings). Perform loops, rolls, figure eights, and more in an open-cockpit biplane and live to tell the grandkids. Or just take it easy, sit back, and fly over the Kona or Kohala Coast, the Volcano area. Classic Aviation also takes you over the luxury resorts. Ride lengths vary from 25 to 60 minutes, minimum two passengers. Reservations required. General admission.

Hawaii Forest and Trails ★★★★
P.O. Box 2975, Kailua-Kona, 96745, ☎ *(808) 322-8881.*
http://www.hawaii-forest.com/
Highly recommended. Renowned naturalist Rob Pacheco leads guided birding expeditions to remote wilderness locations on the Big Island, where the sheer number of native forest birds is astounding. Most tours are on private lands, where individuals have no access. Rates include transportation, continental breakfast, lunch, and gear. Higher rate is for a family or group rate, six maximum per party. Ask about overnight expeditions and rainforest tours. General admission.

Hawaiian Helicopters ★★★
Departs from Kona Airport, Kailua-Kona, ☎ *(808) 877-3900.*
These are no ordinary air tours. Passengers board luxury Astar touring helicopters that feature 180-degree views from all seats, a "total recall" video system, four independently mounted cameras, a CD-audio system and choreographed music. Everyone's "oohs and aahs" are recorded on video for a fond souvenir after each flight. Pickup is from Kona or Hilo Airport. Four tours are offered; the most expensive is the "Kona Island Special," which includes Hilo, the waterfalls along the Hamakua Coast, and Kilauea Crater's Pu'u O'o vent, where molten lava flows along its surface. Reservations required. General admission.

Kona Walking Tours ★★★
From the King Kam Hotel, Kailua-Kona, ☎ *(808) 232-2005.*
Educational tours are led by longtime local residents familiar with the culture, color, and history of Kona. The 1.5-hour tour begins on the grounds of the King Kam Hotel with its own archaeological sites, and restored *heiau*, and wanders through the Village along Alii Drive as far as Hale Halawai, ending on the grounds of the Hulihe'e Palace. The higher fee includes a tour of Hulihee Palace. Reservations can be made at the Historical Society from 8 a.m.–4 p.m., or at the Hulihe'e Palace

Gift Shop at 75-5718 Alii Drive from 9 a.m.–4 p.m. General admission.

Nautilus Semi-Submersibles ★★★
57-5663 Palani Road, across street from Kailua Pier, Kailua-Kona, ☎ *(808) 326-2003.*
This 58-foot boat, unlike the submarine that it resembles, doesn't submerge. It's also a lot less expensive than a sub, and no one has to fight for access to a large viewing window. Guests can also ride topside. The show consists of professional divers leaping into the water and coaxing the fish to come to them, and bringing them directly to the windows. The most-popular critters, especially with kids, are the octopi and spiny sea urchins. Seniors, $28.95; children, $24.95. Ages three and under, free. Leaves daily at 9:30, 10:30 and 11:30 a.m.; and 1:30 and 2:30 p.m. General admission: $39.95.

NavaTrek Explorer Captain Cook Cruise ★★★
Kailua-Kona Pier, Kailua-Kona, ☎ *(808) 326-2999.*
The NavaTrek *Explorer*, the largest American-made rigid inflatable boat, offers snorkeling tours of Kealakekua Bay and the Captain Cook monument, which can only be reached by sea. Operated by Royal Hawaiian cruises, the craft is staffed by a three-man crew and carries 49 passengers. Very comfortable for what it is, the boat features a shade canopy, rest room, and freshwater showers. Seating is on raised bleachers, backseat rails, or directly on the edge of the tube. It travels up to 30 knots and has great maneuverability. Passengers are picked up from various locations and transported to the reservation center near Kailua Pier for breakfast, followed by a four-hour snorkeling trip to Kealakekua Bay, with snorkel gear, lunch and return trip to hotels included. Admission for children ages four through 12 is $65. General admission: $85.

Paradise Safaris ★★★★
P.O. Box 9027, Kailua-Kona, 96745, ☎ *(808) 322-2366.*
Just before sunset, Pat Wright takes visitors on stargazing treks to the 13,796-foot summit outside the Mauna Kea Observatory via a four-wheel-drive wagon. There'll be ample time for photos before sunset transforms the area into an eerie, unearthly spectacle. After sunset, everyone moves to mid-

mountain, where the night sky is explored with a large portable telescope and giant binoculars. A welcome supper of hot soup and sandwiches will be provided, as the average temperature is 30 degrees Fahrenheit, with high wind conditions. Warm, hooded parkas are also thoughtfully supplied. Pregnant women, people with heart or lung conditions, scuba or snuba divers, and children under 13 are discouraged from taking the trip. No alcohol, please. General admission: $130.

Mauna Kea/Saddle Road

Mauna Kea State Park
Parks and Gardens

Mauna Kea State Park ★★★
Saddle Road, 33 miles out of Hilo, Mauna Kea State Park, ☎ (808) 961-7200.
There are seven cabins available at this park, which is 6500 feet above sea level. Bird-watchers love it. Contact the Department of Land and Natural Resources at ☎ *(808) 961-7200* for a permit. General admission.

ITRAVELBOOKS FREEBIE

Mauna Kea Observatory ★★★★
Saddle Road (Highway 200) to 9200 foot elevation, Mauna Kea State Park, ☎ (808) 961-2180. Hours vary. Closed on Tuesdays, Wednesdays, Thurdays.
Located 27 miles out of Hilo at the 9000-foot elevation of Mauna Kea Volcano, the Ellison Onizuka Visitors Center offers graphic displays of why the 13,796-foot summit of the mountain provides the finest conditions for astronomical research. Open Friday from 1 to 5 p.m.; Saturday and Sunday from 8 a.m. to noon, 1 to 2 p.m., and 4 to 5 p.m. The Observatory, which can be visited on Saturdays and Sundays, is one of the island's greatest free attractions, if you can get to it. Meet the guide at the Onizuka Center at 1:30 pm. Four-wheel-drive vehicles are required for trips to the summit. People with heart or lung conditions and pregnant women are discouraged from making the trek. For information, contact **Mauna Kea Support Services**, *177 Maka'ala Street, Hilo, Hawaii 96720.*

North Kohala
Kapa'au
Beaches

Keokea Beach Park ★★
On the way to Pololu Lookout from Kapa'au, Kapa'au.
On weekdays you may have this beach that's on the way to Pololu Valley Lookout all to yourself. Decidedly unflashy, it's still a nice place to go for a picnic, with tables facing the ocean. Plenty of facilities, including showers and a covered pavilion.

Pololu Valley Lookout ★★★★
At the end of Highway 270, Kapa'au.
This gorgeous vantage point overlooks a deserted valley that was once inhabited and lush with taro. It attracts fishermen and campers who want to be left alone. The hike to the valley and the black-sand beach takes about 15 minutes on a trail that can be slippery after recent rains. Not advisable for swimming, due to frequent riptides.

Historical Sites

Kalahikiola Congregational Church ★★★
Highway 270, Kapa'au.
This historic white stone church was built in 1855 by Protestant missionary the Rev. Elias Bond, who is credited with bringing Christianity to Hawaiians living in the Kohala District. Nearby is Bond's home, constructed between 1839 and 1889, where he and his wife and 10 children lived. You can visit the carriage house, carpenter shop, tack room, stable, chicken house, and washhouse. The estate also encompasses the old Kohala Girls' School, which Bond founded for native girls in 1874. It's now a ramshackle hotel that's on the National Historic Register.

Tours

Kohala Carriages, Ltd. ★★★
P.O. Box 1437, Kapa'au, 96755, ☎ (808) 889-5955.
Tour the back roads of North Kohala on a horse-drawn carriage. This low-key, romantic excursion ends with an outdoor picnic lunch in a secret spot. One- and 2.5-hour tours available. General admission: $15–$35.

Kawaihae
Historical Sites

Lapakahi State Historical Park ★★★
Highway 270, between Kawaihae and Mahukona, Kawaihae, 96743, ☎ (808) 889-5566.
Take a self-guided tour to an ancient Hawaiian fishing village, which flourished long before the arrival of Westerners. The spot was chosen because the coral beach was one of the few places along this coast where canoes could be brought ashore year-round. Among the most interesting sights is a small shrine where fishermen sacrificed part of their catch to the fishing god, Ku'ula. Even if you're not an archaeology buff, the walk on the hour-long trail is a very pleasant one.

Pu'ukohola Heiau National Historic Site ★★★
P.O. Box 4963, Kawaihae, 96743, ☎ (808) 882-7218.
http://www.nps.gov/puhe/
Located a few miles south of Kawaihae on the Kohala coast, this temple honoring the war god Kuka'ilimoku was rebuilt by Kamehameha the Great in 1791. Only the platform remains, but efforts are being made to preserve and restore the landmark. For two days in August, a cultural festival is held at the site, featuring Hawaiian food-tasting, arts and crafts workshops, ancient hula, and other cultural demonstrations.

Kohala Ranch
Tours

Kohala Naalapa Trail Rides ★★★
Kohala Ranch on Highway 270, Kohala Ranch,
☎ (808) 889-0022.
This scenic horseback ride meanders through historic Kahua and Kohala ranches. You'll pass cinder cones, ancient Hawaiian ruins, and lush pastures with sheep and cattle. No children under eight or riders over 250 pounds. Reservations 24 hours in advance. General admission: $65–$85.

Puna
Pahoa
Parks and Gardens

Lava Tree State Monument ★★★
Three miles down Route 132, Pahoa.

This ghostly state park was created after the 1790 eruption of Mauna Loa. Hot lava surrounded the fragile *ohia* trees that once stood here, leaving twisted, white molds that stand 12 feet high. You'll find a black-sand beach down a nearby lava rock trail. Turn your vehicle around about three miles back and explore Pahoa, a one-horse town with a raised wooden sidewalk and false-front shops.

Puna
Beaches

Cape Kumukahi ★★★★
Highway 132, Puna.

A dramatic drive down Highway 132 to the easternmost cape in the state. Highlights include a series of relatively new lava flows, each marked with a date. At the end of the highway is a lonely lighthouse, the only thing left standing after a 1960 lava flow decimated the village of Kapoho. Continue on highway 137 to Kaimu for a series of black-sand beaches. The first is Isaac Hale Beach Park, which is well-serviced and has good swimming. Mackenzie State Park is next, offering excellent fishing but dangerous swimming. Kehena is a small, fairly inaccessible black-sand beach popular with nudists. Connect to Highway 130 from Kaimu Beach, a lovely, wild picnic spot (forget about swimming), to what was once Kalapana, site of a housing development and much-missed beach, which was covered over by lava in 1983.

South Kohala

Kamuela
City Celebrations

Waimea Cherry Blossom Festival ★★
Church Row Park, Kamuela, ☎ *(808) 935-5068.*
Hours: 9 a.m.–2 p.m.

A lovely, low-key festival that takes place each February and March in Waimea-Kamuela, home of the Parker Ranch. It's known in these parts as "Hanami," which translates as "a viewing of the flowers of spring." Imported Formosan and Okinawan cherry trees bloom with light- and dark-pink blossoms at Church Row Park. Celebrations include Japanese tea ceremonies, ikebana demonstrations, and art and photo displays. Local specialties are prepared, including teriyaki, saimin, plate lunches and bento boxes, as well as mochi ice cream and manju (both made from azuki bean paste) for dessert.

Museums and Exhibits

Kamuela Museum ★★
Waimea-Kamuela Junction, Routes 19 & 250, Kamuela, 96743, ☎ (808) 885-4724.

Known for its collection of Hawaiian, European, and Oriental artifacts, including royal Hawaiian treasures from Iolani Palace, this is the largest private museum in the state. Take a guided tour with owners Albert and Harriet Solomon (she's a direct descendant of the founder of the Parker Ranch), who are experts in Hawaiiana. The view of the surrounding ranchlands from the building is also outstanding. General admission.

Parker Ranch Historic Homes ★★★★
Parker Ranch Shopping Center, Kamuela, 96743, ☎ (808) 885-5433.

Although Pu'u'opelu and Mana were both homes built in the mid-1800s by John Palmer Parker, founder of Parker ranch, they are two different structures. Mana (which means power), built of koa wood, is designed in a simple, New England-saltbox style, recalling Parker's Massachusetts origins. In contrast, Pu'u'opelo, an 8000-square-foot home with a sweeping lawn and flower gardens, was opulently furnished by Parker's great-great-grandson, Richard Smart, who sang and danced on Broadway stages. Smart lived up to his name and bought up a 100-plus-piece collection of fine French Impressionist art. The home, where Smart lived until he died in 1992, features works by Renoir, Utrillo, Chagall, Corot, Degas, and Dufy. In addition, there are originals by Maurice de Vlaminck, Henri Martin, Bonnard, and Picasso. Among the rare glasswares and porcelains are five Ming Dynasty pieces. Mana, which was formerly located on a slope of Mauna Loa, was moved next to Pu'u'opelu in 1987. General admission: $7.50.

Parker Ranch Visitor Center ★★★
Parker Ranch Shopping Center, Kamuela, 96743,
☎ (808) 885-7655.
Hours: 9 a.m.–5 p.m.

One of the largest ranches in the United States, the Parker Ranch grew over the years from two to more than 225,000 acres. Some 35 cowboys, or paniolos, are in charge of 60,000 head of cattle and 400 horses. Well-laid-out displays in glass cases trace the history of the Parker Family from founder John Palmer Parker, an ex-sailor turned land baron and son-in-law of King Kamehameha I, to his great-great grandson, the late Richard Palmer Smart, who appeared on Broadway stages. Artifacts include a rare Hawaiian-language Bible, photos of various Parkers, and an old tack room and saddlery dating from the late 1800s. General admission: $8.

The Shows

Kahilu Theatre ★★
P.O. Box 549, Kamuela, 96743, ☎ *(808) 885-6017.*
http://www.kahilutheatre.org/
An eclectic mix of entertainment is offered in a bucolic setting on Parker Ranch land. It was founded in part by Richard Palmer Smart. The repertoire runs the gamut from spiritual ensembles to symphony orchestras to brass quartets. Performers have included Die Musik, a chamber quintet, and the Peking Acrobats.

Tours

Hawaiian Walkways ★★★★
P.O. Box 2193, Kamuela, 96743, ☎ *(808) 885-7759.*
This well-established company specializes in custom hiking trips to volcanoes, rainforests, waterfalls, and ancient Hawaiian trails along the coast. Hikes range from easy to challenging, and from short day hikes to three-day, two-night camping trips or the 14-day, 150-mile treks across the entire island. These "Treks across Hawaii" combine walking with backpacking, mountain biking, and sea kayaking. Included are light packs, lunch (for day hikes), support equipment, filled water bottles, and shared camp equipment and food for multi-day trips. Groups are kept small, but a minimum of two is necessary. General admission: $120–$550.

Kohala Coast
Beaches

Hapuna Beach ★★★★
Highway 19, Kohala Coast, 96743, ☎ *(808) 882-7995.*
At 200 feet, this is the island's longest white-sand beach, except

in winter when some of that sand recedes. Families and children love it, but it's big enough that couples and loners can eke out a spot for themselves. Swimming, unfortunately, can be hazardous, and is extremely so in winter due to high surf and rip tides. There's no camping directly on this beach.

> **ITRAVELBOOK TIP:** If you're lucky, you can rent yourself some of the cheapest accommodations on the island, complete with ocean view, for just $15. Situated less than a mile above the beach are six cute but spartan A-frame cabins that sleep four each. Facilities include covered cooking pavilions, enclosed showers, and his-and-her rest rooms. For reservations, call or write to Hapuna Beach Services, P.O. Box 5397, Kailua-Kona, HI 96745; ☎ (808) 882-1095.

Spencer Beach Park ★★★★
Highway 19, past Hapuna Beach Park, Kohala Coast, 96743, ☎ (808) 882-7094.

Although not as famous or picture-perfect as Hapuna, its next-door neighbor, Spencer Beach Park is far safer, with a protected bay that assures fine swimming most of the year. The county-maintained facilities are superior, with barbecue grills, rest rooms that work, a volleyball net, basketball court, even tennis. The park is secured until closing, and there's a lifeguard. Kamehameha I's Pu'ukohola Heiau is a short walk away.

Waikoloa Beach Park/Anaehoomalu Bay ★★★★
Highway 19, Kohala Coast, 96738, ☎ (808) 885-6789.

Just south of Hapuna Beach and adjacent to the Royal Waikoloan Resort, this white-sand, half-moon-shaped beach stretches between ancient fishponds and the ocean. There's a calm lagoon that's usually safe for swimming when other beaches are not. Rest rooms, picnic facilities, and services provided by the hotel.

City Celebrations

Aloha Festivals ★★★★
Mauna Lani Bay Resort and various locations, Kohala Coast, ☎ (808) 326-7820.

For general description, see Aloha Festivals, "Molokai" chapter. The organizers of the Big Island events try to top themselves every year with such wild happenings as the Ms. "Big" Big

HAWAII

Island Contest, held at the Mauna Lani Bay Hotel on the Kohala Coast. To give you an idea, it's open to all *wahines* (women) weighing in at 200 pounds and up.

Winter Wine Escape ★★★
62-100 Kauna'oa Drive, Kohala Coast, 96743,
☎ *(808) 880-1111.*
Held at the Hapuna Beach Prince Hotel in November, this annual event includes food tastings, seminars showcasing the world's finest wines, and a Grand Finale wine reception spotlighting Big Island farmers, aquaculturists, and craftsmen. Meet and mingle with culinary and oenophilic celebrities. Hotel offers special room packages, some including golf. General admission: $50–$65.

ITRAVELBOOK FREEBIES

The Royal Waikoloan Historical Grounds Tour ★★
69-275 Waikoloa Beach Drive, Kohala Coast, 96743,
☎ *(808) 885-6789.*
Hours: 9 a.m. Tuesdays, Thursdays only
Tour the grounds of this 543-room hotel with Armstrong Yamamoto, a "living Hawaiian treasure." Yamamoto has extensive knowledge about many uses of endemic plants.

Historical Sites

Eva Parker Woods Cottage ★★★
One Mauna Lani Drive, Kohala Coast, 96743,
☎ *(808) 885-6622.*
Located on the grounds of the Mauna Lani Bay Hotel, this cottage houses several interesting displays, including fishhooks, ti-leaf raincoats, feather leis, and old photos of cattle shipments from Kawaihae. A free historical/ethnobotanical tour is also offered Tuesdays and Saturdays at 9 a.m. and Thursdays at 3:30 p.m. Along with Kaniela Akaka, the hotel's resident Hawaiian historian, you'll visit shelter caves, a canoe landing, petroglyphs, and natural fish feeding tour at the hotel on Tuesdays, Thursdays, and Saturdays at 10:30 a.m.

Tours

Petroglyph Tours ★★★
The King's Shops, P.O. Box 384330, Kohala Coast, 96738,

☎ *(808) 885-8811.*
More than 12,000 well-preserved petroglyphs are located at easily accessible fields on the Kohala Coast. A knowledgeable local guide takes visitors on 45- to 90-minute free walking tours through petroglyph fields along Anaeho'omalu Bay's Kings' Trail. Meet in front of the food pavilion at Kings' Shops, which is adjacent to the Royal Waikoloan Resort. You can also explore the Puako Petroglyph Archaeological Preserve at Mauna Lani Resort any day of the week on your own. This 1.25-mile walk affords "up close and personal" views of more than 3000 petroglyphs. Wear broken-in footwear, and take along sunscreen and water.

South Kona
Captain Cook
Museums and Exhibits

Kona Historical Society ★★★
P.O. Box 398, Captain Cook, 96704, ☎ *(808) 323-3222.*
http://www.konahistorical.org/
The Kona Historical Society's museum is housed in an old wood-and-stone store named after the Greenwell family, missionaries and ranchers who owned most of the land around Kealakekua from the 1850s to the early 1900s. When the museum was opened in 1985, the exhibits were original items sold in the store during its heyday. Today you'll see an antique bottle collection, photo displays, maps, and manuscripts that explain the history of the Kona area. Guided tours available. Free for children ages 11 and under. General admission.

Parks and Gardens

Amy B.H. Greenwell Ethnobotanical Garden ★★
82-6188 Mamalahoa Highway, Captain Cook, 96704,
☎ *(808) 323-3318.*
Special hours: hours may vary. Call for more information.
http://www.bishopmuseum.org/greenwell/
This agricultural research facility, an adjunct of the Bishop Museum, cultivates more than 250 rare crops that early Hawaiians used for food. New this year is an herbarium that consists of a mounted display of preserved Polynesian plants.

Five of the 10 acres have been set aside as an archaeological site. On the second Saturday of the month, a 90-minute tour is offered at 10 a.m. Plant sales held in March and September.

Holualoa
Tours

Capt. Dan McSweeney's Whale Watch ★★★★
P.O. Box 139, Holualoa, 96725, ☎ *(808) 322-0028.*
http://www.ilovewhales.com/

Captain Dan McSweeney is Kona's only whale scientist, who has spent more than 30,000 hours observing the magnificent mammals, photographing their antics for such publications as *National Geographic* and *Audubon*. His trips are different in that they're conducted year-round, except for a two-month summer break—he guarantees you'll see a whale or get your money back. Sightings are not limited to humpback whales, which only migrate to Hawaii in the winter months. Six other species are found off the Kona Coast, plus five types of dolphins. Two three-hour cruises leave daily in the winter from Dec. 20–April 30; from July 1–Dec. 19, tours leave three to five times a week. A live underwater camera records whales and dolphins playing around the stationary boat, and with the aid of a hydrophone, you'll hear the whales communicate with each other. Included in the price is a professional color guide to Hawaii's whales plus snacks and juices. General admission: $50.

Honaunau
Historical Sites

Pu'uhonua O Honaunau National Historic Park ★★★★★
Off Highway 11, Honaunau, ☎ *(808) 328-2288.*

This 181-acre, national historic site on the Kona Coast, about 20 miles south of Kailua-Kona, is the best-preserved example of a *pu'uhonua*, or city of refuge. *Kapu* (sacred law) breakers in ancient times had no recourse but to attempt to flee here or they face certain death. Eventually absolved by a *kahuna*, or priest, the wrongdoer could return to normal life.

Hookena
Beaches

Hookena Beach Park ★★★
Off Highway 11, adjacent to the City of Refuge, Hookena, 96704,

☎ *(808) 961-8311.*
The road to this beach is twisty, steep, and narrow, and the area around it is slightly seedy, but the sea here is benevolent, making for usually ideal snorkeling and swimming conditions. Facilities are sort of wild and uncared for, with no water and iffy toilets, but there are picnic tables. Tent camping is available with a county permit.

Kealakekua
The Shows
Aloha Performing Arts Center ★★★
Highway 11, Kealakekua, 96750, ☎ *(808) 322-9924.*
This remarkable old theater with a tin roof was built in the 1920s. Call for current schedule. General admission: Varies.

Tours
Captain Jack's Charters ★★
P.O. Box 1018, Kealakekua, 96750, ☎ *(800) 545-KONA.*
Daily deep-sea fishing charters in search of wahoo, marlin, tuna, and mahi are available on the *Notorious,* a 35-foot Bertram. Available on an exclusive or share-boat basis, full- or half-day. Novices as well as seasoned anglers and professionals are accommodated. The boat is also wheelchair-accessible. Captain Jack has 38 years in Kona waters and boasts that his record catch was five marlin in a single afternoon. Also overnighters for $1300. General admission: $85–$475.

Kings' Trail Rides O'Kona ★★★
P.O. Box 1366, Kealakekua, 96750.
http://www.interpac.net/~hit/ktr.html
Kings' Trail Rides O'Kona offers a 4.5-hour horseback ride and snorkeling combo. You'll ride a gentle horse down a mountain trail to the Captain Cook Monument in Kealakekua Bay, followed by snorkeling and a picnic lunch. Some riding experience is necessary. Wedding packages and custom camping/hiking /swimming adventures can be arranged. The meeting point is at the 111-mile marker on Highway 11 in Kealakekua, 15 minutes south of Kailua village. Reservations required. General admission: $125.

Keauhou
Beaches

Kahalu'u Beach ★★★
Ali'i Drive, next to the Keauhou Beach Hotel, Keauhou, 96739,
☎ *(808) 961-8311.*
A gray sand beach with shallow protected bay for excellent snorkeling, swimming, and boogie boarding. Facilities include a lifeguard, picnic facilities, showers, and phones. There's snorkel equipment rental and eateries nearby.

Volcano

Volcano Village
Hiking

Climb Mauna Loa–Sierra Club Outing Department ★★★
Hawaii Volcanoes National Park, Volcano Village, 96720,
☎ *(415) 923-5525.*
http://www.sierraclub.org
Adventurous travelers can make the difficult three- or four-day, 18-mile hike to the summit of Mauna Loa with an experienced Sierra Club outing leader. Also available for booking through the Sierra Club is a "Hidden Hawaii" outing with the John Muir Society, usually held in summer. The various adventures include hikes into rainforests and snorkeling with sea turtles and dolphins on the islands of Lanai and Maui. For information, contact the Sierra Club's Outing Department, 730 Polk Street, San Francisco, CA 94109.

Crater Rim Trail ★★★★
Hawaii Volcanoes National Park, Volcano Village, 96785,
☎ *(808) 967-7311.*
This loop trail begins at park headquarters and circles the summit caldera of Kilauea. An easy, 11-mile trail that's partly paved, it travels through cool rainforest and warm desert, all on the same day. Several other trails branch out from it, including Halemaumau Trail (see Hawaii Volcanoes National Park description). General admission: $10.

Mauna Loa Trail ★★
Hawaii Volcanoes National Park, Volcano Village, 96785,
☎ *(808) 967-7311.*
http://www.sierraclub.org

This strenuous trek starts at 6662 feet from its head, and takes two days to climb to the south rim of the Mokuaweoweo Caldera at 13,250 feet. Most hikers spend the night in a cabin with eight bunks at Red Hill (10,035 feet) and proceed to the summit shelter (12 bunks) on the second day. It takes another half-day to hike around the caldera to the true summit at 13,677 feet. Catchment water for drinking and pit toilets are located at each cabin—but if others have been there before you, and were greedy, there may be NO water at all, so be prepared. Even hardy hikers (no neophytes here, please) have experienced severe headaches and nausea upon reaching the summit. Try to walk on smooth lava; those with humps or ridges have been known to collapse, fragmenting into sharp pieces. For guided hikes contact the Sierra Club's Outing Department, *730 Polk Street, San Francisco, CA 94109,* ☎ *(415) 923-5525.* General admission: $5.

Museums and Exhibits

Thomas A. Jaggar Museum ★★★★
Hawaii Volcanoes National Park, P.O. Box 52, Volcano Village, 96718, ☎ *(808) 967-7643.*
This museum, at the Hawaiian Volcano Observatory, is perched on the rim of the Kilauea caldera, and naturally its focus is on volcanology . One of the finest museums in the finest national park in the world, the Jaggar gives out eruption and volcano information through seismograph machines that measure the Earth's movement. General admission.

Parks and Gardens

Akatsuka Orchid Gardens ★
Highway 11, north of Volcano Village, Volcano Village, 96785, ☎ *(808) 967-8234.*
http://www.islandsource.com/Botanical/Botanical1.htm
This six-acre covered garden features one of the largest orchid collections on the island. Cattleya, vanda, and other varieties can be shipped to the mainland. Also handicrafts and floral-related gifts.

Tours

Hawaii Volcanoes National Park ★★★★★
P.O. Box 52, Volcano Village, 96718, ☎ *(808) 967-7311.*

http://www.nps.gov/havo/

Some wags call this 229,000-acre national park a drive-in volcano. Hawaii Volcanoes National Park is the only park in the world where spectacular eruptions emanating from the perpetually active Kilauea volcano can be observed from its slopes. When that happens, the Chain of Craters road resembles rush hour at a well-known hamburger chain. What could also be said about the park is that its territory is constantly expanding—without benefit of permits.

At present, the park encompasses the southern and eastern flanks of Kilauea Volcano, the slopes of Mauna Loa, and the Kalapana coast. In 60,000 years, a new volcano, Loihi, now some 3,180 feet below sea level, located 30 miles southeast of the Big Island, will join her sisters. Of all the sights in the entire state, the park is one attraction that shouldn't be passed up. Besides the Earth-moving fire and lava show, there's an excellent museum of volcanology, an informative visitor center, an 11-mile circular loop around the Kilauea caldera (crater), hiking trails, camping, an art gallery, and even a hotel, Volcano House, perched right on the crater rim. The Kilauea Visitor Center presents a film of spectacular past volcanic eruptions, and entertaining, educational displays of plants, animals, and volcano lore. Check out the bulletin board for the latest volcanic activity and trail information. Adjacent is the **Volcano Art Center** ☎ *(808) 967-7643*, which features the work of Big Island craftsmen, photographers, woodcarvers, and artists. Thomas A. Jaggar Museum (see listing) overlooks Halemaumau, Kilauea's steaming firepit. If you only have a day at the park, drive the Crater Rim Drive loop road to see the summit caldera, sulfur banks, steam vents, pit craters, recent lava flows, and a "walk-thru" lava tube. If you've ever tried to imagine Dante's *Inferno*, don't miss the three-mile hike to **Halemaumau Crater,** Pele's legendary home—pungent sulphur fumes are emitted from the steaming cracks of the 3000-foot caldera. For those who have a week to spare, the park offers two drive-in campgrounds: Namakani Paio, three miles from the park entrance on Route 11; and Kipuka Nene, which is closed to campers from October to March due to nesting Nene geese. The former has free tent sites with eating shelters and fireplaces available on a first-come, first-served basis. It has flush toilets but no showers. Also, 10 housekeeping cabins sleeping four persons each are operated by the privately held Volcano House hotel. Fees are $35 a night and must be

Sports

Among the Big Island's claims to fame are its renowned **golf courses**—rolling green blankets in the midst of parched lava fields. Most famous are the Robert Trent Jones Sr. course at Mauna Kea Beach Hotel and the Robert Trent Jones Jr. course at Waikoloa Beach Resort. Other top courses are Mauna Lani Resort, Waikoloa Village, Kona Country Club, Makalei Hawaii Country Club, and Hapuna Golf Course. Low on bucks? Try Hilo Municipal Golf Course, Hamakua Country Club, or Discovery Harbor. **Tennis** buffs will find plenty of courts around the Big Island. For high-class play, the Keauhou-Kona resorts are primo—nonguests might want to try the many free school- and county-operated courts around the island.

The Kailua-Kona waters are internationally famous for big-game **fishing**. You'll find tuna, mahimahi, wahoo, and, of course, the highly prized marlin, which can be caught year-round. The **Hawaiian International Billfish Tournament**, the first part of each August, reels in anglers from all over the world. Hit the beaches, forests, valleys or ranch land via **horseback**. A variety of outfitters will guide you on escorted rides to scenic island sites—a ride down to the Captain Cook monument is one company's trademark excursion. Or how about **skiing?** Expert skiers should bring their own equipment, rent a four-wheel-drive vehicle (no ski lifts!), and head for the slopes of Mauna Kea. Came unprepared? **Ski Guides Hawaii** ☎ *(808) 885-4188)* will organize your outing.

Hilo

Hilo Municipal Golf Course ★★
340 Haihai Street, Hilo, 96720, ☎ *(808) 959-7711.*
Hours: 7 a.m.–5:30 p.m.
Popularly priced, this public course three miles from the Hilo airport was established in 1950. It has a nice, flat, wooded setting that might bore some hotshots. Cart rental: $14.50. Facilities include a pro shop, practice green, and driving range. General admission: $25.

Kona
Kailua-Kona

Eco-Adventures ★★★

75-5744 Ali'i Drive, Kailua-Kona, 96740, ☎ (808) 329-7116.
Offers diving adventures and instruction (from beginner to dive master) on board a 42-foot Seattle Delta dive vessel. Morning trips include lunch, beverages, tanks, weights, and guides. Highlights include "Manta Mania" night dives, in which participants are taken to sites where rays come right next to shore to feed on plankton, encouraged by divers' bright lights. Ocean kayaking, snorkeling, and custom fishing charters are available. The company also arranges hiking and bike/hike expeditions. General admission: $45–$1050.

Fair Wind ★★★★

78-7130 Kaleiopapa Street, Kailua-Kona, 96740,
☎ (808) 322-2788.
The Fair Wind II is a state-of-the-art 60-foot catamaran owned by kamaainas Puhi and Mendy Dent. The Dents and their crew like to impart a special "local style" family feeling to their snorkel and dive cruises to historic Kealakekua Bay. There are other cruises to this marine sanctuary accessible only by boat, but this one seems to draw lots of repeat customers. Two cruises depart daily from Keauhou Bay. The deluxe morning excursion lasts 4.5 hours, and includes a yummy breakfast with Kona coffee from the Dents' farm, plus a lunch of barbecued cheeseburgers or gardenburgers. The 3.5-hour afternoon cruise includes snacks; both offer a no-host bar. *The Fair Wind II* has a 15-foot water slide and a high-dive platform. All snorkeling gear, plus instruction if needed, is provided. Scuba (certified and intro) and snuba are optional. General admission: $44–$69.

Makalei Hawaii Country Club ★★

72-3890 Hawaii Belt Road, Kailua-Kona, 96740,
☎ (808) 325-6625.
Hours: 7 a.m.–6 p.m.
Sprawled within the slopes of Hualalai Mountain overlooking Kona, this country club offers unbeatable weather and spectacular golf over terrain ranging from 2100 to 2800 feet. Higher greens fees are for out-of-state players; lowest rates for Big Island residents; $45 for Hawaiian island residents. Cart fee

$25. Facilities include a restaurant and driving range. General admission: $45–$110.

UFO Parasail ★★

P.O. Box 5438, Kailua-Kona, 96745, ☎ *(808) 325-5836.*
Hours: 8 a.m.–4 p.m.

Leaves from Kailua Pier in downtown Kona. See UFO Parasail description in Maui chapter. General admission: $32.50–$48.

North Kohala
Kapa'au

Chris' Adventures ★★★

P.O. Box 869, Kula, HI 96790; Kapa'au, 96790,
☎ *(800) 224-5344.*
Hours: 8 a.m.–6 p.m.
Special hours: Saturdays 8-10 a.m. Closed Sundays.

Chris and his associates offer on- and off-road cycling, hiking, and snorkel adventures (or combos of the three) for small groups daily—morning or afternoon. The varied itineraries include a Kohala-Pololu Venture, in which participants bike "mostly downhill" to the coast, then hike the magnificent Pololu Valley and its black-sand beach. This tour is recommended for riders of all abilities. Tough dudes and dudettes can take the 50-mile "Mauna Loa Challenge" and bike 11,000 feet to sea level via challenging, seldom-traveled roads. The scenery changes from lava fields to lush ranchlands. For experienced riders only. Ask about "Inn-to-Inn" vacations, three- to eight-day biking and/or hiking trips for all levels, with options for the more advanced (or masochistic) participants. Included are all meals, transportation, equipment, lodging, and all extras; price ranges from $200–$275 per day. Call Chris' Adventures tour planner for details, dates, and trip itineraries. General admission: $110–$275.

South Kohala
Kamuela

Mauna Kea Mountain Bikes ★★

P.O. Box 44672, Kamuela, ☎ *(808) 885-2091.*

Choose from eight scenic but hard-core mountain biking and/or hiking trips, although beginners are welcome. Pedal and hoof it through rainforests or coast trails. Gourmet lunch or snacks provided. Front-suspension bikes and rentals available. General admission: $75 and up.

Mauna Kea Ski Corporation ★★★
P.O. Box 1954, Kamuela, 96743, ☎ *(808) 885-4188.*
http://www.skihawaii.com/

Lofty Mauna Kea, an extinct volcano and the world's tallest mountain, isn't called "White Mountain" (translated from the Hawaiian) for nothing. From late November through May, the 13,796-foot summit is usually covered with four to six feet of snow. Prime conditions are between the months of February and March. The world's highest cross-country ski race takes place up here in May, called "Pele's Cup." The area is not maintained for skiing, as its primary use is for observing the heavens. Only experienced skiers should tackle the slopes, as there are no lifts, lodges, or medical services. The Mauna Kea Ski Corporation, formerly called Ski Hawaii, is the only company to conduct guided ski tours. It also provides transportation to the summit by four-wheel-drive vehicle (which also doubles as a ski lodge), lunch, and portable toilets. Must be 14 years or older. Group tours are $150 per person (ski rental extra), or $250 for personal tours (includes equipment and clothing). General admission: $150–$250.

Kohala Coast

Francis H. I'i Brown Championship Course ★★★★
Mauna Lani Resort 68-150 Ho'ohana Street, Kohala Coast, 96743, ☎ *(808) 885-6655.*
Hours: 7 a.m.–6 p.m.

Composed of two courses, both of which look like they belong on an Irish moon. The dazzling, emerald-green fairways of the south course were built on rough lava from a relatively recent flow. This challenging course features ocean and mountain views. The famed 15th hole crosses crashing surf. The North Course, situated atop Pahoehoe lava (smoother and far older) is characterized by rolling terrain and thorny kiawe groves. Feral goats on the fairways present a hazard. Higher greens fees for nonguests, lower fees for guests of the Orchid at Mauna Lani and the Mauna Lani Bay Hotel. Facilities include on-course refreshment carts, bar and lounge, restaurant, pro shop, practice green, and two driving ranges. Lessons and shoe and club rentals. General admission: $80–$150.

Hapuna Golf Course ★★★★
62-100 Kaunaoa Drive, Kohala Coast, 96743,
☎ *(808) 880-3000.*
Hours: 7 a.m.–6 p.m.
Situated next to the Hapuna Beach Prince Hotel, this 18-hole championship links-style course, designed by Arnold Palmer and Ed Seay, was named the "most environmentally sensitive in the state" and "course of the future" by the USGA. Shared cart and tax included in greens fee, higher price is for nonguests. Pro shop, driving range, practice green, restaurant, spa. General admission: $80–$130.

Mauna Kea Golf Course ★★★★
62-100 Mauna Kea Beach Drive, Kohala Coast, 96743,
☎ *(808) 880-3480.*
Hours: 7 a.m.–6 p.m.
Designed by the venerable Robert Trent Jones Sr., Mauna Kea is one of his best courses and possibly the best in the nation. The third hole is considered to be the most difficult, with the ocean between you and the green. Rental cart included in the fee. Facilities include a restaurant, lounge, snack bar, locker room, pro shop, driving range, and practice green. General admission: $80–$130.

Waikoloa Village Golf Club ★★★★
P.O. Box 383910, Kohala Coast, 96738, ☎ *(808) 883-9621.*
Hours: 6:30 a.m.–6:30 p.m.
http://www.unclebilly.com/act14.htm
Established in 1972, this course, designed by Robert Trent Jones Jr., is situated on the slopes of the legendary Mauna Kea Mountain on Parker Ranch land. Rental cart included in greens fees. Facilities include a restaurant, lounge, snack bar, locker rooms, pro shop, driving range, practice green, pool, tennis. There are two other courses bearing the Waikoloa name; these cater to guests of the Hilton Waikoloa Village and Royal Waikoloan resorts, but off-property guests can play too. The Beach course, at *1020 Keana Place, Waikoloa,* ☎ *(808) 885-6060)* was also designed by Robert Trent Jones Jr., who incorporated petroglyph fields, historic fishing villages and, lava formations into the fairways of this par-71 course. Facilities: golf shop, driving range, practice green, restaurant, lounge. Tom

HAWAII

Weiskopf and Jay Morrish designed the 130-acre Kings' Course, at *600 Waikoloa Beach Drive,* ☎ *(808) 335-4647)* on natural lava terrain, with six lakes and 83 traps. It has a golf shop, and complete practice and golf-school facility. General admission: $70.

South Kona
Napoopoo

Kona Kayak Expedition ★★★
Napoopoo, Napoopoo, ☎ *(808) 329-6411.*
Hours: 7:30 a.m.–noon
Paddle across Kealakekua Bay to the famous Captain Cook monument, accessible only by water. You can hike around the monument or take a dip in the fresh-water Queen's Bath. Rate includes a naturalist guide, lunch, snorkel gear, and instruction. For more information, contact Royal Hawaiian Cruises, 2270 Kalakaua Avenue, Suite 708, Honolulu, HI 96815.

Volcano
Volcano Village

Volcano Golf and Country Club ★★
P.O. Box 46, Volcano National Park, Volcano Village, 96718, ☎ *(808) 967-7331.*
Hours: 7 a.m.–5 p.m.
Located in Pele's backyard, this par-72, Jack Snyder-designed course is 4000 feet above sea level. It combines modern facilities with historic character and magnificent natural surroundings. Rental cart included in greens fees. Pro shop, driving range, practice green, restaurant, lounge. General admission: $50.

Where to Stay

It's easy to find accommodations in a wide range of price brackets on the Big Island. Occupancy rate is relatively low, so crowds and overbooking are usually not a problem—except during certain festivals (April's Merrie Monarch Festival, for example). Most of the hotels and condos are spread around Kailua-Kona—the sunny part of the island. The **luxury resorts** are situated close to each other along the Kohala coast. Over on Hilo, there are about half as many rooms, but certainly a lot more rain. Or how about an A-frame cabin at Namakani Paio Campground, in Hawaii Volcanoes National Park?

HAWAII

A **bed-and-breakfast** overlooking Waipio Valley? A **campsite** on a black-sand beach?

Hamakua Coast

Honokaa
Bed-and-Breakfasts

Paauhau Plantation House $75–$140 ★★★
P.O. Box 1375, Honokaa, 96727, ☎ (808) 775-7222.
The Paauhau Plantation House could easily be mistaken for Robin Masters' estate on the "Magnum, P.I." TV series. Guests can mix their own drinks at the wet bar in the TV room, play billiards, or select a book from the library in the main house, which has 12-foot ceilings. The formal gardens are immaculately maintained and overlook the ocean. At 1200 feet above sea level, the house is perpetually cooled by ocean breezes. Honeymooners (or other romantics) will appreciate the peach-and-white bathroom with an ocean view in the master suite with its oval tub (large enough for two) surrounded by mirrors and candles. The suite has a fireplace, color TV, and a large private lanai. A continental breakfast is served at 8 a.m. or as requested. In addition to the main house, there are three cottages on the estate for families or those who wish additional privacy. The entire facility can be rented for seminars or meetings for $400 a day. One drawback is there's no laundry service, and the only phone is in the office. Maid service additional. Amenities: tennis. Six rooms. Credit cards: MC, V.

Waipio Wayside Bed and Breakfast Inn $65–$105 ★★★
P.O. Box 840, Honokaa, 96727, ☎ (800) 833-8849,
☎ (808) 775-0275.
http://www.stayhawaii.com/wayside/wayside.html
The Waipio Wayside Bed and Breakfast Inn was built in 1938 to house executives of a local sugar plantation, and the building has been meticulously restored and furnished to retain the character of that period. Household furnishings are an astute mix of wicker, Chinoiserie, lace, and contemporary artwork. The neat garden, surrounded by a picket fence and established plantings of palm trees, poincianna trees, hibiscus, and bananas, adds to the feeling of Hawaii before Pearl Harbor. Three guest rooms share baths and two have private baths. All rooms have windows that overlook adjacent sugar-cane fields and the

ocean. Several have private decks. If you're an avid reader, book the Library Room; it has a cozy reading nook where you can sit and browse through more than 400 volumes. Amenities: balcony or patio. Five rooms. Credit cards: not accepted.

Kukuihaele
Apartments

Waipio Valley Artworks Vacation Rentals $65–$90 ★★★
P.O. Box 5070, Kukuihaele, 96727, ☎ *(800) 492-4746,*
☎ *(808) 775-0958.*

Waipio Valley Artworks functions as a workshop/gallery/coffee house. An outlet for the work of more than 75 artisans, the majority of whom work in exotic woods, it also offers two comfortable, reasonably priced apartments in this desirable area. Located in a private home, the most expensive one is a two-bedroom, two-bath unit on the top floor. It has a huge lanai with a fantastic waterfall and valley/ocean views, and a complete kitchen with dishwasher and washer/dryer. The other apartment, on the ground floor, offers similar features, less one bedroom and one bath. Both have phones and color TVs. Units can be rented by the week or month. Amenities: balcony or patio. Two rooms. Credit cards: MC, V.

Inns

Hale Kukui $85–$175 ★★★
Box 5044, Kukuihaele, 96727, ☎ *(800) 775-7130,*
☎ *(808) 775-7130, FAX (800) 775-7130.*
http://www.halekukui.com/

The Hale Kukui guest cottage is a perfect destination for those of us who want to get close to nature. It's located in a pristine little postage stamp of a village called Kukuihaele, on bluffs overlooking Waipio Valley, which is only a mile away. It also looks out over the ocean, and on a clear day you can see Maui. Hale Kukui is a perfect base for hiking in the valley. The four-acre spread supports fascinating examples of local flora and fauna. Non-native animals include a Waipio pony and two dogs who never fail to ingratiate themselves with guests. Accommodations consist of one studio, one 2-bedroom, and one 3-bedroom unit. All have living areas, kitchenettes, private full baths, and lanais. The cottage is 150 feet from the hosts' property. Discounts of five percent are available for members of Greenpeace, the Sierra Club, and other national environmental organizations. Amenities: balcony or patio. Three rooms. Credit cards: MC, V.

Papaikou
Bed-and-Breakfasts

Our Place   **$55–$70**   ★★

P.O. Box 469, Papaikou, 96781, ☎ *(808) 964-5250.*

Our Place is a small, well-appointed bed-and-breakfast property with lots of cedar paneling and comfortable beds. Some rooms share baths. The master bedroom has a king-size bed and private bath, and decorating touches include a rolltop desk and a vintage wall clock. Our Place is four miles north of Hilo and six miles from Honomu, which makes it a good place to stay when visiting Akaka Falls. Children over 12 are welcome; no pets. There's a two-night minimum stay. Amenities: balcony or patio. Four rooms. Credit cards: not accepted.

Waipio Valley
Guest Houses

Waipio Treehouse Waterfall Retreat   **$175–$225**   ★★★

Waipio Valley, 96727, ☎ *(808) 775-7160.*

Not for the fainthearted. Guests are met at the Waipio Valley Lookout (cars are left in a secret parking area) and transported in a four-wheel-drive vehicle over "Hawaii's steepest road" to the retreat. Getting there is half the fun and involves fording five streams and a river. Sometimes you won't be able to leave when you want, as the place becomes inaccessible because of high river water. Each of the guest houses has a different feeling. The Waipio Treehouse, as indicated by its name, is located 30 feet up in a monkeypod tree. The Hale has a spectacular waterfall view from the sleeping area in the loft. Shower and toilet are outside. The Kahu is the most traditional of the guesthouses and has a living room, full kitchen, dining area, and loft with waterfall view. Guests must provide their own food. Amenities: Jacuzzi. Three rooms. Credit cards: not accepted.

Hilo
Hotels

Dolphin Bay Hotel   **$50–$85**   ★★

333 Ilahi Street, Hilo, 96720, ☎ *(808) 935-1466.*
http://www.dolphinbayhilo.com/

The Dolphin Bay Hotel is a more-than-adequate no-frills establishment. It doesn't have a pool or restaurant, but it's only three blocks away from Hilo Bay and management is happy to make recommendations. Because of its location in a residential area, parking is not a problem. Four types of rooms are available, including superior studios with large Roman tubs; these units sleep up to four people. All have kitchens, color TVs, and ceiling fans. The Dolphin Bay has a loyal clientele of repeat travelers who eschew glitzy resort living. Amenities: balcony or patio. 18 rooms.

Hawaii Naniloa Hotel   **$96–$144**   ★★★
93 Banyan Drive, Hilo, ☎ *(800) 442-5845,*
☎ *(808) 969-3333, FAX (808) 969-6622.*
http://www.naniloa.com/

The Hawaii Naniloa is Hilo's largest hotel, and may be the best in town—if you like plenty of on-site services, banquet rooms, and restaurants. It also has a spectacular pool area. If you have a choice of which wing to stay in, opt for the Waipio Wing; it has the best ocean views. Amenities: tennis, health club, Jacuzzi, balcony or patio, business services. 325 rooms. Credit cards: A, CB, DC, D, MC, V.

Hilo Bay Resort Hotel   **$77–$91**   ★★
87 Banyan Drive, Hilo, 96720, ☎ *(800) 367-5102,*
☎ *(808) 935-0861, FAX (808) 935-7903.*
http://www.unclebilly.com/hb.html

Operated by Uncle Billy's Resort Hotels, this is Uncle Billy's flagship location, and it's the kind of place they dream about in Lake Wobegon. The lobby sets the tone for the rest of the hotel—lots of dried grass skirts, tapa cloth, flowered material, and white wicker. The hotel is also wedged in between two behemoths on either side, and you may have to lean out the window to see the ocean from your room. Nevertheless, what the Hilo Bay Resort lacks in pizzazz it makes up for in an enthusiastic and friendly staff and good value. The restaurant is family-style buffet, and the free Hula Show is one of the great bargains of Hawaii. (Some of the dancers may be on the mature side, but they look like they're enjoying what they're doing!) All rooms have color TVs, fridge, and private lanais. Some "condo-style" rooms have kitchenettes. Oceanfront swimming pool. Amenities: balcony or patio, family plan. 150 rooms. Credit cards: A, D, MC, V.

Hilo Hawaiian Hotel $99–$315   ★★★
71 Banyan Drive, Hilo, 96720, ☎ (800) 367-5004, ☎ (808) 935-9361, FAX (808) 961-9642.
<http://www.castleresorts.com/HHH>

Renovated in 1992, the Hilo Hawaiian is a vintage 1970s hotel that has done its best to catch up. Some of the rooms have spectacular views over a lagoon, and glass louvers that you can open to let in fresh air. The Wai'oli lounge features nightly entertainment. All rooms are air-conditioned and feature refrigerators, color TVs, coffee makers, and radios. Suites have kitchenettes. On-site services include a banquet facility for 450, laundry room, gift shop, beauty salon, massage, and wake-up service. Golf across from the hotel, nearby tennis courts, two miles to the beach. Amenities: balcony or patio, business services. 283 rooms. Credit cards: A, D, MC, V.

Ka'u

Naalehu
Bed-and-Breakfasts

Becky's Bed and Breakfast $50–$65   ★★
P.O. Box 673, Naalehu, 96772, 64 miles from Hilo, 56 miles from Kona on Highway 11, ☎ (800) 235-1233, ☎ (808) 929-9690, FAX (808) 929-9690.

Becky's is a cheerful green-and-white plantation house that was built before World War II. The front porch is crowded with potted plants, and a hot tub takes pride of place on the back. All rooms are simply furnished and have private baths. Breakfast is an all-you-can-eat affair, but it's served from 6:30-8 a.m., so if you want to eat, you can't sleep in. The village of Naalehu is located on the southern edge of the island, roughly halfway between Hilo and Kona. Sea Mountain, Discovery Harbor, and Volcano golf courses are within easy reach of Naalehu, but a car is a necessity. This place isn't fancy, but there are good reasons to spend a couple of days here. There's a 25 percent discount on stays of four days or longer with prior reservation. Amenities: Jacuzzi. Three rooms. Credit cards: not accepted.

Condos

Colony One at Sea Mountain Condominiums $100–$200   ★★★
Highway 11, 28 miles from Volcanoes National Park, Naalehu, 96777, ☎ (800) 525-5894, ☎ (808) 326-2252.

Colony One at Sea Mountain is a modern condo development overlooking a golf course and the ocean. The unusually attractive units are constructed of wood and local stone. The main attraction for many visitors to this area is golf, and even those who are lukewarm toward the game will be impressed with the par-72 Arthur Jack Snyder golf course. Every hole has a spectacular ocean or mountain view. Hiking trails along the coast lead to hidden coves with black-sand beaches. Sea turtles often feed here, and adjacent tidal pools present a wealth of marine life for the interested observer. Restaurant, conference center. Amenities: tennis, Jacuzzi, sauna, balcony or patio, business services. 76 rooms.

Kona

Kailua-Kona
Bed-and-Breakfasts

Kailua Plantation House   **$145–$205**   ★★★★

75-48 Ali'i Drive, Kailua-Kona, 96740, ☎ *(808) 329-3727.*
Kailua Plantation House will appeal to the sybarite in all of us. Guest rooms have been meticulously appointed, many with queen-size canopy beds and ceiling fans; all have private lanais. The top-of-the-line rooms, Pilialoha and Kai o Lani, feature luxurious platform tubs and glass-enclosed showers with ocean views. After a long day of exploring, the perfect nightcap is a moonlight dip in the oceanfront spa and triangular-shaped dipping pool. No children under 12 accepted. Amenities: Jacuzzi, balcony or patio. Five rooms. Credit cards: A, MC, V.

Kiwi Gardens   **$50–$80**   ★★

74-4920 Kiwi Street, Kailua-Kona, 96740, ☎ *(808) 326-1559, FAX (808) 329-6618.*
http://www.kiwigardens.com
More than 100 exotic fruit-bearing trees and bushes dot the one-acre estate located just a few minutes from the Kona airport and a short drive from the town of Kailua-Kona. One of the most enjoyable features of staying at the Kiwi Gardens is watching the tropical birds in the garden. Some are caged, but many more are free-flying. The house, built in an art deco style, is impeccably maintained, and the 800-foot elevation assures cooler temperatures and breezes. There are two standard rooms and a master suite within the house, with two lanais. A Hawaiian-style guest cottage has a queen bed, and from its

lanai there's an outstanding sunset view over the ocean. Breakfast is included in the room charge, and consists of freshly baked breads every morning, plus fruit picked in the gardens. Amenities: balcony or patio. Four rooms. Credit cards: not accepted.

Three Bears' Bed and Breakfast $65–$75   ★★★
72-1001 Puukala Street, Kailua-Kona, 96740,
☎ *(800) 765-0480,* ☎ *(808) 325-7653.*

A visit to Three Bears' Bed and Breakfast is like staying in a private home. A large common area opens out onto a covered terrace, which overlooks the lush gardens surrounding the house. Both guest rooms have private baths, color TVs, coffeemakers, microwaves, and a small fridge. Full kitchen privileges are available for longer stays. A superior breakfast is provided, much of which is produced on the premises. Papayas, pineapples, and lilikoi from the garden are frequently served, as well as coffee from its own coffee farm. Beach gear provided free to guests. German spoken. Amenities: Jacuzzi, balcony or patio. Two rooms. Credit cards: not accepted.

Condos

Aston Royal Sea Cliff Resort $125–$400   ★★★
75-6040 Ali'i Drive, Kailua-Kona, ☎ *(800) 922-7866,*
☎ *(808) 359-8021, FAX (808) 326-1897.*

This meandering, terraced condominium property overlooks a dramatic, rocky stretch of ocean, but has no beach. The apartments, furnished in wicker and rattan, are BIG, especially the lanais; many have great views. One- and two-bedroom suites have kitchens with microwaves, while lower-priced studios only have fridges, and you'll have to drive a bit to get to a restaurant. Other amenities include an iron and ironing board, washer-dryer, in-room safe and voice mail. Large seawater pool, smaller freshwater pool, barbecue. Free parking, maid service. Amenities: tennis, Jacuzzi, sauna, balcony or patio. 146 rooms. Credit cards: MC, V.

Colony Kona Bali Kai $88–$200   ★★★
76-6246 Ali'i Drive, Kailua-Kona, 96740, ☎ *(800) 777-1700,*
☎ *(808) 329-9381, FAX (808) 326-6056.*

This four-story Colony condominium property overlooks a lava rock beach. Units consist of studio or one- or two-bedroom apartments with fully equipped kitchens, private lanais, and color TVs. Not all rooms are air-conditioned, but all have louvers that can be opened to let in the sea breezes. Nearby attractions include golf courses, deep-sea fishing, snorkeling, scuba diving, tennis, horseback riding, and shopping at the Kona Inn Shopping Center. If you tire of cooking, restaurants of all types and in all price ranges can be found nearby. Pool on premises. Amenities: Jacuzzi, balcony or patio. Credit cards: A, CB, DC, D, MC, V.

Hale Kona Kai — $75–$85 ★

75-5870 Kahakai Road, Kailua-Kona, 96740,
☎ *(800) 421-3696,* ☎ *(808) 329-2155.*

The Hale Kona Kai is ideal for long-term travelers. All the one-bedroom apartments in this three-story building have some kind of ocean view and are equipped with full kitchens and color TVs. On those nights (or days) when cooking lacks appeal, guests can walk next door to the Royal Kona Resort with its restaurants and coffee shops, or walk to Kailua Town and choose from a number of interesting dining establishments. Nearby activities include deep-sea fishing, horseback riding, snorkeling, hiking, golf (five miles from the Keauhou Golf Course), sailing, and hunting. Pool, laundry facilities. Maid service on request. No Sunday or holiday check-in. Amenities: balcony or patio. 39 rooms. Credit cards: not accepted.

Keauhou Resort — $90–$135 ★★★

78-7039 Kam III Road, Kailua-Kona, 96740,
☎ *(800) 367-5286,* ☎ *(808) 322-9122, FAX (808) 322-9410.*

A one and two-level condominium townhouse development that caters to travelers who want to spend an extended period of time in the islands. Almost all have an ocean view, and all have at least one covered lanai. Amenities include full kitchens with microwave, dishwasher and fridge with ice-maker, washer-dryer and cable TV. Two championship golf courses are within walking distance (reduced rates on green fees offered) and two pools, shaded by coconut palms, are available for the enjoyment of those who would rather stay at home. Nearby attractions include snorkeling and/or scuba diving, deep-sea fishing, ancient Hawaiian temples, and shopping in the nearby town of Kailua-Kona with its boutiques, open-air cafés, and historic buildings. A resident manager is on hand to solve any problems and give good advice as to what to do, where to go, and how to get there. Amenities: balcony or patio. 48 rooms. Credit cards: not accepted.

White Sands Village $100–$150 ★★
P.O. Box 4466, Kailua-Kona, 96745, ☎ (808) 329-6402, FAX (808) 326-2401.
http://www.konahawaii.com/wsv.htm
White Sands Village is another good choice for families and travelers who want to stay in one place for a while. The two-bedroom, two-bath apartments in several low-rise buildings feature fully equipped kitchens and washer-dryers. The village has an attractive pool area with lush plantings and is across the street from a namesake white-sand beach. Adjacent to the pool is a game room with a pool table and gas-fired barbecue. Plan on renting a car, though, as it's four miles from Kailua. Amenities: tennis, Jacuzzi, sauna, balcony or patio. 10 rooms. Credit cards: A, MC, V.

Hotels

Keauhou Beach Hotel $98–$415 ★★★★
78-6740 Ali'i Drive, Kailua-Kona, 96740, ☎ (800) 367-6025, ☎ (808) 322-3441, FAX (808) 322-6586.
http://www.ohanahotels.com/details/property.asp?h_id=50
The Keauhou Beach Hotel is a resort that's manageable. There's plenty to do, but not so much that you feel guilty if you just relax and sit in one place. Tennis courts are located on the grounds, and a free shuttle takes guests to the nearby Kona Country Club, where they can play on a world-famous 27-hole golf course. The hotel is right on the beach, with access to Kahalu'u Beach Park from the gardens. On weekends, the seafood buffets are reputed to be the best on the island. Even locals eat here. Depending on the availability of local talent, there's usually a good musical show on weekends. Amenities: tennis, balcony or patio. 318 rooms. Credit cards: A, DC, D, MC, V.

King Kamehameha's Kona Beach Hotel $100–$500 ★★★★
75-5660 Palani Road, Kailua-Kona, 96740,

☎ *(800) 367-6060,* ☎ *(808) 923-4511, FAX (808) 922-8061.*
http://www.konabeachhotel.com/
This old-timer on the Kona Coast is practically self-contained. With a minimum of effort, guests can enjoy golf, tennis, twilight outrigger canoe rides, a stroll in the tropical gardens, a visit to an active volcano, and shopping in 28 boutiques and specialty stores. Luaus on the beach are offered four times a week. Guest rooms are spacious, and attractive wooden-louvered doors lead onto private lanais with either ocean or garden views. Amenities include refrigerators, safes, and color TVs with movies. The King Kam is one of the only hotels to boast a national treasure on its grounds—the faithfully restored *Ahu'ena Heiau* (see "Historical Sights"). Amenities: tennis, Jacuzzi, balcony or patio, business services. 460 rooms. Credit cards: A, MC, V.

Kona Bay Hotel $77–$91 ★★
75-5739 Ali'i Drive, Kailua-Kona, ☎ *(800) 367-5102,*
☎ *(808) 329-1393, FAX (808) 935-7903.*
http://www.unclebilly.com/
Take your cue from the fact that this hotel is operated under the name Uncle Billy's Hawaiian Family Hotels. This generic, budget, Polynesian-style property is sort of like going to visit your Uncle Billy, who's laid-back, awfully nice, and not terribly hip. It's located right in downtown Kailua and a shopping center now separates it from the beach. Rooms tend to be small and renovations seem to be limited to slapping another coat of paint on the aging rattan furniture. But all rooms are air-conditioned and contain private lanais, refrigerators, and color TVs. Bar, pool, children's pool. Amenities: Jacuzzi, balcony or patio, family plan. 123 rooms. Credit cards: A, DC, D, MC, V.

Kona Tiki Hotel $59–$65 ★★
75-5068 Ali'i Drive, Kailua-Kona, 96740, ☎ *(808) 329-1425, FAX (808) 327-9402.*
The Kona Tiki is a no-frills operation with an enviable location in a palm grove right on the (rocky) oceanfront. It's also close to golf courses and Kailua shopping and restaurants. The downside is that the rooms are small, yet they all face the ocean and have private lanais. No TVs or phones. A good place to use as a base of operations for exploring the Kona coast. The man-

agement will be happy to arrange deep-sea fishing trips or boat cruises. Amenities: balcony or patio. 15 rooms. Credit cards: not accepted.

Royal Kona Resort — $195–$1500 ★★★★
75-5852 Ali'i Drive, Kailua-Kona, 96740,
☎ *(800) 44R-OYAL,* ☎ *(808) 329-3111, FAX (808) 661-6150.*
http://www.rkona.com

Your typical "Polynesian" resort, the Royal Kona boasts a private lagoon and a two-level swimming pool overlooking the ocean. Most of the rooms have at least a partial ocean view, and sunset from your own balcony is an unforgettable experience. Food in the Tropics Café is good, and the bartenders in the Windjammer Lounge are especially creative—almost every evening there's a new cocktail to try. Tihati's "Drums of Polynesia" luau is the only oceanfront luau on the Kona Coast. It's a little bit touristy, but a lot of fun. Amenities: tennis, Jacuzzi, balcony or patio, business services. 454 rooms. Credit cards: A, D, MC, V.

Resorts

Kona Surf Resort — $125–$700 ★★★★
78-128 Ehukai Street, Kailua-Kona, 96740,
☎ *(800) 367-8011,* ☎ *(808) 322-3411.*

The Kona Surf Resort and Country Club enjoys a spectacular setting on an ancient lava flow at the entrance to Keauhou Bay. The design of the hotel is stark and modern in the extreme, in dramatic contrast to the lush tropical surroundings. All rooms have views—either of the gardens, the ocean, or both. The oceanfront suites, with their view of the lava cliffs and pounding waves, are especially impressive. All rooms have private lanais, mini-fridges, and private dressing areas. Golfers are invited to play on Kona Country Club courses next door—36 challenging holes between volcanic mountains and the Pacific. Dress is casual. Lighter meals and tropical drinks are served at the poolside Nalu Terrace. Karaoke sing-alongs are a nightly happening at the Puka Bar. A variety of watersports can be arranged. Volleyball, shuffleboard, botanical gardens, wedding chapel, meeting facilities. Amenities: tennis, balcony or patio, business services. 530 rooms. Credit cards: A, CB, DC, D, MC, V.

North Kohala
Kapa'au
Guest House

Hawi Farms Guest House   **$85–$125**   ★★

P.O. Box 640, Kapa'au, 96777, ☎ *(800) 889-0680,*
☎ *(808) 889-0007.*

Hawi Farms Guest House is the place to get away from it all. Located in the hill country of North Kohala, it's 30 minutes from the Parker Ranch and 20 miles from beaches that offer surfing, deep-sea fishing, and snorkeling. In other words, you can get there if you want to, but you'll probably prefer to sit on the guest house lanai and enjoy the scenery and sunsets. Closer to home are the back-to-back towns of Hawi and Kapaau, which up to now have been overlooked by tourists, though they're slowly becoming gentrified. There are several interesting art galleries, restaurants (including the excellent Bamboo), an ice cream shop, and a handful of worthwhile historical sites. Amenities: balcony or patio. One room.

North Kona
Resorts

Four Seasons Resort Hawaii at Hualalai   **$400–$1200**   ★★★★★

8 Queen Kaahumanu Highway, North Kona,
☎ *(800) 332-3442,* ☎ *(808) 325-8000, FAX (808) 325-8100.*
http://www.fourseasons.com/hualalai/

Always known for its attention to detail and comfort, the Four Seasons outdid itself this time with a complex of 32 beachfront and four golf-club bungalows situated on a secluded private beach on the North Kona Coast. Careful planning (each room has an exterior entrance—no corridors!) ensures that each room has an ocean view and a feeling of maximum privacy. Windows that don't look out over the ocean face onto artfully composed views of native vegetation, the Jack Nicklaus golf course, or private plunge pools surrounded by black-lava rock. The resort has eight tennis courts and a pro staff to arrange tournaments and provide group or individual instruction. The 15,000-square-foot Health and Wellness center provides aerobics, massage, treatment rooms, and indoor-outdoor showers in addition to a lap pool, whirlpool, Olympic free weights, and cardiovascular training equipment. There's also a Kids for All Seasons program included in the room rate. Amenities: tennis, health club, exercise room, Jacuzzi, balcony or patio, business services. 243 rooms. Credit cards: A, DC, MC, V.

Kona Village Resort $400–$850 ★★★★★
Highway 19, North Kona, 96745, ☎ *(800) 367-5290,*
☎ *(808) 325-5555, FAX (808) 325-5124.*
www.konavillage.com/

The Kona Village boasts 125 hales and a notable reputation for integrity and service. All have private baths and almost all have lanais (with hammocks). By design, there are no telephones, TVs, or clocks in the rooms. A children's program runs year-round (except September). Aside from arts and crafts, activities include night reef-walking with flashlights (a real winner). The high point of the week is the famous luau, which begins at 9 a.m. with the preparation of kalua pig in an underground *imu* (oven). The resort is a popular wedding site. With advance notice, the hotel will help you select a site, issue the marriage license, and arrange for a minister. Honeymoon packages and special-occasion packages also are available. Other services and features include watersports, use of sailboats, outrigger canoes and kayaks, two freshwater pools. Prices are based on an American Plan of three meals a day and airport transfers. Amenities: tennis, balcony or patio. 125 rooms. Credit cards: A, CB, DC, D, MC, V.

Puna

Kalani Oceanside Eco-Resort $85–$150 ★★★
RR2, Box 4500, Puna, 96778, ☎ *(800) 800-6886,*
☎ *(808) 965-7828.*
http://www.kalani.com

The Kalani Oceanside Eco-Resort is for travelers who really want something different: it's operated as a nonprofit organization. Accommodations range from campsites (from $15) in the orchard to cozy, oceanfront cottages. Meals are vegetarian buffets. The Kalani also doubles as an educational facility and has an exceptionally active list of seminars and conferences. The 1996 offerings were as diverse as yoga retreats, a HeartPower Healing and Celebration, a workshop on Sculpture in Landscape, a retreat entitled Women and Sacred Transitions, or a study of Hula Heritage. Nearby attractions include beaches with dolphins, Hawaii Volcanoes National Park, thermal springs, snorkeling, cave climbing, hiking, and fascinating tidal pools. Dress is casual in the extreme, and the management recommends cotton or rayon fibers. Bring your thongs and sneakers. Facilities include a 25-meter pool. Amenities: tennis, exercise room, Jacuzzi, family plan. 30 rooms. Credit cards: A, MC, V.

South Kohala
Kamuela
Bed-and-Breakfasts

The Kamuela Inn   **$75–$200**   ★★

P.O. Box 1994, Kamuela, 96743, ☎ *(808) 885-4253, FAX (808) 885-8857.*
http://www.hawaii-bnb.com/kamuela.html

The Kamuela Inn is a well-established hostelry in Parker Ranch country; reservations have to be made far in advance. It offers varied accommodations, ranging from comfortable double rooms to third-floor "penthouse" suites. A newly completed wing houses the Executive Suites with full kitchens and private sunrooms; one has a carved rosewood antique bed. All rooms have private baths and cable TVs. A serve-yourself continental breakfast is offered daily on a coffee lanai. It's close to shops, museums, and restaurants. 31 rooms. No credit cards.

Waimea Gardens Cottage   **$150**   ★★★★

P.O. Box 563, Kamuela, 96743, ☎ *(800) 262-9912,*
☎ *(808) 885-4550, FAX (808) 885-0550.*

Waimea Gardens Cottage actually consists of two adjoining wings of a restored historic cottage on a 1.5-acre estate in Parker Ranch country, only eight miles from Kohala Coast beaches and two miles from shopping, restaurants, and museums. Both are meticulously decorated in a picturesque country style that Martha Stewart would admire. The older of the two, the Kohala Wing, is a large studio with a gleaming, complete kitchen. The Waimea Wing, with a kitchenette, has a romantic sleeping alcove, a sitting area with a fireplace, a koa-wood rocker, and a comfy loveseat. Both have private baths, hardwood floors, wainscotting, lace curtains, and French doors opening to brick terraces. Amenities: balcony or patio. Two rooms.
Credit cards: not accepted.

Motels

Waimea Country Lodge   **$100–$250**   ★★

Highway 19, Kamuela, 96743, ☎ *(800) 367-5004,*
☎ *(808) 591-2235, FAX (808) 596-0158.*
http://www.castleresorts.com/WCL

Located within walking distance from the historic country town of Waimea, the Waimea Country Lodge (formerly the Parker Ranch Lodge) offers spiffy, modern accommodations at a reasonable price. High-ceilinged rooms are comfortably rustic, with knotty pine furniture and color TVs hidden in armoires; all have views of the surrounding mountains and horse meadows. Kitchenettes are available for those who want to set up light housekeeping on an extended visit. 21 rooms. Credit cards: A, D, MC, V.

Kohala Coast
Condos

Elima Lani   **$89–$125**   ★★★

68-3883 Lua Kula Street, Kohala Coast, 96743,
☎ *(800) 367-5004,* ☎ *(808) 883-8288, FAX (808) 883-8170.*
Single: $89–$125. Double: $89–$125.

The Elima Lani is a good, reasonably priced option for golfers and their families. Special rates at Waikoloa Village course are offered, as well as to six other courses nearby. The one- and two-bedroom units feature full kitchens and two full baths. There are two swimming pools, jet spas, and barbecue areas at various locations on the grounds. All units have lanais overlooking the Waikoloa Village course. Guests have complimentary use of the tennis courts. Recent redecoration of the suites included Berber carpeting and soft floral print upholstery for the rattan furniture. Ceiling fans keep the air circulating, and high ceilings give a pleasant, open feeling to the units. Amenities: tennis, Jacuzzi, balcony or patio. 216 rooms. Credit cards: A, CB, DC, D, MC, V.

Mauna Lani Point   **$260–$520**   ★★★★

68-1310 Mauna Lani Drive, Kohala Coast, 96743,
☎ *(800) 642-6284,* ☎ *(808) 885-5022, FAX (808) 661-1025.*
Single: $260–$520. Double: $260–$520.

This is how the rich and famous live. One-, two-, or three-bed-

room units overlook either the Francis H. I'i Brown South Golf Course or the ocean. The fairway units are cheaper. The facilities of the Mauna Lani Resort are available to guests of the condominium at reduced rates, including some of the most sophisticated tennis facilities in the Pacific, and players have their choice of hard surface, clay, or grass courts. Amenities: tennis, exercise room, Jacuzzi, sauna, balcony or patio. 116 rooms.
Credit cards: A, D, MC, V.

Resorts

Hapuna Beach Prince Hotel $325–$6000 ★★★★★
62-100 Kauna'oa Drive, Kohala Coast, 96743,
☎ *(800) 882-6060,* ☎ *(808) 880-1111, FAX (808) 880-3112.*
If location, location, location makes a resort, the Hapuna Beach Prince has it all. Its 350 rooms all overlook the Pacific and spill down the mountainside to the ocean, providing unobstructed views. The rooms themselves are on the small side and their decor can best be described as opulent-minimalist. The golf course, consistently ranked among the best in the world, was designed by Arnold Palmer and Ed Seay—a par-72 course, it rises from sea level to 700 feet and wanders 6875 yards between the lava beds and the ocean with dramatic views on every hole. It's no surprise to anyone that the restaurants at the resort are some of the best on the island. Other amenities include ocean sports, summer children's program, Hawaiian arts- and-crafts classes, shuttle service to local hotels and shops, boutiques, beauty salon. Amenities: tennis, health club, Jacuzzi, balcony or patio, business services. 350 rooms. Credit cards: A, CB, DC, D, MC, V.

Hilton Waikoloa Village $210–$3750 ★★★★★
425 Waikoloa Beach Drive, Kohala Coast, 96743,
☎ *(800) HIL-TONS,* ☎ *(808) 885-1234,*
FAX (808) 885-7592.
http://www.hiltonwaikoloavillage.com/
Guests are housed in more than 1200 rooms spread out over three low-rise buildings. No one has to walk anywhere because trams and canal boats (on underwater tracks, a la Disneyland) whisk you from place to place. All have private lanais with sliding glass doors that make the already ample rooms seem larger. In what seems to have been an attempt to improve on nature (the property faces the ocean), a seven-acre artificial lagoon has

been constructed and stocked with tropical fish so guests can snorkel without having to leave the premises. In another lagoon, the hotel sponsors Dolphin Quest, which allows guests to experience direct contact with six of these marine mammals. The Dolphin Discovery program (for children five-12) and the Teen Encounter (for teenagers) require advance reservations. Children's activities get special priority at the Waikoloa Village, including the daily Camp Menehune program for children ages five-12. Adults have a choice of two championship golf courses. There are both clay and hard-surface tennis courts. Workout facilities, aromatherapy, massage (Swedish shiatsu, and lomi-lomi Hawaiian), Jacuzzis, steam rooms, saunas, beauty salon, herbal wraps—it's all here. There are eight main restaurants and as many snack bars/sandwich shops. Amenities: tennis, health club, exercise room, Jacuzzi, balcony or patio, family plan, business services. 1238 rooms. Credit cards: A, CB, DC, D, MC, V.

Mauna Kea Beach Hotel　　　　$280–$500　　★★★★★
62-100 Mauna Kea Beach Drive, Kohala Coast, 96743,
☎ *(800) 882-6060,* ☎ *(808) 882-7222, FAX (808) 882-3112.*
Reopened in late 1995 after renovations, Mauna Kea Beach Hotel has been the standard against which all things top-notch have been compared in Hawaii. Six restaurants will serve you a meal at any time of the day or night. The famous and scrumptious buffet spread at the Terrace/Copper Bar is still going strong; there is also a nightly buffet in the vast Pavilion restaurant overlooking Mauna Kea Beach. If you want to dress up in jacket and tie, the Batik, the resort's premier dining establishment, serves classic Provençal French cuisine. Two special ál fresco dining events are the seafood buffet and clambake on Saturdays at the Hau Tree and the Tuesday evening Luau, featuring performances by Kumu Hula Nani Lim and her award-winning hula *halau* (school). Recreational facilities include the par-72 Mauna Kea Golf Course, which was named the number-one golf course in Hawaii and among America's 100 Greatest by *Golf Digest* in 1995; guests can also play at the newer, "environmentally sensitive" Hapuna Golf Course, which is within walking distance of the Mauna Kea's sister hotel, the Hapuna Beach Prince. Amenities: tennis, horseback riding, health club, exercise room, Jacuzzi, balcony or patio, business services. 310 rooms. Credit cards: A, CB, DC, D, MC, V.

The Mauna Lani Bay Hotel and Bungalows $260–$3970   ★★★★★
68-1400 Mauna Lani Drive, Kohala Coast, 96743,
☎ *(800) 367-2323,* ☎ *(808) 885-6622.*
http://www.maunalani.com

This is a resort in the true sense of the word. The two golf courses, carved from a 16th-century lava flow, will be familiar to TV viewers as the site of the Senior Skins Game. The on-site Tennis Garden has been rated as one of the Top 50 Greatest Tennis Resorts by *Tennis* magazine, and contain 10 plexi-pave courts of varying speeds to suit the needs of players of all levels. Ninety percent of the rooms have an unobstructed view of the ocean. The hotel takes a special interest in children's activities. *Keikis* have their own special beach with small cabanas. Kids lucky enough to be here in the summer can participate in Turtle Independence Day, July 4, when honu, or endangered sea turtles, that have been raised in the hotel fish ponds are released into the sea. Guest rooms at the Mauna Lani range from luxurious to downright opulent. If you can swing it, try for one of the five private bungalows, which are 4000 square feet, with private swimming pools, whirlpool spas, steam baths, and round-the-clock butler service. Meals are a delight here, especially in the evening at the terrific Canoe House restaurant, made famous by now-departed chef Alan Wong, serving inspired Pacific Rim cuisine. Sunsets from its terrace are spectacular. Amenities: tennis, health club, balcony or patio, family plan, business services. 350 rooms. Credit cards: A, D, MC, V.

The Orchid at Mauna Lani $285–$475   ★★★★★
1 North Kaniku Drive, Kohala Coast, 96743,
☎ *(800) 782-9488,* ☎ *(808) 885-2000, FAX (808) 885-8886.*
http://www.orchid-maunalani.com

Formerly the Ritz-Carlton Mauna Lan, this spectacular resort has been renamed The Orchid at Mauna Lani. All guest rooms feature sumptuous marble baths with separate shower, double vanities, and an additional telephone, fully-stocked honor bar with refrigerator, plush terry robes, Crabtree and Evelyn toiletries, in-room safe, color TV, and a 24-hour in-room video service. The Club Level on the top floor, which is an excellent value, is entered via a special key, and guests are provided with a private lounge, continental breakfast, mid-morning snacks, a light lunch of sandwiches and salads, cocktails, pupus, chocolates, and liqueurs. A "Beach Boys Club" features local boys who teach guests about tides, surfing, canoe paddling, celestial navigation, ancient land division system and more. The Orchid's "Spa without Walls" healing-and-wellness package is one of the finest on the island. The program includes t'ai chi classes under palm trees, power walks through ancient lava flows, aqua aerobics in the 10,000-square-foot pool, and yoga on the beach followed by snorkel dives in the Pacific. Guests have privileges at the Francis H. I'i Brown 36-hole championship golf courses as well as five other courses in the vicinity. You might think about hosting a company function here; the resort has very impressive conference facilities. Amenities: tennis, health club, exercise room, Jacuzzi, balcony or patio, family plan, club floor, business services. 539 rooms. Credit cards: A, D, MC, V.

The Royal Waikoloan $184–$650   ★★★
69-275 Waikoloa Beach Drive, Kohala Coast, 96743,
☎ *(808) 885-6789, FAX (808) 885-7852.*
http://www.worldwidevacations.com/hawaii/haw/haw1 11.htm

Located between two of the pricier destinations on the Big Island, the Royal Waikoloan, is a welcome oasis of mid-range pricing. Rooms are a nice size and all have private lanais. This 15-unit, two-suite building overlooks the lagoons. Guests are treated to continental breakfast while meeting other guests. The luau is offered two nights a week, but between times, guests can watch torch-lighting and torch-dancing acts after dark in the beachfront lounge. Activities available to guests are year-round swimming on beautiful Anaeho'omalu Bay, a white-sand beach protected from high surf by a living reef. There's golf at the nearby King's Course and Beach Course (shuttle available), tennis, snorkeling, hiking, tours of petroglyph sites, Hawaiian crafts classes and shopping in the adjacent Waikoloa King's Shops. The helpful and cheerful staff make the establishment one of the best buys on the Big Island. Amenities: Jacuzzi, balcony or patio, business services. 533 rooms. Credit cards: A, D, MC, V.

South Kona
Captain Cook
Hotels

Manago Hotel — $55–$125 ★★

P.O. Box 145, Captain Cook, 96704, ☎ (808) 323-2642.
http://www.managohotel.com/

The Manago is a bare-bones, no-frills operation that will appeal to the type of traveler who doesn't spend a lot of time in his/her room. Rooms have balconies, are spotlessly clean, and have radios but no telephones. The only TV is in the lobby. The original rooms are on the first floor of the old building and are Spartan in the extreme—linoleum floors, shared baths and minimal bedding. The higher-up the room, the more comfortable the accommodation, so the best rooms are on the third floor of the new wing. The most expensive are the Japanese rooms, with tatami mats and furo baths. The dining room is popular with locals and serves home-style Hawaiian meals in copious quantities—pork chops, rice, and lots of gravy is the house specialty. Amenities: balcony or patio. 42 rooms. Credit cards: MC, V.

Holualoa
Bed-and-Breakfasts

Holualua Inn — $125–$165 ★★★★

P.O. Box 222, Holualoa, 96725, ☎ (800) 392-1812,
☎ (808) 324-1121.

This beautiful inn, set in a private country estate overlooking the ocean in the heart of the Kona Coffee Belt, is surrounded by 40 acres of gardens and coffee trees. Its location on the slopes of Mount Hualalai ensures that guests enjoy cool breezes year round. The sprawling, three-story house and each of the four rooms are paneled in polished cedar, the floors of eucalyptus wood. Each guest room has a different theme with platform beds. A stunning pool in the shape of a bird's beak features a flower mosaic at its bottom. Picnic coolers are provided for day trips. The inn prides itself on its pupu platter of fresh fruit and cheese, served in the late afternoon, on request. Guests are encouraged to bring home meals from nearby restaurants and enjoy dining ál fresco in the gardens or rooftop gazebo; later you can use the telescope to get a close look at the stars. No children under 13. Amenities: balcony or patio. Four rooms. Credit cards: A, MC, V.

Honaunau

The Dragonfly Ranch $70–$160 ★★★

*P.O. Box 675, Honaunau, 96276, ☎ (800) 487-2159,
☎ (808) 328-2159, FAX (808) 328-9570.*
<http://www.dragonflyranch.com/>

The owners of the Dragonfly Ranch describe the place as a "tropical fantasy lodging," and if your fantasies involve close contact with nature, then you won't be disappointed. The indoor-outdoor ambience means there's as little between you and the outdoors as possible; if you have a phobia of spiders (they're harmless), this might not be the place for you. The gardens surrounding the guest accommodations are lush with tropical vegetation, and the honeymoon suite features an outdoor waterbed with a mirrored canopy. Fantastic snorkeling is available just two minutes away from the ranch. An added treat is swimming with the dolphins residing in the bay. Besides the honeymoon suite, guest quarters include two rooms in the main house and a writer's studio attached to—but below—the main house, with a private entrance. Suites have wet bars with toaster oven, small fridge, coffee makers, and utensils. Ingredients for a do-it-yourself continental breakfast are supplied. All rooms have private outdoor showers. Four rooms. Credit cards: MC, V.

Kealakekua

Dr. Boone's Bed and Breakfast Lodge $85 ★★

P.O. Box 666, Kealakekua, 96750, ☎ (808) 232-3231.

There's something for everyone on the Big Island, and Dr. Boone's is a haven for bicyclists. The doctor and his wife (a weaver) are avid cyclists themselves who have led tours through China. As longtime residents, they have firsthand knowledge of the back roads of the island. For a nominal fee and with advance notice, they'll pick you up at the airport and help you reassemble your bike. Hearty breakfasts are tailored to athletic tastes (hint: plenty of carbs). The Doc has three rooms with shared baths in his large but simply furnished home. The grounds include a pool and exotic fruit trees. The Boones are very sociable people, so if you vant to be alone, this isn't the place for you. Three rooms. Credit cards: not accepted.

Volcano
Volcano Village

Hale Ohia Cottages   **$75–$95**   ★★★

P.O. Box 758, Volcano Village, 96785, ☎ *(800) 455-3803,* ☎ *(808) 967-7986.*
http://www.haleohia.com/

Once the estate of a wealthy kamaaina family, Hale Ohia maintains its tradition of hospitality in its present reincarnation as one of the better accommodations on the Big Island. The main residence, guest cottage, gardener's cottage, and other buildings have been meticulously restored and provide guests with an exceptional level of comfort and privacy. The gardens of Hale Ohia can be considered a destination in themselves. No earth was moved in their development, and they take advantage of the natural lava formations. A favorite gathering spot is the Japanese soaking tub, or *furo*, behind the main house. The Hale Ohia Cottage is popular with families. It has three bedrooms, a large living room, sitting area, and a fully furnished kitchen. The covered lanai is a favorite place for barbecues. Honeymooners are partial to the Hale Lehua and Ihilani Cottages. The Hale Lehua is the oldest of the cottages and is notable for its lava-rock fireplace. It is very secluded, and visitors can use the limited housekeeping facilities—a microwave, fridge, and hot plate. The covered lanai looks out over the gardens. Amenities: Jacuzzi. Seven rooms. Credit cards: A, CB, DC, D, MC, V.

Kilauea Lodge and Restaurant   **$95–$135**   ★★★

P.O. Box 116, Volcano Village, 96785, 27 miles from Hilo, Junction of Highway 11 and Highway 148, ☎ *(808) 967-7366, FAX (808) 967-7367.*
http://www.kilauealodge.com

The Kilauea Lodge is a comfortable example of pre-World War II Island bungalow construction. It was built in 1938 for the YMCA, and thousands of islanders remember it with affection as the jumping-off point for their explorations of the nearby volcano. In 1986, it was purchased by Lorna and Albert Jeyte and completely refurbished to begin a new reincarnation as a country inn and restaurant. Accommodations are in four separate buildings. There are four rooms in the original building, Hale Maluna; all have fireplaces. Other units include a small, one-bedroom cottage with living room and woodburning stove. Tutu's (Grandmother's) Place is a two-bedroom cottage one block from the main lodge. It's equipped with a full kitchen, living room, and fireplace, and has its own large garden and porch. All rates include a full breakfast served in the main lodge. Amenities: balcony or patio. 12 rooms.

Hotels

Volcano House $105–$175 ★★★

On the north rim of Kilauea Crater, Volcano Village,
☎ *(808) 967-7321.*
http://www.volcanovillage.com/V_house.htm
The only hotel in the Hawaii Volcanoes National Park, a sprawling lodge with a dramatic setting, perched on the northern rim of Kilauea crater. The present structure was built in 1941 after a fire destroyed the original 1800s Victorian-style building; Mark Twain, Franklin D. Roosevelt, and Queen Liliuokalani were among the most distinguished guests. Part of the original section escaped the flames, and is now the Volcano Arts Center, a nonprofit outlet for local artisans. Volcano House features 42 recently redecorated rooms, some overlooking the crater, outfitted with rare koa-wood furniture and Hawaiian-style quilts. The cocktail lounge and restaurant are often engulfed by tour groups during the day, but the hotel is quiet and peaceful at night, and the atmosphere is always casual and low-key. It helps to make reservations at least six months in advance in the winter and three months ahead other times of the year. You might try calling a day in advance to see if there are any vacancies. Amenities: balcony or patio. 42 rooms. Credit cards: A, DC, D, MC, V.

Where to Eat

Dining on the Big Island can range from putting a picnic together from neighborhood-type markets to fine dining. The resorts offer a range of dining options, including scheduled **luaus**. **At Kailua-Kona,** you'll find visitor-oriented **cafés, bistros** and **restaurants. Waterfront Row,** with its **Chart House,** draws heavy tourist traffic. Over on Hilo, dining tends to be more casual—and cheaper—with neighborhood eateries (and the ubiquitous fast food) the big rave. **Waimea** also offers a couple of good options for the inland crowd.

Hamakua Coast

Jolene's Kau Kau Korner $ ★★
Corner of Lehua and Mamane Streets, Hamakua Coast,
☎ *(808) 775-9498.*
Specialties: Hamburgers, beef teriyaki, grilled mahi-mahi.
This cheerfully decorated, family-owned restaurant is located near the Hawaiian Holiday Macadamia Nut Factory. Jolene's is a convenient stop on the way to the Waipio Valley. Several different American and Hawaiian specialties are prepared daily, and everything is available for takeout. Open until 3 p.m. on Saturday. Reservations not accepted.

Hilo

Bear's Coffee $ ★★★
106 Keawe Street, Hilo, ☎ *(808) 935-0708.*
American cuisine. Specialties: Coffee drinks, espresso, Belgian waffles, sandwiches, bagels and lox, ice cream.
For people who are grizzly bears until they have their first morning cup of joe, Bear's is ideal—it's open bright and early at 6:45 on weekdays (8 a.m. on weekends). There are sidewalk tables outside so you can take advantage of the passing Hilo scene while chowing down on souffléed eggs made in the espresso machine, or Bear's famous "busters," sort of a genteel version of the greasy stuff you get at a well-known fast-food joint. If you don't like eggs, there are pastries and Belgian waffles or lox 'n' bagels. Soups, salads, sandwiches, and hot dishes are served at lunch. Picnic lunches available on request. Features: outside dining, own baking. Reservations not accepted.

Broke da Mouth $ ★★★
93 Mamo Street, Hilo, ☎ *(808) 934-7670.*
Specialties: Hawaiian vegetarian dishes.
Closed: Mondays, Sundays.
Non-greasy and absolutely meatless plate lunches are served at this downtown Hilo deli/takeout establishment that was once a fish market. Combinations are surprisingly complex, eclectic and inventive, and nothing is over $10. All produce is grown on a cooperative farm nearby. Even the mustards and salad dressings are homemade. Sample the manapua, traditional dumplings made here with whole-wheat flour and filled with

Chinese eggplant or taro, sweet potato, and green papaya salad. Features: outside dining, own baking. Reservations not accepted.

Café Pesto $$$ ★★★
308 Kamehameha Avenue, Hilo, ☎ *(808) 969-6640.*
Italian cuisine. Specialties: Fresh local seafood, gourmet pizzas, Pacific Rim pastas, and appetizers.
The historic, meticulously restored circa 1912 S. Hata building is the site of this rather stark, contemporary restaurant with a centerpiece exhibition-kitchen that puts out an interesting combination of Italian and Pacific Rim cuisine. The original location is in a shopping center near Kawaihae Harbor, not far from Hapuna Beach. Expansion was possible due to the popularity of the mini-chain's specialty: delectable, wood-fired pizzas and breads made from their own dough mix. Microbrewery beers and a decent wine selection accompany the sparkling cuisine. Espressos, lattes, and homemade "chocoholic" desserts. Reservations recommended. Credit cards: A, MC, V.

Don's Grill $$ ★★
485 Hinano Street, Hilo, ☎ *(808) 935-9099.*
American cuisine. Specialties: Saimin, loco moco, breakfast dishes, teriyaki.
Closed: Mon.
Don's Grill is as plain and no-nonsense as its name. It serves the kind of food that brings tears to the eyes of starving truckers hauling a load down an interstate highway. Only in this case, saimin, loco moco, and teriyaki dishes are interspersed with hearty pork chops and liver-and-onions on the sizable menu. Rotisserie chicken and barbecued ribs are also big sellers, and the place is packed for breakfast on weekends. Credit cards: A, MC, V.

Ken's House of Pancakes $ ★★★
Corner of Highway 11 and Kamehameha Avenue, Hilo,
☎ *(808) 935-8711.*
American cuisine. Specialties: Pancakes, 24-hour breakfasts, Hawaiian dishes.
Providing "good, old-fashioned" service for more than 20 years at the same location, Ken's is also the only place in Hilo

that offers this service 24 hours a day, rain or shine. It's ideal for folks who like to have their pancakes and eggs at midnight. The daily specials include local dishes as well as heart-healthy "lite" cuisine. Features: late dining. Reservations not accepted. Credit cards: A, DC, D, MC, V.

Lehua's Bay City Bar and Grill $$ ★★★
11 Waianeunue Avenue, Hilo, 96721, ☎ *(808) 935-8055.*
American cuisine. Specialties: Charbroiled teriyaki chicken burgers, country pork ribs.
A collection of vintage signs, photos, and memorabilia on loan from various businesses decorates the walls of this downtown Hilo eatery, situated in the 1930s Hilo Drug Company building. The menu is just as old-fashioned, with comforting dishes such as charbroiled chicken teriyaki sandwiches and country pork ribs with paniolo barbecue sauce. No lunch on Sundays. Reservations recommended. Credit cards: A, D, MC, V.

Restaurant Fuji $$$ ★★★
142 Kinoole Street, Hilo, ☎ *(808) 961-3733. Associated hotel: The Hilo Hotel.*
Japanese cuisine. Specialties: Japanese teishoku lunches and dinners, tempura, teriyaki.
Restaurant Fuji, a fixture in the Hilo restaurant scene, is a relaxing, fine-tuned old-timer with a genteel atmosphere, gracious service, and traditional Japanese cuisine. The fish teppanyaki, cooked with assorted vegetables at your table, is the meal of choice. Reservations recommended. Credit cards: A, DC, MC, V.

Roussel's $$$ ★★★
60 Keawe Street, Hilo, ☎ *(808) 935-5111.*
Specialties: Shrimp remoulade, blackened sashimi, soft-shell crab, Cajun prime rib, gumbos, fresh fish.
New Orleans comes to Hilo via this swank Creole restaurant on the ground floor of a turn-of-the-century bank building, one of the first to be restored in an ambitious city gentrification program. Lights are low, ceilings are high and airy—even the bare wooden floors gleam. One of the founders, the late chef Andrew Oliver, was instrumental in getting the Hilo Mardi Gras Festival off the ground. Features: private dining rooms. Reservations recommended. Credit cards: A, MC, V.

Ting Hao Mandarin Restaurant $$ ★★★
Highway 11 at the Puainako Town Center, Hilo,
☎ *(808) 959-6288.*
Chinese cuisine. Specialties: Shrimp with lobster sauce, Kung Pao chicken, shredded pork with garlic sauce, vegetarian dishes.
Closed: Sundays.

Ting Hao is a family-style restaurant that's usually packed with local Chinese, who obviously enjoy the trademark spicy Szechuan and Hunanese specialties served in this shopping-center location not far from the airport. Less-brave souls are treated kindly; they tone down the chilies on request. There's also a gentler menu of dishes from Peking and Taiwan. Veggie specials too. Another branch, Ting Hao Seafood Restaurant, is located in the lower lobby of the Naniloa Hotel, at *93 Banyan Drive* on Hilo Bay. Call ☎ *(808) 935-8888* for information. Reservations recommended. Credit cards: A, MC, V.

Ka'u
Naalehu

Naalehu Coffee Shop $$ ★★
Highway 11, Naalehu, ☎ *(808) 929-7238.*
American cuisine. Specialties: Banana bread, fresh fish.
Closed: Sun.

If you find yourself way down south Naalehu way, drop in to this down-home, linoleum-and-chrome, country restaurant that has surprisingly good food. There are some sophisticated fish dishes among the liver-and-onions and deep-fried items; the source is only a few minutes away in Ka Lae, the southernmost point of the United States. Take some of their famous banana bread with you for on-the-go munchies. Reservations not accepted.

Punalu'u Bake Shop $ ★★
Highway 11, Naalehu, ☎ *(808) 929-7343.*
American cuisine. Specialties: Sandwiches made with Hawaiian sweetbread.

A working bakery in a charming village that's conveniently placed between Hawaii Volcanoes National Park and Ka Lae, the southernmost point of the United States, Punalu'u Bake Shop has a picnic area where you can sample sandwiches made with Hawaiian sweetbread. It's also the place to try chili made with macadamia nuts grown by the Mauna Loa Macadamia

Kona
Kailua-Kona

Banana Bay Buffet $$ ★★
75-5739 Ali'i Drive, Kailua-Kona, 96740, ☎ (808) 329-1398.
Associated hotel: Uncle Billy's Kona Bay Hotel.
American cuisine. Specialties: Breakfast and dinner buffets with free hula show, Sunday brunch.

Uncle Billy, known for his mini-chain of affordable hotels (another in Hilo) also features all-you-can-eat buffets for breakfast and dinner (no lunch). There are more than 20 items available for breakfast, including healthful things such as oatmeal and fruit bars, and local kine chili, stew, and mahi-mahi. Muffins are made fresh daily, and there's a river of Kona coffee constantly flowing. Dinner is a multi-ethnic affair with Hawaiian, Chinese, Korean, and even Mexican food (slightly dubious) to choose from. Also on the list are 14 homemade salads, ribs, fresh pasta, stir fries, and carved roast beef and loin of pork. Management swears you can eat here seven days a week and always find something different. Desserts and beverages extra. There's a free hula show on Saturdays and Sundays from 6–8 p.m. No buffet on Sunday, when there's a brunch offered from 7 a.m. to noon at $6.95 per person. Reservations for large groups only. Features: Sunday brunch. Reservations recommended. Credit cards: A, MC, V.

Buns in the Sun $ ★★
75-5595 Palani Road, Kailua-Kona, ☎ (808) 326-2774.
American cuisine. Specialties: Cinnamon buns, sandwiches, espresso.

An indoor-outdoor deli, bakery, and coffee-shop combination, the saucily named Buns in the Sun features nicely priced (read CHEAP), tasty cinnamon rolls (even low-fat ones), fresh-baked pastries, breakfast sandwiches, deli sandwiches, (try the island ono) and soup or salad. Everything is available for take-out. Reservations not accepted.

Huggo's $$$ ★★★
Ali'i Drive, Kailua-Kona, ☎ (808) 329-1493.

American cuisine. Specialties: Fresh fish, barbecued ribs, steaks.
Dreamy Kona sunsets, live music (different every night), fresh fish, and prime rib ensures a steady stream of customers to this 25-year-old South Seas-style building that juts out over the Pacific. The fresh catch of the day is prepared in a Cajun, Mediterranean, or Pacific Rim style. Barbecued ribs are the specialty on Tuesdays and Thursdays. No lunch on weekends. Features: outside dining. Reservations recommended. Credit cards: A, D, MC, V.

Island Lava Java $
75-5799 Ali'i Drive, Kailua-Kona, ☎ *(808) 327-2161.*
American cuisine. Specialties: Specialty coffee drinks, pastries, Tropical Dreams ice cream, sandwiches.
Although it's open late, Lava Java is particularly popular for breakfast pastries and an excellent imported dark-roast espresso blend. Treat yourself and top it with chocolate or cinnamon. Other menu items include sandwiches, croissants, soups, and Tropical Dreams ice cream. Outdoor tables overlook Oneo Bay. Open until 11 p.m. on Fridays and Saturdays. Features: outside dining, own baking. Reservations not accepted. Credit cards: MC, V.

Jameson's $$ ★★★
77-6452 Ali'i Drive, Kailua-Kona, ☎ *(808) 329-3195.*
American cuisine. Specialties: Fresh seafood, steaks.
Known for steaks and sunset views over Magic (or Disappearing) Sands Beach, Jameson's is, to some, one of the best places to eat on the Big Island. The newly expanded outdoor dining area is a big plus, so more folks can dine on well-prepared island fish and filet mignon while enjoying the sea breezes. At lunch, bring the kids to watch the feeding of the resident moray eels that live in the surf among the black-lava rocks below the deck. Excellent service from old Kona hands. No lunch served on weekends. Features: outside dining. Reservations recommended. Credit cards: A, MC, V.

Keauhou Beach Hotel Buffets $$$ ★★
78-6740 Ali'i Drive, Kailua-Kona, ☎ *(808) 322-3441.*
Associated hotel: Keauhou Beach Hotel.
American cuisine. Specialties: Chinese, Hawaiian, and seafood

buffets.

Three different theme buffets are featured every week in the Kuakini Terrace at the Keauhou Beach Hotel in Kailua. The Hawaiian dinner buffet on Wednesdays and Thursdays is like a luau without the show. For a flat rate, it's an all-you-can-eat feast of traditional goodies such as lau lau, lomi salmon, tako poke, kalua pork, and, of course, poi. Also included is a 25-dish salad bar. Chinese night is on Mondays and Tuesdays, while Seafood buffets are on Fridays, Saturdays and Sundays. Reservations required. Credit cards: A, MC, V.

La Bourgogne $$

77-6400 Nalani Street, Kailua-Kona, ☎ *(808) 329-6711.*
French cuisine.

With only 10 tables, this is an intimate French restaurant, a little gem tucked away in a shopping center three miles from Kailua-Kona. The menu has been updated over the years to include some Pacific Rim-style dishes using fresh local produce. Try the delectable opakapaka in caviar cream sauce. You'll be treated like a special guest by the American chef and his wife, who work the room themselves with very little help and do an admirable job. A winner from the start and getting better all the time. Features: own baking, rated wine cellar, non-smoking area. Reservations required. Credit cards: A, DC, D, MC, V.

Mixed Plate $$ ★★★

Palani Road, in Kopiko Plaza, Kailua-Kona,
☎ *(808) 329-8104.*
Asian cuisine. Specialties: Plate lunches, Korean dishes.

This large, air-conditioned shopping center eatery is popular with local residents, but drop-ins get a warm welcome. The Kim family specializes in 36 lunch and dinner plates, ranging from vegetable tempura to a sizzling 10-ounce New York steak with shrimp. There's an emphasis on Korean dishes such as kalbi ribs, or short ribs marinated in ginger, soy, garlic, and sesame oil, and then grilled. Also bulgogi beef, teriyaki chicken, and steak. Friday night is prime rib night, and it's served until they run out. All dishes are cooked to order. Reservations not accepted.

Ocean View Inn $$ ★★
Ali'i Drive, Kailua-Kona, 96740, ☎ *(808) 329-9998.*
American cuisine. Specialties: Chinese vegetarian dishes, breakfasts, fresh fish, roast pork.
The Ocean View Inn has been in the same location for more than 50 years, and looks it. No attempt has been made to yuppify it, to the relief of many faithful customers. Veteran waitresses (who may be a little ornery at times) take your order from a huge menu that encompasses Chinese vegetarian dishes, fresh fish, teriyaki steak, corned beef and cabbage (!), and the like. If you're the type who has to have rice with your breakfast eggs, this is the place to come. No outside seating, but there is an ocean view from across the sea wall, just like the name says.

Palm Café $$$ ★★★★
75-5819 Ali'i Drive, Kailua-Kona, 96740, ☎ *(808) 329-7765.*
Although Kailua town's main drag bustles below, you'd never know it at this sublime open-air, ocean-view restaurant outfitted in white wicker and crisp linens and cooled by ceiling fans. Some of the Asian-flavored dishes were inspired by the French chef's sojourn in the Philippines, including a signature item, crab lumpia. The menu changes frequently, but you can always count on the fresh fish, perhaps a gentle mahi-mahi malia with lobster and crispy noodles in a creamy coconut sauce. The service here is a perfect blend of unobtrusiveness and efficiency. A casual bistro, Under the Palm, is appropriately located under the Palm. Breakfast is served from 7–11 a.m., and lunch and dinner from 11 a.m.–midnight. Preferred dining is on the open-air patio and sidewalk café, which is great for people-watching. Inventive pizzas, grilled dishes, mouth-watering sandwiches, and desserts are all recommended. Features: outside dining, own baking. Reservations recommended. Credit cards: A, D, MC, V.

Sam Choy's Diner $ ★★★
Frame Ten Center, next to Kona Bowl, Kailua-Kona,
☎ *(808) 329-0101.*
Asian cuisine. Specialties: Plate lunches.
Celebrity chef Sam's second Kona eatery is a diner situated in a shopping center next to a bowling alley in Kailua. Open continuously for breakfast, lunch, and dinner until 10 p.m., the

fare consists of 25 plate lunches, including his signature fried poki, fresh fish in a special sauce, served with plenty of rice. Dishes are dressed with potato/macaroni salad or tossed greens with Sam's Oriental dressing. Reservations not accepted.

Sam Choy's Restaurant $$$ ★★★★
73-5576 Kauhola Street, Kailua-Kona, ☎ *(808) 326-1545.*
Sam Choy's Restaurant is hidden away in the Kaloko Industrial Area near Kona Airport; unlikely neighbors include the Shooter's Choice indoor gun range and a bowling alley, among others. But local boy Sam Choy's creative variations on the humble plate lunch have made him number one with a bullet among his growing legion of fans. Entirely casual (and casually priced) at breakfast and lunch, you'll be served such items as Spam sushi (here called musubi), beef stew, or Kaloko Noodle Mania—beef chow mein in a deep-fried noodle bowl. At dinner, though, the management pretties up the place with white linen and jacks up the prices accordingly. Patrons have to bring their own booze as Sam's has no liquor license; the restaurant passes out the corkscrew. You'll enjoy Sam's award-winning seafood laulau, with fresh fish instead of pork, wrapped in a ti-leaf. Entrées include soup, salad, and fresh bread. Reserve in advance for dinner.

Sibu's $$ ★★★
75-5695 Ali'i Drive, in the Kona Banyan Court, Kailua-Kona, ☎ *(808) 329-1112.*
Asian cuisine. Specialties: Chicken satay, Gado-gado.
Possibly the only eatery to serve Indonesian specialties on the Big Island, the open-air Sibu Café can be found behind a monstrous banyan tree in a mall populated by hungry felines waiting for a handout. It's been a local fixture for almost 10 years, and the exotic offerings—such as chicken satay with peanut sauce, or gado-gado salad with a mound of lettuce, cabbage, potatoes, and sprouts with a peanut-lime dressing—have become old friends. Specify whether you want your meal mild or spicy. No MSG is used, and there's an extensive vegetarian menu. Features: outside dining, wine and beer only. Reservations not accepted.

North Kohala
Hawi

Bamboo Restaurant   **$$$**   ★★★

At the intersection of Highway 250 and Highway 270, Hawi, 96755, ☎ *(808) 889-5555.*

Hawaiian cuisine. Specialties: Chicken satay pot-stickers with sweet chili-mint dipping sauce, coconut milk clam chowder.

The old Takata dry-goods store, which was also once a sugar-cane workers' hotel in the early 1900s, has been transformed into this widely talked-about restaurant. This is the kind of place where customers call the warm-hearted waitresses "auntie" and the chef comes out of the kitchen to sing and dance for guests. The inventive Hawaiian-Pacific Rim cuisine should be more expensive than it is. The menu tries to please everyone, including a separate section for vegetarians, and it usually succeeds. Make it a point to start your meal with a passion-fruit margarita and end it with a dual-chocolate lava mousse. Afterward, check out the Kohala Koa Gallery within the restaurant for beautiful custom-made wooden furniture. No dinner on Sundays. Reservations recommended. Credit cards: MC, V.

Kapa'au

Don's Family Deli   **$**   ★★★

P.O. Box 1463, Kapa'au, 96755, ☎ *(808) 889-5822.*

American cuisine. Specialties: Deli sandwiches, vegetarian dishes, smoothies.

With a landmark such as the King Kamehameha statue across from it, you can't miss Don's Family Deli. True to its name, deli sandwiches are available, as well as bagels and lox. But much of the menu is pretty healthful and darn incredible for these parts, including tofu burgers, mesquite chicken, veggie enchiladas, quiche, toasted crab or peanut-butter-and-guava-jam sandwiches, shepherd's pie, and Portuguese bean soup. The luscious banana-papaya-strawberry smoothies are a meal in themselves. Ask them about Blue Green Algae, if you dare. Reservations not accepted.

Tropical Dreams   **$**   ★★★

Highway 270, Kapa'au, 96755, ☎ *(808) 889-0505.*

American cuisine. Specialties: Homemade ice cream.

Just down the road from Don's Family Deli is this ice cream

emporium with a factory behind it. It's owned by Diane and Warren Wulzen, former California ranchers who pulled up stakes two years ago and decided to fulfill their tropical dreams of trying to make a living in Hawaii. Some of the flavors they've devised will make you delirious—how about Tahitian vanilla, coconut cream, white chocolate ginger, lilikoi sorbet, pikake, and papaya? There are usually 40 ice cream flavors available, as well as 25 sorbets and 10 low-fat yogurts. Also espresso drinks, Italian sodas, pastries, and shave ice. Another location in downtown Hilo, in the historic Kress building, (808) 961-4767. Reservations not accepted.

North Kona

Teshima's $$ ★★★
Highway 11, North Kona, ☎ *(808) 322-9140.*
Japanese cuisine. Specialties: Sashimi, tempura, teriyaki.
You won't find any rock-and-roll sushi chefs at this always reliable Japanese restaurant and small inn situated in the heart of Kona coffee country. Year in and year out, faithful diners can expect the same well-prepared lunches and dinners of sashimi, teriyaki, shrimp tempura, and all the trimmings, nestled in their own little compartments on a black lacquer tray. Yes, there is a Mrs. Teshima, and she's usually on hand to greet customers. A favored spot for local dignitaries.

The Captain Cook Inn $ ★
Highway 11, North Kona, ☎ *(808) 323-2080.*
American cuisine. Specialties: Plate lunches.
A good budget choice in a restaurant-poor area, Captain Cook Inn serves a mixed bag of cuisines, including Korean chicken served by the plate or by the bucket (this was, after all, an old Kentucky Fried Chicken outlet), and fresh fish, burgers, fries, sandwiches, and salads. Reservations not accepted.

The Coffee Shack $ ★★
Highway 11, North Kona, ☎ *(808) 328-9555.*
American cuisine. Specialties: Kona coffee, capuccino, espresso, latte, eggs benedict, pastries.
Connected to the Kahauloa Coffee Co., which has been in business for 20 years, this open-air café features a heady brew made from beans picked straight off the trees, and ground and

roasted in-house. The house specialty is a dark-roast peaberry coffee as well as 100 percent no-foolin' Kona coffee. Decaf available. Accompaniments include eggs benedict, quiche, waffles, or fresh pastries at breakfast or daily specials, pasta, salads, and sandwiches at lunch. Ask for their mail-order brochure or inquire about shipping their product to friends in faraway places.

South Kohala
Kamuela

Hawaiian Style $ ★★
Highway 19, Kamuela,.
American cuisine. Specialties: Loco moco, Belgian waffles, plate lunches, sandwiches.
This owners of this spotless, spiffy café took over Masayo's, an old-time greasy spoon, leased the building next door, and tore the walls down to create more space. The action centers around a circular wood counter, and when you enter, regulars may give you the once-over, but it's a friendly place. Weekly specials include oxtail, shoyu chicken, and the Friday luau plate of laulau, chicken long rice, lomi lomi salmon, kalua pig, rice, and poi for $10.95. Among the regular plate lunches, served with rice and potato-mac salad, are kalbi ribs, teriyaki steak, and broiled mahi-mahi. There are a number of sandwiches, served with fries or mac salad; the ground barbecued pork is huge and delicious. It's closed every last Sunday and Monday of the month. Reservations not accepted.

Island Bistro $$ ★★★
Highway 19 and Kawaihae Road, Kamuela,
☎ *(808) 885-1222.*
International cuisine. Specialties: Waimea sweet potato soup, tamarind roasted leg of lamb with pepper-papaya sauce.
The relaxed decor features an exhibition kitchen. Specials change nightly, but there's always something for vegetarians and pasta lovers. Come for an ál fresco lunch during the week (not served on weekends). The patio offers a majestic view of Mauna Kea, and soups, salads, and sandwiches are mostly under $10. Features: outside dining, own baking. Reservations recommended. Credit cards: D, MC, V.

Maha's Café $ ★★★
P.O. Box 6960, Kamuela, 96743, ☎ *(808) 885-0693.*
American cuisine. Specialties: Smoked ahi with lilikoi salsa, Hawaiian style bread pudding with guava-ginger sauce.
Closed Tuesdays.

This small but delightful country-style café is ensconced in the back of Cook's Discoveries, one of Kamuela's finest island craft stores. Open for light breakfasts, lunch, and afternoon tea, selections are unusual and creative. Breakfasts include poi pancakes with coconut syrup and Maha's granola parfait with fruit, nuts, and yogurt. At lunch, hearty appetites might go for the fresh roast turkey on squaw bread with home-style mushroom stuffing and Ka'u orange and cranberry relish. Light eaters will appreciate the Waipio Ways platter—broiled fresh fish with sliced steamed Waipio taro and sweet potato on a bed of Kahua greens, served "nude" or with a gingered vinaigrette. Folks can drop in for dessert washed down by a cup of the featured Kona coffee flavor of the month. "Maha" is a caterer and pastry chef, so you won't go wrong with any of her old-fashioned sweets, such as Hawaiian-style bread pudding with guava ginger sauce. Maha's homemade honey-curry dressing, green olive pesto, poi bread, banana bread, and papaya coffee cake are available to go. Afternoon tea served from 3–4:30 p.m. Reservations not accepted.

Mean Cuisine $ ★★★
65-1227 A Opelu Road, Suite 4, Kamuela, 96743,
☎ *(808) 885-6325.*
American cuisine. Specialties: Homemade sushi, turkey, and mashed potatoes, chocolate cake with triple raspberry sauce.
Closed: Sun.

The food is the only show at this unpretentious storefront eatery and bakery located just steps away from the highly praised Merriman's in the Opelu Shopping Center. Chef Ann Sutherland has much in common with Peter Merriman: each served as executive chefs at the Mauna Lani resort. Both are energetic overachievers; where Merriman dives for the shellfish on his table, Sutherland is up way before the 6 a.m. opening baking breads, muffins, and pastries and rolling homemade sushi (!), which disappears quickly. All items are available for takeout. Features: own baking. Reservations not accepted.
Credit cards: MC, V.

Merriman's $$$ ★★★★

Highway 19, in Opelo Plaza, Kamuela, ☎ *(808) 885-6822. American cuisine. Specialties: Wok-charred ahi, Kahua ranch lamb, steak with Cabernet Sauvignon, and gorgonzola sauce.*

This is a surprisingly bright, tropical-romantic restaurant in a shopping-center setting. The atmosphere is livened further by the goings-on in a wraparound, open kitchen, where celebrity chef Peter Merriman is usually seen orchestrating the proceedings. Merriman, an expert hiker and all-around athlete, has been known to dive under the sea for the shellfish on your plate. Anything he doesn't catch himself is obtained from local fishermen off Kawaihae harbor, and all produce is grown locally. No lunch on weekends. Features: own baking, rated wine cellar. Reservations required. Credit cards: A, MC, V.

Kohala Coast

Donatoni's $$$ ★★★★

425 Waikoloa Beach Drive, Kohala Coast, 96743, ☎ *(808) 885-1234. Associated hotel: The Hilton Waikoloa Village.*

Donatoni's is the star among the Hilton Waikoloa Village Resort's six restaurants. The elegantly appointed room recalls a villa on the Italian Riviera rather than the volcanic Kohala Coast, but it all works. And you can get here by gondola. Cuisine is Northern Italian, and there's a dress code to match the decor. Try the delicious pizzas, osso bucco, cioppino, and fresh cannoli for dessert. Excellent wine list. Features: own baking, rated wine cellar. Jacket requested. Reservations required. Credit cards: A, DC, D, MC, V.

Hakone $$$ ★★★★

62-100 Kauna'oa Drive, Kohala Coast, 96743, ☎ *(808) 880-1111. Associated hotel: The Hapuna Beach Prince. Japanese cuisine. Specialties: Sukiyaki, nabemono, shabushabu, kaiseki dinners, sushi.*

You'll have to dress a bit to enjoy a wide variety of Japanese specialties at this tranquil, peaceful, yet elegant dining room in the Hapuna Beach Prince Hotel. In addition to a menu (buffet or a lá carte) of traditional sukiyaki, seafood in broth, shabushabu (tabletop cooking), and Imperial court-style kaiseki dinners, there's a separate sushi bar with its own kitchen. Ocean or garden views are included. Jacket requested. Reservations required. Credit cards: A, DC, MC, V.

Roy's Waikoloa Bar & Grill $$$ ★★★
250 Waikoloa Beach Drive, in the King's Shops, Kohala Coast,
☎ *(808) 885-4321.*
International cuisine. Specialties: Dim sum-style appetizers, imu oven pizzas, fresh fish, dark chocolate souffle.
Roy's Waikoloa features a regular menu of appetizers, individual imu pizzas, pasta, fresh salads, and entrées side-by-side with a nightly special sheet. Some items might include Puna papaya and hibachi beef salad with julienne veggies and hoisin sesame vinaigrette, "local style" Portuguese sausage pizza with Maui onions and cheddar, or a mixed plate of lemongrass shutome and blackened ahi. Among the desserts are Roy's signature original dark chocolate soufflé with a liquid center (a must for chocoholics), or Big Island style sundae with tropical sauces and ginger candy. Reservations recommended. Credit cards: CB, DC, D, MC, V.

The Bistro $$$ ★★★★
62-100 Kauna'oa Drive, Kohala Coast, 96743,
☎ *(808) 880-1111. Associated hotel: The Hapuna Beach Prince. Closed: Mondays and Tuesdays.*
Renowned for a prodigious wine cellar, the luxurious, intimate Bistro is subtly decorated in an elegant English hunt-club style. Many dishes are prepared at tableside, and patrons are expected to dress in "evening resort attire." The Bistro recently switched from Mediterranean cuisine to a contemporary American menu of grilled steaks, fresh seafood, and poultry, enhanced by fresh local produce. Features: own baking, rated wine cellar. Jacket requested. Reservations required. Credit cards: A, DC, MC, V.

The CanoeHouse $$$ ★★★★
68-1400 Mauna Lani Drive, Kohala Coast, 96743,
☎ *(808) 885-6622. Associated hotel: The Mauna Lani Bay Hotel.*
Gourmet cuisine. Specialties: Fresh coriander crusted ahi with curried eggplant, kiawe smoked five-spice duck with mango relish. Closed on Tuesdays.

Even if the name of the restaurant is all stuck together, this gleaming, open-air, beachfront dining room in the Mauna Lani Bay Hotel is one of the most beautiful on the island. Dinner here is pure romance, with magnificent views of the splendid sunsets, twinkling stars, and waves lapping the sand right outside. Try the signature rare peppered ahi (tuna) accompanied by a bottle of champagne. A must for a special-event dinner, and definitely worth the price. Features: outside dining, own baking, rated wine cellar. Credit cards: A, DC, MC, V.

The Coast Grille $$$ ★★★★
62-100 Kauna'oa Drive, Kohala Coast, 96743,
☎ *(808) 880-1111. Associated hotel: The Hapuna Beach Prince. Seafood cuisine. Specialties: Oyster bar, fresh seafood.*
This circular-shaped dining room in the Hapuna Beach Prince allows almost all diners a view of fabulous Hapuna Beach and the ocean; suffice it to say that sunsets can be wonderful from this vantage point. The chef uses local ingredients, such as tender ahi (Pacific yellowfin tuna) and fresh Big Island produce in his Hawaiian Regional cuisine. Seafood is the star here, including a tantalizing steamed whole fish wrapped in a banana leaf, but meat dishes are also served. Features: rated wine cellar. Reservations required. Credit cards: A, DC, D, MC, V..

South Kona
Captain Cook

Aloha Café $$ ★★★★
Highway 11, Captain Cook, ☎ *(808) 322-3383.*
American cuisine. Specialties: Breakfasts, baked goods, coffee drinks.
Since good restaurants of any substance are few and far between in this area, this small but terrific indoor/outdoor café in the lobby of the Aloha Theater, a circa 1920s building and home to the Aloha Community Players theater troupe, is a welcome relief. Locals and tourists in the know head here to sit on the covered, wrap-around lanai for hearty breakfasts and steaming-hot Kona coffee sprinkled with chocolate. All pastries, desserts, and muffins are homemade. If you're here for lunch and dinner, fresh fish is the best bet, prepared with light, healthful sauces. Features: outside dining, own baking. Reservations not accepted. Credit cards: MC, V.

Holualoa Café $ ★★★
76-5901 Mamalahoa Highway, Captain Cook,
☎ *(808) 322-2233.*
American cuisine. Specialties: Kona coffee, pastries, smoothies.
Closed on Sundays.

A charmer of a coffee house/gift shop, with a garden for outdoor seating, Holualoa Café is in the heart of the Kona coffee belt. This café's house blend is served with whipped cream if you desire. Homemade pastries and friendly service, as well as live music on Thursdays from 7–10 p.m. Features: outside dining, own baking. Reservations not accepted.

Kay's Kitchen $ ★★
Four miles above Keahole Airport, Captain Cook,
☎ *(808) 325-1086.*
Specialties: Loco moco.

Primarily used for takeout, this family diner with four outdoor tables is in a somewhat out-of-the-way location next door to a small market. Locals don't mind making the drive for the familiar rib-sticker, loco moco, a freshly ground meat patty topped with brown gravy and served with an egg, or hamburger steak. Call *(808) 325-7797* for a recording of daily specials. Features: outside dining. Reservations not accepted.

Keauhou

Edward's at the Terrace $$$ ★★★
78-261 Manukai Street, Keauhou, 96739, ☎ *(808) 322-1434.*
Associated hotel: Kanaloa at Kona Condominiums.
Mediterranean cuisine. Specialties: Medallions of pork with prunes, Bastia, fresh fish, homemade desserts.

The poolside terrace of the Kanaloa at Kona condominiums, overlooking the ocean, is the setting for this lovely restaurant serving Mediterranean cuisine with a touch of the Middle East. If you've maxxed out on Pacific Rim fare, sample the Moroccan bastia, Cornish game hen wrapped tenderly in phyllo pastry. Features: outside dining, own baking. Reservations recommended. Credit cards: A, CB, DC, MC, V.

Volcano
Volcano Village

Kilauea Lodge and Restaurant $$$ ★★★

Old Volcano Road (between Haunani & Wright Roads), Volcano Village, 96785, ☎ *(808) 967-7366. Associated hotel: Kilauea Lodge.*

European cuisine. Specialties: Broiled marlin with mango relish, game dishes, vegetarian specialties, macadamia nut pie.

European specialties with a local touch are served in a baronial, high-ceilinged dining hall with polished hardwood floors and koa tables. A historic rock "fireplace of friendship" glows constantly in the center of the room. Located in the Kilauea Lodge, this is the favored choice for dining in the Volcano area, and chef-innkeeper Albert Jeyte (together with wife, Lorna) make all the soups, breads, and desserts from scratch daily. Features: own baking. Reservations recommended. Credit cards: A, MC, V.

Nightlife

The Big Island doesn't offer a whole lot of heel-kicking action after nightfall. The resorts and large hotels feature lounge acts and various other entertainment, including **luaus** and **Polynesian revues.** Two **discos** to try on the **Kona coast** are the **Eclipse Restaurant,** in Kailua, and the **Second Floor**, within the Hilton Waikola Village. Don Drysdale's Club 53, Jolly Roger, and Under the Palms are popular lounges for drinking and hanging out. Over at **Hilo** (which is *really* dead after dark), you can practice **country dancing** at Fiascos or Lehua Bay City Bar and Grill, **disco** at D'Angoras or do the **karaoke** thing at KK Tei's Lounge; the bar at the Hilo Seaside Hotel draws the locals who entertain themselves. There are **movie theaters** in Kailua-Kona, Hilo, and Pahoa, and **legitimate theater** in Kainaliu, Hilo, and Waimea.

Hilo

Fiascos ★★

Highway 11 near Banyan Drive, Hilo, 96720,
☎ *(808) 935-7666.*

Line dancin' in Hilo Thursdays from 8 p.m. to midnight; Live Hawaiian music on Friday and Saturdays from 9 p.m. General admission: Varies.

Kona
Kailua-Kona

Eclipse ★★

75-5771 Kuakini Highway, Kailua-Kona, 96740,
☎ *(808) 329-4686.*

A Kona hot zone, with '90s style-disco dancing on weekends. Big-band and country-western the rest of the week.

Huggo's ★★

75-5828 Kahakai Road, Kailua-Kona, 96740,
☎ *(808) 329-1493.*
Closed: Sundays.

A "smorgasbord" of live music accompanies the good eats at this Kona bayfront institution. "Sound Effects" plays oldies from the '50s and '60s on Friday nights, slinky salsa by "Kona Blend" on Saturday nights, "island attitude" music (whatever that is) on Mondays. Tuesday, karaoke and dancing. Wednesday, contemporary; Thursday, jazz.

Island Breeze Luau ★★★

75-5660 Palani Road, Kailua-Kona, 96740,
☎ *(808) 326-4969.*
Closed: Mondays, Fridays, Saturdays.

Although most luaus have similar menus and entertainment, this one is special in that it's set at King Kamehameha I's restored Kailua Bay beachfront estate, Kamakahonu. The revue commences with the arrival of the royal court, replete with ceremonial headdresses and "feather" *kahili*. Among the 22 dishes served are some vegetarian items. It's also offered four nights a week and is reasonably priced. General admission: $60.

King Kamehameha's Kona Beach Hotel ★★

75-5660 Palani Road, Kailua-Kona, 96740,
☎ *(808) 329-2911.*

The poolside Billfish Bar at this beachfront hotel offers live music entertainment to accompany the gorgeous sunsets; it's relatively uncrowded, and pupus and cocktails are served. Warble to the karaoke machine on Friday and Saturday nights at Paddlers Grille, also on the hotel grounds.

Kona Bowl Lounge ★★
75-5586 Ololi Road, Kailua-Kona, 96740, ☎ *(808) 326-2695.*
Hours: 7 p.m.–2 a.m.
Karaoke with deejay "J.J." Kapele every evening; if you stink, at least the rolling balls will drown you out. On the other hand, if you're great, the room will be so quiet you can hear the pins drop.

The Puka Bar/Kona Comedy Club ★★
78-128 Ehukai Street, Kailua-Kona, 96740,
☎ *(808) 322-3411.*
Hours: 8 p.m.–2 a.m., Wednesdays. only.
The nightly karaoke song fest is interrupted one night a week when the Kona Comedy Club takes over the bar on Wednesdays at 8 p.m. Good for a couple of belly laughs.

North Kona

Kona Village Resort Luau ★★★★
P.O. Box 1299, North Kona, 96740, ☎ *(808) 325-5555.*
Hours: 6:45–9 p.m., Wednesdays. only.
The Kona Village luau, a tradition for 30 years, has been consistently judged by luau connoisseurs as the best all around. The exclusive resort opens up its guarded gates to anyone who can afford to attend the feast. Preparations start as early as 9 a.m. on Fridays when 20 hot cooking stones are put inside the traditional *kalua* pig. At 6:45 p.m., guests are invited to witness the unveiling of the pig at a special ceremony, when chefs remove the stones with their bare hands. The luscious menu features sushi, fresh crab, and teriyaki beef, as well as the usual Hawaiian dishes. The fiery Polynesian revue includes Hawaiian hula, rhythmic chants, and a Samoan fire dance. No price.

South Kohala
Kohala Coast

Mauna Kea Beach Hotel Luau ★★★★
Mauna Kea Beach Hotel, Kohala Coast, ☎ *(808) 882-7222.*
Closed: Mon., Wed., Thur., Fri., Sat., Sun.
The newly reopened Mauna Kea Beach Hotel presents an authentic luau on the North Pointe Lawn every Tuesday at 6 p.m. The special entertainment is provided by Kumu Hula

Nani Lim and dancers from her hula halau, winners of the prestigious Merrie Monarch hula competition. No price.

Petroglyph Bar ★★★
*69-275 Waikoloa Beach Drive, Kohala Coast, 96743,
☎ (808) 885-6789.*
Located on the rooftop of the Royal Waikoloan Hotel, this relaxing spot offers uninterrupted views of gorgeous Anaeho'omalu Bay, ancient fishponds, and Mauna Kea in the distance. A favored sunset sojourn, the tropical drinks are choice, and the Hawaiian music is live and romantic.

Shopping

Both Kona and Hilo have enough **malls and shopping centers** to please even the most fixated visitors. Waimea and Captain Cook also have their own—albeit small—shopping areas. The strip along **Alii Drive,** in Kailua-Kona, is geared toward visitors who crowd in to pick up souvenirs, resort wear, gift items, and arts and crafts. Selections of **local arts and crafts**—jewelry, pottery, weavings, glasswork, carvings, beadwork, feather work, etc.—can be viewed and purchased at Volcano Art Center (within Hawaii Volcanoes National Park) and at galleries in **Holualoa, Kapaau,** and **Kainalu.**

Hilo

Basically Books ★★
*46 Waianuenue Avenue, Hilo, ☎ (808) 961-0144.
Hours: 9 a.m.–5 p.m.*
Specializes in books about the islands, including out-of-print vintage Hawaiiana. The adjoining map shop has a large selection of travel guides and maps of Hawaii.

Dan de Luz's Woods Inc. ★★★★
*760 Kilauea Avenue, Hilo, ☎ (808) 935-5587.
Hours: 9 a.m.–5 p.m.*
Collector's-item wood bowls made by famed island artist Dan de Luz, who has a workshop in the back that guests are invited to tour. Visit his Waimea-Kamuela shop at *64-1014 Mamalahoa Highway, (808) 885-5856,* daily 9 a.m.–5 p.m.

Panaewa Homestead Farmers Market ★★
Puainako and Ohuohu Streets, Hilo, ☎ *(808) 959-2726.*
Hours: 6 a.m.–noon
Saturdays only.
This market was established recently by local farmers from Hilo's Panaewa area. It's a colorful distribution point for a variety of produce and foodstuffs. Also check out Hilo's main farmer's market at the corner of Kamehameha Avenue and Mamo Street on Wednesdays and Saturdays from 6 a.m.–1 p.m.

Sig Zane Designs ★★★
122 Kamehameha Avenue, Hilo, 96720, ☎ *(808) 935-7077.*
Hours: 9 a.m.–5 p.m.
Sig Zane features locally designed, 100-percent-cotton clothing, original fabrics to buy by the yard, bedding, and gifts.

Kona
Kailua-Kona

Hula Heaven ★★★
75-5744 Ali'i Drive, Kailua-Kona, 96740, ☎ *(808) 329-7885.*
Hours: 9 a.m.–9 p.m.
This shop in the Kona Inn Shopping Village will assuage any pangs people have for the romantic era of mid-1900s Hawaii. Hula Heaven features Matson Line menu art (up to $500 for those in mint condition), and Aloha shirts worth as much as an Italian haute couture original.

Island Preservations ★★
75-5660 Palani Road, Kailua-Kona, 96750,
☎ *(808) 329-7770.*
Hours: 9 a.m.–5 p.m.
Located in King Kamehameha's Kona Beach Hotel, this unique shop uses real blossoms from the Big Island, including orchids, pikake, and roses, and preserves them whole in a unique, dye-free, secret process. The flowers are then mounted and placed in a Plexiglass case to protect them from ultraviolet light, trimmed with copper foil, and placed in a handsome koa frame (some back-lit). Amazingly, some of the orchids are more than 10 years old but look freshly picked. A lava-rock-like urethane foam is sculpted into a human torso to display leis. Prices range

from $65 to $1250 depending on size and complexity. Shipping available worldwide.

Kona Farmers Market ★★★
Kona Inn Shopping Village, Kailua-Kona.
Hours: 6 a.m.–3 p.m., Wednesdays and Saturdays only.
Rare orchids and heliconias, papayas, Ka'u oranges and other tropical flowers and fruits as well as island-style food, coffee, and macadamia nuts are featured at this lively market.

Noa Noa ★★★
75-5744 Ali'i Drive in the Kona Inn Shopping Center, Kailua-Kona, 96740, ☎ (808) 329-8187.
Hours: 9 a.m.–9 p.m.
All original, hand-painted batik clothing in natural fabrics from Indonesia for men, women, and children. Also a fine collection of Pacific Island artifacts including Ikat weavings, basketry, masks, and ceramics.

North Kohala
Hawi

As Hawi Turns ★★★
Downtown Hawi 96719, ☎ (808) 889-5023.
Hours: 10 a.m.–6 p.m.
Vintage clothing, crafts and "wild things," all in the heart of downtown Hawi.

Hawaiian Moon Gallery ★★★
P.O. Box 1469, Hawi, 96755, ☎ (808) 889-0880.
Hours: 9 a.m.–5 p.m.
This eclectic gallery in rustic Hawi exhibits the works of talented local potters, artists, sculptors, and jewelers. Also featured are handcrafted wood furniture by the owner's husband, and distinctive, one-of-a-kind clothing.

Kohala Koa Gallery ★★★
Junction of Highway 250 and 270, Hawi, ☎ (808) 889-0055.
Hours: 9 a.m.–5 p.m.
Located within the Bamboo Restaurant, a restored old general store. Robin and Michael Felig have amassed a unique collec-

tion of locally crafted wall art, pottery, jewelry, baskets, koa clocks, boxes, bowls, and custom furnishings and accessories made of Hawaii's native woods.

Kapa'au

Ackerman Gallery ★★★
P.O. Box 961, Kapa'au, 96755, ☎ *(808) 889-5971.*
Hours: 10 a.m.–5:30 p.m.
Owned by Gary Ackerman, a Paris-trained artist with a distinguished reputation, this restored old auto showroom and gas station features canvases, hand-blown glass pieces, wood sculptures, hand-painted silks, and original works by Hawaii's leading artists, including Greg Pontius, Leimana Pelton, John Flynn, and Wilfred Yamazawa, a Kapa'au resident famous for petroglyph jewelry displayed at the Bishop Museum. Also Oriental antiques and primitive artifacts.

South Kohala
Kamuela

Cook's Discoveries ★★★★
Highway 19, in the Waimea Center, Kamuela, 96743,
☎ *(808) 885-3633.*
Hours: 10 a.m.–6 p.m.
Shopping here is truly a discovery: you get to explore several rooms full of genuine koa carvings, jewelry, clothing, toys, and confections made by artists with taste. Cook's Discoveries is also an excellent location for authentic hula implements (sorry, no ukuleles). It's located in the restored Spencer House, an old general store built in 1850.

Parker Square ★★★
Highway 19, one block past Edelweiss Restaurant, Kamuela.
Hours: 9 a.m.–5 p.m.
The eight shops and galleries in this rustic-chic shopping center in a country setting are fun to just browse through. Hawaiian, Polynesian, Asian and primitive art, antique baskets, jewelry, and koa bowls at Gallery of Great Things, ☎ *(808) 885-7706;* Antique Japanese, Korean, and Chinese furniture, porcelains, and textiles from Silk Road Gallery; Gourmet kitchen accessories, gift cards, Hawaiian books, candles, blankets, linens, and Crabtree and Evelyn products at Waimea

General Store, ☎ *(808) 885-4479;* Kamuela Goldsmiths for gold and gemstones, country furnishings, teddy bears galore, woven throws and quilts; Christmas collectibles at Bentleys; and meditation supplies, beads, and incense at Sweet Wind. Relax with aromatic coffee and a snack at Waimea Coffee Company, ☎ *(808) 885-4472.*

Princess Kaiulani Fashions ★★★
Waimea Center, Kamuela, 96743, ☎ *(808) 885-2177.*
Hours: 10 a.m.–6 p.m.
Don't think you can hide under these designer muumuus—the elaborate shoulders and scoop necklines recall the Victorian era of the real Princess Kaiulani. Also a full line of distinctive women's clothing. Opens at 9 a.m. on Saturday.

South Kona
Holualoa

Studio 7 ★★★
Mamalahoa Highway, Holualoa, ☎ *(808) 323-2877.*
The old coffee town and art colony of Holualoa is home to Studio 7, where woodblock prints, paintings, sculptures, and pottery by contemporary Big Island artists Hiroki and Setuko Morinoue are displayed.

Keauhou

Alapaki's ★★★
Keauhou Shopping Center, Keauhou, ☎ *(808) 322-2007.*
Hours: 9 a.m.–6 p.m.
Enter this dramatic shop through a unique lava rock archway where Alapaki and Josie Tampos have collected Hawaiian crafts by more than 100 local artists. The woodwork is incredible, including bowls, jewelry, and poi pounders. Feather *uli-uli* rattles, coconut *pahu* drums, and other Hawaiian musical instruments make great gifts. Open Sunday from 10 a.m.–5 p.m.

Volcano
Volcano Village

Farmer's Market ★★
Cooper Center, P.O. Box 600, Volcano Village, 96785,
☎ *(808) 967-7121.*
Hours: 8:30–11 a.m.

Closed: Saturdays.
Fresh produce, herbs, flowers, and coffee grown by volcano farmers are the main attractions at this local-style market. Also used clothing, books, and fresh baked goods, including *malasadas* (Portuguese donut holes).

OAHU

Many island-bound visitors no doubt believe Oahu *is* Hawaii. They land at Honolulu International Airport, shuttle over to Waikiki, crowd together on the sand, elbow each other in the shops, ogle Diamond Head in the distance, pay respect at Pearl Harbor, do a luau and see a real hula dancer, then go back to the airport and head home.

In many ways, Oahu is indeed the perfect island—a place with plenty of everything to do, as well as room to escape from it all—with contrasts that can't help but startle and amaze even jaded tourists. Yes, there is the tourist mecca of Waikiki with its crowds, malls, hotels, restaurants, street vendors, flash and fervor, schlock and gawd—all mesmerizing, even if it is *not* your style. But blink hard, and you'll also be gazing at a booming city with overdeveloped communities, rural villages, highly visible military power, sugarcane and pineapple fields, cultural presence and sinful practices, cranes and bulldozers, world-class surfing and bubbling streams, claustrophobic beaches and wide-open spaces. Nicknamed the "Gathering Place," Oahu's 826,231 residents (about 80 percent of the state's population) are quite happy, thank you, with this "gathering" of elements.

Oahu more or less slipped through the cracks of the early settlement days, only becoming *really* noticed in 1795 when King Kamehameha the Great swooped in on his island-unification quest. It wasn't long before Honolulu, with its attractive harbor, became the islands' center of commerce, and Pearl Harbor, with its deep waters, became the focal point of U.S. military might.

Once King Kamehameha shifted the capital from Lahaina to Oahu, the island became something of a royal playground, with the kings and queens growing more and more enchanted with their new home *and* that strip of beach known as Waikiki. Many members of the royal family set up residence near the beach (Kamehameha's IV and V, Lunalilo, Kalakaua, Liliuokalani, and Kaiulani). Did someone say, "island, beach, remote, paradise—women?"

The influx of visitors meant, of course, that they needed places to stay. The building began. First came a barrage of beach cottages but, come the turn of the century, a hotel just *had* to go up. The Sheraton Moana Surfrider (then known as the Moana) became Oahu's first hotel, followed in 1927 by the luxurious Royal Hawaiian Hotel (or the "Pink Palace of the Pacific"). It didn't take

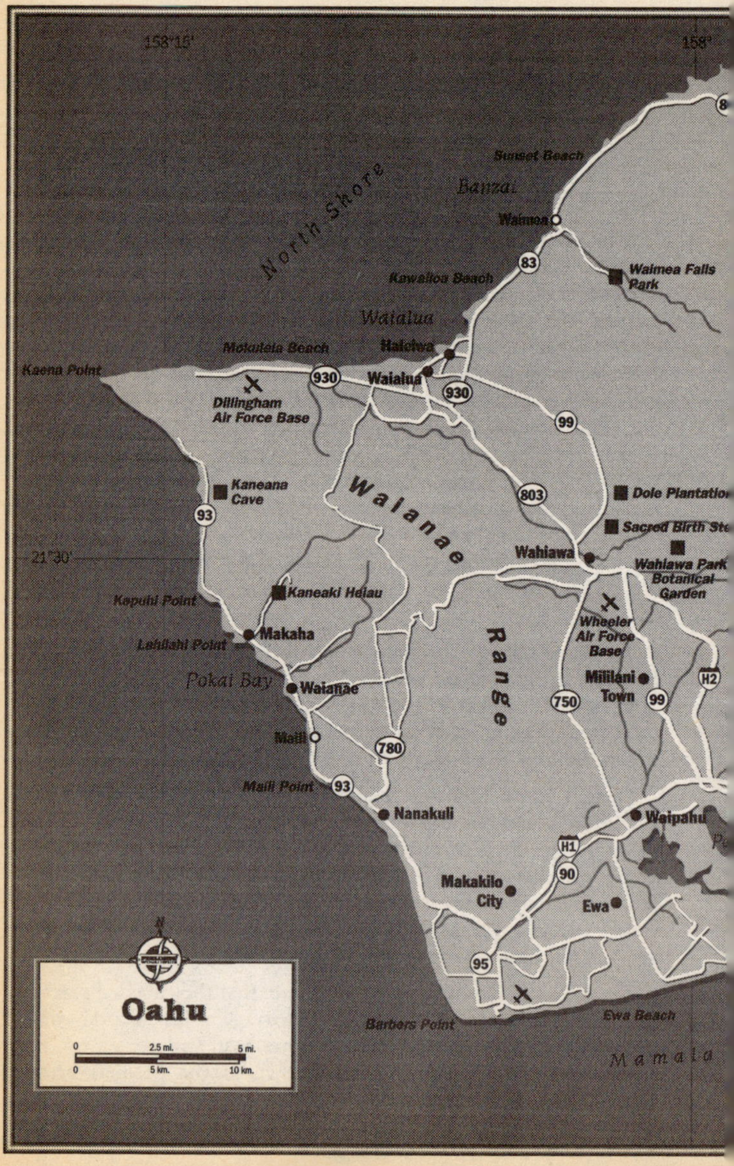
158°15'
158°
Sunset Beach
Banzai
North Shore
Waimea
83
Waimea Falls Park
Kawailoa Beach
Waialua
Mokuleia Beach
Haleiwa
Kaena Point
930
Waialua
930
Dillingham Air Force Base
99
Kaneana Cave
Waianae
803
Dole Plantation
93
Sacred Birth Sto
21°30'
Wahiawa
Wahiawa Park Botanical Garden
Kaneaki Heiau
Kepuhi Point
Wheeler Air Force Base
Makaha
Lahilahi Point
Range
Pokai Bay
Waianae
Mililani Town
H2
750
99
Maili
780
Maili Point
93
Nanakuli
Waipahu
H1
90
Makakilo City
Ewa
95
Barbers Point
Ewa Beach
Mamala
Oahu
0
2.5 mi.
5 mi.
0
5 km.
10 km.

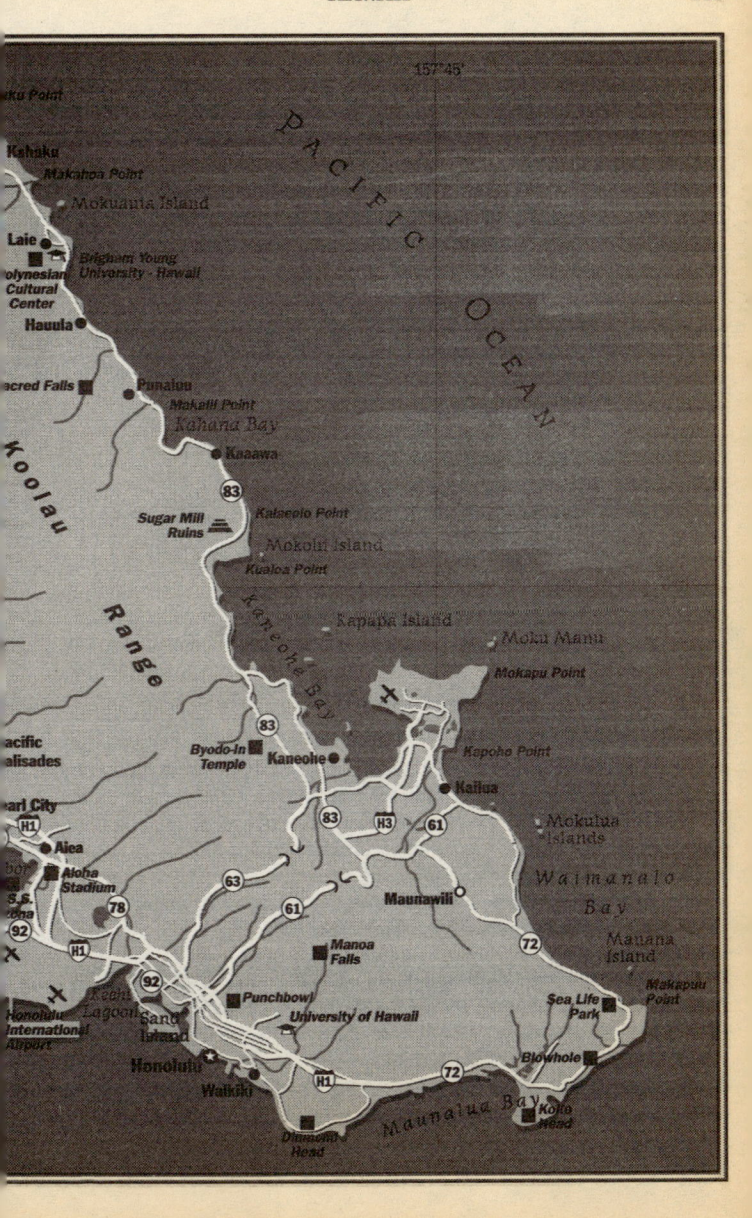

HAWAII

143

long before Waikiki became known as a visitor destination *par excellence*. But tourists weren't the only ones to visit Oahu—the Japanese made a surprise appearance on December 7, 1941, making their presence felt by bombing Pearl Harbor.

Within a decade, the island was ready again to welcome the paradise-seeking masses. More hotels went up, followed by resorts, followed by condos, and today's visitors can now choose from about 130 hotels and condos, and approximately 34,000 rooms.

Oahu Facts

A.k.a.	The Gathering Place
Main city	Honolulu
Flower	Llima
Color	Yellow
Area	594 square miles
Length	44 miles
Width	30 miles
Population	826,231
Highest point	Kaala Peak (4003 feet)

Honolulu Survival Guide

Getting There

Honolulu International Airport, about nine miles west of Waikiki, is one of the nation's busiest, serving about 1000 flights each day. The main terminal caters to international and domestic flights, while the inter-island terminal serves the commuter and island-hopping trade. Both terminals provide plenty of facilities for travelers: information centers, car rental booths, gift and souvenir shops, newsstands, restaurants, snack bars, cocktail lounges, lockers, baggage claim areas, and ticket counters. Domestic airline are:

AMERICAN AIRLINES	(800) 833-7600
AMERICAN TRANS AIR	(800) 833-0074
CANADIAN AIRLINES	(800) 839-2244

from Vancouver:

CONTINENTAL AIRLINES	(800) 523-0000
DELTA AIRLINES	(800) 833-8281
HAWAIIN AIRLINES	(800) 838-1555
NORTHWEST AIRLINES	(800) 955-2255
TRANS WORLD AIRLINES	(800) 221-2000
UNITED AIRLINES	(800) 547-2211

Interisland airlines are:

AIR MOLOKAI	(800) 521-0090
ALOHA AIRLINES	(800) 484-1111
ISLAND AIR	(800) 484-2222
MAHALO AIR	(800) 833-5555

A large number of **foreign carriers** also serve Honolulu, though they are prohibited by law from transporting passengers from other U.S. cities. See previous chapter for website information.

Various **cruise ships** call into Honolulu throughout the year. Among the cruise lines that make Honolulu a regular stop are Cunard Line, P&O, Princess Cruises, Royal Cruises and Royal Viking. American Hawaii Cruises' SS *Independence* stops at Honolulu on its scheduled inter island excursions.

Getting Around

Taxis will be waiting outside baggage claim at the airport; a ride into Honolulu will run $20–25. Many island hotels and resorts will send their own **airport shuttles** (ask when booking your room), otherwise you can use **Trans-Hawaiian Services** *((808) 533-8765);* fare is about $8 into Waikiki. The public bus, known as **TheBus,** will take you from the airport to anywhere on the island for a piddly 85 cents, but no baggage is allowed.

146　　　　　　　　　　　　　HAWAII

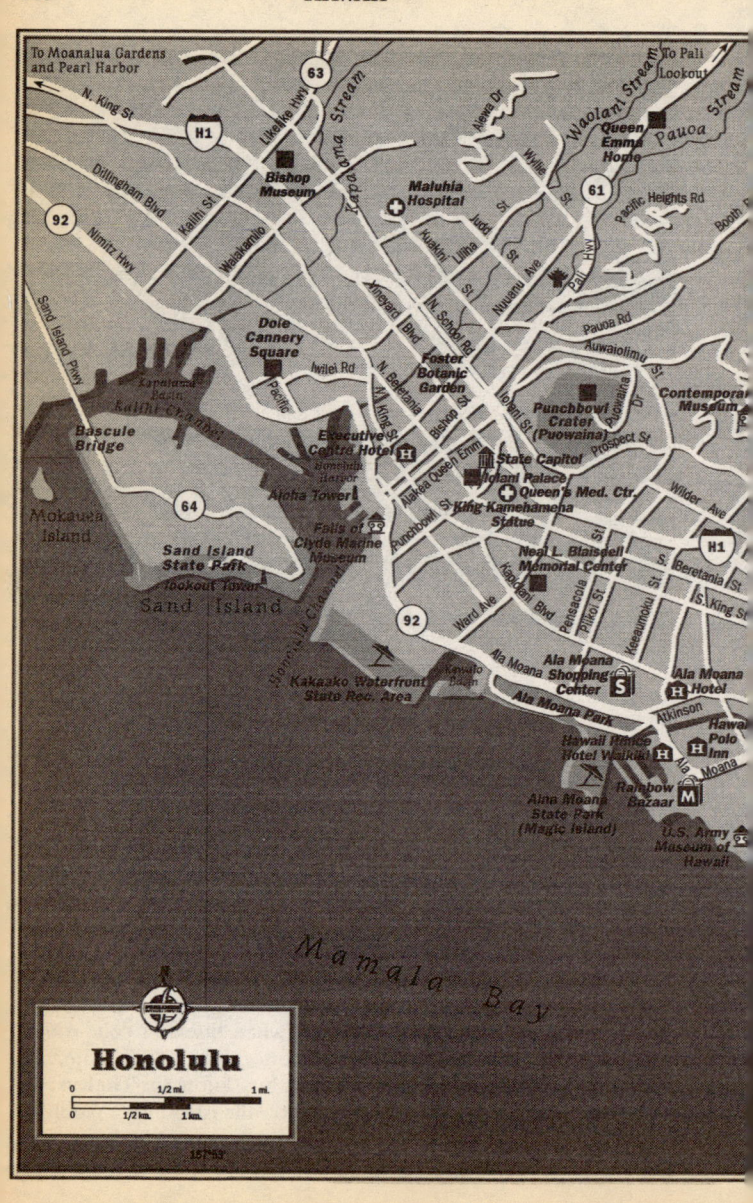

Honolulu

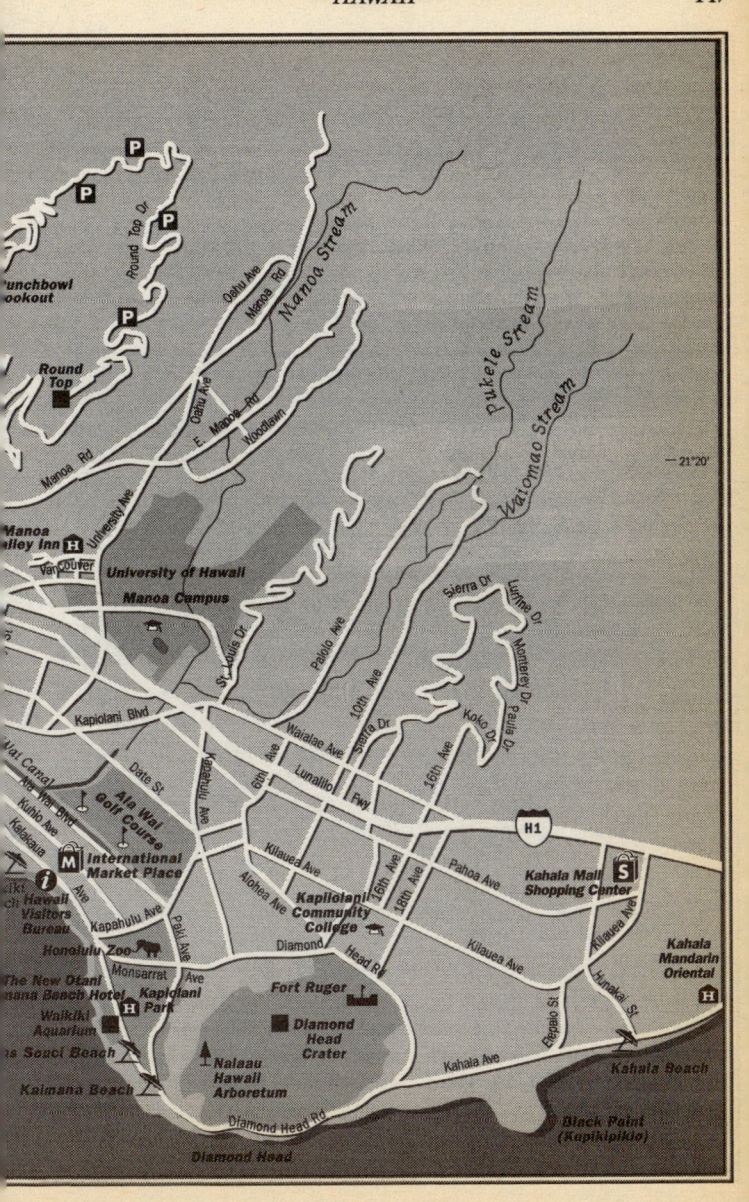

HAWAII

Map labels:

- Punchbowl Lookout
- Round Top Dr
- Round Top
- Oahu Ave
- Manoa Rd
- Manoa Stream
- Pukele Stream
- Waiomao Stream
- E. Manoa Rd
- Woodlawn
- 21°20'
- Manoa Valley Inn
- University Ave
- Vancouver
- University of Hawaii Manoa Campus
- St. Louis Dr
- Paloa Ave
- Sierra Dr
- Lurline Dr
- Monterey Dr
- Paula Dr
- Kapiolani Blvd
- Waialae Ave
- 10th Ave
- Sierra Dr
- Koko Dr
- Date St
- 6th Ave
- Lunalilo Fwy
- 16th Ave
- Ala Wai Canal
- Ala Wai Blvd
- Kuhio Ave
- Kalakaua
- Ala Wai Golf Course
- International Market Place
- Kapahulu Ave
- Kilauea Ave
- Alohea Ave
- Pahoa Ave
- H1
- Kahala Mall Shopping Center
- Hawaii Visitors Bureau
- Honolulu Zoo
- Paki Ave
- Monsarrat Ave
- Kapiolani Park
- Kapiolani Community College
- Kilauea Ave
- 18th Ave
- Kilauea Ave
- Kahala Mandarin Oriental
- The New Otani Kaimana Beach Hotel
- Waikiki Aquarium
- Diamond Head Rd
- Fort Ruger
- Diamond Head Crater
- Elepaio St
- Hunakai St
- Sans Souci Beach
- Kaimana Beach
- Nalaau Hawaii Arboretum
- Kahala Ave
- Kahala Beach
- Diamond Head Rd
- Diamond Head
- Black Point (Kupikipikio)

Baggage hassles aside, **TheBus** is quite some deal—85 cents (exact change necessary) is the fare to anywhere on the route, and the route goes all around the island, into the interior and to most of Oahu's towns and villages. On top of that, you can get one free transfer if you request it when boarding. Long-term visitors might want to spring for a monthly bus pass ($20). For information, call (808) *848-5555*.

You'll find plenty of **car rental agencies** at the airport and in Honolulu and Waikiki—with a number of small independents groveling alongside the big names. Rental agencies with airport counters and 24-hour service include:

ALOMA	833-4585
AVIS	834-5536
BUDGET	836-1700
DOLLAR	831-2330
HERTZ	831-3500
NATIONAL	831-3800

Driving is easy on Oahu. One road (which changes names depending on where you are) hugs most of the coast, while another (which doesn't change names as often) slices through the interior. The main roads in Honolulu are King and Beretania streets; in Waikiki, the major ones are Kalakaua and Kuhio avenues. Rush-hour hell (the worst in Hawaii) is normally 6:30–8:30 a.m. and 3:30–5:30 p.m. on weekdays. Locals are unusually courteous drivers who will slow down and let you turn in front of them—don't honk unless it's an emergency, and smile and wave your appreciation. Parking spots around Waikiki and central Honolulu are not particularly easy to find, though you should be able to nab a space in a public garage or shopping complex.

Taxis are not allowed to cruise and, for all legal purposes, must be booked ahead (they're often waiting at hotels). Fares are about $1.50 for the flag-fall, $1.50 for each additional mile. Companies to try are **Aloha State Taxi** *((808) 847-3566)*, **Charley's** *((808) 531-1333)*, **SIDA of Hawaii, Inc.** *((808) 836-0011)* and **TheCab** *((808) 533-4999)*.

Aside from the super-developed areas, Oahu has excellent conditions for both **mopeds** and **bicycles**. For bicycle rentals, try the following Waikiki- or Honolulu-based companies: **Aloha Funway Rentals** *(2025 Kalakaua Avenue, (808) 946-2766)*, **The Bike Way** *(250 Ward Way, (808) 538-7433)*, **Blue Sky Rentals** *(1920 Ala Moana Boulevard, (808) 947-0100)* or **Fun and Sun Scooters** *(37 Olohana Street, (808) 946-2424)*. Motorcycles and mopeds are available from **Aloha Funway Rentals, Blue Sky Rentals, Fun and Sun Scooters** (above) or **Discount Moped Rentals** *((808) 941-3623)*, **Island Scooters** *((808) 924-9331)* and **Two Wheel Ventures** *((808) 943-0223)*. You'll need a valid motorcycle license to rent scooters, and a driver's license for mopeds.

Limousine lovers can arrange for airport transportation and island tours with **Cloud Nine Limousine Service** *((808) 524-7999)*, **Lowy Limousine Service** *((808) 455-2444)*, **Rocy's Limousine** *((808) 949-8001)*, or **Your Royal Highness** *((808) 941-4418)*.

Visitor Information

You'll find visitor information booths at Honolulu International Airport, or call into the Waikiki branch of the **Hawaii Visitors Bureau** *(2270 Kalakaua Avenue, 8th Floor, Honolulu 96815, (808) 923-1811)*.

Bird's-Eye View

At 594 square miles (44 miles long, 30 miles wide), Oahu holds the position of third-largest Hawaiian island. The famous stretch of beach known as Waikiki (on the dry, sunny side of the island) measures about two miles—between Diamond Head and the Ala Wai Canal—and is filled with hotels, tourists, restaurants, tourists, malls, tourists, street vendors, and tourists (hard to believe it was once filled with swamps and ducks!). Nearby Honolulu is the island's main city, the state capitol, and the political, cultural, and commercial heart. Few visitors miss a trek over to Pearl Harbor, west of Honolulu, home of the USS *Arizona* Memorial. The Koolau Range (highest point is 3150-foot Puu Konahuanui), behind Honolulu, runs north and south across most of Oahu, slicing the island into windward and leeward sides, and is traversed by the Pali Highway (Highway 61). The center of the island is planted with acres of sugarcane, pineapples, bananas, flowers, and fruit trees. Main communities on the fairly uncrowded windward shore are Kailua and

150   HAWAII

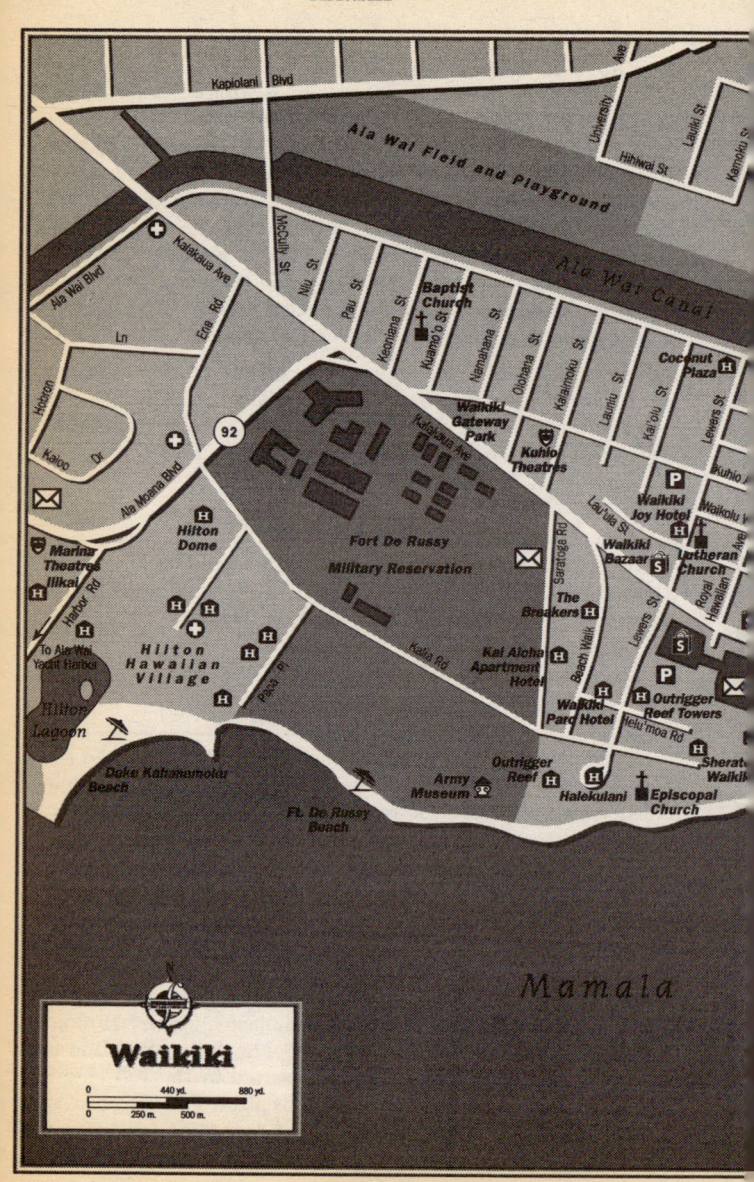

Waikiki

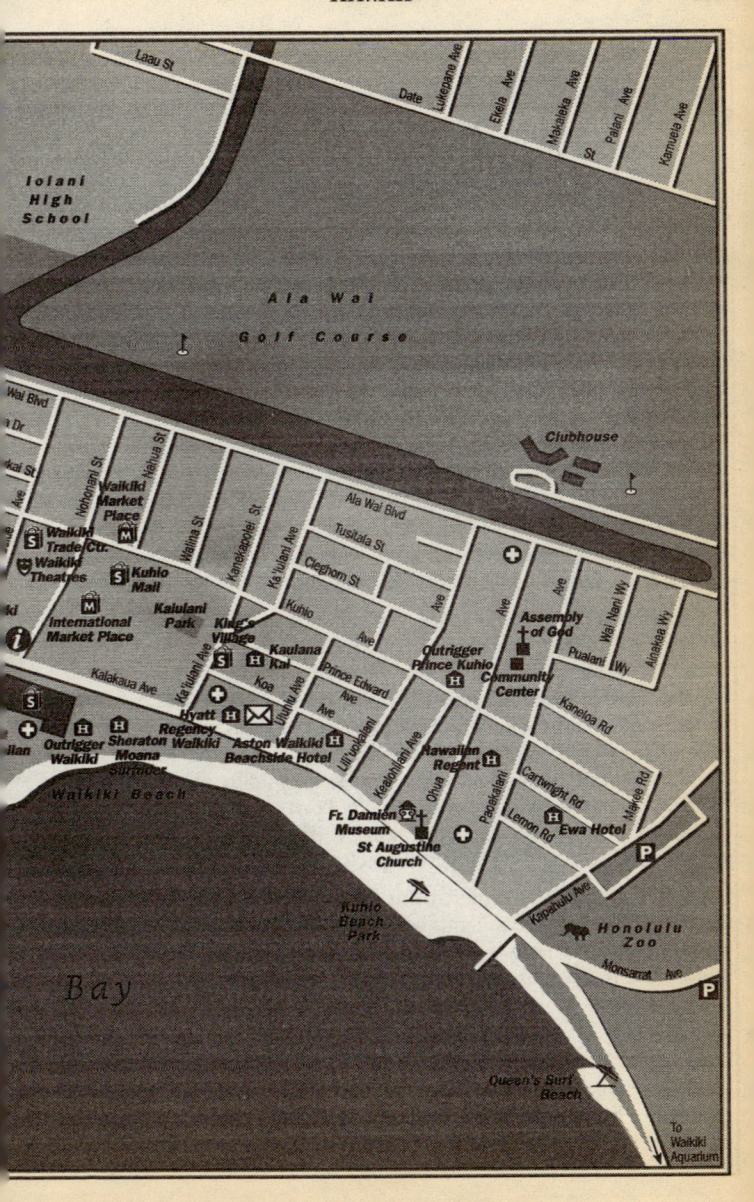

HAWAII

Map of Waikiki area

- Iolani High School
- Laau St
- Lukepane Ave
- Date St
- Eliela Ave
- Makiela Ave
- Palani Ave
- Kamuela Ave
- Ala Wai Golf Course
- Clubhouse
- Ala Wai Blvd
- Nohonani St
- Nahua St
- Walina St
- Kanekapolei St
- Ka'iulani St
- Tusitala St
- Cleghorn St
- Kuhio Ave
- Pualani Wy
- Wai Nani Wy
- Ainakea Wy
- Waikiki Trade Ctr.
- Waikiki Theatres
- Waikiki Market Place
- Kuhio Mall
- International Market Place
- Kaiulani Park
- King's Village
- Kaulana Kai
- Koa Ave
- Prince Edward
- Liliuokalani Ave
- Outrigger Prince Kuhio
- Community Center
- Assembly of God
- Kaneloa Rd
- Kalakaua Ave
- Hyatt Regency
- Outrigger Waikiki
- Sheraton Waikiki
- Moana Surfrider
- Aston Waikiki Beachside Hotel
- Hawaiian Regent
- Paoakalani Ave
- Cartwright Rd
- Lemon Rd
- Marke Rd
- Ewa Hotel
- Waikiki Beach
- Fr. Damien Museum
- St Augustine Church
- Ohua Ave
- Kapahulu Ave
- Kuhio Beach Park
- Honolulu Zoo
- Monsarrat Ave
- Bay
- Queen's Surf Beach
- To Waikiki Aquarium

151

Kaneohe, suburban towns that break up the almost end-on-end run of gorgeous beaches. Continuing northwest, the area around Waiahole offers sleepy villages and taro fields and, beyond, more great beaches, Kahana Valley State Park, Sacred Falls, and the Polynesian Cultural Center. Curving around Kawela Bay, the North Shore area features the world-famous Banzai Pipeline, Waimea Bay, Sunset Beach, and Kaena Point, with artsy communities and Dillingham Airfield situated in-between. The Waianae Coast, along the northwestern shores, is Oahu's last frontier, a region savored by locals who did not take well to the huge Koolina Resort recently built in Kapolei. More top surfing beaches sit along this coast (Makaha hosts annual surfing championships), along with the towns of Makaha, Waianae, Maili, and Nanakuli. Backdrop to the coast is the Waianae Mountain Range and 4003-foot Mount Kaala—Oahu's highest point.

Nature Guide

Flora and fauna on crowded Oahu? This island, in fact, is one gigantic tropical paradise endowed with almost every species of flower, fruit, tree, and shrub that Hawaii has to offer.

Around the cities and beaches, you can spot such feathered friends as sparrows, bulbul, and munia, plus upland forest game birds such as the Japanese quail, ring-necked pheasant, and dove. Less visible are the marine birds—Laysan albatross and various species of tern. In the forests and mountain ranges you might sight native dwellers such as the *'i'iwi* and *pueo* (Hawaiian owl). True bird enthusiasts should visit one or both of Oahu's national wildlife refuges (Pearl Harbor National Wildlife Refuge, at Pearl Harbor, and James Campbell Wildlife Refuge, near the North Shore) which attract many introduced and endangered species.

Oahu's unique and prolific plant life can be enjoyed throughout the island, but animals are another story. You might hear the call of a feral goat or wild pig if you're hiking in the mountains; otherwise you'll have to be content with suburban puppies and kitties.

Beach Finder

Most people, when they think of "Waikiki Beach," envision it as one distinctive stretch of sand. The two-plus-mile strip is actually a clump of beaches that stretch between the dramatic Diamond Head and the bustling Hilton Hawaiian Village Resort. The island of Oahu is laced with more than 100 different beaches, ranging from crowded tourist haunts to remote bays and international surfing haunts. Check with local authorities before you venture into the water, especially along the North Shore.

Waikiki

Kahanamoku Beach
In front of the Hilton Hawaiian Village.
A gentle lagoon that is favored by families with children and novice swimmers. Rest rooms, showers, surfboard rentals, volleyball, snack bar.

Fort DeRussy Beach
In front of Fort DeRussy and the Hale Koa Hotel.
Offers good snorkeling and is targeted mostly by beach-going military personnel. Rest rooms, showers, snack bars, volleyball.

Gray's Beach
In front of the Halekulani Hotel.
A narrow stretch with good surfing. Rest rooms, surfboard rentals, snack bars, catamaran and canoe excursions.

Kahaloa and Ulukou beaches
In front of the Royal Hawaiian Hotel and Sheraton Moana Surfrider.
Strictly a tourist stretch (there's even a police station!). Rest rooms, showers, snack bar, surfing lessons, catamaran and canoe excursions.

Kuhio Beach Park
Between the Waikiki Beach Center and the seawall.
Good for surfing and bodysurfing, but the occasional deep spot makes it a bit too treacherous for kids and other inexperienced swimmers.

Queen's Surf
Across from the Honolulu Zoo.
Frequented by an odd mix of families, locals, and gay men who come to picnic, frolic, and watch the sun go down. Rest rooms, showers, picnic area.

San Souci
In front of Kapiolani Park.
Favored by experienced swimmers, training triathletes, canoeists, kayakers, kids, and near-naked sunbathers. Rest rooms, showers, picnic area, volleyball.

Ala Moana Beach Park
In Honolulu, northwest of Waikiki (in front of the Ala Moana Mall).
One of the island's most popular tourist beaches. Calm surf, jogging tracks, picnic and games areas, and plenty of oiled-up bodies set the scene. Rest rooms, showers, snack bars, lifeguards, tennis courts.

Diamond Head to Makapuu Point

Waialae Beach Park
Off Kahala Avenue (near the Kahala Hilton).
Draws windsurfers. Rest rooms, showers, picnic area.

Hanauma Bay
East of Hawaii Kai.
A marine preserve and a popular site for snorkeling and scuba-diving lessons. Rest rooms, showers, equipment rental, snack bar.

Sandy Beach
Two miles east of Hanauma Bay.
Brings the younger (somewhat rowdy) crowd who like to tempt fate by swimming in the treacherous surf. Rest rooms, showers.

Along Windward Oahu

Makapuu Beach Park
Across from Sea Life Park.
Suitable only for strong swimmers and lazy sunbathers. Rest rooms, showers.

Waimanalo Beach Park
South of Waimanalo town.
Has gentle surf but is quite obviously local turf. Rest rooms, showers, picnic area.

Bellows Field Beach
Near Waimanalo town.
An Air Force beach, available to others on weekends for good swimming and bodysurfing. Rest rooms, showers, picnic area, parking.

Kailua Beach Park
Near Kailua town.
A long, usually crowded stretch with ideal windsurfing conditions. Rest rooms, showers, picnic area, snack bar.

Kualoa Regional Park
North of Waiahole town.
Features superb bay and mountain views and grassy picnic areas. Rest rooms, showers, picnic and camping areas.

Around the Fabulous North Shore

Sunset Beach
South of Waialee (and the Turtle Bay Hilton).
A wide beach with wild winter surf and calm summer swimming. No facilities.

Ehukai Beach Park
About two miles southwest of Sunset Beach.
This beach is long and wide and features a great view of the fabled Banzai Pipeline. Rest rooms, showers.

Waimea Bay Beach Park
A few miles north of Haleiwa.
This is the world-famous beach that reels the world's top surfers into its humongous 25-foot waves—steer clear unless you're one of them or you've come in summer when the surf is calm.

Haleiwa Beach Park
North of Haleiwa town.
Another big-winter-surf, gentle-summer-waves spot. Rest rooms, showers, grassy areas.

On the Waianae Coast

Makaha Beach Park
Northwest of Makaha town.

Sought out by locals as well as winter surfers. Rest rooms, showers.

Yokohama Bay
North of Makaha.
Another beach favored mainly by locals. Rest rooms, showers.

Adventure Guide

Want to do something a tad more active than shopping or tanning? Oahu has a variety of more action-packed activities to offer.

Trekkers will most likely start off at **Diamond Head**, where the trail will take you from the center of the crater up to the summit. The **Maunawili Demonstration Trail**, off Pali Highway (beyond Pali Lookout), leads through tropical forest along the windward edge of the Koolau Mountains. Also on the windward side, the **Hauula Loop Trail** winds through gorgeous plant life, ironwood forest, and Norfolk pine groves to a ridge-top with dynamite views. Various trails branch out from the top of **Tantalus** and **Round Top** drives, taking you to panoramic lookouts over the **Makiki Valley.** A favorite hike (during dry weather!) is into **Sacred Falls**, on the windward coast. Start off in the morning for the trek along Kaluanui Stream, into a narrow canyon, a deep pool, and the dramatic falls. For super-remote, isolated hiking on Oahu, go up to **Kaena Point,** at the western tip of the island. Casual hikers might want to try **Peacock Flat Trail** through the Mokuleia Forest Reserve, while serious trekkers go for the **Dupont Trail,** which leads up to Mount Kaala.

Camping is allowed at state, county, and private campgrounds dotted around the island. State park sites include **Kahana Valley State Park, Keaiwa Heiau State Recreation Area, Malaekahana Bay State Recreation Area** and **Sand Island State Recreation Area.** Many of Oahu's beautiful beach parks are designated county sites. Campers should be forewarned that some (maybe even *many*) locals might not be particularly happy to see you spreading out on "their" land. If the situation feels uncomfortable at a camping area, you might consider bedding down elsewhere. Permits and reservations are necessary for state and county facilities.

For information on Oahu's hiking trails and designated campsites, contact the **Hawaii State Department of Land and Natural Resources** *(Division of State Parks, 1151 Punchbowl Street, Honolulu 96813, (808) 587-0300);* or **City and County of Honolulu,**

HAWAII

Department of Parks and Recreation *(650 South King Street, Honolulu 96813, (808) 523-4525)*. For additional info on trails and hiking conditions, contact the **State Division of Forestry and Wildlife** *(1151 Punchbowl, Room 35, Honolulu 96813, (808) 587-0166)*. To join an organized hike, try the **Sierra Club** *(1111 Bishop Street, Honolulu 96813, (808) 538-6616)*.

Oahu offers **diving and snorkeling** opportunities for all levels. **Kahuna Canyon,** near Mokuleia, features an amphitheater full of octopi, crabs, spiny lobsters, and unicorn fish. If wrecks are your thing, the **Waianae coast** shelters sunken ships. Green sea turtles are the main attraction at **Maunalua Bay,** near Diamond Head, while the North Shore's **Shark's Cove** offers summer diving into sunlit caverns. The underwater park at **Hanauma Bay,** east of Koko Head, is a top **snorkeling** spot, with abundant tropical fish and sea turtles. Get advice and rent equipment from local dive shops, or sign up for an organized excursion. Waimea Valley's **Waimea River-to-Waimea Bay** is a favorite with **ocean kayakers.** Or sign up for a **sailing or parasailing** adventure (parasailors fly over the shores of **Ala Moana** and **Waikiki**). Oahu is paradise to **surfers** of every level—novices hit the gentle currents at **Waikiki,** while international pros hunt the perfect wave at the North Shore's **Waimea Bay** and **Banzai Pipeline.** Surfing lessons and rental boards are readily available. **Bodysurfers** frequent the waters of Kailua, Makapuu, and Sandy beaches, while **windsurfers** and **sailboarders** pretty much stick to Kailua Beach Park (instructions and equipment are available).

What Else to See

Beaches, sunsets, and **shops** rank as **Waikiki's** top attractions, along with people-watching, people-dodging, and people-avoiding. Boat-lovers might be interested in the colorful craft anchored over at **Ala Wai Yacht Harbor.** The enormous **Hilton Hawaiian Village** is Hawaii's largest hotel, with many restaurants, bars, and shopping outlets. On Kaila Road, the **U.S. Army Museum of Hawaii,** housed inside a 1911 bunker, displays war memorabilia and exhibits. Art and history lovers should check out the huge murals in the **First Hawaiian Bank** as well as the Hawaiian-colonial architecture of the **Gump Building,** both on Kalakaua Avenue. The landmark **Halekulani Hotel** (on Kailia Road) and **Royal Hawaiian Hotel** (on Kalakaua Avenue) reflect images of old elegance in chaotic contemporary Waikiki. Pick up your Versace gown and Hermés scarf in the **Royal Hawaiian Shopping Center,** then ogle the handicrafts and souvenirs at the **International Market Place.** The four **wizard stones** in front of the bronze statue of surfing champ Duke Kahanamoku (next to the Sheraton Moana Surfrider Hotel) were supposedly bequeathed with healing power by four 16th-century Tahitian *kahuna* (priests). The small two-room **Damien Museum,** on Ohua and Kalakaua avenues, pays tribute to the life of Father Joseph Damien of Belgium, who showed great compassion for lepers. **Kapiolani Park,** southwest of Diamond Head, is a 220-acre recreational area with the usual game and picnic fun, plus the site of the **Honolulu Zoo, Waikiki Aquarium, Waikiki Shell Amphitheater,** and the finish line for December's world-famous **Honolulu Marathon.** At the end of Kalakaua Avenue, the 1927-built, 1990s-decrepit **Waikiki War Memorial Natatorium** is a decaying tribute to World War II's dead. When Kalakaua Avenue becomes Diamond Head Road, you have left Kapiolani Park and are on the road to **Diamond Head.**

In the hustle-bustle of **Honolulu**—Hawaii's commercial and legislative hub—you'll be immersed within both contemporary culture and the historic past. Explore the 300-acre **University of Hawaii** campus in Manoa Valley, almost as noteworthy for its eclectic mix of architectural styles as for its curriculum. Up Manoa Road, you can ooh and aah at hundreds of plants in the **Lyon Arboretum,** then take a break at nearby **Manoa Falls.** The **Punahou School,** founded in 1841 and alma mater of many important Hawaiians, sits on Punahou Street. Much of the state's best art is exhibited at **Honolulu Academy of Arts,** on Beretania Street. Shopping fiends will be satiated at **Ala Moana Shopping Center** (Hawaii's largest mall), **Ward Centre,** or **Ward Warehouse,** all on Ala Moana Boulevard. Join local trendies for a meal on **Restaurant Row,** bounded by Ala Moana Boulevard and Punchbowl, Pohukaina, and South streets. Up the road, the **News Building** cranks out Hawaii's two dailies—the *Honolulu Advertiser* and the *Honolulu Star-Bulletin*. The 1840s **Kawaiahao Church** (South King and Punchbowl streets) welcomes the public to its services; **King Lunalilo's Tomb** is near the church entrance, and the bones of several other dignitaries are resting in the churchyard. Other South King Street sites include the 1821 **Mission Houses Museum** (Hawaii's first frame house), the 1929 **Honolulu City Hall,** the **King Kamehameha I Statue,** and **Iolani Palace** (the nation's only royal palace).

Hawaii's governor and state legislators work out of the **State Capitol,** a wondrous piece of architecture bounded by South

Beretania, Richards, and Punchbowl streets. Statues of **Father Damien** and **Queen Liliuokalani** are nearby. Across from the State Capitol, **Washington Place** was the home of American John Dominis and his wife, the future Queen Liliuokalani. These days it's the governor's mansion. **St. Andrew's Cathedral,** founded by King Kamehameha IV, is situated on Queen Emma Square. Two "Big Five" headquarters are located at the 1929 **Alexander and Baldwin Building** (on Bishop Street) and the 1930 **C. Brewer Building** (on Fort Street). Learn all about Hawaii's seafaring days at the **Hawaii Maritime Center,** on Honolulu Harbor. A couple of piers away, **Aloha Tower Marketplace** draws locals and visitors to its restaurants and shops. Over on Maunakea Street, you can wander amid the flower-scented **lei workrooms** or the Asian-food-scented **Maunakea Marketplace. Hotel Street,** between Bishop and River streets, is the city's famed red-light district (though attempts are being made to clean the place up).

Punchbowl Crater (National Memorial Cemetery of the Pacific), off Tantalus Drive, welcomes visitors to its 115-acre cemetery commemorating those who died in wars from World War I through Desert Storm. Continuing up **Tantalus Drive** will take you to some great viewpoints and trailheads. Back in town, **The Contemporary Museum,** on Makiki Heights Drive, houses a selection of works by world-famous contemporary artists and sculptors including Tom Wesselmann and David Hockney. On the other side of Tantalus Drive, you'll find the **Royal Mausoleum**—burial place for most of Hawaii's royal family. Take a tour of **Queen Emma's Summer Palace** (on the Pali Highway), the **Dole Pineapple Cannery** (on Iwilei Road) or the **Hilo Hattie Garment Factory** (on Nimitz Highway). Soak up everything Hawaiian in the extensive **Bishop Museum,** on Bernice Street.

The island's **southwest** area consists of heavily urbanized Pearl City and newly urbanized Kapolei. Sites to be seen are the famed **USS *Arizona* Memorial, USS *Bowfin* Submarine and Park, Moanalua Gardens,** and **Pearlridge Center** (another shopping experience). In Kapolei, you won't miss the **Koolina Resort.** In sharp contrast, you won't find much along **West Oahu's Waianae Coast** other than some bays, beaches, and very-native villages. (Be forewarned: this section of the island is reputedly not particularly hospitable to visitors, who should lock their vehicles and watch their backsides.) In **Oahu's Central District, Schofield Barracks** (headquarters of the U.S. Army's 25th Infantry Division) and **Dole Plantation** (pineapple heaven) are the noteworthy attractions.

Fielding OAHU

PEARL HARBOR

On December 7, 1941 the Japanese launched a surprise attack on the U.S. Pearl Harbor Naval Station. The offensive sunk or damaged nineteen ships, killing 2300 Americans and forced the U.S. into WWII. Pearl Harbor has since earned the distinction of being the only U.S. naval base to be honored as a national historic landmark.

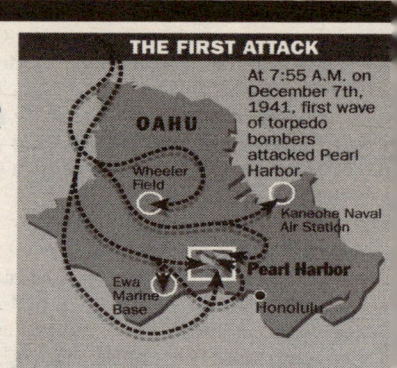

THE FIRST ATTACK

At 7:55 A.M. on December 7th, 1941, first wave of torpedo bombers attacked Pearl Harbor.

- OAHU
- Wheeler Field
- Kaneohe Naval Air Station
- Ewa Marine Base
- Pearl Harbor
- Honolulu

H1

U.S.S Utah Memorial

FORD ISLAND

PEARL HARBOR

The U.S.S. *Utah* memorial honors the fifty-eight crew members that died when their ship was struck by two torpedoes and sank. The ship can be seen from a viewing platform containing a flagpole and plaque dedicated to the ship's crew.

U.S. NAVAL RESERVATION

PEARL HARBOR ENTRANCE

U.S. NAVAL RESERVATION

HAWAII

The U.S.S. *Arizona* was sunk in the Pearl Harbor attack, entombing 1102 crew members in her hull. To honor the crew, the U.S.S. *Arizona* Memorial was built above the ship which lies, in tact, on the floor of the harbor.

One wall of the U.S.S. *Arizona* memorial contains 1178 engraved names of all the sailors who died aboard the ship.

Stack remains exposed

The U.S.S. Arizona as it looked before the attack

U.S.S Arizona Memorial

Submarine Memorial Park

EAST LOCH

Ferry

U.S.S Arizona Memorial Visitor Center

Aloha Stadium

Salt Lake Blvd.

Halawa Gate

CAMP CATLIN NAVAL RES.

North Rd.

Makalapa Gate

Nimitz Gate

HONOLULU →

You'll find various beaches, parks, and even a blowhole along the **southeast** section of Oahu. **Sea Life Park** features all types of sea critters and marine amusements, including a Touch Pool and Whaling Museum. Continuing along the **windward coast**, you (and thousands of other sightseers) will come to **Nuuanu Pali Lookout**, a windy outlook on windward Oahu. Visit the tropical **Haiku Gardens** and **Byodo-in Temple**, in Kaneohe, and **Senator Fong's Plantation and Gardens**, in Kahuluu.

Heading up the **North Shore**, the **Polynesian Cultural Center** at Laie will introduce you to Pacific Island culture through a variety of performances and demonstrations. Unless you're Mormon, don't expect admission to the **Mormon Temple** (though you can visit the grounds). Two Arnold Palmer-designed golf courses are the main attraction at **Turtle Bay Hilton and Country Club** in Kahuku. Watch cliff-divers as they plunge over the 45-foot falls at **Waimea Falls Park**, then gasp and squeal as surfers hang ten on humongous winter waves at **Sunset** and **Waimea beaches**.

Aiea/Pearl City

Aiea
Children's Activities

Ice Palace ★★

4510 Salt Lake Boulevard, in Stadium Mall, Aiea,
☎ *(808) 487-9921.*
Hours vary widely, call for schedule.
Hawaii's only ice-skating rink! Admission includes skate rentals. Ask about the birthday package, where your tot and eight pals receive skate rentals, a large pizza, two pitchers of soda, and a table for two hours. The birthday celebrant even gets a specially wrapped gift. Pandemonium on weekends. General admission: $6.50-$10.

City Celebrations

Hawaii State Fair ★★

Aloha Stadium, 99-500 Salt Lake Boulevard, Aiea,
☎ *(808) 488-3389.*
Late May. This two-day event, running for almost 60 years, features rides, carnival games, food booths, exhibits, and entertainment.

Hula Bowl Football All-Star Classic ★★★
Aloha Stadium, Aiea, ☎ *(808) 947-4141.*
Held in mid-January. Sponsored by "Hooters" restaurant chain, this post-season college football all-star game spotlights the nation's top college athletes. Parties, a championship golf tournament, and boat parades go on before and after the big event.

NFL Pro Bowl ★★★
Aloha Stadium, Aiea, ☎ *(808) 486-9300.*
Held in early February. This annual all-star game features the top stars from the National Football League.

Hiking

Aiea Loop Trail ★★★
Aiea Heights Drive, from Highway 78, Aiea.
Closed: Wednesdays, Thursdays.
This 4.8-mile (round trip) loop trail is in Keaiwa Heiau State Park, north of Pearl Harbor. Keaiwa Heiau was an herbal healing center as well as a temple site for native Hawaiians some 300 years ago. Views of the harbor and the Koolau Mountains can be seen on this hike, along with the wreckage of a World War II cargo plane. A variety of native trees, including lehua, ohia, and koa, grow heavily on the path, and in season, guavas are free for the picking. The park is a popular campsite. Rest rooms, shower, phone, drinking water available.

Central Oahu

Wahiawa
Museums and Exhibits

Tropic Lightning Museum ★★
Schofield Barracks, Wahiawa, 96857, ☎ *(808) 655-0438.*
Hours: 10 a.m.–4 p.m.
Closed: Mondays, Sundays.
http://www.museumsusa.org/data/museums/HI/115725.htm
Artifacts, photos, and archival material document the history of Schofield Barracks and the 25th Infantry Division.

Tours

Dole Plantation ★★
64-1550 Kamehameha Highway, Wahiawa, 96786,
☎ *(808) 621-8408.*
Hours: 9 a.m.–6 p.m.
http://www.dole-plantation.com/
Believe it or not, the pineapple industry is dying in Hawaii—so get here while you can. Among the attractions: fresh fruit, a variety garden, the "Story of Pineapple" exhibit, a goodies and gifts store, and "Dole Whip" tastings. And yes, the Dole Plantation store is one of only two—count 'em, two—Dole stores in the world.

Honolulu
Downtown
City Celebrations

Chinese New Year/Narcissus Festival ★★★
Chinatown Cultural Plaza, Maunakea Street, downtown,
☎ *(808) 533-3181.*
Held in late January through the first week of February. Although you have to pay to get in to some of the events preceding Chinese New Year (the Narcissus Queen Pageant and Coronation Ball), there are loads of freebies. The exciting "Night in Chinatown" features lion and dragon dances, arts and crafts and food booths, and stage performances. Festivities begin with a parade that starts in the late afternoon in front of the State Capitol, followed by more of the same at the Chinatown Cultural Plaza.

First Night Honolulu ★★★
Honolulu and Chinatown, downtown,
☎ *(808) 532-3131.*
January 31. An alcohol-free block party (*ho'olaule'a*) featuring performing arts, cultural shows, games, parades, a fireworks display, and ethnic food booths. Family afternoon at the Honolulu City Hall (*Hale*) from 2:30–6 p.m.

Great Aloha Fun Run ★★★
Aloha Tower, downtown, ☎ *(808) 528-7388.*
http://www.greataloharun.com/events.php3
Held in late February. One of the largest of its kind in the

country, this charity 8.2-mile fun run begins at dawn at the Aloha Tower in downtown Honolulu and ends at the Aloha Stadium in the Aiea-Halawa Valley near Pearl Harbor. Entry fee.

Honolulu Marathon ★★★
Aloha Tower to Kapiolani Park, downtown, ☎ *(808) 734-7200.*
http://www.honolulumarathon.org/
Held in December. One of the largest marathons in the world, with more than 30,000 competitors. The 26.2-mile run begins at dawn from Aloha Tower in downtown Honolulu and ends at Kapiolani Park in Waikiki. Free to spectators.

King Kamehameha Celebration ★★★
Iolani Palace, King and Richards streets, downtown,
☎ *(808) 586-0333.*
http://www.loc.gov/bicentennial/propage/HI/hi_s_aka ka1.html
This is one of Hawaii's biggest state holidays (June 11) honoring Hawaii's greatest monarch, Kamehameha I. In Oahu, a statue-decorating ceremony across from Iolani Palace and a floral parade from downtown Honolulu to Kapiolani Park are held prior to the date. But the main event is a hula competition in late June, with participants entering from as far away as Japan. Most events are free.

Taste of Honolulu ★★★★
Honolulu Hale (City Hall), 530 S. King Street, downtown,
☎ *(808) 536-1015.*
http://www.eastersealshawaii.org/taste/
Two days in late June. At this tasty fest, you can accomplish in a weekend what would usually take a year to do—sample dishes from more than a dozen of Honolulu's best restaurants. Come with an empty tummy and a full wallet. Wine tastings, musical entertainment. Although admission is free, there's a tasting fee.

The Dole Pineapple Story ★★
650 Iwilei Road in Dole Cannery Square, downtown,
☎ *(808) 548-6601.*
Hours: 9 a.m.–5 p.m.

Although the downtown cannery has ceased operations, the history of King Pineapple lives on by means of a multimedia presentation on nine screens shown every 30 minutes. There's also a museum of pineapple history, and a hands-on, arts/science/cultural museum for children that has nothing to do with pineapples. The children's museum is open from 9 a.m.–1 p.m. Tuesday-Friday; Saturday-Sunday from 10 a.m.–4 p.m. Free samples, and free transportation from Waikiki and Ala Moana Center from 8 a.m.–4 p.m. Look for buses marked "Dole Cannery" and "Hilo Hattie." Admission.

ITRAVELBOOK FREEBIES

Mayer's Aloha Friday Music Break ★★★
Tamarind Park, corner Bishop and King streets, downtown.
☎ *(808) 527-5666.*
Fridays at noon.
Celebrate *"Pau Hana"* (end of work)—well, almost—at this parkside concert where the music—Hawaiian, jazz, soul, rock, country, whatevah—changes each week.

Royal Hawaiian Band Concerts ★★★
Iolani Palace, King Street, downtown, ☎ *(808) 922-5331.*
The famed band, the only full-time municipal band in the country presents an entertaining hour-long show of musical faves each Friday at 12:15 p.m. on the palace grounds and on Sundays at 2 p.m. at Kapiolani Park in Waikiki.

Historical Sites

Iolani Palace ★★★★
King and Richards streets, downtown, 96813,
☎ *(808) 522-0832.*
Guided tours Wednesdays–Saturdays. Closed: Mondays, Tuesdays, Sundays.
http://www.hawaii-nation.org/palace.html.
Surrounded by an elaborate Victorian iron fence in downtown Honolulu, this is the only government building in the United States that was once a royal palace. Iolani Palace was also the state capitol until 1969. Built in 1882 by King Kalakaua after his voyage around the world, the palace is a polyglot of things that impressed him on the voyage. Among other features, it had electric lights before our own White House was wired up,

telephone service, hot-and-cold running water, and flush toilets. While waiting for the tour of the palace, the grounds are worthy of scrutiny. The barracks of the Royal Household Guards are located here, looking like a squat medieval castle and containing the ubiquitous gift shop. The domed pavilion and bandstand were built for the coronation of King Kalakaua. The governors of the state of Hawaii are still sworn into office here. The palace received a multimillion-dollar restoration in 1969, when the seat of government moved next door. Tours are given every 15 minutes from 9 a.m.–2:15 p.m. Reservations necessary. Children under five years not permitted. General admission: $8.

Kawaiahao Church ★★★
Punchbowl Street at King Street, downtown.
http://www.hvcb.org/islands/oahu/point51.html
Oahu's oldest church was built to replace the original thatched structure built by the missionaries upon their arrival in 1820. Constructed of coral-block between 1837 and 1842 in the New England Congregationalist style, its clock was donated by Kamehameha III. The rear seats are still reserved for descendants of Hawaiian royalty and are marked by feather kahili standards and velvet kneeling pads. Outside the church you can see the tomb of King Lunalilo, who held the distinction of being Hawaii's only elected monarch. Sunday services at 10:30 a.m. are held in both English and Hawaiian.

Museums and Exhibits

Damien Museum ★★
130 Ohua Avenue, downtown, 96815, ☎ *(808) 923-2690. Hours: 9 a.m.–3 p.m.*
http://maxpages.com/damienmuseum
This humble, small, two-room museum and archive commemorates Belgian priest Father Damien de Veuster, who devoted his life to the shunned victims of Hansen's disease (leprosy) in their permanent forced exile at Kalaupapa, Molokai. Displays include Damien's handwritten letters and photos of Kalaupapa and its residents. Visitors can watch an informative video about the life of the priest who died of the disease himself at the age of 49. Father Damien's proper title is now "Blessed" Damien. He was beatified by Pope John Paul in 1995 and is just one step from sainthood. Although his body is buried in Belgium, his

hand has been returned to Kalaupapa, and is contained in a reliquary at the church he founded there.

Hawaii Maritime Center ★★★
Pier 7, Honolulu Harbor, downtown, 96813,
☎ *(808) 536-6373.*
Hours: 8:30 a.m.–5 p.m.
http://holoholo.org/maritime/
Near the Aloha Tower and situated at Pier 7 at Honolulu Harbor, this museum has an interesting potpourri of nautical displays, the best of which may be the whaling section. A new exhibit features a rare humpback whale skeleton, only one of two on display in the world. There are two distinctive vessels docked outside the museum. One is the 266-foot, iron-hulled, square rigger *Falls of Clyde* (once owned by Matson Shipping Company), which was on the Hilo-to-San Francisco run, carrying passengers and sugar. When it's not cruising the Pacific, the *Hokulea*, a twin-hulled Hawaiian sailing canoe, is moored at the museum. Famous for its long-distance voyages to destinations as far as New Zealand using traditional methods of navigation, it just completed a successful round-trip journey to Tahiti. General admission: $7.50.

Honolulu Academy of Arts ★★★
900 S. Beretania Street, downtown, 96814, ☎ *(808) 532-8701.*
Hours: 10 a.m.–4:30 p.m.
Special hours: Sundays, 1–5 p.m.
http://www.honoluluacademy.org/
If you're into Asian art, this museum is a must-see. Dedicated in 1927, the 33,000-piece collection includes priceless Japanese prints, furniture, and Chinese bronze dishes from the 11th century B.C. Also notable are traditional and contemporary European (Pisarro, Van Gogh, Gauguin) and American (Maron's "Grand Canyon of the Yellowstone") masterpieces. There is also a small but select grouping of Hawaiian and Pacific artifacts. It is architecturally pleasing as well, with open courtyards, tiled fountains, and an enclosed garden with a lily pond. The museum is also a cultural center. The Academy Theatre presents popularly priced classic films and concerts. Gift shop, library, café. General admission: $8.

Mission Houses Museum ★★★
553 S. King Street, downtown, 96813, ☎ *(808) 531-0481.*
Hours: 9 a.m.–4 p.m.
Closed: Mondays, Sundays..
http://www.lava.net/~mhm/
Built between 1821 and 1841, this trio of New England-style, salt-box buildings formed the headquarters of the Sandwich Islands Mission. The oldest one was actually a prefabricated wooden dwelling brought around the Horn by the missionaries. The Chamberlain House, built in 1831 of coral block, served as the store room and contains examples of the supplies necessary to support the missionary families. The Printing Office still houses the lead-type press that was used to print a Hawaiian Bible. The Mission Houses Museum offers the popular Christmas Candlelight Tours, and a "living history" tour with authentically costumed actors playing roles of 19th-century missionaries. Admission to the museum is free the fourth Saturday of each month. Reservations required. General admission: Free–$10.

Music

Hawaii Opera Theatre ★★★
987 Waimanu Street, downtown, ☎ *(808) 596-7858.*
http://www.hawaiiopera.org/
Hawaii's only resident opera company presents three to four grand operas annually in the *Neal Blaisdell Theater, 777 Ward Avenue*. Performances are in the native language with an English translation. Call the hotline from 10 a.m.–5 p.m., Monday-Friday. General admission: $25 and up.

Parks and Gardens

Foster Botanical Gardens ★★★
50 N. Vineyard Boulevard, downtown, 96817,
☎ *(808) 522-7066.*
Hours: 9 a.m.–4 p.m.
The nation's largest collection of tropicals are spread out over 14 acres. Among the orchids and bromeliads are some peculiarly bizarre species: the fruit of the Coco de Mer palm weighs more than 50 pounds. That's some strange fruit. Tours on weekdays at 1 p.m. by reservation. A peaceful place to picnic. General admission: $10.

The Shows

Hawaii Theatre Center ★★★★
1130 Bethel Street, downtown, ☎ *(808) 528-0506.*
http://www.hawaiitheatre.com
In its heyday, the Hawaii Theatre was the flagship theater of the state's largest movie company. It featured an 1800-seat auditorium, a mural by the famed Hawaii artist Lionel Walden, and a five-ton Robert Morgan organ with 1128 pipes, even the first known theater "air conditioning" system. Employees would fan the air over big blocks of ice below the stage to cool off the delighted audience. The "new" theater, which includes a state-of-the-art electronic sound system, wider seats, and an enlarged orchestra pit, is now a multi-use facility booking everything from symphony orchestras to trade shows. One of the highlights of the three-day opening extravaganza was a musical concert—featuring a "new" Robert Morgan organ—salvaged from the unfortunately demolished Princess Theatre. General admission: Varies.

Honolulu Academy of Arts Academy Theatre ★★★
900 S. Beretania Street, downtown, ☎ *(808) 532-8700.*
Movies at 4 p.m. and 7:30 p.m., shows at 7:30 p.m
http://www.honoluluacademy.org/theater/events.htm
Within Hawaii's oldest and largest art museum, the Academy Theatre features classic art-house movies, and music performances by eclectic acts. General admission: Varies.

Honolulu Theatre for Youth ★★★
2846 Ualena Street, downtown, ☎ *(808) 839-9885.*
http://www.htyweb.org/
Entertaining and educational theater produced for youth and their families. Performances in various venues including the Richardson Theatre at Ft. Shafter. General admission: Varies.

Kumu Kahua Theatre ★★★
46 Merchant Street, downtown, ☎ *(808) 536-4441.*
http://www.kumukahua.com/
A showcase for the diverse ethnic cultures that make up Hawaii, this eclectic group produces plays mostly written by, and for, local audiences. Ticket prices are low, too. This is the place to feel the grime under the glitter. General admission: Varies.

Theme/Amusement Parks

The Outer Edge ★★
Aloha Tower Marketplace, downtown, ☎ (808) 528-5564.
Hours: 10 a.m.–1 a.m.; Fridays and Saturdays to 2 a.m.
We think 9000 square feet of virtual reality rides and games should keep the cyberkids occupied for hours, don't you? Located at Pier 10.

Tours

Chinatown Historical Walking Tour ★★★★
Asia Mall, 1250 Maunakea Street, downtown,
☎ (808) 521-3045.
Hours: 10 a.m.–noon.
Closed on Sundays.
Open-air markets, lei stands, herbal shops, a cleaned-up red-light district, historical sites (including the "new" Hawaii Theatre Center)—everything you can wiggle a wonton at are part of this exciting two-hour walking tour of Honolulu's revitalized Chinatown, which is one of the oldest in the United States. The Society also conducts an afternoon Temple Tour from 1–2 p.m. It covers Chinese temples, a Japanese Shrine, Chinatown Cultural Plaza, and more. General admission: $10.

Honolulu Hale (State Capitol) ★★
530 S. King Street, downtown, ☎ (808) 547-7000.
Hours: 8:30 a.m.–1:30 p.m.
http://www.pixi.com/~infotech/
An example of late '60s "theme architecture," the state Capitol symbolizes the triumph of form over function—its legislative chambers are cone-shaped to represent volcanoes, while the open-air rotunda has supporting columns meant to denote palm trees. Encircling the entire building is a reflecting pool symbolizing the Pacific Ocean. Tours are given daily at 8:30 a.m., 10:30 a.m., and 1:30 p.m.

Honolulu Time Walks ★★★★
2634 S. King Street, downtown, ☎ (808) 951-8878.
Hours: 7–11 p.m., Tuesdays only.
It's reported that ghosts (of the past, that is) have been sighted in downtown Honolulu. Raconteur Glenn Grant conducts "Haunted Honolulu" tours every Tuesday at 7 p.m.; after a

stroll with him you'll be spooked, too. Includes pub refreshment. General admission: Varies.

Top Gun Tours ★★
P.O. Box 25204, downtown, 96825, ☎ *(808) 396-8112.*
Hours: 6:15 a.m.–1:45 p.m.
A great experience for history and military buffs, as well as kids. Also called Home of the Brave Military Base Tours. An experienced and knowledgeable guide dressed in an authentic World War II Army Air Corps uniform takes visitors to as many as five military bases/sites, including Pearl Harbor and the *Arizona* Memorial, all in one day. Routes and sites are subject to change without notice, depending on base operations. On a typical itinerary, you'll visit Hickam Air Force Base, Wheeler Army Airbase, Schofield Barracks, Punchbowl National Memorial and downtown Honolulu. Glenn Miller music and authentic broadcasts of FDR's fireside chats and his declaration of war accompany narration on the tour bus. Lunch (not included in the tour price) is held at an officer's club. Vets and their families are encouraged to share experiences. General admission: $75, varies for seniors, veterans, and children.

Greater Honolulu
Beaches

Ala Moana Beach Park ★★★
1201 Ala Moana Boulevard, Greater Honolulu.
http://www.aloha.com/~lifeguards/alamoana.html
Just five minutes away from Waikiki, across the street from the Ala Moana Shopping Center, Ala Moana Beach Park is a favorite with local residents. Waters are clear, the sand is soft, and there are numerous picnic facilities on a large, grassy area. From some vantage points, you'll have million-dollar views of Diamond Head. Swimming is perfect in the sandy, shady lagoon protected by an offshore reef. Adjacent is Magic Island Beach, a failed resort turned into a park. Families with small children frequent the calm swimming cove. Lots of parking, but still gets crowded on weekends.

City Celebrations

Cherry Blossom Festival ★★
1525 Bernice Street, Greater Honolulu, ☎ *(808) 949-2255.*
January to March. A celebration of Japanese contributions to Hawaii's cultural life. Events are held at the Bishop Museum and other locations. General admission: Varies.

Hawaiian Song Festival ★★★
McCoy Pavilion, Ala Moana Park, Greater Honolulu,
☎ *(808) 266-7654.*
Mid March. Perpetuates Hawaiian music and culture with a song competition.

Na Wahine O Hawaii ★★
McCoy Pavilion, Ala Moana Park, Greater Honolulu,
☎ *(808) 239-4336.*
Held in early July. For several years, the best *wahine* (women) in music and dance have performed their works at Ala Moana Park.

ITRAVELBOOK FREEBIES

Concerts at Ala Moana Centerstage ★★★
1450 Ala Moana Boulevard, Greater Honolulu,
☎ *(808) 946-2811.*
Hours: 9:30 a.m.–9 p.m., Sundays, 10 a.m.–5 p.m.
A wide variety of free entertainment—drama, music, dance—are presented by top talent (Honolulu Theatre for Youth, the Royal Hawaiian Band, etc.) on an outdoor stage each day. Showtimes are noon, 2 p.m., and 7 p.m., Monday-Saturday; Sundays, noon and 2 p.m.

Historical Sites

Aloha Tower ★★★
Pier 9, Nimitz Highway, Greater Honolulu, ☎ *(808) 528-5700.*
http://www.alohatower.com
Originally built in 1926, the Aloha Tower was the tallest building in Oahu. Emblazoned with the words "Aloha," the clock tower welcomed passenger liners when all tourists arrived by ship on "Boat Days." After a period of restoration, the Tower was reopened in 1994 as the centerpiece of the Aloha Tower Marketplace, a shopping area that dominates Pier 9 at the foot of Fort Street. There are spectacular views on all four sides of

the 10th-floor observation deck, reached via a tiny, slow elevator. Claustrophobics beware. Recently, the fanfare of "Boat Days" has been attempted, if not exactly re-created. Every Friday, hula dancers with fresh leis bid farewell to the hokey *Windjammer* cruise boat as it departs Pier 9 at 7 p.m.

National Memorial Cemetery of the Pacific ★★★
2177 Puowaina Drive, Greater Honolulu, 96813,
☎ *(808) 566-1430.*
http://www.interment.net/data/us/hi/oahu/natmem/
A sobering pilgrimage, the National Memorial Cemetery of the Pacific, situated in the Punchbowl Crater, is the final resting place of more than 30,000 U.S. Armed Services personnel (from World War II to Vietnam) and their families. Astronaut and native son Ellison S. Onizuka is also buried here. Known to the ancient Hawaiians as the "Hill of Sacrifice," the cemetery contains a monument with the names of all the youth lost in action in the Pacific carved in marble. A lookout surmounts the crater from which Diamond Head can be seen among the highrises in Honolulu. The American Legion conducts hour-long walking tours by appointment only. Call ☎ *(808) 946-6383* by 8:00 a.m. the day the tour is desired. Cost is $25. There's a road behind the memorial for those who can't make the stairs. Open Sept. 30–March 1, 8 a.m.–6:30 p.m.; March 2–Sept. 29, 7 a.m.–7 p.m.

Royal Mausoleum ★★★
2261 Nuuanu Avenue, Greater Honolulu, 96817.
Hours: 8 a.m.–4 p.m.
The most sacred burial ground in the islands, the Royal Mausoleum is the resting place for six of eight Hawaiian monarchs, including King Kalakaua and Queen Liliuokalani. King Kamehameha I is notably missing; he was the last of the Hawaiian kings to be buried in secret, which was the ancient way. Also on the three-acre site is a chapel built in 1922.

Museums and Exhibits
Bishop Museum and Planetarium ★★★★
1525 Bernice Street, Greater Honolulu, ☎ *(808) 422-0561.*
Hours: 9 a.m.–5 p.m.
http://www.bishopmuseum.org

Set on 10 acres, the Bishop Museum is perhaps the finest repository of Pacific and Hawaiian artifacts in the world. It was a gift to the people of Hawaii by Charles Bishop in memory of his wife Bernice Pauahi Bishop, a direct descendant of Hawaiian royalty. The central building is made of dressed volcanic stone, and is said to be the oldest structure of this type on the island. Its interior is highlighted by elaborate marble floors and fantastic koa woodwork, which seems to only get better with time. The core collection is in the multi-storied and balconied Hawaiian Hall. Here can be seen the original feathered cape worn by Kamehameha I when he completed the conquest of the islands, bowls adorned with human teeth, and, perhaps most interesting of all, actual wooden gods worshiped by the ancient Hawaiians, carved in the Kona style. Very few of these have survived to this day, because most were burned or destroyed when Hawaiian royalty converted to Christianity. In adjacent halls are other collections of Pacific island cultures, whaling artifacts, a Science Center, and Planetarium. In February 1990, the museum opened its first major exhibit area in 90 years, the Castle Memorial Building, which houses changing exhibitions. The first Sunday of the month is Family Sunday, a cultural celebration with Hawaiian entertainment, food, displays, and demonstrations. Free admission for children ages five and under. General admission: Varies.

Pacific Aerospace Museum ★★
Honolulu International Airport, main lobby, Greater Honolulu, 96819, ☎ (808) 839-0777.
Hours: 9 a.m.–6 p.m.
Special hours: Fridays, to 9 p.m., Saturdays to 10 p.m. Closed: Sundays.
http://www.cyberspacemuseum.com/pamsp.html
A good way to kill time at the airport, if the Honolulu traffic hasn't caused you to almost miss your flight. Three theaters cover separate aspects of navigation and aviation, one of which recreates the attack of Pearl Harbor with holograms. Don't miss the life-size replica of the *Challenger* flight deck. Many of the displays are interactive and friendly. General admission: $10.

HAWAII
The Shows

Aloha Tower Ice Theatre ★★
101 Ala Moana Boulevard, Greater Honolulu,
☎ *(808) 528-5700.*
This ice rink at the Aloha Tower Marketplace cost a cool million and features three performances with 34 of the world's top figure skaters. "Skate, Rattle, and Roll" and "Land of Ice" run 30 minutes, and are presented several times a day. Admission is $10.95 and up.

Kennedy Theatre ★★★
1770 East-West Road, Greater Honolulu, ☎ *(808) 956-2598.*
The University of Hawaii at Manoa's 600-seat theater presents a seasonal mix of classics, experimental theater, Grand Kabuki, Peking Opera, children's theater and, to a lesser extent, musicals. Avant garde adult offerings play late at night in the Earle Ernst Lab Theatre.

Manoa Valley Theatre ★★★
2833 E. Manoa Road, Greater Honolulu, 96822,
☎ *(808) 988-6131.*
http://www.manoavalleytheatre.com/
Features the best contemporary works from Broadway and off-Broadway. Very popular. General admission: varies.

Tours

Kapiolani Community College Walking Tours ★★★
4303 Diamond Head Road, Greater Honolulu, ☎ *(808) 734-9211.*
Special hours: call for schedule.
Kapiolani Community College sponsors fascinating two-hour walking tours of some of Honolulu's oldest neighborhoods. Itineraries change frequently, and most tours are given on weekends. For information, call ☎ *(808) 538-3952.* General admission: Varies.

Makiki Heights
Children's Activities

Hawaii Nature Center ★★★
2131 Makiki Heights Drive, Makiki Heights,

☎ *(808) 955-0100.*
Hours: 8 a.m.–4:30 p.m., Sundays 1:30–4:30 p.m.
The Center sponsors terrific programs for kids that include everything from group hikes to fishing expeditions to the hands-on study of birds, bugs, and other beasties. Everything is geared for an in-depth understanding of nature and the environment in a fun, non-boring, user-friendly way. Special programs for the physically challenged. Memberships available. General admission: Varies.

Hiking

Makiki Valley Loop Trail ★★★
Tantalus Drive, and Makiki Heights Drive, Makiki Heights.
These are three interconnecting trails (Makiki Valley Trail, Maunalaha, and Kanealole) that begin at Tantalus Drive. The entire loop is about three miles long and begins at the Territorial Nursery, Hawaii's first native tree nursery. The Makiki Valley Trail itself affords views of Honolulu while you see and taste guava and mountain apples in season (usually summer).

Waikiki
Beaches

Waikiki Beach ★★★★
From the Ala Wai Canal to Kapahulu Avenue, Waikiki.
Yes, this is the world's most famous stretch of beach, and yes, you'll feel like the third sardine in a tin can while lying on the sand at the height of the day. If you're an early bird, take a peaceful morning stroll or run at 6 a.m. It's possible to walk the whole length from the Sheraton Waikiki at its core to Sans Souci Beach at the Diamond Head end. The population count seems to be highest at the center of the beach in front of the Sheraton Waikiki, or the Royal Hawaiian Hotel, less so at the outer fringes (the Hilton Hawaiian Village, or the New Otani Kaimana Beach). Swimmers share the waters with catamarans, inflatable rafts, outrigger canoes, inflatable floats, and watercycles with enormous wheels in neon colors, just in case you can't see them. Learn to surf here from the legendary beach boys (the real thing, not the Wilson brothers). Try the rental stand in front of **Kuhio Beach Park,** *2453 Kalakaua Avenue;* look for the bronze statue of Duke Kahanamoku.

Children's Activities

Snooze at the Zoo ★★★★
Honolulu Zoo, next to Kapiolani Park, Waikiki,
☎ *(808) 971-7174.*
Special hours: 6 p.m.–9 a.m., Friday evening to Saturday morning.

Once or twice a month, kids and their parents can pack up their sleeping bags and spend the night at the Honolulu Zoo. The price of admission includes a light dinner, snacks, storytelling around a campfire, "after dark" tours of animal exhibits, and breakfast the next morning. Limited to only 25 participants, so reserve in advance. Much better than a hotel room. But wait, there's more. Before, during, and after a full moon, attend a "Zoo by Moonlight" behind-the-scenes tour of the nocturnal habits of zoo animals. Includes refreshments and a "hoary bat game." General admission: $30.

City Celebrations

Aloha Festivals ★★★
1201 Ala Moana Boulevard, Waikiki, ☎ *(808) 944-8857.*
This statewide cultural festival, the only one in the United States, celebrated its 50th anniversary in 1996. Held over a two-month period (September–October). Oahu celebrates with a floral parade from Ala Moana Park to Kapiolani Park, concerts at the Waikiki Shell, and a Royal Ball. For general description, see "Molokai" chapter.

Great Hawaiian Rubber Duckie Race ★★★
Ala Wai Canal, Waikiki, ☎ *(808) 538-6789.*
Late March. To raise money for this "quacky" fund raiser for the United Cerebral Palsy Association, 20,000 people sponsor 20,000 rubber ducks and race them down the Ala Wai Canal. Free to spectators.

Hawaii International Sport Kite Championships ★★
Kapiolani Park, Waikiki, ☎ *(808) 922-5483.*
Early March. Sport kite-flyers from around the world compare air toys and perform high, speed acrobatics in this annual event. Food booths and entertainment.

Honolulu International Bed Race ★★★
Kapiolani Park and various locations, Waikiki,
☎ *(808) 735-6092.*
http://www.bedraceusa.com/aboutus.html
Two days in late April. These crazy Waikikians will do anything for charity—including racing beds in their 'jammies alongside Kapiolani Park. A must-see. Other events include electric-light parades, á la Disneyland, and a fireworks show.

Lei Day/Annual May Day Concert ★★★
Waikiki and various locations, Waikiki, ☎ *(808) 924-8934.*
Held on May 1. May Day is Lei Day in Hawaii, an islandwide celebration of the fragrant floral necklace of nostalgia and aloha. There are lei-making contests, pageants, music, arts and crafts, and a Lei Queen competition. The finale is the annual May Day Concert at the Waikiki Shell in Kapiolani Park. Not to be missed.

Prince Lot Hula Festival ★★
Moanalua Gardens, Waikiki, ☎ *(808) 839-5334.*
Hours: 9:15 a.m.–4 p.m.
Held on July 20. Authentic ancient and modern hula, as well as demonstrations and arts and crafts, honoring Kamehameha V.

ITRAVELBOOK FREEBIES

Art Mart ★★
Montserrat Avenue, Waikiki.
Hours: 10 a.m.–4 p.m.
Closed: Mon., Wed., Thurs., Fri.
On weekends, the fence along the perimeter of the Honolulu Zoo becomes a colorful display of good, bad, mediocre and, in rare instances, superb works by local artists.

Japanese Tea Ceremony ★★
245 Saratoga Road, in the Urasenke Foundation, Waikiki,
☎ *(808) 923-3059.*
Hours: 10 a.m.–noon each Wednesday.
The intricate rituals of the Chado—Japanese Tea Ceremony— are painstakingly explained, gesture by gesture, in this authentic teahouse maintained by a foundation with branches all over

the world. The ceremony is free, but samples of green tea and accompanying delicacies are $5 per person. The foundation asks that guests wear long pants, socks (no holes, please—you'll upset the delicate balance), or hose.

Kodak Hula Show ★★★
Waikiki Shell in Kapiolani Park, Waikiki, ☎ *(808) 627-3300.*
Hours: 10–11:15 a.m. Tuesdays and Wednesdays.
www.kodak.com/cluster/global/en/consumer/events/hula Show.shtml
This beloved freebie has only been around since 1927 and still draws the crowds. Many of the endearing aunties dancing the hula have been doing it since 1927. Even the most jaded among you will yell out "Aloha" with everyone else, guaranteed. Also worth going to is the Hilton Hawaiian Village's popular hula show accompanied by a fireworks display, which caps off the King's Jubilee, held every Friday, beginning at sunset; call ☎ *(808) 949-4321* for information. Mall wiggles at the Royal Hawaiian Shopping Center, Mondays, Wednesdays, and Fridays from 6:30-8 p.m., *2201 Kalakaua Avenue,* ☎ *(808) 922-0588.*

Lucoral Museum ★★
2414 Kuhio Avenue, Waikiki, ☎ *(808) 922-1999.*
Hours: 9:30 a.m.–5:30 p.m.
http://www.hawaii.edu/hga/urban00/lucoral.html
Gemstones, rocks, and minerals mingle with eccentric curiosities such as a dinosaur egg from China and a fish fossil from, of all places, Saudi Arabia. Jewelry-making classes, tours (reservations required), and a gift shop.

Royal Waikiki Historical Walk ★★
Hyatt Regency Waikiki ☎ *(808) 923-1234.*
Hours: 9 a.m.–10 p.m.
Gather at the Sharing Room, on the second floor behind the waterfall, where a professional storyteller leads one-hour walks on and near the grounds and beach where royalty lived and played. Hear about Princess Kaiulani and Ainahau, her nearby garden estate, her friend Robert Louis Stevenson, and Duke Kahanamoku. Reserve 24 hours in advance.

Hiking

Diamond Head Trail ★★★
Montserrat Avenue, Waikiki, ☎ *(808) 587-0300.*
Hours: 6 a.m.–6 p.m.
The climb to the top of this 760-foot-tall volcanic crater (don't worry, it's extinct) and symbol of Waikiki is only 0.7 miles long, but it takes an hour to go up and half an hour to come down. Really for intermediate hikers, it involves climbing two staircases, one with 76 steps, the other 99. Various other thrills and chills involve snaking your way through a dark 300-foot tunnel (part of World War II military installation) and peering through long-unused gun embattlements. Upon reaching the summit, you'll be rewarded with a 360-degree view of Waikiki and Honolulu. There are also a number of observation points on the way. Wear a hat and a pair of reliable boots, but no slippers or sandals. Bring water—you'll need it. A flashlight for the tunnel will prevent gouged knees and dinged-up foreheads. If you'd like a guided tour, The Clean Air Team offers fully narrated hikes every Saturday. No reservations necessary. Meet at 9 a.m. at the front entrance of the Honolulu Zoo. Rest rooms, picnic tables, phones, and drinking water available at the site.

Hanauma Bay to Toilet Bowl ★★★
7455 Kalanianaole Highway, Waikiki.
This is a two-mile coastal hike past Hanauma Bay Beach Park. Toilet Bowl is a unique tide pool with a 10-foot-deep hole at its bottom. Wave action causes it to fill and flush. Certain daredevils enjoy getting flushed in, but have to scramble out before it fills again. On the other side of the bay, about 10 minutes away, is Witches' Brew, a cove with turbulent waters. Take a hint from the name and go for the view of Koko Crater and the green sand made of olivine crystals.

Judd Memorial Trail ★★★
Nuuanu Pali Drive, Waikiki.
The highlight of this 1.5-mile hike is the Jackass-Ginger Pool, which is less than 15 minutes from the head of the trail. An easy family outing, it passes Nuuanu Stream (you might have to get your feet wet), a bamboo thicket, eucalyptus grove, and Norfolk pines, which local residents use for Christmas trees. When it's wet enough, kids like to slide down several mud

chutes on plastic sheets, aping Hawaiian *ali'i*, who used large ti leaves. Take Pali Highway to Nuuanu Pali Drive about half a mile to the Reservoir No. 2 spillway.

Historical Sites

Pali Lookout ★★★★
Pali Highway, Waikiki.
Many tourists come here to see how many articles of clothing will be blown off their bodies by the high winds. A few do know it (and respect it) as a historical site. It was here where Kamehameha the Great defeated Oahu chief Kalanikupele in 1795, thereby unifying the islands under one ruler. A majority of the chief's men were forced off the precipice to their deaths. Not a pretty picture. A prettier one is the sight of the lush windward coast in the distance.

Museums and Exhibits

The Contemporary Museum ★★★
2411 Makiki Heights Drive, Waikiki, ☎ *(808) 526-1322.*
Hours: 10 a.m.–4 p.m.
Special hours: Sundays, noon-4 p.m. Closed: Mondays.
http://www.tcmhi.org/
Way up in Makiki Heights is Hawaii's only museum dedicated to modern art. Among the seven galleries of rotating exhibits is a permanent collection by David Hockney. Some say the gorgeous 1.5-acre gardens of this estate-turned-museum are better than the collections. There are more than 80 varieties of flowers and trees—magnolia, kukui, monkeypod, banyan, breadfruit, and mango. Docent guided tours of the gardens by appointment only. Guided museum tours at 1:30 p.m. daily except Monday. Admission waived on the third Thursday of each month. General admission: Varies.

U.S. Army Museum of Hawaii ★★
Corner of Kalia and Saratoga Roads, Waikiki, 96815,
☎ *(808) 438-2821.*
Hours: 10 a.m.–4:30 p.m.
Closed: Mondays.
If you need a break from the Waikiki Beach heat, try the cool interior of the U.S. Army Museum. It's housed in Battery Randolph, at Fort deRussy, which occupies a prime piece of

beachfront real estate. It probably survives only due to the fact that its massive construction makes it too difficult to remove. Built in 1909 and completed in 1914, it was one of several coastal artillery positions built for the defense of Oahu. Originally, it mounted a pair of 14-inch guns, which fired 2000-pound projectiles 18 miles away. The gift shop has some cool "Rosie the Riveter"-type T-shirts for sale.

USS Bowfin Submarine Museum & Park ★★★
11 Arizona Memorial Drive, Waikiki, 96818,
☎ *(808) 423-1341.*
Hours: 8 a.m.–5 p.m.
http://www.bowfin.org/
Moored near the USS *Arizona* Memorial Visitor's Center is the *USS Bowfin*, an 1800-ton World War II diesel fleet submarine that sank 44 enemy ships during its career and received a Presidential Citation before the end of the war. A walk through its cramped exterior can leave one with the realization that it took a special type of person to inhabit such a small space with 80 other men on war patrol for months at a time. Children under four not allowed in the sub. General admission: Varies.

Music

AT&T Wildest Show in Town ★★★
Honolulu Zoo, Waikiki, ☎ *(808) 971-7171.*
Actually a very tame event. This twilight concert series features top island musical entertainers. Picnicking is allowed, but don't feed the animals. Held every Wednesday from early June through August.

Parks and Gardens

Honolulu Zoo ★★★★
Kapiolani Park, Kalakaua Avenue, Waikiki, 96815,
☎ *(808) 971-7171.*
Hours: 9 a.m.–4:30 p.m.
http://www.honoluluzoo.org/
Founded in 1914, the Honolulu Zoo has grown from a small animal shelter to a large zoological and botanical garden with more than 1500 animals. Highlights are a simulated African savannah that encompasses 10 acres, some of the first Galapagos tortoises to be hatched in captivity, and a number of

rare Hawaiian wildlife, including the state bird, the nene goose. The zoo also sponsors a number of exciting activities including a family sleep-over (see above), "full-moon" walks, art shows, and free twilight concerts. A great place. General admission: $6-$12.

Lyon Arboretum ★★★
3860 Manoa Road, Waikiki, ☎ *(808) 988-7378.*
Hours: 9 a.m.–3 p.m.
http://www.hawaii.edu/lyonarboretum/
A division of the University of Hawaii-Manoa, Lyon Arboretum is as noteworthy for its otherworldy aura as it is for its 196 acres of tropical plants. Located high up above the city, the gardens are often shrouded in mist. Reservations required for 90-minute guided tours offered on the first Friday and the third Wednesday of each month at 1 p.m., and the third Saturday at 10 a.m. The admission is actually a donation. General admission: Varies.

Waikiki Aquarium ★★★★
2777 Kalakaua Avenue, Waikiki, 96815, ☎ *(808) 923-9741.*
Hours: 9 a.m.–5 p.m.
http://waquarium.otted.hawaii.edu/
Located across from the tennis courts at Kapiolani Park. Among the newest and noteworthy of the 64 exhibits at this nearly century-old aquarium is the Hawaiian Monk Seal Habitat, dedicated to the study and hopeful propagation of these slowly-disappearing (only 1500 are left) mammals. For people unable to snorkel Hanauma Bay, the Edge of the Reef Display or the Reef Machine may be the next best thing. It's an outdoor living-coral-reef ecosystem where visitors can make eye-to-eye contact and play touchy-feely with sea cucumbers, sea stars, and other marine life. Current films are shown at the Sea Visions Theater. Support the aquarium in its efforts by purchasing a memento in the Natural Selection Shop. General admission: Varies.

The Shows

Aloha Showroom/Legends in Concert ★★★
2233 Kalakaua Avenue, Waikiki, ☎ *(808) 971-1400.*

Hours: 5–8:30 p.m.
Vegas' all-star superstar impersonator revue has landed in Waikiki, which is actually the Vegas of the Pacific. Features Broadway-caliber performers, who actually sing, not lip-synch, and a few of them, including "Little Richard" and "The Performer Formerly Known as Prince," look uncannily like the real thing. Two shows daily, dinner optional. Performer lineup varies. Watch for the free previews given daily in front of the Royal Hawaiian Shopping Center. General admission: $33–$135.

Diamond Head Theatre ★★★
520 Makapuu Avenue, Waikiki, 96816, ☎ *(808) 734-0274.*
http://www.diamondheadtheatre.com/
A professional regional theater company, Diamond Head Theatre has been in existence for 82 years. It specializes, and does very well at, crowd-pleasing Broadway musicals made possible with talent and a 400-plus seat theater. General admission: $10 and up.

Honolulu Comedy Club ★★
2045 Kalakaua Avenue, Waikiki, ☎ *(808) 922-5998.*
Hours: 8–9 p.m.
Special hours: Fridays and Saturdays, 10 p.m. Closed on Mondays.
This standup comedy showcase features both locals and mainlanders. Two-drink minimum. Reservations suggested. General admission: Varies.

Polynesian Palace ★★★★
227 Lewers Road, Waikiki, ☎ *(808) 923-7469.*
Closed: Sundays and Mondays.
The puckish Frank DeLima, known as Waikiki's Crown Prince of Comedy, and baby-faced Glen Medeiros, a Kauai native who had several Top 40 hits on the pop charts, are the "Pocho Knights," an affectionate island term for two wild-and-crazy Portuguese guys. The pair are the Martin and Lewis of Waikiki, with Medeiros playing straight man to the zany de Lima, in a series of musical-comedy routines that gently poke fun at Hawaii's diverse ethnic cultures. One show at 9:15 p.m., price includes one cocktail. When she's in town, Charo, the self-described "belle of coochie-coochie" and accomplished Spanish flamenco guitarist, performs at 7:15 p.m. Dinner seat-

ing at 6:15 p.m.; cocktail seating at 6:45 p.m. General admission: $25–$55.

The Magic of Polynesia ★★★★
2005 Kalia Road, in the Hilton Dome, Waikiki,
☎ *(808) 941-0924.*
http://www.waikikibeachcomber.com/magic.html
One of Honolulu's top-paid performers, illusionist John Hirokawa has been compared to David Copperfield and Siegfried and Roy—not surprising, he has trained with them. Two dinner shows nightly at 6:30 and 8:45 p.m. General admission: $30–$56.50.

The Society of Seven ★★★★
Outrigger Main Showroom, 2335 Kalakaua Avenue, Waikiki,
☎ *(808) 922-6408.*
Lovingly called "SOS" by the legions of *kamaiianas* and visitors who flock to see them, year after year. Ensconced in this spot for the last 26 years, this truly talented group of musicians/comics/charmers specialize in elaborate Broadway numbers. Each one is an accomplished solo performer as well. Routines change frequently. Shows at 7:15 p.m. Wednesday–Saturday, and 9:15 p.m. Monday–Saturday. Higher admission includes a buffet dinner and one drink; lower includes one drink and a parking discount (!). General admission: Varies.

Tours

Atlantis Submarines ★★★
2005 Kalia Road, Hilton Hawaiian Village, Waikiki,
☎ *(808) 973-9811.*
Hours: 7 a.m.
Although Atlantis Submarine rides are available on the Big Island and Maui, only on Oahu will you find the Atlantis XIV, the latest in high-tech underwater exploration. The 100-foot-long, 160-ton sub submerges to a depth of 150 feet. Each of the 64 passengers gets one porthole. Souvenir guidebook included. Leaves from Port Hilton, beachfront at the Hilton Hawaiian Village. General admission: $69–$148, varies by age and trip.

HAWAII

Round Top Road/Tantalus Drive ★★★
Starts at the end of Makiki Street, Waikiki.
The best overall view of Honolulu that's closest to the teeming city is from this vantage point. From the end of Makiki Street, the road makes a circle around Round Top Mountain—stop along the way for excellent views of Manoa Valley. The dense, dripping vegetation is punctuated by bursts of scarlet and fuschia, in the form of hibiscus and bougainvillea. At the apex is Puu Ualakaa State Wayside Park with a virtually unimpeded vista of half the island.

USS Arizona Memorial ★★★★
One Arizona Memorial Place, off Kamehameha Highway, Waikiki, ☎ *(808) 422-0561.*
Hours: 8 a.m.–3 p.m.
Special hours: closed Thanksgiving, Christmas, New Year's.
http://www.nps.gov/usar/
A must-see for all visitors to Oahu. Dec. 7, 1941, marks a historical divide between a distant innocence and the world of today. After six decades, the loss of the *USS Arizona* and its crew is perhaps the most salient memory of that day. Half of the 2300 fatalities of the Japanese attack on Pearl Harbor died on this one ship in a matter of moments; 1100 of the *Arizona* crew members remain entombed in her broken hull. The visitor center and the museum contain a theater that shows an orientation film before a Navy launch takes visitors to the off-shore memorial. The memorial is above, but does not touch, the sunken hull, which can be clearly seen through the water. Next to the National Memorial Cemetery of the Pacific (Punchbowl), this is the most visited monument in the state, with more than 1.5 million visitors a year. Visits to the memorial are on a first-come, first-served basis, and waits of up to three hours are not uncommon. Early mornings are best, with the shortest lines. Don't leave Oahu without a visit.

Waikiki Trolley ★★
Royal Hawaiian Shopping Center, Waikiki, ☎ *(808) 596-2199.*
Hours: 8 a.m.–4:30 p.m.
http://www.waikikitrolley.com/
A convenient way to see downtown Honolulu is via this old-fashioned trolley that leaves every 15 minutes from the Royal

Hawaiian Shopping Center. One- or five-day passes available. The 20 stops along the route include the Bishop Museum, the Hawaii Maritime Center, and Chinatown. Get on and off at any point and re-board when you're good and ready. The Trolley can be hired for private events. General admission: Varies.

Leeward Oahu

Ewa
The Shows

Paradise Cove Luau ★★★
Ko Olina Resort, Ewa, ☎ *(808) 973-5828.*
Call for hours.
http://www.paradisecovehawaii.com/
The food isn't the only star at this luau. Located in a private village on a 12-acre beachfront site, Paradise Cove likes to immerse visitors in island culture first. Before chowing down, watch and/or join in a lei-making or coconut-husking demonstration, play Maori stick games, or try Hawaiian bowling. Before the pig is removed from the underground *imu* oven, everyone gets to pull in a traditional *hukilau* fish net from the sea. Then guys with iron-cast hands remove the pig from the oven in an *imu* ceremony. The show climaxes afterwards with the exciting fire-knife dance. Price includes round-trip transportation from Waikiki. General admission: Varies

Waianae
Beaches

Makaha Beach Park ★★★
84-369 Farrington Highway, Waianae.
Beautiful, uncrowded beach on Oahu's laid-back, very local westside, Makaha has perfect winter surf. Usually calm in summer months, folks must use caution while swimming at any time due to dangerous shore breaks. Snorkeling, scuba diving off shore. No parking, but there's a picnic area, rest rooms, phones, and a lifeguard.

Waipahu
Tours

Hawaii's Plantation Village ★★★
97-695 Waipahu Street, Waipahu, 96797, ☎ *(808) 677-0110.*

Hours: 9 a.m.–3 p.m.
http://www.hawaiiweb.com/html/hawaiis_plantation_village.html
This is a fascinating museum of authentically furnished, re-created dwellings of eight ethnic groups that worked the sugar plantations of the early 19th century. Set in a three-acre garden, with labeled medicinal plants, there is also an original cookhouse and a historical museum with photos, artifacts, and documents. Guided tours every hour from 9 a.m.–3 p.m. The admission fee is actually a "donation." General admission: $3–$5.

North Shore
Haleiwa
Beaches

Ehukai Beach Park ★★★
59-337 Ke Nui Road, Haleiwa.
Across from Sunset Beach Elementary School in Haleiwa, Ehukai is more famously known as the Banzai Pipeline. This is a tube formed by monstrous waves breaking in a hollow fashion. Surfers disappear inside the tube, and hopefully emerge seconds later—surfing's ultimate maneuver. Calm and safe in summer, Banzai has wide stretches of sand for strolling or tanning. Lifeguard, rest room, showers, picnic areas.

Haleiwa Beach Park ★★★
62-449 Kamehameha Highway, Haleiwa.
Located just past rustic Haleiwa Town on the fabled north shore. Beginner surfing is good here, waves are gentle, swimming is calm in summer. Pros, look elsewhere. Scuba and snorkeling in a coral reef nearby. Also jet-ski and windsurfing lessons. Plenty of facilities: a small boat harbor, playing field, basketball courts, picnic tables, rest rooms.

Ke Iki Beach ★★★
Ke Iki Road, off Kamehameha Highway, Haleiwa.
This "secret" North Shore beach has no official name; Ke Iki comes from the access road. Located a mile from Waimea Bay, it has a long, broad shore, often deserted. Swimming is not advisable due to the strong surf, so stroll, loaf, or use your

imagination. No facilities, but you can use neighboring **Pupukea Beach Park,** *59-727 Kamehameha Highway,* with a parking lot, rest room, and picnic area.

Sunset Beach ★★★
59-104 Kamehameha Highway, Haleiwa.
Aptly named for its spectacular sunsets, this is the site of the World Cup of Surfing. The rad surfers come out in the winter, but milder activities such as swimming and snorkeling are fine in summer, when things calm down a bit. Lifeguard, but no facilities.

Waimea Bay Beach Park ★★★
61-031 Kamehameha Highway, Haleiwa.
In winter, the world's largest ridable waves (30-footers) pound Waimea. Watch professional surfers do their thing. Glassy calm in summer, Waimea is beautiful all year. A great escape from Waikiki crowds, with its thick sand and wide beach. The ocean floor and reefs are clearly visible below the crystalline waters, which make it an excellent dive spot.

City Celebrations

Morey World Bodysurfing Championship ★★
59-337 Ke Nui Road, Haleiwa, ☎ *(808) 396-2326.*
Held in January at Ekuhai Beach, home of the "Banzai Pipeline." Top bodyboarders compete for the best waves and try to outdo and outmaneuver each other for fame, glory, and money.

Triple Crown of Surfing ★★★
Haleiwa, various locations, Haleiwa, ☎ *(808) 377-5850.*
November-December. An exciting series of events pits top professional surfers against each other for a total of $215,000 in prize money.

Theme/Amusement Parks

Waimea Valley/Waimea Falls Park ★★★
59-864 Kamehameha Highway, Haleiwa, 96712,
☎ *(808) 638-8511.*
Hours: 10 a.m.–5:30 p.m.

Waimea Falls Park is one of the only botanical gardens in the world that incorporates ancient archaeological sites and ridge-rides on an ATV (four-wheel-drive all-terrain vehicle). Attractions are laid out fairly methodically throughout the bosky 1800-acre spread. Guests can follow a well-planned route on foot or by tram; a detailed pictorial map is provided. Start perhaps by visiting a *Kauhale*, or Hawaiian living site. You're encouraged to go back 300 years while a native Hawaiian guide recreates activities common to daily life. Close by is the *Hale Iwi*, discovered by the park's resident archaeologist in 1976. Translated to "house of bones," it contained two burials and was believed to be the temple of an *ali'i*. Afterward, watch a performance of the Waimea Valley Dancers, the park's hula *halau* (troupe). One of the events nobody misses is the cliff-diving show. Divers plunge over the park's 45-foot waterfall, which feeds into a shallow pool. The aforementioned ATV rides, plus mountain biking and kayaking, can be arranged at the Visitor Center. The park also has a snack bar and two restaurants. The Proud Peacock is open until 9 p.m. General admission: $25 and up.

Kaena Point
Hiking

Kaena Point Trail ★★★

At the end of Route 930, Kaena Point.
This remote, wildly beautiful state park is the end of the road for both the north and west shorelines. The four-mile trail is fairly strenuous, as well as hot and dusty, but there are swimming holes along the way. You'll see coastal dunes, native plants, seabirds, and perhaps a school of spinner dolphins or a Laysan albatross. The views of the coast are spectacular. To get here, drive to the end of the paved road from Route 930 on the North Shore or Route 93 on the West Shore. Follow the jeep trail to Kaena Point.

Waialua

Pacific International Skydiving Center ★★★
68760 Farrington Highway, Waialua, 96712,
☎ *(808) 637-7472.*
Hours: 8 a.m.–5 p.m.
<http://www.pacific-skydiving.com/>

Takes off from Dillingham Airfield in Mokuleia. Participants receive basic on-ground skydiving instruction followed by a tandem jump, where the student is attached to an experienced tandem-master's harness from exit until landing. Discounts for 10 or more souls jumping at the same time. Tandem jumps are made from at least 8500 feet and go up as high as 13,000 feet. After you've survived this, you're ready for an accelerated free-fall course—you'll perform seven tandem dives until they feel you can go it alone, falling from 3000 to 4000 feet. Course price varies with the season. Gear rental and lift tickets are extra. Students must be at least 18 years of age and under 200 pounds. Also at the Airfield is Skydive Hawaii, ☎ *(808) 637-9700*. Tandem dives start at $225. If you're staying in Waikiki or near there, you can arrange for a pickup. General admission: $175–$862.

Southeast Oahu
Hawaii Kai
Hiking

Koko Head Trail ★★
Kalanianole Highway, at the Hanauma Bay entrance, Hawaii Kai.
Although this trail is not always open, it's short (one mile), fun for the family, and fairly easy. The short hike to the summit of Koko Head gives one a superb view over Hanauma Bay, Diamond Head, Hawaii Kai, the Koolau Mountains, and sometimes the island of Molokai, 200 miles across the channel.

Sandy Beach
Beaches

Sandy Beach ★★★
8801 Kalanianaole Highway, Sandy Beach.
Just around the bend from Hanauma Bay, and 30 minutes from Waikiki, Sandy Beach is the ultimate (advanced only) bodysurfing site on Oahu. Others can walk on the sand and savor the action from shore. The ocean here is a seductive temptress, beautiful but dangerous. Beware the strong undercurrents and large waves. Showers, phones, lifeguard, parking, rest rooms.

Waialae
City Celebrations

United Airlines Hawaiian Open ★★★
Waialae Country Club, Waialae, ☎ *(808) 526-1232.*
Held for four days each year in mid-February. In a sea of avocado green and mai-tai pink, top pro golfers swing and putt their hearts out for $12 million worth of prize money. It's also a way for spectators to get into the exclusive, old-money Waialae Country Club.

Upper Manoa Valley
Manoa Valley
Hiking

Manoa Falls Trail ★★★
End of Manoa Road, Manoa Valley, ☎ *(808) 587-0166.*
Less than a mile long, this trail is well-maintained and takes about 30 minutes each way. The hike is deeply forested, and glimpses of the falls can be seen on various points on the trail. Small, but steep and picturesque, Manoa Falls is a perfect picnic spot, surrounded by lush, junglelike vegetation most of the year, especially after a rain. Although tempting, it's not advisable to hike above the falls. Take Manoa Road all the way to the entrance of Lyon Arboretum, then make a sharp left to a dirt road and parking area. Note: The parking at the Arboretum is for patrons only.

Windward Oahu
Hauula
Hiking

Sacred Falls State Park ★★★
Off Kamehameha Highway, south of Hauula
☎ *(808) 587-0300.*
This one is a good workout. Recommended for surefooted hikers with some experience. An old cane road passes the slippery Kaluanui stream into a narrow valley leading up to the waterfall. The falls, which drop some 80 feet, may be a bit of a disappointment when you get to them. The area is subject to flash floods, even in sunny weather. If there are any warning signs up, take them very seriously. The hike is about 4.5 miles round-trip and takes 1.5 hours to complete.

Kailua
Beaches

Kailua Beach Park ★★★★
Kalaheo Road, in downtown Kailua, Kailua.
A two-mile stretch of white sand sloping gently outward to deeper water, Kailua Beach is one of the country's most beautiful beaches. Also known as Oahu's windsurfing capital for its steady breezes; perfect for beginners. Schools nearby give lessons and rent equipment. Generally safe for swimming (no riptides); kayaking, walking, and sunning are alternate activities. Located five miles past Waimanalo, and 50 minutes from Waikiki. There's a big parking lot, but it still gets full, especially on weekends. Rest rooms, showers.

Lanikai Beach ★★★★★
South of Kailua Beach Park, Kailua.
This beach, not far from Kailua Beach Park, is so spectacular that the Australian Tourist Board took a picture of it and tried to pass it off as one of theirs. The unbelievable turquoise water is shot with flashes of purple and the sand is absolutely pure and white. Lanikai is almost a private beach for the residents who have homes right on the water's edge. On the horizon are two offshore islands, both called Mokulua, and you can kayak or sail to them. No facilities or parking.

The Shows

The Lanikai Mortgage Players ★★
Between Kaiolena Drive and Aalapapa Drive, Kailua,
☎ *(808) 261-6469.*
This enterprising group performs for their health and to help maintain Lanikai Park—which is the group's main venue. Material is primarily old-fashioned melodramas, with wacky vaudeville routines and barbershop quartets thrown in. General admission: Varies.

Kaneohe
Beaches

Kualoa Regional Park ★★★
49-479 Kamehameha Highway, Kaneohe.
Only 35 minutes from Waikiki, Kualoa is the viewpoint for Chinaman's Hat island, named for the straw hats Chinese plan-

tation workers wore in the late 19th and 20th centuries. There's good snorkeling around the coral reef. Kite-flying is among the favored dry activities. Good camping, lifeguard, tons of parking, with lots of speed bumps, rest rooms, showers, picnic grounds.

Parks and Gardens

Byodo-In Temple ★★
47-200 Kahekili Highway, Kaneohe, 96744, ☎ *(808) 239-8811. Hours: 9 a.m.–4 p.m.*
http://www.hawaiiweb.com/html/byodo_in_buddhist_temple.html
Situated in the Valley of the Temples Memorial Park (a cemetery) at the foot of the Koolau Mountains, this is a replica of a 900-year-old temple in Uji, Japan. Its bright-red exterior is a striking contrast to the chiseled and verdant cliffs that serve as a backdrop. Carp swim in the pool in front of it, and in the interior is a nine-foot-high gilded Buddha statue. Don't be bashful about ringing the three-ton bronze bell at the entrance—everyone else does it. Gift shop. General admission: $3–$5.

Senator Fong's Plantation and Gardens ★★★
47-285 Pulama Road, Kaneohe, 96744, ☎ *(808) 239-6775. Hours: 10 a.m.–4 p.m.*
http://www.fonggarden.net/
After he retired from public life, Senator Hiram Fong opened his family's 725-acre plantation to the public. There are more than 100 different edible fruits and nuts grown in its orchards. Panoramic views of the windward coast can also be seen. Guided trams tour the property until 3 p.m. With 24-hour notice, guests can engage in paintball games, hike, go mountain climbing, or take Jeep rides into a rainforest. General admission: $5–$15.

Laie
Beaches

Malaekahana Recreation Area ★★★★
Kamehameha Highway, north of Laie, Laie.
Once a well-kept secret, this beautiful, sandy beach, protected by a coral reef, is becoming more popular, but it's fairly empty

during the week. Local residents like to camp here on weekends. There are two islands across the reef from the beach, and it's possible to walk across to the closest one, Mokuauia (Goat Island), a bird refuge, at low tide. Wear reef walkers. Rest rooms, parking, picnic tables, camping.

Theme/Amusement Parks

Polynesian Cultural Center ★★★★
55-370 Kamehameha Highway, Laie, 96762,
☎ *(808) 293-3333.*
Hours: 12:30–9 p.m.
http://www.polynesia.com/

One of Oahu's most popular attractions, the Polynesian Cultural Center takes at least one day to see. The core of the complex is seven authentically replicated islands that make up Polynesia and Melanesia. Walk over to "Tonga," and a smiling woman will demonstrate how a piece of tapa cloth is made from bark. In "Samoa," a youth clambers up a coconut tree and husks and opens the fruit at warp speed. Visitors are meant to stroll and explore at their own pace. Within eight hours, you may have learned at least the rudiments of the Tahitian otea dance, or the basics of the Maori stick game *tititorea*. The center is constantly adding features and attractions—for example, a state-of-the-art IMAX theater, and a lavish new evening show. Better than any luau show you've ever seen, the "Horizons" extravaganza has more than 100 performers covering a four-tiered stage cut out of the side of a "volcano." Songs, dancing, and other revelry follow. The finale is an astounding fire-knife show (the center hosts the annual Fire Knife Dance Championships). A $1.4 million shopping village, "The Treasures of Polynesia," opened in 1995. By the center's accounting, it has the world's largest selection of Polynesian handicrafts. Admission fees depend on ticket packages purchased; the lowest price is for admission only, the highest includes admission, the luau, IMAX, and the night show. General admission: $27–$92.

Waimanalo
Beaches

Makapuu Beach Park ★★★
41-095 Kalanianaole Highway, Waimanalo.

Known for advanced body/boogie-boarding. Waters are calm for reasonably safe swimming during the summer. Showers, phones, lifeguard, parking, picnicking, camping.

Waimanalo Beach Park ★★★
41-741 Kalanianole Highway, Waimanalo.
Long and wide, Waimanalo encompasses at least five beach parks, so there's plenty of room for everyone. It's great for learning how to bodysurf or boogie-board because of the small, gentle waves. Great for picnicking. Located two miles past Sea Life Park. Picnic area, rest room, phones, lifeguard.

Theme/Amusement Parks

Sea Life Park ★★★
41-202 Kalanianaole Highway, Suite 7, Waimanalo, 96795, ☎ (808) 259-7933.
Hours: 9:30 a.m.–5 p.m.; Fridays to 9:30 p.m.
http://www.sealifeparkhawaii.com/
Founded in 1964, Sea Life Park is both an amusement center and marine conservation/education enterprise. Animal shows are its main draw, but there are a number of breeding and treatment centers for endangered species. These programs are incorporated into a number of exhibits, including the Penguin Habitat and the Hawaiian-monk-seal care center. Sea Life Park has the world's only known "wholphin," named Kekaimalu, the result of a union between a false killer whale and an Atlantic bottlenose dolphin. Visitors can observe Kekaimalu being trained. One of the most popular attractions is the 300,000-gallon Hawaiian reef tank, with sharks and stingrays among the 4000 inhabitants. Children are drawn to the Touch Pool, where they can tickle a sea cucumber or stroke a spiny seastar. Good fun for a good cause. General admission: $12-$24.

Tours

Hideaway Tours ★★★
41-127 Nalu Street, Waimanalo, 96795, ☎ (808) 259-9165.
Hours: 7 a.m.–3:30 p.m. Mondays, Wednesdays, and Fridays.
Spend a day in little-known Waimanalo with Darren Keawekaopuaokalani Akau on his Hana ("action") tour of Oahu. Akau, a former tour director, wanted to go on his own and show tourists the "real Hawaii." On a visit to a five-acre

native Hawaiian family plantation, guests will make plumeria and ti-leaf leis, play Hawaiian games, and identify native plants. Also boogie-boarding and snorkeling at two separate beaches—if you've never done one or the other before, Akau, a certified lifeguard, will provide instruction. Tour includes hotel pickup, lunch, use of boogie boards, picture postcards, and a ti-leaf-wrapped gift. General admission: Varies.

Sports

More than 30 **golf courses** are sprinkled around Oahu, ranging from relatively inexpensive public courses to world-class (and big-priced) resort courses. The most-sought-after public courses include par-72 **Hawaii Kai Golf Course,** par-72 **West Loch Municipal Golf Course,** par-72 **Pali Golf Course,** and par-70 **Ala Wai Golf Course.** For exceptional resort courses, try the 18-hole, Arnold Palmer-designed **Links at Kuilima** or the George Fazio-designed, nine-hole course at the **Turtle Bay Hilton** and the two 18-hole courses at the **Sheraton Makaha Resort and Country Club.** The world's best golfers take to the links at Waialae Country Club (around the end of January) for the **Hawaiian Open Invitational Golf Tournament.** More than 150 county-run tennis courts are available to visitors, plus those at hotels, resorts, and country clubs. Free public courts in the Waikiki district are at **Ala Moana Park, Diamond Head Tennis Center,** and **Kapiolani Tennis Courts.** Please be advised that all court and greens fees are subject to change.

Oahu's waters draw fishers to the Waianae Coast, where they try their luck with marlin, mahi-mahi, ahi, and other game fish. Hop on board in Honolulu Harbor (Kewalo Basin) or Pokai Bay on the Waianae coast. Catch bass, Chinese catfish, sunfish, and other **freshwater** species at **Nuuanu Reservoir** above Honolulu, or **Wahiawa Pubic Fishing Area** around Wahiawa town. **Horseback riders** can choose from a variety of trails at the 4000-acre **Kualoa Ranch** in Kaneohe, on the windward coast. Both guests and nonguests can rent horses at the **Sheraton Makaha Lio Stables** for rides into Makaha Valley, or the **Turtle Bay Hilton** for a trot around the resort's property (which includes a private beach).

Central Oahu
Wahiawa

Hawaii Country Club ★★★
1211 Kunia Road, Wahiawa, ☎ *(808) 621-5654.*
http://www.hawaiicc.com/index-e.html
A semi-private club in the center of Dole Pineapple country. Course is 18 holes, par-72. Greens fees for U.S. citizens on weekdays are $10–$25; weekends, $35–$37. Foreign visitors: weekdays, $65; weekends, $69. Twilight for citizens and foreign visitors: weekdays, $7, with cart, $14; weekends, $9, with cart, $18. Pro shop, restaurant, driving range, putting green. General admission: Varies.

Honolulu
Downtown

Hans Hedemann Surf ★★★
350 Ward Avenue, Suite 106, downtown, ☎ *(808) 591-7778.*
Hours: 8 a.m.–6 p.m.
http://www.hhsurf.com/
One- and two-hour private and group surf lessons are taught by Hedemann, a world pro-tour competitor for the past 17 years, and co-owner Tim Groh. Includes water safety, wave selection, and location. All equipment and ground transportation provided. Also bodyboarding for $40 an hour, $60 for two hours. Student discounts are offered. Location is arranged at time of booking. General admission: Varies.

Hawaii Bicycling League ★★★
P.O. Box 4403, downtown, 96812, ☎ *(808) 735-5756.*
http://www.hbl.org/
Outside of Honolulu/Waikiki, coastal roads are relatively level, but traffic is frequent and heavy at times, especially along Kamehameha Highway on the windward coast past Kaneohe through the small hamlets of Laie, Kualoa, and Kaawa. There have recently been a rash of accidents, with impatient drivers trying to pass slow vehicles on the left, with sticky results. A few tough hills, too, including the 1000-foot saddle between the Koolau and Waianae mountain ranges (windward and leeward). The Hawaii Bicycling League will provide you with buds and good tips. Its free weekend rides are open to all. The on- or off-road beginner rides meet on the first Sunday of each month.

Riders must wear helmets and bring water bottles. A free newsletter is distributed in bicycle shops. Bicycle rentals are available from **Planet Surf,** *421 Nahua Street,* in Waikiki near the **Outrigger West Hotel,** ☎ *(808) 926-2060;* and on the North Shore, *59-051 Pupukea Road,* next to Foodland, ☎ *638-7167.* Also recommended in the Waikiki area is **Blue Sky Rentals,** *1920 Ala Moana Boulevard.* Full range of bikes, and mopeds available. Rates vary.

Greater Honolulu

Ala Wai Golf Course ★★★

404 Kapahulu Avenue, Greater Honolulu, ☎ *(808) 733-7387. Hours: 6 a.m.–6 p.m.*

http://www.co.honolulu.hi.us/depts/aud/golf/alawai.htm

This 18-hole, par-70 course right in the heart of Waikiki is probably one of the most-played courses in the world. So it'll probably be a while before you get to scuff up the greens. Cart rental is $20. Half-price after 4 p.m. Large driving range, two putting greens, two pro shops, snack shop, lessons available. General admission: $50 and up.

Atlantis Reef Divers ★★★

1085 Ala Moana Boulevard, Room 102, Greater Honolulu, ☎ *(808) 973-9811.*

Dive Atlantis Reef from a 72-foot Rainbow catamaran, or from the Explorer, a 60-footer with a huge enclosed cabin, spacious dive deck, and hot-water shower. Introductory scuba dives and two-tank guided tours for certified divers. Two-day dive packages take participants to the *Mahi,* a World War II minesweeper, wrecked off the Waianae Coast. Try Club Atlantis, a three-hour cruise off Waikiki. Scuba, snorkel, boogie-board, play water basketball (using an innertube as a basket), or just lay in the sun. The rate includes a barbecue lunch. Massages are extra. Cruises leave from Port Hilton off the beach in front of the **Hilton Hawaiian Village,** *2005 Kalia Road,* in Waikiki. General admission: $100–$250.

Renaissance Ilikai Hotel Sports Center ★★★

1777 Ala Moana Boulevard, Greater Honolulu, ☎ *(808) 944-6300.*

Hours: 7 a.m.–10 p.m.

The Renaissance Ilikai has one of the largest private tennis centers in Waikiki. There are five courts, including one lit for night play. Registered guests, of course, have priority. A pro is on hand for lessons. General admission: Varies.

Waikiki

Hawaii Kai Golf Course ★★★
8902 Kalanianaole Highway, Waikiki, ☎ *(808) 395-2358.*
Hours: 6 a.m.–6 p.m.
http://www.hawaiikaigolf.com/

Public suburban course features two courses. The Championship course is a a par-72, 18-hole course. Greens fee weekdays is $85, weekends $95. The Executive Course is a par-54, 18-hole course. Greens fee weekdays is $37, weekends $42, cart $23.50. Driving range, pro shop, restaurant, putting green. General admission: Varies.

Tradewind Charters
1833 Kalakaua Avenue, Suite 612, Waikiki, 96815,
☎ *(808) 973-0311.*
http://www.tradewindcharters.com

Offers half-day sail and snorkeling excursions daily year-round. Guests can take turns at the helm if they choose, sailing down the Honolulu coastline and sipping cool ones while watching dolphins, flying fish, and sea turtles. Cap it all off with snorkeling at Rainbow reef. All beverages and gear are provided. In season, a morning or afternoon four-hour whale-watching excursion is available on an uncrowded sailing yacht. Also private sailing lessons. You can charter one of the 32- or 72-foot sailing yachts for overnight and interisland cruises. Ask about weddings and burials at sea. General admission: $65 and up.

Leeward Oahu
Kapolei

Ko Olina Golf Club ★★★★
92-1220 Aliinui Street, Kapolei, 96707, ☎ *(808) 676-5300.*
Hours: 6 a.m.–6 p.m.
http://www.koolinagolf.com/

Ted Robinson designed this 18-hole, 6867-yard, par-72 course that opened in February 1990. The rolling course is laid out along a dry coastal plain, with thousands of rare trees, including coconut palm, banyan, monkeypod, and firecracker plants. Robinson created eight water features on eight holes. The whole place is larger than life, with an enormous practice range, a fabulous clubhouse, and a bar overlooking the tough 18th hole with its own lake and waterfall. A team of golf pros are at your service. Greens fees $65 after 2:30 p.m.; $35 after 4 p.m. General admission: $95–$145.

Waianae

Rainbow Diver II ★★★
Pier 8, Waianae Boat Harbor, Waianae, ☎ *(808) 625-7190.*

Lee and Dinah Rodgers operate the only glass-bottom dive boat in Hawaii. It leaves from Waianae Boat Harbor on the leeward coast, far away from the madding crowds in Honolulu. This location makes it a lot easier to get to the to the *Mahi* shipwreck off Maili Point and Makaha Caverns, a popular site for experienced divers. The wreck is now the habitat of sea turtles, eels, and colorful Hawaiian tropical fish. There are more than 20 other dive sites to choose from, including ones with intriguing names such as Jurassic Park, Land of Oz, and Pray for Sex (!). Rainbow Divers offers PADI four-day certification and two-day advanced certification dives, and a "scuba discovery" one-tank dive with an instructor for $100 (not a certification). Also two-tank dives ($65–$75), three-tank sunset/night dives for $125 (48-hour advance reservations required). Snorkelers and ride-alongs allowed (gear included) for $25. Ask about snorkel cruises. The *Rainbow Diver* II has a sundeck and solar shower. Free soft drinks and snacks included. Waikiki hotel pickup and rentals available. General admission: Varies

North Shore
Haleiwa

Raging Isle Sports ★★★
66-250 Kamehameha Highway, Haleiwa, ☎ *(808) 637-7700.*

For exploring Haleiwa's new 3.5-mile beachside hike-and-bike trail, you'll need the right equipment. It's all available from this exclusive shop. Also rentals and repairs. Bikes also available from **Planet Surf**, *59-051 Pupukea Road*, next to Foodland, ☎ *(808) 638-7167.* Call for daily and weekly rates.

Surf & Sea Inc. ★★★
62-595 Kamehameha Highway, Haleiwa, ☎ *(808) 637-9887.*
Hours: 9 a.m.–6 p.m.
Offers surf instruction for all levels. Teaches basic etiquette, wave-riding, safety, and how to recognize currents. Surfboards are provided for beginning lessons. A two-hour, semi-private lesson is $65, with three persons per instructor. Also body-boarding, windsurfing, and scuba diving (certified and non-certified). General admission: Varies.

Kahuku

Happy Trails Hawaii Ltd. ★★★
Kahuku, past Waimea Valley, Kahuku, ☎ *(808) 948-1235.*
Hours: 8 a.m.–5 p.m.
Catering to newbies and first-timers, this out-of-the-way North Shore company specializes in small, intimate trail rides through a 380-acre private ranch above Waimea Valley. Rides meander through eucalyptus and ironwood groves, with panoramic views of the ocean and coast past Kaena Point. Three times daily, at 8:30 a.m., 10:15 a.m. and 3:30 p.m. Reservations required, and some weight restrictions may apply. General admission: Varies.

Turtle Bay Hilton & Country Club ★★★
57-091 Kamehameha Highway, Kahuku, 96731,
☎ *(808) 293-8811.*
Hours: 7 a.m.–5 p.m.
This secluded beachfront resort on 808 acres on Oahu's North Shore features two courses. The resort's newest course, The Links at Kuilima, is an 18-hole, par-72 course designed by Arnold Palmer, Ed Seay, and Erik Larsen. Greens fee $125, guests $50, weekends $75. The older course, the Turtle Bay Country Club Course, is a nine-regulation-holes par-36, with two sets of tees offering a full 18-hole challenge. $25 greens fee. General admission: $25–$175.

Turtle Bay Hilton–Nick Bolletieri Tennis Academy ★★★
57-091 Kamehameha Highway, Kahuku, 96731,
☎ *(808) 203-8811.*
Hours: 8a.m.–7 p.m.
The Turtle Bay Hilton offers 10 Plexipave courts, four of them

lighted, on its 808-acre North Shore resort. A Tennis Center rents equipment and ball machines. Since 1991, the Nick Bolletieri Tennis Academy has maintained a campus on the resort, featuring intensive clinics and programs for all levels. Private lessons are $45 per hour; semi-private $22.50; group, $15. Expect somewhat windy conditions. General admission: $12–$25.

Windward Oahu
Kaaawa

Kualoa Activity Club/Secret Island ★★★
49-560 Kamehameha Highway, Kaaawa, 96730,
☎ *(808) 237-8515.*
Call for hours.
Located on a 4000-acre ranch on Oahu's windward coast. One-hour trail rides every afternoon, and two-hour rides on weekends. If you're pressed for time, you can choose from a bevy of activities offered by the ranch, from a helicopter tour, a historic trolley ride, target shooting, dune cycling, mountain-bike riding, snorkeling, scuba (the ranch also owns a private islet), and more, all packed into an 8.5-hour day. This is one of those places you expect Tattoo to come running out yelling, "Boss, boss, zee plen, zee plen." Reservations required. General admission: Varies.

Kailua

Naish Hawaii ★★★
155-A Hamakua Drive, Kailua, ☎ *(808) 262-6068.*
http://www.naish.com/
What better place to learn windsurfing (also known as sailboarding) than on Oahu's prime windsurfing spot, Kailua Beach? Windsurfing champ Robbie Naish or one of his associates teaches three-hour introductory group lessons plus private lessons. All boards and sails are custom-made in the shop, so you can buy or rent gear here. They'll deliver everything to the beach for you. Also recommended is Kailua Sailboard Co., 130 Kailua Road, ☎ (808) 262-2555; General admission: $55–$75.

Kaneohe

Pali Golf Course ★★★

45-050 Kamehameha Highway, Kaneohe, ☎ *(808) 266-7612. Hours: 6:30 a.m.–6 p.m.*

Highly popular 18-hole, par-72 municipal course. Use of cart adds $14 to the greens fee. Half-price after 4 p.m. Putting green, snack bar. General admission: $40.

Where to Stay

The choices are many—condo bliss (or hell), nondescript highrises, classic hotels, sprawling resorts, homey bed-and-breakfasts, beachy campsites, budget hostels, no-tell motels...with an equally wide range of price brackets and amenities. You'll find an enormous selection of accommodation options in and around Waikiki. In other areas of the island, however, your choices are somewhat (blissfully) limited. For historic and elegant ambiance, Waikiki's **Halekulani Hotel** (circa 1931) or **Royal Hawaiian Hotel** (circa 1927) are hard to beat. Other luxurious digs include the **Sheraton Moana Surfrider, Hilton Hawaiian Village** and **Hawaii Prince Hotel Waikiki** (all in Waikiki), the newly renovated **Kahala Mandarin Oriental Hotel** (Honolulu), **Ihilani Resort and Spa** (Waianae Coast), and **Turtle Bay Hilton** (on the North Shore). The **Outrigger** hotel group offers good value at its various properties. Peak travel months are January, February, and August, and the best (and cheapest) rooms might be difficult to come by unless you've booked way ahead. Don't forget the ubiquitous package deals (ask your travel agent or scour newspaper travel sections) that include airfare, accommodations, and rental cars in one (usually low) price. And, remember, rooms right *on* the beach are a lot more expensive than rooms a block or so away.

Honolulu

Greater Honolulu
Bed-and-Breakfasts

Manoa Valley Inn $99–$190 ßßßß

2001 Vancouver Drive, Greater Honolulu, 96822,
☎ *(800) 535-0085,* ☎ *(808) 947-6019, FAX (808) 946-6168. Single: $99–$190. Double: $99–$190.*
http://www.aloha.net/~wery/mvbroch.htm

By Honolulu standards, its location is off the beaten path—in a residential neighborhood just a block from the University of Hawaii campus—but still convenient to downtown. Rooms are furnished with antiques; three share baths. For more privacy, you might want to book the Alexander Cottage (all accommodations are named after prominent missionary families) or the Guild one-bedroom suite. Sunsets are gorgeous. Highly recommended, except for children under 12 or family pets. Smoking allowed on the lanai only. Amenities: balcony or patio. 8 rooms. Credit cards: A, DC, MC, V.

Hotels

Ala Moana Hotel $105–$185 ★★★
410 Atkinson Drive, Greater Honolulu, 96814,
☎ *(800) 367-6025,* ☎ *(808) 955-4811, FAX (808) 944-2974.*
http://www.alamoanahotel.com/

The Ala Moana Hotel is big, but even with 1200 rooms, the staff here pays admirable attention to detail, and the result is an elegant, smoothly running, international hotel with a large repeat clientele. Business travelers appreciate its close proximity to downtown and government centers. The Ala Moana Shopping Center, one of the largest in the Pacific, is located across the street (a sky bridge is provided for shopaholics), as is Ala Moana Park. The hotel has no fewer than six restaurants, including Tsukasa, which serves Japanese cuisine for breakfast, lunch, and dinner, and the Royal Garden, which offers Chinese dishes in an elegant setting for lunch, dinner, and a late-night snack. Accommodations are generally spacious and modern, but vary somewhat in amenities. Lanais are available in the Waikiki Tower only. Amenities: Jacuzzi, balcony or patio, family plan, club floor, business services. 1200 rooms. Credit cards: A, DC, D, MC, V.

Executive Centre Hotel $125–$180 ★★★
1088 Bishop Street, Greater Honolulu, 96813,
☎ *(800) 949-EXEC,* ☎ *(808) 539-3000, FAX (808) 523-1088. Rated restaurant: Centre Court.*
http://www.hawaii-waikiki.com/executive-centre-hotel.html

As its name implies, the Executive Centre Hotel is one of the increasingly popular all-suite hotels catering to business travelers. The Executive Centre is close to state office buildings, courts, city government buildings, the Iolani Palace, and the

Aloha Tower Market Place. It's also conveniently located to the airport (the Pali Highway becomes Bishop Street, the hotel is on the right). Studio- and one-bedroom suites have either mountain or ocean views (a fabulous view of the harbor) and private whirlpool baths. One-bedroom suites contain full kitchens and a washer and dryer. Complimentary continental breakfast, free local calls (a terrific deal, believe us!) and a daily newspaper are included in the rate. All units have large desks, three telephones, private voice mail, and there's a 24-hour business center on the premises. The Centre Court restaurant is handy for private dining or business entertaining. The hotel also offers an Executive Pass for frequent visitors. Discounts on parking, rooms, and dining in the restaurant are part of the package. Amenities: business services. 114 rooms.

Hawaii Polo Inn $75–$145 ★★
1696 Ala Moana Boulevard, Greater Honolulu, 96815,
☎ *(800) 777-1700,* ☎ *(808) 949-0061.*
http://www.hawaiipolo.com/

Located at the Yacht Club end of Waikiki, the reasonably priced Hawaii Polo Inn offers easy access to shopping at the Ala Moana Shopping Center and leisurely strolls at the Ala Moana Beach Park. Kitchenettes available in mini-suites and suites. Some suites have harbor views. Amenities: balcony or patio. 72 rooms. Credit cards: A, CB, DC, MC, V.

Kahala Mandarin Oriental $260–$560 ★★★★★
5000 Kahala Avenue, Greater Honolulu, 96816,
☎ *(800) 367-2525,* ☎ *(808) 734-2211, FAX (808) 737-2478.*
Rated restaurant: Hoku's.
http://www.mandarin-oriental.com/

Longtime visitors to Hawaii will be gratified to know that the Kahala Mandarin Oriental, which opened in March of 1996, is the much-loved Kahala Hilton with a face-lift and some much-needed ($75 million worth) renovations. Located 10 minutes from Waikiki, it seems today—as it did when it opened—to be on another island. Visitors used to wall-to-wall bodies will find themselves almost alone on the hotel's gorgeous 800-square-foot beach, with lots of grassy areas for those who don't want sand between their toes. Other amenities are a Keiki Club for the kids, a fully equipped business center, and a fitness center replete with steam room, sauna, and Jacuzzi. Amenities: health club, Jacuzzi, sauna, balcony or patio, business services. 370 rooms. Credit cards: A, DC, D, MC, V.

The New Otani Kaimana Beach Hotel $99–$240 ★★★
2863 Kalakaua Avenue, Greater Honolulu, 96815,
☎ *(800) 733-7949,* ☎ *(808) 923-1555, FAX (808) 922-9404.*
http://www.kaimana.com/

In our opinion, The New Otani Kaimana Beach Hotel is what a hotel in the tropics should be. History and nostalgia buffs will be interested to find that Robert Louis Stevenson spent time here in the 1890s, when it was called the Sans Souci Hotel. The Kaimana Beach is located on Sans Souci Beach, another name for the section of Waikiki which is under Diamond Head. The hotel is surrounded by Kapiolani Park, and all rooms have excellent views either of the ocean or of the park and the city beyond (incredibly lovely at night). Besides the normal tourist activities, guests or other visitors can purchase kites in the Kite Fantasy shop located on the premises—the park is a perfect place to fly them. The Diamond Head Climbers Hui (club) was founded here, and takes people up the 1.7-mile trail to the top of the old volcano. Public tennis courts and golf course nearby. Amenities: exercise room, balcony or patio. 125 rooms. Credit cards: A, MC, V.

Waikiki
Condos

Ilima Hotel $82–$104 ★★★
445 Nohonani Street, Waikiki, 96815, ☎ *(800) 367-5172,*
☎ *(808) 923-1877, FAX (808) 924-8371.*
http://www.ilima.com/

Only two blocks from Waikiki Beach, the Ilima is a condominium/hotel offering one of the best values for families on long stays. Accommodations range from studios (530 square feet) to 770-square-foot suites. Be warned, though, that the one- and two-bedroom suites are about the same size. The Executive Suites contain king-size "waveless" waterbeds, or a regular mattress, whirlpool bath, entertainment center, extra large desk, extra phones, and dataports. Amenities: exercise room, sauna, balcony or patio. 99 rooms. Credit cards: MC, V.

Hotels

Alana Waikiki   **$140–$180**   ★★★

1956 Ala Moana Boulevard, Waikiki, 96815,
☎ *(800) 367-6070,* ☎ *(808) 941-7275, FAX (808) 951-3114.*
http://www.alana-doubletree.com/

Located at the entrance to Waikiki Beach on Ala Moana Boulevard, Alana Waikiki Hotel is for sophisticated travelers, not tourists, who desire something more than surf and sand. This boutique hotel, part of the Doubletree chain, is one of the only lodgings we know that has a complete business center with everything from fax machine rentals to translation services, plus a contemporary Museum Gallery AND a 30-piece collection of Picasso ceramics, all under one roof. Commissioned works by distinguished local artists are placed in each guest room. The Alana's two restaurants, Café Picasso and Harlequin, serve Pacific Rim and Mediterranean cuisine in spare but stylish surroundings. The hotel has no beach, but there's a pool, and the concierge can arrange for any watery desires you might harbor. Amenities: exercise room, balcony or patio, family plan, club floor, business services. 313 rooms. Credit cards: A, DC, D, MC, V.

Coconut Plaza Hotel   **$95–$150**   ★★★

450 Lewers Street, Waikiki, 96815, ☎ *(800) 882-9696,*
☎ *(808) 923-8828, FAX (808) 923-3473.*
http://www.hawaii-waikiki.com/hotel-coconut-plaza.html

With 80 rooms, this particularly gay-friendly boutique hotel can offer many of the "touches" found in the mega-hotels and still maintain the personalized service that the larger hotels have lost. The Coconut Plaza is located three blocks from Waikiki and overlooks the Ala Wai Canal. Its main view from the lanais is the Koolau Mountains—not your usual Honolulu tourist view, but one that is nonetheless beautiful. All but the standard rooms (with wet bar) have kitchen facilities with mini-fridge, microwave, and a complete set of cooking utensils. Ten executive suites contain a parlor with a queen-size sofabed, adjacent to the bedroom. The Club Room on the penthouse floor comes complete with a service kitchen, full bar, a living area seating 40 persons, state-of-the-art sound system, and a large-screen TV and VCR. It's ideal for parties, receptions, and company functions. A complimentary continental breakfast is served daily in the lobby. Amenities: exercise room, club floor. 80 rooms. Credit cards: A, DC, D, MC, V.

Diamond Head Beach Hotel $170–$190   ★★
2947 Kalakaua Avenue, Waikiki, 96815, ☎ *(800) 367-2317,*
☎ *(808) 922-3861, FAX (808) 924-1982.*
http://www.marcresorts.com/diamondhead.html
The Diamond Head Beach Hotel is probably about as far from the crowds as it's possible to get in the Waikiki area. Situated at the end of Kalakaua Avenue near the base of Diamond Head, this tall and skinny 14-story building varies considerably in appointments. All but the hotel rooms have full kitchens, and the only ones with lanais are the one-bedroom apartments and suites. The standard and deluxe rooms have to make do with a balcony, but at least the latter have a glimpse of the ocean. Although the property faces the ocean, there's no beach or pool. For travelers who don't want to be where the action is, this is a good choice. Included in the rate is a daily continental breakfast and watersports equipment. In-room safes and parking costs extra. Amenities: balcony or patio. 57 rooms. Credit cards: A, DC, D, MC, V.

Ewa Hotel $77–$100   ★★
2555 Cartwright Road, Waikiki, 96815, ☎ *(800) 359-8630,*
☎ *(808) 922-1677, FAX (808) 923-8538.*
http://www.choicemall.com/hotelwaikiki/
The eight-story Ewa is located on the Kapiolani Park end of Waikiki, about a block from the beach. It's not far from the Ala Wai Golf Course or the lighted tennis courts in Kapiolani Park. All but the standard rooms feature lanais and kitchenettes. There's a rooftop recreation deck where you can crane your neck to see the ocean over the hotel's taller neighbors, but it's fine for sun-worshiping. Given its location, the Ewa offers comfort, a certain measure of style, and good value. Amenities: balcony or patio. 90 rooms. Credit cards: A, DC, D, MC, V.

Halekulani $290–$470   ★★★★★
2199 Kalia Road, Waikiki, 96815, ☎ *(800) 367-2343,*
☎ *(808) 923-2311, FAX (808) 926-8004.*
http://www.halekulani.com/home2.asp
The legendary Halekulani, in one guise or another, has been

welcoming guests to Honolulu since 1907, when it was a residential hotel consisting of a house and five bungalows, situated on Waikiki Beach. In the late 1920s, the original house was torn down and replaced with a more fashionable plantation-style mansion. The mansion was in turn restored and became an integral part of the 1983 renovation. Today the Halekulani consists of five buildings ranging in height from two to 17 stories set among many of the original turn-of-the-century groves and plantings. It's also one of the world's greatest hotels, famed for understated luxury and exemplary services. A personal concierge takes new arrivals to their rooms to register. From then on, all guests are addressed by name. Most rooms have ocean views, and large lanais. Dining facilities at the Halekulani range from the informal House Without A Key to the ultra-sophisticated La Mer. There's a fully equipped fitness center with personal trainer available, and regular running sessions and aerobic classes are scheduled. The Beach Center arranges outrigger canoe rides, surfing lessons, and more. Amenities: exercise room, balcony or patio, family plan, business services. 412 rooms. Credit cards: A, DC, D, MC, V.

Mariott Waikiki Beach Resort (formerly the Hawaii Regent)
$150–$295 ★★★
2552 Kalakaua Avenue, Waikiki, 96815, ☎ (800) 367-5370, ☎ (808) 922-6611, FAX (808) 922-5222.
<u>http://marriotthotels.com/HNLMC</u>
Completely renovated in 2001, this new member of the Mariott chain takes up a whole block on Ohua Avenue between Kalakaua Avenue and Kuhio Avenue, which means there is plenty of space for shops and courtyards. Ask about location before you book your room. Suites run $260–295. Amenities: tennis, balcony or patio, family plan. 1346 rooms. Credit cards: A, MC, V.

Hawaiian Waikiki Beach Hotel $110–$200   ★★★
2570 Kalakaua Avenue, Waikiki, 96815, ☎ (800) 877-7666, ☎ (808) 922-2511, FAX (808) 923-3656.
The Hawaiian Waikiki Beach Hotel is across the street from the beach, on the Diamond Head end of Waikiki. It's within minutes of the zoo, the Waikiki Aquarium, and the Waikiki Shell. If a view or glimpse of the ocean is important to you, consider the hotel's Main Tower—it enjoys enough of a setback from its

neighbors that almost all of the rooms have an ocean view. Be warned that very few rooms in the smaller, adjacent Mauka Tower have this advantage, but the prices are low by Waikiki standards. All units have voice-mail, safes, color TVs, and pay movies; some have mini-fridges. The hotel sets an attractive Sunday brunch in the Captain's Table Restaurant (including omelettes made to order). Lounge with live entertainment in the evenings. Amenities: family plan, business services. 715 rooms. Credit cards: A, MC, V.

Hyatt Regency Waikiki $200–$345   ★★★★
2424 Kalakaua Avenue, Waikiki, 96815, ☎ *(800) 233-1234,* ☎ *(808) 923-1234, FAX (808) 923-7839.*
http://waikiki.hyatt.com/

By now everyone knows that no hotel can claim to be a Hyatt unless it has a multi-story glassed-in atrium. The Hyatt Regency Waikiki is no exception. The building itself is two 40-story towers joined by a three-story atrium replete with foliage, waterfalls, ponds, lava rock and dendrobium orchids in season. Is it Hawaiian? We wouldn't presume to say, but it is impressive, and there is no question that you are in a Hyatt. The hotel boasts that its rooms are oversized, and they don't exaggerate. The color scheme in the rooms, a restful combination of tones of dusty terra-cotta and natural wood, is a welcome relief from the inevitable beiges, tans, and cremes found elsewhere. The upper floors of the Diamond Head Tower have been turned into the Regency Club, an area of superior service and extra attention for vacationers and business travelers. Guests in this section enjoy the services of a concierge during business hours, the use of a private lounge, complimentary breakfast with daily newspapers, daily cocktails from 5–7:30 p.m., and a sun deck with Jacuzzi, plus a 360-degree view of the city. Hint: if you can, locate a copy of the booklet called "101 Wonderful Things To On Oahu." In it are the recommendations of the Regency Club Concierges, who tell you where to find antique Aloha shirts, who makes the best *malasadas* (Portuguese doughnuts), and how to locate a Chinese herbal pharmacy. In keeping with the current revival of interest in Hawaiian tradition and culture, the Hyatt Regency is taking pains to offer guests first-hand experience with authentic Hawaiian music, crafts, food, and more. Visit Hyatt's Hawaii, a historical center, on the second floor. Quilts, tapa work, feather work, and ancient artifacts are just a few of the exhibits. You may even hear Hawaiian spoken by hotel employees, who are encouraged to use the language as they go about their tasks. As you might expect in a hotel this size, guests have a number of options for dining. Ciao Mein, despite its consciously cute name, is really a good restaurant offering diners the option of Italian or Chinese dinners served family-style. The chefs have made a conscious effort to avoid heavy sauces and high fat. The Colony Seafood and Steak House is exactly what its name implies. Guests can select their fresh fish, chicken, beef, or seafood from a refrigerated display case. It's then charcoal broiled to your taste. Mushashi offers sushi plus traditional and contemporary Japanese dishes. Amenities: Jacuzzi, balcony or patio, family plan, club floor. 1230 rooms. Credit cards: A, DC, D, MC, V.

Kai Aloha Apartment Hotel $65–$100 ★★
235 Saratoga Street, Waikiki, 96815, ☎ (808) 923-6723, FAX (808) 922-7592.
The Kai Aloha Apartment Hotel is an old-fashioned, air-conditioned lodging for people who want to be within walking distance of Waikiki Beach (it's about a block away) and not pay exorbitant prices. It offers studios with private lanais and an itty-bitty kitchenette; a much better deal are the spacious one-bedroom apartments, with separate living areas, front and rear porches, and full kitchens. These sleep up to five people. Rates include daily maid service, private phone, radio (but no TVs), iron and ironing board, and a coin-op laundry. Note: Saratoga Street is noisy. Amenities: balcony or patio. 18 rooms. Credit cards: A, MC, V.

Kaulana Kai $99–$250 ★★
2425 Kuhio Avenue, Waikiki, 96815, ☎ (808) 922-7777, FAX (808) 922-9473.
Conveniently located within walking distance of the beach and the Ala Wai Golf Course, the Kaulana Kai was once a rather run-down hotel that has been given a new lease on life. Recently renovated, it's now a boutique-style hotel, spruced up considerably with wood and marble accents. The spacious guest rooms, done up in dusty rose and beige tones, feature refrigerators and in-room safes. Some have kitchenettes or full kitchens. Complimentary breakfast and a shuttle to nearby attractions in Waikiki are among the amenities. There's a pool,

and a washer-dryer on several floors. All in all, a good value for families and couples on a budget. Amenities: Jacuzzi, sauna, balcony or patio. 69 rooms. Credit cards: A, DC, MC, V.

The Outrigger Waikiki $175–$305 ★★
2335 Kalakaua Avenue, Waikiki, ☎ (800) 688-7444. Rated restaurant: Duke's Canoe Club
http://www.outrigger.com/

The Outrigger chain of hotels and resorts was founded by Roy Kelley, Jr. with the intention of bringing paradise within reach of the middle class. If your idea of paradise is being in the midst of the pack on Waikiki Beach, then the jumping, lively, Outrigger Waikiki (right on the beach) will be your ideal destination. Rooms are reasonably priced and reasonably sized. They have a few of the frills that the larger resorts have, but the emphasis is on value over luxury. What the Outrigger Waikiki does have is an outstanding entertainment offering in the Main Showroom where the Society of Seven presents a long-running spectacular that is a judicious and carefully extemporaneous combination of Broadway numbers, skits, and audience participation. They've hit on a winning formula and it's been going on for years. Contemporary Hawaiian music is performed free each evening from 4–6 p.m. and from 10 p.m.–midnight at the hotel's legendary Duke's Canoe Club, a nostalgically decorated restaurant perched on the sand. Amenities: exercise room, Jacuzzi, balcony or patio, club floor, business services. 530 rooms.

Sheraton Moana Surfrider $230–$395 ★★★★
2365 Kalakaua Avenue, Waikiki, 96815, ☎ (800) 782-9488, ☎ (808) 922-3111, FAX (808) 923-0308.
http://www.moana-surfrider.com/

In the beginning there was the Moana. Built by the Matson Navigation Company, the Moana opened its doors on March 11, 1901, and has emerged relatively unscathed after the hotel closed for two years in 1987 for a much-needed, $50-million restoration. We would definitely recommend that you request the Historic Banyan Ocean rooms, or even the City View rooms in the old building. All the modern conveniences are available, including TVs, video-cassette players, refrigerators, mini-bars, and safes hidden in wooden armoires. The modern wings are well-appointed but lack the charm of the original, but most have lanais and ocean views. The older wing has lanais on only two floors. Memorabilia from the hotel's past is displayed in special cabinets in various public rooms. Among them are the christening dress of the first child born in the hotel (silent screen star Julia Moana Kuhn), newspaper clippings pertaining to the death (under ambiguous circumstances) at the hotel of Mrs. Leland Stanford, and an invitation to a dance given in the ballroom by the officers of the *USS Arizona* on September 22, 1941. The tour leaves at 11 a.m. from the Concierge's Desk in the main lobby. It's free and highly recommended. Facilities include four restaurants; the atmospheric Banyan Court is a delightful and traditional place for a buffet breakfast, afternoon tea, cocktails, or Sunday Brunch. Amenities: balcony or patio, business services. 791 rooms. Credit cards: A, DC, D, MC, V.

Sheraton Princess Kaiulani   **$155–$250**   ★★★
120 Kaiulani Avenue, Waikiki, 96815, ☎ (800) 782-9488, ☎ (808) 922-5811, FAX (808) 923-9912.
http://www.princess-kaiulani.com/
The hotel, located in the heart of Waikiki, is a thoroughly modern behemoth, and popular with tour groups. The smallish rooms are hotel-bland, modern, and characterless. Your best bet might be the Junior Suites in the Ainahau Wing. They have the best views and are furnished with a wet bar, ice maker, and whirlpool tub. Among the public rooms are four restaurants, including a Minute Chef for burgers and pizzas, and a Japanese eatery, Momoyama, which is popular with local residents for lunch. The hottest attraction is the Spectacular Polynesian Revue, with dancers from Tahiti, Samoa, Fiji, New Zealand, and Tokelau. The show is offered twice nightly in the Ainahau Lounge. Amenities: balcony or patio. 1149 rooms. Credit cards: A, DC, D, MC, V.

Sheraton Waikiki Hotel   **$210–$380**   ★★★
2455 Kalakaua Avenue, Waikiki, 96815, ☎ (800) 782-9488, ☎ (808) 922-4422, FAX (808) 922-9567.
http://www.sheraton-waikiki.com/
Humongous. Bustling. With 1852 rooms, that's the only way to describe the 25-year-old Sheraton Waikiki. It's aimed at travelers who want the resort experience without a huge price tag, and for the most part, it delivers. The Sheraton has a full program of activities that include fun runs, aerobics, a walking tour through Waikiki to point out the area's history, arts and crafts

programs, and cooking demonstrations. Entertainment includes soloists in the Lobby Bar, jazz and the best views in town at the penthouse-level Hanohano Room (where it's great fun to ride to the top in a glass elevator), popular Hawaiian music pool-side, and dancing at the Esprit nightclub. There's also a program for kids ages five–12. Because of the incredible beachfront location, a whopping 70 percent of the rooms have ocean views. Along with private lanais, all have color TVs and first-run movies, mini-bars and refrigerators, toiletries, coffee makers, and in-room video check-out. Amenities: balcony or patio, family plan, business services. 1852 rooms. Credit cards: A, DC, D, MC, V.

The Aston Waikiki Beachside Hotel $175–$305 ★★★

2452 Kalakaua Avenue, Waikiki, 96815, ☎ (800) 321-2558, ☎ (808) 931-2100.

http://www.aston-hotels.com

The Aston Waikiki Beachside Hotel prides itself on attentive personal service and has many repeat visitors. It was magically converted from a Motel 6 in the 1960s into an intimate European boutique property where the owners wanted to convey the feeling of an elegant kamaaina home of the 1900s. Rooms are extremely well-appointed and decorated with hand-painted tiles in dusty rose, beige, and cream, with hand-painted Oriental screens on the walls. Custom-designed armoires hide mini-fridges, TVs, and videotape players. Pink-and-white applique bedcovers are used instead of heavy bedspreads, which gives it a finished look, and the goosedown pillows were imported from England. To our minds, the elegant trappings make up a lot for the smaller-than-average-sized quarters, which resemble staterooms on luxury cruiseships. They are also amazingly quiet, even though the hotel is in the heart of the Waikiki Beach action. Oceanfront rooms have lanais and great views of Kuhio Beach Park. Others are actually windowless; some have windows that look onto brick walls. There is no restaurant, but an authentic English or Hawaiian tea (the only one in the state) is served in the courtyard by an Italian fountain daily, and continental breakfast is included in the rates. Amenities: balcony or patio. 79 rooms. Credit cards: A, DC, D, MC, V.

The Breakers $88–$98   ★★

250 Beach Walk, Waikiki, 96816, ☎ *(800) 426-0494,*
☎ *(808) 923-3181, FAX (808) 923-7174.*
http://www.breakers-hawaii.com/

An older hotel located half a block from Waikiki, the Breakers will appeal to those who want a little less-formal environment than the newer high-rises. Rooms are reasonably sized, and have electric kitchenettes and air conditioning. The snack bar/lounge at poolside isn't fancy, but the drinks are very cold, and the burgers are some of the best in town. 49 rooms. Credit cards: A, MC, V.

The Renaissance Ilikai Hotel Waikiki $185–$280   ★★★

1777 Ala Moana Boulevard, Waikiki, 96815,
☎ *(800) 645-5687,* ☎ *(808) 949-3811, FAX (808) 941-1523.*
http://www.ilikaihotel.com/

The Ilikai's location near the yacht harbor combines the best of both worlds—it's just a few minutes away from Honolulu's business district, and is also perched ever-so-closely to the edge of Waikiki. Situated in this spot since 1964, it was a familiar landmark to old-time visitors. Its cachet faded a bit with the advent of newer, more exciting hotels, but a $50 million renovation in 1991 put it back on track. Most of the Ilikai's rooms have lanais and are exceptionally large, some of them almost 600 square feet. More than 200 rooms also feature full kitchen facilities, great for families and long stays. As you get to the upper floors, if the view seems familiar, it probably means that you still watch "Hawaii Five-O" reruns on television. Remember the opening shot with Jack Lord as Steve McGarrett, with McGarrett standing with his back to the Honolulu skyline? It was shot from the Ilikai penthouse balcony, and the view is just as spectacular now as it was then. Amenities: tennis, exercise room, business services. 800 rooms.

The Radisson Prince Kuhio $135–$195   ★★★

2500 Kuhio Avenue, Waikiki, 96815, ☎ *(800) 688-7444.*
Rated restaurant: Trellises.
http://www.radisson.com

Terrific for business travelers, the Radisson Prince Kuhio, formerly the Outrigger, has recently undergone an extensive refurbishment that includes converting the 34th and 35th floors of the hotel into the Kuhio Club with concierge service, complimentary continental breakfast, evening hors d'oeuvres, and a guest library. Business travelers to the Kuhio Club have access to laser-printing facilities (for use with laptops), and postal and handling fees are waived for club members using the hotel business center. The hotel has also installed a Meridian Mail voice-messaging system that is among the most-advanced in the world. Guests are able to record their own messages on the voice-mail system or take advantage of pre-recorded greetings in English, Japanese, Korean, or German. Incoming messages are held in the guest's private mailbox until they are retrieved via remote touch-tone phones from anywhere on the island. Located a block from the beach, the Radisson Prince Kuhio has ocean views on one side and views of the Koolau Mountains on the other. Most rooms have private lanais, marble baths, and wet bars. Complimentary coffee is offered daily in the lobby. Amenities: balcony or patio, club floor, business services. 625 rooms. Credit cards: A, DC, D, MC, V.

The Outrigger Reef — $145–$275 ★★

2169 Kalia Road, Waikiki, ☎ *(800) 688-7444,*
☎ *(808) 922-2887.*
<http://www.outrigger.com>

The Outrigger Reef, which opened its doors in 1955, was one of Roy Kelley's earlier undertakings on Waikiki. It has recently undergone a $50 million renovation. They are now furnished in washed white wicker with pale-brown carpets, and have floral print bedcovers. Most rooms have lanais, and at least a partial view of the ocean. If you forgot to bring something with you, you can buy a replacement locally in one of the 15 shops and boutiques located in the lobby. Amenities: business services. 885 rooms. Credit cards: A, DC, D, MC, V.

The Outrigger Reef Towers — $95–$100 ★★

227 Lewers Street, Waikiki, 96815, ☎ *(800) 688-7444,*
☎ *(808) 923-9861.*
<http://www.outrigger.com>

The Outrigger Reef Towers has become something of a landmark in the Waikiki area simply because it's been there so long (by Honolulu standards). First opened in 1959, it was another of Roy Kelley's successful attempts to market Hawaii to the masses. By today's standards, the rooms are a little on the small side. Most have balconies, but the heavy full-length drapes give the rooms a needlessly heavy look, yet are useful for keeping the light out in the morning after a rollicking night out on the town. Furniture is institutional rattan, and the room we saw was done in tones of blue—blue carpets, blue drapes, blue floral print on the beds, blue lamps—all it lacked was Elvis singing "Blue Hawaii." The Reef Towers' Polynesian Palace night club offers nightly entertainment. The local singing/comedy team of Frank DeLima and Glenn Medeiros (a Hawaiian Martin and Lewis) are immensely popular with residents. When she's in town, Charo (the "belle of cootchie cootchie") offers a cross-cultural experience as she offers a program of Latin comedy, dance, and Spanish flamenco guitar under the palms. 480 rooms. Credit cards: A, DC, D, MC, V.

The Royal Garden at Waikiki   **$120–$500**   ★★★★
440 Olohana Street, Waikiki, 96815, ☎ (800) 367-5666, ☎ (808) 943-0202, FAX (808) 946-8777.
http://www.royalgardens.com/
Opened in 1993, the Royal Garden is a tower of luxury located about a half-block from the beach. The lobby is a cool expanse of marble and brass and crystal chandeliers. The focal points are the terraced gardens surrounding the two swimming pools. A waterfall splashes above the main pool. Fronting the waterfall is the hotel's signature restaurant, Cascada, where you dine on Mediterranean-French cuisine under a hand-painted ceiling. The guest accommodations range from standard rooms to royal suites, and feature lanais, sitting rooms, "closet space for kings," marble baths, and wet bars. All have some kind of ocean view; the vista gets better and the prices higher on the uppermost floors. Continental breakfast is included in the rates. Amenities: exercise room, Jacuzzi, sauna, balcony or patio, club floor, business services. 230 rooms. Credit cards: A, CB, DC, D, MC, V.

The Royal Hawaiian Hotel   **$275–$505**   ★★★★
2259 Kalakaua Avenue, Waikiki, 96815, ☎ (800) 325-3535, ☎ (808) 923-7311, FAX (808) 924-7098.
http://www.royal-hawaiian.com/
Recognized for its "plumeria pink" facade, The Royal Hawaiian is one of the hotels constructed by the Matson Navigation Company in the days when Honolulu was seven days away

from Los Angeles or San Francisco. If you crave nostalgia, ask for a room in the original building (circa 1927), which retains its high ceilings, native wooden paneling, and views out into the tropical gardens. Expect a riot of pink everywhere you look, including the ironing boards and terry bathrobes. For fun, take a ride in the "Bathers Elevator." The newer and more expensive Tower Oceanfront rooms are in a modern addition. They are completely luxurious, and feature lanais, but lack the charm of the older section. The beachfront Surf Room, the hotel's main dining room, has been a gathering place for world travelers and locals for years. Here, freshly baked pink cookies are a traditional after-dinner treat, and a mai tai from the Mai Tai Bar right on the beach is like none other. Amenities: balcony or patio, business services. 526 rooms. Credit cards: A, DC, D, MC, V.

The Waikiki Joy Hotel — $150–$205 — ★★★
320 Lewers Street, Waikiki, ☎ *(800) 922-7866,* ☎ *(808) 923-2300.*
http://www.purpleroofs.com/waikikijoy.html
The former Sherry Waikiki, this intimate, gay-friendly boutique hotel IS a joy. Each guest room, nicely decorated with new berber carpets and light-blue-and-pink color schemes, is equipped with entertainment centers with state-of-the-art JVC Bose sound systems, as well as an oval Jacuzzi and a refrigerator. If you want a lanai, you'll have to book one of the suites, located in an adjacent tower next to the pool. The Executive Suites have the largest ones, as well as full kitchens that include a rice cooker. Club Suites have a microwave and wet bar. Located off the veranda, where a daily complimentary breakfast is served, is Capuccinos Café, a coffee bar with a limited menu of finger sandwiches and pastries. In the summer of 1996, the hotel was to venture boldly into cyberspace with the addition of computers and modems so guests can surf the Internet. Amenities: sauna. 94 rooms. Credit cards: A, DC, D, MC, V.

Waikiki Parc Hotel — $160–$245 — ★★★★
2233 Helumoa Road, Waikiki, 96815, ☎ *(800) 422-0450,* ☎ *(808) 921-7272, FAX (808) 923-1336.*
http://www.waikikiparchotel.com/
The Waikiki Parc Hotel appeals to those who are searching for "affordable luxury." It has a great location, about 100 yards from the beach, but is about half the price of the Halekulani,

its sister hostelry across the street. The rooms, which could be termed a little snug, are decorated in a clean, spare style. Amenities include a mini-fridge and well-stocked honor bar, flashlight, hair dryer, custom toiletries, and an in-room safe ($3.50 per day). Bath towels are nice and thick. There's a pool and sundeck on the eighth floor and a sundry shop off the lobby. The Waikiki Parc has two restaurants—the Parc Café, a local favorite, which serves four kinds of buffets (great homemade potato chips), and Kacho, which features a sushi counter in addition to table seating for Japanese meals. Amenities: balcony or patio. 298 rooms. Credit cards: A, DC, D, MC, V.

Resorts

Hilton Hawaiian Village   **$155–$335**   ★★★★
2005 Kalia Road, Waikiki, 96815, ☎ *(800) HIL-TONS,* ☎ *(808) 949-4321.*
http://www.hawaiianvillage.hilton.com/

The Hilton Hawaiian Village is for sociable types who don't want to get away from it all. The resort is the largest in Hawaii and has more than 2500 rooms. At any given time, there are probably 4000 guests registered, and there's something going on 24 hours a day. It consists of several high-rise towers, has its own shopping centers, a Thai temple, a Japanese *minka* (farmhouse), and a 50-foot replica of a Japanese pagoda. The builders constructed a beach by blasting and dredging the rocky shoreline and replacing it with 30,000 cubic yards of sand. The main swimming pool, the 10,000-square-foot "superpool," is surrounded by waterfalls and lava rock, often super-busy with kids. The grounds are home to 25 species of birds, and the artificial lagoon and ponds are stocked with Japanese carp selected for their brilliant coloring. The resort's most-luxurious accommodations, and well worth the expense, are in the Ali'i Tower, consisting of 348 beautifully decorated rooms and suites. The hotel's flagship restaurants are The Bali, which features Pacific Rim cuisine, and The Golden Dragon, which has been serving Cantonese dishes since the hotel opened. Amenities: spa, exercise room, Jacuzzi, balcony or patio, family plan, club floor. 2542 rooms. Credit cards: A, DC, D, MC, V.

Leeward Oahu

Kapolei

Resorts

JW Marriott Ihilani Resort and Spa $275–$550   ★★★★★
*92-1001 Olani Street, Kapolei, 96707, ☎ (800) 626-4446,
☎ (808) 679-0079, FAX (808) 679-0080.*
http://www.ihilani.com/

Rated one of the top five resorts in the world (*Conde Nast Traveler*), this spectacular spot, although it is just twenty-five minutes away from the Honolulu Airport, is far removed from urban chaos. It forms part of the 640-acre Ko Olina Resort and enjoys a gorgeous artificial beach-lagoon teeming with marine life. About 85 percent of the rooms in the 15-story tower have ocean or lagoon views. The rooms are generously proportioned at 680 square feet or more, and have large lanais. One of the major attractions of the resort is its 18-hole Ko Olina Golf Course, designed by Ted Robinson and voted one of the top 75 courses in the United States by *Golf Digest*. Morning tee times are reserved for hotel guests. The other major attraction is the hotel's health and fitness spa. Great use is made of seawater (it's one of the two places in the country to offer authentic Thalasso treatments) and seaweed therapies. Men's and women's massage rooms are available. Herbal wraps using Hawaiian herbs are a house specialty. Diners have a number of choices at Ihilani. Azul, serving Mediterranean cuisine, is the premier restaurant. The Naupaka Terrace presents "cross-cultural" cuisine in a relaxed setting with views over the lagoon and pool area, while Ushio-tei is a traditional Japanese restaurant with a sushi bar and some tatami rooms. The children's program, The Keiki Beachcomber's Club, is run by enthusiastic people who love what they do. Amenities: tennis, health club, exercise room, Jacuzzi, sauna, balcony or patio, family plan, business services. 387 rooms. Credit cards: A, DC, D, MC, V.

North Shore

Haleiwa

Rentals

Ke Iki Hale $85–$145   ★★★
Haleiwa, 96712, ☎ (808) 638-8229.

K'e Iki Hale is for people who don't mind roughing it—a little. Alice Tracy's beach compound consists of tidy, thatched, one- and two-bedroom oceanside cottages on an acre-and-a-half on wild and secluded K'e Iki Beach, located between Shark's Cove (great for snorkeling) and Ehukai Beach (home of the Banzai Pipeline). Units have large picture windows, and kitchens and are stocked with towels and utensils. Outdoor showers hang from coconut trees. Other attractions include the nearby Polynesian Cultural Center, Waimea Falls Park, numerous restaurants, and the hammocks in the yard. Units available by the week. 12 rooms. Credit cards: MC, V.

Kahuku
Resorts

The Turtle Bay Hilton $200–$285   ★★★
57-091 Kamehameha Highway, Kahuku, 96731,
☎ *(800) HIL-TONS,* ☎ *(808) 293-8811,*
FAX (808) 293-1286.
http://www.hilton.com

The Turtle Bay Hilton, built in 1972, is located on the end of Kuilima Point, which juts out over roiling waves on Oahu's fabled North Shore. One of the resort's two beaches is a sandy crescent protected by an offshore reef. There are 27 holes of championship golf, including the Links at Kuilima, which was ranked fourth among *Golf Digest's* top 10 picks for best new courses. Other recreational pursuits range from a game on one of 10 Plexipave tennis courts or a clinic at the Nick Bolletieri Tennis Academy to daily trail rides from the resort's stables. All accommodations have ocean views, some with lanais, and while the rooms are comfortable and clean, they are also a bit dated. Closet space is surprisingly ample. Amenities include coffeemakers ($3 per packet), cable TV with free HBO and pay-per-view movies. Amenities: tennis, horseback riding, exercise room, balcony or patio, family plan. 485 rooms. Credit cards: A, MC, V.

Windward Oahu

Kailua
Bed-and-Breakfasts

Papaya Paradise Bed and Breakfast $70   ★★
395 Auwinala Road, Kailua, 96734, ☎ *(808) 261-0316.*
http://www.bnbweb.com/Papaya.html

Far from the madding crowd on Waikiki, Papaya Paradise Bed and Breakfast is 20 miles away on the windward side of the island, just a short walk from one of the country's best white-sand beaches, Kailua Beach Park. Your hosts are Jeannette and Bob Martz, who offer two units in their contemporary bungalow. Although small, both have private entrances and private baths, and are furnished in tropical rattan and wicker. Each has two beds, two lounge chairs, ceiling fans and air conditioning, phone and cable TV. Units open onto a poolside lanai, where papaya, of course, is served for breakfast along with pancakes, eggs, and home fries. There's also a Jacuzzi and a well-tended tropical garden. Beach gear, including coolers, are provided. Guests are free to use the refrigerator and microwave, as well as a small library. Free parking. Children under six are accepted, and there is a cat on the premises. Amenities: sauna. Two rooms. Credit cards: not accepted.

Rental

John Walker's Beach House $495 ★★★★
572 Kailua Road, Suite 201, Kailua, 96734,
☎ *(808) 261-7895.*
http://www.lanikaibb.com/ricrai.htm

John Walker was an adventuresome Scot who came to Hawaii in the 1870s. He became a contractor, and among his buildings are the Bishop Museum and Honolulu *Hale* (City Hall). This white bungalow with a stone wall and screened-in porches was his weekend retreat, one of the first to be built fronting the pristine white sands of the otherwordly Lanikai Beach. It's furnished with a comfortable mix of period furniture and functional rattan. It has three bedrooms, two baths, a kitchen, sauna, and cabana. There's also a two-bedroom, one-bath cottage (at additional cost). The two buildings share a courtyard, while the main house has its own picnic/patio area. Amenities: sauna, balcony or patio. Five rooms. Credit cards: MC, V.

Kaneohe
Bed-and-Breakfasts

Ali'i Bluffs Windward Bed and Breakfast $55–$65 ★★★
46-251 Ikiiki Street, Kaneohe, 96744, ☎ *(808) 235-1124.*
http://www.hawaiiscene.com/aliibluffs/

The Ali'i Bluffs Windward Bed and Breakfast enjoys a privileged location overlooking Kaneohe Bay. A private home with bedrooms to let, it's a bed-and-breakfast in the true sense of the word—in fact, co-host Donald Munro learned the art of running one from his mother, who had one in Scotland. The decor is an interesting combination of Victorian pieces juxtaposed with collectibles from various periods. The Victorian Room (with attached private bath) has a walk-in closet and a double bed. The Circus Room (with a private bath across the hall) has extra-long twin beds. Late-afternoon tea is served in the living room, and ice and glasses are placed there in the evening for guests to make their own nightcaps. The house has a pool and beach gear, coolers and road maps are provided for trips to Kailua Beach Park, one of the state's best beaches, which is only 15 minutes away. No pets, please, as Munro and his partner De, an artist and retired fashion designer, have two small Maltese terriers (who, by the way, get along great with all the guests). Two rooms. Credit cards: not accepted.

Where to Eat

You'll find everything your stomach will ever desire in Oahu, where hotels and resorts routinely recruit some of the world's finest chefs. As with accommodations, there's food for every pocketbook—from cheap and filling plate lunches for a beach-side picnic to silver-service fine dining on gourmet cuisine by candlelight. Feast on creative Pacific Rim specialties, traditional Polynesian favorites, fresh-from-the-sea fish, Japanese saimin or American Spam, a spectacular array of ethnic specialties (especially Chinese and Japanese), fast-food galore, or just-picked fruits, nuts, and veggies. The dining scene is centered mostly around Waikiki and Honolulu, though you won't go hungry anywhere on the island. Try one or more of the excellent restaurants in Honolulu's **Restaurant Row** (on Ala Moana Boulevard) or **Aloha Tower Marketplace,** and don't miss out on a meal at one of the branches of **Keo's Thai Restaurant** or at **Orchids** (in the Halekulani Hotel).

Aiea/Pearl City
Aiea

Bandito's Cantina $ ★★
98-151 Pali Momi Street, Aiea, (808) 488-8888.
Mexican cuisine. Specialties: Blackened chicken tacos, seafood enchiladas.

A fine spot to dine while shopping at Pearlridge Center, Bandito's makes some attempts to get creative with a few southwestern and Baja-style selections scattered among the usual combo plates. Decor is bright and corny, with wahines dressed up like señoritas from south of the border. It's great. Credit cards: MC, V.

Honolulu
Downtown

A Little Bit of Saigon $$ ★★

1160 Maunakea Street, downtown, ☎ *(808) 528-3663.*
Asian cuisine. Specialties: Pho, coconut chicken, green-papaya-and-shrimp salad.
BYOB

Terrific Vietnamese cuisine at this otherwise plain little Chinatown eatery. But most people bypass the dull decor in favor of staring into a cavernous bowl of *pho*—beef in a signature broth. Accompanying this small masterpiece are fresh basil leaves, onions, and an array of appropriate condiments that you add as you like—bean sprouts for crunch and jalapeno peppers for ouch. If it's too hot for soup, another specialty, green-papaya-and-shrimp salad, is appropriately zingy, with a happy blending of cool mint, lip-puckering limes, garlic, and chiles. If just an appetizer will do, the spring rolls with crabmeat and shrimp are recommended. Credit cards: MC, V.

Big Island Steak House $$$ ★★

101 Ala Moana Boulevard, Suite 279, downtown, 96813,
☎ *(808) 537-4446.*
American cuisine. Specialties: Black-and-Blue ahi, steaks, prime rib, fresh local seafood, Mauna Kea brownie.

Steak, chicken, fish, all delicious, all at good prices. Decked out in a luxe beach-hut style, with steamer trunks, hula dolls, and a wooden canoe, all that's missing from the dining room of this '40s Waikiki-style restaurant at the Aloha Tower Marketplace is a sarong-clad Dorothy Lamour swaying and singing to a corny old song. Everything is high camp to the max, including the pupu and cocktail menus written on coconuts. To immerse yourself in the whole experience, order the Mauna Kea brownie for dessert—this clever concoction is covered with ice cream, raspberry lava sauce, and browned meringue, and brought to the table erupting in flames. The kids'll love it. Features: outside dining, own baking.

Buddhist Vegetarian Restaurant $ ★★★
100 North Beretania Street, Chinatown Cultural Plaza, downtown, ☎ *(808) 532-8218.*
Chinese cuisine. Specialties: Cantonese vegetarian entrées, dim sum.
Exactly as its name implies, the Buddhist Vegetarian Restaurant serves zingy dishes in the Cantonese vein without a trace of meat, in simple, Zen-like surroundings. This eatery's repertoire is surprisingly huge and inventive—tofu and seaweed are fashioned to resemble a fish fillet; the Hawaiian staple, taro, is sculpted into a receptacle cupping perfectly cooked veggies. Dim sum is rolled around on carts, the choices awaiting your selection. Not a few have exotic (perhaps revolting) ingredients such as moss and tree fungus mixed in with more prosaic carrots, broccoli, mushrooms, and pine nuts. But don't be fearful—they're delicious. It's best to come here with a group, but be aware that there are only 12 tables. Open 8 a.m.–2 p.m. and 5:30–10 p.m. on Saturdays and Sundays. Reservations recommended. Credit cards: A, MC, V.

Gordon Biersch $$$
101 Ala Moana Boulevard, in the Aloha Tower Marketplace, downtown, ☎ *(808) 599-4877.*
American cuisine. Specialties: House-brewed beers, fish, steak, lobster.
Gordon Biersch does double duty as a restaurant/hot spot with music and a full-fledged brewery. Two burly varieties (Marzen and dark Dunkel) plus a mellow Export our German friends would admire are concocted within the million-dollar, industrial-size, stainless-steel vats right within the establishment. Garlic fries are a perfect accompaniment, along with a host of other *ono* pupus. Added to the list of steaks and fish are some daring nightly specials from the "contemporary Pacific Rim" school of cookery. Most tables have great views of the Honolulu Harbor, especially from the open-air lanai, if you look up from partying long enough to notice. Features: outside dining, own baking. Reservations recommended. Credit cards: A, CB, DC, MC, V.

Indigo $$$ ★★★★

1121 Nuuanu Avenue, Suite 105, downtown,
☎ *(808) 521-2900.*
Asian cuisine. Specialties: Goat cheese wontons with four-fruit sauce, fiery-explosions-to-heaven shrimp, Madame Pele's Mousse.
Creative appetizers are the specialty here, including goat-cheese won tons with four-fruit sauce, vegetarian spring rolls, grilled spice chicken with Indigo peanut sauce, or lobster pot-stickers, so don't be afraid to graze. Features: own baking, non-smoking area. Reservations recommended. Credit cards: A, DC, D, MC, V.

Pacific Vegetarian Café $ ★★

Aloha Tower Marketplace, downtown, ☎ *(808) 536-6767.*
Specialties: Vegetarian dishes with an international flavor, salads, sandwiches, soups.
The Pacific Vegetarian Café offers an intriguing takeout menu of luscious-sounding international vegetarian specialties, all reasonably priced. Called World Food, you can pick from five kinds of plate lunches or dinners from five countries. Be transported to Morocco, for example, with a taste of pastillas, traditional "special occasion" pies baked with a tofu, almond, and onion filling with a touch of honey. Accompaniments include tabouleh, hummus, salad greens, and chips. Items on the salad menu come in half or whole sizes. Sandwiches (falafels, gardenburger, soy "sloppy joes") and soups (Hawaiian style miso with tofu) are also alternatives. Those less-hungry can opt for a baked potato or Indian samosas from a list of light(er) bites. The Café is located on the second floor of the Aloha Tower Marketplace, in the Makai Food Lanai. Reservations not accepted. Credit cards: A, D, MC, V.

People's Café $ ★★

1300 Pali Highway, downtown, ☎ *(808) 536-5789.*
Specialties: Hawaiian plate lunch, kalua pig, pipikaula.
Closed on Sundays.
In a setting that's older than Don Ho's Polynesian revue, eating at this authentic Hawaiian coffee shop is like attending a neighborhood luau. The pipikaula (a type of beef jerky) served here is the definitive version. You can order it á la carte, but it also comes with the Kalua Plate, a generous serving of appro-

priately smoky shredded pork, lomilomi salmon, chicken long rice, white rice, and poi. If you're the more adventurous type, sample the squid luau or oxtail stew. Reservations not accepted.

Greater Honolulu

3660 On The Rise $$$ ★★★★
3660 Waialae Avenue, Greater Honolulu, ☎ *(808) 737-1177.*
Asian cuisine. Specialties: Pan-seared rock shrimp and taro cake, topped with banana salsa, osso buco Asian style.
Closed on Mondays.
http://www.3660.com/
Recipient of several distinguished dining awards, this "cross-cultural" (mostly Asian and European) restaurant is also one of the best places on the island to dig your fork into a choice steak. A signature dish of this type is pan-seared New York steak Alaea, seasoned fearlessly in secret house spices, and topped with crisp onions. Delicious, mind-bogglingly creative fare. The restaurant also hosts cooking classes every other month, as well as wine dinners. Note: the owners also operate a gourmet (natch) plate lunch place, **Kakaako Kitchen,** *1216 Waimanu Street,* between Pensacola and Piikoi Streets, Honolulu, ☎ *(808) 596-7488.* It's open Monday-Friday from 6:30 a.m.–2 p.m. Freshly baked pastries and desserts are a highlight. Features: own baking, rated wine cellar. Reservations recommended. Credit cards: A, CB, DC, MC, V.

A Pacific Café–Oahu $$$ ★★★★
1200 Ala Moana Boulevard, in Ward Centre, Greater Honolulu, ☎ *(808) 593-0035.*
Specialties: Appetizer bar, Caesar salad over parmesan mozzarella pizza bread, Toasted Hawaiian.
Located on the third floor of Ward Centre, A Pacific Café-Oahu has even jaded Honolulu gourmands all agog. Opened in April 1996, it features Hawaii's first-ever pupu (appetizer) bar. Situated next to the main dining room, the bar has an inviting open kitchen outfitted with a wood-burning oven and a sushi area. Although both lunch and dinner menus change with the seasons, a signature lunch item is smoked-salmon pizza with herb cream cheese and arugula salad; at dinner, patrons might try porcini and fresh herb-crusted island opakapaka with fennel

and dry tomato Israeli couscous and baby vegetables. The magnificent desserts include the "Toasted Hawaiian" — a steamed white-chocolate cake layered with haupia, toasted-macadamia-nut mousse served with caramel sauce and Tahitian-vanilla-bean creme anglaise. Features: own baking, rated wine cellar. Reservations recommended. Credit cards: A, CB, DC, D, MC, V.

Alan Wong's $$$ ★★★★

1857 South King Street, McCully Center, 5th Floor, Greater Honolulu, ☎ *(808) 949-2526.*
International cuisine. Specialties: Kalua pig on wonton nachos with refried taro, avocado salsa, and chili sour cream.

Alan Wong is the much-lauded and ultra-creative former chef of the acclaimed dining duo the CanoeHouse/Le Soleil at the Mauna Lani Bay Hotel and Bungalows on the Big Island's Kohala Coast. Recent menu items have included "Da Bag," steamed clams with kalua pig, shiitake mushrooms, and spinach in a foil bag, or "Poki Pines," crispy ahi poke balls on avocado sashimi with wasabi sauce. And these are just appetizers. The entree list encompasses a wide variety of fresh-fish dishes such as furikake salmon with ume chiso rice cream on linguine, or seared peppered yellowfin ahi with a crispy Asian slaw and soy vinaigrette. The hoof-and-horn set will appreciate some incredible combinations ranging from braised veal shank with "smashed" taro in poi sauce with crab and corn, grilled New York steak with roasted garlic au jus, or roasted pork tenderloin medallions with coconut ginger sweet potato puree, pineapple, water chestnut, and macadamia nut relish. Features: own baking. Reservations recommended. Credit cards: A, MC, V.

Auntie Pasto's $$ ★★

1099 South Beretania Street, Greater Honolulu, ☎ *(808) 523-8855.*
Italian cuisine. Specialties: Seafood pasta, eggplant parmesan, pasta carbonara, chicken marsala.

There's always a line to get in, and the decibel levels are so high you'll want to cover your ears, but the superior quality and huge portions of Italian food (especially pasta with a variety of sea creatures) make whatever discomfort you feel worth the trouble. Terrific appetizers and salads with fresh ingredients; marinated vegetable antipasto and fresh-baked crusty bread accompany all entrées. The service is remarkably efficient and friendly for all the guff the staff has to put up with. Reservations not accepted. Credit cards: MC, V.

Ba-Le Sandwich Shops $ ★★
333 Ward Avenue, Greater Honolulu, ☎ *(808) 533-2843.*
Asian cuisine. Specialties: Vietnamese sandwiches.
Closed on Sundays.
Although other items are available at this tiny shop with two or three tables and a deli case, the tasty Vietnamese sandwiches are as far as most people get. Ham, turkey, and chicken are available as fillings, but the most traditional are head cheese, pâté, or steamed pork. But what spices up these otherwise ordinary meats are the accoutrements: crispy fresh French rolls; a marinade of vinegar, soy and garlic, pickled carrots and turnips; and sprigs of cilantro. Features: own baking. Reservations not accepted.

Coffee Haven $ ★★
1026 Kapahulu Avenue, Greater Honolulu, ☎ *(808) 732-2090.*
American cuisine. Specialties: Coffees, Italian sodas, teas, sandwiches, pastries.
Coffee Haven is a mellow place that offers Internet access along with live guitar music and light meals. When not on-line or munching, patrons can sprawl on a couch (provided for that purpose) in a room that's decorated in a thrift-shop mode. Although coffee is the beverage of choice, there's an entire array of liquid treats, including ultra-sweet Italian sodas, fruit essences flavored with cream and fizzed up with soda water, New-Age teas, including Envy, a mix of green tea with "notes of lemon, mint, and desire." When the munchies hit, have a bagel with cream cheese-pesto spread, smoked ahi or veggie sandwiches, or one of the daily specials, which range from eggplant parmigiana to curry chicken with rice. Scones, carrot cake and cheesecake are baked in-house. Features: outside dining, own baking, non-smoking area.

Crepe Fever/Mocha Java $ ★★★
1200 Ala Moana Boulevard, in Ward Centre, Greater Honolulu, ☎ *(808) 591-9023.*
French cuisine. Specialties: Omelettes, frittatas, crepes, vegetarian entrées, espresso, specialty coffees.
A sprightly café where filled things are a specialty. Crepe Fever

serves many purposes; it's perfect for a coffee break or snack (try the espresso milkshake), a quick breakfast (or any meal) at the counter, or a languid chew-and-gaze at the passing scene in the pseudo-posh, constantly-under-construction Ward Centre (note the British spelling) from a seat at an outside table. Breakfasts are the thing here, though, served all day, including a number of meatless offerings, and they're good, too. A particular favorite is a melange of eggs, potatoes, and vegetables served with an Indian *chapati* (unleavened bread). A host of vegetarian dinner specials are offered daily except Sunday (when the place closes at 4 p.m.) from 5–9 p.m. Friday nights feature live "coffee house" music from 8–10 p.m., and an open mike night on Saturdays at the same time. Features: outside dining, own baking. Reservations not accepted. Credit cards: MC, V.

Down to Earth Deli $ ★★
2525 South King Street, Greater Honolulu, ☎ *(808) 947-7678.*
Specialties: Ethnic vegetarian entrées, salad bar.

A well-respected health-food store, Down to Earth Deli offers cheap sustenance to a variety of neo-hippies, UH students, a few kooks here and there, and other alternative-lifestyle types. It's loved for its salad bar stocked with stellar veggies and produce, and homemade dressings, as well as made-to-order international vegetarian entrées. Items change daily, but the Thai, Middle Eastern, and Indian dishes are recommended. No meat, fish, or poultry, but dairy products, including cheese, are served. You can get things to go , or eat in, cafeteria-style. Seating is at a counter with fewer than 10 seats, or in a cozy loft. Features: own baking. Reservations not accepted.

Hanatei Bistro $$$ ★★★★
6650 Kalanianaole Highway, Greater Honolulu,
☎ *(808) 396-0777.*
French-Asian cuisine. Specialties: Charred ahi coated with seven Japanese spices with shoyu lilikoi sauce, bouillabaisse.

A fabulous Contemporary French-Asian restaurant designed like an indoor Japanese garden, replete with bridges and running streams. Start your meal with wild mushrooms served au gratin with parmesan and fresh herbs, and proceed to bouillabaisse, the chef's own interpretation of the classic dish, combining salmon and opakapaka with lobster, clams, and shrimp in a broth redolent of saffron, lemongrass, and plum tomatoes. Many entrées can be ordered in smaller portions. Features: own baking, Sunday brunch. Reservations required. Credit cards: A, MC, V.

Hoku's $$$ ★★★

5000 Kahala Avenue, Greater Honolulu, 96816,
☎ *(808) 739-8888. Associated hotel: Kahala Hilton*
Oriental Mandarin cuisine. Specialties: Sushi, oysters, fresh Hawaiian fish, chicken and lamb kebabs.

After the Mandarin Oriental Group purchased and refurbished the Kahala Hilton, one thing they noticed was the lack of a restaurant with a view. A two-story addition was built to house Hoku's, the hotel's kicky new multi-level signature dining establishment, which has panoramic views of the Pacific, the beach, and sunsets from every table. Located just off the lobby, Hoku's features Honolulu's most extensive oyster and sushi bar, with the freshest seasonal oysters flown in regularly from all over the globe: Belon from France and rock oysters from Sydney, as well as good ole' boys from the Texas Gulf Coast. In addition, guests can feast on a number of ethnically diverse dishes, such as ahi sashimi with wasabi pesto spread on seaweed naan bread, made in the open kitchen's tandoor oven. One floor below is the open-air Plumeria Beach Café, with all-day casual dining, and American and Japanese-themed buffets at breakfast, lunch, dinner, and Sunday brunch. Features: own baking, rated wine cellar. Reservations recommended. Credit cards: A, MC, V.

I Love Country Café $ ★★★

451 Piikoi Street, Greater Honolulu, ☎ *(808) 596-8108.*
American cuisine. Specialties: Plate lunches, vegetarian offerings, stir-fries, homemade carrot cake.

You won't hear George Jones sobbing into his drink from a jukebox at this no-nonsense café situated in a mall near Ala Moana Center. I Love Country has nothing to do with country, except perhaps where the lone chef wishes he was after sweating over the stoves all day. It's not a place to linger; the place prides itself on preparing fresh food as quickly as possible. Vegetarian dishes are a specialty, including stir fries and brown rice, spinach-stuffed ravioli, and Philly cheese steaks made with mushrooms (or sizzling steak) and served on crunchy French rolls with sauteed onions. Also available are plate lunches, sandwiches, salads and fruit smoothies. Features: own baking. Reservations not accepted.

India Bazaar Madras Café $ ★★
2320 South King Street, Greater Honolulu, ☎ *(808) 949-4840. Indian cuisine.*

Catering to a college crowd (it's near UH Manoa), this airy Indian cafeteria and grocery features at least six tasty curries per day. Hefty portions are dished out on metal trays with compartments for the entrées and condiments. A generous pile of steaming saffron rice is the focal point of everything; to it is added chicken masala, tandoori, or a trio of vegetable curries. Side dishes are always a stellar part of this type of meal, and India Bazaar's selection doesn't disappoint—the *samosas* (fried turnovers with meat or vegetables), *chapati* (unleavened bread), cooling cucumber raita, and spicy *dal* (lentils) are just fine.

Keawe Kafé $ ★★
327 Keawe Street, Greater Honolulu, ☎ *(808) 531-5930. Specialties: Plate lunches.*

A bright spot in a dull area, the Keawe Kafé is a real find in an industrial section off of Ala Moana Boulevard. Not totally unknown, there's usually a crowd waiting along with you for the daily special: one or two kinds of internationally themed plate lunches. One day, there may be a Jamaican plate complete with jerk chicken, barbecued mahimahi AND shrimp. Another time it'll be Greek or Filipino, or... Plates are served with "two-scoop" rice, and a choice of salad; the macaroni is the traditional option, and it's appropriately eggy and mayonnaisy, the way a respectable mac salad should be. Sandwiches are hefty; there's also homemade soup and crispy french fries. Open early for breakfast, the Kafé offers a full range of coffee drinks. Reservations not accepted.

Keo's at Kapahulu $$ ★★★
625 Kapahulu Avenue, Greater Honolulu, ☎ *(808) 737-8240. Thai cuisine. Specialties: Lemongrass soup, curries, satay, salad, spicy rolls.*

Keo Sananikone is not a shy man—he's a world-class name-dropper who loves to have his picture taken with visiting celebrities, and he'll even provide a list of those who've eaten at his restaurant since its opening almost 20 years ago. But he must be credited for breaking the stereotype of a typical humble, storefront Thai eatery. His three Keo's restaurants (this one is the original) are silky, pastel boudoirs filled with art, orchids, and exotic greenery, all lit by soft track lighting or lanterns. Long before the advent of Hawaii Regional Cuisine, Keo introduced exciting items, including his signature "Evil Jungle Prince"—a cabbage salad with chicken and fresh basil, coconut milk, and chilis. It's little wonder he's been written up and lauded repeatedly by every major publication in the world, as well as by *Honolulu Magazine* and *Honolulu Weekly*. All produce, herbs, and flowers are grown on two farms he owns on the island. Other locations: *1486 S. King Street,* ☎ *(808) 947-9988,* and at Ward Centre at 1200 Ala Moana Boulevard, ☎ *(808) 596-0020.* Features: rated wine cellar. Reservations recommended. Credit cards: A, DC, MC, V.

Kincaid's $$ ★★★
Ward Warehouse, Greater Honolulu, ☎ *(808) 591-2005.*
American cuisine. Specialties: Fresh island fish, prime rib, rack of lamb Hunan style, hot Dungeness crab appetizer.
Lauded for its seafood, Kincaid's also has some delicious salads at lunch, including a classic pea straight out of a Midwest farmhouse (only the water chestnuts give it away) or shrimp on romaine lettuce tossed with Maytag blue cheese dressing. Getting back to the fish, try the macadamia nut, stuffed prawns with mango-banana chutney. And if that wasn't rich enough for you, don't leave without lapping up one of the desserts, such as burnt cream—rich vanilla custard with fresh eggs and whole cream, topped with a caramelized, crackling, sugar crust. Sunset menu served from 5-5:45 p.m. Features: own baking. Reservations recommended. Credit cards: A, CB, DC, MC, V.

L'Uraku $$$ ★★★
1341 Kapiolani Boulevard, Greater Honolulu,
☎ *(808) 955-0552.*
Seafood cuisine. Specialties: Sashimi, baked oysters with uni, steamed fresh clams.
One of Honolulu's newest East-West restaurants, L'Uraku specializes in elegant, understated Euro-Japanese cuisine, with an

emphasis on seafood. Chef Hiroshi Fukui's credentials are impeccable: he spent a number of years in Japan preparing the imperial court dinners known as kaiseki. L'Uraku is also one of the few places in town that's not a coffee shop that serves a late supper menu from 10:30 p.m.–2 a.m. It's a great place to slip into when you get a craving for sashimi or baked oysters with uni at 1 a.m. Features: late dining. Reservations recommended.

Old Waialae Road $ ★★
2820 South King Street, Greater Honolulu, ☎ *(808) 951-7779.*
Asian cuisine. Specialties: Korean plate lunches, kimchi.
BYOB
Formerly Ted's Kim Chee To Go, new owners have put in enough seating for 40 bodies at small tables, so you can eat in as well as take food out. Some Italian specialties have been added to the Korean menu, but the most popular items remain the garlicky barbecue Koreans do so well, plus man doo— stuffed, deep-fried dumplings. Steamed rice, mac salad, and crunchy veggies accompany most orders, as well as a small portion of an incendiary kim chee that gave the place its name. If you choose to eat here, you can BYOB. Features: outside dining.

Ono Hawaiian Foods $ ★★
726 Kapahulu Avenue, Greater Honolulu, ☎ *(808) 737-2275.*
Hawaiian cuisine. Specialties: Laulau, kalua pig, Hawaiian plate lunches.
Closed on Sundays.
Many local residents agree that Ono prepares the best authentic Hawaiian food anywhere. Excellent beef stew, kalua pig, and raw fish dishes (*poke*), but the laulau is the thing. Service is particularly warm and welcoming. It's mostly a takeout business, but there are about 10 tables inside if you want to people-watch. Also recommended is Aloha Poi Bowl, 2671 S. King Street, ☎ (808) 944-0798. Try the squid luau. Reservations not accepted.

Roy's $$$ ★★★★
6600 Kalanianaole Highway, Hawaii Kai Corporate Plaza, Greater Honolulu, 96825, ☎ *(808) 396-7697.*
Hawaiian Regional cuisine. Specialties: Wood-roasted Szechuan

baby back ribs, rack of lamb with rosemary potatoes in kiwi butter sauce.

Roy Yamaguchi, the founding father of Hawaii Regional Cuisine (and he's barely in his 40s!) opened this handsome space overlooking Maunalua Bay, beneath Koko Head, in Hawaii Kai in 1988. It's now the flagship operation of a mini-empire of Roy's Restaurants (including one in the Philippines). It's hard to fault any of his appetizers (except that they disappear too quickly) or fresh-fish preparations. At least six kinds of different ones are available nightly, including onaga, mahi-mahi, or ahi, usually seared in a dry cast-iron skillet at high heat, and tossed lightly with outrageous sauce combinations that never fail to work. Pass up Roy's Chocolate Soufflé and you'll never forgive yourself. Features: own baking. Reservations recommended. Credit cards: A, CB, DC, D, MC, V.

Tai Pan on the Boulevard $$$ ★★★★

1680 Kapiolani Boulevard, Greater Honolulu, 96814,
☎ *(808) 943-1888.*
Euro-French cuisine. Specialties: Live seafood wok fried with udon noodles and black-bean sauce, salmon tartare.

Enjoy excellent Euro-French cuisine without the noise and fuss found in many other foodie havens. In a serene atmosphere, you might want to start with the restaurant's signature salmon tartare, a beautifully presented dish of fresh salmon mixed with green onion, lemon juice, sesame oil, and spices, topped with enoki mushrooms, black sesame seeds, and red caviar. It's served with a pungent wasabi mayonnaise and toast triangles. Also recommended are the baked jumbo prawns stuffed with clam soufflé, bearnaise sauce, and creamed orso, or a grilled seafood brochette with lobster, prawns, and scallops. Features: own baking. Reservations recommended. Credit cards: A, D, MC, V.

The Old Spaghetti Factory $

1050 Ala Moana Boulevard, Greater Honolulu,
☎ *(808) 591-2513.*
Italian cuisine. Specialties: Spaghetti with browned butter and mizithra cheese, mud pie, Italian cream sodas.

Located on the second floor of the Ward Warehouse, this is one of an international chain of spaghetterias decorated in a Roaring '20s motif, with plenty of brass and frosted glass. A great place to take fussy kids. Features: own baking. Credit cards: A, DC, D, MC, V.

Waiola Store — $ — ★★
2135 Waiola Street, Greater Honolulu, ☎ *(808) 949-2269.*
Specialties: Shave ice.
This neighborhood market touts itself as the "King of Shave Ice," and in Honolulu at least, not many people dispute this fact. There are more than 30 flavors of homemade syrup available daily, poured onto ice that's as soft and fine as newly fallen snow. They have icky things such as bubble gum for the kids, but adults gravitate towards the mango, lilikoi, and *haupia* flavors. Try the li hing mui (preserved plum) if you really want to blend in.

Waikiki

Acqua — $$ — ★★★
2552 Kalakaua Avenue, Waikiki, ☎ *(808) 924-0123.*
Associated hotel: Hawaiian Regent Hotel.
Mediterranean cuisine. Specialties: Phyllo-wrapped swordfish baked with white and balsamic vinegars, lamb encrusted with herb mustard.
Closed on Sundays.
A remarkable establishment, featuring intriguing Hawaiian-Mediterranean dishes that include rock-shrimp risotto, bouillabaisse, and garlic sesame ahi pasta. Live salsa music is featured nightly from Thursday–Saturday. Features: own baking, late dining. Reservations recommended. Credit cards: A, D, MC, V.

Cascada — $$$ — ★★★
440 Olohana Street, Waikiki, ☎ *(808) 943-0202. Associated hotel: Royal Garden at Waikiki.*
International cuisine. Specialties: Moroccan-style veal shank, salmon tartar, peach melba.
Cascada is a fanciful dining experience in the heart of bustling Waikiki Beach. Named after an artificial waterfall that fronts the restaurant, the best seats in the house are on a marble terrace under a hand-painted ceiling. The kitchen turns out an intriguing mix of Cal-Asian pupus, pastas, Moroccan entrées, and ancient French desserts. Features: outside dining, own baking. Reservations recommended. Credit cards: A, MC, V.

Ciao Mein $$ ★★★
2424 Kalakaua Avenue, Waikiki, ☎ *(808) 923-2426.*
Associated hotel: Hyatt Regency Waikiki.
Chinese and Italian cuisine. Specialties: Spicy kung pao chicken, Szechuan eggplant, petti di pollo, tiramisu.

Ciao Mein serves both Chinese and Italian dishes in a stylish, sexy, and fun environment. You'll know you're on to something different when handed a mint-scented menu (at first we thought it was the server's aftershave). Breadsticks as long and curly as a witch's fingernails come next, along with addictive cheese-herb rolls. These are accompanied by assorted East-West dippers, garlic pesto, and olive oil from Marco Polo land as well as Chinese red pepper chili sauce. It's customary to order "family style," with a series of plates placed on the table and shared by all diners. For folks confused by the choices at hand), the kitchen prepares a daily "cultures collide" combo on one platter. Black-clad servers, sans attitude, don't hesitate to offer suggestions. From the Chinese side, the award-winning wok-fried eggplant in spicy Szechuan sauce, served as an appetizer, is suitably smoky and meaty, and the whole steamed fish with soy ginger sauce is sublime and perfectly cooked. One recommendation off the Italian menu is petti di pollo—sauteed breast of chicken on provolone, garlic, cheese, and prosciutto For dessert, there's a sinful tiramisu, or an assortment of ice creams—lychee, ginger, espresso, etc.—dolloped onto an artfully enameled tray. Sunday brunch served from 10 a.m.–2 p.m. Features: own baking, Sunday brunch. Reservations recommended. Credit cards: MC, V.

Hau Tree Lanai $
2863 Kalakaua Avenue, Waikiki, ☎ *(808) 921-7066.*
Associated hotel: New Otani Kaimana Beach Hotel.
American cuisine. Specialties: Eggs Benedict, fresh fish, seafood, steaks.

This postcard-lovely spot, shaded by umbrellas and a leafy hau tree of indeterminate age, juts out onto Sans Souci Beach, on the Diamond Head side of Waikiki. It's somewhat farther away from the crowds than most seaside eateries. Particularly favored for breakfast (ooh, those Eggs Benedict!), the Hau Tree, lit by tiki torches, is also gorgeous at sunset and in the evenings. Features: outside dining, Sunday brunch. Reservations recommended. Credit cards: A, CB, DC, MC, V.

La Mer $$$ ★★★★★
2199 Kalia Road, Waikiki, 96815, ☎ *(808) 923-2311.*
Associated hotel: Halekulani.
French cuisine. Specialties: Ahi tartare and caviar, roasted Big Island lobster with couscous, Hawaiian vintage chocolate surprise.
The ultra-sophisticated and oh-so-French La Mer, located on the second floor of the hotel, serves sublime dishes that are an engaging combination of Provencal flavors and the freshest island produce. Local seafood is a specialty, and we enjoyed the charbroiled opakapaka (pink snapper) with ginger. Other entrées included roasted barbarie duck with Hayden mango (the huge ones that are about the size of a football) and beef with Pacific oysters. For dessert, try the excessive Hawaiian Vintage Chocolate Surprise, a chocolate crust filled with warm chocolate sauce, or the mousseline of champagne with rhubarb and fresh berries. Features: outside dining, own baking, rated wine cellar, private dining rooms. Reservations required. Credit cards: MC, V.

Nick's Fishmarket $$$ ★★★
2070 Kalakaua Avenue, Waikiki, ☎ *(808) 955-6333.*
Associated hotel: Waikiki Gateway Hotel.
Seafood cuisine. Specialties: Lobster, fresh Hawaiian fish, Australian rack of lamb.
Diners have a choice of sweet Atlantic Tristan rock lobster tails, slipper lobster from Brazil, and Florida Keys whole lobster, as well as lobsters flown in live from Maine. These choice crustaceans can be tackled solo or combined with fresh Hawaiian fish, which changes nightly depending on availability. Other specialties include giant calamari steak, Alaskan king crab legs, roast chicken, and Australian rack of lamb. Oysters Rockefeller and the now, ubiquitous seared ahi sashimi are some of the options. Salads are popular items, particularly Nick's Special Salad—bay shrimp with a secret spinach dressing. Raspberry cheesecake is what most people order for dessert. Nick's also has a thriving bar scene; the Café Lounge features dancing and live music nightly. The restaurant is open until 11 p.m. Fridays and Saturdays. Late-night menu offered weekdays until midnight, and until 1 a.m. on Friday and Saturday. Features: own baking, rated wine cellar, late dining. Reservations recommended. Credit cards: A, CB, DC, D, MC, V.

Orchids $$$ ★★★

2199 Kalia Road, Waikiki, ☎ *(808) 923-2311. Associated hotel: Halekulani.*
American cuisine.
Closed on Sundays.

Although there are a number of spots to take in Diamond Head and Waikiki Beach scenes, few would dispute that Orchids' vantage point is one of the loveliest, especially when the sun goes down. Naturally the covered patio is the choicest spot, where only a stretch of lawn and a fence separate it from the calm waters of Waikiki Beach. No other meals are served on Sunday except brunch, from 9:30 a.m.–2:30 p.m. Features: outside dining, own baking, Sunday brunch, rated wine cellar. Reservations recommended. Credit cards: A, CB, DC, MC, V.

Sarento's–Top of the Ilikai $$$ ★★★

1777 Ala Moana Boulevard, Waikiki, ☎ *(808) 955-5559.*
Italian cuisine. Specialties: Lamb chops Mediterranean, opakapaka Italiano.

A romantic aerie atop one of Waikiki's older hotels, Sarento's replaces the old Top of the "I" that operated up here for ages. The main draws are the intimate booths separated by decorative glass partitions that allow for a little (or a lot) of impromptu smooching between courses. The views of Diamond Head and the Waikiki skyline are spectacular; on a velvet night, the string of high-rises are lit up like gems. Cuisine is mostly high-rent Italian with Mediterranean touches; the juicy lamb chops are served with feta cheese, kalamata olives, and sautéed onions. Features: outside dining, own baking. Reservations recommended. Credit cards: A, D, MC, V.

The Jungle Restaurant $ ★★

311 Lewers Street, Waikiki, ☎ *(808) 922-7808.*
American cuisine.

A neighborhood bar and dance emporium with a state-of-the-art sound system, Jungle Restaurant is for those who like their music loud. It also happens to serve good food. Named by a local newspaper as one of the best places in town to have dinner under $10, the menu includes "wild" green salads with homemade dressings, pastas, chicken Dijon, and a spicy Jungle burger served with garlic fries. A different bread pudding is prepared every evening, as well as chocolate cheesecake Grand Marnier, Snickers pie and whiskey pudding. Decent wines are available by the glass. No lunch served on weekends. Features: own baking.

The Parc Café $$$ ★★★
2233 Helumoa Road, Waikiki, ☎ *(808) 921-7272. Associated hotel: Waikiki Parc Hotel.*
International cuisine. Specialties: Four kinds of buffets.
Local residents love the unpretentious atmosphere that goes along with the gourmet buffets at this contemporary, light-filled restaurant in the Waikiki Parc Hotel. At lunch, you might expect to find a taco station, an international array of salads, a create-your-own-sandwich bar, herb-roasted chicken, at least three kinds of cakes and pies, plus a frozen yogurt bar with toppings. The whole idea started with a Sunday brunch, which was later extended to include breakfast, lunch, and dinner. An all-seafood spread is featured at night. No lunch Sunday or Monday. Features: own baking, Sunday brunch. Reservations recommended. Credit cards: A, CB, DC, D, MC, V.

The Tea Cozi $ ★★★
2452 Kalakaua Avenue, Waikiki, ☎ *(808) 931-2100. Associated hotel: Aston Waikiki Beachside.*
English cuisine. Specialties: Hawaiian and British Tea and pastries.
Closed on Mondays.
It might be an odd notion to sit down to a "veddy British" tea in the heart of Waikiki Beach, but Hawaiian monarchs enjoyed this tradition for many years before the overthrow of the kingdom (the royals were brought up in the European style). Today, there are several locations in Honolulu where you can enjoy this delightful, and totally civilized, afternoon treat. Tea is served in a courtyard, where nothing is heard but a gurgling Italian stone fountain. Hawaiian fruit was advertised, but was apparently unavailable that day, as we received a plate of long-stemmed strawberries. One advantage of opting for the English tea ($12) is the variety—more than a dozen types, from Earl Grey and rosehip to decaf English breakfast, are listed. Scones with Devonshire-style cream come with both versions; the Hawaiian *kine* gets lilikoi butter served with them; the English,

strawberry preserves. In any case, the service is sweet and unobtrusive—after the teapots and a fancy-tiered stand with the goodies are presented at your table, you are left alone to enjoy a few hours of bliss. Tea hour is 3 p.m. on Sunday. Features: own baking. Reservations recommended.

Leeward Oahu
Kapolei

Azul $$$ ★★★★
92-1001 Olani Street, Kapolei, 96707, ☎ *(808) 679-0079. Associated hotel: Ihilani Resort and Spa.*
Mediterranean cuisine. Specialties: Grilled marinated lamb chops with couscous and walnut garlic mayonnaise, chocolate mystique.
Azul, the Ihilani Resort & Spa's signature restaurant, is a cool, sophisticated haven of mellowed native woods, immense wall paintings, and massive flower arrangements. Service, though warm, is formal and correct. In contrast, the cuisine served here, developed by the now-departed executive chef "Suki" Sugiura, is inspired by sunny Mediterranean climes. Choice meats, fresh Hawaiian fish, and fresh breads are prepared in a wood-burning oven and grill. Features: outside dining, own baking, rated wine cellar, private dining rooms. Reservations required. Credit cards: MC, V.

Waianae

Masago's $ ★
85-915-A Farrington Highway, Waianae, ☎ *(808) 696-7833. Pacific Rim cuisine. Specialties: Hawaiian plate lunches, Japanese dishes.*
Closed on Mondays.
Masago's is a rare find in a sea of fast-food joints on this stretch of highway—hidden away next to an auto parts store, it serves a companionable mix of Japanese and Hawaiian specialties, along with burgers and such. The pork eggplant is legendary. Features: outside dining. Reservations not accepted.

North Shore
Haleiwa

Flavormania $ ★★★

66-145 Kamehameha Highway, Haleiwa, ☎ *(808) 637-9362.*
American cuisine. Specialties: Ice cream.
Closed on Mondays.

Despite the silly name, this is the place in Haleiwa, and maybe the world, for homemade ice creams. Try the coconut macadamia, cherries in paradise, or the "chocolate sin." Salads, sandwiches, hotdogs, and smoothies are also on the menu. Open until 10 p.m. on weekends. Reservations not accepted.

Kua Aina Sandwich $ ★★★

Kamehameha Highway, Haleiwa, ☎ *(808) 637-6067.*
American cuisine. Specialties: Burgers, mahimahi burgers.

Some of the most delicious burgers in the world emanate from this no-nonsense sandwich shop on the main drag of Haleiwa town. What makes these thick, cooked-to-order beauties (in one-third- and one-half-pound sizes) so fine is their quality ingredients, fresh buns, juicy tomatoes, Manoa lettuce, hot grilled onions, and a splash of Vermouth. All are cooked to order and come with your choice of cheese (including provolone) and bun. And the pastrami is even better. The hand-cut french fries are extra. Other non-burger items include tuna and avocado, BLTs, mahi-mahi, and roast beef. The best place to eat your sandwich is on one of the benches outside, where you can watch the streetside activity. The violently air-conditioned dining area has several booths, stained-glass windows, and circa 1900 photos of old Haleiwa. Features: outside dining, non-smoking area. Reservations not accepted.

L & L Drive Inn $ ★★

66-197 Kamehameha Highway, Haleiwa, 96712,
☎ *(808) 637-4700.*
American cuisine. Specialties: Plate lunches, grilled pork chop with brown gravy, hot and spicy blackened New York steak.

Starting from just one small drive-through plate-lunch place in 1976, partners Eddie Flores Jr. and Kwock Yum Kam expanded their business to include 24 additional locations, mostly in shopping malls. It's one of those great places that appears out of nowhere when you're tired and hungry. Local residents have recommended L&L as an economical place to eat for under $10. The Haleiwa branch, situated in the Haleiwa Shopping Center, serves up a mean and hearty BBQ mix plate of short ribs, chicken, and teriyaki steak, piled on top of two scoops of rice and accompanied by a rather bland macaroni salad. There are a few booths for eating in, but the place does a brisk take-out service. Although called a plate lunch, all items are served until closing. Chinese food is also served. Reservations not accepted.

Matsumoto Shave Ice $ ★★
66-087 Kamehameha Highway, Haleiwa, ☎ *(808) 637-4827.*
American cuisine. Specialties: Shave ice.
Matsumoto's, a little general store in Haleiwa founded in 1951, is probably the only establishment of its ilk to make the glossy pages of *Gourmet Magazine*. Its especially fine-grained ice, set at the right notch on the machine (syrups are commercially made), is also served with azuki beans and ice cream. Among the 19 flavors are Rainbow (strawberry, lemon, and pineapple) and the Hawaiian Special (Pineapple, banana, and coconut). You can also buy souvenir T-shirts and gaze at the photos of local and international celebrities on the walls. Down the road, and less well-known, is **Aoki's**, *66-117 Kamehameha Avenue,* ☎ *(808) 637-4985,* which some fans say surpasses Matsumoto's. Unlike other establishments, Aoki's makes its own syrups, including the "Volcano," which is lilikoi and banana with a "splash" of strawberry. Cones and cups are less than $2. Open noon–5:30 p.m. Closed Monday and Tuesday.
Credit cards: A, CB, DC, D, MC, V.

Kahuku

Ahi's $ ★★★
Main Camp Road, Kamehameha Highway, Kahuku, 96762, ☎ *(808) 293-5650.*
Seafood cuisine. Specialties: Shrimp from local shrimp farms, fresh fish, teriyaki steak.
Closed on Sundays.
Named for native Hawaiian owner Ahi Logan, not the fish, Ahi's should actually be called "Shrimpy's." Its specialty is fresh shrimp that's aquacultured at the Kahuku Shrimp Farm next door. Shrimp is served cocktail, tempura, and scampi-style. There's also a platter served all three ways. Dishes are served with lots of starch—bread with butter, macaroni salad, AND

rice or creamy mashed potatoes. If the surroundings look stark, it may be because Ahi's was once an army barracks. Very downhome, it's a local favorite for lunch or dinner under $15. Also Chinese dishes, burgers. Features: outside dining.

Windward Oahu
Kailua

Buzz's Original Steakhouse $$$ ★★★
413 Kawailoa Street, Kailua, ☎ *(808) 261-4661.*
American cuisine. Specialties: Steaks, seafood.
When you're ready to come out of the sun, buzz over to Buzz's, conveniently located across from Kailua Beach Park. In an unabashedly corny Polynesian atmosphere (thatched roof, tiki torches), Buzz's offers tall cool ones in bright colors, plus simply grilled steaks, burgers, and fresh fish. The all-you-can-eat salad bar, loaded with fresh ingredients, is acclaimed. Features: outside dining. Reservations not accepted.

Kaneohe

Kin Wah Chop Suey $ ★★
45-588 Kamehameha Highway, Kaneohe, (808) 247-4812.
Chinese cuisine. Specialties: Char siu, seafood.
This busy, bustling place serves excellent Cantonese food, and is one of Kaneohe's favorite family eateries. It's one of the few restaurants where a delicacy such as birds' nest or shark's fin soup can be sampled without robbing Fort Knox. Also recommended are sizzling platters and char siu (barbecued pork). A group of three could easily have dinner for under $30. Reservations not accepted. Credit cards: MC, V.

Nightlife

Oahu makes up for all the other Hawaiian islands combined in the nightlife department, with Honolulu and Waikiki (no surprise) the center of the action. Internationally known bands and traditional entertainers, hula and disco dancing, rowdy bars and ramshackle saloons, luaus and sunset cruises, heavy metal and soft jazz, country-western and down-home blues, full-on Polynesian spectacles, theater, ballet, and the symphony all provide diversion for your non-beach time. Bars shut down at 2 a.m., but places with special cabaret licenses are allowed to keep pouring the booze until 4 a.m. (so long as live music stays on). Try **Anna Bannana's** (Honolulu) for lots of fun and live music; **Banyan Veranda** (Sheraton Moana Surfrider), for Hawaiian entertainment; **Rumors** (Ala Moana Hotel) for disco; **Pecos River Café** (Aiea) for country and western performers; **Don Ho** (Waikiki Beachcomber Hotel) for Hawaiian nostalgia; **Nick's Fishmarket** (Waikiki Gateway Hotel) for upmarket meat market; and **Hotel Street** (Honolulu) for prostitution and sleaze.

Honolulu
Downtown
Bars

Sand Island R&B ★★
197 Sand Island Access Road, downtown, ☎ *(808) 847-4274.*
Hours: 11 a.m.–2 a.m.
Frequented by aging bikers. Blues and R&B is the music of choice. Cover when mainland bands perform.

The Pier Bar ★★★
Aloha Tower Marketplace, downtown, ☎ *(808) 536-2166.*
Hours: 9 p.m.–12:30 a.m.
Closed: Mondays and Sundays.
This is a laid-back, outdoor waterfront bar with live music that's a local fave. Styles vary from rock to jazz or Hawaiian.

Clubs

Sloppy Joe's ★★
Aloha Tower Marketplace, downtown, ☎ *(808) 528-0007.*
Hours: Noon–1 a.m.
Closed: Mondays, Tuesdays, Sundays.
Fashioned like its namesake Hemingway hangout in Key West, with pics of Papa all over the place, Sloppy Joe's features live music and dancing four nights a week along with chili, Jamaican chicken, burgers and, natch, sloppy joes Caribbean-style. Cover applies after 8 p.m. only. General admission: Varies.

Nightlife

The Fast Zone ★★
1154 Fort Street Mall, downtown, ☎ *(808) 536-1035.*
Hours: 10:30 a.m.–midnight; Saturdays and Sundays 6 p.m.–2 a.m.
Deliberately un-stylish, this club specializes in live punk and reggae played by local bands and caters to a starving student clientele. Like a dorm room, there's not much in the way of decor. General admission: Varies.

Greater Honolulu
Clubs

Anna Bannanas ★★
2440 S. Beretania Street, Greater Honolulu, ☎ *(808) 946-5190.*
Hours: 11:30 a.m.–2 a.m.
College students share brewskis with profs at this "venerable" club that's been popular for—gasp—30 years. Ultra-casual in a studied way. Loud music (reggae, blues, alternative) reigns upstairs; serious drinkers congregate in the downstairs bar. General admission: Varies.

Coconuts Nightclub ★★
1777 Ala Moana Boulevard, Ilikai Hotel Nikko, Greater Honolulu, ☎ *(808) 949-3811.*
Hours: 9 p.m.–1 a.m.
Special hours: Mondays, 8:30–11:30 p.m. Closed on Sundays.
Weekend island-music jams; Monday is big-band jazz night; sizzling salsa on Wednesdays. Other evenings you'll just have to settle for pool, aiming at an electronic dart board, and live shower-singing at the karaoke bar. Cocktails and pupus served. No drink minimum, validated parking. General admission: Varies.

Rumours ★★
410 Atkinson Drive, in the Ala Moana Hotel, Greater Honolulu, ☎ *(808) 955-4811.*
Hours: 5 p.m.–2 a.m.
Special hours: Thursdays–Sundays to 4 a.m. Closed on Mondays.
Elegant, dressy,'70s-style hotel nightclub with smooch booths. Mostly local crowd, mainstream, Top 40 playlist. To give you an idea, something called "Big Chill Friday Dance Night" has been a fixture here for more than two years. It's nice to know

some things never change. Also ballroom dancing on Wednesday and Sunday; call for details. General admission: Varies.

Studebaker's ★★
500 Ala Moana Boulevard, Greater Honolulu, ☎ *(808) 531-8444.*
Hours: 5 p.m.–2 a.m.
Special hours: Open until 3 a.m. on Saturdays; Sundays, 6 p.m.–2 a.m.
Named after the vintage auto outside, this diner/club features "American Graffiti"-style entertainment until 9 p.m., when the place flips over into a "contemporary" mode (and all night Saturday). Country-line dancing on Monday. General admission: Varies.

Nightlife

Blue Zebra Café ★★
500 Ala Moana Boulevard, Greater Honolulu, ☎ *(808) 538-0409.*
Hours: 9 p.m.–4 a.m.
Special hours: Saturdays and Sundays from 10 p.m.
Not too many tourists make their way to this Restaurant Row dance club, where everything but Top 40 is played, either live or on disc. But that shouldn't stop you. Acid-jazz on Friday–Saturday. Higher cover for weekends. Sunday free for over 21, $5 for others. General admission: Varies.

Boomer's Live House ★★
1130 N. Nimitz Highway, Greater Honolulu, ☎ *(808) 533-0334.*
Hours: 5 p.m.–2 a.m.
A haven for folks in the 35–49-year-old age bracket who still like to listen to music. Hip hop, house, and acid jazz lovers need not apply. A lot of up-and-coming local acts attempt to get discovered here on Monday and Tuesday nights. Also comedy/magic on Wednesdays, Hawaiian on Thursdays, '50s and '60s dance music Friday and Saturday, and jazz on Sundays. General admission: Varies.

Waikiki
Bars

House Without A Key ★★★★
Halekulani Hotel, Waikiki, ☎ *(808) 923-2311.*
Hours: 6 a.m.–10 p.m.
This legendary beachfront restaurant/cocktail lounge is one of the last vestiges of old Hawaii. Perfect for sunset watching with a cold mai tai in hand while a steel guitar plays in the background. Top-notch Hawaiian music and dancing under the stars. Also in the Halekulani is the Lewers Lounge, for late-evening fare and jazz nightly.

Joy Square ★★
2005 Kalia Road, Waikiki, ☎ *(808) 944-2525.*
This karaoke fun palace features 11 private karaoke rooms, food, a massive video arcade, and a refreshment bar for the kids. People like to celebrate birthdays here.

Punani's Bar ★★
1315 Kalakaua Avenue, Waikiki, ☎ *(808) 946-0000.*
Hours: 4 p.m.–2 a.m.
Live Hawaiian music from 9:30 p.m. Local style, lively, popular. Karaoke, dartboards, full bar, "heavy pupus."

The Jungle ★★
311 Lewers Street, Waikiki, ☎ *(808) 922-7808.*
Hours: 11 a.m.–4:00 a.m.
Special hours: weekends from 6 p.m.
By day, The Jungle is just a neighborhood tavern, with bare wood floors and a fully stocked bar against one wall, softened somewhat with tropical greenery. After 10 p.m., it reverts to a dance club. Progressive, house, and techno music is played, very loudly, from a notorious, state-of-the-art sound system. Features live music occasionally, plus '70s disco on Sundays.

Clubs

Duke's Canoe Club ★★★
2335 Kalakaua Avenue, Suite 116, Waikiki,
☎ *(808) 922-2268.*
Hours: 7 a.m.–midnight.

This beautiful beachfront club/restaurant, decorated in retro '30s and '40s Waikiki Beach revival, is dedicated to the great Duke Kahanamoku. Live Hawaiian music on weekends draws a local crowd.

Eurasia ★★
2552 Kalakaua Avenue, Waikiki, ☎ *(808) 921-5335.*
Hours: 9 p.m.–4 a.m.
Special hours: sports bar, 2–9 p.m.
One of Waikiki's newest hot spots, located on the second floor of the humongous Hawaiian Regent Hotel. Sort of like a Top 40 station, it features nightly "contests." No cover before 10 on Friday and Saturday evenings.

Hula's Bar & Lei Stand ★★
2103 Kuhio Avenue, Waikiki, ☎ *(808) 923-0669.*
Hours: 10 a.m.–2 a.m.
An established gay dance club, Hula's is democratic and open to everyone, except skinheads and homophobes. Al fresco environment, with music videos playing constantly.

Maharaja ★★
2555 Kuhio Avenue, Waikiki, ☎ *(808) 922-3030.*
Hours: 9 p.m.–4 a.m.
This gilded danceteria, with headquarters in Tokyo, is probably what Imelda Marcos' private disco looked like in her former New York townhouse. It's overmarbled, overbrassed, overglassed and overcrowded. Flee if you hate "Boyz 2 Men." Delicious but expensive food is served. Dress code for men. In the Waikiki Trade Center. General admission: Varies.

North Shore
Kahuku
Nightlife

Old Plantation Restaurant ★★
56-565 Kamehameha Highway, Kahuku, ☎ *(808) 293-7427.*
Hours: 11 a.m.–2 a.m.
Special hours: dancing from 10 p.m.
Dancing and live music is offered Fridays and Saturdays at this restaurant in the Kahuku Sugar Mill Complex.

Windward Oahu
Kailua
Clubs

Jaron's Restaurant Kailua ★★
201A Hamakua Drive, Kailua, ☎ *(808) 262-6768.*
Hours: 10 p.m.–1:30 a.m.
One of Kailua's few nightspots is this restaurant, which features live music on Fridays and Saturdays only. General admission: Varies.

Shopping

Shopping in Oahu can easily be considered "sub-paradise" within the Big Paradise. You'll find malls and shopping centers throughout Honolulu, Waikiki, Pearl City, and other major and minor population centers, plus scads and scads of small shops and boutiques tossed in along streets and shorelines, inside hotels and resorts. **Ala Moana Shopping Center,** in Honolulu, is Hawaii's largest, and houses a Liberty House department store as well as branches of Louis Vuitton, Chanel, and Gucci. Other Honolulu-area shopping centers include **Ward Warehouse, Ward Centre,** and **Aloha Tower Marketplace** (all on Ala Moana Boulevard). You'll no doubt notice the **ABC** stores around the Waikiki district—sundry shops that sell everything from sunscreen to potato chips.

Aiea/Pearl City
Aiea

Aloha Flea Market ★★★
Aloha Stadium, Aiea, ☎ *(808) 486-1529.*
Hours: 6 a.m.–3 p.m.
Special hours: open most holidays. Closed: Mondays., Tuesdays, Thursdays, Fridays.
Held in the gargantuan parking lot of the Aloha Stadium, this tri-weekly flea market has clocked in some 30,000 visitors on busy weekends. Composed of two sections—new merchandise on one end and garage sale items on the other—locals and tourists alike can get excellent deals on gift items that are overpriced elsewhere Also toys, clothing, housewares, jewelry, books, fresh flowers and produce. If you've been to an event

like this before, you know it's best to get here as early as possible. Haggling permitted. Examine before you buy, as all sales are final. Some merchants take cash only. General admission: 35 cents.

Kam Super Swap Meet ★★★
98-850 Moanalua Road, Aiea, ☎ *(808) 483-5933.*
Hours: 5:30 a.m.–3 p.m.
Special hours: open most holidays. Closed: Mondays., Tuesdays, Thursdays, Fridays.
Across from Pearlridge Center in the parking lot of the Kam Drive-In Theaters. This is where local residents go for below-market-priced fresh fish, produce, and flowers (orchid plants for under $10). Many vendors have been renting stalls for years and have regular customers. Get there early, as most items are gone by noon.

Pearlridge Center ★★
231 Pearlridge Center, Aiea, ☎ *(808) 488-0981.*
Hours: 10 a.m.–9 p.m.
Special hours: Sunday to 5 p.m.
http://www.pearlridgeonline.com
The Ala Moana Center of the suburbs, Pearlridge Center is patronized by local residents and military families stationed near Pearl Harbor. A sprawling, two-part complex, it even has a monorail, á la Disneyland, to travel from one section to the other. It's almost as big as the Ala Moana Center, at 1.4 million square feet, and features the same anchor stores: Liberty House, J.C. Penney, and Sears. There's also the requisite multi-screen movie complex and food court. For a tasty local treat, try the "Hurricane," an East-West mix of buttered popcorn and mochi crunch (Japanese rice crackers and seaweed) from the Cosmic Candy/Popcorn Planet in Phase II.

Honolulu
Downtown

Chinatown ★★★★
Between River and Bethel Streets, downtown.
Honolulu's Chinatown reminds us of the Cole Porter song, "Come To The Supermarket In Old Peking." Cole wrote that you could buy everything from seaweed soup to gizzard cakes

to an egg that was "more or less decayed," even a "pill to kill your mother-in-law." We're not attesting to the last item, but all other things on his list can be procured in this historic nerve center that's one of the oldest of its kind in the country. The place that most resembles Porter's musical concoction is the **Oahu Market,** *145 N. King Street,* a landmark collection of stalls, shops, bargain produce, and Asian recipe ingredients. Local residents and chefs come for the fresh papio and lomi lomi salmon, as well as Dungeness crab. Chinatown is the best place to shop for Asian cooking ingredients. Come early for the best deals. Open 6 a.m.–3 p.m., Monday-Saturday; until noon on Sundays. Call ☎ *(808) 841-6924.* Street parking only. Other worthwhile stops include **Asia Mall** in the Chinatown Cultural Plaza, *1250 Maunakea Street* ☎ *(808) 521-3045,* open 9 a.m.–9 p.m. daily. The Chinatown Historical Society walking tours take off from here. The Mall is an indoor flea market with a thrift shop, restaurants, jewelry and antique stores, even acupressure and acupuncture specialists. Nearby is **Maunakea Market Place,** *1120 Maunakea Street* ☎ *(808) 524-3409,* with 70 stalls. Open daily 6 a.m.–6 p.m. All along Maunakea Street are some heady shops where residents buy their special-occasion flower leis. Some of them are: **Aloha Leis and Flowers,** *1145 Maunakea,* ☎ *(808) 599-7725,* open Monday-Sunday, 8:30 a.m.–9 p.m.; **Cindy's Lei and Flower Shoppe,** *1034 Maunakea,* ☎ *(808) 536-6538,* open Monday-Saturday, 6 a.m.–9 p.m. Prices go as high as $20 depending on the exotic quality of the blooms.

Chinatown Historical Society Thrift Shop ★★
1250 Maunakea Street, downtown, ☎ *(808) 521-3044.*
Hours: 9:30 a.m.–2 p.m.; Tuesdays and Thursdays.
Shop for a good cause at this thrift shop that benefits the Chinatown Historical Society. Also recommended: The Punahou Thrift Shop open Mondays, Wednesdays, and Fridays from 9 a.m.–3 p.m. The campus is located at *1 Slade Drive,* ☎ *(808) 944-5848.* They also have a white elephant bazaar called **The Tank,** open from April-December; for information ☎ *(808) 944-5752.* **The Owl's Nest Thrift,** *2445 Ka'ala Street,* on the campus of the Mid-Pacific Institute, is open Tuesdays, Wednesdays, Fridays, and Saturdays from 9 a.m.–1 p.m., ☎ *(808) 973-5122.* Proceeds benefit the Ronald McDonald House as well as the University. The University of Hawaii's

thrift shop, ☎ *(808) 956-7418,* is open 10 a.m.–1 p.m. Tuesdays and Wednesdays; Thursday, noon–3 p.m. One-hour validated parking.

Island Provision Company ★★
900-A Maunakea Street, downtown, ☎ *(808) 531-5592.*
Hours: 10 a.m.–5:00 p.m.
Hours: Saturdays, to 2 p.m.
http://www.islandprovision.com
This small, Chinatown-area shop fashions unique Hawaiian-style gift packages from woven lauhala or oversize coconut shells, which are then filled with island herbs, produce, sweets, coffee, and condiments. Most are compact enough to take back home on the plane.

Macadamia Classic ★★
2660 Waiwai Loop, downtown, ☎ *(808) 836-8007.*
Hours: 9 a.m.–4 p.m.
If you despise, or are allergic to, chocolate, these tasty morsels will satisfy your sweet tooth. Macadamia nuts are covered with fresh, preservative-free guava, passion fruit, coconut pineapple, and something called Hawaiian espresso. Everything is color-coded, so you know what you're biting into.

Greater Honolulu

Ala Moana Center ★★★
1450 Ala Moana Boulevard, Greater Honolulu,
☎ *(808) 946-2811.*
Hours: 9:30 a.m.–9 p.m.; Sundays, 10 a.m.–5 p.m.
http://www.alamoana.com/
At 1.5 million square feet, this open-air shoparama is touted as the state's largest, with an annual visitor count of 56 million. Many tourists head straight here right off the plane; some are reported missing in action. With 200 shops, it has surprisingly little kitsch, and a lot of class. The Center Court caters to Japanese tourists with such label-intensive procurers as Salvatore Ferragamo, Cartier, Dior, Fendi, Tiffany & Co., and so on. The mall is still anchored by midwestern stalwarts such as Sears , J.C. Penney, and Hawaii's own Liberty House. A vast, tempting display of prepared foods, including sushi and

French-style baked goods, awaits at Shirokiya's, a branch of the Tokyo mid-market department store. Among the smaller shops and specialty stores, visit Crack Seed Center, featuring a dizzying array of mouth-puckering prepared plums and fruit sold by the pound. Free entertainment is a regular occurrence at the Center Stage on the Street Level. If you're faint from hunger, the Makai Market Food Court will make you faint with indecision; it resembles one of those new international buffets in some Las Vegas casinos. Relief can come from a walk across the center to Ala Moana Beach Park.

Aloha Tower Marketplace ★★★
101 Ala Moana Boulevard, Greater Honolulu,
☎ *(808) 528-5700.*
Hours: 9 a.m.–9 p.m.; Fridays and Saturdays to 10 p.m.
http://www.alohatower.com/
With the historic Aloha Tower as its symbol and centerpiece, this atmospheric, 180,000-square-foot waterfront complex opened in 1994 to help revitalize the Honolulu Harbor area. Among the 120 shops is a retail outlet for the finely crafted koa (and other fine wood) furniture of Martin and MacArthur, Hawaii's premier cabinetmakers. A select collection of locally crafted vases, bowls, clothing, and Aloha shirts (including the renowned Sig Zane line) and quilts are also represented. Of the seven restaurants and bars, many of them have waterfront views, and run the gamut from a branch of Seattle's Gordon Biersch Brewery to the Rodeo Cantina, which has the only tortilla-making machine in Hawaii, and six shelves containing more than 80 varieties of incendiary sauces. There's also an informal food court on the second level. Live entertainment daily and *Pau Hana* (end of work) concerts on Fridays.

Changes ★★
2716 S. King Street, Greater Honolulu, ☎ *(808) 944-1039.*
Hours: 10 a.m.–6 p.m.
Special hours: Saturdays until 5 p.m. Closed: Sundays.
Stylish consigned clothing and accessories in good condition. If you want to unload some of your resort apparel, the owners will pay you cash up front. Also in the area is **Consigned Designs and Consign It For Kids!** *2885 S. King Street,* ☎ *(808) 942-2885,* which caters to working women and young families. Wedding gowns are a specialty item. Open

Monday–Saturday, 10 a.m.–5:30 p.m.; Sundays, 11 a.m.–3 p.m.

Na Lima Mili Hulu No'eau ★★
762 Kapahulu Avenue, Greater Honolulu, ☎ *(808) 732-0865.*
Hours: 9 a.m.–9 p.m.
Special hours: Saturdays to 5 p.m. Closed: Sundays.
Auntie Mary Lou Kekuewa and her daughter Paulette run this store, which translates to "skilled hands touch the feathers." You'll find feather leis (head, neck, hat band), combs, instruction books and lauhala hats. Also offered are feather classes, two hours' minimum to get the basics.

Needlepoint, Etc. ★★★
1030 Kapahulu Avenue, Greater Honolulu, ☎ *(808) 737-3944.*
Hours: 10 a.m.–5 p.m.
Special hours: Saturdays to 4 p.m. Closed: Sundays.
If you're nuts for needlepoint, head to this well-regarded shop that specializes in Hawaiian and Oriental needlepoint designs hand-painted on canvas. Instruction books and fabrics. Needlepoint, Etc. is located in Kilohana Square, a little warren of Oriental art galleries, restaurants, a coffee house, and other amusements worth looking into.

Nohea Gallery ★★★
Ward Warehouse, Greater Honolulu, ☎ *(808) 596-0074.*
Hours: 10 a.m.–9 p.m.
Special hours: Saturdays to 6 p.m.; Sundays to 5 p.m.
On the ground floor of the Ward Warehouse. This well-regarded gallery and repository of local crafts carries woodblock prints by Dietrich Varez, pottery by Gail and Bunky Bakutis, plus stained glass, original paintings, jewelry, and native wood bowls. More than 400 items are represented.

Nui Mono ★★★
2745 South King Street, Greater Honolulu, ☎ *(808) 946-7407.*
Hours: 9:30 a.m.–5:30 pm
The mother-and-daughter team of Elaine Costello and Lue Zimmerman creates hand-sewn, exotic, and vividly colored custom clothing from antique kimonos and selected Japanese cottons. Also eyeglass cases, pillows, bags, and toys.

R. Field Wine Company ★★★
1200 Ala Moana Boulevard, Greater Honolulu,
☎ *(808) 596-9463.*
Hours: 10 a.m.–9 p.m.
Special hours: Fridays, Saturdays to 10 p.m., Sundays to 5 p.m.
http://www.foodland.com/rfield/rfield.html
Along with fine wines, cigars from Brazil and Nicaragua, Petrossian caviar and boar meat, Richard Field is one of the few gourmet specialty shops to carry an extensive selection of foodstuffs from Hawaii's specialty growers. There are few places that you can buy Kulana Organic Beef from Kahua Ranch on the Big Island, exotic tropical fruit trees and fresh herbs from Frankie's Nursery in Waimanalo, lettuce from Sun Bear Produce in Kona, coffee from Langenstein Farm, or Puna Goat cheese. And Field is the sole U.S. retailer for Kona-grown Hawaiian Vintage Chocolate. Much in demand by top chefs, HVC is the only organically farmed cocoa in the world. R. Field also sponsors a food festival every summer, with wine seminars, tastings, cooking demos, and samplings. Gourmet foods are also on display. Free to the public.

The Pacific Handcrafters Guild ★★★
Ala Moana Park and other locations, Greater Honolulu,
☎ *(808) 254-6788.*
http://www.alternative-hawaii.com/profiles/crafters/phg.htm
For really special gifts, residents turn to scores of craft fairs all over the island. The best resource is the Pacific Handcrafters Guild, the state's only juried membership organization for crafters. Almost 140 members display wares at four annual fairs in May, July, October, and December at Ala Moana Park and Thomas Square. The **Island-Wide Handcrafters Christmas Fair** is the state's largest, with 300 vendors. Usually November 29–December 1 at the Neal S. Blaisdell Exhibition Hall, *777 Ward Avenue*, Honolulu, ☎ *(808) 623-4050.*

Turnstyles ★★★
P.O. Box 90663, Greater Honolulu, 96835, ☎ *(808) 674-0238.*
Modern-day craftsman Michael Lee is well-known for fashioning rare island woods such as koa, milo, and kamani into beautiful calabashes. The entire process takes more than a year,

including the final shaping and sealing—that's why prices can edge up to $600 per piece. More affordable are Lee's lathe-turned and hand-decorated pens for $25–$55 each.

Vue Hawaii, Inc. ★★
1022 Kapahulu Avenue, Greater Honolulu, ☎ *(808) 735-8774. Hours: 10 a.m.–5 p.m.*
Located in Kilohana Square. Distinctive island gifts, clothing, Hawaiian art, and koa-wood items and bowls.

Ward Centre ★★★
1200 Ala Moana Boulevard, Greater Honolulu,
☎ *(808) 591-8411.*
Hours: 10 a.m.–9 p.m.
Special hours: Saturdays and Sundays to 5 p.m.
This cluster of shops near the Ala Moana Center focuses more on glossy restaurants, cafés, and a limited-but-noteworthy collection of gourmet and specialty-food stores. Delectable bonbons can be had at The Honolulu Chocolate Company. Proprietor Richard Field of R. Field Wine Company proffers good advice along with escargot eggs, boar meat, Petrossian caviar, fine cigars, liquors, and wines. Sample the Li Hing Wild Strawberries (a confection that's a cross between a gumdrop and crack seed) and the Banzai Mix at the Candy Company. Slinky models glide blankly past the ladies who lunch at weekly fashion shows in selected eateries on Wednesdays.

Ward WarehouseWard Centre
1050 Ala Moana Boulevard, Greater Honolulu,
☎ *(808) 591-8411. Hours: 10 a.m.–9 p.m.*
Special hours: Saturdays and Sundays to 5 p.m.
Facing Kewalo Basin and busy Ala Moana Boulevard, the two-story Ward Warehouse is low-slung and low-key, an altogether pleasant place to shop. It also has some of the nicest clothing boutiques in town, and a number of eclectic, tasteful craft stores and galleries. Among the former are Pomegranates in the Sun, for locally designed casual clothing and accessories, and Mamo Howell, for muumuus with flair. Kincaid's, Orson's, the Chowder House, and an outdoor food court are among the dining options if you get the munchies. Across the street is the **Ward Farmers Market,** *1020 Auahi Street,* ☎ *(808) 591-8411,* open Monday–Saturday, 7 a.m.–6 p.m.; Sundays to 1 p.m.

Local food to go, as well as fresh fish, produce, and tropical fruits from 13 vendors.

Waikiki

Antique Alley ★★★
2145 Kuhio Avenue, Waikiki, ☎ *(808) 924-3649.*
Features 35 vendors, including Hula Hands and Aloha Antiques, offering a unique selection of Hawaiian wares, including menu covers from the Matson liners *Lurline* and *Matsonia*. Given away as souvenirs, these romantic depictions of Hawaiian women, legends, and lore are now all the rage among collectors of '30s and '40s Hawaiiana. Full sets in mint condition run about $450.

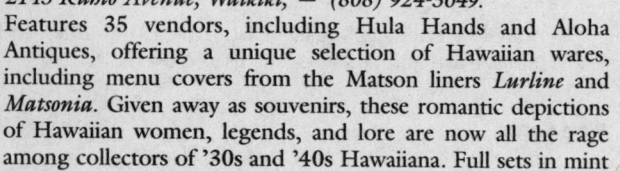

Body & Soul ★★★
131 Kaiulani Avenue, Waikiki, ☎ *(808) 926-2550.*
Hours: 9 a.m.–11 p.m.
Located in The King's Village Shopping Center. Probably the only shop in Hawaii to carry the NARS line of cosmetics created by make-up-artist-to-the-models Francois Nars. Also features the terminally hip and terminally expensive fashions of New Yorkers Betsey Johnson and Anna Sui and London's Todd Oldham, among others.

Ettore Bugatti Boutique ★★★
2174 Kalakaua Avenue, Waikiki, 96815, ☎ *(808) 949-4131.*
The Bugatti family designed automobiles, furniture, airplanes and trains. Now in Waikiki are two floors of quality merchandise inspired by these latter-day Leonardos. Among the clothing, silverware, handbags, luggage, and watches is a Bugatti EB110, the fastest car in the world, and, at $400,000, one of the most expensive. And it's not for sale. Attached to the store is a coffee house with indoor-outdoor seating.

Royal Hawaiian Shopping Center ★★★
2201 Kalakaua Avenue, Waikiki, ☎ *(808) 922-2299.*
Hours: 9 a.m.–10 p.m.
Special hours: Sundays to 9 p.m.
http://www.shopwaikiki.com/index.shtml
Billed as the "Rodeo Drive of Honolulu," this self-consciously upscale swankery with 150 shops is heavy into designer rags

such as Hermes, Cartier, Sonia Rykiel, Ferragamo, Prada, and Van Cleef and Arpels. It's for people who don't want to deal with the Ala Moana Shopping Center, which has the same kind of label-intensive shops in its Center Court. The Royal Hawaiian Hotel is sadly dwarfed behind it, so you have to go through the center to get to it from Kalakaua Avenue. It has six Asian restaurants (one is a kiosk)—the best one and the priciest is Restaurant Suntory. The hot dog stand on the ground floor serves New England lobster roll. The center offers a karaoke bar and a shooting club as between-shopping amusements. Also: hula lessons, ukulele lessons, lei-making, quilt-making, and a Polynesian mini-show with dancers from the Polynesian Cultural Center.

The Military Shop of Hawaii ★★
1833 Kalakaua Avenue, at Ala Wai Boulevard, Waikiki,
☎ *(808) 942-3414.*
Hours: 9 a.m.–6 p.m.
Collectors of military patches will go gaga at this shop that has the widest selection in town. Also insignia memorabilia, books, "survival candy," and apparel. Worth a stop to gaze at the "Great Wall of Patches."

Leeward Oahu
Waipahu

Waikele Center ★★
94-790 Lumiaina Street, Waipahu, ☎ *(808) 676-5858.*
Hours: 9 a.m.–9 p.m.
Special hours: Sundays, 10 a.m.–5 p.m.
It had to happen—the outlet factory mall has landed in Hawaii. Because of the "only available on the mainland" cachet, it's been a big hit with bargain-hunting residents. Off-price designer clothing is the main draw, but you can also purchase luggage, china, kitchenware, furniture, crystal, chocolate, and more, at what a lot of people think are good deals. Harassed moms can drop dad and the kids off at the Discovery Zone, a family fun center. There's a food pavilion, restaurants, and a trolley that shuttles bedazzled shoppers around the complex. Stores include: Off Fifth (Saks), DKNY, Anne Klein, Nine West, Fragrance Outlet, Guess, Levi's Outlet by Most, McInerny Designer Outlet, Mikasa, Tommy Hilfiger, and Guess Kids.

North Shore
Haleiwa

Silver Moon Emporium ★★★
66-037 Kamehameha Highway, Haleiwa, ☎ *(808) 637-7710.*
Hours: 10 a.m.–6 p.m.
Open for several years, this North Shore boutique in a tropical garden setting is owned by a professional model and make-up artist. The sexy and stylish merchandise includes one-of-a-kind designer clothing in silks and velvets, bustiers, retro-earrings, *pareus*, hats, jewelry boxes, umbrellas, and candles.

Southeast Oahu
Kahala

Kahala Mall ★★
4211 Waialae Avenue, Kahala, ☎ *(808) 732-7736.*
Hours: 10 a.m.–9 p.m.
Special hours: Sundays to 5 p.m.
Just a few minutes away from the heart of Waikiki is this unpretentious mall catering to residents of the high-rent Kahala district. There are more than 90 shops, including a branch of Liberty House, an eight-screen movie multiplex, specialty boutiques, Hawaiiana gift stores, an espresso bar, even a New York-style deli (Bernard's). The Following Sea ☎ (808) 734-4425, is a good source for one-of-a-kind handicrafts and gift items by Hawaiian artists.

Windward Oahu
Kailua

Elizabeth's Fancy ★★★
767-B Kailua Road, Kailua, 96734, ☎ *(808) 262-7513.*
Hours: 10 a.m.–4:00 pm
Closed: Mondays and Sundays.
Wall hangings, pillows, patterns, books, Christmas ornaments, whatever island quilter Elizabeth Root fancies—more than 300 of them are to be found within this tiny shop in Kailua. Most are inspired by her original designs. She carries a few selected items created by local artists and small manufacturers. You'll find a number of gift ideas priced under $20.

Kaneohe

Kauila Maxwell ★★★
46-056 Kamehameha Highway, Kaneohe, 96744,
☎ *(808) 235-8383.*
Hours: 9:30 a.m.–9 p.m.
Special hours: Sundays 10 a.m.–5 p.m.

A showcase for authentic Hawaiian gifts on the windward coast, Kauila Maxwell is located at Windward Mall. All merchandise, from bowls, jewelry, art objects, soaps, and T-shirts must past muster from dedicated owner Susan Fernandez Kopper. All items are tagged with explanations about their significance in Hawaiian culture. The store also carries its own line of T-shirts and stationery. Prices from $3–$5000.

MAUI

It is common for Hawaii-bound visitors to completely bypass too-touristy Honolulu and head straight for almost-too-touristy Maui, the island running nearly neck-in-neck with Oahu as the Number One destination.

Known both as "The Valley Isle" and "*Maui no ka oi*" (or "Maui is best"), the island features plenty of beauty for its 91,361 residents and ever-increasing numbers of visitors—rainforest, jungle valleys, miles and miles of swimmable beaches, and the world's largest dormant volcano. Couple the natural features with history, culture, posh resorts, exciting restaurants, and a growing plethora of man-made attractions and it's easy to see why the place is so popular. Maui, in fact, boasts more millionaires than many other resorts-of-the-rich-and-famous, including Palm Springs and the French Riviera. If you want golf, hiking, biking, swimming, snorkeling, off-roading, fabulous food, and glitz, glamour, and the rich folks who go with it, Maui is for you.

Beginning in the late 1700s, *everyone* seemed to descend upon the island, making Lahaina the base of operations. Before the whites took over, however, an internal battle was waged. In the 1770s, Maui had two rulers: King Kalaniopuu of Hawaii had charge over the Hana District, while King Kahekili controlled the rest of Maui. In a grab to get Kahekili's piece of the action, Kalaniopuu—in 1776—made an unsuccessful invasion. Kahekili and his fierce warriors prevailed, only to lose out in 1790 to King Kamehameha the Great, who built his palace at Lahaina around 1802. The town already had been seeing action—French Commander La Perouse and his expedition visited in 1786; Captain Vancouver and entourage followed in 1793. In 1819 the whalers began stopping by, doing both their business and partying in Lahaina. Partying? In came the missionaries several years later to clean things up, convert the natives to Christianity, and put a stop to as much frivolity as possible. The whalers, of course, didn't take well to this intrusion but, after vehement and occasionally violent protests, gave up the fight, if not their supposed vices. Within the next 40 years, Maui had celebrated its first Catholic Mass, written its first constitution, built its first royal palace, and inaugurated its first steamship service. It was also during this period that Kamehameha III shifted Hawaii's capital from Lahaina to Honolulu. Sugar, however, made Maui all the sweeter.

In 1849, George Wilfong planted the first successful sugar plantation on the island, followed by the creation of James Campbell's sugar mill in 1861. But it was Claus Spreckels ("The King of Sugar") who really established Maui as a sugar capital. Spreckels managed to buy cheap land from the natives, win water rights by gambling with Kamehameha III, and build the Haiku Ditch to irrigate his crop. By the early 1900s, the island's center of activity shifted from Lahaina (which had long since lost its "capital" status to Honolulu) over to Paia, the designated plantation town. The island remained relatively quiet until the 1960s, when all of Hawaii became more tourist-friendly and Maui was "rediscovered."

Possibly Maui has been discovered a little too much. Though Old Lahaina and other historical sites continue to be preserved, developers have swooped in and thoughtlessly desecrated some parts of the island. Kihei, on the south shore, is a prime example—a once pristine area that has been turned into an ugly condo jungle.

Maui continues to flourish through agriculture such as sugar, pineapples, cattle, flowers, and truck crops such as russet potatoes and sweet Maui onions—along with the illegal-but-abundant *pakalolo* (marijuana). Tourism, however, continues to be the island's primary economic stronghold, with approximately 4 million visitors arriving annually—some of whom never leave.

Maui Facts

A.k.a.	The Valley Isle
Main city	Wailuku
Flower	Lokelani
Color	Pink
Area	729 square miles
Length	48 miles
Width	26 miles
Population	91,361
Highest point	Haleakala (10,023 feet)

Maui Survival Guide

Getting There

Most Maui-bound flights stop first at Honolulu International Airport, though United, Delta, and Hawaiian Air run direct flights to Maui from the mainland. Kahului Airport, two miles east of cen-

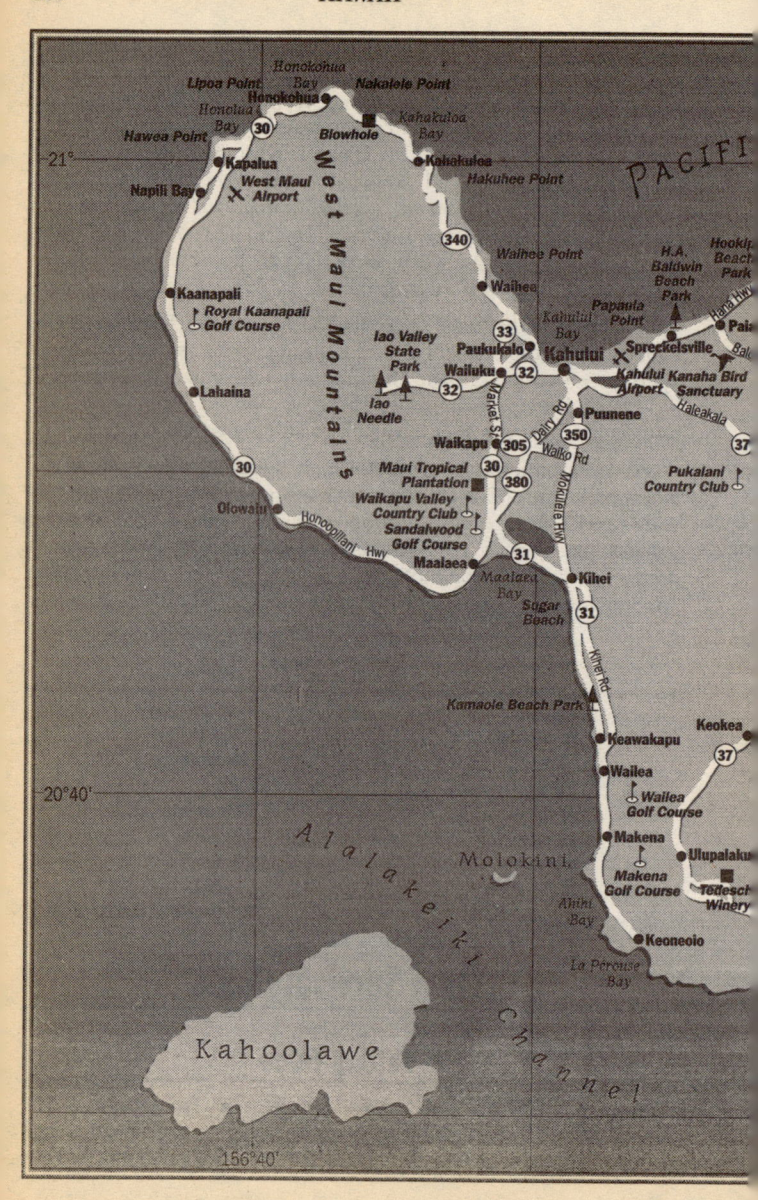

HAWAII

Maui

tral Kahului, is the island's principal airport (servicing approximately 100 flights per day) and offers a full range of airport facilities. Airlines are:

ALOHA	(808) 244-9071	HTTP://WWW.ALOHAAIR.COM/
AMERICAN	(808) 244-5522	HTTP://WWW.AA.COM/
DELTA	(808) 871-0882	HTTP://WWW.DELTA.COM/
HAWAIIAN	(808) 871-6132	HTTP://WWW.HAWAIIANAIR.COM/
ISLAND AIR	(808) 877-5755	
MAHALO AIR	(808) 877-7444	HTTP://WWW.ISLANDER-MAGAZINE.COM/MAHALOSCHEDULE.HTML/

About 50 flights per day operate out of **Kapalua-West Maui Airport**, situated between Kaanapali and Kapalua resort areas, and the best airport for West Maui visitors. Airlines served include **Air Molokai** *(808) 877-0026* and **Island Air** *(808) 877-5755*.

Very small **Hana Airport**, just east of Hana, is a remote airstrip serving visitors to Hana.

Two **ferry services** operate out of Maui: **Expeditions** *(808) 661-3756* runs between Lahaina and Lanai five times daily; The **Maui Princess** *(808) 661-8397* travels once daily between Lahaina and Molokai.

Getting Around

Maui has no public transport and, unless you plan to stay put in one hotel or resort, a rental car is the best way to travel around the island. If you fly into Kahului Airport, you can take shuttles between the airport and Kihei, Wailea and South Maui. For taxi service, contact:

YELLOW CAB OF MAUI OR A-1 TAXI	(808) 877-7000, (808) 667-5675

To Kaanapali resort and other West Maui areas contact:

AKINA TOURS	(808) 879-2828
TRANS-HAWAIIAN SHUTTLE	(808) 877-7308

HAWAII

Fares are high: $30 to Wailea, $50 to Kaanapali, $65 to Kapalua. Car rental agencies are:

ALOMA	(808) 871-6235	HTTP://WWW.GOALMO.COM/
AVIS	(808) 871-7575	HTTP://WWW.AVIS.COM/
BUDGET	(808) 871-8811	HTTP://WWW.BUDGET.COM/
DOLLAR	(808) 877-2731	HTTP://WWW.DOLLAR.COM/
HERTZ	(808) 877-5167	HTTP://WWW.HERTZ.COM/
NATIONAL	(808) 871-8851	HTTP://WWW.NATIONALCAR.COM/
THRIFTY	(808) 871-7596	HTTP://WWW.THRIFTY.COM/

A **free trolley** shuttles between **Kapalua-West Maui Airport** and Kaanapali hotels. **Taxis** should be waiting outside the baggage claim area. Fares are $7 to Kapalua, $12 to Kaanapali, and $60 to Wailea. Courtesy phones inside the terminal summon car-rental companies.

The Hotel Hana Maui shuttles its guests to and from isolated **Hana Airport**. There are no taxis and no buses. **Dollar Rent-a-Car** *(808) 248-8237* and **Word of Mouth Rent a Used Car** *(808) 877-2436*—a local company—are the two car-rental options in town.

Before renting a car, determine if you will need a **four-wheel-drive** vehicle. Many car-rental firms won't cover your off-the-beaten-path or upcountry excursions. Some of the standard companies, such as Hertz, carry four-wheel-drive vehicles, or try **Maui Jeep Rental** *((808) 877-6626,* **http://www.online-catalog.com/jeep/**). Expect to pay a lot more than you would for a conventional car.

> **ITRAVELBOOK TIP:** IF YOU PLAN TO DO ANY OFF-ROADING, IT'S ADVISABLE TO GO WITH A REPUTABLE ORGANIZATION. SOME TRAVELERS ASSUME THAT ANY FOUR-WHEEL-VEHICLE WILL INSURE THEIR SAFETY ON RUTTED MOUNTAIN ROADS; NOTHING COULD BE FURTHER FROM THE TRUTH. OFF-ROADING CAN BE FUN, EXHILARATING, AND EXTREMELY DANGEROUS, SO ERR ON THE SIDE OF CAUTION.

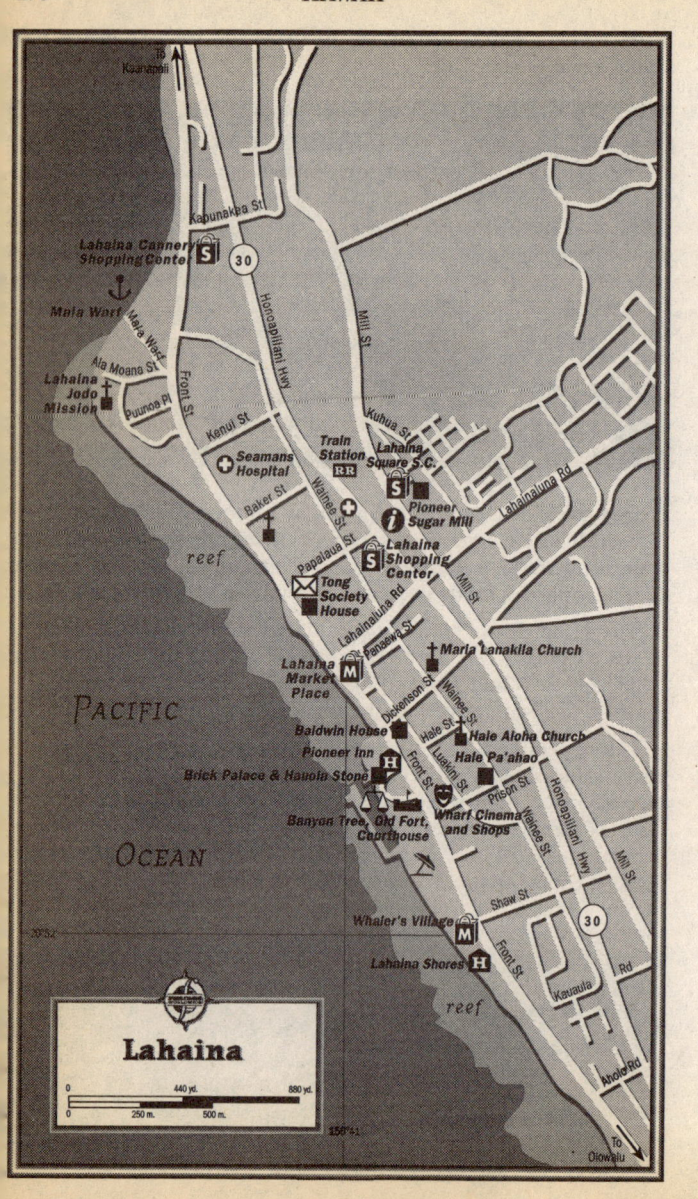

HAWAII

Lahaina

Roads in Maui are good, and parking is easy. Several major byways traverse the island. The Mokulele Highway (Highway 350) will get you from the Kahului Airport down to Ihei, Wailea, and Makena on East Maui. The Honoapiilani Highway (Highway 30) runs from Wailuku down to Maalaea and along the coastal towns of Olowalu, Lahaina, Kaanapali, Kahana, and Kapalua. For travel between Kahului and Haleakala, take the Haleakala Highway (Highway 37). And, of course, the most talked-about road on Maui is the **Hana Highway** (Highway 36) between Kahului and Hana—a 56-mile super-scenic route with more than 50 bridges and 600 twists and turns.

Taxis on Maui are metered and *not* cheap. They're suitable really only for short trips between hotels and shops or restaurants. Call ahead for service. Some of the 20 or so companies are **Yellow Cab of Maui** *((808) 877-7000, Kahului Airport)*, **West Maui Taxi** *((808) 667-2605, Lahaina)*, **Resorts and Kaanapali Taxi** *((808) 661-5285)*, **Alii Cabs** *((808) 661-3688, Lahaina)*, **Kahului Taxi Service** *((808) 877-5681)*, **Kihei Taxi** *((808) 879-3000)* and **Wailea Taxi** *((808) 874-5000)*.

Mopeds and bicycles are great for most Maui travel, though some of the bigger hills can be difficult to negotiate, and heavy traffic and narrow shoulders can wreak havoc for cyclists. Rent mopeds from **Fun Rentals of Maui** *((808) 661-3053, Lahaina)*, **A&B Moped Rental** *((808) 669-0027, Honokowai)* or **Go Go Bikes** *((808) 661-3063, Kaanapali)*. For bicycle rentals, contact **Fun Rentals** *((808) 661-3053, Lahaina)*, **South Maui Bicycles** *(874-0068, Kihei)*, **Maui Mountain Bike Adventures** *((808) 669-1169, Honokowai)* or **Kukui Activity Center** *((808) 875-1151, Kihei)*.

And, on the other end of the transportation spectrum, how about a chauffeured **limousine**? Call **Arthur's Limousine Service** *((808) 871-5555, Kahului)*.

Visitor Information

Get local information from the **Maui Visitors Bureau** *(1727 Will Pa Loop, Wailuku 96793, (808) 244-3530)* or the **Maui Chamber of Commerce** *(26 Puunene Avenue, Kahului 96732, (808) 871-7711)*. You'll also find **information kiosks** located at Kahului Airport.

HAWAII

Bird's-Eye View

Maui, the second-largest of the major Hawaiian islands (after the Big Island), is situated about 70 miles southeast of Oahu and measures a comparatively whopping 729 square miles (48 miles long and 26 miles wide). Created from two volcanoes connected by a low, sugarcane-planted, seven-mile wide isthmus, the island is basically divided into West Maui and East Maui, along with a few other defined regional areas. West Maui was formed by 5779-foot Puu Kukui (the oldest volcano) and is the smaller side—make that *much* smaller. Size obviously doesn't make a difference to visitors (the majority of which flock to this side) nor to residents (most of whom live there). The west (also dubbed "The Golf Coast") has the most stuff for the moneyed crowd and those who need civilization-away-from-civilization. Along with golf (and more golf), the west offers tropical forests, sugarcane fields and pineapple plantations, a long string of gorgeous beaches, a rugged east side, the newer resort community of Kapalua, the already-famed Kaanapali resort area, and the old whaling capital at Lahaina, center of tourist action and the local arts-and-crafts scene. From the town of Olowalu, on the Auau Channel, you can sight the islands of Kahoolawe, Lanai, Molokai, and a glimpse of the Big Island. The isthmus—or Central Maui—contains Kahului (location of the principal airport) and the government seat of Wailuku, both highly populated commercial centers, and the small port area at Maalaea. East Maui, created by 10,023-foot Haleakala (the world's largest dormant volcano), is about four times larger than its sibling to the west and features an astounding array of terrain—farmland, mountains, jungle, desert, beaches, and lava land. Most of the resorts are situated on the southwest area between Kihei (with the condo atrocities) and its antithesis, the comparatively well-designed town of Wailea. Whoop-it-up cowboy towns dot the countryside beyond, while wealthy celebrities and other VIPs reside in the hills around Kipahulu. The Hana Coast, on the eastern shore, is accessed by the infamous Hana Highway, a spectacular scenic drive that will take you across more than 50 bridges and around more than 600 curves. Upcountry Maui is composed of rural farms and ranches (sugarcane, pineapple, flowers), a winery, and the majestic Haleakala, Maui's highest point.

Nature Guide

Dazzling flowers, trees, and plant life are prolific throughout the island and easily seen in rainforests, reserves, parks, gardens, and nurseries. Unfortunately, most of what you'll see is of the introduced variety—as on the other islands, Maui's indigenous flora is on the way out. Distinctive flowers include carnations (grown in the Kula area), *panini* (prickly pear cactus, found in the pasture land of Haleakala's windward slope), a rather magnificent assortment of protea (look on Haleakala's leeward slope) and the *ahinahina* (silversword, in and around the crater itself).

The *'i'iwi* and *amakihi* are two of Maui's most commonly found native birds. Among endangered species are the *akohe'kohe* (crested honeycreeper) and parrotbill, both found on the slopes of Haleakala around the 5000-foot mark; the dark-rumped petrel hangs out around the Haleakala Crater visitors center. Other indigenous birds include the white-tailed tropic bird, wedge-tailed shearwater, American plover, and the nearly extinct *poouli*. The *alae ke'oke'o* (Hawaiian coot) and *ae'o* (Hawaiian stilt) are two of the island's more common waterbirds.

Many visitors come to Maui just to see the migration of the humpback whales. Come during the season—late November to early May—and find a vantage point just about anywhere along Maui's south coast.

Beach Finder

With more than 150 miles of coastline—and about one-fifth of that harboring good beaches—you won't have a problem finding a spot to sun or swim. Maui, in fact, has more swimmable beaches than any of the other islands. Again, beware of strong currents and high surf—it's best to check with locals about conditions before plunging into the sea. Also, watch out for falling coconuts.

Beginning at the top of West Maui and moving down along the **southwest coast**:

D.T. Fleming State Park
A top spot for winter surfing and bodysurfing and year-round sunning and picnicking, though swimming is dangerous due to strong currents. Showers, rest rooms, parking, picnic facilities.

Kapalua Bay (The Beach Formerly Known as Fleming)
Just beyond the Napili Kai Beach Club.
A lovely palm-sheltered (usually crowded) bay with safe swimming and snorkeling. Showers and rest rooms.

Kaanapali Beach

This beach fronts a strip of condos and hotels but is otherwise a superb spot for summer swimming and year-round people-watching.

Black Rock

In front of the Sheraton Hotel.
Tops for snorkeling. Showers, beach-equipment rentals.

Olowalu Beach

South of Lahaina.
A wonderful sandy area with good swimming and terrific snorkeling. No facilities.

Kamaole Beach Parks I, II, and III

At the south end of Kihei.
Safe for swimming and snorkeling, and popular with locals. Rest rooms, showers, picnic facilities.

Ulua Beach

In Wailea.
Another popular (i.e., crowded) beach, good for swimming, snorkeling, and body-surfing (in the right conditions). Rest rooms, showers.

Makena Beach

Southwest of Wailea.
A secluded "alternative" beach. The "Big Beach" area offers good snorkeling and swimming when the water is calm, while the "Little Beach" to the south is an unofficial nude beach. No facilities, and definitely no changing rooms.

Over in **Central Maui** the beaches are fairly unremarkable.

Kanaha Beach Park

At Kahului Bay.
White sands, shady lawns, very popular with local families. Facilities include rest rooms, showers, picnic tables, and parking. (Take precautions against theft at this one.)

Hookipa Beach

Just east of Paia.
Draws the world's top windsurfers with its up-to-15-foot

waves. Rest rooms, showers, picnic facilities, and parking are all available.

The **Hana District** is rife with beautiful beaches. Two of the best are:

Waianapanapa State Park

Four miles north of Hana.

With fine snorkeling and swimming, as well as the legendary cave where the occasionally red tide-pool pays tribute to the demise of suspected adulteress Popoalaea. Facilities include picnic facilities, rest rooms, showers, parking, and a hiking trail.

Kaihalulu Beach (also known as "Red Sand Beach")

Striking red sand indeed, and a beautiful cove for swimming and snorkeling. No facilities are on hand.

Adventure Guide

Maui offers scads of **hiking** possibilities, particularly in the mountainous, remote Upcountry district. Trekking within the **Haleakala National Park** is the not-to-be-missed hiking opportunity, with 30 miles of trail leading through the crater. **Sliding Sands Trail** starts along the rim at about 9800 feet and drops to the crater floor, offering 10 miles of cinder-cone and lava-flow closeups; **Kaupo Trail** leads through Kaupo Gap, past Kaupo Ranch, into Kaupo town; **Halemauu Trail** is a 10-mile hike from park headquarters to the crater floor, and links up with the Sliding Sands Trail. Scenery along the way includes lava flows, volcanic vents, cinder cones, red and black lava, and interesting vegetation. Stop at park headquarters for information, and be prepared for drastic changes in the weather—it can get very cold and nasty at 10,000 feet!

> **ITRAVELBOOKS TIP:** MOST VISITORS TO HAWAII DON'T ASSOCIATE HIGH ALTITUDE WITH TROPICAL PARADISE. IN FACT, WITH HIKES BEGINNING AT 9800 FEET AND ABOVE, EVEN THE HARDIEST HIKERS WILL BE HUFFING AND PUFFING. IF YOU'RE PLANNING ON HIKING ABOVE 6000 FEET, DRINK PLENTY OF WATER — BEFORE, DURING, AND AFTER — YOUR ADVENTURE. IF YOU BEGIN TO EXPERIENCE HEAD OR STOMACH ACHES, NAUSEA, OR YOU FEEL FAINT, TURN AROUND IMMEDIATELY. AND ALWAYS BE PREPARED FOR DRASTIC CHANGES IN THE WEATHER.

The **Polipoli State Park**, within the 21,000-acre Kula and Kahikinui Forest Reserve on the Haleakala slope, offers a variety of trails—from easy to rough—through magnificent forests of native *koa, mamane,* and *ohia* trees as well as redwood, Monterey cypress, pine, eucalyptus, and other introduced species. Many of the trails mix and mingle with each other, forming loops.

Along the coast, the three-mile **Hana-Waianapanapa Coastal Trail** is an easy trek past caves, blowholes, ancient *heiau,* and clusters of *lauhala* trees. Or retrace ancient history on the **King's Highway Coastal Trail**, down at the island's southernmost point, for views, stone ruins, and remnants of Maui's last volcanic eruption in 1790.

Low energy? Just about anyone can do the cushy half-mile paved trail in **Iao Valley**, offering views of the Iao Needle.

For more **hiking information**, contact the **Hawaii State Department of Land and Natural Resources** *(State Parks Division, P.O. Box 1049, Wailuku 96793, (808) 243-5354, http://www.state.hi.us/dlnr/)*, the **State Division of Forestry and Wildlife** *(52 South High Street, Wailuku 96793, (808) 243-5352, http://www.state.hi.us/dlnr/dofaw/)*, or **Haleakala National Park** *(P.O. Box 369, Makawao 96768, (808) 572-9306, http://www.haleakala.national-park.com/weather.htm)*. Some of Maui's best **walking tours** are organized by **Hike Maui** *(P.O. Box 330969, Kahului 96733, (808) 879-5270, http://www.hike-maui.com/)*.

Camping is prevalent on Maui, with an excellent range of campsites and cabins available near most of the scenic areas and along the beaches. A variety of campsites are up for grabs at **Haleakala National Park**. You can set up on the south rim, along the coastal road, near park headquarters, or even at the bottom of the crater. Permits and maximum-stay regulations vary. For more information, contact Haleakala National Park at the address above. Overnight camping is allowed at both **Polipoli Springs State Recreation Area** and **Waianapanapa State Park**. Permits and reservations are necessary. Contact the **Maui Division of State Parks** *(54 South High Street, Wailuku 96793, (808) 243-5354)*. For information and permits to camp at Maui's **beach parks**, get in touch with the **Department of Parks and Recreation** *(Recreation Division, 1580 Kaahumanu Avenue, Wailuku 96793, (808) 243-7389)*.

Just about any of your favorite **watersports** can be indulged in Maui's glorious waters, with their plethora of coral reefs and bathing-bath temperatures. The usual rules apply—check with locals before plunging into the sea, and watch for strong currents and high waves. One of the best—and most popular—spots for **scuba and snuba diving** is at the 160-foot-wide **Molokini Crater**, an underwater park with plenty of marine activity. The next-most-popular dive site is the world-famous **Cathedrals**, off the south coast of Lanai, which are a church-like network of coral-latticed caves. Experienced divers only should attempt the area around the **Seven Sacred Pools** and areas along the back of West Maui. Other beaches that draw **snorkelers** and **divers** include **Waianapanapa State Park** near Hana, **Baldwin Beach Park** in Paia, **Ulua** and **Wailea** beaches in Wailea, **Kamaole Parks I, II and III** in Kihei, **Olowalu Beach** and **Black Rock** in Kaanapali and the **Marine Conservation District** at Honolua Bay.

The "windsurfing capital of the world" is located at **Hookipa Beach**, east of Paia, and lures top international **windsurfers** to the March and April championship events. Other windsurf-friendly areas are **Kealia Beach** in Kihei and **Kanaha Beach Park** in Kahului. The **Kihei Coast** is a favorite for **ocean kayaking**, while **boaters** like to set sail for **Lanai** or **Molokai**. Thrill seekers can sign up for **waterskiing, parasailing,** or **jet skiing**.

Board surfers can ride the waves at **Honolua Bay, Maalaea, Hookipa, Lahaina Harbor, Napili Bay, Baldwin Park,** and **Lower Paia Park**, while **bodysurfers** catch them at **Mokuleia Beach** ("Slaughterhouse" to locals), **Makena, Wailea, Ulua, Napili Bay,** and **Baldwin Park**.

What Else to See

Central Maui consists of the commercial/industrial/business town of **Kahului** (where you'll probably arrive at the airport) and the county seat of **Wailuku**. Most visitors don't even bother to stop at either place, preferring instead to ensconce themselves at one of the resorts. **Kaahumanu Center**, on Kaahumanu Avenue in Kahului, is the one-stop mall and cineplex fix. You can view Hawaiian crafts and artifacts at the **Bailey House**, on Main Street, then bone up on sugarcane history at **Alexander & Baldwin Sugar Museum**, on Hansen Road. Highway 320 will take you into **Kepaniwai Park and Heritage Gardens** and, at the end of the road, **Iao Valley State Park** with its 2250-foot high stone Iao Needle. Adventurous sorts might want to head west along the very narrow Highway 340 that runs from Wailuku to Honokohau.

West Maui is the side of the island most frequented by tourists. Poised at the top of the Honopiilani Highway is the protected **Marine Life Conservation District,** consisting of **Honolua and Mokuleia bays,** underwater reserves filled with tropical fish. Head down to **Kapalua Bay Hotel** or **Ritz-Carlton Kapalua** to bask in elegance (or a round on one of the three courses at **Kapalua Golf Club**), or skip the dress-up act and scoot over to **Kapalua Beach** for a picnic and safe swim. Try not to be disgusted at the glut of condos as you pass through the communities of **Napili, Kahana,** and **Honokowai.** For a special meal, stop in Kahana at **Roy's Kahana Bar & Grill** or **Roy's Nicolina**. On a budget or a diet? Then hit town on Monday or Thursday for island-fresh produce at the **Farmer's Market.** At **Kaanapali Beach Resort**, you can visit a handful of big hotels.

The old capital and rowdy one-time whaler's town of **Lahaina** is, these days, the centerpoint for Maui visitors who flock to the clubs, restaurants, shops, and galleries, most of which are on or around **Front Street**. The whole town was designated a National Historic Landmark in 1962. The old **Seamen's Hospital,** on Front Street, has been restored but is not open to the public. See the 12-foot-high Buddha at **Jodo Mission**, next to Mala Wharf. James Campbell's **Pioneer Sugar Mill** stands on Lahainaluna Road, and just to the north, the old **Sugarcane Train** operates out of Lahaina Station. View implements and artifacts relating to the Chinese immigrant laborers at **Wo Hing Temple**, on Front Street. **The Hawaii Experience Dome Theater**, on Front Street, presents hourly shows that include a closer-than-you'll-ever-want-to-get volcanic eruption. Imagine the hanky-panky that went on inside the 1860s **Lahaina Inn** on Lahainaluna Street (David Paul's **Lahaina Grill**, inside the once-decadent bar, is one of the trendiest restaurants in town). At the northeast end of Lahainaluna Road, the restored 1830s **Hale Pai (House of Printing)** stands as a reminder of the Protestant missionary presence. The 50-foot-plus **Banyan Tree**, on Front Street, was planted in 1873 (when it was just eight feet tall) and is the largest banyan in Hawaii. Nearby, **505 Front Street** has been decked out to look like a New England whaling town—within are shops, restaurants, and boutiques. The old **Lahaina Courthouse**, built in 1857 and reconstructed in 1925, now houses the **Lahaina Arts Society** and a couple of galleries. The turn-of-the-century **Pioneer Inn** is a good place to stop for a drink or burger while soaking up local atmosphere. Just across from the Pioneer Inn, the Brig *Carthaginian II* is the world's only true-to-the-original restored brig. Watch the action, or engage in reminisces of bygone whaling days, at **Lahaina Harbor**. The **Baldwin Home,** on Front Street, is the one-time home of missionary Dwight Baldwin and Lahaina's oldest standing building.

Continuing south **from Lahaina,** you'll arrive at the seaside community of **Olowalu,** notable both for the 1790 Olowalu Massacre and the present-day **Chez Paul Restaurant. Olowalu Beach** is a tourist and snorkeler's favorite. Heading inland from Maalaea Harbor, along the Honopiilani Highway, **Maui Tropical Plantation** will knock you out with its 112 acres of Hawaiian flowers, fruits, nuts, sugarcane, and other agricultural delights. A string of atrocious condos, sunny beaches, and ritzy resorts line the route from Kihei to Makena.

The biggest attraction of rural **Upcountry Maui** has got to be 27,284-acre **Haleakala National Park** and the enormous crater. Other Upcountry sights to see include **Tedeschi Vineyards,** the nine-mile scenic **Olinda Drive** and the cowboy-turned-artsy-town of Makawao.

Highlight of the **Hana Coast** is definitely the view-, twist-, and plant-a-thon **Hana Highway** between Kahului Airport and Hana. Enroute are plenty of nature walks, beaches, waterfalls, caves, and scenic lookouts. Stop off at **Keanae Arboretum** to view wonderful displays of plant life, and investigate the caves, coves, pools, and beaches of **Waianapanapa State Park.** In Hana, check out the changing exhibits at **Hana Cultural Center**, do a safe swim at **Hana Beach Park**, hang with the locals at **Hasegawa General Store,** and explore the **Seven Sacred Pools.**

Central Maui
Kahului

Kaahumanu Center
275 Kaahumanu Avenue, Kahului, ☎ *(808) 877-3369.*
http://www.kaahumanu.net/
Only five minutes from Kahului Airport, it features more than 60 stores and restaurants. Favorite for residents, with Sears, Liberty House, J.C. Penney, and the Japanese counterpart, Shirokiya. Frequent free activities and entertainment.

Beaches

Kanaha Beach Park ★★
Amala Place, near Kahului Airport, Kahului.
A popular windsurfing spot near the airport with picture-perfect white sand, the only drawback being the loud planes flying overhead. Fine for swimming, with barbecue pits, picnic tables, showers, and phones.

City Celebrations

Art Maui ★★★
340 Kahului Beach Road, Kahului.
Closed: Mondays.
http://www.artmaui.com
One of Hawaii's most prestigious juried art shows, held in March at the Kazuma International Gallery, at the Maui Arts and Cultural Center. Showcases a variety of art representing Maui County. Painting, drawing, prints, photography, fiber arts, collages, and sculpture must all have been created within the past two years. Artists interact with attendees.

Hiking

Hike Maui ★★★★
P.O. Box 330969, Kahului, 96733, ☎ (808) 879-5270.
http://www.hikemaui.com
Ken Schmidt is the granddaddy of hiking guides, and he's spawned many imitators. Schmidt, a naturalist who lived in the wilderness for three years, leads guided natural-history excursions and hikes to rainforests, waterfalls, and the Haleakala Crater. **MAKE RESERVATIONS WAY IN ADVANCE, AS THESE HIKES ARE VERY POPULAR.** Half- and full-day itineraries include lunch, waterproof day packs, rain ponchos, first-aid gear, water bottles. Maximum group size is six to eight people. Call for prices.

Kanaha Pond Waterfowl Refuge ★★★★
Haleakala Highway 36, Kahului, 96732, ☎ (808) 243-5352.
Just east from Kahului Airport, heading towards Paia, is this nesting site for migratory waterfowl and native birds, including Hawaiian heron, coot, and stilt. Sketch, photograph, or just observe these fine-feathered friends while walking on one of two circular trails, each a mile long. Permits required.

Museums and Exhibits

Paper Airplane Museum ★★
Maui Mall, 70 East Kaahumanu Avenue, Kahului,
☎ *(808) 877-8916.*
http://www.flex.com/~edynray/museum/museum.htm
Situated next to the House of Pancakes in Maui Mall, the Paper Airplane Museum is reputed to be the only facility of its kind in world. More than 2000 aircraft models and kits can be found, from postage-stamp size to one with a wing span of six feet. All are made from at least 95 percent paper. Numerous items made from Hawaiian juice cans. Regular construction demos scheduled. Great for kids.

The Shows

Maui Arts & Cultural Center ★★★★
Maui Central Park, Kahului, ☎ *(808) 242-2787.*
http://www.mauiarts.org/
Private citizens raised $11.3 million to help build this visually friendly yet technically sophisticated community arts and theater center. The 12-acre complex features the 1200-seat Castle Theater (James Taylor and Carlos Santana performed here recently) and the more intimate, 300-seat McCoy Studio Theater. Both the Maui Community Theater (Maui OnStage) and Maui Academy of Performing Arts call the Center home. Also on the grounds are an outdoor amphitheater, and *a pa hula*, or earthen platform, used exclusively for ancient Hawaiian chants. The 4100-square-foot Kazuma Gallery houses a valuable collection of arts and crafts commissioned especially for the center.

Tours

Alex Air ★★★
P.O. Box 330626, Kahului, 96733, ☎ *(808) 871-0792.*
http://www.mauionabudget.com/alexair.htm
The founder of this family-owned company helped develop the Hughes 300 helicopter, and today the AlexAir fleet includes 11 helicopters and 14 airplanes. Ten kinds of helicopter tours are offered on four-passenger Hughes 500 'copters. Window seats are guaranteed. Flights longer than 30 minutes include a free video, "choreographed" to Alpine stereo music. AlexAir rarely

cancels flights; heavy rain means more waterfall activity and light tradewinds. Reservations three to five days in advance. Ask for repeat-visitor and *kamaaina* rates.

Biplane Barnstormers ★★★
Kahului Airport, Kahului, ☎ *(808) 878-2860.*
http://www.airnav.com/airport/OGG/BIPLANE_BARNSTORMERS
Wayne Wagner, who's been flying folks around for more than 30 years, offers five sightseeing tours for one or two passengers, or a thrilling aerobatic ride for one in an authentic reproduction of a 1935 WACO open-cockpit biplane. Wagner communicates with his passengers via intercom (kinda hard to yell up there). For an authentic experience, wear a leather helmet, goggles, and silk scarf, and pretend you're the Red Baron.

Blue Hawaiian Helicopters ★★★
Kahului Airport Hangar 105, Kahului, 96732,
☎ *(808) 871-8844.*
http://www.bluehawaiian.com/
There are no helicopter companies in Molokai, so if you want to fly over the spectacular Kalaupapa Peninsula, you might want to try Blue Hawaiian's Molokai-West Maui air tour, a 65-minute flight that takes you over the isolated former leper colony separated from the rest of the island by the world's highest sea cliffs. Blue Hawaiian's new ASTAR helicopters are reportedly stable, spacious, and fairly quiet (plus they provide special Bose headsets that cancel all cabin noise), offering 180-degree views for all passengers. This company, in business for 12 years, employs ex-military aviators with at least 11,000 logged hours and 20 years experience each. Twenty-four-hour cancellation notice required.

First Class Yacht Charters ★★
107 Kahului Heliport, Kahului, 96732, ☎ *(808) 667-7733.*
Along with whale-watching and sunset sails, this company offers a unique experience: a 1.5-hour competition sail adventure. This journey simulates an America's Cup, style race, with two trained crews on equally matched 65-foot yachts challenging each other to finish first. You get to watch while on board and take in incredible views. **NO SAILING EXPERIENCE NECES-**

sary, but prepare to get wet. Not for the easily nauseated.

Maui Downhill Bicycle Safaris ★★★
199 Dairy Road, Kahului, 96732, ☎ *(808) 871-2155.*
http://www.paradisemaui.com/NEWactivities/mauidownhill.html
Former VP Dan Quayle and his flock chose to bike down Haleakala Volcano with this outfit, which provides "safari" bikes with heavy-duty brakes, helmets, windbreakers, and gloves. It starts at the 10,023-foot summit of the volcano. You can choose from among six rides, which range from 22 to 38 miles; longer ones include continental breakfast at the Kula Lodge and lunch. It's a lot of fun, although you look kinda funny dressed in a space suit following other funny-looking people down the mountain. It's something the whole family can enjoy, with only 400 yards of pedaling involved. Includes two guides, escort van. The cheapest ride doesn't include round-trip transportation.

Makawao
Hiking

Nature Conservancy Hikes Maui ★★★
P.O. Box 1716, Makawao, 96768, ☎ *(808) 572-7849.*
Conservancy guides lead monthly hikes to Waikamoi and Kapunakea preserves every month. Kapunakea, in the West Maui mountains, protects many types of rare Hawaiian plants, animals, and natural communities. Hikes are along a historical trail on the lower edge of Honokawai Valley. Not for people with a fear of heights (or hikes!). Space is very limited. Reserve hikes way in advance. The $25 donation helps to defray costs; non-members receive a one-year membership including all benefits.

Museums and Exhibits

Hui Noeau Visual Arts Center ★★★★
2841 Baldwin Avenue, Makawao, 96768, ☎ *(808) 572-6560.*
Closed: Mondays.
http://www.huinoeau.com/
Meaning "Club of Skills," this is Maui's first art league formed by missionary descendant Ethel Baldwin and her circle of

friends. The group grew to become a prestigious visual arts organization, bringing the world's leading artists to Maui for exhibits, classes, lectures, and workshops. Hui Noeau is now housed in the gracious old Baldwin estate, Kaluani, and hosts important island shows in its gallery. The small gift shop is a treasure trove of some of the best island-made arts, crafts, clothing, and jewelry. Offers more than 400 art programs each year, most of them hands-on studio classes. **IF YOU'RE HERE AT CHRISTMAS, DON'T MISS THE ANNUAL HOLIDAY CRAFTS FAIR, FEATURING HANDMADE ITEMS MADE ON MAUI.**

Tours

Open Eye Tours ★★★
P.O. Box 324, Makawao, 96768, ☎ (808) 572-3483.
http://www.openeyetours.com/
Custom-designed, half-day (up to five hours) and full-day (up to 10 hours) tours by photographer Barry Fried, who's led Elder Hostel tours, been a volunteer educator with the Hawaii Nature center, and is a PADI-certified scuba instructor. Active types can tour rainforests, craters-or wildlife reserves. Or if you're not particularly outdoorsy, he'll take you to an exotic garden, a cultural center, an artist's studio, or show you where the best local eateries are. **CATERS MOSTLY TO SOLOS AND COUPLES.** Tours available on all islands.

Paia
Beaches

Hookipa Beach ★★
Hana Highway, east of Paia, Paia.
If your bod hasn't seen the sun lately, approach this beach with extreme trepidation. This turf is dominated by bronzed, buffed godlets who are top-class (or wannabe) windsurfers from around the globe (mostly Europe), plus a few weatherbeaten fisher-folk who couldn't care less. **HOOKIPA IS THE BOARD-SAILING CAPITAL OF THE WORLD,** and site of two major world-class competitions, awarding purses of up to $180,000. The small beach is rock-strewn, and the swimming? Forget it. Picnic area, phone, showers.

Tours

Cruiser Bob's Original Downhill Bike Tour ★★★
99 Hana Highway, Paia, 96770, ☎ *(808) 579-8444.*
Cruiser Bob started it all: now there's Snorkel Bob, Windsurf Bob, you name it, but there's only one Bob Kiger, originator of the 38-mile downhill bicycle coast from Haleakala Crater to his exclusive base lodge in a Chevron station in Paia. Three tours, but the most popular is the Sunrise Tour, with a hotel pickup at (yeow!) 2 a.m. SERVICE IS EXCELLENT.

Pu'unene
Museums and Exhibits

Alexander and Baldwin Sugar Museum ★★★
3957 Hansen Road, Pu'unene, 96784, ☎ *(808) 871-8058.*
Closed on Sundays.
http://www.sugarmuseum.com/
While no longer king of Maui agriculture, sugar is at least a princeling (and it still rots your teeth). Not far away from this converted factory superintendent's home-turned-museum is the actual mill itself, still chugging away. One of two mills operated by Alexander and Baldwin on Maui (the other is in Paia), it processes some of the 36,000 acres of sugarcane grown on the island by the 125-year-old company. In each of the AWARD-WINNING MUSEUM's six rooms, the exhibits, documents, and photographs focus on the humble plantation worker rather than trumpet the achievements of the bosses.

Waikapu
Parks and Gardens

Maui Tropical Plantation ★★
Honopiilani Highway, Waikapu, ☎ *(808) 244-7643.*
http://www.mauionline.com/activityland/plantation.html
Six miles from the Kahului Airport, this 150-acre plantation and agricultural extravaganza is campy but fun. All kinds of produce, including flowers, veggies, nuts, sugarcane, bananas, and pineapples, are on display for your perusal and/or purchase. THERE'S ALWAYS SOMETHING TO CATCH YOUR EYE; in one corner someone is stringing a lei, husking a coconut, or cutting up pineapple. A film on the sugar industry is constantly on view in the Pavilion. The kids can have their picture taken

with "Joe" the Hawaiian horse (who wears a flower lei around his neck).

Wailuku
Hiking

Iao Valley ★★★★
West Main Street to end, park in lot, Wailuku, 96793,
☎ *(808) 243-5354.*

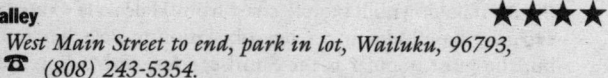

The famous Iao Needle is a 2250-foot lava-rock pinnacle covered with lush foliage that points a velvet finger at the sky. A lovely park is built around it, where visitors can stroll, viewing many varieties of exotic flowers and trees, or climb the path to a sheltered lookout. The trail begins at the parking lot and climbs 500 feet to the valley overlook. You can also take a side trail up to Iao stream, but the rocks near the stream are slippery. Along the road to the valley is Kepaniwai Park, where gardens and replicas of ethnic dwellings can be seen. Parking, picnic facilities, rest rooms.

Waihee Ridge Trail ★★
Camp Maluhia Kahekili Highway, Wailuku, 96793,
☎ *(808) 243-5352.*

This tough trail climbs 2.5 miles to a peak overlooking Wailuku, with lush jungle views of cliffs, gorges, and a wet native-scrub forest. Wear long pants, rain gear, and hiking boots—NO SNEAKERS. Pick up a free plant-photo guide and maps from the Department of Land and Natural Resources weekdays at *54 S. High Street, Room 101, Wailuku,* ☎ *(808) 243-5352.*

Museums and Exhibits

Bailey House Museum ★★★
2375-A Main Street, Wailuku, 96793, ☎ *(808) 244-3326.*
http://www.mauimuseum.org

Once the home of missionary Edward Bailey, this restored 1833 building is run by the Maui Historical Society. Docents provide fascinating running commentary while showing off an EXCELLENT COLLECTION OF HAWAIIAN ARTIFACTS, including rare examples of *kapa* (bark cloth) clothing and period furniture. Of particular interest is a collection of landscape paintings done by Bailey himself.

Parks and Gardens

Kepaniwai Cultural Park ★★
Iao Valley Road, Wailuku, 96793, ☎ (808) 243-7389.
At this pleasant park located on the bank of Iao Stream, you can see representative dwellings, gardens, and sculptures of most of the diverse ethnic mix of peoples that live in Hawaii. You'll also see living examples in the families that picnic and barbecue in the park. There's also a public swimming pool.

Maui Zoological and Botanical Gardens ★★
Kanaloa Avenue, Wailuku, 96793, ☎ (808) 243-7337.
Not worth going out of your way for, but it's a nice place to stroll and take the kids; BEST OF ALL, IT'S FREE. If you missed seeing a *nene* goose in Haleakala National Park, here's your chance. The botanical section features more than 150 species of native Hawaiian plants.

The Shows

Maui OnStage ★★
68 North Market Street, Wailuku, 96793, ☎ (808) 244-8680.
http://www.maui.net/~onstage/
Also known as the Maui Community Theater, this company is housed in two venues: the $28 million Maui Art and Cultural Center, and the historic old Iao Theater. While the group has no specific season, at least eight major productions and two experimental plays are staged each year. Call for schedule and prices.

Tours

Maui Molokai Sea Cruises ★★★
831 Eha Street, Wailuku, 96793, ☎ (808) 242-8777.
http://www.mvprince.com/home.html.
Year-round snorkeling adventures to Molokini Crater on the *M.V. Prince Kuhio*, the largest cruise vessel in Maui waters. The vessel seats 250, but takes only 150 passengers. The typical crew includes a NAUI-certified snorkel instructor. Both the upper viewing deck and air-conditioned lower deck have full-service bars. A 12-foot bowsprit extends out over the water for a thrilling ride. INCLUDES EVERYTHING BUT TOWELS. Also private charters, theme parties for groups, and sunset dinner sails. Pick-up from selected hotels. General admission: varies.

East Maui
Hana
Beaches

Hamoa Beach ★★★★
Left on coast road, three miles south of Hotel Hana Maui, Hana.
This crescent-shaped, 100-foot-wide beach has sand that looks like someone forgot to put the top on the pepper shaker. It has an **IDYLLIC, LUSH SETTING,** inspiring James Michener to call it "the only beach I have ever seen that looks like the South Pacific—and it's in the North Pacific." (Or something like that). Used by the Hotel Hana Maui's guests, but it's public. Facilities include rest rooms, shower, snack bar, benches, lounges, and lifeguard.

Red Sand Beach (Kaihalulu) ★★★
Hana.
This beach, whose Hawaiian name means "roaring sea," is reached by a trail that starts at the Hana Community Center and wraps around the coast of Kauiki Hill. The path is well-trod but narrow, steep, and perilous. Beware. Its red sands were formed by hot-cinder fallout from an exploding volcano. When you reach it, you'll be surrounded by red cinder walls and natural rock jettys. Great for sun, snorkel, locals, hippies, and tourists. **USED FOR NUDE SUNBATHING. SOME OF THE ROUGHEST SWIMMING ON THE ISLAND.** No facilities. Park on street by softball diamond next to hotel.

Waianapanapa State Park ★★★★
Three miles north of Hanna, ☎ *(808) 243-5354.*
http://www.alohafrommaui.com/wainapanapa.htm
Three miles from Hana town, this ruggedly beautiful beach park has it all. Activities include **HIKING ON FOOTPATHS TROD BY HAWAIIAN KINGS**, swimming in lava-tube caves, or setting out a beach mat on a black, sand beach (swimming is unsafe). **THE CHOICE OF CAMPING FACILITIES INCLUDE 12 CABINS AND TENT SITES WITH OCEAN VIEWS.** The cabins house six people each and are equipped with linens, cooking facilities, and utensils. Cost is $5 per person for six people, and $10 for a single camper (less for children under 11). Maximum stay is

five nights. Reservations taken a year in advance, and they are extremely hard to get. For information, write to the Division of Parks, 54 South High Street, Wailuku, HI 96793. General admission: $5–$10.

City Celebrations

Maui Food Festivals ★★★★
Hana and various locations, Hana.

IF YOU TIMED IT RIGHT, YOU COULD SPEND A YEAR EATING FAIRLY CHEAPLY AND EXTREMELY WELL FROM BOOTHS AT MAUI'S VARIOUS FOOD AND WINE FESTIVALS, where top island chefs perform culinary wizardry before your eyes. Pretend it's spring and we're in Hana for the East Maui Taro Festival. Here's your chance to sample taro pancakes, taro tempura, or poi balls. When you look up from your plate, there's a farmer's market, poi-pounding demos, and Hawaiian games to look forward to. For more info, call ☎ *(808) 248-8972*. In April, the question on everyone's lips is "Are you going to the Ulupalakua Thing?" That's local talk for the Maui County Ag Trade Show, held at the Ulu Ranch and Tedeschi Winery. The focus is on up-country produce, but the food booths feature munchies from just about everywhere. Amateur chefs can participate in a Fresh Fruit contest. Information, ☎ *(808) 875-0457*. Every weekend in July the Kapalua Bay Hotel and Villa sponsors the Kapalua Wine and Food Symposium. Functions include seminars, demos, discussions, and tastings. It culminates in a Chefs' Seafood Festival, where 10 of Hawaii's premier chefs prepare an oceanside gourmet banquet. For information, call ☎ *(808) 669-0244*. The Maui Onion Festival, held in August at the Whalers Village Shopping Village in Kaanapali, honors the island's famous sweet onion grown in Upcountry Kula. Watch cooking demos or enter an onion recipe cook-off. You'll have an opportunity to nosh at a farmer's market and from a food court offering plenty of Maui onion concoctions. For information, call ☎ *(808) 661-4567*. Top chefs from more than 30 restaurants try to outdo each other in September, when A Taste of Lahaina takes place. There's continuous entertainment, and beer and wine flows like rain. Make arrangements to attend the gala dinner under the stars that kicks off this two-day grande bouffe. ADMISSION IS FREE; guests purchase scrip for tasting at food booths. For information, call ☎ *(808) 667-9175*.

Historical Sites

Fagan Memorial ★★
On a hilltop across from the Hotel Hana-Maui, Hana.
The people of Hana erected this 30-foot-high lava rock cross on a hilltop in 1960 after the death of Paul Fagan, founder of Hana Ranch and the Hotel Hana-Maui. THE VIEWS OF THE HANA COAST FROM THE TOP OF THE MEMORIAL ARE ABSOLUTELY TOPS!

Museums and Exhibits

Hana Cultural Center ★★
Box 27, Hana, 96713, ☎ (808) 248-8622.
Hours: 10 a.m.–4 p.m.
http://planet-hawaii.com/hana/
Although small, this museum is packed with rarities, including a 100-year-old fishing net made of woven vines, turtle shell fishhooks, koa canoe paddles, poi boards, baskets, turtleshells and quilts, as well as photo and bottle collections. These will, keep you occupied for hours.

Tours

Hana Highway ★★★★★
Hana Highway (360), Hana.
Just remember while you're stuck behind someone going 10 miles an hour down this road: Getting there is half the fun. With this mind-set, the 51-mile route (from the Kahului Airport), involving 617 curves and 56 one-lane bridges, won't be so aggravating. Relax and take in the sights, slowly. Highlights include TWIN FALLS, JUST PAST THE TWO-MILE MARKER, WITH A GREAT SWIMMING HOLE; Kaumahina State Wayside Park, at sea level, where you can explore tide pools; and Keanae Arboretum (at mile marker 16), with six acres of native trees, bamboo, and indigenous Hawaiian crops. The twisty, curvy highway straightens out just before Hana, but before you explore the town proper, you can take the coast route past the Hana Airport to Waianapanapa State Park, with its incredible black-sand beach. Back in town, enjoy the waterfront and beach area, have lunch at Tutu's, a beach shack serving good mahi burgers and haupia (coconut pudding) ice cream. DON'T PASS UP THE HASEGAWA GENERAL STORE,

where you can pick up an official "I Survived the Hana Road" T-shirt. After a few hours here you can return the way you came or continue past Kipahulu and the Pools of Oheo, on the eastern side of Haleakala National Park. Ask a ranger about road conditions along this end; if it isn't washed out, continue the back way out of Hana. After four miles of potholes and dirt, the road eventually becomes paved again. The desert-like terrain is nothing like the road you just came on, but it'll get you back to Kahului.

> ITRAVELBOOKS TIPS: THE FOLLOWING ARE THE MAIN PRECAUTIONS FOR THE HANA HIGHWAY: CALL FOR A WEATHER REPORT. THIS ROAD IS NO FUN IN A SQUALL. TRAVEL ON A WEEKEND. THERE WILL BE FEWER DELIVERY TRUCKS, COMMUTERS AND LESS ROAD WORK. TANK UP BEFORE YOU GO. THERE ARE NO GAS STATIONS BETWEEN KAHULUI AND HANA. ALLOW AT LEAST THREE HOURS TRAVEL TIME EACH WAY, AND AN ADDITIONAL HOUR IF YOU'RE TRAVELING TO KIPAHULU.

Keanae
Parks and Gardens

Keanae Arboretum ★★★
On Hana Highway, between Huelo and Keanae, Keanae.
THIS HIKE IS FOR HARDY BEGINNERS, but the whole family will enjoy it. The complete hike is 2.3 miles, with a 200-foot elevation. You'll see a variety of native and introduced plants and trees, many of which are identified. Paths are wide and well-kept, and when the stream has enough water in it, you can soak your feet or swim. Bring good walking shoes and bug repellent, and DON'T DRINK FROM THE STREAMS.

Kipahulu
Hiking

Waimoku Falls ★★★★
Highway 31 between Hana and Kipahulu 96713,
☎ *(808) 248-7367.*
Situated in the East Maui section of Haleakala National Park, the trail to the falls is two miles long, past a gate that's 100 yards south of the Pools of Oheo. The well-maintained trail includes wonderful views of the upper falls. You'll pass through a beautiful bamboo forest. FUN FOR THE WHOLE FAMILY, WITH

Historical Sites

Lindbergh's Grave ★★★
Piilani Highway, 10 miles south of Hana Town, Kipahulu.
The great aviator, who lived in Hana for the last years of his life, is buried under a block of Vermont granite in the graveyard of Palapala Hoomau Congregational Church. Somewhat out of the way, the church is reached via a rutted, gravel drive off the Piilani Hwy about a quarter-mile past Oheo Gulch. Sometimes a sign is nailed up to a tree about 100 feet from the church driveway, but it's best to ask a local for directions.

Parks and Gardens

Pools of Oheo ★★★★
Piilani Highway, south of Hana, near Kipahulu 96713,
☎ *(808) 248-7375.*
This is the new Hawaiian name for the long-controversial SEVEN SACRED POOLS, a gulch and stream that flows through some 22 pools in Kipahulu, which is part of Haleakala National Park, reached on a potholed road past Hana. This delightful spot is for everyone who has always dreamed of bathing under a waterfall. At the Pools of Oheo, not one, but several waterfalls spill into tiered pools leading to the sea where you can swim. Rangers conduct nature walks and proffer advice on nearby hiking trails that you can do yourself.

Tours

Ohe'o Stables ★★★
Kipahulu Ranch, Star Route 1, Box 151A, Kipahulu, 96713,
☎ *(808) 667-2222.*
http://www.mauihorse.com/
This refreshing horseback ride is unusual in that it is the only one that traverses the Kipahulu section of Haleakala Park, which is one mile past the Pools of Oheo. The three-hour mountain ride takes in panoramic views of Waimoku falls and five to seven smaller ones. Weight limit is 250 pounds, "no exceptions." Rides leave promptly at 11:30 a.m. and 2:30 p.m. Remember that it's three hours from West Maui and Kihei to Kipahulu; leave at 7 a.m. for the early ride. Don't forget your

Northwest Maui
Kahakuloa

Kianna Kai
Kahakuloa, ☎ *(808) 575-9165.*
THE ONLY DEEP-SEA FISHING CHARTER TO OPERATE OFF THE SCENIC NORTH SHORE. Couples sightseeing with angling. Shares a cut of the catch. Charter aboard 21-foot Alii Kai, caters to small groups. Captain is "ono King" Chris Ingrisano. General admission: varies.

> I TRAVELBOOK TIP: MANY HOTEL RESTAURANTS WILL PREPARE YOUR FRESHLY-CAUGHT FISH FOR A SMALL FEE. BE SURE TO ASK IF YOU FANCY DINNER THAT YOU'VE CAUGHT YOURSELF.

South Maui
Kihei
Beaches

Kamaole Beach Parks ★★★
Along South Kihei Road, Kihei.
These are three consecutive, top-flight beach parks located across the street from Dolphin Plaza and Rainbow Shopping Mall, on South Kihei Road. Depending on weather conditions, all are GREAT FOR SWIMMING, SNORKELING, KAYAK LAUNCHING, SAILING, WHALE-WATCHING, AND BOOGIE-BOARDING. Parking is plentiful and close, with spacious picnic areas for family gatherings. ARGUABLY, THE BEST OF THE TRIO IS KAMAOLE III, WITH THE FINEST SAND. At its end is Peace Park, with only a few trees, lots of grass, and a fairly gentle slope. You'll see a lot of kite-flying activity in the afternoon, due to trade-wind activity. Facilities include a lifeguard, BBQ grills, phone, and showers. One drawback is the high wind factor, especially in the afternoon, which creates fast currents and blowing sand. Watch for the red-flag alert.

Hiking

Kealia Pond National Wildlife Refuge ★★★
On both sides of Route 31 between Routes 30 and 350, Kihei.
This protected, 691-acre federal refuge and sanctuary for 30 or more species of birds can be toured via an easy, two-mile hike (each way) that's just a short drive from Kihei. Because the route follows the coast and beach, you can walk the shoreline and even swim in the surf, if you wish. FABULOUS FOR BIRDERS: along with birds such as the ae'o, a black-necked stilt, or the black-crowned night heron, there are frequent sightings of the hawksbill turtle between July and December. These rare creatures, with long, narrow beaks, often get as big as 200 pounds. The females come here to nest—unfortunately, crossing a busy highway to do so. Recently, officials have posted roadside warning signs to alert motorists. Kealia is also a good vantage point for whale sightings in November–April. Begin the hike at the turnout at the three-mile marker on the ocean side of Route 31. Plenty of parking. Information, refuge office at *101 N. Kihei Road.*

Outfitters Maui ★★★
2439 South Kihei Road, Kihei, ☎ *(808) 875-4848.*
Hiking tours brought to you by Michael and Melissa McCoy, owners of South Pacific Kayaks. "Maui Hiking Adventures: Streams and Waterfalls," three to four hours, both morning and afternoon tours available. You'll see native birds and learn about flora and fauna. Includes snacks and backpack. Bring hiking shoes, hat, visor. Easy. "Hidden Treasures," six to seven hours. Takes you to a less-accessible area, including waterfalls, deep valleys, and crystal-clear pools. Easy to moderate. Includes lunch, beverage, and backpack. Bring bottled water. "The Bamboo Forest Tour," in the Hana/Kipahulu area, traverses swimming holes, Waimoku Falls, and a singing bamboo forest. Easy to moderate, nine to 11 hours, includes lunch. Reservations required. On mainland call ☎ *(800) 776-2326* for more information and rates.

Tours

Ocean Activities Center ★★★
1847 South Kihei Road, Kihei, 96753, ☎ *(808) 879-4485.*
<http://www.mauioceanactivities.com/>
The first company to offer group snorkeling trips to Molokini

islet, ONE OF MAUI'S FINEST SNORKELING SPOTS, and thanks to other imitators, now the most crowded. Offices are located in resorts and hotels all over the island. Books a variety of activity packages, from sunset dinner cruises to deep-sea sport-fishing charters to whale-watching. There are two excellent Molokini snorkel cruises, including a deluxe package with a continental breakfast and deli lunch, mai tais, gear, instruction, and shuttle transportation. Leaves 7:15 a.m. and returns 12:15 p.m. from Maalaea harbor slip 58. Call for more information.

Pacific Whale Foundation ★★★
101 North Kihei Road, Kihei, 96753,
☎ *(808) 879-8811.*
http://www.pacificwhale.org/
This nonprofit scientific research foundation offers 10 humpback whale-watching cruises out of Lahaina and Maalaea Harbors. Trips are guided by knowledgeable marine naturalists, most of them involved with whale research. Both of the whale-watching vessels, the *Manute'a*, a 50-foot sailing catamaran, and *Whale II*, a 50-foot sailing yacht, or the *Whale One*, a 53-foot motor vessel, offer a combination of sunny observation decks and protected, shady cabins. Scientific hydrophones enable you to hear the whales' songs. All profits support the Foundation's efforts to save the whales. Ask about other trips.

Maalaea Bay
Tours

Navatek II ★★★★
Maalaea Harbor, Maalaea Bay, ☎ *(808) 661-8787.*
Navatek II has revolutionized ocean travel in Hawaii with its patented motion-control technology developed by Lockheed. EVEN SENSITIVE PASSENGERS CAN FORGET ABOUT SEASICKNESS. This luxurious vessel features a spacious tanning deck with lounge chairs, air-conditioned main cabin, and amphitheater seating. The company's main offering is the "Lanai Voyage of Discovery," where guests are taken to a secluded bay off the Lanai coast to snorkel. Includes a gourmet waffle-bar breakfast, barbecue lunch, full-service bar, and a marine life naturalist providing expert narration on the history and legends of Lanai. You don't even need snorkel gear; even prescription masks are provided. Optional: snuba, therapeutic massage, video services.

A fabulous way to enjoy the water! General admission: varies. and hours of operation.

Makena
Beaches

Maluaka Beach ★★★★
In front of the Maui Prince Hotel, Makena.
A beautiful white-sand beach next to the Keawalai Church and fronting the Maui Prince Hotel in Makena, south of Kihei. You can swim to a turtle reef about 100 yards off the south end. Good for swimming and boogie-boarding. Phone and showers.

Oneloa Beach ★★★
Beyond the Maui Prince Hotel at Makena Resort, Makena, 96753.
Also called Makena, or Big Beach, for its miles and miles of soft, golden, unbelievable sand. Waters are always clear, clean, and of varying turquoise hues. But SWIMMING CAN BE TREACHEROUS, as waves crash right onto the beach and can be very dangerous. In winter, humpbacks frolic in the channel fronting the beach. Some snorkelers have experienced hearing the whales' songs while underwater. No facilities, and it gets pretty hot due to lack of shady trees. Directions: Take Highway 31 or Piilani Highway to Wailea Resort. Follow Wailea Alanui to Makena Alanui past the Maui Prince, turn right on a dirt road that runs down to a parking lot at the beach.

Puu Olai Beach ★★★
Past the Maui Prince Hotel, Makena.
One mile south past the Maui Prince Hotel, you can't help but notice a 360-foot-high, red-cinder cone overlooking the ocean. This is Puuolai, one of Haleakala's craters, under which is a large cave, said to be the sacred dwelling place of Mano, the ancestral shark deity. At the north end of the cinder cone is a trail leading up a cliff and over to a gorgeous beach that's an UNOFFICIAL "BATHING SUITS OPTIONAL" stretch. It's patrolled occasionally, so beware. Snorkeling and bodysurfing are great. No facilities.

Sacred Beach
Makena.

Sunbathe and snorkel or do something unmentionable at this ROMANTIC, OFF-THE-BEATEN, TRACK BEACH where weddings often take place. Directions: Go on Wailea Alanui Drive about eight miles south of the Kea Lani Hotel and turn into the beach parking lot marked Paipu Beach. Walk north over a sand dune and you'll come out on a very secluded beach.

Tours

Makena Stables ★★★
7299 South Makena Road, Makena, 96753, ☎ *(808) 879-0244.*
http://www.makenastables.com/

Located a mile from the Maui Prince Hotel, Makena Stables OFFERS THREE-HOUR MORNING AND SUNSET GUIDED RIDES THAT INCLUDE REFRESHMENTS SERVED ON A HILL OVERLOOKING THE LAVA FLOWS AND THE ISLANDS OF MOLOKINI AND KAHOOLAWE. On clear days, the snowcapped peaks of Mauna Kea Volcano on the Big Island can be seen through the clouds. A six-hour ride takes visitors to the heart of Ulupalakua Ranch and to Tedeschi Vineyards. Picnic lunch included. SOME FAMILIARITY WITH HORSES RECOMMENDED. Trail is dusty, wild, and sometimes desolate. Windy at dusk. Weight limitation is 250 pounds; age limit 12 years. General admission: varies..

Wailea
Beaches

Wailea Beaches ★★★★
Kihei Road in front of the Wailea Resorts, Wailea, 96753,
☎ *(808) 879-4461.*

Five gorgeous white-sand beaches indent the shores of this posh, master-planned community on 1500 acres. Wailea, Ulua, Polo, Mokapu, and Keawapuku beaches are considered some of the finest, with excellent swimming, snorkeling, scuba, and sunbathing conditions year-round. Each winter, humpback whales are often breaching just offshore. ONE GREAT FREE ACTIVITY IS THE WAILEA BEACH WALK, a public path overlooking all the beaches and ocean in front of the big resorts.

City Celebrations

Celebration of Whales ★★★
3900 Wailea Alanui Drive, Wailea, ☎ *(808) 874-2221.*
You won't find any "nuke the whales" bumper stickers on Maui; along with two whale museums, there are countless commercial cruises taking visitors on whale-watch expeditions during the humpback whales' annual migration from Alaska to Maui to breed, give birth, and nurse their young. Not only are whales big business, people here sincerely love them. This annual, four-day festival, held around the last week of January, features video screenings, art exhibits, educational workshops, and naturalist-narrated whale-watching tours. Cost varies according to activity.

Upcountry

Haleakala National Park
Parks and Gardens

Haleakala National Park ★★★★★
P.O. Box 369, Makawao, Haleakala National Park, 96768, ☎ *(808) 572-9306.*
http://www.haleakala.national-park.com/
The "House of the Sun," a mammoth, dormant 10,023-foot volcano, offers great hiking and camping, and is inarguably THE BEST PLACE TO WATCH THE SUN WAKE UP in the morning from several vantage points. Just before the entrance to the park is Hosmer Grove, A PERFECT PICNIC, CAMPING, AND HIKING AREA SURROUNDED BY EUCALYPTUS, CEDAR, JUNIPER, AND SPRUCE TREES. On Mondays and Thursdays at 9 a.m., there's a three-hour, ranger-led hike into a rainforest that begins at the Grove. The first viewpoint, at 8800 feet, is Leleiwi Overlook, which is not for people afraid of their own shadow. In late afternoon, on cloudy days, you might see your image reflected in the mist. Kalahaku Overlook, at 9325 feet, showcases a garden of silverswords—unique plants found only in Hawaii. A 10-mile drive from headquarters takes you to the House of the Sun Visitors Center, with its interesting geological exhibits, and to Pu'u 'Ula'ula Overlook, at the crater summit, where panoramic views of Maui and other islands may be seen on clear days. From the visitor center there are several trails that allow you to

explore the crater. While traversing Sliding Sands Trail (yes, it's slippery and S-T-E-E-P; watch those knees) you're sure to feel intimidated by the 1000-foot cinder cones you'll pass on the way to the crater floor. This trail meets midway with Halemauu Trail, a semi-tough route that's five miles each way from the crater floor to the rim. The Kaupo Trail descends 6100 feet out of the crater after only 8.5 miles, with weather changing from wet to broiling in less time. It winds up in the isolated, southeastern coast town of Kaupo; recommended for overnight trips; all trails are recommended for experienced hikers only. If you want to camp, there are also three remote cabins in the crater that are reached by hiking between four and 10 miles on two trails. The cabins are equipped with 12 bunk beds, a woodburning stove, cooking utensils, toilets, and a limited amount of drinking water and firewood (for which there is an additional fee). Because of high demand, reservations are made on a lottery basis on the first day of the month two months prior to your proposed stay. Winners are notified by mail; three-night maximum, only two nights may be spent in any one cabin. There are also 15–20 free tentsites available every day on a first-come, first-served basis. Check in at park headquarters from 7:30 a.m.–5 p.m. A schedule of daily talks and guided hikes is posted on the bulletin board. Call ☎ *(808) 572-7749* for information on daily weather conditions, tours, and programs. **DRESS IN LAYERS WHEN YOU VISIT THE PARK; IT GETS COLD UP THERE.**

Kula
Hiking

Polipoli Springs State Park ★★★
Waipoli Road, Kula, 96790, ☎ *(808) 243-5354.*
http://www.hawaiiweb.com/maui/html/sites/polipoli_s prings_state_recreational_area.html
Camping, hiking, and picnicking opportunities are available at this damp, 10-acre park in upcountry Maui at 6200 feet. Although warm enough during the day, the park is always cold at night and often drops to below freezing in winter. With more than 51 inches of rain falling here annually, mildew is a factor. Pitch your tent among pine and cypress trees; there's space for about 20 campers. Parking, barbecues, but only one toilet, no showers. Bring your own water, as what's available is not potable. There's a separate campsite behind a locked gate

with a lone cabin that requires a four-wheel-drive vehicle to reach. Cabin sleeps 10. Maximum stay is five nights. Reservations taken a year in advance. For information, write to Division of State Parks, 54 South High Street, Wailuku, HI 96743.

Parks and Gardens

Kula Botanical Garden ★★★
Kekaulike Avenue, Route 377, Kula, 96790, ☎ *(808) 878-1715.*
Not just a prime picnic spot, this six-acre garden boasts more than 1700 tropical plants; it takes at least two hours to appreciate it all. EVERYTHING CAN BE SEEN ON A GARDEN WALK, AND THERE ARE PAVED WALKWAYS WITH WHEELCHAIR ACCESS. Protea, introduced in the 1960s from its native South Africa, flourishes here. The Educational Garden, featuring plants indigenous to Hawaii, including the increasingly rare sandalwood tree, is a learning experience. Don't forget your camera. Gift shop.

Tours

Aloha Bicycle Tours ★★★
P.O. Box 455, Kula, 96790, ☎ *(808) 249-1564.*
http://www.mauibike.com/
Marc Friezner, a two-time Haleakala Hill Climb and Hawaii State Bicycling champion with many years experience, conducts small, relaxed bike rides in the Volcano and Kula area. Friezner and his wife Karen offer both downhill and "rolling hill" rides. The Volcano Bike Adventure Tour, which takes about seven hours, combines a ride down 21 switchbacks through Haleakala Ranch with sightseeing tours of the Sunrise Protea Farm, Silver Cloud Ranch, and wine tasting at Tedeschi Winery. Riders may go at their own pace, and nonriders can follow along in the tour van. Snacks and refreshments provided. Includes 21-speed mountain bikes and safety gear. Some kind of mountain-biking experience required. Gnarlier, off-road suspension tours for more-experienced riders are available; tour routes depend on ability of riders. Limited to four persons. For both rides, participants must be at least 4-foot-10; no pregnant women or those with heart conditions allowed. Rides leave from Harold Rice Park in Kula. General admission: varies.

Crater Bound ★★★
P.O. Box 265, Kula, 96790, ☎ *(808) 878-1743.*
Owner Craig Moore and his staff offer hikes, mule rides, and overnight camping trips into Haleakala crater, Oheo in Kipahulu or combinations of both. Guests travel from Haleakala summit to Paliku Campground for two nights. After a hike to Kaupo Gap, they're driven to Kipahulu for camping near waterfalls and pools. Guides and wranglers are state-certified tour guides that are trained through the park service. General admission: varies.

Pony Express Tours ★★★
Crater Road (Highway 378), Kula, 96790, ☎ *(808) 667-2200.*
<http://www.ponyexpresstours.com/>
This company offers ONE OF THE FEW HORSEBACK RIDES IN THE WORLD THAT VENTURE INTO A DORMANT VOLCANO CRATER. Rides are also available on the largest working cattle ranch in Maui. The most intensive adventure lasts all day, covers 12 miles, and goes all the way to the crater floor. It's advised for those who "feel at ease on the saddle." A short, one-hour ride on the Haleakala ranch, with stops at Haleakala National Park, Tedeschi Winery, and protea farms, is also available. Deli or picnic-style lunches are included in the longer rides. Guides are experienced wranglers with a broad knowledge of plant life, geology, and crater legends. Riders must be at least 10 years of age, under 65, in good health for elevation levels up to 10,000 feet, and weigh under 235 pounds. Advance reservations highly recommended. General admission: varies.

Ulupalakua Ranch
ITRAVELBOOK FREEBIE

Tedeschi Winery Tasting Room ★★
Ulupalakua Ranch, Ulupalakua Ranch, ☎ (808) 878-6058.
Hours: 9 a.m.–5 p.m.
Special hours: tours between 9:30 a.m.–2:30 p.m.
http://www.alternative-hawaii.com/profiles/trade/tedeschi.htm

You might not like the pineapple wine, called Maui Blanc, that's grown on this 22-acre, Upcountry winery, but you'll certainly love the ambience of the tasting room, a weathered old brick building that served as a jailhouse for the 20,000-acre Ulupalakua Ranch. There are several other interesting products to sample, including Plantation Red, the first red table wine developed by the winery, and Maui Brut champagne, which made its debut at the inaugural banquet of President Reagan. In addition, you can see how the wine is processed and bottled during a half-hour tour of the winery and the manicured grounds; daily between 9:30 a.m. and 2:30 p.m. Just before arriving at the vineyard, stop in at the Ulupalakua Ranch Country Store—it's the one with the wooden cowboys on the porch, carved by the ranch's resident sculptor. Located about 10 miles past the junction of Highways 377 and 37, up the slopes of Haleakala volcano.

West Maui
Kaanapali Beach
Beaches

Kaanapali Beach ★★★
Kaanapali Resort, Honopiilani Highway, Kaanapali Beach, 96761.
http://www.kbhmaui.com/

Built in the 1960s and '70s, the resort is nestled at the foot of rolling canefields. **SOME OF THE BEST SNORKELING ON MAUI CAN BE HAD IN THE TURQUOISE OCEAN AROUND BLACK ROCK.** Colorful reef fish are tame and even ask for tips. A stroll along the beach from the Hyatt Regency past the Maui Marriott and the Westin Maui brings you to Whalers Village, a collection of fancy shops and restaurants. In general, the ocean here, while bathtub warm, is better for sunbathing than swim-

HAWAII

ming, due to frequent shore breaks. A red, flag warning system is there in lieu of lifeguards.

Museums and Exhibits

Hale Kohala Whale Museum
2435 Kaanapali Parkway, Kaanapali Beach, 96761,
☎ *(808) 661-9918.*

One of two whaling museums in the Whalers Village. Devoted to evolution of humpback whale, the museum features see-and-touch displays, computer terminals where visitors may punch up whale facts, a theater showing videos on such topics as the humpback's migratory patterns, and impressive whale models, including a 16-foot model of a baby humpback skeleton. Gift shop with everything from crystal whale figurines to the latest ecology books. Admission.

Whalers Village Museum of the Pacific ★★
Whalers Village Shopping Center, Building G, Kaanapali Beach, third floor, ☎ *(808) 661-5992.*

This engaging museum on the third floor of Whaler's Village that WILL DELIGHT THE KIDS as well as mom and dad features more than 100 whaling implements, a six-foot model of a whaling ship, scrimshaw, harpoons, sailors' journals, tools, and historic photographs. Also in Whaler's Village is the Hale Kohala Whale Museum and Pavilion at the entrance (how can you miss it?). The museum zeroes in on the evolution and migratory patterns of the humpback whale, Maui's most-welcome winter visitor. Humpy factoids are accessed on computer terminals, and kids aren't snarled at for touching the life-size marine models–especially a 16-foot humpback calf and its favorite food, the squid (here in 3-D). Admission.

The Shows

Auntie Aloha's Breakfast Luau ★★★
Kaanapali Beach Hotel Plantation Room, Kaanapali Beach,
☎ *(808) 661-0011.*

This fun luau is presided over by Auntie Aloha, a big lady with an infectious smile who proclaims, "You can suck 'em up, cuz in Hawaii mo' big, mo' better, mo' beautiful." The only one of its kind in Hawaii, this breakfast luau features mai tais along with your Special Ks. Also live music, dancing, tips on Maui, and a side-splittin' slide show called "Auntie's Comedy Activities Review." All-you-can-eat breakfast of taro pancakes, sweet-bread French toast, coconut and passion fruit syrups, Portuguese sausage, fruits, and homemade breads. Call for hours. **THE MOST INEXPENSIVE LUAU IN TOWN, IN MAUI'S MOST HAWAIIAN RESORT.**

Tours

Westin Maui Botanical Tours ★★★
2365 Kaanapali Parkway, Kaanapali Beach, 96761,
☎ *(808) 667-2525.*
Fridays only.
http://www.westinmaui.com/
Botanical tours of the hotel grounds by David Simons, Maui native and horticulturist. The vast collection includes flora of most of the HOT spots of the world, including Southeast Asia, the American Tropics, Barbados, Madagascar, Brazil, and Polynesia. You'll see seven species of palms, three varieties of ferns, including a tree fern unique to Hawaii used for making leis, and a 40-foot-tall Singapore plumeria.

Westin Maui Wildlife Tour ★★★
2365 Kaanapali Parkway, Kaanapali Beach, 96761,
☎ *(808) 667-2525.*
Closed: Tuesdays, Thursdays, Fridays and Saturdays.
http://www.westinmaui.com/
The 12-acre water wonderland of the Westin Maui is home to loads of colorful birds that squawk and talk, including Kolohe, a rose-breasted cockatoo that sings and hops on people's hands. You'll see most of them in this fascinating avian tour that meanders all over the property. Most intriguing is the collection of swans—among them a pair of European mutes—the jealous male can be seen protecting his mate from humans.

Kahului
City Celebrations

Maui Marathon ★★
P.O. Box 330099, Kahului, 96733, ☎ *(808) 871-6441.*
http://www.mauimarathon.com/
Hawaii's oldest point-to-point marathon celebrated its 25th anniversary in March 1995. The race starts at Maui Mall in

Kahului and ends at Whaler's Village in Kaanapali. The usual limit is 1000 runners, and proceeds support Maui charities.

Kapalua
Beaches

Kapalua Bay ★★★★
Lower Honoapiilani Road, Kapalua.
A SPECTACULAR WHITE-SAND BEACH with great coral and lots of fish that's perfect for snorkeling, with fabulous views of Molokai and Lanai. It's protected from wind and waves by an ancient lava flow that extends well out into the ocean at the north end of the beach. Facilities include: rest rooms, showers, a landscaped path to the beach, lifeguard. Directions: Drive south from the Kapalua Bay Hotel (1 Bay Drive) to the first shoreline access sign, turn right toward the ocean to a public lot. If parking lot is full, go back to the main road and turn right, park on the road across the street from the Napili Kai Beach Club, and walk down to the beach via the shoreline access through the tunnel.

ITRAVELBOOK FREEBIE

Celebration of the Arts ★★★
One Ritz-Carlton Drive, Kapalua, 96761, ☎ *(808) 669-6200.*
http://www.celebrationofthearts.org/
More than 40 Hawaiian-island artists and hula *halaus* (hula schools) offer lessons and demonstrations of the traditional and contemporary arts of Hawaii each year during the Easter weekend on the grounds of the Ritz-Carlton, Kapalua. The only "hands-on" workshop in Maui, participants can attend free workshops on hula and chant, lei-making, lauhala-weaving, basket-weaving, and other crafts. Art supplies and instructions are also complimentary. Admission is charged for a Hawaiian food celebration and concert.

Lahaina
Beaches

Wahikuli Beach ★★
Highway 30, beyond Lahaina, Lahaina.
Wahikuli Beach is popular for those seeking a more serene scene than its neighbor, glitzy Kaanapali Beach. SCUBA DIVERS

FAVOR ITS SAFE WATERS TO TEACH BEGINNERS. Picnic tables, showers, toilets, parking. Across from the police station.

City Celebrations

Aloha Festivals ★★★★
Under the Banyan Tree, Lahaina, ☎ *(808) 944-8857.*
Visitors and residents get together under the famous old Banyan Tree (the largest in the state) to share ethnic food and festivities, including music, dance, arts, and crafts.

> **ITRAVELBOOK FREEBIE**
>
> ### Aloha Friday Arts and Crafts Fair ★★★
> *Lahaina Center, Lahaina,* ☎ *(808) 667-9216.*
> *Hours: 3–8 p.m., Fridays.*
> Local artisans and "aunties" sell wares; also a Polynesian review with an authentic drum dance, as well as Tahitian and Hawaiian hula.

Friday Night is Art Night ★★★
Front Street, Lahaina, ☎ *(808) 667-9175.*
With dozens of galleries packed easel-to-easel on this rejuvenated downtown Lahaina street, it's hard to separate the art from the drek. But every Friday evening, merchants compete in a friendly way for your attention, providing demonstrations and gallery shows, complimentary wine, and hors d'oeuvres, while roving musicians of various abilities play lively tunes. Many artists are on hand to sign autographs and go one-on-one with visitors. In June, there's a block party and juried art show. The Mardi Gras-like atmosphere is heightened on Halloween, when Front Street is closed off to car traffic. The action culminates in a wild costume contest.

Hula Shows ★★
1221 Honoapiilani Highway, in the Lahaina Cannery, Lahaina, ☎ *(808) 661-5304.*
The Lahaina Cannery shopping center presents a *keiki* (children's) hula show every Sunday at 1 p.m., and on the first Thursday of each month at 7 p.m., ancient songs and dances are interpreted by members of the hula *halau* (school) Ho'oulu

o Ka'ula. Other free shows are featured at the Whalers Village in Kaanapali, ☎ *(808) 661-4567* every Wednesday and Sunday at 1 p.m. A complete open-air Polynesian revue plus a fashion show (of grass skirts?) is offered at the Wailea Shopping Village, ☎ *(808) 879-4474,* Tuesdays at 1 p.m.

Historical Sites

The Brick Palace and Old Fort Ruins ★★
Wharf Street, Lahaina.
Sharing the same lot as the Banyan Tree are the ruins of a palace commissioned by Kamehameha I and built by two ex-convicts from Australia; it was the first Western building in the islands. Next to the excavated foundations are the remnants of a fort built of coral blocks brought in from the reef in the 1930s to guard missionaries from angry whalers mad at them for introducing stringent moral rules and spoiling their fun. The original fort covered one acre and was approximately 20 feet high. In the same area, closer to the Banyan Tree, is the Old Courthouse, built of stones from Hale Piula, an unfinished two-story palace originally built for Kamehameha III.

The Pioneer Inn ★★★
Hotel and Wharf Streets, Lahaina.
http://www.pioneerinn-maui.com/
Now a Best Western—and the only hotel in West Maui until the late 1950s—the Pioneer Inn's facade dates from 1901, as do the comical house rules still posted in the public rooms, including, "If you wet or burn you bed, you going out." **A PRIME TOURIST ATTRACTION**, especially for its colorful, rowdy bar. Across the street is the equally famous Banyan Tree, which is more than 60 feet high, casting shade on two-thirds of an acre, great on a hot Lahaina day, the original "Lahaina Cooler." The tree was planted in April 1873, to mark the 50th anniversary of the beginning of Protestant missionary work in Lahaina.

Waiola Church and Cemetery ★★★
Wainee Street, near Shaw Street, Lahaina.
Originally called Waine'e, this was the first stone church in the islands (1828–1832), built by natives for the Protestant mission. Sundays were a lively scene, with 3000 Hawaiians packed together on the floor, ringed by calabash spittoons for tobacco-

chewing chiefs and ships' masters. Native royalists burned it in 1894 to protest the annexation of Hawaii by the United States. Rebuilt several times after another fire (due to unknown reasons) and a whirlwind blew it down, it was rebuilt to its present state in 1951 and renamed Waiola, or "Water of Life." Tombs were marked with glass-framed pictures. Among the dead are Queen Ke'opuolani, the first royal Christian convert and the wife of Kamehameha I.

Museums and Exhibits

Baldwin Home Museum ★★★
Front and Dickenson Streets, Lahaina, 96767,
☎ *(808) 661-3262.*

In the early 1960s, the Lahaina Restoration Foundation lovingly restored the 150-year-old clapboard-and-coral-stone residence and office of Revered Dwight Baldwin, a Protestant medical missionary. Old furniture and antique buffs will most likely covet the 1860 piano, koa bed, and kapa quilts in the various rooms. Other items of interest include THE FIRST TOILET USED ON MAUI and a collection of medical instruments. Narrated tour. Admission.

Brig Carthaginian II ★★
Lahaina Harbor, Lahaina, 96761, ☎ *(808) 661-3262.*
http://www.hiohwy.com/c/carthagi.htm

A floating maritime museum berthed in Lahaina Harbor, this 93-foot, two-masted replica of a 19th-century sailing ship features an entertaining video on (you guessed it) whales. Admission. Kids get in free.

HAWAII

TRAVELBOOKS FREEBIE

Lahaina Whaling Museum ★★★

865 Front Street, Lahaina, ☎ *(808) 661-4775.*

This free museum, located in the Crazy Shirts' outlet in Lahaina, has a small but unique collection of rare 19th-century whaling artifacts. Crazy Shirts' tycoon Rick Ralston acquired his treasures both on Hawaii and on numerous scouting trips to New England seaports over a 33-year period. The collection of scrimshaw, carved by lonely sailors for loved ones at home, is outstanding. Try to forget that these are carved from genuine whales' teeth and bone, and just enjoy them for the artistic value. You'll see ivory clothespins, jewelry, and even a swift, an expanding whalebone-and-ivory marvel used to wind yarn for knitting. Also interesting is a huge ship's figure from the *Carthaginian,* a replica of a 19th-century, square-rigged bark, used in the movie *Hawaii.*

Wo Hing Temple Museum ★★

858 Front Street, Lahaina, 96761, ☎ *(808) 661-3262.*
http://www.lahainarestoration.org/temple.html

Among the photos and displays of Chinese culture and their contributions to the Hawaiian economy is a Taoist shrine affiliated with the Chee Kung Tong, a Chinese fraternal society with branches all over the world. Those interested in the history of cinema will be pleasantly surprised to find regularly scheduled showings of Thomas Edison's 1898 and 1906 films of old Hawaii in an adjacent building. Donation requested.

Parks and Gardens

Jodo Mission and Buddha ★★★

Near Mala Wharf, Lahaina.

The 3.5-ton statue of Buddha at the oceanfront Jodo Mission Park near Mala wharf was erected to mark the 100th anniversary of the arrival of the first Japanese plantation laborers in 1868. The grounds and building of the mission are open to the public.

The Shows

The Hawaii Experience Domed Theater ★★★
824 Front Street, Lahaina, 96761, ☎ *(808) 661-8314.*
If you didn't get up in time to greet the sunrise at Haleakala National Park, you can experience it vicariously at this giant domed theater with surround sound. The current feature, shown on a 180-degree, wrap-around screen, is "Hawaii, Islands of the Gods," a cinematic voyage around the islands. Shows every hour on the hour. General admission: varies.

Tours

Atlantis Submarines ★★★
Leaves from Pioneer Inn on Front Street, Lahaina, 96761,
☎ *(808) 667-6604.*
http://www.goatlantis.com/default.htm
This well-known company gives travelers a voyage to the bottom of the sea (well, not quite) on a comfortable, battery-powered, 80-ton, 48-passenger sub. You won't get the bends or ear infections; in fact, you won't even get wet. There are three one- and two-hour narrated rides available. General admission: varies.

Ironwood Ranch ★★★
5095 Napili Hau Drive, Lahaina, 96761, ☎ *(808) 669-4991.*
http://www.ironwoodranch.com/
Friendly ranch hands take everyone from beginners to advanced riders on several horseback-riding excursions; the lowest priced is through a pineapple plantation. Also private rides. General admission: varies. Call for prices and excursion details.

Kawika's Aina Tour Company ★★★
505 Front Street, Suite 231, Lahaina, 96761,
☎ *(808) 667-2204.*
Special hours: sunset tours available.
Pricey, but worth it, for a van tour. This company specializes in tours to Kahakuloa, an isolated valley on Maui's seldom-visited northwest shore about 28 miles from Lahaina, HOME TO FEWER THAN 75 RESIDENTS, MOST OF THEM OF HAWAIIAN ANCESTRY. The valley has deserted beaches for snorkeling, but the main draw is the people you'll meet, who still live off the

land and fish for food. Although homes have electricity, most prefer to use lanterns for lighting and gas generators for washing machines and fridges. There's one roadside vendor, so it's advisable that you bring a picnic. General admission: varies. Call for prices.

Lahaina-Kaanapali & Pacific Railroad ★★★
Honoapiilani Highway, P.O. Box 816, Lahaina, 96767,
☎ *(808) 661-0089.*
http://www.sugarcanetrain.com/
This fun, 1890s-era, steam-powered locomotive shuttles tourists between Kaanapali and Lahaina, where the parking situation can be horrendous. Also called the "Sugar Cane" Train, it puffs merrily through a real sugar plantation, while a conductor prattles on (and sometimes sings) knowingly about King Sugar's history and its impact in the islands. Ask about two-for-one deals with the Hawaii Experience Domed Theater and Nautilus Maui. General admission: varies. General admission: varies.

Luckey Strike Charters ★★
P.O. Box 1502, Lahaina, 96767, ☎ *(808) 661-4606.*
http://www.luckeystrike.com
This sport-fishing charter company run by Tad and Cindy Luckey, who have 20 years experience, leads customers to marlin, mahi-mahi, tuna, wahoo, shark, and other big fish. You and your party can have the *Lucky Strike II*, a 50-foot Delta equipped with state-of-the-art electronics and computerized downriggers all to yourself, for half-, three-quarter- or full-day trips. Maximum six passengers on private charters. Share-boat trips can be arranged. In addition, a smaller sportfishing boat, the 31-foot. Uniflite Sport Fisher *Kanoa*, is available for charter (maximum six passengers). No license required. All equipment, bait, and ice provided; bring your own lunch, beverages, and sun protection. Boats leave from Slips 50 and 51 at Lahaina Small Boat Harbor. General admission: varies. CAN BE EXPENSIVE call for prices.

Nautilus Semi-Submersibles ★★★
From Slip 10 in Lahaina Harbor, Lahaina, 96761,
☎ *(808) 667-2133.*

Although these vessels resemble subs, the 58-foot boats don't submerge, which makes a trip a lot less expensive than submarine tours. While the vessel itself stays on the surface, the spacious viewing cabin is under the waterline. Passengers can also choose to ride topside part of the way. After direct boarding from Lahaina Harbor, the boat sets out for a shallow coral reef outside of Lahaina. This is when **DIVERS LEAP OVERBOARD AND BRING SEA URCHINS, OCTOPUS, AND OTHER MARINE CREATURES RIGHT TO WINDOWS BEFORE RELEASING THEM.** While this is happening, outboard cameras video the action around the vessel so no one misses a thing. Carries up to 34 passengers. General admission: varies. General admission: varies.

Zip-Purr Charters ★★★
P.O. Box 12256, Lahaina, 96761, ☎ (808) 667-2299.
http://www.playmaui.com/zippur.html
Capt. Mike "Turk" Turkington and Julie operate this 47-foot sailing cat with a large covered cabin. Mike, a former firefighter and professional surfer born on Oahu, designed the boat himself. From January-April they offer a six-hour, Lanai Snorkel Sail/Whale-Watch expedition. **THE TRIP STOPS AT TWO PRISTINE SNORKEL SPOTS, INCLUDING TURTLE REEF.** Limited to 35–37 passengers. Ask about a two-hour Sunset Cocktail Sail/Whale Watch. Tours leave from the Hula Grill restaurant in Whalers Village, Kaanapali Beach. A 24-hour cancellation notice is required. General admission: varies. General admission: varies.

Sports

Maui is practically synonymous with **golf** and **tennis**. Golfers will find clubs and courses at the ritzy resort areas of Wailea and Kaanapali. Big names include Kapalua Golf Club, Makena Golf Course, Maui Country Club, Pukalani Country Club, Royal Kaanapali, Sandalwood Country Club, Silversword Golf Course, Waiehu Municipal Golf Course, Waikapa Valley Country Club, and Wailea Golf Club. Or come for one of the **tournaments**: Asahi Beer Kyosan Golf Tournament at the Wailea Golf Club (February), Kaanapali Classic Senior PGA Golf Tournament at the Royal Kaanapali (October), Isuzu Kapalua International Golf Championship at Kapalua Golf Club (November) and the Kirin Cup World Championship of Golf (December).

HAWAII

You'll find **tennis courts** all over the island—some are attached to resorts and hotels, some are private clubs, others are free public courts. For more information on public courts, contact **Maui County Department of Parks and Recreation** *(200 South High Street, Wailuku 96793,* ☎ *(808) 243-7232,* http://www.co.maui.hi.us/departments/Parks/*)*. The big tennis event is the Kapalua Open, held on Labor Day weekend.

Anglers can sign up with a charter at Lahaina or Maalaea harbors to try your luck with Maui's various game fish such as marlin, mahi-mahi, and tuna. Maui is a fantastic place for **horseback riding**, with stables and trails around the island offering excursions into virtually every type of terrain, from tropical forests and remote beaches to pineapple fields and the Haleakala Crater. **Cyclists** thrill to the ride down Haleakala, while **joggers** can't wait to run up the volcano during the annual (August) 36-mile **Haleakala Run to the Sun**. The **Maui Marathon** (March) is another top running event.

Central Maui
Kahului

Hawaiian Island Windsurfing ★★★★
415 Dairy Road, Kahului, 96732, ☎ *(808) 871-4981.*
http://www.windsurf.cc/windsurf/
This retail store and rental facility is also known as Windsurfing West, one of the best windsurfing schools on the island. IT WILL RENT YOU EVERYTHING YOU NEED, EVEN A CAR-ROOF RACK. Other full-service outfits include Hawaiian Sailboarding Techniques, *444 Hana Hwy, Kahului, 96732,* ☎ *(808) 871-5423*, open Monday–Saturday, 9 a.m.–5 p.m. owned by top champion Alan Cadiz. Hunt Hawaii, *P.O. Box 989, Paia, 96779,* ☎ *(808) 575-2300*, offers rentals, lessons, and accessories. Open 9 a.m.–6 p.m.. Maui Windsurf Co. and Maui Magic Windsurfing Schools, *520 Keolani Place, Kahului, 96732,* ☎ *(808) 877-4696.* 8:30 a.m.–5:30 p.m.

Makawao

Hiking Paradise ★★
P.O. Box 1582, Makawao, 96768, ☎ *(808) 573-0464.*
http://www.maui.net/~arrowhd/paradise/
Custom half- or full-day rainforest, waterfall, or mountain hiking trips. Ponchos, backpacks, snacks (for half-day trips), and

lunch (full-day only) provided. Advance booking required; 10 percent discount for those reserving two weeks in advance. From the mainland, call ☎ *(808) 227-7741*. General admission: varies..

Makawao Rodeo ★★
Oskie Rice Arena, Olinda Avenue, Makawao,
☎ *(808) 572-9928.*
No cardboard cowpokes here, no sir. This is the real thing, with barrel racing, calf roping, bull riding, and more, all part of the annual Makawao rodeo. It's a skill test for all qualified contenders from throughout the state, including little 'uns. Held over the Fourth of July Weekend, it's kicked off by a colorful parade.

Waiehu

Waiehu Golf Course ★★
Waiehu, Northwest of Wailuku, Waiehu, 96793,
☎ *(808) 243-7400.*
On the old Hawaii north shore, with a very tranquil setting, this par-71, 6330-yard course is the **CHEAPEST OF THREE MUNICIPAL GOLF COURSES**. Lower price is for weekday play. General admission: $33–$38.

Waikapu

Grand Waikapu Country Club ★★★★
2500 Honoapiilani Highway, Waikapu, 96793,
☎ *(808) 244-7888.*
http://www.hiohwy.com/g/grwacocl.htm
VERY HIGH END, despite it's peculiar architecture: designed by Frank Lloyd Wright, this extravagant country club looks like a Taos pueblo as conceived by George Lucas. Within is a restaurant with a 180-degree view of Maui and Haleakala. Associated with the Grand Wailea Resort, the Club's literature boasts how this $140 million course is **"THE MOST EXPENSIVE IN THE U.S."** and that it's the only course in Hawaii that uses "two million gallons of water per day." The hilltop setting is 1000 feet above sea level, and every hole has panoramic views. Takes only a limited number of players per day, so that every golfer can enjoy a round. Caddy service. Spa Grande facilities included in the greens fee, $30 for non-players. Regular fee is, again,

"the most expensive in the U.S." General admission: varies., and be sure to have the smelling salts handy.

South Maui
Kihei

Ed Robinson's Diving Adventures ★★★
P.O. Box 616, Kihei, 96753, ☎ *(808) 879-3584.*
http://www.mauiscuba.com/erd1.htm
This highly recommended company, which CATERS TO CERTIFIED DIVERS ONLY, is operated by Ed Robinson, a widely published underwater photographer and dive master. Professional, experienced divers come to Maui expressly to dive with Ed. Robinson knows where all the out-of-the-way sites are, and customizes each dive trip depending on the skill level and interest of the participants. Ask about the three-day "Ultimate Dive Package," where divers choose among trips to Lanai, Molokini, and Maui's south shore, as well as a two-tank Sunset/Night dive and a progressive three-tank adventure trip. A 10-percent discount is offered with this package. Trips leave from Kihei Boat Ramp, usually at 6:45 a.m. Photography courses available. General admission: varies.

Kelii's Kayak Tours ★★★
Kihei, 96753, ☎ *(808) 874-7652.*
Experienced local guides take small groups on ocean-kayaking and snorkeling trips to inaccessible, out-of-the-way shoreline areas and coves. YOU'LL PROBABLY HAVE AN ENCOUNTER OR TWO WITH GREEN SEA TURTLES, OR SEE WHALES AND DOLPHINS IN SEASON. Tours include: Maui's South Shore-Makena, Ahihi Bay, LaPerouse; 2.5 hours, two departures daily 7:30–11 a.m. from Makena Landing. This is a leisurely paddle in gentle ocean conditions. The price includes snorkel equipment and light refreshments. Also caters to corporate groups. General admission: varies.

Makena

Makena Resort Golf Courses ★★★
5415 Makena Alanui Drive, Makena, 96753,
☎ *(808) 879-3344.*
These two 18-hole golf courses, designed by Robert Trent Jones, Jr., are located in the Makena Resort in front of the

Maui Prince Hotel in a rustic, oceanfront setting south of Wailea. The North Course, a 6567-yard, par-72 course, features breathtaking views of Haleakala Crater and natural obstacles that add to the challenge. The 6629-yard, par-72 South Course features natural rolling fairways, undulating greens, and **CAPTIVATING OCEAN AND MOUNTAIN VIEWS**. The signature 16th hole runs parallel to the ocean and is rarely described as easy. Pro shop, and a restaurant on the 19th hole that serves the best saimin on Maui. An **ON-SITE GOLF SCHOOL INCLUDES A ROOM/GOLF PACKAGE WITH FIVE NIGHTS AT THE HOTEL, THREE DAYS OF INSTRUCTION, INCLUDING 10 HOURS OF PRIVATE LESSONS, WITH A PRO PLAYING ALONG FOR NINE HOLES, UNLIMITED GOLF AND PRACTICE BALLS, AND HIGH-TECH VIDEO ANALYSIS.**

Wailea

Wailea Golf Club ★★★★
100 Wailea Golf Club Drive, Wailea, 96753,
☎ *(808) 875-5111.*
http://www.waileagolf.com/
Composed of three award-winning courses, Blue, Gold and Emerald. Gold, designed by Robert Trent Jones, Jr., is Wailea's claim to golfing fame. **NATURAL HAZARDS INCLUDE ANCIENT LAVA-ROCK WALLS BUILT BY EARLY HAWAIIANS THAT WERE LEFT IN PLACE AND INCORPORATED INTO THE COURSE.** Players also have to contend with the breathtaking scenery, which makes it hard to keep your mind on the ball. Facilities include a clubhouse, complete pro shop, and the SeaWatch restaurant, with a spectacular view. The Blue course, meandering through the resort amidst million-dollar homes, is the Club's grande dame, designed by Arthur Jack Snyder. **IT'S A COURSE FOR EVERYONE, WITH WIDE FAIRWAYS FOR THE HIGH HANDICAPPER.** Facilities: clubhouse and fairway restaurant. New in 1995, Wailea Emerald has a tropical look. Also designed by Robert Trent Jones, Jr., it has great views of Mount Haleakala, the ocean, and lush gardens. Has a double green shared by the 10th and 17th holes. Separate chipping and putting areas, practice bunker, driving range with three built-in target greens surrounded by traps. General admission: varies.

Wailea Tennis Club ★★★★
131 Wailea Ike Place, Wailea, 96753, ☎ *(808) 879-1958.*
http://www.waileagolf.com/
Called "Wimbledon West," this club caters to Wailea resort guests and features 11 Plexipave courts, three of them lit for night play. IT'S THE ONLY CLUB IN HAWAII WITH THREE GRASS COURTS AVAILABLE TO THE PUBLIC. Daily tennis clinics. Court rental, $10/day guests and owners, $15 nonguests. Grass court rental, $20/day for guests and owners, $25 nonguests. General admission: $10–$25.

Upcountry
Pukalani

Pukalani Country Club ★★
360 Pukalani Street, Pukalani, 96768, ☎ *(808) 572-1314.*
http://www.pukalanigolf.com/cgi-bin/e-commerce/pgc.pl?page=home
It's just a short cruise up Haleakala Highway to this 160-acre club with a par-72 championship course designed by Bob Baldock. Lovely upcountry setting with cool climate and panoramic views. The driving range is open until 9:30 p.m. The clouds ringing Haleakala often break here, creating a hole, hence the name "pukalani." Offers a good restaurant serving Hawaiian plate lunches. General admission: varies.

Ulupalakua Ranch

Papaka Sporting Clays ★★
Ulupalakua Ranch, Ulupalakua Ranch, ☎ *(808) 879-5649.*
http://www.tombarefoot.com/maui/papaka.html
Learn the fine art of clay target shooting, a veddy British sport that has recently come to Maui. Papaka Sporting Clays is situated in an old cinder cone on the 20,000-acre Ulupalakua Ranch. Participants shoot at colored clay targets representing different game birds (and one rabbit). There are 35 scenarios you can choose from, to suit all levels of expertise, from greenhorn to James Bond. The most difficult is a klutz's nightmare, where a computer picks several targets that whiz through the air at different speeds and positions, and you have to shoot them all at the same time. The price includes use of either a semi-automatic Browning, Remington 8, or Beretta shotgun, a padded vest and other protective gear, 75 targets, 75 shells, and

shooting instruction. Guests are picked up and returned from the Maui Prince in Makena and other hotels at the Wailea resort. Corporate and *kamaaina* rates available. Two daily sessions; morning 8:30 to 11:30 a.m., afternoon 1 to 4:30 p.m. Reservations required. Age limit: 11 years. General admission: varies.

West Maui
Kaanapali Beach

Kaanapali North and South Courses ★★★★
Kaanapali Resort, Kaanapali Beach, 96761,
☎ *(808) 661-3691.*
http://www.kaanapali-golf.com/
These championship courses serve the Kaanapali Resort area. Kaanapali North, an 18-hole, par-72, 6305-yard course, was laid out by Robert Trent Jones, Sr. The 18th hole demands a shot over water and is said to be one of the TOUGHEST HOLES IN THE ISLANDS. The South Course, an 18-hole, par-72, 6250-yard course, was a piece-of-cake executive layout until Arthur Jack Snyder put in a water hazard. Good for all levels. HIGHER PRICE FOR NON-RESORT GUESTS. Pro shop. General admission: $90–$110.

Kapalua

Kapalua Resort Golf Courses ★★★★
Kapalua Resort, 300 Kapalua Drive, Kapalua, 96761,
☎ *(808) 669-8044.*
http://www.kapaluamaui.com/
The Kapalua Golf Club is known as one of the finest in the world with three championship courses. The Bay Course, opened in 1975, was designed by Arnold Palmer and Francis Duane and incorporates magnificent ocean panoramas, lush tropical terrain, and the beaches of Kapalua. The signature hole extends onto an ocean-framed black-lava peninsula. The Village course, designed by Palmer with Ed Seay, rises into the West Maui mountains, and travels through eucalyptus and Cook pine trees, past a lake, and alongside ridges plummeting hundreds of feet into deep green valleys. IT'S COMPLEX ENOUGH FOR SEASONED PROS AND ENJOYABLE FOR BEGINNING GOLFERS. The Plantation course, designed by Bill Coore and Ben Crenshaw, is set on 240 acres of dramatic natural terrain,

and is home to the Lincoln-Mercury Kapalua International. It's the most challenging of the three. Lessons, video taping, and more.

Kapalua Tennis Garden and Village Tennis Center ★★★★
100 Kapalua Drive, Kapalua, 96761, ☎ *(808) 665-0112.*
http://www.kapaluamaui.com/activities/tennis/
Located steps from the Ritz Carlton, this is ONE OF THE FINEST CLUBS IN THE COUNTRY, and is actually comprised of two facilities, The Tennis Garden and the Village Tennis Center. Each feature 10 Plexipave courts for day and night play. Also full-service pro shops, snack bars, lounge areas. Home of Wilson Kapalua Open. Private lessons, rentals, tennis program, matchmaking (!). Lower fee for resort guests. Children under 18 free when playing with parents. General admission: varies.

Lahaina

Extended Horizons ★★
Box 10785, Lahaina, 96761, ☎ *(808) 667-0611.*
Dive Lanai on *Extended Horizons II*, a 36-foot, custom aluminum dive boat. Limited to small groups, including 13 divers, the captain, and a dive crew of two, with six divers maximum per guide, all of whom are professional naturalists. All dive gear provided. There are 60 dive sites available, with average depths of 60–70 feet, and divers' requests are taken into consideration. The crossing to Lanai takes as little as 30 minutes. Refreshments provided. Ask about night dives, a PADI introductory course, and open-water referrals. Departure from Mala Wharf, Lahaina. Reservations required. Call for rates and hours of operation.

Lahaina Divers Turtle Charter ★★★
143 Dickenson Street, Lahaina, 96761, ☎ *(808) 998-DIVE.*
http://www.lahainadivers.com/charters.htm
A new offering from Lahaina Divers, Maui's first five-star PADI dive center and instructor training center, is the "Turtle Reef Dive Charter," a snorkel/dive/seminar combo. Prior to your trip, instructors give you the skinny about the rare Hawaiian green sea turtle, one of the company's favorite "dive buddies." The four-hour expedition leaves from Lahaina Harbor daily at 12:30 p.m. HIGHER PRICE FOR CERTIFIED AND INTRODUCTO-

RY DIVERS; LOWER PRICE FOR SNORKELERS.

Maui Surfing School ★★
Lahaina Harbor behind Kam III School, Lahaina,
☎ *(808) 875-0625.*
http://www.maui.net/~mol/activitysea/surfsch.html
ANDREA THOMAS GUARANTEES THAT YOU'LL LEARN TO SURF IN ONE LESSON OR YOU'LL GET YOUR MONEY BACK. Her method was developed for beginners, cowards, and non-swimmers. Two-hour group lessons, or private sessions. Custom "surfaris" for competent surfers who want insider tips on different breaks. Equipment provided. General admission: varies.. On the mainland, call ☎ *(800) 851-0543.*

Nancy Emerson School of Surfing ★★
Lahaina, ☎ *(808) 244-7873.*
http://www.surfclinics.com/
Nancy, a former surfing champion, claims along with rival Andrea Thomas that she created the method of teaching people to surf in one lesson. We don't want to start a fight between the two, so you decide. Emerson developed her technique in 1973, and has operated schools for beginners since 1980. All instructors are personally trained by Nancy. Two-hour group or private lessons. Bring your camera and the kids. General admission: varies. Call for rates and hours of operation.

Where to Stay

Next to Oahu, Maui has the most rooms for visitors in its hotels, resorts, B&Bs and condos—plenty of condos. Unfortunately, this island also averages out as the most expensive of the Hawaiian islands in terms of accommodation. Price, obviously, is determined by where you decide to stay and, in most cases, the time of year you visit. The low season generally runs from after Easter to before Christmas, and rooms can be discounted 25 percent or more during this period. On **West Maui**, where most of the tourists stay, you can choose from more than 80 hotels and condo units. The major resorts are the **Kaanapali Beach Resort** and the **Kapalua Bay Resort**, both crammed with high-class condo complexes and hotels such as the Westin Maui, Marriott, and Hyatt Regency. There are a few condos and some funkier hotels in Lahaina, and more condos around **Maalaea Bay**. On **East Maui**, you can't miss the hideous sea of condos (popular with vacationing families) at **Kihei**, while down the coast **Wailea** offers more luxury hotels and tasteful condos. A variety of accommodations, from rustic to flash, can be found in **Hana**. And don't overlook **Kahului**, in **Central Maui**, for convenience and value.

Central Maui

Haiku
Bed-and-Breakfasts

Halfway to Hana House $85   ★★

100 Waipio Road, Haiku, 96708,
☎ *(808) 572-1176, FAX (808) 572-3609.*
http://www.maui.net/~gailp/

A REAL FIND, Halfway to Hana House is a cozy studio unit in a private home set in the country 30 minutes from Kahului airport. Colorful tropical plants and flowers, fruit trees, and herb gardens surround the property. ONLY A SHORT WALK TO FRESHWATER POOLS AND WATERFALLS, HORSEBACK RIDING, AND COUNTRY TRAILS FOR HIKING, THE B&B IS A GOOD POINT OF DEPARTURE FOR BOTH HANA TOWN AND HALEAKALA VOLCANO. The host, Gail Pickholz, is a longtime resident (more than 25 years) and outdoor enthusiast, and she'll be happy to be a personal resource guide to secret places away from the tourist trail. The light and airy accommodation has its own entrance and bath, a double bed, mini-kitchen, and outdoor covered patio with an ocean view. Amenities: balcony or patio. One room. Credit cards: not accepted.

Pilialoha Bed and Breakfast Cottage $110-150   ★★★

2512 Kaupakalua Road, Haiku, 96708, ☎ *(808) 572-1440, FAX (808) 572-4612.*
http://www.pilialoha.com/index.html

GUESTS RAVE about the genuine sense of Aloha they receive during their stay at this aptly monikered property, which means "friendship" in Hawaiian. The hostess, Machiko Heide, an artist, is as sweet as her name, and the little B&B cottage on her two-acre spread is decorated with lots of personal touches, including hand-painted bed pillows and artful arrangements of anthuriums and other exotic blooms. Evidence of her green thumb is everywhere, including 100 bug-free rose bushes, all labeled for your edification. The two-bedroom cottage has one room with a queen bed and another with a twin. The living room has a queen-size sofa bed, and extra futons are kept in the closet. Up to six people can be accommodated, but it is more comfortable for two. It also has a fully equipped kitchen, living room with cable TV and phone, washer/dryer, and iron. The Heide's will also loan you beach gear. Fresh fruit, homemade bread, pastry or muffins, and beverages are supplied daily; all you have to do is dish them up. **THE UPCOUNTRY LOCATION IS CONVENIENT TO SEVERAL INTERESTING AREAS, INCLUDING THE COWBOY-RODEO TOWN OF MAKAWAO, THE SUMMIT OF HALEAKALA NATIONAL PARK, AND MAUI'S WINDSURFING CAPITAL, HOOKIPA.** There's a minimum two-night stay. One room. Credit cards: not accepted.

Cottages

Maui Dream Cottages/ Halelea $490 ★★★

265 West Kuiaha Road, Haiku, 96708, ☎ *(808) 575-9079, FAX (808) 575-9477.*

VERY EXPENSIVE, BUT WORTH EVERY PENNY if you have the dough and the inclination. The two stand-alone cottages that compose Maui Dream Cottages are on a two-acre estate on a hilltop on the north shore of Maui, 12 miles from the Kahului Airport. These very private retreats are fenced in, and there are 1.5 acres of open lawn for relaxing or for active kids to play on. Hammocks are stretched between palm trees. **YOU COULD LIVE ON THE HUGE VARIETY OF FRUIT THAT DROPS OFF THE TREES ON THE ESTATE—THESE INCLUDE COCONUTS, BANANAS, AVOCADOS, PAPAYAS, MANGOES, EVEN PASSION FRUIT—THE LIST GOES ON AND ON.** The closest beach for swimming is five minutes from the house, and management recommends that the surrounding pineapple fields (Haiku used to be an old plantation town) are great for long runs or just walking. The handsomely furnished and roomy cottages are fully equipped with designer kitchens with microwave, washer-dryer, phone, TV, and VCR. It sleeps from two to five people comfortably. Also available for rent by the same owners is a private residence, *Halelea* (House of Joy), which is on the point of Tavares Bay on 10,000 square feet of land near Paia and Hookipa Beach Park. For $385 per night, you get 3650 square feet of antique and art-filled living space with three bedrooms, four baths, and a self-contained pool house/cottage with kitchen and bath. The main bath is a replica of an old Japanese bath house, with a Jacuzzi offering ocean views. Reservations should be made early, for obvious reasons, as many people book a year in advance for all these dream properties. Amenities: Jacuzzi, sauna, balcony or patio, family plan. Two rooms.

Kahului
Hotels

Maui Seaside Hotel   **$78–$140**   ★
100 Kaahumanu Avenue, Kahului, 96732,
☎ *(800) 367-7000,* ☎ *(808) 877-3311,*
FAX (808) 922-0052. Rated restaurant: Vi's
http://www.sand-seaside.com/maui_hotels.htm
An informal, family-owned oceanfront hotel on Kahului Bay, the Maui Seaside is three miles from Kahului Airport. Each room (none have ocean views) features two double beds, ceiling fan as well as air conditioning, refrigerator, and color TV. Vi's, the on-site restaurant, offers a mid-priced, varied menu of local and international dishes. **THE HOTEL CATERS TO SENIORS AND OTHERS LOOKING FOR A COMFORTABLE, HOMEY BARGAIN.** Amenities: exercise room. 190 rooms. Credit cards: A, MC, V.

East Maui
Hana

Heavenly Hana Inn   **$185–$250**   ★★
4155 Hana Highway, Hana, 96713, Five minutes from Hana Airport, ☎ *(808) 248-8442, FAX (808) 248-8442.*
http://www.heavenlyhanainn.com/
This Japanese-style inn, although miles away from anything, is **A DELIGHT FOR LOVERS OF ASIAN ART.** Two stone lions, symbols of luck and well-being, greet guests at the front gate. The central lobby and lounge feature Tonsu-type furniture and brand-new eucalyptus wood flooring, installed shortly after new owners bought the property from longtime proprietor Alfreda Wurst. Guests sleep on queen-size platform futons, and new bathrooms have vanities and deep-soaking tubs big enough for two. **ONE UNFORTUNATE CHANGE IS THE REMOVAL OF THE KITCHENETTES; NO MEALS EXCEPT A CONTINENTAL BREAKFAST ARE SERVED, AND THERE ARE NO**

RESTAURANTS IN THE IMMEDIATE VICINITY. Three rooms. Credit cards: not accepted.

Condos

Hana Kai-Maui Resort Condominiums $125–$195 ★★
1533 Uakea Road, Hana, 96713,
☎ *(800) 346-2772,* ☎ *(808) 248-8426, FAX (808) 248-7482.*
http://www.hanakaimaui.com/

Nestled in a sheltered cove facing the black-sand Papolana Beach, the Hana-Kai Maui Resort Condominiums consists of a pair of two-story structures housing 18 simple, but fairly spacious and neatly kept, studio and one-bedroom units. All have oceanfront views and lanais with a molded plastic table and chairs. Complete kitchens (sans dishwashers) are thoughtfully provided, as Hana's grocery stores are shuttered by 6:30 p.m. and there are only a sprinkling of eateries in the area. THERE ARE NO TVs OR RADIOS; THE ONLY MUSIC YOU HEAR IS YOUR SIGNIFICANT OTHER WHISPERING IN YOUR EAR AND THE SOUND OF THE SURF BEATING AGAINST THE WAVES OUTSIDE YOUR QUARTERS. Amenities: balcony or patio, family plan. 18 rooms. Credit cards: A, MC, V.

House Rentals

Blair's Original Hana Plantation Houses $90–$200 ★★★
P.O. Box 249, Hana, 96713,
☎ *(800) 228-HANA,* ☎ *(808) 248-7686,*
FAX (808) 248-8240.

A TERRIFIC ALTERNATIVE FOR THOSE WHO WANT TO AVOID BIG (OR SMALL) HOTELS. For more than 10 years, Blair Shurtleff has been offering "alternative" (and very affordable) accommodations for travelers looking for the real Hana experience. His unique collection of rentals includes the Garden House, three miles from the town of Hana. The tropical-style dwelling offers two units, including a downstairs studio with a private entrance, and is suitable for two persons. It has a queen-size bed with combination bath, plus a full kitchen and cable TV. Available for a bit more is Lani Makaalae Studio, which has a whirlpool tub/shower on an outdoor deck under plumeria trees. One of Blair's most upscale properties (for $200 per night) is the solar-powered Waikoloa Beach Cottage, situated on a half-acre lot just steps from a black-sand beach. Sleeping up to five guests (there's also a separate Japanese sleeping room for two), the cottage is decked out in exotic woods and has large picture windows overlooking Hana Bay. All houses feature fully equipped kitchen facilities, barbecue grills, and beach access. Blair and his associates are all longtime residents and will help arrange such head-clearing activities as yoga/stretch classes, massages, and more. **EXTREMELY-GAY FRIENDLY; ACTUALLY, VERY FRIENDLY TO JUST ABOUT EVERYONE.** Amenities: Jacuzzi, balcony, or patio. 12 rooms. Credit cards: A, MC, V.

Rentals

Ekena $185–$600 ★★★

P.O. Box 728, Hana, 96713,
☎ (800) 262-9912, ☎ (808) 248-7047.
http://www.maui.net/~ekena/

Two apartments are available in this spacious, two-story hillside home above Hana. Its prime attraction is wrap-around decks affording awesome 360-degree views of the ocean, the Hana coast, and the surrounding hills. The lower-level (and lower-priced) unit features 1700 square feet of living space, and includes one or two bedrooms, two baths, a fully equipped kitchen, dining room, TV and VCR, and washer/dryer. The 2000-square-foot, skylit, second-story apartment offers the same amenities and facilities. The hostess has a green thumb; her tropical blooms are everywhere in evidence. Amenities: balcony or patio. Two rooms. Credit cards: not accepted.

Resorts

Hotel Hana–Maui $235–$1500 ★★★★

At Hana Ranch, off Highway 31, Hana, 96713,
☎ (800) 325-3535, ☎ (808) 248-8211, FAX (808) 248-7202.
Rated restaurant: Hana Ranch Restaurant
http://www.hotelhanamaui.com

For close to 50 years, the Hotel Hana Maui has been drawing a legion of repeat visitors despite several changes of ownership. The 66-acre property, located on what was once a cattle ranch, hasn't really changed much, despite a top-to-bottom renovation by the Rosewood Corporation of Dallas in the mid-'80s. Accommodations are in 97 rooms and suites housed in a series of single-story, plantation-cottage style buildings. Hardwood floors gleam, and artful flower arrangements are everywhere, even in the hand-tiled baths, which feature deep-soaking tubs overlooking private gardens. Latticed lanais offer sea views. Amenities include wet bars, refrigerators with ice-makers, and Kona coffee beans with a grinder. You'll also find a brolly for sudden rain squalls, but no TVs, radios, telephones, or clocks are anywhere in evidence. One could live very happily and permanently in one of the top-of-the-line Sea Ranch Cottages (reached by shuttle). Each has an outdoor spa and deck, and are considerably larger than other dwellings. If you can be lured out of your lodgings, partake in some of the outdoor activities, which are a big thing at the resort, including horseback riding, picnics, and barbecues on nearby Hamoa Beach. Amenities: tennis, horseback riding, health club, Jacuzzi, balcony or patio, family plan. 97 rooms. Credit cards: A, MC, V.

Huelo Point
Bed-and-Breakfasts

Huelo Point Bed and Breakfast $95–$275 ★★★

P.O. Box 1195, Huelo Point, ☎ *(808) 572-1850.*

This has got to be THE MOST UNUSUAL B&B ACCOMMODATION IN MAUI—a secluded, glass-walled gazebo, perched atop a 300-foot cliff, directly overlooking Waipio Bay, where whales spawn. The property, located on a flower farm, INCLUDES AMENITIES SUCH AS A HOT TUB, OUTDOOR SHOWER, ROCK-LINED POOL and, of course, the view. From here, you can explore hiking trails to private waterfalls. The hosts, Guy and Doug, live on the property in a palatial home, which they also rent out for $2000 a week (that's the day rate some resorts charge for a suite). Despite the back-of-beyond location, it's only a few minutes' drive to Paia, where restaurants, shops, and beaches abound. Also, you're halfway to Hana. Amenities: Jacuzzi, balcony or patio. One rooms. Credit cards: not accepted.

South Maui
Kihei
Bed-and-Breakfasts

Aloha Pualani $89–$159 ★★

15 Wailana Place, Kihei, 96753,
☎ *(800) 782-5264,* ☎ *(808) 874-9265, FAX (808) 874-9127.*
http://www.alohapualani.com/

Aloha Pualani, situated 100 feet from Maalaea Bay beach, is A

BED-AND-BREAKFAST/CONDOMINIUM/RESORT COMBO offered by hosts Keith and Marina Dinsmoor. The Dinsmoors, who live on the property, maintain five two-story units surrounding a heated pool and tropically landscaped courtyard. **EXCELLENT VALUE.** All are one-bedroom suites with 1.5 baths and a living/dining area. Amenities include fully equipped kitchens, washer and dryer, color cable TV, phone, and ceiling fan. Best of all is an oceanfront lanai upstairs. Amenities: balcony or patio. Five rooms. Credit cards: MC, V.

Ann and Bob Babson's Vacation Rentals $90–$150   ★★★
3371 Keha Drive, Kihei, 96753, In Maui Meadows, just above Wailea,
☎ *(800) 824-6409,* ☎ *(808) 874-1166, FAX (808) 879-7906.*
For more than four years, Ann and Bob Babson, an enthusiastic couple transplanted from Northern California, have run a bed-and-breakfast operation from their contemporary wooden home in Maui Meadows, a residential suburb above Wailea. The house, on a half-acre of land, is landscaped with tropical fruit trees and flowers, including avocado, papaya, plumeria, and red ginger. Many guests enjoy just sprawling in the double hammock and taking it all in, even though Kihei beaches are a mere five-minute drive away. The bed-and-breakfast units, on the second floor of the house, include the one-bedroom, one-bath Bougainvillea Suite, which offers both ocean and mountain views. The 450-square foot Molokini Suite, decorated in a tasteful but spare Oriental style, also has a small fridge, a king-size bed with a skylight above it, and a rocking chair. The large bathroom has double sinks and a whirlpool tub/shower combination. On the ground floor is the Hibiscus Hideaway, a one-bedroom, one-bath apartment. It has a private entrance and its own garden. Adjacent to the main house is the Sunset Cottage, with two bedrooms (it sleeps six, with a sofa bed in the living room) and two baths. Special touches include a cathedral ceiling and covered lanai off the living room where you can see whales doing their thing in season. The Cottage and the Hideaway have kitchen facilities. Guests who opt for breakfast are provided with an "all you can eat" repast of juice, coffee, fruit, homemade granola, muffins, and scones. Sometimes a hot, freshly prepared item such as quiche, pancakes, french toast, or coconut waffles is on the menu. Unfortunately for slugabeds, the Babsons serve breakfast fairly promptly at 7:30

a.m., as the couple feel most guests like to get up and go. Also, **Ann and Bob are vegetarians, so don't expect any meat dishes.** All units have cable TVs and telephones. A laundry basket is provided in the rooms, and the Babsons will do your laundry for a nominal fee. Beach chairs and towels are also provided. **The Babsons delight in their guests discovering bed-and-breakfast living for the first time, whether they're honeymooners or seniors.** If you don't have an itinerary planned for Maui, when you ask for their brochure Ann and Bob will send you several pages of things to do and places to eat on the island. **They also run an interisland reservation service, and are happy to match people with other hosts in Maui when they're full.** Notice to animal-lovers: no pets are allowed, as Ann and Bob have two frisky indoor cats (they also have two outdoor cats and a pair of birds). Amenities: balcony or patio. Four rooms. Credit cards: MC, V.

Condos

Hale Hui Kai — $150–$300 ★★

2994 South Kihei Road, Kihei, 96753, On Keawakupu Beach, ☎ *(808) 879-1219, FAX (808) 879 -0600.*
http://www.beachbreeze.com/

A mile-long beach extends from the front door of the Hale Hui Kai (meaning "House by the Sea") to the Wailea resort area. You can literally fall out of your room to the sand from one of the two-bedroom, two-bath apartments at this fairly tasteful property, a series of wood-shingle buildings, some with Polynesian peaked roofs. Units are spacious and individually appointed, with wall-to-wall carpeting and twin or queen-size beds and full kitchens featuring a dishwasher and refrigerator. **Adjacent to the property is Carelli's, one of Maui's best Italian restaurants. Instead of going on a whale-watching cruise, you can save money by staying here and watching the great humpbacks cavorting just outside your front door.** Amenities: balcony or patio, family plan. 40 rooms. Credit cards: not accepted.

Hale Kamaole — $100–$182 ★★

2737 South Kihei Road, Kihei, 96753,
☎ *(800) 367-2970,* ☎ *(808) 879-1221.*
http://www.crhmaui.com/unit_hale.html

Hale Kamaole is a low-rise condo complex with beach access from a two-lane road across from the property. Spacious lawns, with palm trees, hibiscus, plumeria, and other tropical plants, give it a garden-like setting. All of the individually owned and decorated one- or two-bedroom units contain fully equipped kitchens, cable TVs and telephones, and most have queen or king beds and a sofa bed in the living room, but some one-bedroom apartments only have twin beds. A few upper-level, two-bedroom units possess lofts. All have lanais, except for ground-floor accommodations, which have to make do with a parcel of concrete with some tables and chairs. On-site facilities include two swimming pools with barbecue grills, and a tennis court. Amenities: balcony or patio, family plan. 187 rooms. Credit cards: MC, V.

Kamaole Beach Royale Resort $120–$250 ★★★
2385 South Kihei Road, Kihei, 96753,
☎ *(800) 421-3661,* ☎ *(808) 879-3131, FAX (808) 879 -9163.*
http://www.mauikbr.com/
Situated across from Kamaole Beach Park I, this unremarkable-looking, six-story stucco building with aqua accents features rather attractive one-, two-, or three-bedroom apartments. Furnishings are the requisite wood and rattan, but the pieces here are of good quality, and some include swivel rockers with ottomans in the separate living areas. Some bedrooms have wicker chests at the foot of the beds for storage. All have private lanais, some with views of neighboring islands; all have vistas of Haleakala. Amenities include ceiling fans, color cable TV, and telephones. Full kitchens with dishwashers and washer/dryers are provided. Five-day minimum stay required. Amenities: balcony or patio. Credit cards: not accepted.

Kamaole Sands $101–$410 ★★★
2695 South Kihei Road, Kihei, 96753,
☎ *(800) 367-5004,* ☎ *(808) 874-8700, FAX (808) 879 -3273.*
A fairly large complex of staggered mid-rise white concrete buildings, the Kamaole Sands nevertheless offers nicely landscaped gardens and rock pools with fountains as a cooling touch. But no one spends much time on the grass, as THIS PROPERTY SITS ACROSS FROM ONE OF MAUI'S MOST FAMOUS BEACH PARKS, KAMAOLE III. Accommodations, with separate living, dining, and sleeping areas, are much larger than you'd

expect, and well-kept, with light rattan and wood furniture. All studios and one-, two-, or three-bedroom units have private lanais, color cable TVs, and fully equipped kitchen facilities. Ceiling fans compensate for the lack of air conditioning. There's a pool, including a wading pool for tots, two whirlpool spas, four tennis courts, a sundeck, and barbecues. Ask about Internet specials. Amenities: tennis, Jacuzzi, balcony or patio. 440 rooms. Credit cards: A, MC, V

Mana Kai Maui — $70–$250 ★★
2960 South Kihei Road, Kihei, 96753,
☎ *(800) 367-5004,* ☎ *(808) 879-1561, FAX (808) 874-5042.*
Rated restaurant: Five Palms Beach Grill
http://www.mauimanakai.com/

This eight-story property is **CONVENIENTLY LOCATED ON AN EXCELLENT WHITE-SAND BEACH ON A QUIET STRETCH OF SOUTH KIHEI THAT'S PERFECT FOR SWIMMING**. Although billed as a condo resort, the Mana Kai Maui also offers hotel rooms with twin beds as well as spacious one- and two-bedroom suites decorated in easy-on-the-eye taupes and beiges, twin or king beds with quasi-Hawaiian quilts, and light, tropical, woven-rattan furniture. Private lanais are wide enough for a table and chairs. Fully equipped kitchens have plenty of storage space and contain a counter with bar-stool seating. All have color TVs. The two-bedroom units can sleep up to six people; these are ideal for families. Facilities include an open-air restaurant and lobby lounge and a pool. Included in the rates are a rental car; breakfast is supplied for hotel guests only. Amenities: balcony or patio. 67 rooms. Credit cards: A, MC, V.

Maui Isana Resort — $70–$90 ★★
515 S. Kihei Road, Kihei, 96753,
☎ *(800) 633-3833,* ☎ *(808) 879-7800, FAX (808) 874-5321.*
http://windsurfari.com/Pages/property/Isana.html

The Maui Isana, with a location just a short walk from the beach, will **APPEAL TO LOVERS OF JAPANESE FOOD AS WELL AS WINDSURFERS AND DIVERS**. This small complex of white, concrete buildings with pink-tile roofs has its own dive/sport shop with instructors on hand, and a restaurant specializing in Teppanyaki-style cooking. It also has a sushi bar. The one- and two-bedroom apartments have separate living areas, with lanais separated by louvered glass windows and sliding doors. All suites have attractive spic-and-span kitchens with blue-tiled floors, plus a washer and dryer, color TVs, and radios. A free-form pool and jacuzzi is situated in the center of the complex. An in-house activity desk will book tours for you upon request. Amenities: Jacuzzi, balcony or patio. 50 rooms. Credit cards: A, MC, V.

Punahoa Condominiums $90–$195 ★★
2142 Iliili Road, Kihei, 96753, Near Kalama Park,
☎ *(800) 564-4380,* ☎ *(808) 879-2720.*
Small and intimate, ALL OF THE 15 APARTMENTS IN THIS THREE-STORY PROPERTY FACE THE OCEAN. You have your choice of studios or one- or two-bedroom units, all with living rooms with sofa beds, large lanais (some corner units have two), fully equipped kitchens (including full sets of dinnerware), color cable TVs, and phones. The beach, while not directly in front of the Punahoa, is only 50 feet away, so you won't miss the lack of a pool unless you don't like saltwater. Beach towels are provided in rooms. There's not much else to do here, but if you use the place as a base to explore the Kihei area, you'll be happy with the prices; in low season, a studio for two runs as low as $66 a night! MANAGEMENT WILL GLADLY ASSIST YOU WITH CAR-RENTAL DEALS. Minimum stay is five nights. Amenities: balcony or patio, family plan. 15 rooms. Credit cards: not accepted.

Rentals

Kathy Scheper's Maui Accommodations $100 ★★
1587 North Alaniu Place, Kihei, 96753,
☎ *(800) 645-3753,* ☎ *(808) 879-8744, FAX (808) 879 -9100.*
Kathy Scheper offers several alternatives for your Maui beach vacation, ALL AT AN EXCELLENT PRICE. All accommodations are just steps away from world-class strands in the Kihei area. A TERRIFIC DEAL IS A CUSTOM-DESIGNED COTTAGE THAT KATHY SAYS IS PERFECT FOR HONEYMOONERS. The cottage is air-conditioned and features color cable TV, stereo, fully equipped kitchen, washer and dryer, and complete bedding. Also available are beach mats and coolers. Enjoy the warm evenings on a private patio with an umbrella-table set and Webber barbecue grill. Private covered parking is just outside the front door. Also on offer is a studio apartment for a single traveler or a couple on a budget. All bedding and towels are

provided, as are color cable TV and a radio. Kathy also offers an apartment that sleeps four in the Kai Nani Beach Condominiums, which is just across the street from Kamaole II beach park. It has a large master bedroom and private lanai, color cable TV, stereo, and full kitchen with utensils; bedding, beach gear, and even golf clubs and tennis rackets are supplied. Ask about monthly rates. There is a two-week minimum stay over the Christmas holidays. Amenities: balcony or patio. Three rooms. Credit cards: not accepted.

Ma'alaea Village
Condos

Makani A Kai $125–$200 ★★★

280 Hauoli Street, Ma'alaea Village, 96793, Near Ma'alaea Harbor, a few miles away from Kihei,

☎ (800) 367-6084, ☎ (808) 244-7012, FAX (808) 242-7476. http://www.extremezone.com/~maui/makani/makani.htm

This handsome low-rise condominium development in a tropical garden setting is one of the nicest of seven such properties situated side-by-side near the Maalaea Boat Harbor. **THE MAKANI A KAI SITS ON THE QUIETEST STRETCH OF A LOVELY FIVE-MILE BEACH THAT IS OFTEN NEGLECTED BY TOURISTS.** All of the one-, two- or three-bedroom units, set around a courtyard, have some views of the sea, but the most desirable oceanfront properties are often booked solid, especially in high season. Nearest to the Makani a Kai is the Hono Kai, with a half-moon-shaped pool right at the ocean's edge. There are laundry rooms on every floor, which is good for families with kids. Only two-bedroom apartments are available at the Kanai A Nalu, next door to the Hono Kai. Its palm-tree-lined courtyard features a waterfall, barbecues, and a freshwater pool. Common to all these sister properties are completely furnished kitchens with microwaves and dishwashers, color TVs, lanais, and direct-dial phones. The harbor location is **CONVENIENT TO WHALE-WATCHING, SNORKELING, FISHING, OR SUNSET DINNER CRUISES, AS WELL AS RESTAURANTS, A DELI AND STORE, AND EVEN A FRESH-FISH MARKET.** The hustle and bustle of Kihei is only 20 minutes away. Minimum stay is five nights. Amenities: balcony or patio. 24 rooms. Credit cards: MC, V.

Makena
Bed-and-Breakfasts

Vi & Boogie's Makena Landing Studios $95 ★★★
5100 Makena Road, Makena, 96753, Two miles from Wailea resorts, 18 miles from Kahului Airport,
☎ *(808) 879-6286.*

READERS RAVE ABOUT THIS OCEANFRONT B&B THAT DRAWS TONS OF REPEAT VISITORS. About a mile from Makena's famous Big Beach, Makena Landing Studios is situated in an enviable location with its expansive front lawn and concrete deck facing a lava-rock coastline. Close to the Wailea resorts, it's also AN EXCELLENT VANTAGE POINT FOR SPOTTING HUMPBACK WHALES IN SEASON. But the main reason for visiting is the warm welcome from owners Vi and Boogie Lu'uwai, a native Hawaiian couple who rent out two studio apartments with private entrances on opposite ends of the second floor of their comfortable cedar-wood home. They're also great cooks, providing a homemade gourmet breakfast each morning, plus snacks (three-night minimum stay required). The comfy studios have a queen-size bed, combination baths (including bathroom supplies), sparkling white kitchens with refrigerator, microwave, coffee maker and utensils, color TVs and private telephone, and oceanfront lanais. For all this bounty, is it so surprising that Vi and Boogie need prospective guests to reserve at least four months in advance? Amenities: balcony or patio. Two rooms. Credit cards: not accepted.

Resorts

Maui Prince Hotel $310–$1500 ★★★★★
5400 Makena Alanui Road, Makena, 96753,
☎ *(800) 321-MAUI,* ☎ *(808) 874-1111,*
FAX (808) 879-8530.
http://www.princeresortshawaii.coml

The Maui Prince Hotel, three miles from Wailea, is designed in a V-shape so that all of its guest rooms and suites have ocean views from their private lanais. Facing one of Maui's best—and surprisingly uncrowded—beaches, the hotel enjoys a tranquil sense of isolation. There's 24-hour room service from one of five excellent restaurants, including the award-winning Prince Court. Kaiseki dinners and sushi are both stellar in the traditionally decorated Hakone restaurant. Lighter meals are available álfresco at Café Kiowai. Besides splendid and uncrowded golf (36 holes) and tennis facilities (six courts), there are two oval pools (no waterslides), a catamaran to take guests to Molokini atoll, and a full-service ocean-activity center. The Prince Kids Club keeps youngsters (guests and nonguests) occupied. Complimentary shuttle to the neighboring Wailea resorts. Amenities: tennis, horseback riding, balcony or patio, family plan. 310 rooms. Credit cards: A, DC, MC, V.

Wailea
Condos

Maui Polo Beach Club $270–$380   ★★★
3750 Wailea Alanui Drive, Wailea, 96753,
☎ *(800) 367-5246,* ☎ *(808) 879-1595, FAX (808) 874-3554.*
http://www.polobeach.com/
The exterior of this staggered, white, eight-story condominium looks rather like a county hospital on the beach, but the designer interiors of the one- or two-bedroom apartments are handsomely furnished with overstuffed chaise lounges and couches in muted tones of white, beige, and taupe. All the better to set off the gorgeous ocean views from the wide lanais, which are roomy enough to contain another chaise lounge, this time in white wicker, as well as a table and chairs. All bedrooms have marble baths, and some have walk-in closets. Full kitchens and washer and dryer in all units. The complex is named after Polo Beach (no turf club in sight, however), a sheltered cove once named Dead Horse Beach; the new name is somewhat more palatable. **THERE'S EXCELLENT SNORKELING NEARBY**, and swimming is good in summer, but the Polo Beach Club also provides guests with an oceanfront pool and spa. Other facilities include a barbecue area; and special golf rates are available at Makena Resort. Daily concierge and maid service. Three-night minimum. Amenities: balcony or patio, family plan. 71 rooms. Credit cards: A, MC, V.

Wailea Ekahi Village $139–$319   ★★★
3750 Wailea Alanui Drive, Wailea, 96753,
☎ *(800) 367-5246,* ☎ *(808) 879-1595, FAX (808) 874-3554.*
http://waileaekahivillage.com/
Wailea Ekahi Village, a 34-acre property on handsome, half-mile-long Keawakupu Beach, is **ONE OF THE LOWEST-PRICED CONDOMINIUMS IN THIS SWANKY AREA**, but that doesn't trans-

HAWAII

late as low-quality. The studios and one- and two-bedroom apartments are situated on a terraced hillside, and all units come with a private lanai, fully equipped kitchens with microwaves, and washer and dryer. Some units are air-conditioned. Facilities include your choice of four pools, with one facing the ocean, two paddle tennis courts, and shuffleboard (do people really play shuffleboard anymore?). Special golf rates available at the neighboring Makena and Wailea resorts. Daily concierge and maid service. Three-night minimum stay. Amenities: balcony or patio. 55 rooms. Credit cards: A, MC, V.

Wailea Elua Village $285–$800   ★★★
3750 Wailea Alanui Drive, Wailea, 96753,
☎ *(800) 367-5246,* ☎ *(808) 879-1595, FAX (808) 874-3554.*
A LUXURIOUS, PRIVATE, AND GATED 24-ACRE CONDOMINIUM COMPLEX, Wailea Elua Village is located JUST STEPS AWAY FROM INTIMATE ULUA BEACH, which is frequented by film stars on holiday. Some of the spacious, high-ceilinged one-, two-, and three-bedroom condominiums have wraparound lanais with barbecue grills, perfect for private entertaining. All are centrally air-conditioned and equipped with full-size kitchens with all the amenities, as well as a washer and dryer. If you tire of the beach (beach chairs and cooler provided), which is ONE OF THE BEST SWIMMING, SNORKELING AND BODYSURFING STRETCHES IN WAILEA, there are two freshwater pools. Other facilities include a paddle tennis court, putting green, and beachfront pavilion with gas barbecue grill. Special golf rates are available at the neighboring Wailea and Makena resorts. You can also swing the old racket at one of the 14 professional courts (three grass) at the Wailea Tennis Club, called "Wimbledon of the West," which is adjacent to the Wailea Elua's sister property, the Grand Champions Resort. A beachfront walkway provides easy access to world-class restaurants and shopping. The hotel's concierge is on hand to arrange other amusements. There's a three-night minimum stay. Amenities: Jacuzzi, balcony or patio. 61 rooms. Credit cards: A, MC, V.

Wailea Grand Champions $195–$350   ★★★
3750 Wailea Alanui Drive, Wailea, 96753,
☎ *(800) 367-5246,* ☎ *(808) 879-1595, FAX (808) 874-3554.*
http://www.drhmaui.com/grand.htm

These classy, spacious condominium apartments on 11 rather crowded acres are sandwiched between the Wailea Tennis Club and Wailea Blue Golf course, so they're ideal for aspiring champions in either sport. The buff-colored two- and three-story buildings contain one- and two-bedroom apartments with either a garden view or partial ocean view from private lanais. Full of light from wide windows, the units have separate living areas with plush carpeting and rattan furniture (including swivel chairs), enhanced by potted plants. All are air-conditioned, and feature fully equipped kitchens with microwave, and a washer/dryer. Daily maid service. Facilities include two pools, two spas, and barbecue areas. **SPECIAL GOLF RATES AVAILABLE AT WAILEA AND MAKENA RESORTS.** Ask about tennis packages. Amenities: Jacuzzi, balcony or patio, family plan. 27 rooms. Credit cards: A, MC, V.

Resorts

Outrigger Wailea Resort   **$245–$1350**   BBBB
3700 Wailea Alanui Drive, Wailea, 96753,
☎ *(800) 321-2558,* ☎ *(808) 879-1922.*
http://www.outrigger.com/details/property.asp?code=owr

Formerly the Aston Wailea Resort and the Maui Inter-Continental, this is a 20-year veteran of the Wailea resort scene. Although already well-entrenched in its lovely 22-acre oceanfront spot, Outrigger aims to continue to preserve the property's tradition of being the most "Hawaiian" resort on this platinum coast. There are more than enough facilities to go around, including the beach, **THREE FRESHWATER SWIMMING POOLS** and a spa, two restaurants (**THE WHIMSICALLY NAMED HULA MOONS IS AN AWARD-WINNER**), a lounge, and championship tennis and golf nearby. Guest rooms and suites are spread out among seven rosy-roofed, low-slung buildings and a seven-story tower. Generously oversized, even a standard room measures at least 436 square feet. Each has a separate dressing and bath area. There are 46 suites with five floor plans. Mini-suites have a separate bedroom and living room, while the top-of-the line Ali'i Suite features two bedrooms, two baths, a living room, and dining room. Although not loaded with amenities, both suites and rooms include private lanais, mini-fridges, and color TVs with in-room movies. The Wailea has no health spa, but massage and body-care service are available on an on-call basis. Recommended for jet-lagged guests is a combination of Swedish, Oriental, and Shiatsu techniques. **A CHILDREN'S PROGRAM, CALLED CLUB GECKO, GIVES PARENTS A BREAK THURSDAY–SATURDAY.** The resort puts on an award-winning traditional luau every Tuesday, Thursday, and Friday from 5–8 p.m. Amenities: Jacuzzi, balcony or patio, business services. 516 rooms. Credit cards: A, DC, MC, V.

Four Seasons Resort Maui at Wailea $315–$5000 ★★★★★
3900 Wailea Alanui Drive, Wailea, 96753,
☎ *(800) 334-6284,* ☎ *(808) 874-8000, FAX (800) 874-6449.*
Rated restaurant: Seasons.
http://www.fourseasons.com/maui/index.html

This elegant beachfront property was the prestigious Four Seasons chain's first foray in the islands, and it's designed with architectural sensitivity, blending serenely within its environment. Several subtly colored buildings with pale-blue roofs, no higher than eight stories each, are oriented around the water, with stunning views from the public areas and guest rooms. Adjoining the lobby is an elegant bar-lounge overlooking the Pacific on one side and the West Maui mountains on the other. There are three additional restaurants, all facing the sea. Seasons, a special-occasion type of place, showcases American regional cuisine. Service has always been a hallmark of the Four Seasons; sometimes it's carried to an extreme here. Attendants spritz guests with Evian water at the cabana-dotted beach or by the pool(s). Chilled towels and ice water are replenished to prevent heat-stroke. Children are well looked after; the Kids for All Seasons program includes year-round supervised activities for youngsters ages five to 12. **EACH OF THE ROOMS AND SUITES ARE AT LEAST 600 SQUARE FEET**, with 85 percent boasting ocean views. All have private lanais, some have two. Soothing decor schemes include soft-cushioned rattan and wicker furnishings in peach and blue pastels, ceiling fans, wood shutters, and teak armoires. Striated marble baths include an eight-foot counter with double vanities, soaking tub, and separate shower. The activities desk can arrange everything from sport fishing to horseback adventures. Golf and additional tennis nearby. Amenities: tennis, health club, exercise room, Jacuzzi, sauna, balcony or patio, family plan, club floor, business services. 380 rooms. Credit cards: A, DC, MC, V.

Grand Wailea Resort Hotel and Spa $380–$3000   ★★★★
3850 Wailea Alanui Drive, Wailea, 96753,
☎ *(800) 888-6100,* ☎ *(808) 875-1234, FAX (808) 874-5143.*
http://www.grandwailea.com/

The Grand Wailea, an oceanfront spa resort completed at a cost of $600 million in 1991, is THE MOST EXPENSIVE HOTEL EVER BUILT IN HAWAII. The 42-acre oceanfront property (where even the employees get lost) is designed around a garden atrium with a marvelous excess of fountains, waterfalls, pools, and interconnecting waterways. You might opt for a chamber in the 100-room Napua Tower, with a 700-square-foot club room that starts at $580 a night. Prices go up to $1400 for a one-bedroom suite; the 5500-square-foot Grand Suite, where the hotel's billionaire owner usually resides when he's in town, is only a mere $10,000 a night. Actually a self-contained hotel within the resort, the Napua Tower features two lounges, where a complimentary continental breakfast, afternoon tea, and evening cocktails are served. But even if you can only afford a lower-echelon Terrace room ($380 per night), it will be at least 650 square feet, and all guest wings are positioned to face the ocean in some capacity. All are spectacular, with separate living, dining, and sleeping areas, louvered wooden windows, tile or polished wooden floors, Oriental carpets, and custom furnishings that include antique sculpture and porcelain pieces, inlaid-wood desks, and pencil-post two-poster beds. Huge tiled baths have plenty of counter space, sunken tubs, and separate shower areas. Amenities common to all include three phones, "inter-active" TVs, mini-bar, coffee maker, and lanais. THERE ARE EIGHT RESTAURANTS AND 12 LOUNGES, 14 TENNIS COURTS, SIX LANDSCAPED GARDENS (ONE FOR EACH WING), AND PROBABLY THE MOST TALKED-ABOUT BODY OF WATER ON THE ISLANDS, THE WAILEA CANYON ACTIVITY POOL. Sort of a Disneyland ride in miniature, the 2000-foot-long pool has valleys, water slides, waterfalls, caves, a rope swing, white water rapids, grottos, a Jacuzzi, and sauna. Amenities: tennis, health club, exercise room, Jacuzzi, sauna, balcony or patio, family plan, club floor, business services. 767 rooms. Credit cards: A, CB, DC, MC, V.

Kea Lani Hotel Suites & Villas $304–$2200   ★★★★★
4100 Wailea Alanui, Wailea, 96753, 25 minutes from Kahului Airport,

☎ *(800) 882-4100,* ☎ *(808) 875-4100, FAX (808) 875-1200.*
http://rghonline.com/articles/kealani.asp
The central feature of the resort are two huge, free-form, lagoon-style swimming pools connected by a 140-foot waterslide; one has a swim-up bar. Tented cabanas protect virgin skin from the sun's rays. The resort's beach activities center offers snorkel sets, boogie boards, floats, and more for rent. Whale-watching, deep-sea fishing, and other water-related activities can be arranged here. Beach butlers proffer cold towels, juices, snacks, and sightseeing tips. When you feel the need to crash, you'll have a lot of elbow room to do it in; accommodations are either in one-bedroom suites of at least 840 square feet of living space, or the dreamy split-level villas with one, two, or three bedrooms. Suites, some with ocean views, all have separate living areas with sofa beds and two private, double lanais. Amenities are legion; how about an entertainment center with a 21-inch TV and VCR plus a CD/DVD setup? There's an additional 19-inch TV in the bedroom, and laser discs and videos are available in the lobby. Add to that list a two-line phone with modem hook-up, wall safe, wet bar and refrigerator, microwave, and coffee maker. If you opt for a villa that sleeps up to eight adults (**MANY AFFORDABLE PACKAGES ARE AVAILABLE, INCLUDING USE OF A LUXURY CAR OR MINIVAN**), you'll get the same amenities as above, plus a private plunge pool and sun-deck, two marble bathrooms, gourmet kitchen with all the trimmings, and a washer-dryer. A Villa manager will take your order for groceries prior to check-in and have everything stocked for you when you arrive. Dining options include the Kea Lani Restaurant, offering Pacific cuisine in an open-air setting; Caffe Ciao, an upscale bakery-deli, and Polo Beach Grille and Bar, with a casual menu. Amenities: exercise room, Jacuzzi, balcony or patio, family plan, business services. 413 rooms. Credit cards: A, MC, V.

Renaissance Wailea Beach Resort   **$269–$400**   ★★★★
3550 Wailea Alanui Drive, Wailea, 96753, 17 miles from the Kahului Airport,
☎ *(800) 468-3571,* ☎ *(808) 879-4900, FAX (808) 874-5370.*
http://renaissancehotels.com/dpp/PropertyPage.asp?MarshaCode=HNMRN
Formerly owned by Stouffers (and now owned by Renaissance/Marriott), the Renaissance Wailea Resort is a trio

of six-story buildings set in a lushly overgrown and extensive tropical garden fronting semi-private, golden-grained Mokapu Beach, which is EXCELLENT FOR BATHING AND SNORKELING, AND RARELY USED BY ANYONE OTHER THAN HOTEL GUESTS. The 15.5-acre property also offers access to an impressive array of sporting activities, including the NEARBY WAILEA GOLF CLUB AND ITS THREE TOP-RATED, 18-HOLE GOLF COURSES, Blue, Gold, and Emerald. The Wailea Blue Course, designed by Arthur Jack Snyder, has been RATED BY GOLF DIGEST AS ONE OF THE STATE'S TOP FIVE. Amenities include three phones, two with fax-modem capabilities, cable TV and VCRs in armoires, mini-bar, and in-room safe. All have sitting areas with a loveseat and chaise lounge, and deluxe bath treats include double vanities, hair dryer, lighted makeup mirror, and his-and-her *hapi* (short Japanese robe) coats. Some suites have Jacuzzi tubs. The most desirable accommodations are in the Mokapu Beach Club, consisting of 26 beachfront rooms in three wings. In addition to the amenities offered in the regular rooms and suites, these choice spots also feature terry robes and a complimentary continental breakfast served on the private lanais. A plethora of dining and entertainment, all within arm's reach, is available at four restaurants and a lounge. Amenities: tennis, health club, exercise room, Jacuzzi, balcony or patio, family plan, business services. 347 rooms. Credit cards: A, DC, MC, V.

Upcountry
Kula

Bloom Cottage   **$125**   ßßß

229 Kula Highway, Kula, 96790,
☎ *(800) 262-9912,* ☎ *(808) 878-1425.*
http://www.hookipa.com/bloom_cottage.html

Surrounded by an herb and flower garden, this cute-as-a-button, white country cottage with green shutters on a one-acre property is A TERRIFIC DEAL. For $125 ($300 deposit required), you get the whole two-bedroom dwelling for yourself, including books and magazines, videos for the VCR, and a sewing basket in case you pop a button. The living room has a beamed ceiling, floral curtains, a big, wide, rattan couch with comfy pillows to sprawl out on, and a **FIREPLACE**! In the bedroom, the bamboo four-poster bed is topped with a handmade quilt, and room decor includes Victorian prints and a heritage koa rocking chair. Fresh, seasonal herbs scent the air. See

HAWAII

you there! **No children under 10 years** or pets. Amenities: balcony or patio. One room. Credit cards: not accepted.

Puluke's Farm $75 ★★
203 Wahelani Road, Kula, 96790,
☎ *(808) 878-3263, FAX (808) 878 -3263.*

The entrance to Haleakala Volcano Park is 10 minutes from the door of this B&B. Your accommodation is a studio with a queen-size bed on the second floor of a private home with a wrap-around deck overlooking the West Maui mountains on one side and an open valley with a patchwork quilt of farmer's fields on the other. The newly decorated unit has a private entrance (your hosts, the Lepolstats, live on the property), and is equipped with its own kitchen, full bath, and laundry facility. There's a color TV and VCR to keep you amused. The refrigerator is stocked with muffins, rolls, or croissants, as well as fresh fruit, juice, milk, and coffee so you can prepare your own breakfast. Because you're on a 3500 foot elevation, the temperature at night often drops to the low 50s (it rises rapidly to 75 degrees once the sun rises, though) so bring some warm clothes, which you'll need if you're going to visit the volcano. Puluke's Farm is a place where you won't need an alarm clock, as roosters crow at dawn to roust you out of bed. **Daily rates drop if you book the studio for three nights or more.** There's no maid service. Amenities: balcony or patio. One room. Credit cards: not accepted.

Inns

Kula Lodge and Restaurant $100–$175 ★★
On Highway 377, on the way to Haleakala Volcano Park, Kula, 96790, ☎ *(800) 233-1535,* ☎ *(808) 878-1535, FAX (808) 878 -2518.*
http://www.kulalodge.com/main_p.htm

Stellar views of the West Maui mountains plus a good restaurant are the main draws to this popular upcountry retreat, which has five rustic but comfortable cabins, some with fireplaces, available for your lounging pleasure. **Reservations should be made at least three months in advance, and if a fireplace is important to you, make sure you reserve Chalets No. 1 or 2.** The aforementioned chalets have queen-size beds, a private porch, and stairs leading to a loft with twin beds; these are the nicest and priciest. Next in line are Nos. 3 and 4, which are fun for kids and adults masquerading as kids, as they have a ladder leading to a sleeping loft with a set of futon beds. It also has queen beds and a private porch. The fifth Chalet has only one story, plus a queen-size bed and private porch. None of the chalets have TV or phones. The front desk will take messages, and there is fax service as well as public phones on the premises. **THE KULA LODGE RESTAURANT IS ONE OF THE LAST DINING PLACES ON THE WAY TO THE SUMMIT OF HALEAKALA.** As you would expect, early-morning sunrise breakfast and sunset supper times are the most desirable, so get there early (it's open from 6:30 a.m. to 9 p.m. daily). **A FABULOUS, REASONABLY-PRICED ACCOMODATION FOR THOSE WHO HATE THE HUSTLE AND BUSTLE OF LARGER ESTABLISHMENTS.** Amenities: balcony or patio. Five rooms. Credit cards: MC, V.

Ranches

Silver Cloud Upcountry Guest Ranch $85–$150 ★★★

Old Thompson Road, Kula, 96790, 35 minutes from Kahului Airport, ☎ *(808) 878-6101, FAX (808) 878 -2132.*
http://www.silvercloudranch.com

A SPECTACULAR VALUE. Silver Cloud Ranch, in the Ulupalalua area of upcountry Maui, was originally part of Thompson Ranch, which was founded in 1902. The nine-acre property, with 11 rooms and suites located in the former plantation house and a cowboy bunkhouse plus a self-contained cottage, is a **FINE ALTERNATIVE VACATION CHOICE FOR THOSE WHO THINK THE BEACH AREAS ARE TOO CROWDED.** The guest rooms in the Plantation Home have private baths, many with their own entrances. The spacious, second-floor King Kamehameha and Queen Emma suites command breathtaking panoramic views. The Paniolo (cowboy) Bunkhouse apartments feature roomy studios with kitchenettes, large bathrooms, and lanais providing views of the ocean or the mountain. The Haleakala Suite, with both ocean and mountain views, is a special part of the Paniolo Bunkhouse, with a separate living and bedroom area, fireplace, full kitchen, and lanai. The romantic and private Lanai Cottage, surrounded by its own flower gardens, has a private porch where you can greet the sun or bid it adieu daily. Warmed indoors by a wood-burning stove, it has a king-size bed, complete kitchen, and a big red bathtub (there's no shower) that you can fill up with bubble bath. Everyone gets breakfast, which is served in a garden sunroom adjacent to the kitchen in the Plantation Home; YOU'RE ALSO WELCOME TO USE THE KITCHEN TO PREPARE LUNCH OR DINNER. None of the accommodations has phones, but messages are posted on a bulletin board, and there's a common telephone in the living room. Fax service is available. In keeping with the ranch ambience (it's no longer a working ranch), Silver Cloud has a lot of furry and four-footed friends, including three horses, a pot-bellied pig named Rupert, Daisy the cow, hens that lay eggs, and some very friendly cats. You might be tempted to take them into your room, but the hosts advise against this, since fellow guests may have allergies. The owners live in the caretaker's cottage next to the Plantation Home and are almost always on hand if you need them or have any questions. Maid service is provided after the fourth day of your visit. Amenities: balcony or patio. 12 rooms. Credit cards: MC, V.

West Maui

Honokawai
Condos

Papakea Oceanfront Resort $119–$204 ★★
3543 Lower Honoapiilani Highway, Honokawai, 96761, Between Kapalua and Kaanapali Beach,
☎ *(800) 367-7052,* ☎ *(808) 669-4848, FAX (808) 661-4683.*
PERFECT FOR FAMILIES AND COUPLED VACATIONERS, this establishment is a low-key, low-rise condominium on 13 well-tended acres offering two pools and a sauna to make up for its lack of a good swimming beach. But the sparkling sands of Kapalua and Kaanapali are close by, so if you're the type who doesn't need to step directly into the ocean from your room, this property may suffice. The setting is quite lovely, with three of its 11 red-roofed buildings situated almost directly on the seawall. An activities desk is on hand to assure that guests don't get bored, and there are weekly happenings planned, including island orientations, "swimmercize classes," putting tournaments (on two 18-hole putting greens), tennis clinics, and round robins (three lighted tennis courts). Individually furnished apartments range from studios with sofa beds and baths with shower only to two-bedroom suites with deluxe combination baths and king or double beds. All have fully equipped kitchens, spacious private lanais, washer/dryer, ceiling fans (no air conditioning), and color TV. Daily maid service is provided,

which is ideal for families with kids. Amenities: tennis, Jacuzzi, balcony or patio. 364 rooms. Credit cards: MC, V.

Kaanapali

Aston Kaanapali Shores $175–$1000   ★★★
3445 Honoapiilani Highway, Kaanapali, ☎ *(800) 922-7866.*
http://www.kaanapalishores-maui.com/
Aston's most complete resort on a strategic stretch of Kaanapali Beach, this nine-story property offers a wide range of units FOR COUPLES AND FAMILIES, AS WELL AS A YEAR-ROUND CAMP PROGRAM FOR CHILDREN. Air-conditioned accommodations include lanai-less hotel rooms with refrigerators only, and studio, one-, and two-bedroom condominium apartments with gourmet kitchens, washer-dryers, and private lanais. Amenities include color TVs and in-room safes. There's daily maid service. Free tennis, putting green, video game room, beauty salon, gift/apparel shop, restaurant, guest activities desk. Amenities: tennis, health club, Jacuzzi, sauna, balcony or patio, family plan, business services. 430 rooms. Credit cards: MC, V.

Maui Kaanapali Villas $162–$342   ★★★
45 Kai Ala Drive, Kaanapali, 96761,
☎ *(800) 922-7866,* ☎ *(808) 667-7791.*
http://www.hotels-maui.com/maui-kaanapali-villas/
This bright, attractive Aston property on an 11-acre oceanfront estate is surrounded by pools and gardens. Featured are hotel rooms and condo units. All rooms are air-conditioned and feature refrigerators, while spacious studios and one-bedroom condo suites have complete kitchens. Amenities include three pools, a restaurant, shuffleboard, and shuttle to nearby golf. Note: Since all condo units are individually owned, the number of available units at any one time varies. Amenities: Jacuzzi, balcony or patio, family plan. 200 rooms. Credit cards: A, DC, MC, V.

Resorts

Embassy Suites Resort $329–$1500   ★★★★
104 Kaanapali Shores Place, Kaanapali, 96761,
☎ *(800) 462-6284,* ☎ *(808) 661-2000, FAX (808) 667-5821.*
http://www.embassy-maui.com/
This trio of flamingo-pink towers, located on north Kaanapali Beach, was the first to offer the all-suites concept to Hawaii

HAWAII

when it opened in 1988. It's proven to be a wild success, especially with families looking for the space associated with condo living plus the added amenities and services of pricier resorts. The one- and two-bedroom suites, at 820 and 1100 square feet, respectively, are nearly twice the size of most first-class hotel rooms. Decor standards (as well as prices) are much higher than comparable Embassy Suites on the mainland. A minikitchen is equipped with a microwave, refrigerator with ice maker, wet bar, and coffee maker, with Kona coffee replaced daily. Lanais can be accessed from either the living area or bedroom. Included in all this largesse is a complimentary breakfast buffet of fruit, pastries, cereals, and juices, as well as cooked-to-order omelettes. Unlike most Embassy Suites hotels, where the morning repast is all that's offered, lunch and dinner—as well as snacks and to-go items—are available from three venues. The offerings at the white-napkin North Beach Grille, with an oceanfront vista, run the gamut from seafood to pasta, and what the resort calls "Maui's finest salad bar." At poolside is the Ohana Grill (no "e"), where homemade pizza can be eaten in bathing attire. Adjacent to the lobby is the Deli Planet, where sandwich makings or picnic baskets can be prepared for meals on the run. What do to for fun on-site? Shoot into the one-acre pool via a water slide, rent snorkeling equipment, take a windsurfing lesson, or luxuriate in the spa. **THERE'S A SEVEN-DAY, YEAR-ROUND "BEACH BUDDIES" PROGRAM FOR KIDS (AGES 4–10).** Amenities: exercise room, Jacuzzi, balcony or patio, family plan, business services. 413 rooms. Credit cards: A, CB, DC, D, MC, V.

Hyatt Regency Maui $315–$900   ★★★★★
200 Nohea Kai Drive, Kaanapali, 96761,
☎ *(800) 233-1234,* ☎ *(808) 661-1234, FAX (808) 667-4498.*
http://www.mauihyatt.com

The Hyatt Regency Maui was first in a series of increasingly spectacular "mega-resorts" that have popped up in profusion all over the islands. Three connecting **TOWERS OVERLOOK FANTASTIC GARDENS**, including the vast swimming pool with its network of waterfalls, a grotto, 130-foot water slide, rope swing, and swim-up cocktail bar. **A TOURIST ATTRACTION IN AND OF ITSELF, THE RESORT ALSO HAS ITS OWN WILDLIFE PARK**, a collection of Asian and Pacific Art valued at more than $2 million, teak-paneled and Chinese-carpeted elevators, and a special, rooftop, deep-space telescope, called "Big Blue." Guests and the general public are treated to a guided tour of the Hawaiian skies three nights a week in a popular show presented by the Hyatt's resident "Director of Astronomy." The resort offers a bountiful array of services, including **"CAMP HYATT" (A CHILDREN'S PROGRAM)**, watersports, game room, library, six hard-surface tennis courts, access to championship golf courses, bike rental, and shops. There are a number of excellent, but pricey, restaurants and lounges, including the Lahaina Provision Company, featuring a Chocoholic Bar, and the Swan Court, winner of a Travel Holiday award and named one of the **TOP 10 MOST ROMANTIC RESTAURANTS** in the world by "Lifestyles of the Rich and Famous." Amenities: tennis, health club, exercise room, Jacuzzi, sauna, balcony or patio, club floor, business services. 815 rooms. Credit cards: A, DC, MC, V.

The Westin Maui $325–$3500 ★★★★★

2365 Kaanapali Parkway, Kaanapali, 96761, Three miles west of Lahaina, ☎ *(800) 228-3000,* ☎ *(808) 667-2525, FAX (808) 661-5764.*
http://www.westinmaui.com/

Set upon a fine stretch of Kaanapali Beach, The Westin Maui's two guest towers and public rooms are surrounded by an extensive series of water gardens and lagoons and a vast pool area that's really an aquatic playground, with two waterslides, waterfalls, and a swim-up Jacuzzi hidden in a grotto. The poshest quarters are in the Royal Beach Club, sort of a penthouse within a luxury hotel, **PERFECT FOR EXECUTIVES WHO FEEL GUILTY ABOUT LEAVING THEIR OFFICES**. Unique to the Westin (and Hawaii) is the **JAPANESE GUEST SERVICES DEPARTMENT**, providing separate check-in and translation services. Honeymooners will be gratified to know that the resort also has an **ON-SITE DIRECTOR OF ROMANCE, THE ONLY ONE IN THE STATE**. Guests and nonguests alike are invited to tour the 12-acre property's wildlife, botanical, and art collections; call the concierge for information. Additional services include a children's program and camp, ocean activities center, watersports, massage services, **HIKING AND HISTORICAL TOURS,** and shuttle to off-site tennis and golf. Amenities: health club, Jacuzzi, sauna, balcony or patio, family plan, club floor, business services. 761 rooms. Credit cards: A, CB, DC, MC, V.

Kaanapali Beach
Condos

The Whaler — $220–$645 ★★★

2481 Kaanapali Parkway, Kaanapali Beach, 96761,
☎ *(800) 367-7052,* ☎ *(808) 661-4861, FAX (808) 367-7052.*
http://www.the-whaler.com/Oceanside Resorts/Whaler/

Right NEXT DOOR TO THE SHOPPING WONDERS OF WHALERS VILLAGE and ACROSS THE STREET FROM THE ROYAL KAANAPALI GOLF COURSE, the Whaler is a beachfront condominium where you won't have to go far to amuse yourself. But if neither of the above activities turns your crank, you can take a dip in the pool or luxuriate in the spa that separates the complex's two 12-story buildings. Other diversions include an exercise room and sauna, five tennis courts with a pro shop and, of course, there's the beach, which is divine for swimming. A beach-activities center is adjacent for renting gear or arranging a scuba, snorkeling, or sailing expedition. Accommodations consist of studios, one- and two-bedroom apartments, and a presidential suite. Some have full or partial ocean views, others garden vistas, but all are spacious enough (largest ones can sleep six), and designer standards are high, with a remarkable lack of the usual floral print fabrics. The Whaler offers guests plenty of conveniences, including 24-hour desk and switchboard, wake-up calls, daily maid service, concierge, coin-laundry, dry cleaning, mini-mart, and lots of free underground parking. IF YOU MUST STAY IN A HIGH-RISE, THE WHALER IS A GOOD CHOICE. Amenities: tennis, Jacuzzi, sauna, balcony or patio, family plan. 360 rooms. Credit cards: A, CB, DC, MC, V.

Hotels

Kaanapali Beach Hotel — $165–$595 ★★★

2525 Kaanapali Parkway, Kaanapali Beach, 96761,
☎ *(800) 262-8450,* ☎ *(808) 661-0011, FAX (808) 667-5978.*
http://www.kbhmaui.com/resort/rates.html

In case you're wondering, part of Old Hawaii does exist on Kaanapali Beach's gold coast, in the form of this U-shaped, old-fashioned, and nicely time-weathered resort hotel, where employees are asked to attend regular classes (on company time, no less) on Hawaiian culture and values. In turn, staff members share with guests what they've learned, in the form of ti-leaf skirt-making, lauhala weaving, and even pineapple-cutting instruction. **ONE OF THE HOTEL'S LOVELIEST TRADITIONS IS THE FRIDAY NIGHT SPIRIT OF ALOHA,** at which employees from different departments sing traditional songs, dance the hula, and present hand-fashioned crafts. Delighted by complimentary coffee parties and other sincere gestures, some returnees couldn't even dream of staying anywhere else. Accommodations, spread over four guest wings, are decidedly unflashy, but generally satisfying. Some have two queen beds or one king bed and marble combination baths (except in the older Molokai Wing). Some have ocean or partial ocean views; lower-priced units have vistas of the courtyard or garden, but all have private lanais. Amenities include refrigerators, in-room safes, coffee makers, and color TVs with movies. Besides a whale-shaped pool, the hotel has a beach-activities center and offers **FREE SCUBA LESSONS.** Boogie boards and other gear can be rented here as well. Whalers Village and other shopping centers are close by, but there are a couple of on-site stores for souvenirs and such. Among the hotel's three eateries is the affordably priced Mixed Plate (formerly the Koffee Shop), which offers all-you-can-eat buffets three times a day. The Tiki Terrace is open daily for breakfast and dinner and features Hawaiian specialties, plus a Sunday Champagne brunch. Snacks and drinks by the pool can be had at the Tiki Grill and Tiki Bar, respectively. If you're still hungry for more, **AUNTIE ALOHA'S RAUCOUS BREAKFAST LUAU IS A REGULAR HAPPENING.** Amenities: balcony or patio, family plan, business services. 431 rooms.

Resorts

Maui Marriott   **$240–$400**   ★★★★
100 Nohea Kai Drive, Kaanapali Beach, 96761, Off Highway 30 from Lahaina,
☎ *(800) 228-9290,* ☎ *(808) 667-1200, FAX (808) 667-2047.*
<http://www.marriott.com>
Unsurprising, reliable, and comfortable, the 720-room Maui Marriott resort is composed of two multi-windowed, white, mid-rise buildings situated around an open-air courtyard planted generously with lush foliage and tropical flowers. **ONE OF ITS BIG DRAWS IS ITS LOCATION:** The resort sits on a choice stretch of sugary white sand smack dab (or darn close to) the center of Kaanapali Beach. Almost all the oversized rooms and

suites are positioned to face the sea. There are plenty of dining and entertainment options, including Banana Moon, Maui's only video disco. Lava rock waterfalls splash through two freeform, interconnecting swimming pools, and there are a twin pair of whirlpool spas. **CHILDREN HAVE THEIR OWN POOL AND KEIKI PROGRAM IN THE SUMMER.** Off-site activities include 36 holes of championship golf at the adjacent Royal Kaanapali Golf Course. Souvenirs, gifts, and forgotten items can be picked up at 18 retail shops on the premises. **ONE WARNING: THE OCEAN DIRECTLY IN FRONT OF THE HOTEL MAY BE LOVELY, BUT ISN'T GREAT FOR SWIMMING, DUE TO RIPTIDES, POWERFUL SHOREBREAKS, AND OTHER NASTY THINGS.** Amenities: tennis, exercise room, Jacuzzi, balcony or patio, family plan, business services. 720 rooms. Credit cards: A, CB, MC, V.

Kahana
Condos

Kahana Sunset $150–$235 ★★★

4909 L. Honoapiilani Highway, Kahana, 96761,
☎ *(800) 669-1488,* ☎ *(808) 669-8011, FAX (808) 669-9170.*
These are fairly luxurious condos situated on tropical gardens planted with hundreds of exotic plants, flowers, and shrubs. **IT FRONTS A HIDDEN, REEF-PROTECTED BAY AND A SAFE, SANDY BEACH.** On offer are one-bedroom, one-bath apartments, and two-bedroom, two-bath townhouses with ocean and garden views, as well as split-level "executive" oceanfront townhouses with two bedrooms and 2.5 baths. All have private lanais, but the townhouses have lanais on both levels. Amenities common to all include ceiling fans, color cable TV, fully equipped kitchens with microwaves, refrigerators with ice-makers, and a washer and dryer. There's a garden-side pool and barbecue pits on the property, but not much else; sightseeing and entertainment are within a short driving distance away. Amenities: balcony or patio. 79 rooms. Credit cards: MC, V.

Kahana Village $185–$355 ★★★

4531 Honoapiilani Road, Kahana, 96761,
☎ *(800) 824-3065,* ☎ *(808) 669-5111, FAX (808) 669-0974.*
http://www.maui.net/~village/kahana.html
These low-rise, two-story condominium apartments, facing a quiet cove and reef-protected white sand beach, **OFFER A LOT**

OF AMENITIES FOR YOUR VACATION DOLLAR. Lots of space, for one thing. All ground-level apartments are 1700 square feet, with two or three bedrooms and two full baths with a sunken tub in the master bath, plus a study and wet bar. The second-floor units are a bit smaller, at 1200 square feet, but they all have at least two bedrooms and two full baths; the second bedroom is a loft. **CONSIDER THESE IF YOU LIKE A LOT OF SUNSHINE, SINCE THEY FEATURE SKYLIGHTS AND OPEN-BEAM CEILINGS.** Large private lanais with loungers offer partial or prime ocean views. Other amenities include a washer-dryer and telephone. Most apartments can accommodate up to six persons. Designers didn't stint on the facilities outside the rooms, either. The 40-foot oval pool features an oversize deck, and there's a beachside pavilion and private entertainment center with a Jacuzzi and barbecue. The property is positioned somewhat away from the rest of Kahana, but is a short drive from championship golf and tennis and the shopping and restaurant opportunities in Kaanapali and Lahaina. There's a five-day minimum stay. Amenities: Jacuzzi, balcony or patio, family plan. 42 rooms. Credit cards: not accepted.

Mahina Surf $110–$190 ★★★

4057 Lower Honoapiilani Road, Kahana, 96761,
☎ *(800) 367-6086,* ☎ *(808) 669-6068.*
http://www.mahinasurf.com/

The Mahina Surf is situated on a two-acre spread facing a handsomely designed lawn and a big, oceanfront pool with barbecue facilities. These **BUDGET CONDOMINIUM APARTMENTS ARE IDEAL FOR FAMILIES** and include one-bedroom units that sleep from two to four people, and two-bedroom, 1.5, or two-bath units that accommodate up to six comfortably. Features available throughout the complex include separate living areas, full-size, kitchens with all the appliances needed for a carefree vacation (unless you're the chef). All have phones and color TVs and VCRs. There's a three-night minimum stay, and extra persons, including children, are charged $8 per night. Amenities: balcony or patio. 56 rooms. Credit cards: MC, V.

Noelani $87–$170 ★★★

4095-L Honoapiilani Road, Kahana, 96761,
☎ *(800) 367-6030,* ☎ *(808) 669-8374, FAX (808) 669-7904.*
http://www.noelani-condo-resort.com/

Adjacent to a **PERFECT SANDY COVE WITH A SMALL BEACH FOR SUNNING AND SNORKELING**, all of the 50 privately owned oceanfront condos at Noelani have private lanais. Studios and spacious one-, two-, and three-bedroom units are comfortably furnished in light pastels and wood-and-rattan furnishings. All have complete kitchens; studios have microwaves and access to laundry facilities, while the larger apartments feature a washer and dryer and dishwashers. Amenities include ceiling fans, color cable TV, and VCRs. Linen and guest supplies are provided, and a maid comes in to clean midweek. Recreational facilities include two partially hand-tiled seaside pools with barbecues, where new guests are treated to continental breakfast and an island "orientation." **ASK ABOUT SPECIAL CAR-RENTAL PACKAGES AND OFF-SEASON RATES.** Extra person charge is $7.50 per day. Amenities: balcony or patio. 50 rooms. Credit cards: A, MC, V.

Polynesian Shores $135–$245 ★★★
3975 Lower Honoapiilani Road, Kahana, 96761,
☎ *(800) 433-MAUI,* ☎ *(808) 669-6065,*
FAX (808) 669-0909.
http://www.maui.net/~polyshor/

A fun, partylike atmosphere permeates from this airy, pleasantly designed, two-acre property consisting of several staggered, two-story wooden buildings separated from each other by a heated pool and a well-tended lawn. Besides the lovely (but **ROCKY) OCEANFRONT LOCATION (A SANDY BEACH IS NEARBY)**, the focal point is a wide redwood deck at the water's edge supplied with barbecues and tables and chairs. Lit by tiki torches in the evening, this is where management passes out appetizers (pupus) so all guests may partake and meet one another. These affairs happen in winter, when humpback whales put on a show directly in view of the revelers. The pleasantly furnished, one-, two-, and three bedroom units (some with lofts, cathedral ceilings, and three baths) are reached by neatly landscaped pathways. All feature wide, wrap-around lanais with excellent views. They are fully furnished and have complete kitchens, including microwave, dishwasher, toaster, blender, and coffee maker, as well as all utensils. Cable TV and direct-dial phones in all units. A coin-operated laundry is on the premises. **CONTACT THE MANAGEMENT FOR PREFERRED CAR-RENTAL RATES.** Three-night minimum stay, deposit required. Amenities: balcony or patio, family plan. 52 rooms. Credit cards: D, MC, V.

Kapalua
Resorts

Kapalua Bay Hotel & Villas $350–$4500   ★★★★

*One Bay Drive, Kapalua, 96761, 10 miles north of Lahaina,
☎ (800) 367-8000, ☎ (808) 669-5656, FAX (808) 669-4694.*
<http://www.kapaluabayhotel.com/>

The 1800-acre property's somewhat-isolated location, on a private pineapple plantation fronted by ONE OF HAWAII'S (AND POSSIBLY THE WORLD'S) MOST BEAUTIFUL BEACHES, draws seasoned travelers who welcome the quiet, understated elegance of the hotel's design, a series of low-rise structures surrounded by beautifully landscaped tropical grounds, The ivy-draped, open-air lobby is particularly pleasant, with views of the ocean and a profusion of orchids. SERVICE SEEMS TO BE A STRONG POINT, with new arrivals greeted like VIPs by smiling staff members offering leis (the floral kind), perfumed towels, and glasses of guava juice. The subtlety in decor is carried on to the 194 oversized (more than 500 square feet) rooms and suites with ocean or garden views. While sleeping quarters are comfortable enough, the marble baths are spectacular, supplied with thoughtful features such as his-and-her vanities, robes, hair dryers, make-up mirrors, and a selection of skin products. Clustered nicely on a hillside, the resort's 100 one- and two-bedroom villas offer even more space and a modicum of independent living, with fully equipped kitchens and washer/dryers, in addition to the same features offered in the hotel rooms. VILLA GUESTS ENJOY THE SERVICES, RESTAURANTS, AND LEISURE FACILITIES OF THE HOTEL, BUT ALSO HAVE THEIR OWN POOLS. Grocery delivery is available. ALWAYS A GOLFER'S RETREAT, THE RESORT OFFERS THREE CHAMPIONSHIP 18-HOLE COURSES. Two, the oceanview Bay Course and the Village Course, which rises into the scenic Maui Mountains, were designed by Arnold Palmer. The Plantation Course, the newest of the trio, was designed by Ben Crenshaw and Bill Coore. Tennis enthusiasts aren't neglected either, with a choice of 20 Plexipave courts lit for night play. Lazier types can sun or swim on one of three white-sand beaches, snorkel, scuba-dive, and attack the waves on a boogie board; a beach-activities center rents gear and arranges watersports and lessons. Two pools provide freshwater relief. There are stables nearby for horseback riding. A CHILDREN'S PROGRAM, KAMP KAPALUA, IS OFFERED TO YOUNGSTERS AGES FIVE–12. For $25 per child ($45 for two), a whole week's worth of supervised fun is planned (Monday–Friday only), including Hawaiian games, a nature walk, snorkeling, exotic fruit-tasting, and more. Other features: shopping adjacent to hotel, beauty salon, resort and airport shuttle, baby-sitting. Amenities: tennis, exercise room, balcony or patio, family plan, business services. 294 rooms. Credit cards: A, MC, V.

The Ritz-Carlton Kapalua $350–$2800 ★★★★★
One Ritz-Carlton Drive, Kapalua, 96761,
☎ *(800) 241-3333,* ☎ *(808) 669-6200, FAX (808) 665-0026.*
http://www.ritzcarlton.com/

A TRULY SPECTACULAR ACCOMODATION, The Ritz-Carlton Kapalua is one of the newer additions to the Kapalua luxury resort scene, designed in the traditional Hawaiian style of the late 19th century. Located on a stunning 37-acre hillside property sloping down to a lovely white-sand beach, the resort, consisting of two six-story wings, features oversized guest rooms with private lanais; 80 percent overlook the sea. The 58 extra-spacious suites are the most desirable accommodations, but common amenities include marble bathrooms with separate tub and stall shower, double vanities, make-up mirror, hairdryer, phone, plush terry his-and-her bathrobes, fully stocked honor bar and refrigerator, color TV, and in-room safe. Extra services and a sense of privacy can be yours in the deluxe Ritz Carlton Club, on the top three floors of the Napili wing. A specially cut key opens the elevator to this exclusive enclave with a private lounge staffed by a concierge. Guests can repair here several times a day for complimentary continental breakfast, afternoon tea, evening hors d'oeuvres, and after-dinner chocolates. Cocktails and beverages are served continuously. The Ritz-Carlton GLADLY WELCOMES AND CATERS TO LARGE GROUPS, with a 143-seat amphitheater (the only one in a Maui hotel), two ballrooms, and two boardrooms with fireplaces. The Kapalua Golf Club, surrounding the hotel, offers 54 championship holes. Rates include complimentary use of the on-site health facility. Some activities, such as power walking and aqua aerobics, are free; others, including yoga classes, massage therapy, aromatherapy, and reflexology, require an extra charge. ONE OF THE AREA'S BEST DINING ROOMS, the Anuenue Room (formerly The Grill), is on resort property, serving light island cuisine, with herbs grown in the Ritz-Carlton garden. It has piano entertainment nightly. There are five other eateries and lounges, including the Beach House and Bar, for casual snacks, lunches, and cocktails. If you are thinking of getting hitched on Maui, be aware that THE RESORT EMPLOYS ITS OWN "HONEYMOON COORDINATOR." She can work with potential newlyweds as long as two months in advance of arrival. Additional amenities and facilities include: Artists in Residence Program, "RITZ KIDS" CHILDREN'S PROGRAM DAILY EXCEPT SUNDAY, 24-hour room service, nightly turn-down, valet service, complimentary airport shuttle, car rental, baby-sitting, shops, beauty salon. Amenities: tennis, health club, exercise room, Jacuzzi, sauna, balcony or patio, family plan, club floor, business services. 550 rooms. Credit cards: A, CB, DC, MC, V.

Lahaina
Bed-and-Breakfasts

Blue Horizons $99–$119 ★★★

3894 Mahinahina Street, Lahaina, 96761,
☎ *(800) 669-1948,* ☎ *(808) 669-1965, FAX (808) 661-1896.*
http://www.bluehorizonsmaui.com/

Jim and Beverly Spence, originally from Atlanta, welcome guests from all over the world to their two-story custom home located between Kahana Beach and Honokawai Beach Park. Convenient to Kaanapali and Kapalua resort areas, this B&B offers FIVE AFFORDABLE ROOMS AND SUITES, ALL WITH PRIVATE BATHS. All accommodations are air-conditioned, with color TVs. The Spences provide a large breakfast spread every day except Sunday, and everyone is welcome to use their gourmet kitchen, which is fully equipped with a dishwasher, microwave, and coffee maker. When not out seeing the sights, guests can barbecue, swim in the tiled pool, or lounge in the spacious, high-ceilinged living room with a VCR and videotape library. For beach forays (just a short stroll away), the Spences loan out beach gear. They can also assist with activity advice and CAR-RENTAL DISCOUNT PACKAGES. Additional amenities include a washer and dryer and iron and ironing board. Amenities: balcony or patio. Five rooms. Credit cards: A, MC, V.

Garden Gate Bed and Breakfast $69–$125 ★★

67 Kaniau Road, Lahaina, 96761,
☎ *(808) 661-8800, FAX (808) 667-7999.*

http://www.gardengatebb.com/
PERFECT FOR THE BUDGET-MINDED TRAVELER AND LOCATED JUST TWO BLOCKS FROM THE BEACH and a few minutes from Lahaina Town, this serene B&B on a quarter-acre consists of a 475-square-foot Garden Studio, suitable for up to four people with a queen-size bed, queen sleeper-sofa, sitting room with TV, telephone, and private combination bath. A wide private deck overlooks the ocean. If you stay in the studio, which has its own kitchen, you'll find it stocked with local fruits, cereals, Kona coffee, and other breakfast fixin's for you to dish up when you please. Your hosts, Ron and Welmoet Glover, deliver fresh-baked French pastries, muffins, or a loaf of bread to your door daily. The Glovers are more than willing to recommend fun stuff to do in Maui. There's a three-night minimum stay. Smoking allowed outdoors only. Amenities: Jacuzzi, balcony or patio. Two rooms. Credit cards: not accepted.

Old Lahaina House $69–$205   ★★
PO Box 10355, Lahaina, 96761,
☎ *(800) 847-0761,* ☎ *(808) 667-4663, FAX (808) 667-5615.*
http://www.oldlahaina.com/
If you like REASONABLY PRICED B&B living, Old Lahaina House could be the perfect place to stay on Maui. Only two blocks away from the hubbub of Lahaina Town, it's in a quiet, peaceful neighborhood, just ACROSS THE STREET FROM A BEACH POPULAR WITH LOCAL SURFERS. All rooms are air-conditioned, and feature TVs and phones. Breakfast consists of fresh pastries from a French bakery, fruit, juice, hot beverages, and locally made jams and jellies. Lots of socializing goes on in and around the pool area, where guests can splash around with the assorted water toys provided. Amenities: balcony or patio. Five rooms. Credit cards: A, MC, V.

The Guesthouse $55–$89   ★★★
1620 Ainakea Road, Lahaina, 96761,
☎ *(800) 621-8942,* ☎ *(808) 661-8085, FAX (808) 661-1896.*
More than half the guests at this DELIGHTFUL B&B are repeat visitors, and some never leave, including a local tour operator who booked a room and is still there after two years. The Guesthouse is situated in a one-mile stretch of residential homes between Lahaina and Kaanapali Beach. All suites have a queen-size bed (three have an additional twin bed), color TV

with remote control, refrigerator, phone, and private lanai. Bargain-hunters can opt for a room that shares a bath with the hosts. It has most of the amenities the suites have, except for the spa and lanai. Guests are allowed free rein in the quiet living room, which has floor-to-ceiling windows overlooking an attractive pool. Picnic and beach supplies are provided in the laundry room. Breakfast includes Hawaiian coffee, home-baked bread, and tropical fruits and juices, in addition to a hot repast of French toast or banana pancakes. When they aren't busy attending to guests, **YOUR HOSTS ALSO OPERATE A TOUR COMPANY AND CAN OFFER SPECIAL CAR-RENTAL RATES AND DISCOUNTS ON ISLAND ACTIVITIES. NOT SUITABLE FOR CHILDREN UNDER 12.** Amenities: Jacuzzi, balcony or patio. Five rooms. Credit cards: A, D, MC, V.

Condos

Honokeana Cove Resort Condominiums $103–$200 ★★

5255 Lower Honoapiilani Road, Lahaina, 96761, Eight miles north of Lahaina, one mile north of Kapalua Resort,
☎ *(800) 237-4948,* ☎ *(808) 669-6441, FAX (808) 669-8777.*
http://www.honokeana-cove.com/

SNORKELING FANS WILL DELIGHT IN THE PRIVATE COVE TEEMING WITH TROPICAL FISH AND SEA TURTLES right in front of this peaceful condominium property. Personable and small, Honokeana Cove offers 38 units contained in a series of naturally weathered brown-shingled buildings, some with ocean views. Management stresses that staying here is like being a guest in someone's second home instead of "an impersonal hotel room," and in each individually decorated one-, two-, and three-bedroom unit (some with a loft) you'll find a blender and microwave in the kitchen, a VCR, and cable TV. Families (or couples who like their space) will probably appreciate a townhouse apartment with three baths. Besides the snorkeling cove, the only other on-site diversion is the pool where, if you're feeling friendly, you can join up with other guests at the weekly pupu (appetizer) parties. If a crescent-shaped, sandy beach is your thing, Napili Bay is only a five-minute walk away. The Kapalua Resort's tennis facilities and three championship golf courses are less than a mile north of the property. There's a three-night minimum. Amenities: balcony or patio. 38 rooms. Credit cards: MC, V.

Hotels

Pioneer Inn $115–$225 ★★

658 Wharf Street, Lahaina, 96761, Behind the Lahaina Small Boat Harbor,
☎ *(800) 457-5457,* ☎ *(808) 661-3636, FAX (808) 667-5708.*
http://www.pioneerinn-maui.com/

Now part of the Best Western chain, the once-dowdy (and cheap) guest rooms of this plantation-era historic hotel, built in 1901, were extensively renovated in January 1995, although the rowdy atmosphere in the famous ol' Bar and Grill hasn't changed a whit. After all, the place has a reputation to protect, with a location looking out to Lahaina Harbor. KEEP IN MIND THAT IF YOU STAY HERE, YOU'LL HAVE TO PUT UP WITH LOOKY-LOOS WANDERING THE PUBLIC AREAS OF THE ESTABLISHMENT, WHICH IS A TOURIST ATTRACTION IN ITSELF. The aforementioned Bar and Grill, for example, trimmed with gleaming dark woods, with a mural of leaping dolphins over the bar, features a plethora of nubile maidens on canvas, and THERE'S STILL A POSSIBILITY THAT A BRAWL MAY ERUPT NOW AND THEN. But we wouldn't want to discourage the management's efforts to gentrify the place—it does have a pretty dining room, called Snug Harbor, with a reasonably elegant and romantic setting overlooking the ocean and harbor. Surrounded by bougainvillea, the courtyard is also a nice place to sip a drink and set for a spell under wide umbrellas. Guest rooms and suites are now air-conditioned, and all feature private baths (you used to have to share a bath) and lanais. There are souvenir and gift shops, but not much else in the way of facilities, since all the action in the harbor and in town is just a step away from your front door. Amenities: balcony or patio. 50 rooms. Credit cards: A, MC, V.

Inns.

Lahaina Inn $109–$1691 ★★★

127 Lahainaluna Road, Lahaina, 96761,
☎ *(800) 669-3444,* ☎ *(808) 661-0577, FAX (808) 667-9480.*
http://lahainainn.com/

It's hard to believe that the Lahaina Inn, a pristine example of quiet Victorian splendor, was a beat-up old dive until 1989. That's when Crazy Shirts, Inc. owner Rick Ralston (whose hobby is architectural restoration) took it in hand. Most guests feel transported into another world once behind the doors of the two-story, cream-colored wooden structure, located right smack in the middle of bustling Lahaina Town. After checking in, you ascend a carved wooden staircase to one of the 12 individually decorated guest rooms on the second floor. A continental breakfast, consisting of orange juice, warm croissants, and freshly brewed Kona coffee is supplied on a sideboard outside the rooms each morning. All rooms are cooled by ceiling fans and air conditioning (partly due to street noise from partygoers outside) and have modern, tiled private baths and telephones. There are no TVs, but classical music is piped in. No children under 15 years accepted. Smoking on lanais only. At street level, where an old salt carved in wood stands guard, is the ACCLAIMED DAVID PAUL'S LAHAINA GRILL, WHICH HAS CONSTANTLY BEEN RATED AS THE BEST MAUI RESTAURANT. Amenities: balcony or patio. 12 rooms. Credit cards: A, D, MC, V.

The Plantation Inn $152–$245 ★★★
174 Lahainaluna Road, Lahaina, 96761,
☎ *(800) 433-6815,* ☎ *(808) 667-9225, FAX (808) 667-9293.*
http://www.theplantationinn.com/

The two-story property, with lacy verandas surrounding a courtyard and hand-tiled pool, appears to have been transported from New Orleans. Most of the guest rooms are contained in the annex behind this lovely structure, but no matter where you're lodged, you'll be impressed with the attention to detail: all quarters have hardwood floors, brass or canopy beds, brass fixtures, Craftsman-like wood detailing, and ceiling fans (central air conditioning is provided). Amenities include remote-control TVs, VCRs, and refrigerators; some suites have kitchenettes. Note that the pool (with an attached spa) is 12 feet deep, and meant for aspiring divers. The first floor of the inn is given over to Gerard's Restaurant, A HIGHLY RATED ESTABLISHMENT SERVING FRENCH CUISINE embellished with Hawaiian produce. Just down the street is one of Maui's best restaurants, David Paul's Lahaina Grill (in the Lahaina Inn), so you can have a moveable feast. Amenities: Jacuzzi, balcony or patio. 19 rooms. Credit cards: A, MC, V.

Napili
Condos

Napili Sunset $85–$249 ★★
46 Hui Drive, Napili, 96761,

☎ *(800) 447-9229,* ☎ *(808) 669-8083, FAX (808) 669-2730.*
http://www.napilisunset.com/
LOCATION, LOCATION, LOCATION—that's what makes this otherwise unprepossessing (but reasonably priced) condominium **A GOOD VALUE**—a sugary stretch of beautiful Napili Beach lies just behind the property. The more desirable one- and two-bedroom beachfront apartments are furnished in pale pink, beige, and white fabrics, with art to match. Lanais are large enough to contain a table and chairs; it's a lovely place for a sunset supper or sunrise breakfast. The lower-priced garden-view studios are in a separate building away from the beach, but all units boast fully equipped kitchens with microwaves, ceiling fans (**NO AIR CONDITIONING**), and cable TVs. There's daily maid service. Facilities include a pool, library, and barbecue pits. For other recreational activities, Kapalua Resort's tennis, golf, dining, and shops are only a short walk away. There's a minimum three-night stay. Amenities: balcony or patio, family plan. 42 rooms. Credit cards: MC, V.

Hotels

The Mauian $140–$195 ★

5441 Lower Honoapiilani Road, Napili, 96761,
☎ *(800) 367-5034,* ☎ *(808) 669-6205, FAX (808) 669-0129.*
http://www.mauian.com/

A beachfront hotel for traditionalists who eschew the bright lights and glitz of Kaanapali and Wailea resorts, the Mauian has been drawing the same clientele for more than 30 years. **BEAUTIFUL, UNDERRATED, HALF-MILE WIDE NAPILI BAY IS JUST OUTSIDE THE LOW-RISE PROPERTY'S FRONT DOOR,** although a pool with a pretty garden is provided. The hotel touts proudly that it has "no TV or phones in the rooms," which are otherwise equipped with all-electric kitchens with microwaves and utensils, and lanais with ocean views. Guest rooms are actually studios, which are nicely and tropically furnished with wicker and rattan, cooled by ceiling fans and sea breezes. **IDEAL FOR FAMILIES**, it has two twin beds as well as a queen-size bed. No charge for children under 12. Two public phones, one courtesy phone. Amenities: balcony or patio, family plan. 44 rooms. Credit cards: MC, V.

Napili Bay
Resorts

Napili Kai Beach Club   **$210–$735**   ★★★

5900 Honoapiilani Road, Napili Bay, 96761, Nine miles north of Lahaina,
☎ *(800) 367-5030,* ☎ *(808) 669-6271, FAX (808) 669-0086.*
http://www.napilikai.com/

Encompassing a respectable 10 acres on a dreamy stretch of beach, the Napili Kai Beach Club is a monument to unpretentiousness. For more than 30 years, this resort has hosted a number of repeat visitors who wouldn't dream of staying anywhere else, although fancier facilities are available in more-fashionable areas for about the same price. The difference is the genuine Aloha spirit, including the Friday night Polynesian show featuring local *keikis* (kids) who study Hawaiian dance, history, language, and legends through the resort's Napili Kai Foundation. STAYING HERE CAN BE AN ENDLESS ROUND OF FUN, IF YOU'RE THE SOCIABLE TYPE—there are weekly coffee and tea parties, putting parties (on the 18-hole putting green, with 50-cent cocktails), and Wednesday Mai Tai parties. A boon for families is an array of FREE CHILDREN'S ACTIVITIES (ages six–12) held on Easter and Christmas and from June 15 through August 31. Those who like to be left alone can snorkel quietly in Napili Bay (snorkeling equipment provided free) or stroll along the beach. Freshwater fans have a choice of four pools to swim in. Quiet time can also be spent on your own private lanai, all with ocean views. Of the 162 accommodations, the second-level suites are especially nice, with beamed ceilings, ceiling fans, plenty of seating areas, shoji screens, and soothing, tasteful furnishings. Some have deluxe, tiled kitchenettes with microwaves and dishwashers. All have color TVs. NOT EVERY ROOM HAS AIR CONDITIONING, so keep this in mind when making a reservation. Facilities include two 18-hole putting greens (golf privileges nearby), shuffleboard courts, and barbecue pits. Tennis court adjacent to hotel (hotel provides complimentary tennis rackets). Free use of beach gear and equipment. A minimum of seven nights is required for stays over the Christmas holidays (December 20–January 1). Amenities: Jacuzzi, balcony or patio, family plan. 162 rooms. Credit cards: MC, V.

HAWAII

Where to Eat

No one will go hungry on Maui, no matter what they like to eat. Sophisticated tastes are appeased at any number of gourmet restaurants—most of which are attached to a hotel or resort—where Pacific Rim, Hawaiian Regional, and Nouvelle Hawaiian cuisines are served in style. Best bets for the fancy set include **Seasons** (The Four Seasons, Wailea), **The Grill** (Ritz-Carlton Kapalua), **The Grand Dining Room** (Grand Wailea Resort), **Prince Court** (Maui Prince Hotel, Makena), **Swan Court** (Hyatt Regency Maui, Kaanapali Beach Resort), **Gerard's** (Plantation Inn), and **Bay Club** (Kapalua Bay Resort). You'll also find a large number of trendy restaurants dotted around Maui. Just some of the noteworthy are **David Paul's Lahaina Grill** (Lahaina), **Chez Paul** (four miles south of Lahaina), **Avalon Restaurant and Bar** (Lahaina), **Longhi's** (Lahaina), and **Haliimaile General Store** (near Pukalani). Call well in advance for reservations at the fine-dining restaurants (men should be prepared to don jacket and tie at some). You can pick and choose from a veritable slew of "ordinary" local spots and mom-and-pop establishments, where you can feast relatively inexpensively on everything from sandwiches and fresh fish to ethnic cuisine (Asian, Mexican, Italian, etc.). Vegetarians and health-fooders will be well taken care of at a number of natural-food shops and delis. And don't pass up the **fresh produce** at **fruit stands** and **farmer's markets**. LASTLY, YOU ABSOLUTELY MUST DO A LUAU NIGHT WHILE ON MAUI. The evening includes a stuff-your-face feast, open bar, and Hawaiian entertainment for a cost of $50–60. Two of the most authentic presentations are at **Stouffer's Wailea Beach Resort** and **Old Lahaina Luau**.

Central Maui
Haliimaile

Haliimaile General Store   **$$$**
900 Haliimaile Road, Haliimaile, ☎ *(808) 572-2666.*
Asian cuisine. Specialties: Szechuan barbecued salmon, Peking duck salad, pina colada cheesecake, chocolate macadamia fudge pie.
http://www.haliimailegeneralstore.com/main.html
The Haliimaile General Store is situated in a tin-roofed, salmon-hued, false-front building that's reached via a cane road in an off-the-beaten-path location just a few miles from

Kahului. This very "in" restaurant features eclectic Asian-inspired entrées created by caterer and chef Beverly Gannon. Gussied up (but not too much) to re-create the ambience of the plantation store it once was, it's a lot of fun for the eye as well as the palate. Along one wall is a deli-bakery case, on the other, a tall shelf full of colorful Italian crockery. Ingredients are simple, but of the best quality, and enhanced by tricky and flavorful seasonings that Beverly has conjured. Diners rave about succulent paniolo pork ribs served with mashed potatoes or Szechuan barbecued salmon, among other things. Also recommended for a bountiful Sunday brunch served from 10 a.m.–2:30 p.m. Features: own baking, rated wine cellar, nonsmoking area, private dining rooms. Reservations recommended.

Kahului

Lucy's Cyber Restaurant $ ★★
161 Alamaha Street, Kahului, ☎ *(808) 871-1135.*
American cuisine. Specialties: Espresso, pupus, sandwiches, plate specials, computer classes, Net-surfing.

Also called the Katchi-Katchi Espresso Bar, for reasons unknown, Lucy's, located in the old Lopaka Bar and Grill, offers computers for classes and Internet surfing, along with low-tech amusements such as a dart board, pool table, and jukebox. If you can tear yourself away from your monitor, cups of a robust, special Spanish coffee, overstuffed sandwiches, plate specials, and pupus are available on a small but diverse menu. An ethnic-vegetarian buffet is offered twice a week on Sunday and Monday at 6 p.m. for $15.

Marco's Grill and Deli $$ ★★
444 Hana Highway, Suite M, Kahului, 96732,
☎ *(808) 877-4446.*
Italian cuisine. Specialties: Chocolate cinnamon French toast, omelettes, pastas, pizza.
http://www.mauimenusonline.com/restaurants/marcos/menu.html

The DeFanis family, who hail from New Jersey, of all places, have set up shop in a fairly new restaurant strategically located on the route to and from the Kahului Airport. Ideal for an early breakfast before (or after) flights, patrons can choose from a number of interesting omelettes served with oven-roasted potatoes. A big menu of hot and cold sandwiches, salads, appetizers, pizza, pastas, and generally Italian specialties are on order for lunch or dinner; try the seafood rustica, a hollowed-out crusty bread filled with mahi-mahi, clams, scallops, shrimp, and crab meat in a light cream sauce. Marco's is open from 7:30 a.m. on Saturdays and Sundays. Features: own baking, Sunday brunch, wine and beer only. Credit cards: MC, V.

Makawao

Casanova Italian Deli $$$ ★★★
1188 Makawao Avenue, Makawao, ☎ *(808) 572-0220.*
Italian cuisine. Specialties: Wood-fired pizza, fresh pasta, island fish.
http://www.casanovamaui.com/.
The management at this upcountry Italian deli and restaurant wants you to eat here because "Dining in Rome is too far away." **WE DON'T THINK WE'VE HAD A PIZZA IN ROME (OR IN ITALY) THAT WAS AS GOOD AS THE WOOD-FIRED CREATIONS THEY SERVE UP HERE.** Yummy antipasti, pasta, fresh fish, and desserts, including the omnipresent tiramisu. Pizza served until 11 p.m. The adjoining deli is open daily from 8 a.m.–6:30 p.m. There's dancing nightly on Maui's "biggest dance floor," and the bar is open until 1 a.m. Features: own baking. Reservations recommended. Credit cards: MC, V.

Crossroads Café $$ ★★★
3682 Baldwin Avenue, Makawao,.
American cuisine. Specialties: Ethnic vegetarian dinners, coffee drinks, desserts.
Heaven for vegans and skeptics alike, this cozy, **NO-BOOZE, NO-RED-MEAT,** no-foolin' cowtown café does draw the granola and sprouts crowd—but also features excellent vegetarian dinners with different themes every evening. Surprise chefs often don the apron here and whip up heavenly things that even die-hard carnivores will appreciate. Live music performances on Saturday nights. Open from 9 a.m.–5 p.m. on Sundays. Features: own baking, non-smoking area. Reservations not accepted.

Paia

Mama's Fish House $$$ ★★★
799 Poho Place, Paia, 96779, ☎ *(808) 579-8488.*
Seafood cuisine. Specialties: Raw fish salad.
http://www.mamasfishhouse.com/

Located in a grove of coconut palms between Paia and Hookipa Beach, Mama's is a **PERFECT DINING DESTINATION FOR THOSE DRIVING TO HANA.** Situated in a pretty, breezy, converted beach house with sliding windows and a low, wood-slatted ceiling, Mama's was the first fresh-fish house in Hawaii when it opened in 1973. Fishermen deliver their catch right to the door. Inside, walls are decorated with old photos, tables are covered with tapa cloths. Fish is served all manner of ways—pan-fried with Maui onion and chili; sautéed with bananas, tropical fruit and coconuts, or raw, as in the fresh marinated poki salad, served with taro chips. Also terrific is ahi sashimi with spicy wasabi and soy sauce dip. There are a few chicken and steak dishes, as well as sandwiches and salads. One drawback is that, despite the low-key setting, **MAMA'S IS VERY EXPENSIVE, ALTHOUGH PORTIONS ARE GENEROUS.** Features: outside dining, private dining rooms. Reservations required. Credit cards: A, CB, DC, D, MC, V.

Picnics $ ★★
30 Baldwin Avenue, Paia, 96779, ☎ *(808) 579-8021.*
American cuisine. Specialties: Spinach Nut Burger.
http://www.aloha.net/~picnics/

When it first opened 16 years ago, this **LOCAL HANGOUT MADE THE MOST OF ITS POSITION AS THE LAST STOP FOR FOOD AND GAS ON THE ROAD TO HANA.** The clever marketing ploy was to specialize in selling picnic lunches to go, called the "Holo Holo Pikinike." Hence, its name. Picnics still continues the moveable feast tradition, replete with a cooler loaded with ice and a "Road to Hana" cassette tape (deposit required), beverages, salads, and fresh cookies or muffins, depending on how many are in your party. Provided free of charge is a guide to Hana. Although not included in the packed lunch deal, don't miss Picnics' original-recipe spinach nut burger. Even veggie-haters will love this savory concoction of chopped nuts, sesame seeds, and secret spices, mixed with Popeye's delight, all topped with cheddar cheese on a fresh baked roll. Add crisp bacon and Swiss cheese, and it becomes the Windsurfer, which is the restaurant's most popular item. Other offerings are Hawaiian pancakes with tropical fruit mixed into the batter, fish tacos, fresh salads made with Haiku greens, frozen yogurt, low-fat shakes, sundaes, and coffee drinks. Features: own baking. Reservations not accepted.

Wunderbar Restaurant $$ ★★★
89 Hana Highway, Paia, ☎ *(808) 579-8808.*
International cuisine. Specialties: Breakfast dishes, salads, sandwiches on flatbread, fresh seafood.
Wunderbar has an Austrian chef, and there are a few German and Swiss items on the huge menu, but this is not strictly an Old World restaurant. In fact, the eclectic menu traverses the globe, with sashimi, Greek salad, and eggs with "two-scoop rice" making regular appearances. POPULAR WITH PAIA SAILBOARDERS AND SURFER DUDES AND DUDETTES, Wunderbar is open for early breakfast, so they can carbo-load before hitting the waves. Pancakes range from one to three stacks of blueberry, coconut banana, and even chocolate varieties, all served with homemade peach butter. There are also three preparations of eggs benedict, called "bennies," either regular kine, veggie, or a spicy Cajun fish version. All sandwiches, even burgers, are served on fresh flatbread. One salad offering, Grilled North Shore ono and Maui avocado on Kula greens with lemon butter vinaigrette, WON FIRST PLACE IN THE TASTE OF LAHAINA FOOD FEST. Children's menu available. Features: outside dining, own baking. Reservations recommended. Credit cards: A, DC, MC, V.

Pukalani

Pukalani Country Club $ ★★
360 Pukalani Street, Pukalani, 96768, ☎ *(808) 572-1325.*
American cuisine. Specialties: Hawaiian plate lunches, breakfasts, sandwiches.
Located in a lovely upcountry setting, this restaurant in the Pukalani Country Club is perfecto for après golf. Extremely popular at lunch, with locals and tourists jamming together for attention. Authentic Hawaiian plate lunches are served with poi or rice, chili pepper, fresh Maui onions, and haupia. Good ole American breakfasts and sandwiches are also available, as well as drinks and pupus at "Happy Hangover Time" and dinners.

Wailuku

Maui Bake Shop and Deli $ ★★
2092 Vineyard Street, Wailuku, ☎ (808) 242-0064.
European cuisine. Specialties: European-style pastries.
Radiating an olde-world European ambience, THIS EXCELLENT BAKERY provides yummy breads and pastries, as well as sandwiches and quiches perfect for a light and cheap breakfast or lunch. Try a veggie quiche or a piping-hot stuffed pizza bread. Whole pies and tortes are available for takeout. Saturday hours: 7 a.m.–5 p.m. Features: own baking. Reservations not accepted.

Maui Boy $ ★★
2102 Vineyard Street, Wailuku, ☎ (808) 244-7243.
Polynesian cuisine. Specialties: Teriyaki, roast pork plate.
Sometimes the mayor and other notables show up at this humble but clean and OH-SO-GOOD LOCAL WATERING HOLE that's famous for its teriyaki chicken plate lunches. Accompanied by two scoops of rice and potato/mac salad, it'll fill you up very cheaply. Equally mouthwatering is the roast pork and Hawaiian plates with poi, lau-lau, lomi-lomi salmon, and kalua pig for just a dollar or so more. Also worth knowing about for hearty breakfasts of French toast made with Portuguese sweet bread, omelettes, or pancakes. Reservations not accepted. Credit cards: MC, V.

Sam Sato's $ ★★
1750 Wilipaloop, Wailuku, ☎ (808) 244-7124.
Japanese cuisine. Specialties: Manju, saimin.
Sam Sato's, a Maui institution founded in 1932 and recently relocated to an industrial park in Wailuku called the Millyard, is FAMOUS FOR SWEET PASTRY BUNS OF JAPANESE ORIGIN, CALLED MANJU. Traditionally filled with a mashed red paste made from azuki beans (an acquired taste), local versions feature everything from pineapple (natch) to coconuts and even white-bread apple. Sam's specialty is a prized white lima bean concoction originally made by his mother, Mite. Even if you don't like manju, buy a couple of boxes (they're only about 50

cents each) to give as gifts to island friends, who love them. Sato's also makes a mean bowl of saimin, as well as tasty, low-priced plate lunches. Features: own baking, non-smoking area. Reservations not accepted.

East Maui
Hana

Café at Hana Gardenland $ ★★★

Hana Highway and Kalo Road, Hana, ☎ *(808) 248-7340. American cuisine. Specialties: Hanamole and chips, steamed eggs and salsa.*

Located at the end of the drive along the Hana coast, this refreshing café, nestled inside the Hana Gardenland nursery, offers a small but comprehensive menu of healthful dishes for **BREAKFAST AND LUNCH ONLY**. Aside from being one of the few places in tiny Hana to get a meal outside of the Hotel Hana-Maui, this eatery's claim to fame is the 1993 visit of First Lady Hillary Rodham Clinton. Apparently eating light, Mrs. Clinton ordered the steamed eggs and salsa served with Maui crunch toast, and so too can you. Also recommended by satisfied diners is the ahi tuna salad sandwich, or "hanamole" (guacamole Hana-style) served with taro chips. No alcohol. Features: outside dining, non-smoking area. Reservations not accepted. Credit cards: A, MC, V.

South Maui
Kihei

A Pacific Café $$$ ★★★★

Azeka Place II, South Kihei Road, Kihei, ☎ *(808) 879-0069. Pacific Rim cuisine.*

Cookbook author and celebrity chef Jean-Marie Josselin has arrived in Maui in a big way. Flush with his successes on Kauai, he has taken over a big chunk of Azeka Place 2, the Kihei mini-mall. The restaurant encompasses an outré trio of dining rooms with seating for 200 patrons. Special features include a wood-burning grill and even a tandoori oven. A signature appetizer is tiger eye sushi tempura with Chinese mustard sauce. For a soup course, choices include such diverse items as red Thai coconut curry soup with Hawaiian fish and calamari, to southwestern tortilla soup with tomato onion salsa and smoked tomato aioli. A version of Caesar salad features blackened ahi. Throughout the menu, you'll find pastas and risottos as well as crisp roasted "peking-style" duck with Asian greens, garlic mashed potatoes, and kumquat sauce. If you'd like to try these wonders at home, pick up a copy of Jean-Marie's book, *Taste of Hawaii*, which is for sale at the restaurant. If he's there, Jean-Marie will sign it for you personally. Features: own baking, rated wine cellar. Reservations required. Credit cards: A, MC, V.

Alexander's $$ BB
1913 South Kihei Road, Kihei, Across from the whale at Kalama Park, ☎ *(808) 874-0788.*
American cuisine. Specialties: Fish and chips, chicken, ribs.
Alexander's motto (since 1990) has been **"GREAT FOOD FAST AT GREAT PRICES"** (under $10 a person). At Alexander's you have a choice of fish for the tempura-batter-dipped fish and chips, including mahi-mahi, ono, and ahi. This treatment is available for an assortment of shellfish; if you're watching calories, anything (except clams and calamari) can be served broiled. Ribs, chicken, and fish can be ordered by the piece or in various combinations. American-style pupus (onion rings, buffalo wings, etc.) and sandwiches are also available. It's mostly takeout, but there's a covered lanai outside if you want to eat in. Features: outside dining. Reservations not accepted.

Carelli's on the Beach $$$ ★★★
2980 South Kihei Road, Kihei, ☎ *(808) 875-0001.*
Italian cuisine. Specialties: Zuppa di Frutta di Mare, Carelli's famous pizza, Tiramisu.
By no means is Carelli's a self-effacing establishment. The management blatantly lists the number of celebrity guests who dine here regularly, including Sly Stallone. Among the plethora of virtues are an enviable location **RIGHT ON THE EDGE OF KEAWAKAPU BEACH**, professional service, incredible sunset views, wonderful homemade pastas and seafood dishes, and some of the best Mai Tais on the island. Other features include a wood-burning pizza oven (try the house special, homemade Italian sausage with roasted red peppers, sauteed maui onions, and provolone cheese). Cocktails and a "mangia" menu are served until 11 p.m. Features: outside dining, own baking, private dining rooms. Reservations required. Credit cards: A, MC, V.

Five Palms Beach Grill $$$ ★★
2960 South Kihei Road, Kihei, ☎ *(808) 879-2607.*
American cuisine.

You can't get much closer to the beach than in this open-air, oceanfront restaurant in a Kihei condo complex. SIGH OVER THE SUNSETS OR CHEER WHALE ANTICS WHILE DINING ON A SERVICEABLE MENU OF BURGERS, FISH TACOS, SALADS, PIZZAS, AND PRIME RIB OR RIBS FOR LUNCH AND DINNER. Four to six specials are prepared each day as well. If you want to save some money, sit in the bar, where inexpensive sandwiches are available. There's also poolside service. Breakfast is available on weekends only, from 8 a.m.–2 p.m.; on Saturdays and Sundays, the restaurant stays open until 10 p.m. for dinner. Features: outside dining, Sunday brunch, private dining rooms. Reservations recommended. Credit cards: MC, V.

La Pastaria $$ ★★
41 East Lipoa, Suite 4A, Lipoa Shopping Center, Kihei,
☎ *(808) 879-9001.*
Italian cuisine. Specialties: Gourmet herb-dough pizza, fresh pasta.

Nothing fancy here, but everything is freshly made, including pastas and sauces, pizzas, calzones, salads, and a changing list of desserts prepared nightly by an in-house pastry chef. Diners have their choice of 12-inch traditional or gourmet pizzas; try the grilled eggplant made with red bell peppers, sun-dried tomatoes, feta, mozzarella, and pesto. Also children's menu, specialty coffees, and smoothies. A FAVORITE WITH THE KIHEI CONDO CROWD AND LOCAL RESIDENTS. Features: own baking. Reservations recommended. Credit cards: DC, D, MC, V.

Stella Blues Café $$ ★★
1215 South Kihei Road, in Long's Center, Kihei,
☎ *(808) 874-3779.*
American cuisine. Specialties: Breakfasts, deli items, coffee drinks, vegetarian specialties.

Stella Blues is a cheerful, neighborly café in a shopping-center setting with indoor-outdoor seating. An outdoor patio is planted with flower boxes. Inside is a high-ceilinged room with plastic chairs, floral cloths under glass-topped tables, and a deli case in one corner. All dishes are prepared using fresh ingredients from Kula growers. On the breakfast and lunch menu, you'll find **SCRAMBLED TOFU AND TEMPEH BURGERS AS WELL AS PASTRAMI OR CORNED BEEF ON RYE.** A little on the politically correct side, the place announces that it serves "dolphin-safe" albacore. At dinner there are meatless pastas, steaks, chicken, ribs, and Alaskan crab cakes. Desserts change daily. Flavored espresso drinks are served until closing. Good, live local entertainment Wednesday through Saturday. Features: outside dining, own baking, Sunday brunch. Reservations recommended. Credit cards: MC, V.

Maalaea Bay

Buzz's Wharf $$$ ★★★

Honoapiilani Highway, Maalaea Bay, Turn right at Maalaea sign, look for blue roof, ☎ *(808) 244-5426.*

American cuisine. Specialties: Prawns Tahitian, surf-and-turf combos, 16-ounce porterhouse on a sizzling platter, fresh fish.

A local favorite, this old-Hawaiian-style restaurant overlooks Ma'alaea Harbor, where the sunset views are picture-postcard perfect. From your table, you can watch fishermen deliver the catch-of-the-day to the front door. **MENU ITEMS ARE UNIFORMLY EXCELLENT, AND WONDERFUL IN THEIR SIMPLICITY.** Juicy New York steaks are served with lobster, crab, prawns, or shrimp. Depending on what the chef thinks is good that day, fresh fish ranges from mahi-mahi to spearfish. Shellfish offerings include fresh Pacific pan-fried oysters, shrimp tempura, and Maui-grown rainbow trout. Buzz's even has a bowl of Saimin humbly thrown in with an array of appetizers. Sharp serving staff. Features: outside dining. Reservations recommended. Credit cards: A, MC, V.

Maalaea Waterfront Restaurant $$$ ★★★

50 Haouli Street, Maalaea Bay, ☎ *(808) 244-9028.*

American cuisine. Specialties: Baked prawns Wellington, Colorado roasted lamb rack.

http://www.waterfrontrestaurant.net/

Located in the Maalaea yacht basin, this oceanfront restaurant is definitely a family affair. Chef Ron Smith mans the burners, while he depends on his mom and two brothers to manage the front room. They must be doing a wonderful job; **THE RESTAURANT WAS TWICE KNIGHTED BY THE *MAUI NEWS* FOR HAVING THE "BEST SERVICE" IN TOWN.** Chef Ron keeps up the quality control by personally selecting the fresh catch as it halts by his front door. At least five kinds of fish, prepared nine ways from Sunday (whew!), are on the nightly menu, including grilled ahi, yellowfin tuna paired with Hawaiian Amaebi shrimp in the shell, and "two-scoop" jasmine rice, sauteed scallions and shiitake mushrooms sauced with shrimp, and ginger-coconut milk. Features: outside dining, own baking, Sunday brunch, rated wine cellar. Reservations recommended. Credit cards: A, MC, V.

Makena

Hakone $$$ ★★★★
5400 Makena Alanui Drive, Makena, 96733,
☎ *(808) 874-1111. Associated hotel: Maui Prince Hotel.*
Japanese cuisine. Specialties: Sushi bar, sukiyaki, kaiseki dinners.
Masterful chefs were imported from Japan to prepare excellent, expensive sushi and kaiseki dinners in an understatedly elegant room in the Maui Prince Hotel. Service is particularly thoughtful and gracious. There are two other branches statewide, but this is probably the best one. Features: own baking, private dining rooms. Reservations recommended. Credit cards: A, CB, DC, MC, V.

The Prince Court $$$ ★★★★
5400 Makena Alanui Drive, Makena, ☎ *(808) 875-5888. Associated hotel: Maui Prince Hotel.*
Pacific Rim cuisine.
The Prince Court, the Maui Prince's signature restaurant, is elegant enough for a family of royals, but still welcoming to lesser mortals with its tradition of polished, unobtrusive service. Starters include carpaccio of opakapaka and ahi with osetra caviar or smoked duck salad. Continue your feast with kiawe-roasted Thai free-range chicken or seared peppered salmon sashimi. A dessert that will remain long in your memory and on your waistline is the chocolate caramel brittle flan. If you or your wallet can't make it for dinner, there's always the Brodbigdanian Sunday brunch (from 9:30 a.m.–1 p.m.), a Friday-night seafood buffet, and Saturday prime rib buffet, as well as a soup-and-salad bar. Features: own baking, Sunday brunch, rated wine cellar, private dining rooms. Reservations recommended. Credit cards: A, CB, DC, D, MC, V.

Wailea

Bistro Molokini $$$ ★★★
3850 Wailea Alanui Drive, Wailea, 96753, ☎ (808) 875.1234.
Associated hotel: Grand Wailea Resort.
Italian cuisine. Specialties: Pizzas, sandwiches, salads.
An open-air café with an Italian twist overlooks both the formal pool of the Grand Wailea Resort and the Pacific Ocean. Not a bad spot for pizzas, sandwiches, and "Italian home cooking" emanating from an exhibition kitchen and wood-burning oven. Also open for pupus and specialty cocktails. Features: outside dining, own baking. Reservations required. Credit cards: A, MC, V.

Café Kula $$ ★★★
3850 Wailea Alanui Drive, Wailea, 96753, ☎ (808) 875-1234.
Associated hotel: Grand Wailea Resort.
cuisine. Specialties: Ahi tuna sandwich with grilled pineapple, Kula tomatoes and Maui onions.
An open-air terrace restaurant with counter-style service at the Grand Wailea Resort, Café Kula specializes in **"SPA NOUVELLE"** cuisine. Guaranteed to remove the rubber tires around your waist acquired from the resort's famed luau. Fresh produce is delivered daily from Maui farmers. The menu is heavy on Kula tomatoes and Maui onions, fresh herbs, black beans, and seafood, and light on fats and salt. **OFFERED TO GUESTS ARE WEEKLY COOKING CLASSES TO APPLY THESE GUILT-FREE TECHNIQUES TO THE HOME STOVE.** Features: outside dining, own baking. Credit cards: A, MC, V.

Humuhumunukunukuapua'a $ ★★★
3850 Wailea Alanui Drive, Wailea, 96753, ☎ (808) 875-1234.
Seafood cuisine. Associated hotel: Grand Wailea Resort.
A SPECTACULARLY ORIGINAL IDEA IN AL FRESCO DINING. Named after the unpronounceable (to us Haoles) state fish, "Humu" is a cluster of South Seas-style thatched roof huts on a tropical fish-filled, one-acre lagoon in the Grand Wailea Resort. The handcrafted restaurant, with fanciful railings made of *ohia* wood, serves Pacific Rim cuisine with an emphasis on (natch) seafood. The adjoining cocktail lounge boasts Maui's largest aquarium and an unbeatable sunset view. Features: outside dining, own baking. Reservations required. Credit cards: A, MC, V.

Kea Lani Restaurant $$$ ★★★★
4100 Wailea Alanui Drive, Wailea, ☎ *(808) 875-4100. Associated hotel: Kea Lani Hotel.*
International cuisine. Specialties: Chicken-coconut soup with kaffir lime leaf and kha ginger, petite filet mignon with venison sausage.

Overlooking the ocean, the Kea Lani Hotel's dressy, southern-Mediterranean-style restaurant is open to the breezes. It offers gourmet dining and similar service, and indoor and outdoor tables are designed to face the setting sun. **VERY ROMANTIC.** The restaurant features new menus monthly, and includes dewy-fresh organic produce grown on the grounds of the resort. Several vegetarian selections are available each evening. Try the chef's four-course tasting menu. Service is polished and extremely knowledgeable. Features: outside dining, own baking. Reservations required. Credit cards: MC, V.

Kincha $$$ ★★★★
3850 Wailea Alanui Drive, Wailea, 96753, ☎ *(808) 875-1234. Associated hotel: Grand Wailea Resort.*
Japanese cuisine. Specialties: 14-course kaiseki dinners, filet of salmon en papillote.

Descend one flight below the main lobby of the Grand Wailea Resort to this tranquil re-creation of a Japanese *ryokan* that features rocks blasted out of Mt. Fuji. You may never see a restaurant outside of Japan like this again, due to both economic and technological reasons. Indeed, aside from elaborate 14-course kaiseki dinners, a new Continental menu has been added. For "only" $45 or so, you can taste grilled Angus tenderloin and shrimp Provençal with duchess potatoes, or a delectable sauteed snapper on wild mushroom bordelaise with roasted pinenut and rice croquettes. There's also a sushi and tempura bar. Features: own baking, private dining rooms. Reservations required. Credit cards: A, MC, V.

Pacific Grill $ ★★★★
3900 Wailea Alanui Drive, Wailea, 96753, ☎ *(808) 874-8000. Associated hotel: Four Seasons Resort Wailea.*
Asian cuisine.

Go for the bountiful breakfast or salad-laden lunch buffets if you can't afford dinner. But you may miss out on the wonderful pan-Asian cuisine served in front of you at the ORIENTAL EXHIBITION KITCHEN. Seaside views, especially from a patio seat, are as delicious as the food. Features: outside dining, own baking, Sunday brunch, rated wine cellar. Reservations recommended. Credit cards: A, CB, DC, D, MC, V.

Sea Watch Restaurant $$$ ★★★★
100 Wailea Golf Club Drive, Wailea, 96753,
☎ *(808) 875-8080.*
Pacific Rim cuisine. Specialties: Molokai French Toast, fresh fish several ways.
http://www.bestofmaui.com/seawatch.html

WITH PERHAPS THE BEST VIEW IN MAUI, the Sea Watch is actually the clubhouse restaurant for the Wailea Golf Course. For those who been exposed to many dreadful, rubbery meals in golf clubs over the years, this indoor-outdoor eatery is a fabulous exception. Specializing in Pacific Rim cuisine, the Sea Watch also serves local-style breakfasts until 3 p.m. Eggs and things are accompanied by "two-scoop" rice. You can also have ono French toast made with Kanemitsu Bakery bread from Molokai. If you eschew breakfast, how about a fish sandwich? No ordinary fish filet here—you get whatever's fresh that day, served with ginger-scallion mayonnaise. At dinner, just try to get past the scrumptious appetizers such as Chinese five-spice crab cakes, smoked salmon Napoleon layered with Maui onions, endive salad, and dill *creme fraiche,* or pot-stickers filled with scallops and shrimp, stir-fried shiitake mushrooms, tobiko caviar, and orange sesame butter sauce. The chef is masterful with seafood, but there are also lamb, beef and chicken dishes. Just a sampling of the dessert cheesecakes: lilikoi with macadamia nut crust, or vanilla bean with crunchy almond crust. Features: outside dining, own baking. Reservations recommended. Credit cards: A, CB, DC, D, MC, V.

Ferarro's at Seaside $$$ ★★★
3900 Wailea Alanui Drive, Wailea, 96753, ☎ *(808) 874-8000.*
Associated hotel: Four Seasons Resort Wailea.

The Four Seasons Resort recently invested $1 million to transform the poolside Cabana Café into Maui's only "full-beachfront" restaurant. Among the new additions is a rotisserie where island chickens are roasted whole and served with olive oil, rosemary, and caper mashed potatoes. New executive chef

George Mavrothallasitis is all excited about the unusual varieties of fish brought to his kitchen by Maui fishermen. Chef Mavro, one of the founders of Hawaiian Regional Cuisine, believes in handling the seafood as little as possible, "using fresh herbs and seasonings to bring out the true flavors." Sample the tombo, or fresh albacore tuna, served with a light sauce of capers, black olives, and oregano tomatoes. For dessert, we recommend apple tart with rhubarb ice cream or chilled cheesecake souffle with lilikoi sauce. An excellent array of sandwiches (even a $9 jumbo hot dog), salads, vegetarian dishes, and frozen yogurt are available at lunch. An extensive pupu menu is available from 3 p.m.–6 p.m. Features: outside dining, own baking, rated wine cellar. Reservations recommended. Credit cards: A, CB, DC, MC, V.

Seasons $$$ ★★★★
3900 Wailea Alanui Drive, Wailea, 96753, ☎ (808) 874-8000.
Associated hotel: Four Seasons Resort Maui.
Gourmet American cuisine.
SERVICE, AMBIENCE AND VIEWS ARE ALL SUBLIME at this, the Four Seasons' main dining room. The regionally influenced menu showcases contemporary U.S. cuisine. What was already a good thing can only reach the stars since renowned chef George "Mavro" Mavrothalassitis took over the resort's kitchens. Dancing every evening until 10:30 p.m.. Features: outside dining, own baking. Jacket requested. Reservations recommended. Credit cards: A, MC, V.

Upcountry
Keokea

Grandma's Coffee House $ ★★
End of Highway 37 on the way to Tedeschi Vineyard, Keokea, ☎ (808) 878-2140.
American cuisine. Specialties: Coffees, pastries, sandwiches.
A cute, family-operated coffee house in a little hamlet near Haleakala Volcano GETS A BIG THUMBS-UP from many visitors and locals. Besides the coffee drinks (cappuccino, caffe latte), Grandma's has yummy soups, sandwiches, and fresh-baked desserts. Also food to go. Features: own baking. Reservations not accepted.

West Maui
Kaanapali

Hula Grill $$$ ★★★★
2435 Kaanapali Parkway, in Whalers Village, Kaanapali, 96761, ☎ *(808) 661-3894.*
Seafood cuisine. Specialties: Wok charred Ahi, homemade ice cream sandwich.

Peter Merriman, a founding member of the Hawaii Regional Cuisine chef's society, offers **SOME OF THE BEST FISH ON MAUI IN A LOVELY BEACH HOUSE SETTING** off Kaanapali Beach. On summer evenings, just before the sun sets, there's no better place for dining than in the outdoor Barefoot Bar (open from 11 a.m.–11 p.m.), which is right on the sand. A number of appetizers, sandwiches, salads, and pizzas from a kiawe-wood-fired oven are served here. Seafood is showcased throughout the large menu; a typical starter is a dim sum of scallop mousse and chunks of lobster, folded in a gyoza wrapper, then poached and sautéed and served with guava plum sauce. Fish-haters will gravitate toward the small but hearty selections of steak, chicken, and pork chops. Merriman swears that he offers absolutely "the best" prime New York steak, served with herb butter, roasted tomato, and Maui onion rings. For lunch, choices salads, sandwiches, and pizza from the kiawe-wood-fired oven; these go as low as $6.95 for a pineapple and jalapeño pizza with mozzarella and provolone. Save the best for last: the homemade ice cream sandwich, which consists of ice cream between two brownies covered with raspberry sauce. See if you can stand up afterwards. Sometimes free desserts are offered to repeat visitors. Features: outside dining, own baking, private dining rooms. Reservations recommended. Credit cards: MC, V.

Kaanapali Beach

Cook's at the Beach $ ★★★
2365 Kaanapali Parkway, Kaanapali Beach,
☎ *(800) 937-8461. Associated hotel: The Westin Maui.*
American cuisine.

Accented by a **FREE POLYNESIAN REVUE EACH EVENING** (except Sunday), this is a casual, poolside restaurant. A salad bar plus a choice of fish, chicken, and other dishes are included in an all-you-can-eat special. Japanese specialties and a "health conscious" menu are alternative choices. Features: outside dining, own baking, late dining. Credit cards: A, MC, V.

Lahaina Provision Company $$$ ★★★
200 Nohea Kai Drive, Kaanapali Beach, 96761,
☎ *(808) 661-1234. Associated hotel: Hyatt Regency Maui.*
Seafood cuisine.

The "provisions" in this super-nosher's delight is the **CHOCOHOLIC BAR** in the evening and the tropical seafood spread and salad bar at lunch. Add to that an alfresco garden setting overlooking two of the Hyatt's fantasy pools PLUS the blue Pacific. Are we in heaven yet? Sandwiches and grilled steaks are also featured. Attire is casual, but flip-flops are the minimum footwear. Features: outside dining, own baking, non-smoking area. Reservations recommended. Credit cards: A, MC, V.

Leilani's on the Beach $ ★★★
2435 Kaanapali Parkway, Kaanapali Beach, 96761,
☎ *(808) 661-4495.*
American cuisine. Specialties: Fresh fish, steak.

In Whaler's Village, Leilani's has its own kiawe-wood-fired ovens where ribs, chicken, and fish are smoked daily. The seafood menu contains the freshest catch of the day, sizzled in lava-rock broilers along with meats and fowl. **VIEWS ARE SPLENDID.** The service staff treats everyone like family. Light meals are served downstairs from 11:30 a.m. Features: outside dining, late dining. Reservations recommended. Credit cards: A, MC, V.

Mixed Plate $ ★★
2525 Kaanapali Parkway, Kaanapali Beach,
☎ *(808) 661-0011. Associated hotel: Kaanapali Beach Hotel.*
American cuisine. Specialties: International buffets.

Located in the former Koffee Shop at the Kaanapali Beach Hotel, Mixed Plate is **ONE OF THE BETTER DINING BARGAINS** on Maui. **FOR ONLY $10.95**, which includes a salad bar, beverages, and dessert, you get to choose from a buffet of international specialties that change depending on the day of the week (kids eat for $6.95). For example, Tuesday is Japanese Day, with tempura, chicken katsu-and stir-fry dishes on the menu. If you want to try Hawaiian food without going to an expensive luau, show up on Aloha Friday, when you'll get to taste poi and laulau. On weekends, a combo of all cultures can be sampled. Reservations not accepted. Credit cards: MC, V.

The Villa Restaurant $$$ ★★★★
2365 Kaanapali Parkway, Kaanapali Beach, 96761,
☎ *(808) 667-2525. Associated hotel: The Westin Maui.*
Seafood cuisine.

A VISUALLY STUNNING RESTAURANT in a visually stunning resort, the Villa is a waterland of lagoons where pink flamingos play. The tropical libations are just as colorful. A special place for a dream date. Oh, and the food? It's Pacific Bistro cuisine and fresh, top-notch island seafood. WEAR YOUR FANCIEST DUDS. Features: outside dining, own baking, Sunday brunch, rated wine cellar. Reservations recommended. Credit cards: A, MC, V.

Kahana

Erik's Seafood Grotto $$ ★★★
4242 Lower Honoapiilani Highway, Kahana,
☎ *(808) 661-3123.*
Seafood cuisine. Specialties: Cioppino, ahi salad, burgers, steamed clams.

Open for lunch and dinner every day, Erik's has been catering to area diners and lucky Kahana Villa condo dwellers for nearly 15 years. The seafood-heavy menu hasn't changed much since the days of the late owner, Erik Jakobsen, who formulated many of the original dishes, including clam steamers and coco pie. THERE'S AN ATTACHED OYSTER BAR where you can stay put or start your meal with steamed clams, a sashimi platter, oysters "a la Erik," or barbecue shrimp. The main restaurant menu features bouillabaisse or Italian cioppino served atop a steamy mound of fettuccine. Lighter eaters will enjoy the seared ahi salad with wasabi dressing. Meat-eating friends won't be disappointed in the hefty burgers served on French rolls, filet mignon, or rack of lamb. Erik's is open for early-bird specials from 5–6 p.m. Another branch has opened in Kihei, at the Kamaole Shopping Center. Reservations recommended. Credit cards: A, MC, V.

Roy's Kahana Bar and Grill $$$ ★★★

4405 Honoapiilani Highway, in the Kahana Gateway Center, Kahana, ☎ *(808) 669-5000.*
International cuisine. Specialties: Dark chocolate soufflé, Roy's grilled Szechuan baby back ribs, smoked and peppered duck.

With the opening of Roy's Kahana Bar and Grill (on the second floor of the Kahana Gateway Center), superstar chef Roy Yamaguchi declared he was "returning home" to Maui, where he visited his grandparents as a child. Obviously, hungry Mauians enthusiastically welcomed him back; **SHORTLY AFTER OPENING, ROY'S WAS DECLARED MAUI'S "OVERALL BEST" RESTAURANT.** Like its big brother in eastern Honolulu, the high-ceilinged, 140-seat restaurant wraps around a copper-enclosed open-view kitchen. Decor includes handmade koa wood tables and a changing exhibit of local art. A huge menu includes innovative starters, salads, "imu-baked" pizzas, meats, game, and pastas. On the dessert tray one may find such belt-busters as "peachy apple" cobbler, pineapple cheesecake, and a fabulous dark-chocolate soufflé. Features: own baking, rated wine cellar, non-smoking area. Reservations recommended. Credit cards: MC, V.

Roy's Nicolina Restaurant $$$ ★★★

4405 Honoapulani Highway, in the Kahana Gateway Center, Kahana, Just north of the Kapalua Airport, ☎ *(808) 669-5000.*
Pacific Rim cuisine. Specialties: Original Dark Chocolate Souffle, individual baked imu pizzas.

Opened by Roy Yamaguchi, the godfather of Pacific Rim (he calls it "Euro-Asian") cuisine, Roy's Nicolina is the twin sister to, and sits side-by-side with, Roy's Kahana Bar and Grill. Both of these shopping-center locations share the same seasonally fixed menus and high-energy atmosphere, but each offers its own nightly specials and great, **GREAT FOOD.** Some of the innovative toppings on their famed "imu-baked" pizzas include Kula tomato, basil and brie with caramelized onions, and spinach and seafood marinated in tequila with black beans, cheddar, and chunky guacamole sauce. Don't leave without visiting what the restaurant calls "Pastry Land." The devilish original dark chocolate soufflé (20 minutes preparation time) with a liquid chocolate center is killer good. Features: own baking, rated wine cellar, non-smoking area, private dining rooms. Reservations required. Credit cards: A, MC, V.

Kapalua

Sansei the Sushi Bar $ ★★★

115 Bay Drive, in the Market Shops, Kapalua,
☎ *(808) 669-6286.*
Asian cuisine. Specialties: Sushi, Asian-style grazing menu.

Sansei the Sushi Bar, which opened in the old Market Café location at the Kapalua Shops, brings some LIGHT-HEARTED (AND LOW-PRICED) FUN to this rather tony, staid resort area. Not strictly a sushi bar (raw-fish haters, come back!), Sansei offers a number of traditional Japanese as well as Euro-Pacific dishes served family style, to share at the table. Among the yummy items are shrimp and pork pot-stickers, fried Maryland soft-shell crab, seared ahi over Kula greens, and crispy Long Island duck with homemade apricot chutney and Szechuan peppercorn salt. It's also one of the few places in the area that stays open way past the witching hour (sushi served until 1 a.m.). We hope this grazer's paradise will thrive. Features: late dining. Reservations recommended.

The Anuenue Room $$$ ★★★★

One Ritz-Carlton Drive, Kapalua, 96761, ☎ *(808) 669-6200.*
Associated hotel: The Ritz-Carlton Kapalua.
French-Hawaiian. Specialties: oven roasted onaga, grilled Kona lobster, paniolo glazed lamb rack.

VOTED "BEST SERVICE" BY ZAGAT'S (2000), this spectacular room features a unique Hawaiian/French Provençal menu offering dishes that utilize the freshest local ingredients. A changing exhibit of island art enhances the gorgeous room with a landscaped patio and three sliding glass walls that offer views of Oneloa Bay, Molokai, and the third hole of the Bay course. Expensive, but well worth it. Features: outside dining, own baking, rated wine cellar. Reservations required. Credit cards: A, MC, V.

The Bay Club $$$ ★★★

1 Bay Drive, Kapalua, ☎ *(808) 669-8008. Associated hotel: Kapalua Bay Hotel & Villas.*
Seafood cuisine.

Established in 1977, this BEAUTIFUL, AWARD-WINNING seafood restaurant sits above Kapalua Bay, which was VOTED THE UNITED STATES' BEST BEACH. Both lunch and dinner in the newly renovated dining room or terrace offer a spectacular view of Molokai and Lanai. Lunch features salads tossed at tableside, including regular or seafood Cobb, with bay shrimp, scallops, smoked salmon, diced avocado and more with an herb dressing, or Caesar served as is or with grilled chicken or shrimp. You can also order from a tempting sandwich menu. Come nightfall, whatever fresh fish the chef has prepared is recommended. One recent offering included kiawe-smoked grilled swordfish, portobello mushrooms, and Maui onions, served with shoestring "Yukon Gold" potatoes, covered with a light sauce of Calvados cream. There's also a small menu of meat and poultry dishes. **SERVICE IS EXCELLENT.** Features: outside dining, own baking, rated wine cellar. Reservations required. Credit cards: A, MC, V.

Lahaina

Avalon Restaurant $$$ ★★★★
844 Front Street, Lahaina, 96761,
Pacific Rim cuisine. Specialties: Chili-seared salmon tiki-style, Avalon summer rolls with Asian pasta, Caramel Miranda.
Quite a few slumming celebrities show up from time to time to nosh at this noisy eatery facing a courtyard, where tables are a little close together, and the service is sometimes pretentious. But Avalon's **HEALTHY CUISINE IS CONSISTENTLY GOOD,** and no more over-the-top than some of its competitors in the Pacific Rim arena. Most feature local produce from nearby farms. Prices are also reasonable for a trendy operation. Go all-out and order the house signature dish, chili-seared salmon, tiki style, which is a layered salad of mashed potatoes, eggplant, salmon, greens, island and tomato salsa with plum vinaigrette. Angus steak, Australian rack of lamb, and fresh fish of the day are also good choices. Patrons rave about the fresh-fruit mai tais. Well-chosen wine list; also wine by the glass. Features: outside dining, own baking, rated wine cellar, non-smoking area, late dining. Reservations recommended. Credit cards: A, MC, V.

David Paul's Lahaina Grill $$$ ★★★★
127 Lahainaluna Road, Lahaina, 96761, ☎ *(808) 667-5117.*
Associated hotel: Lahaina Inn.
International cuisine. Specialties: Tequila shrimp and firecracker rice, kalua duck.
http://www.lahainagrill.com/

LOADED WITH AWARDS AND ACCOLADES, this friendly and noisy Pacific Rim-Italian-Mexican-what-have-you (chef David Paul Johnson calls it "New American") restaurant is located in the sedate Lahaina Inn. The voluminous menu of tantalizing delights changes with the seasons, but returning diners (and they are faithful) can always expect such signature dishes as tequila shrimp with firecracker rice and fried maki sushi. The former wickedly combines rice, vanilla beans, chili oil, tequila, brown sugar, and other spices with five fat tiger prawns. In the latter, prawns and a julienne of vegetables are wrapped in seaweed and quickly deep-fried. Entertainment on Friday and Saturday from 8:30 p.m.–11 p.m. Features: own baking, rated wine cellar, non-smoking area, late dining, private dining rooms. Reservations required. Credit cards: A, MC, V.

Gerard's $$$ ★★★★
174 Lahainaluna Road, Lahaina, ☎ *(808) 661-8939.*
Associated hotel: Plantation Inn.
French cuisine.

A gracious little gem of a restaurant comfortably ensconced in a stylish inn that recalls New Orleans' French Quarter. Gerard's features Euro-Pacific cuisine backed by chef Gerard Reversade's classic French culinary techniques. Dining is especially lovely on the covered veranda or in a garden patio. The whole restaurant, including the dining room, has the feel of an old plantation, with white-wicker chairs and tables covered by tutti-frutti pink cloths. The seasonally changing menu is enhanced by a well-chosen wine list and a palate-cleansing sorbet served between courses. **DON'T MISS ANYTHING PREPARED WITH WILD MUSHROOMS,** including the signature dish of shiitake and oyster 'shrooms in puff pastry. Features: outside dining, own baking, rated wine cellar. Reservations required. Credit cards: A, MC, V.

Kimo's Restaurant $$$ ★★★
845 Front Street, Lahaina, ☎ *(808) 661-4811.*
American cuisine. Specialties: Prime rib, fresh fish, Original Hula Pie.
http://www.kimosmaui.com/.

Well-established on the Maui restaurant scene, Kimo's occupies two floors in a building facing the water. The open-air, oceanfront lanai is a popular party spot, with its romantic sunset views. Lunch is mainly hearty sandwiches and salads; at dinner, a crowd of carnivores overwhelms the place for monster portions of prime rib, which goes fast. There's also a substantial fresh-fish menu. Another signature specialty is the **ORIGINAL HULA PIE**, which the management swears is what "sailors swam to shore for." Kimo's isn't cheap, but all dinners come with Caesar salad, a basket of freshly baked carrot muffins, sour herb rolls, and steamed rice. Children's menu and vegetarian specialties available. Features: outside dining, Sunday brunch, private dining rooms. Reservations recommended. Credit cards: MC, V.

Moose McGillycuddy's $$ ★★
844 Front Street, Lahaina, 96761, ☎ *(808) 667-7758.*
American cuisine. Specialties: Breakfast, burgers, fish and chips, fajitas, fish tacos.

The Moose isn't subtle—not with such tongue in cheek (we think) menu items as the Lassie Omelette, containing Kal Kan, liver snaps, and bone chips that "must be eaten outside in a bowl." But it's **A GREAT PLACE TO PARTY**, and the **FOOD IS SOME OF THE MOST REASONABLE IN MAUI** (two other locations on Oahu). Aside from the poochie special, there are 21 types of omelettes, all made with at least four eggs, ono (delicious) pupus, burgers, sandwiches, and "Specialties of the Moose," which include fish and chips, fajitas, and fish tacos. For dessert? Chocolate Moose—what else? The bar scene starts with happy hour daily from 3-6 p.m., when drinks are only a buck each. Reservations not accepted. Credit cards: MC, V.

Old Lahaina Café and Luau $$$ ★★★
505 Front Street, Lahaina, ☎ *(808) 667-1998.*
Polynesian cuisine. Specialties: Kalua pig, mahi-mahi, haupia.

This **RENOWNED, AUTHENTIC HAWAIIAN FEAST AND ENTERTAINMENT EXTRAVAGANZA** is even popular with local residents. Held on beachfront property that was once a royal estate, the Old Lahaina Luau features pretty good food, with kiawe-wood-grilled steaks along with the expected kalua pig (roasted in an underground imu). Sit on the ground on woven mats and gaze out to sea while dancers arrive, seemingly out of nowhere, the old-fashioned way, in torchlit canoes. A fabulous experience. Beverages extra. Features: outside dining. Reservations required. Credit cards: A, MC, V.

Napili

Koho's Grill and Bar $$ ★★
5095 Napilihau Street, Napili, ☎ *(808) 669-5299.*
American cuisine.
Relaxed and casual, Koho's offers two shopping center locations, one in Napili and the other in Kahului, at 275 Kaahumanu Avenue. Both are combination sports bar/restaurants with a family atmosphere; the Napili eatery also has a new game room where patrons can throw darts and play pool. Pupus, plate lunches (with two-scoop rice), Mexican dishes, sandwiches, old-fashioned milk shakes, and burgers are served all day. After 5 p.m., a fancier steak, chicken, and seafood menu is offered, served with soup or salad. Gooey, rich desserts are on the order of something called a Kilauea Snowball, which is vanilla ice cream rolled in graham cracker crumbs, deep-fried and served in a cinnamon tortilla with honey and walnuts. The Kahului location is open for breakfast daily from 7 a.m. Reservations not accepted. Credit cards: MC, V.

Maui Tacos $ ★★
5095 Napilihau Street, Napili, ☎ *(808) 665-0222.*
Mexican cuisine. Specialties: Mexican fast food, soft-shell tacos.
CHEAP EATS, indeed. Maui Tacos grew from one Napili location to four; all are located in high-trafficked shopping malls. Brilliant. For under $7 (average $2 or $3), you can feast on a variety of enchiladas, tostadas, quesadillas, nachos, burritos, and oh, yes, Maui tacos. What's a Maui taco? It's a double soft-shell tortilla served with a base of whole black or pinto beans. Fillings include chicken, steak (only Montana "natural pride" beef is featured), fish, or veggies. You can also have a single-shell taco, as well as an old-fashioned "hard taco," the kind that bursts into pieces after one bite. Also available are guacamole and chips, "surf" burritos named after Maui beaches, and a taco salad. All dishes are served à la carte. Reservations not accepted.

Olowalu

Chez Paul $$$ ★★★
Olowalu Village Road, Olowalu, Four miles south of Lahaina,
☎ *(808) 661-3843.*
French cuisine.

Although it looks a little like a dive, guess again: this quiet, classic French restaurant in out-of-the-way Olowalu is considered **ONE OF THE BEST ON THE ISLAND.** The owner-chef is Lucien Charbonnier, and a single item on the menu, Waterzooi de Homard au Champagne, shows off his Belgian origins. Here is one of the few places left in Maui where you can order *escargots,* served like they do in the mother country—in their shells, with garlic butter. Only two seatings per night are available, so make sure you reserve. Features: rated wine cellar, private dining rooms. Reservations required. Credit cards: A, DC, MC, V.

Nightlife

You'll find more to do in the evenings on Maui than you would, say, on Kauai or the Big Island, but not nearly as much as over in Waikiki. Lahaina is the center of night life for the youthful set, with venues that include the **Hard Rock Café** and **Moose McGillycuddy's.** Try **Blackie's Bar** (also in Lahaina) for hot jazz. Big names such as Mose Allison and Willie Nelson play at **Casanova Italian Restaurant,** in Makawao. Kaanapali has more to do for a broader range of ages, with much of the activity focused at the various hotels and resorts. One of the island's hottest **discos** is in the **Inu Inu Lounge** at Wailea's Maui Inter-Continental Hotel. For giggles, hit the Monday night **Comedy Club** at Maui Marriott (Kaanapali Beach Resort). The old **Pioneer Hotel** in Lahaina is a good drinkin' bar. **Maui Arts and Cultural Center,** in Kahului, is the venue for large concerts and other live entertainment. The **Maui Community Theatre, Baldwin Theatre Guild,** and **Maui Youth Theatre** stage plays throughout the year, and various musical presentations are scheduled by the **Maui Symphony Orchestra** and **Maui Philharmonic Society.** During the summer, the **Kapalua Music Festival** brings fine musical groups to the island. Art lovers should visit Lahaina's galleries on **Art Night** (Fridays, 7–9 p.m.) when artists are on hand, along with drinks and snacks. Film buffs should plan to come in late November and early December when the **International Film Festival** is on—most of the larger towns have local cinemas as well. Other entertainment consists of **Polynesian revues, luaus,** and **sunset cruises**.

South Maui
Kihei

La Pastaria ★★
41 East Lipoa Street, Kihei, ☎ *(808) 879-9001.*
Jazz piano entertainment nightly except Fridays, when the mood changes to hip-hop and funk; Saturdays it's mellow time again with folk guitar.

Makena

Molokini Lounge BB
5400 Makena Alanui Drive, Makena, 96753,
☎ *(808) 874-1111.*
Hours: 5–10:30 p.m.
Relaxing, comfortable lounge at the Maui Prince Hotel. Low-key Hawaiian-style music daily. Entertainment alternates between a solo guitarist and a mellow duo.

Wailea

Aston Wailea Resort Luau ★★★
3700 Wailea Alanui Drive, Wailea, 96753, ☎ *(808) 879-1922.*
Hours: 5–8 p.m.
This oceanfront luau at Wailea's oldest resort (formerly the Maui Intercontinental-Wailea) is a recipient of the Hawaii Visitors Bureau's prestigious Kahili Award for perpetuating the "essence of Hawaii." Preceding a hula show and a performance by a world-champion fire-knife dancer, there's an *imu* (underground oven) and torch-lighting ceremony. Tariff includes an open bar with tropical libations. General admission: $26–$52.

Tsunami ★★★
3850 Wailea Alanui, Wailea, ☎ *(808) 875-1234.*
Hours: 9 p.m.–2 a.m.
Dance the night (or at least part of it) away at Tsunami, the hottest and most-expensive club in the most-expensive resort in Hawaii, the Grand Wailea. It boasts laser lights, video monitors, and a hydraulic dance floor. Stylish decor with an electrified ceiling casting a pinkish glow over everyone. Karaoke on Sundays and Mondays, free admission. Cover charge on Fridays and Saturdays when the club stays open until 4 a.m. Admission.

West Maui

Kaanapali Beach
Clubs

The Comedy Club ★★★
100 Nohea Kai Drive, Kaanapali Beach, 96761, ☎ (808) 667-1200.
Hours: 8:30–11:30 p.m., Mondays only.
Local comics hit the boards and try to get you to laugh every Monday at the Lobby Bar of the Maui Marriott Resort; sometimes they succeed. The action moves to the Sports Page in Kihei on Tuesday at 8 p.m.

Nightlife

Makai Bar ★★
100 Nohea Kai Avenue, Kaanapali Beach, 96761,
☎ (808) 667-1200.
Hours: 4:30 p.m.–midnight.
This popular local watering hole, nestled darkly within the Maui Marriott Resort, has a reputation for having the best pupus in town. Oh, and there's live music nightly.

Maui Marriott Luau ★★★
100 Nohea Kai Drive, Kaanapali Beach, 96761,
☎ (808) 661-5828.
Hours: 5–8 p.m.
One of the better hotel luaus, the Maui Marriott's feast offers preshow entertainment, including lei-making, coconut cutting, ti leaf skirt-weaving, and hula lessons. Copious all-you-can-eat buffet includes an open bar. A highlight is the fire dance performed by a Samoan chief. Admission.

Tour of the Stars ★★★
200 Nohea Kai Drive, Kaanapali Beach, 96761,
☎ (808) 661-1234.
Hours: 8–10 p.m.
Nightly astronomy show atop the Hyatt Regency Maui, where guests can gaze through binoculars and a special, deep-space telescope (called "Big Blue") for a personal guided tour of the Hawaiian skies. Before the show, the hotel's "Director of Astronomy" gives everyone an orientation of what they're

Lahaina
Clubs

Blue Tropix ★★★
Lahaina Center, Lahaina, ☎ *(808) 667-5309.*
Hours: 6 p.m.–2 a.m.
Closed: Tuesdays
This eclectic dance club and restaurant on the wharf in Lahaina features recorded music with a DJ Wednesday through Saturday and live reggae every Monday. Gender-bender reviews (in other words, Gay night) on Sundays. Who knows what will happen? Admission.

Nightlife

Pacific'o ★★★
505 Front Street, Lahaina, 9, ☎ *(808) 667-4341.*
Hours: 9 p.m.–midnight.
Closed: Mondays-Wednesdays, Sundays.
Local publications have deemed the live jazz on the beach at Pacific'o restaurant the best on the island. The location is somewhat hidden away behind the New England-style 505 Front Street shopping center.

Shopping

Malls and **shopping centers** are poised in the larger towns such as Lahaina, Kahului, Wailuku, and Kihei, and feature icons such as **Sears** and **Longs Drug Store.** Front Street, in Lahaina, is the tourist mecca of arts-and-crafts galleries, schlock souvenir shops, unique boutiques, and one-of-a-kind specialty stores. **Wailea Shopping Village,** near Wailea Resort, houses a variety of upmarket shops and boutiques. **Whalers Village**, in Kaanapali, is home to about 65 exclusive outlets, including the Maui branches of **Louis Vuitton** and **Tiffany.** In addition, all of the large hotels and resorts have their own shopping arcades. Although Lahaina boasts a large number of sleek art galleries, Paia—on the other side of the island—is the center for less-commercial local works. Aloha and **resort wear**

can be purchased everywhere from Sears and Liberty House to small specialty shops. Pick up native **Hawaiian crafts** at **Lahaina General Store** (Lahaina), **Lahaina Scrimshaw** (Lahaina), **John of Maui & Sons** (Haiku, in Upcountry Maui), **Maui Crafts Guild** (Paia), **Lahaina Printsellers Ltd.** (six island locations), and elsewhere around the island. Take some Hawaiian taste home with you by purchasing already-passed-agricultural-inspection fruits, coconuts, macadamia nuts, Maui potato chips, and other goodies—**Take Home Maui** (Lahaina) and **Paradise Fruit** (Kihei) are two reliable companies.

Central Maui
Kahului

Kahului Swap Meet ★★★
Puunene Road, Kahului.
Hours: 6:30 a.m.–noon, Saturdays only.
An almost-free activity, this lively swap meet next to the Post Office in Kahului is where locals come to buy and sell everything you can think of, including clothing and jewelry. Way below normal retail, no overhead. Admission.

Makawao

Maui Hands ★★
3620 Baldwin Avenue, Makawao, ☎ (808) 877-0368.
Made-on-Maui arts and crafts by 150 local artisans. Wares range from fine art and prints to basketry, ceramics, woodwork, and handcrafted jewelry. Another location in Kahului at the Kaahumanu Center, 275 Kaahumanu Avenue, Kahului, (808) 877-3369.

Paia

Katie's Place Gifts and Collectibles ★★
Corner of Hana Highway and Baldwin Avenue, Paia, 96779, ☎ (808) 579-8660.
Linen, lace, antique hula girls, and Hawaiian-themed items are on offer here as well as Maui Polo Club shirts. From August through October, stop by Maui Polo Club outdoor field, where first chukker is at 1:30 pm.

Maui Crafts Guild ★★★
43 Hana Highway, Paia, 96779, ☎ (808) 579-9697.
Hours: 9 a.m.–6 p.m.

A co-op of about 30 island artists operates out of a restored old sugar plantation store in Paia. The pottery, jewelry, baskets, and other crafts are some of the best you'll find on Maui.

Wailuku

Bailey House Museum Gift Shop ★★★
2374-A Main Street, Wailuku, 96793, ☎ (808) 244-3326.
Hours: 10 a.m.–4 p.m.

Tired of gaudy T-shirts and velvet paintings of whales that glow in the dark? For some truly distinctive souvenirs of your trip, the Bailey House Museum's gift shop offers the largest selection of books on Hawaiian history and culture, plus koa jewelry and lauhala baskets you won't see anywhere else.

Wailuku Antique Row ★★★
North Market Street, Wailuku, 96793.

This is a quiet business district that's virtually tourist-free. Locals come here to dig up vintage treasures in stores sandwiched between banks and pawn shops. Some of the better stores include Ali'i Antiques, at #158, for Hawaiiana as well as quality Asian, European, and early American antiques ☎ (808) 244-8012. Traders of the Lost Art, at #159, specializes in ritual carvings, masks, and musical instruments from New Guinea. Also paintings, furniture, jewelry, and clothing. Open 1 p.m.–6 p.m. ☎ (808) 242-7753. Memory Lane, at #130, is the place to come for rare Aloha shirts ☎ (808) 244-4196. Jovian Gallery, at #7, is not your father's gift shop! Distinctive cards, one of a kind T-shirts and clothing, jewelry. Also a local artists' showcase. You'll leave with something. Open Mondays–Saturdays 10 a.m.–6 p.m. ☎ (808) 244-3660.

East Maui
Hana

Hana Coast Gallery ★★
Hotel Hana-Maui, Hana, 96713, ☎ (808) 248-8636.
Hours: 9 a.m.–5 p.m.
Special hours: 9 a.m.–9 p.m. Wednesday-Saturday.

This 2500-square-foot gallery showcases the work of more than 50 of Hawaii's finest artists—many from Hana. There's quantity here as well as quality; bronze sculptures, featherwork, oil paintings, and lauhala jewelry.

Hasegawa General Store ★★★
On Hana Road, opposite the Chevron station, Hana, 96713, ☎ *(808) 248-8231.*
Hours: 8 a.m.–5:30 p.m.
Special hours: 9 a.m.–3:30 p.m. Sundays.
Completely rebuilt after a fire, the Hasegawa General Store features the town's only automated teller machine, which was a big deal when it was installed in the old location just a stone's throw away. As much a historic landmark as it is a shopping resource, the store has been owned and operated by the same family since its founding in 1910 by the current owner's grandfather and granduncle. "As you walk through the doorway what a great surprise, there's a wonderful variety of merchandise"—so goes the song written by Paul Weston about the store, which is crammed with a maze of merchandise everywhere you look. You can even buy three cassette versions of the Hasegawa General Store song, books, sarongs (one of Maui's largest selections), and most important, an oft-imitated, original custom-printed T-shirt proclaiming "I survived the Hana Highway." Celebrity sightings are common.

Northwest Maui
Kahakuloa

Kaukini Ranch Gallery and Gift Shop ★★
On Route 340, east of Kahakuloa, ☎ *(808) 244-3371.*
Hours: 10 a.m.–5 p.m.
A pleasant route on a previously unpaved road near the secluded Hawaiian valley of Kakahuloa leads you to a gallery shop owned and operated by the affable Karen Lei Noland. The gallery, which is situated in a ranch house owned by Noland's family since 1943, is a showcase of jewelry, ceramics, and paintings by more than 40 Maui artisans and artists, including Noland herself. Drop in and "talk story" with Karen, who can answer your queries about the untrammeled north shore of west Maui. It's about an hour away from Lahaina.

South Maui
Kihei

Kihei Farmers Market ★★
61 South Kihei Road, Kihei.
Hours: 1:30–5 p.m., Tuesdays and Fridays only.
A farmer's market with an oceanfront setting, offering fresh produce as well as T-shirts, jewelry, and more.

Upcountry
Kula

Curtis Wilson Cost Gallery ★★★
Haleakala Highway, Route 377, Kula, 96790,
☎ *(808) 878-6085.*
Hours: 8:30 a.m.–4:30 p.m.
Located in the Kula Lodge, on the highway to Haleakala National Park, this gallery features the work of Maui's foremost traditionalist painter, Curtis Wilson Cost. Although his originals are expensive, Cost's reflective, peaceful, detailed landscapes of Upcountry life and its denizens are available in limited-edition prints, serigraphs, laser prints, T-shirts, sweatshirts, and notecards at very reasonable prices.

Sunrise Market and Protea Farm ★★
Highway 378 off Keakulike Avenue, Kula, ☎ *(808) 876-0200.*
A refreshing stop on the way to the summit of Haleakala Crater. This market and flower farm features colorful protea growing in a walk-through garden. The fresh varieties last for weeks, and through the farm's unique process, dry beautifully, retaining their amazing colors. Purchase and ship home fresh flowers, dry wreaths, baskets, and dolls.

Upcountry Harvest ★★
P.O. Box 480, adjacent to the Kula Lodge, Kula, 96790,
☎ *(808) 575-6470.*
Under new ownership, the former Kula Protea Gift Shop offers a wide range of protea flowers, both fresh and dried. These unusual flowering plants, from an ancient strain, are named after the Greek god Proteus, who, myths say, could assume many forms. About 50 varieties have been introduced to the

slopes of Haleakala, where they flourish in the rich volcanic soil, warm cloudy days, and cool nights. At Upcountry Harvest, owner Neil Waldo takes dried protea and forms these unworldly blooms into wreaths, flower arrangements, and even hula dancers. Prints by some of Maui's leading artists, jewelry, ceramics, baskets, books, and a variety of interesting items are for sale.

West Maui
Kaanapali Beach

Ka Honu Gift Gallery ★★
2435 Kaanapali Parkway, in Whaler's Village, Kaanapali Beach, 96761, ☎ *(808) 661-0173.*
Hours: 9 a.m.–10 p.m.
This well-established (28 years), family-owned gift shop specializes in handmade island products, wood items, unique koa-wood music boxes that play Hawaiian tunes, traditional quilts and pillow kits, soaps, perfumes, and Maui potpourri. It's also Christmas here all year with a perennial collection of more than 3000 locally made ornaments, including a cute Santa in a grass skirt carrying a surfboard.

Whalers Village ★★★
Kaanapali Resort, Kaanapali Beach, ☎ *(808) 661-4567.*
Hours: 9:30 a.m.–10 p.m.
Recently expanded and renovated to the tune of $3 million, this shopping center features more than 70 shops and restaurants, and due to its location, many of them are on the posh side. Just added to the Chanel, Coach, Tiffany and Co., Louis Vuitton, and Hunting World flock are Maui branches of the European leather lords Salvatore Ferragamo and Gucci. About 14,000 square feet of floor space has been added to accommodate new stores, ousting Chico's Cantina, one of Maui's most popular Mexican restaurants. Six existing stores, including a branch of Maui Divers and Elephant Walk, have been given face-lifts, whether they were needed or not. Whalers Village is also home to the Whale Center of Pacific's two free museums.

Kapalua

Honolua Store ★★★
502 Office Street, Kapalua, 96761, ☎ *(808) 669-6128.*
Hours: 6 a.m.–8 p.m.
In 1983, after 65 years of business and the retirement of Mr. Hew, the 72-year-old manager, this old pineapple plantation store was in danger of being shut down. But the owners of the Kapalua Resort kept it going, fixed it up (a lot) but kept the homey front porch. It sells everything from fresh fish to logo shirts as well as golf-related items. Condo owners and hotel guests stop in for vintage wines and gourmet takeout. You can also buy inexpensive (nothing over $6) breakfasts, sandwiches, and plate lunches; when construction workers were building up the resort, the kitchen served up 489 lunches in a single day. Outside seating.

Lahaina

Hunt Gallery ★★
143 Lahainaluna Road, Lahaina, 96761, ☎ *(800) 538-3247.*
Hours: 10 a.m.–10 p.m.
This year-old gallery, located about a half-block from Front Street, features changing exhibits, original oils, acrylics, bronze sculptures, woodcarvings, ceramics, and soapstone works by island artists.

Lahaina Arts Society ★★
649 Wharf Street, Lahaina, 96768, ☎ *(808) 661-0111.*
Hours: 10 a.m.–5 p.m.
Special hours: Saturday–Sunday, 10 a.m.–4:30 p.m.
This gallery operated by a consortium of Maui artists brings a plethora of generally fine art to the people. Housed in the historic old courthouse at the east end of Front and Wharf streets, you can also watch artists at work (and perhaps buy something) under the Banyan Tree on weekends and holidays.

Lahaina Printsellers ★★★
1221 Honoapiilani Highway, in the Lahaina Cannery, Lahaina, 96761,
☎ *(808) 667-7843.*
A well-known purveyor of antique maps and old prints, Lahaina Printsellers also offers hand-painted reproductions of

the currently in-vogue menu covers made popular by Eugene Savage on the Matson liners *Lurline* and *Matsonia* in the 1930s. Every Monday, Wednesday, and Friday, at 2 p.m., artist Stephen Strickland gives free demonstrations of antique engraving and printing.

Lahaina Scrimshaw ★★
845 Front Street, Lahaina, ☎ *(808) 661-8820.*
Did you know that more scrimshaw (carved designs on whale bone, teeth and ivory) is found and purchased on Maui than anywhere in the world? Now you do. Find a complete selection of the real thing at this shop, including genuine whales' teeth, men's and women's jewelry, and framed original pieces. Also in Whaler's Village.

KAUAI

This island was known to the ancient Hawaiians as *Kauai-a-mamo-ka-la-ni-po*, which translates to "the fountainhead of many waters from on high and bubbling up from below" (a phrase that doesn't exactly roll off the tongue). A lot of modern-day Hawaiians from the other islands refer to Kauai—not flatteringly—as a place for "the newly wed or nearly dead." Well, of *course* a place called "The Garden Isle" is going to attract a fair percentage of romantics and retirees, but it also lures Eden-seekers, New Agers— and Hollywood film crews who have long used this plot of paradise as a movie set. And it certainly lured Madame *Pele*, the volcano goddess herself, who made the island her first home. Kauai is, geologically, the oldest of the Hawaiian islands and the first to be populated (current tally is 50,947).

Kauai's first known settlers, the pre-Polynesian *Menehune*, were apparently anything but romantic or retiring. They were reputedly short (two- to three-feet tall), muscle-bound South Pacific elfin creatures (possibly remnants from Lemuria, the legendary lost continent) who possessed amazing engineering skills—which they practiced only between dusk and dawn—and harbored supernatural powers. Their mysterious disappearance is still a subject bandied about from classrooms to cocktail parties.

Captain James Cook's arrival and departure is no mystery. In 1778, Cook cruised into Waimea Bay on the south shore—the first Hawaiian island he stopped at—and it didn't take long before the whole cruel world knew about the islands. When Kamehameha the Great went on his "unifying" spree, Kauai was the last holdout—the island farthest from all the others and, therefore, saved from the ravages of warfare. When the island was turned over to the king, it was through negotiation with King Kaumualii of Kauai, *not* the result of bloody battles. Eventually, Kaumualii ended up throwing Niihau into the deal.

The 1800s brought all kinds of goings-on: a Prussian smooth-talker convinced Kaumualii to build a Russian fort overlooking Waimea Bay (its remains still remain); the missionaries arrived— Protestants *and* Roman Catholics; the first sugar was planted on the island at Koloa in 1835, followed by the islands' first successful sugar refinery; and leprosy made its unwelcome appearance.

Kauai came out of World War II relatively unscathed, taking a minimal hit at Nawiliwili Harbor, but not much else. Agriculture continued to thrive, sweetened not only by sugar production but by successful tries with beef, papaya, sugar, taro, macadamia nuts, coconuts, fruit, and other crops. Life went on peacefully until the 1960s, when developers set their sights on the island, first constructing a hotel in Wailua, then spreading out to Poipu, Princeville, and other areas. The economy continued to be fueled by agriculture, the military machine, and especially by the influx of tourists (no matter what their reason for visiting).

In 1992 Hurricane Iniki wreaked havoc all over the island, and threatening to all but demolish tourism. The islanders rallied to the cause, banding together to put their Garden Isle back in shape, the outcome being a re-energized destination and big plans for the future. Before Iniki hit there had been a strong anti-development movement on the island. Afterwards, however, many residents realized they badly needed those tourist dollars coming in and tried to be more amenable. The fairly-agreeable-to-all solution has been to favor low-rise developments, clustered in pockets (rather than spread abysmally from one side of the island), and to steer visitors toward ecotourism and local culture.

The island has bounced back to its lush, green, exquisitely beautiful, Garden-Isle condition—good enough to please all you romantics and retirees.

Kauai Facts

A.k.a.	The Garden Isle
Main city	Lihue
Flower	Mokihana
Color	Purple
Area	549 square miles
Length	35 miles
Width	25 miles
Population	50,947
Highest point	Kawaikiki Peak (5243 feet)

Kauai Survival Guide

Getting There

Lihue Airport, about two miles from central Lihue, serves interisland traffic and is Kauai's principal airport. The gleaming new ter-

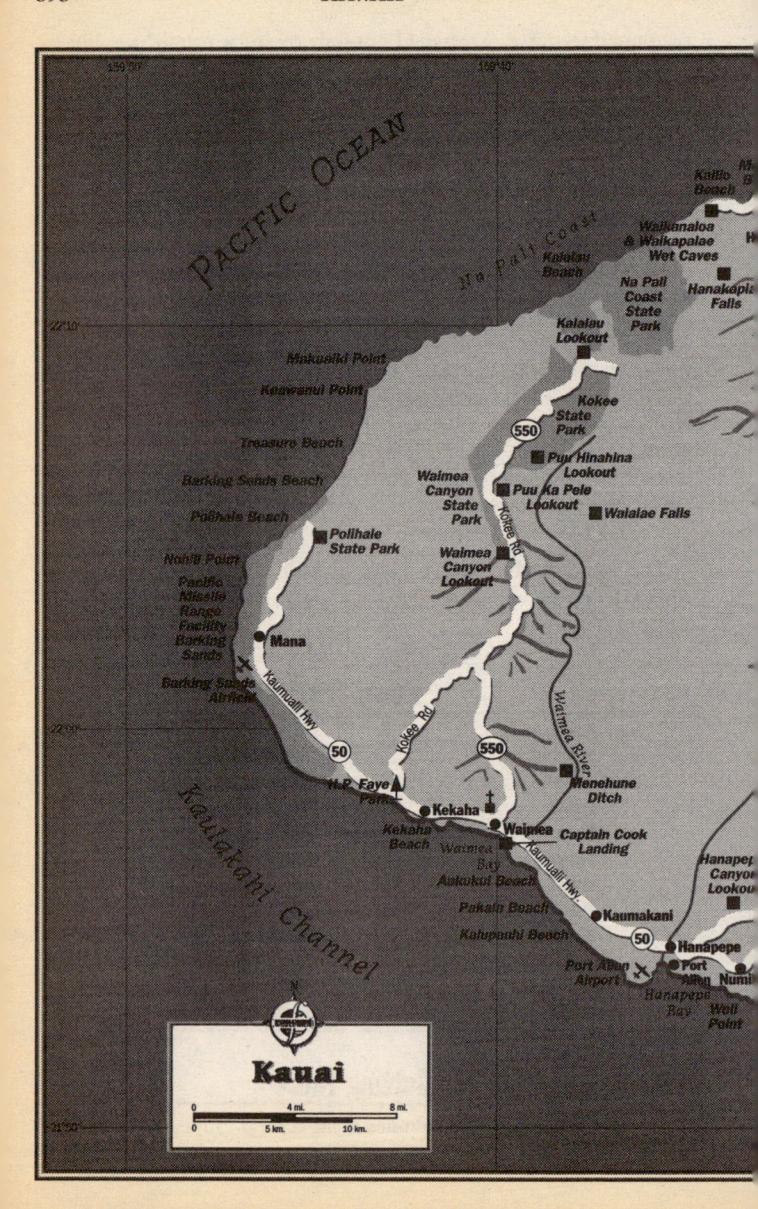

HAWAII

Kauai

Pacific Ocean

- Kaílio Beach
- Waikanaloa & Waikapalae Wet Caves
- Kalalau Beach
- Na Pali Coast
- Hanakapiai Falls
- Na Pali Coast State Park
- Kalalau Lookout
- Makuaiki Point
- Keawanui Point
- Kokee State Park
- Treasure Beach
- Puu Hinahina Lookout
- Barking Sands Beach
- Puu Ka Pele Lookout
- Poöhale Beach
- Waimea Canyon State Park
- Walalae Falls
- Nohili Point
- Polihale State Park
- Pacific Missile Range Facility Barking Sands
- Waimea Canyon Lookout
- Barking Sands Airfield
- Mana
- Kaumualii Hwy
- Kokee Rd
- (550)
- Waimea River
- (50)
- H.P. Faye Park
- Kekaha
- Kekaha Beach
- Waimea
- Menehune Ditch
- Waimea Bay
- Captain Cook Landing
- Aakukui Beach
- Kaumualii Hwy
- Pakala Beach
- Kaumakani
- Kahupouhi Beach
- Hanapepe Canyon Lookout
- Port Allen Airport
- Hanapepe Bay
- Port Allen
- Hanapepe
- Numi
- Well Point

Kaulakahi Channel

0   4 mi.   8 mi.
0   5 km.   10 km.

HAWAII

399

minal features a gift shop, car-rental booths, a restaurant and cocktail lounge, and various other concessions. Airlines are:

Hawaiian	(808) 245-1813
Aloha	(808) 245-3691
Mahalo Air	(808) 246-3500

(See previous chapters for web information.)

Tiny one-terminal Princeville Airport, just east of Princeville, is used mainly for commuter, charter, and sightseeing flights. The basic amenities consist of a café and lounge, a couple of car-rental desks, and rest rooms. The primary interisland commuter airline is **Island Air** *(808) 826-7969*.

Getting Around

Iniki Express *(808) 241-6410* is a bus service that operates between Kilauea and Kekaha from 6 a.m. to 6 p.m. every day except Sunday. You can take it from Lihue Airport into either Kilauea or Kekaha. Otherwise the only transportation from Lihue or Princeville airports is by taxi or rental car. Rental car agencies with booths at Lihue Airport are:

Alamo	(808) 46-0646
Avis	(808) 245-3512
Budget	(808) 245-1901
Hertz	(808) 245-3356
National	(808) 245-5636

The main road along the coastline is **Kuhio Highway** (Highway 56) north of Lihue, changing to **Kaumualii Highway** (Highway 50) when traveling west of town. Roads are generally good throughout the island and parking is rarely a problem.

ITRAVELBOOK TIP: IMPATIENT DRIVERS SHOULD AVOID RUSH-HOUR TRAFFIC BETWEEN LIHUE AND KAPAA.

Metered **taxis** are always on hand at Lihue Airport. Taxi companies include:

Kauai Cab, in lihue	**(808) 246-9554**
A-1, in poipu	**(808) 742-1390**
North Shore Taxi, in hanalei	**(808) 826-6189**
Akiko's, in wailua	**(808) 82-3613**

Be prepared to wait—if you're headed for the airport, allow plenty of time (Hawaiian time).

Kauai is a great ride for **cyclists,** except for the steep road up to Kokee State Park and some of the narrow bits along the North Shore. Also, the roads tend to get very crowded during high season. Bring your own or rent from local shops such as **Bicycle Kauai,** Kapaa *(808) 822-3315,* **Pedal and Paddle,** Hanalei *(808) 826-9069,* **Bicycle John's,** Lihue *(808) 245-7579,* and **Kapaa** *(808) 822-3495,* or **Outfitters Kauai,** Poipu Beach *(808) 742-9667.* For **mopeds and scooters,** try **Pedal and Paddle** (above) or **South Shore Activities,** Poipu Beach *(808) 742-6873.*

Visitor Information

Get local information at the local **Hawaii Visitors Bureau,** *3016 Umi Street, Lihue 96766 ((808) 245-3971,* http://www.kauaivisitorsbureau.org/).

Bird's-Eye View

Round-shaped Kauai, the fourth-largest and northernmost of the major Hawaiian islands, lies about 100 miles northwest of Oahu and has the distinction of being the only island without a view of any other land. Sitting at the center are Mount Kawaikiki (5243 feet), the island's highest spot, and Mount Waialeale (5148 feet), the "wettest spot on earth" with an average rainfall of about 470 inches per year! Geologically the oldest of the Hawaiian islands, 549-square-mile Kauai (35 miles long and 25 miles wide) is also geologically the most stunning tribute to Mother Nature, Madame *Pele,* or *whomever,* a land of magical beauty at almost every turn. Most of the Kauai's mushy, wet, and steep interior is inaccessible, and there is no road encircling this island, either. Located on the sunny south coast is Lihue, the principal town and main airport location; the Poipu resort area; popular white-sand beaches; a barrage of sugar plantation towns; Waimea, Captain Cook's landing place; and spectacular, rainbow-hued Waimea Canyon (also known as the "Grand Canyon of the Pacific"). Above the canyon is cool (sometimes cold) Kokee State Park. The 14-mile-long Na Pali Coast, on the western slopes of Waimea Canyon, is a rugged, dramatic area of 4000-foot-high sea cliffs that tower above wild surf—with no way to get to it except by boat, helicopter, or some very narrow (and arduous) trails. Above Lihue, along the east coast (or coconut coast), are Wailua town and its Wailua River (Hawaii's only navigable river) and Wailua River State Park (with the Fern Grotto and Wailua Falls, two faves on the tourist circuit), more glorious beaches, the Coco Palms Resort, Kapaa and other sleepy towns, and Anahola Beach Park—a top choice on the swimming and camping circuits. Up on the north coast, in the Hanalei district, are Kilauea Point (the northernmost place of all the major Hawaiian islands), a frenzy of exquisite beaches, taro fields, semi-circular Hanalei Bay, and the chic (i.e., quiet and expensive) Princeville resort area. Ahead are the wet and dry caves, the village of Haena and Haena State Park, and beaches that double as movie sets.

Nature Guide

The Garden Isle (also called "Garden of Eden") lives up to every expectation of bloom and birdie. Plant life and feathered friends thrive in the lush greenery, and even many endangered species still dwell on Kauai, particularly inland areas around Alakai Swamp and Mount Waialeale. Unfortunately, the indigenous flora and fauna must compete for space with—like the other islands—the many species that have been introduced over the past couple of centuries.

Search the upper forests for the nearly extinct *nukupu'u*, the *i'iwi*, and the *pueo* (Hawaiian owl). The Alakai Swamp shelters species such as the o'u and Hawaiian creeper, while the indigenous elepaio can be found around Kokee. Waterbirds include the *alae ula* (Hawaiian gallinule), *alae ke'oke'o* (Hawaiian coot), *ae'o* (Hawaiian stilt), *moli* (Laysan albatross), *ua'u kani* (wedge-tailed shearwater), great frigate bird, white-tailed tropic bird, and red-footed booby. House finches, the golden plover, the cattle egret, the western meadowlark, the common mynah, and the northern cardinal are among the common introduced species.

Introduced fauna includes black-tailed deer, feral pigs and goats, ring-necked pheasants, doves, quails, and that highly destructive mongoose.

Beach Finder

Kauai's fabulous, drop-dead beaches were made more so by the demon Hurricane Iniki, which swooped in, cleaned them up, and plumped them full of fresh white sand. This is the dream island for beach lovers—beaches to surf, swim, snorkel, comb, and hide away at. The stuff movies are made of, or—in this case—at. Scenes from *The Thorn Birds*, *Jurassic Park*, and *South Pacific* were all filmed on Kauai sands.

The sunny south shore beaches are best in winter for swimming, surfing, bodysurfing, and snorkeling, as summer months can see high surf. The opposite applies on the north shore (where the movies were made) when winter months pull wild surf conditions and hazardous swimming. In summer, however, the north shore becomes a favorite swimming spot. Eastern shore beaches are best left alone, particularly in winter, when rip currents and rough surf roll in. Before you hit the water, ask locals or contact the **State Department of Land and Natural Resources** *(808) 241-3446* or the **County Department of Parks and Recreation** *(808) 241-6670*.

Kalapaki Beach
Located near Lihue.
ONE OF KAUAI'S BEST with a sheltered bay, gentle waves and A GOOD PLACE TO LEARN OR BRUSH UP ON SURFING, BOOGIE BOARDING OR WINDSURFING. Lifeguards, rest rooms, and showers are on hand.

Hanamaulu Bay
A little farther up the coast, this is a less crowded option.

Around Wailua

Lydgate Beach Park
A GOOD PICK FOR FAMILIES who want to beachcomb, picnic, snorkel, and swim (if it's not too windy). Facilities include rest rooms, showers, and a playground.

Kapaa Beach and Waipouli Beach
Near Kapaa.
These are beaches are on either side of town.

Donkey Beach
Offers a bit more seclusion at the end of sugarcane road, with white sands, good surfing, DANGEROUS SWIMMING IN WINTER MONTHS, and no facilities.

Anahola Beach Park
FOR SAFE SWIMMING AND SNORKELING, try this beach at the south edge of Anahola Bay. Rest rooms, showers, and camping with permit are available.

On the South Shore

Poipu Beach Park
THE FAVORITE OF THE RESORT CROWD, with white sands, shady palms, and good surfing, swimming, and snorkeling. Showers, rest rooms, lifeguards, nearby deli, and (usually) lots of people.

Salt Pond Beach Park
In Hanapepe.
ANOTHER FAMILY FAVORITE FOR SAFE SWIMMING, WINDSURFING, AND PICNICKING. Rest rooms and showers.

Kekaha Beach Park
West of Kekaha.
Offers more good swimming, surfing, snorkeling, and—horrors!—*dune buggying* (watch out where you lay your body down!). No facilities.

Polihale Beach
Through the sugarcane fields at the end of a dirt road.
AFFORDS GREAT VIEWS OF THE MASSIVE NA PALI CLIFFS, but the rip currents are usually too strong for anything else. Again, watch out for those dune buggies! No facilities.

Along the North Shore

Kalihiwai Beach
North of town.
Usually a good swimming and bodysurfing venue. No facilities.

Anini Beach
On the Hanalei side of Kalihiwai Bridge.
A PERFECT SPOT FOR BEGINNING WINDSURFERS, SWIMMERS, AND SNORKELERS. Rest rooms, showers, picnic area.

Hanalei Beach Park
North of Hanalei
A choice spot for Na Pali coast views, experienced surfers, and anyone who would like to just laze their life away. Rest rooms, showers.

Lumahai Beach
West of Hanalei.
THIS IS WHERE MITZI GAYNOR, IN THE MOVIE *SOUTH PACIFIC*, WASHED SOME MAN OUT OF HER HAIR—though she could've saved some time by throwing him into the treacherous rip currents (swimming in summer months *only*). No facilities.

Haena State Park
Just beyond Haena.
OFFERS PRIME SURFING IN WINTER AND SWIMMING IN SUMMER. Rest rooms, showers; Tunnels Beach, near Haena at the end of a dirt road, is a good bet for swimming and snorkeling. No facilities.

Ke'e Beach
Where the road comes to an end.
This beach marks the head of the Kalalau Trail and is popular for summer swimming and snorkeling and winter oohing and aahing. Rest rooms, showers.

Adventure Guide

Kauai's drop-dead gorgeousness and profusion of natural features make it a winner for adventure both on land and in the sea.

Treks, particularly into the remote wilderness, should be at the top of the list for any avid hiker. Kauai's most famous *de rigeur* excursion is the rather strenuous **Kalalau Trail,** an 11-mile (one way) trek leading from near **Ke'e Beach** to **Kalalau Beach,** on the **Na Pali Coast.** On the way to this spectacular beach, you'll pass the lushest of lush—rainforest, deep valleys, steep cliffs, clear streams, choruses of birds, a botanical garden's worth of flora and heart-stopping views upon views.

> **ITRAVELBOOK TIP:** AS WITH ANY ACTIVITY, HIKERS SHOULD TAKE APPROPRIATE PRECAUTIONS, INCLUDING SIGNING IN AT TRAILHEADS WHENEVER POSSIBLE, AND BRINGING SUITABLE QUANTITIES OF WATER.

You'll be able to choose from a wide variety (about 45 miles) of trails in **Kokee State Park** above **Waimea Canyon**. Take the 100-yard **Cliff Trail** for a fantastic ogle at the multi-colored canyon, or continue along the 1.5-mile **Canyon Trail,** past waterfalls and forests, to an even *more* impressive lookout. Experienced hikers might want to take the 2.5-mile **Kukui Trail** down to the canyon floor and then along the three-mile **Koale Canyon Trail** that traverses the Koale Canyon's southern reaches. The 3.5-mile **Kawaikoi Stream Trail** will take you along a trout stream, old cedar and redwood groves, and plenty of stunning scenery. Another strenuous hike is the 3.5-mile **Alakai Swamp Trail** into Hawaii's largest swamp that will reward you with a close-up look at indigenous bird and plant life, as well as a lot of bog, rain, and mud. Check in with **park headquarters** before attempting *any* hikes.

Obtain information of trail conditions as well as free maps from the **Department of Land and Natural Resources** *(State Parks Division, 3060 Eiwa Street, Lihue, HI 96766, (808) 241-3444).*

Campers can choose from free areas on **State Division of Forestry** trails, those under the auspices of **county and state parks** (which include Kokee State Park, Polihale State Park, and several beach parks) or one of the "unofficial" sites tucked along hideaway beaches. Keep in mind that those official sites require campers to have tents, as well as permits. Get information and permits for state parks from the **Department of Land and Natural Resources** (above), or for county parks, contact the **Division of Parks and Recreation** *(4193 Hardy Street, Lihue, HI 96766, (808) 241-6670).*

Check the calendar before **diving and snorkeling**. If it's winter, you'll probably be limited to the more docile south shore but, come summer, don't miss the premier waters of the north shore. Off Poipu, **Sheraton Caverns** affords divers archways and lava tubes to explore (watch for turtles and bright Hawaiian lobsters). Northwest of Hanalei Bay, **Oceanarium's** cove is filled with archways, ridges, and pinnacles teeming with brilliantly colored tropical fish and coral. **Cannon's Reef,** also on the north shore, is another good spot with lava tubes, passing turtle parades, and plate coral to be discovered. **Snorkelers** should try the waters at **Poipu Beach Park, Salt Pond Beach Park, Haena State Park, Ke'e Beach, Anini Beach, Pakala Beach,** and **Kekaha Beach. Windsurfers** lean toward **Anini Beach** and **Kalapaki Beach,** while **sailboarders** favor **Anini Beach** and **Haena State Park** as well as **Poipu Beach Park. Ocean kayakers** paddle the **Huleia River** (leading into the wildlife sanctuary) or around **Hanalei Bay** (or brave the Na Pali Coast). **Boating** is popular (and often the only way) for exploring **Wailua State Park, Menehune Fish Pond,** the **Fern Grotto** (good for water-skiing), **Hanalei** and **Huleia National Wildlife Refuges,** and a variety of other no-other-way-accessible areas. Organized excursions are available for most of the above water adventures (see "Sports" below).

Surfers should talk to locals and heed all warnings—the sea can be dangerous and demonic during those winter months, particularly on the north shore (with, of course, the best surfing). Top spots include **Tunnels, Donkey Beach, Anahola Beach, Pakala Beach,** and the east end of **Hanalei Bay.** For surf conditions, call **KUAI Surfline** *(808) 335-3611*.

What Else to See

Natural attractions are the big sightseeing lure on Kauai—canyons, swamp land, steep cliffs, verdant valleys, rainbows, prisms, grottoes, and such. If you're looking for tropical glitz, stick to Honolulu and Waikiki.

Around **Lihue,** you can explore the "downtown" section of this old plantation town and commercial and government center. **Kauai Museum** presents displays relating to the island's history, culture, and geology. Pleasure craft and U.S. Navy vessels call in at **Nawiliwili,** over in the harbor, while sunners and swimmers drop in to nearby **Kalapaki Beach.** View an 1860s homestead at **Grove Farm,** settled by George Wilcox, a descendant of intrepid New England missionaries. Heading southwest from Lihue, you'll come to the **Menehune Fish Pond,** along the Huleia River—an engineering feat created by those leprechaun-esque *Menehune* dwellers. Close by is **Kilohana Estate,** a sugar-plantation-turned-visitor attraction, with carriage rides, tours, arts-and-crafts galleries, and various shops.

Along the **south shore,** Kauai's first sugar mill—circa 1835—sits at **Koloa,** along with a variety of other restored 19th-century structures. Check out thousands of varieties of plants (including those growing in an authentic Hawaiian garden) at **Kiahuna Plantation Resort and Gardens.** Next is the condo-land resort community at **Poipu,** along with **Poipu Beach Park** and a few other noteworthy beaches. Watch water shoot from an ancient lava tube at **Spouting Horn Park.** Slightly inland, the **National Tropical Botanical Garden** protects almost 200 acres filled with plant life. **Kukuiolono Park,** above Kalaheo, affords great views of the area. Historic **Hanapepe Valley** and **Canyon Lookout** allow you to glimpse bits of days past, while the town of **Hanapepe** lets you see a setting from "The Thorn Birds" miniseries. The ancient Hawaiians harvested their special "Hanapepe" salt at the ponds near **Salt Pond Beach Park,** where swimming and fishing are more the activities of today. You'll be departing from **Burns Field,** near the ponds, if you've signed on for a helicopter tour of **Niihau**—just a 12-minute flight away.

West of Hanapepe, the remnants of **Fort Elizabeth** (or Russian Fort), built in 1817, immortalize the antics of German doctor Georg Anton Schaeffer. The **Menehune Ditch,** across Waimea River bridge, is a reminder of the intriguing engineering skills of those busy little elves. At **Waimea,** you're standing in the steps of Captain Cook, who made this his first Hawaiian landing site back in 1778. The missionaries followed in the early 1800s, and constructed **Waimea Christian Hawaiian and Foreign Church.** Finally, you've reached **Waimea Canyon,** the 10-mile-wide "Grand Canyon of the Pacific," rife with multicolored walls and sun and shadow play—and a *must* on the Kauai pilgrimage list. A few miles from the canyon lookout, **Kokee State Park** offers 4345 acres of nature-filled everything, with 45 miles of hiking trails covering the area. Catch a fantastic view (come early before it mists up) from 4000-foot-high **Kalalau Valley Lookout.** Ride the dirt road through sugarcane fields to reach remote **Polihale State Park,** an isolated beach that kisses the Na Pali Coast.

On the **eastern shore,** north of Lihue, **Wailua Falls** are twin waterfalls used as backdrop for the now-defunct "Fantasy Island" opening shots. You'll be able to spot *heiau* (ancient temple) ruins around the town of **Wailua** on the Wailua River. Family oriented **Lydgate Beach Park** is a good place to take a break for swimming and picnicking. Catch a cruise (with Hawaiian sing-alongs) from **Wailua Marina** for a jaunt into the very touristed **Fern Grotto.** See another plunging cascade at **Opaekaa Falls,** then blast your brain into reality at Kapaa, Kauai's largest town. Up to the north,

Anahola Beach Park is another popular swimming and picnicking area.

Along the more remote northern coast, first stop is the old plantation town of **Kilauea,** and nearby **Kilauea Point National Wildlife Refuge** (home to endangered birds, including the *nene,* Hawaii's state bird) and **Kilauea Lighthouse.** Ogle more glorious views at **Kalihiwai Valley Overlook,** then hit the sands or protected waters at **Anini Beach.** Next is **Princeville Resort** with its high-end hotel, condos, restaurants, and golf courses. **Hanalei Valley Overlook,** across from the shopping center, lets you peek into taro fields and wildlife refuge from high above. Cross the one-lane, circa-1912 bridge into **Hanalei,** where you can visit the 1830s **Waioli Mission** and get a feel of the missionary lifestyle. Re-live your favorite *South Pacific* movie moments at **Hanalei Bay, Lumahai Beach,** and **Haena State Beach Park** (but beware the strong currents). Near Haena, you'll no doubt want to explore the **Maniniholo Dry Cave** and **Waikapalae** and **Waikanaloa Wet Caves. Kee Beach** marks the end of the road, as well as the beginning of the famous 11-mile **Kalalau Trail.** Visit the stone ruins of **Lahiau's Hula Helau,** former dance floor of Laka, goddess of the hula. Continuing along Kalalau Trail, venture two miles to **Hanakapiai Beach,** or go whole-hog into the remotest-of-remote **Na Pali Coast State Park.**

East Shore

Kapaa
Beaches

Donkey Beach ★★★

Highway 56, just past the 11-mile marker, Kapaa.

This secluded, SWIMSUIT OPTIONAL, white-sand beach is accessible only by foot, a casual 20-minute walk through sugarcane fields on a dirt road, or by mountain bike (eight minutes). A local hangout, one used to be able to drive to it when the road was maintained by the Lihue Plantation Company, which still owns the land but no longer cultivates sugarcane. They've closed the road, even rolled boulders in front of the entry, and put up "No Trespassing" signs everywhere, so come at your own risk. A popular gay beach in the '70s (it used to be a hippie beach), Donkey Beach is dangerous for swimming due to shore breaks and other hazards, but SURFERS AND SUNBATHERS LOVE IT.

Kealia Beach ★★★
Highway 56, north of the 10-mile marker, Kapaa.
Located between Kapaa Beach Park and Donkey Beach on Highway 56, this 150-foot-wide, half-mile-long beach is excellent for surfing, boogie boarding (on the north end), bodysurfing, and frolicking in the sand. Very large sandbar.

Museums and Exhibits
Kauai Historical Society
4-241 Kuhio Highway, Kapaa, 96746, ☎ *(808) 822-3373.*
Special hours: by appointment only.
Closed: Saturdays, Sundays.
www.kauaihistoricalsociety.org/
Books, photos, archival material relating to Kauai. Learn how tourism and growth affects the island.

The Shows
Kauai Coconut Beach Resort Luau ★★★
Coconut Plantation, Kapaa, 96746, ☎ *(808) 822-3455.*
Closed: Mondays, Wednesdays, Fridays.
www.hawaiihotels.com/Web/Main/Kcb/KCB_Luau.cfm?Orig=HHR

The Hawaii Visitors Bureau awarded the coveted Kahili award to the Kauai Coconut Beach Resort for excellence in luauing. The festivities actually begin in the morning with the *imu* ceremony (guests are invited to watch). Here is where the pig, or *pua'a*, is prepared and buried in an underground oven, covered with banana and ti leaves to provide moisture and the delectable smoked *kalua* flavor. The pig is left to cook for the remainder of the day. The next time you'll see the porker is in the evening, sometime after 6:30 p.m., when it's removed from the *imu* after a torchlighting ceremony. The luau feast, besides the pig, includes cocktails and drinks, poi, sweet potato, lomilomi salmon, beef teriyaki, mahi-mahi, and a variety of salads. The dessert spread features coconut cake and fresh fruit, as well as haupia. Top-of-the-line, authentic entertainment follows, choreographed by Kumu Hula Kawaikapuokalani Hewitt, a renowned hula teacher, so you know you won't get schlock. General admission.

Smith's Tropical Paradise Luau ★★★
174 Wailua Road, Kapaa, ☎ *(808) 822-4111.*
Closed: Tues.days, Thursdays, Saturdays, Sundays.
www.hawaiian.net/~zx/smith/
A little commercial (they all are), Smith's version is pleasant nonetheless, and reasonably priced for what you get. Walk through a 30-acre botanical garden, watch the *imu* ceremony, quaff cocktails and fruit juices, and pick through the buffet. The show is held at an open-air lagoon theater called a *halau*. The stage seems to float on a lagoon, with a volcanic backdrop, and as the "volcano" erupts, Madame Pele rises out of the inferno. Included are dances from Hawaii, Tahiti, New Zealand, and our favorite, the Samoan fire dance (How do they do it? Why do they do it?). General admission.

Tours

Smith's Tropical Paradise ★★
174 Wailua Road, Kapaa, 96746, ☎ *(808) 822-4654.*
Smith's provides a combo thrill of walking through, or taking a tram through, a pleasant 30-acre garden and lagoons with a nightly luau and Polynesian show. It's also a departure point for Wailua River cruises to the Fern Grotto (9 a.m.–3:30 p.m.) Times and prices below are for the gardens only. General admission: $5–$8.

Lihue
Beaches

Kalapaki Beach ★★★★
In front of the Kauai Marriott Resort, Lihue.
A half-moon-shaped, white-sand beach, Kalapaki Bay Beach, surrounded by Nawiliwili Harbor, is NOT THE PLACE TO COME FOR SOLITUDE OR PEACE AND QUIET. Still, it's a perfect place for a swim, as any rogue wave action is tempered by a jetty. A FAVORITE FAMILY BEACH. Lifeguard, free parking.

City Celebrations

Aloha Festivals ★★★
Rice Street, Lihue, ☎ *(808) 955-8411.*
http://www.alohafestivals.com/
This statewide, two-month-long fall festival honors the

makahiki, the ancient Hawaiian time of music, dance and feasting, when war was not permitted. But there's also a not-so-hidden agenda: the festivals are meant to attract visitors to the islands after the summer rush. A big parade, block parties, luaus, children's events, hula competitions, and brass-band concerts are just some of the fun events.

Museums and Exhibits

Kauai Museum ★★★
4428 Rice Street, Lihue, 96766, ☎ *(808) 245-6931.*
Special hours: to 1 p.m. Saturdays. Closed: Sundays.
www.kauai-hawaii.com/lihue/kauai_m.html

More than 35 years old, this is the largest historical museum in the outer islands. Collections are housed in two adjacent structures: The Wilcox Building, the city's former public library, was built in the 1920s. It contains offices, the Museum Shop, and five galleries used for temporary exhibits. Depending on your visit, you might see some fascinating photographic displays of historical photographs from the sugar plantation days, or Japanese woodblocks, ceramics, lacquerware, and textiles, or perhaps some rare Hawaiian quilts. The Museum Shop is a destination by itself, and can be visited on its own (admission is therefore waived). **ONE OF THE BEST ON THE ISLANDS, IT'S A REPOSITORY OF HAWAIIAN BOOKS, QUILTS, WOODWORK, NIIHAU SHELL LEIS, MAPS, AND MORE.** Next door, the Rice Building contains a permanent collection, called "The History of Kauai." It manages to cover the geologic formation of the island, its changing cultures—from the ancient Hawaiians who lived off the land, to the history of sugar—all on two floors. A valuable community resource, Kauai Museum conducts classes in lauhala-weaving or quilt-making, hosts an **ANNUAL SUMMER CRAFTS FAIR, AND SPONSORS ACTIVITIES FOR KIDS.** Children under six free. General admission.

The Shows

Kauai Community College Performing Arts Center ★★★
P.O. Box 343, Lihue, ☎ *(808) 245-3408.*
www.kauaiarts.org/

The Kauai Community Players and the Kauai Concert Society have a new home in this 550-seat theater. The $12 million cen-

Tours

Air Kauai Helicopter Tours ★★★
3651 Ahukini Road, Lihue, 96766, ☎ *(808) 246-4666.*
www.airkauai.com/
Chuck DiPiazza, the owner-pilot, is the only guy that gets to fly the company's six-passenger ASTAR jet helicopter (why not—it's his ship!). **ONLY ONE FLIGHT A DAY IS OFFERED.** Called an executive tour, the hour-long adventure is as comfortable as it is exhilarating. The air-conditioned helicopter is equipped with a Bose noise-cancelling headphone system, so you can hear the onboard narration clearly. All seats are forward-facing. Chuck has a perfect safety record, and readers who've flown with him say the ride is definitely worth it. General admission: $175 and up.

Fly Kauai/Kumulani Air ★★★
Leaves from the Commuter Terminal, Lihue Airport, Lihue,
☎ *(808) 246-9123.*
Those who don't dig helicopters but would like to see Kauai's inaccessible wonders via an aerial tour can opt for a comfy ride in a sleek, deluxe, twin-engine Cessna 402 (up to nine passengers) or 206 (up to five passengers). There are no middle seats! Prices start as low as $60 for a 45-minute complete island tour, a "Jurassic special" that covers various sites seen in the movie of the same name, and a Three Island Tour flyby over Kauai, Niihau, and Lehua Island (north of Niihau). General admission: $60 and up.

Grove Farm Homestead ★★★
Highway 58, one mile southeast of Lihue 96766,
☎ *(808) 245-3202.*
Special hours: tours 10 a.m. and 1 p.m.; Mondays, Wednesdays, Thursdays.
Closed: Tues.days, Fridays, Saturdays, Sundays.
www.kauai-hawaii.com/lihue/grove_fhm.html
Founded in 1864, Grove Farm, the old homestead of George Wilcox, scion of Kauai's wealthiest sugar-growing family, is now an 80-acre living history museum. Wilcox, the son of missionaries, applied his Yale degree to revolutionizing agriculture.

He was the first to use irrigation in the cultivation of sugar, and transported cane to the mill by means of railcars (until he came along, oxen did the laborious, tedious work). George's last descendant, his niece Miss Mabel, willed upon her death in 1978 that the homestead would be opened to the public as a "living" museum. In 1980, the first visitors saw the home the way she left it, including beautiful but well-used furniture, the kind no one has the time to make anymore. The homestead and its grounds are a window to a tranquil past (at least from the owners' perspective), when Big Sugar was the center of the island's economy. **TOURS BY RESERVATION ONLY; RESERVE AT LEAST TWO WEEKS IN ADVANCE.** Closed federal holidays and Jack Hall Day (January. 2). General admission.

Kauai Mountain Tours ★★★
P.O. Box 3069, Lihue, 96766, ☎ *(808) 821-0010.*
http://www.alohakauaitours.com/kmt/
THE ONLY CONCESSIONAIRE TO TAKE TRAVELERS EXPLORING THE BACK ROADS AND INTERIOR DEPTHS OF NA PALI KONA FOREST RESERVE AND WAIMEA CANYON, Kauai Mountain Tours utilizes comfy, air-conditioned four-wheel-drive vans with seating for no more than 11 passengers. The seven-hour tour includes a continental breakfast and deli-style lunch. Not much walking required, but have broken-in shoes, a jacket, camera, and binocs. Reserve at least a day in advance. General admission: $100 and up.

Puhi
Tours

Kilohana Plantation ★★★
Highway 50, Puhi, ☎ *(808) 245-5608.*
Regular hours: 11 a.m. to 6:30 p.m., daily
Special hours: to 5 p.m. Sun.
Once the centerpiece of a 27,000-acre sugar tract, Kilohana (which translates as "not to be surpassed") is the name of both the grand estate and manor house belonging to grower Gaylord Parke Wilcox and his family. Built in 1935, the 15,000-square-foot Tudor-style house was the most expensive (if not the showiest) home ever built in Kauai. Painstakingly restored from vintage photographs, the main house and attendant structures have been given over to retail shops, art gal-

leries, and a restaurant named after the old patriarch. **Visitors can wander for free (and freely) through 35 acres of tropical gardens the former sugar workers' camp and farm.** Herbs and vegetables from the garden are used in the restaurant. Did you know that it takes a ton of water to produce a pound of sugar? You'll learn this and more on hour-long tours of the sugarcane fields in a horse-drawn wagon available Tuesdays, Thursdays, and Saturdays at 11 a.m. and 2 p.m for a fee.

Wailua
Beaches

Lydgate Beach Park ★★★
Highway 56 to Leho Drive, Wailua.
An ideal family beach, Lydgate Beach Park **features a huge enclosed-stone seawater pool excellent for swimming year-round.** What this means is that the open ocean beyond should be avoided for its strong currents and heavy surf. Don't scoff—many lives have been lost due to drownings. The beach itself is wide and sandy. Playground, changing rooms, rest rooms, showers, picnic facilities.

Hiking

Nounou (Sleeping Giant) Trail ★★★
Kuhio Highway to Haleilio Road, Wailua.
After doing this hike, your kids can claim they had a picnic on a giant's chest! Along the way you can tell them the story about the friendly (but always hungry) giant who befriended the *Menehunes*, Kauai's original "little people." In exchange for as much poi as he could eat, he hung around to protect his friends from their enemies. One day, full of food as usual, he lay down to nap and was out cold during a surprise attack by unfriendlies. The *Menehunes* tried to rouse him by throwing stones at him; he inadvertently swallowed one and choked to death. The climb to this famous landmark is about 1.75 miles through a native Hawaiian forest and takes two hours round trip to complete. **It helps to be in fairly good shape to do this hike, as it can get slippery.** Ocean, mountain, and river views; strawberry guavas to pick and eat reward the intrepid.

Tours

Waialeale Boat Tour/ Fern Grotto Cruises ★★
Up the Wailua River, Wailua, ☎ *(808) 822-4908.*

Waialeale Boat Tours is one of two companies that offer trips up the Wailua River, to **THE LEGENDARY FERN GROTTO, THE SITE OF MANY MARRIAGE CEREMONIES** (the other company is Smith's Motorboat Company). The slightly clunky, oversize, flat-bottom riverboats leave daily from the Wailua River Marina on the south shore of the river. The ride to the Grotto is a pleasant, relaxing, 40-minute trip. Guides point out sights along the way, including their namesake mountain. **YOU'LL PROBABLY BE TOLD THAT FILMS LIKE ELVIS'** *BLUE HAWAII* **AND** *ISLANDS IN THE STREAM* **(FROM A HEMINGWAY BOOK) WERE FILMED ON THIS ROUTE.** At the Grotto, guests take an easy, five-minute walk on a paved walkway to the mouth of the cave, dripping naturally with ferns. The natural acoustics enhance the obligatory performance of the "Hawaiian Wedding Song" and other ditties. Guides also relate ancient Hawaiian historical facts and legends through music and hula, and give an informative lecture about the plants and history of the area. The company also offers kayak rentals. General admission: $15 and up.

North Shore
Anini
Beaches

Anini Beach County Park ★★★★
Anini Beach Road, Anini.

A shallow lagoon surrounded by a protected, exposed reef **ALLOWS FOR YEAR-ROUND SWIMMING**, which makes Anini unique on Kauai. Also a **PRIME WINDSURFING SPOT, ESPECIALLY FOR BEGINNERS,** who find the calm, steady breezes keep both them and their sails afloat. Campsites, BBQ pits, showers, and pavilions. From April through early September, catch a polo game every Sunday at 3 p.m. at the Kauai Polo Field, just beyond the park toward the mountains. For more information on this "sport of kings," call ☎ *(808) 826-6177.*

Hanalei
Beaches

Hanalei Bay ★★★★
Highway 56 to Weke Road, Hanalei.
A two-mile sandy crescent just behind the town of Hanalei, this gorgeous bay encompasses Waioli Beach Park, Hanalei Pavilion Beach Park, and Black Pot Beach Park. All are excellent for swimming (exercise caution in winter), surfing, bodyboarding, and sailing. Facilities include picnic tables, showers, rest rooms, and parking. Lifeguard on duty.

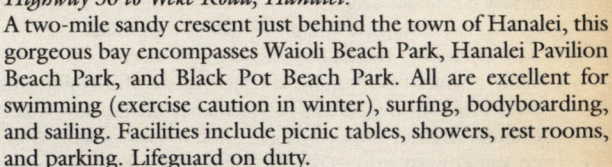

Ke'e Beach ★★★★
From Hanalei, take Kuhio Highway to its end, Hanalei.
A PRIMO SNORKELING BEACH at the end of the road that leads to the Na Pali Coast State Park. There's more fish to be found here than anywhere on the north shore. The sandy-bottomed lagoon is surrounded by a coral reef that protects snorkelers from the ornery ocean. FABULOUS FOR SWIMMING IN THE SUMMER; exercise caution in winter (and at all times). Rest

> ITRAVELBOOK TIP: HAWAII'S BEACHES ARE NOTORIOUSLY BEAUTIFUL, BE THEY LAVA, WHITE SAND, OR BLACK SAND. BUT ALWAYS BE ADVISED — NO MATTER HOW STRONG A SWIMMER YOU ARE — THAT THE SURF IS ALMOST ALWAYS TREACHEROUS IN THE WINTER. EXERCISE EXTREME CAUTION: LOOKS ARE DECEIVING.

rooms, shower, parking lot, lifeguard.

Lumahai Beach ★★★★
A few miles past Hanalei Bay, Hanalei.
Gather your love some puka and other delicate shells for a necklace on this fabulous white-sand North Shore stretch. Aside from strolling and picture-taking, this is about the only safe activity on the beach WHERE MITZI GAYNOR "WASHED THAT MAN RIGHT OUT OF HER HAIR" IN *SOUTH PACIFIC*. DANGEROUS FOR SWIMMING AT ALL TIMES (WHICH IS WHY MITZI WASN'T IN THE WATER), ESPECIALLY SO IN WINTER. Mighty waves break directly on the shore here, and there's no lifeguard to bail you out. To get there from Kuhio Highway, pull over at the west end of the point just beyond Hanalei Bay

Museums and Exhibits

Waioli Mission House Museum ★★★
Highway 56, Hanalei, 96766, ☎ *(808) 245-3202.*
Closed: Mondays, Wednesdays, Fridays, Sundays.
One of Kauai's first American-style houses, the Waioli Mission House was built in 1837 as the residence of the Rev. William P. Alexander. Before that, Alexander and his wife, Mary Ann, had tried valiantly to fit in with their Hawaiian flock by living in a grass hut for two years. Later, other missionaries lived in the house, including Abner and Lucy Wilcox, who taught out of here for two decades. Their descendants eventually became the dominant landholders on the island. The Mission House was turned into a museum in 1952, and is on the list of the National Register of Historic Places. Also part of the original mission compound is the Waioli Social Hall, just in front of the house. This is the original mission church, built in 1841, and ONE OF THE BEST EXAMPLES OF HAWAIIAN ARCHITECTURE.

Parks and Gardens

Limahuli Garden ★★★★
Off Kuhio Highway, past Haena Beach Park, Hanalei, 96714, ☎ *(808) 826-1053.*
Closed: Mondays, Saturdays.
www.ntbg.org/limahuli.html
This magical, well-organized garden at the base of ancient cliffs was donated to the National Botanical Garden in 1994 by private owners. Part of a 900-acre forest reserve, Limahuli nurtures more than 300 varieties of endangered Hawaiian plants, some thought to be extinct, within its 17 acres. Highlights include the virginal Limahuli Stream, ancient taro patches, and a 300-foot overlook to the ocean. You can wander on your own for two hours through a well-marked half-mile-long loop trail, helped along by a pamphlet and identification markers. Guided tours are $20. Reserve in advance, as the gardens are limited to a dozen visitors per day. General admission: $20 and up.

Tours

Captain Zodiac ★★★
Box 456 (in Ching Young Village), Hanalei, 96714, ☎ *(808) 826-9371.*
http://www.planet-hawaii.com/zodiac/

In the 1970s, Clancy Greff (alias "Captain Zodiac") started taking groups of people along the Na Pali Coast on a sturdy, 23-foot, inflatable Zodiac boat. Schools of imitators have spawned since then and have even improved on this idea (power catamarans that can maneuver into sea caves, etc.), but the Cap is still da "original." Offered are three- to four-hour morning and afternoon excursions along the fabled North Shore coast, venturing into sea caves, with a stop for snorkeling (weather conditions permitting). The most popular trip is the five-hour expedition, which adds on a visit to Nualolo Kai, site of an ancient Hawaiian fishing village, AN EXCELLENT SNORKELING SPOT. In season, whale-watching (December–April) and sunrise and sunset cruises (May–September) are available. Backpackers tackling the Kalalau Trail can take advantage of the Captain's drop-off and pick-up service (from Kalalau Beach) offered once a day in summer. General admission: $65–$115.

Na Pali Eco Adventures ★★★
Departs from Hanalei Bay, Hanalei, ☎ *(808) 826-6804.*
http://www.napali.com/

In February 2001, this eco-friendly touring catamaran played host to a breaching baby whale — who greeted guests by jumping out of the water and landing on an unsuspecting tourist. Nevertheless, it is an immensely safe way to travel the Na Pali Coast. The power catamaran is designed to travel in and out of sea caves, and is also swift, allowing more time for exploring the area. All seats are forward-facing and have comfortable back rests. The politically correct tours are conducted by crews who are trained naturalists and environmentalists. Choose from a two-hour sightseeing adventure/dolphin-watching cruise (beverages provided), or a four-hour "Ultimate Snorkel Adventure," with instruction and snorkeling equipment, snacks, and beverages included. General admission: $65–$110 and up.

Kalihiwai
Beaches

Kalihiwai Beach ★★★★
Off Kalihiwai Road west of Kilauea, Kalihiwai.
Although Kauai has a bevy of gorgeous strands, THIS BAY BEACH WITH GOLDEN SAND IS A WOW. There are no facilities, and it's usually uncrowded, used mostly by local residents. Kalihiwai is like a warm bathtub in summer, perfect for sissy swimmers. A different story in winter, when surfers, bodysurfers, boogie-boarders, and such take over the place. Rinse off the salt in a clear stream conveniently located at the end of the bay. Note: there are two Kalihiwai Roads off of Kuhio Highway; take the first one, or you'll have to ford the stream. Also off Kalihiwai Road (turn right off the first dirt road, you'll see a number of cars parked in a dirt lot) is not-so-secret Secret Beach, reached via a steep path that takes about 15 minutes (or five if you're a goat). ONE OF KAUAI'S BEST "CLOTHING-OPTIONAL" BEACHES, AND NO WONDER—SECLUDED AND LUSH, THE SURROUNDINGS ARE DISTINCTLY GARDEN OF EDEN-LIKE. Miles of golden sand for strolling, swimming (in summer only), snorkeling, surfing. No facilities.

Kilauea
Museums and Exhibits

Kilauea Point National Wildlife Refuge ★★★
One mile north of Kilauea 96764, ☎ *(808) 828-1413.*
Special hours: call to make sure they're open. Closed: Saturdays, Sundays.
http://www.hvcb.org/islands/kauai/point5.html
A seabird and mammal refuge maintained by the U.S. Fish and Wildlife Service, the focal point is the historic lighthouse, built in 1913. THIS VENERABLE STRUCTURE GUIDED COMMERCIAL SHIPS BETWEEN HAWAII AND THE ORIENT FOR 62 YEARS. Standing 52 feet high, the lighthouse's original oil lamp and Fresnel lens created a 250,000-candlepower beam that guided ships to shore from as far as 21 nautical miles away. It was replaced by an automatic version in 1976. The cliffs and hillsides off the point are home to the largest colony of seabirds in the main Hawaiian islands. Common sightings include increasingly rare redfooted boobies, nene geese, wedge-tailed shearwaters and, occasionally, a Laysan albatross. FROM DECEMBER TO MAY, VISITORS CAN BE ENTERTAINED BY MIGRATING

HUMPBACK WHALES, AND PERHAPS A SCHOOL OF PLAYFUL SPINNER DOLPHINS PLAYING COURT JESTER. General admission.

ITRAVELBOOKS FREEBIE

Guava Kai Plantation ★★
Kuhio Highway, Kilauea, ☎ *(808) 828-1925.*
Hours: 9 a.m.–5 p.m.
www.hiohwy.com/g/guakaipl.htm

Out of our way, Anita Bryant: If you've got the blahs, nothing's better for you than Vitamin C-packed guava (higher than oranges, even), a delectable yellow fruit with a pink interior and tons of seeds. At the 480-acre Guava Kai Plantation, where sugarcane once flourished, these babies are processed into juice (free samples), made into jams and jellies, and more. Plant tours given in summer only (off-season you can take a short nature walk that's pleasant but nothing special). Gift shop.

Na Pali Coast
Hiking

Kalalau Trail ★★★★
Haena State Park, Na Pali Coast, ☎ *(808) 241-3444.*

If you've hiked this trail, you've seen the "real" Kauai. The difficult, 22-mile (round trip) hike over five valleys will reward you with UNPARALLELED VIEWS OF THE NA PALI COAST, MAGNIFICENT WATERFALLS, AND ANCIENT HAWAIIAN RUINS. Some folks settle for the abbreviated-but-still-strenuous hike from Ke'e Beach two miles to Hanakapiai Valley. Hanakapiai Beach has oceanfront campsites, a fresh-water stream, and caves to explore. Swimming is pretty dangerous year-round. Those going the whole hog can spend the night here and go on four more miles to Hanakoa Valley the next day; then it's five more miles to Kalalau Valley at the end of the trail. Must-sees along the up-and-down trek include a wet foray to spectacular Hanakapiai Falls, with a natural pool—but beware of flash floods in inclement weather, and debris and fallen trees at all times. Before the trail ends at Kalalau Valley, there are three smaller valleys to traverse, such as Waiahuakua Valley, where ancient terraces farmed by Hawaiians now provide well-needed shelter. NOTE: RECOMMENDED FOR SUREFOOTED (IT HELPS TO HAVE HOOVES), EXPERIENCED BACKPACKERS IN GOOD TO

EXCELLENT SHAPE, BUT EVERYONE MUST BE PREPARED FOR MUDDY, SLIPPERY CONDITIONS THROUGHOUT THE ENTIRE TRAIL; STURDY BOOTS WITH GOOD TREAD ARE A NECESSITY, AS ARE PLENTY OF SUNSCREEN, INSECT REPELLENT, BACKPACKING EQUIPMENT, A WATERPROOF TENT, AND DRINKING WATER—OR BOIL WATER FOR FIVE MINUTES. Permits are required for Hanakapiai, Hanakoa, and Kalalau Valleys and are available from the Division of State Parks.

Princeville
City Celebrations

Prince Albert Music Festival ★★★
Princeville Hotel, Princeville, ☎ *(808) 826-2286.*
Held in late May. Now in its second year, the two-day Prince Albert Music Festival is dedicated to the memory of Prince Albert, the only child of King Kamehameha IV and Queen Emma. The tragic prince died at age four in 1862. Featured are performances by classical musicians from around the world, masters of slack-key guitar, and a statewide hula competition for boys. General admission: $25–$60.

South Shore
Koloa
City Celebrations

Koloa Plantation Days ★★★
Old Koloa Town, Koloa, ☎ *(808) 332-9201.*
Mid-July through August 4. This week-long celebration honors the birth of sugar plantations in Hawaii, with a parade, entertainment, crafts, games, sports tournaments, cooking demonstrations, and a luau.

Tours

Capt. Andy's Sailing Adventures ★★★
Box 1291, Koloa, 96756, ☎ *(808) 822-7833.*
www.capt-andys.com/
Cruise aboard the *Spirit of Kauai,* a posh, modern, custom-designed sailing catamaran with teak-trimmed modern cabins and freshwater showers. Leaving from Port Allen in Hanapepe

(on Highway 541) or from Kukuiula Harbor by Spouting Horn, Capt. Andy's company was one of the first to conduct tours of the Na Pali Coast. Half-day winter whale-watching/snorkeling with state-of-the-art hydrophonic sound system to hear the whales' songs; Na Pali cruises in summer. Includes snorkeling equipment, instruction, buffet lunch (salads, sandwich makings, fruit, beverages). General admission: $40–$65.

Poipu
Beaches

Mahaulepu Beach ★★★
Three miles from the end of Poipu Road, Poipu.
Hours: 7:30 a.m.–6:30 p.m.
To get to this remote, uncrowded, two-mile-long, white-sand beach, you'll have to drive through a rough cane road three miles east of Poipu Beach on Poipu Road. Turn right after the road "T's," pass the first turnoff leading to a gravel quarry, and pull up to the McBryde Sugar Plantation Guard Booth, where you sign a waiver. Actually three beaches in one (Kawailoa Bay, Haula Beach, and Gillin's Beach), Mahaulepu was once an ancient Hawaiian fishing village. In 1796, King Kamehameha landed here to capture the island from Chief Kaumalii (he failed, but got his revenge later). Kawailoa is the first beach you come to; just south of Kawailoa past a lava field is Haula Beach and the Aweoweo sand dunes. North of Kawailoa is Gillin's Beach. About 200 yards past a stream is a natural amphitheater. No facilities anywhere except for an unpaved parking lot.

Poipu Beach Park ★★★
Hoona Road, Poipu, 96756, ☎ (808) 742-6722.
Poipu Beach Park offers CRYSTAL-CLEAR WATERS, NEAR-SHORE SNORKELING, SAFE SWIMMING, WADING, AND SURFING. Families and the faint of heart love the natural kiddie wading pool. The palm-tree-shaded lawn at the park is great for picnics or just relaxing. Surfing spots are slightly off-shore, where a reef provides perfect waves for beginner, intermediate, and advanced surfers. Facilities include bathrooms, showers, picnic tables, and pavilions. Brennecke's Beach Broiler operates a convenience store across the street.

Shipwreck Beach (Keoneloa) ★★★
On Poipu Road, in front of the Hyatt Regency Kauai, Poipu.
Fronting the Hyatt Regency Kauai, the beach is wide, broad, and beautiful, but the ocean here is generally unsafe for swimming most of the year. It's best left for advanced surfers and windsurfers. Excellent for sunbathing and strolling; covered walkway if you'd prefer not to get sand between your toes. **PARTICULARLY ROMANTIC IN THE EVENING ON A CLEAR NIGHT** after a few drinks and jazz music at the Hyatt's Stevenson's Library.

Tours

Lawai and Allerton Gardens ★★★
Tours leave from Spouting Horn Park, Poipu, 96765,
☎ *(808) 332-7631.*
www.ntbg.org/allerton.html
Allerton, the first stop on the fully narrated tour, is a 100-acre, former oceanfront estate garden that belonged first to Queen Emma, wife of King Kamehameha IV in the 1800s, and later to Robert Allerton, who landscaped it with his son over a period of 20 years. Together, they built an amazing assemblage of lawns, pools, gazebos, statues, and a mermaid fountain. Lawai Garden, which some visitors have called "too technical," boasts the **LARGEST COLLECTION OF NATIVE HAWAIIAN PLANTS IN THE WORLD ON ITS 186 ACRES. NOTE FOR MOVIE BUFFS: THE GIGANTIC MORETON BAY FIG TREES WERE USED AS A DINOSAUR-LAYING GROUND IN *JURASSIC PARK*.** Tours of Allerton are given in antique communal taxicabs called sampans, while Lawai is traversed on foot. Despite the high price tag, these tours (both are included in the rate) are always booked solid, so reserve well in advance. The 2.5-hour tours are given five times a day. General admission: $40-60.

Outfitters Kauai
Poipu Plaza, 2827 A Poipu Road, Poipu, 96756,
☎ *(808) 742-9667.*
www.outfitterskauai.com/
This Poipu Beach-based company will take you on guided kayaking, bicycling, and snorkeling trips, or combinations of both. Popular areas include Poipu Beach (of course), the Wailua River, the Na Pali Coast, and Waimea Canyon. Half-

West Shore

Hanapepe
Beaches

Salt Pond Beach Park ★★★
Off Highway 50 at the west end of Hanapepe, Hanapepe.
Probably the driest beach on the island (it rarely rains here), SALT POND ALSO HAS THE MOST SUBLIME WATER, MAKING IT POPULAR WITH FAMILIES WITH SMALL CHILDREN. Hawaiian families cultivate salt pans nearby (they've been doing it for generations). Other activities include shelling, snorkeling, and tide pool exploring. Also surfing and windsurfing on an outside reef. Facilities for camping and picnicking, showers, rest rooms. Lifeguard on duty.

Kalaheo
Parks and Gardens

Olu Pua Botanical Gardens and Plantation ★★★
At the intersection of Highway 50 and Highway 540, Kalaheo, 96741, ☎ *(808) 332-8182.*
www.kauai-hawaii.com/south/olupua_gp.html
Perhaps overshadowed a bit by Kilohana Plantation, Olu Pua Gardens shares a similar history. This 12-acre estate surrounds the home of the former plantation manager of Alexander and Baldwin's Kauai Pineapple Company. Designed by the great C.W. Dickey in 1900s, it was the site of many balls, fetes, and galas. THE ESTATE HAS BEEN TURNED INTO A BOTANICAL GARDEN LUSH WITH ORCHIDS, HELICONIA, FLOWERING HIBISCUS, GINGER, AND MORE. Six guided tours, which include a visit to the old homestead, are given daily, 9:30 a.m.–2:30 p.m. General admission.

Kekaha
Beaches

Polihale Beach ★★★★
Highway 50 past Kekaha, Kekaha.
This huge (15 miles), isolated, endlessly windy (but certainly

not unknown) beach marks the west end of the Na Pali Coast. An unworldly place, with sand dunes and immense sawtooth cliffs that tower over you, Polihale is near an area the ancient Hawaiians believed was the departure point for Po, the underworld of the dead (Brrrr!). Sometimes the wind is so fierce, flying grains feel like ant bites on exposed skin. But there are nice covered pavilions to picnic in, and it's one of the best areas for sunset watching. **NEVER GO IN THE WATER, EVEN IN SUMMER** (when we were there last, the only person we saw in the ocean was a lone windsurfer, obviously an expert). Facilities include showers and rest rooms. No lifeguard on duty. To get here, take Highway 50 past Kekaha and the Pacific Missile Range Facility; bear right at Mana. Follow signs inland to dirt roads running north in the sugar cane fields. Head north five miles to the end of the road. Park in the state lot and walk to the beach.

Kokee State Park
Hiking

Alakai Swamp ★★★

Kokee Road, Kokee State Park, 96796, ☎ *(808) 335-5871.*

Kauai's rainforest, the largest wetland area in the state, is **A BIRD-LOVER'S HEAVEN,** and a mud-hater's hell. Come to photograph rare avian creatures, including the nearly extinct Hawaiian *iiwi* bird, which can only be found on Hawaii. Natural wonders include almost 30 waterfalls. **A BOARDWALK HAS BEEN ERECTED RECENTLY ON THE SEVEN-MILE-LONG (ROUND TRIP) TRAIL TO PROTECT HIKERS FROM THE MID-THIGH MUD—BUT YOU WILL GET DIRTY, SO BE PREPARED.** It's about a five-hour trek. Off Camp 10 Road (Mohiki Road) in Kokee State Park, a four-wheel-drive road, or park in the Puu O Kila Lookout lot and walk to the trailhead.

Awaawapuhi Trail ★★★

Route 550, Kokee State Park, Kokee State Park, 96796, ☎ *(808) 335-5871.*

Although it's a seven-mile round trip, this trail through a pristine forest reserve may be worth the trouble. **THE APEX IS A *DIZZYING* PROMONTORY AT THE 2500-FOOT ELEVATION THAT OVERLOOKS THE INACCESSIBLE NA PALI COAST.** These are views people pay big bucks to see from a helicopter. There's also a welcome picnic spot at the end of the trail, and the way back via the Nualolo Trail is a piece of cake. Be sure to pick up a plant guide from the Division of Forestry and Wildlife, although many species are marked. The trailhead begins just before the 17-mile marker on Highway 550; look for a telephone pole numbered "4/2P/152."

Halemanu Kokee Trail ★★★
Off Halemanu Road, Kokee State Park, Kokee State Park.
ANOTHER PLEASANT FAMILY-TYPE OUTING, this is a 1.2-mile hike and self-guided nature trail through the Halemanu forest and its native species of trees, flowers, and plants, including the pesty-but-beloved banana poka and blackberry. Bring binoculars and a field guide to identify Hawaiian birds such as *iiwi*, *apapane*, and *elepaio*.

Museums and Exhibits

Kokee Natural History Museum and Gift Shop ★★
Kokee State Park, Kokee State Park, 96752, ☎ (808) 335-9975.
www.aloha.net/~kokee/
Adjacent to Kokee Lodge, the Kokee Museum is an interesting stop while exploring Kokee State Park and Waimea Canyon. The small building contains natural history and cultural exhibits, where you'll learn some interesting factoids about Pacific weather systems. A COMPILATION OF HEART-STOPPING FOOTAGE TAKEN BY LOCAL RESIDENTS (A DON'T-MISS) DURING HURRICANE INIKI CAN BE VIEWED ON VIDEO, AS WELL AS A MORE LIGHTHEARTED ASSEMBLAGE ON HAWAIIAN BIRDS. The museum gift shop offers a surprisingly comprehensive selection of koa wood bowls, tapa cloth-inspired ornaments, prints of rare birds, slack key guitar instruction books, cassettes, cookbooks, jewelry, and kappa quilt pillow covers. Donations gratefully accepted. Adjacent to Kokee Lodge. Guided hikes are given in summer for a nominal fee.

Makaweli
Tours

Niihau Helicopters ★★★★
P.O. Box 370, Makaweli, 96769, ☎ (808) 335-3500.
THE MOST EXPENSIVE BEACH EXCURSION IN HAWAII and perhaps the world is a no-frills visit to two golden shores on the "forbidden" island of Niihau, sans barbecue lunches, glib

guides, or even bottled water. For $250 per person, you get a blissful three hours on Keamano Beach (with superb snorkeling, swimming, and whale-watching) and Keanahaki Beach (lousy swimming, but great for beachcombing, especially for Niihau shells). Bring all supplies, including water, and a small wad to buy a Niihau shell necklace from locals ($100 and up). The only way to get here is by helicopter, which takes off from Burns Field on Lele Road in Kauai; Burns Field is off Highway 50 in West Kauai, between Hanapepe and Waimea. Reservations required. General admission: $250.

Waimea
Hiking

Iliau Nature Loop/Kukui Trail ★★★
Waimea Canyon State Park, Waimea.
Accessible via the Kukui Trail, which is on the western edge of the canyon. Named for the *iliau* plant, which is related to the silversword, this easy, quarter-mile loop trail is fun for the whole family, and there's plenty to see for such a short walk. A fair number of other native plants are identified for your edification. This trail is a terrific vantage point into the canyon. You can also venture 2000 feet into the heart of the canyon from here, a short but tough 2.5-mile hike. Some choose to spend the night at Wiliwili Camp at the end of the trail. Just remember, if you make this a day trip, it's a long (three hours) uphill trek from the bottom.

Waialae Canyon Trail ★★★
Waimea Canyon State Park, Waimea.
Accessible via the Kukui Trail, following the east rim of Waimea Canyon, this rugged, steep, 1.5-mile trail will reward you with a refreshing swim and picnic at Waipoo Falls, a 3200 foot waterfall amid rare birds and native plants. You'll need a full day, especially if you venture six miles beyond the Falls to Canyon and Kumuwela Trails, which returns to Highway 550 via the Halemanu–Kokee trail.

Historical Sites

Russian Fort/Fort Elizabeth ★★
Highway 50, just southwest of Waimea River Bridge, Waimea.
A Russian fort in Kauai? All that remains today is a foliage-cov-

ered, eight-sided wall that once stood 12 feet high and 300 feet wide. It housed a magazine, armory, barracks, officers' quarters, and a sandalwood trading house. At one time, the Russians and the Hawaiians had a sandalwood-trading operation going (until the supply ran out). The project was started in 1816 by Anton Schaeffer, a German physician-diplomat-charlatan, who involved Kauai's King Kaumualii in a revolt against King Kamehameha. Fort Elizabeth is only one of four forts built in Kauai. One, Fort Alexander, was built on Puu Poa Point, where the Princeville Hotel now stands. After Kaumualii wisely backed down, Schaeffer was thrown out, and the Hawaiians finished the fort in 1817, ultimately using it for ceremonial purposes. It was declared a national historic monument in 1966, but plans to build a historic park in 1970 when the state acquired it have not happened.

Parks and Gardens

Waimea Canyon ★★★★
Route 550 (Kokee Road) or Waimea Canyon Road, Waimea.
This 25-square-mile chasm in the earth is part of the 1866-acre Waimea Canyon State Park. **MARK TWAIN DEEMED IT THE "GRAND CANYON OF THE PACIFIC,"** and on clear days, many would agree with the old curmudgeon. The park is a playland of camping, hiking, great scenery, even fishing. The curvy 20-mile road to the canyon traverses forests of koa, silver oak, eucalyptus, and the lehua tree groves sacred to Pele. From the Waimea Canyon lookout point at 3400 feet, you can see into a 10-mile, 3657-foot gorge, an artist's palette of purples, greens, and blues. The canyon changes hues depending on time of day. The late afternoon is best, especially when the sun isn't obscured by clouds–the dramatic wall-of-fire effect is caused by the sun's rays blasting on exposed orange volcanic walls. Don't forget a jacket; it gets cool up here.

Tours

Liko Kauai Cruises ★★★
P.O. Box 18, Waimea, 96796, ☎ *(808) 338-0333.*
www.liko-kauai.com/
The captains and crews of this company are all raconteurs familiar with Hawaiian legends, history, and lore—well-trained by the native Hawaiian owners. Test out their knowledge while

exploring sea caves, waterfalls, uninhabited valleys, and other wonders on a Na Pali Cliffs Adventure tour on a 38-foot cabin cruiser, the *Na Pali Kai* (takes up to 32 persons, but limited to 24) or the *Kihele Kai*, a 27-foot, six-passenger power catamaran. Also whale-watch cruises in season. Both boats have padded seating, shaded twin viewing decks, freshwater shower, and rest room. **INCLUDES SNORKELING AND EQUIPMENT, DELI LUNCH, AND GAME FISHING.** Cruises leave daily from Kikiaola Harbor in Waimea at 8:30 a.m. and return at 1 p.m. The two-hour whale-watch cruises leave at 2 p.m. Both vessels are available for charter. Free for children under three. General admission: $60–$95.

Sports

Kauai has long beckoned **golfers** to its links faster than Bloody Mary was able to pawn off her "Younger Than Springtime" flesh. The primo fix is **Princeville Resort's Makai Course** (par 36) and **Prince Course** (par 72), both awesome and challenging and designed by the illustrious Robert Trent Jones, Jr. **Kaiahuna Golf Club**, next to Poipu Beach Resort, offers another Jones creation at its par-70 course. Junior also had his hand at the drawing board for the newer par-72 **Poipu Bay Resort Golf Course**. At **Kauai Lagoons Resort**, you can select either the par-72 Lagoons course or the Kiele course (designed by Jack Nicklaus). The par-72 **Wailua Municipal Golf Course**, next to the Wailua River, is an excellent—and inexpensive—public course.

If **tennis** is your game, you'll find 20 lighted public courts and numerous private facilities at hotels and resorts. Resorts that allow public access include **Hanalei Bay Resort, Holiday Inn Kauai Beach, Poipu Kai Resort, Kiahuna Beach and Tennis Resort,** and **Princeville Resort and Complex.** Public courts are located in **Hanapepe, Kekaha, Kalahea, Kapaa, Koloa, Lihue, Wailua,** and **Waimea.** For a complete list of county tennis courts, contact the **Kauai County Parks and Recreation Department** *(4193 Hardy, Lihue 96766,* ☎ *(808) 241-6670).*

Fish are plentiful off shore- and in-stream. A number of charter companies take anglers **deep-sea fishing,** particularly in the area around **Niihau** and along the **north coast. Freshwater streams** near Kokee and Waimea Canyon are well-stocked with bass and trout. For information, contact the **Department of Land and Natural Resources** *(Division of Aquatic Resources, P.O. Box 1671,*

HAWAII

Lihue 96744, ☎ (808) 241-3400). For fishing licenses (not necessary for recreational ocean angling), contact the **Department of Land and Natural Resources** *(Division of Aquatic Resources, 1151 Punchbowl Street, Honolulu 96815, ☎ (808) 587-0077).*

Explore Kauai's beaches, valleys, and vistas by **horseback** on various escorted rides, or arrange a private ride through one of the stables.

East Shore
Kapaa

Bubbles Below Dive Charters ★★★
6251 Hauaala Road, Kapaa, 96746, ☎ (808) 822-3483.
http://www.aloha.net/~kaimanu/

Ken and Linda Bell were the first to take divers on regularly scheduled trips to Niihau. Offered once a week in the summer, these three tank dives are for experienced divers with a spirit of adventure (YOU MAY HAVE TO SHARE THE WATER WITH SHARKS). Another extraordinary summer dive is a two-tank, six-hour trip to Mana Crack, a sunken barrier reef with a drop-off range of 50–90 feet. At most times of the year, four-hour morning and afternoon dives in the waters around Kauai are available, as is a 2.5-hour night dive. Equipment, snacks, drinks, and a dive computer are included. The number of divers per trip are usually limited to six or 10 people. General admission: $70–$200.

Lihue

Gent-Lee Fishing Charters ★★★
P.O. Box 1691, Lihue, 96766, ☎ (808) 245-7504.
Special hours: departures at 7 a.m. and 1 p.m.

Deep-sea fishing for marlin, ahi (yellowfin tuna), mahi-mahi, ono, barracuda, and aku on a fully-equipped (three to five fighting chairs), 36-foot Radoncraft Sportfisher. Rates are based on four- and six-hour share charters for four–six people, and four-, six-, and eight-hour exclusive charters for up to 16 people. Half price for spectators. Includes tackle, ice, and non-alcoholic beverages. Gent-Lee retains the right to the fish, but everyone gets a share, and the crew will even filet the catch. SERVICES AVAILABLE FOR THE PHYSICALLY CHALLENGED, but not advisable for pregnant women. 24-hour cancellation policy. Leaves daily from Nawiliwili Harbor. Ask about overnight fishing excursions to Niihau. Also recommended is **Sport Fishing**

Kauai, *P.O. Box 1195, Koloa, 96756,* ☎ *(808) 742-7013* or ☎ *(808) 639-0013,* or **Anini Fishing Charters,** *Anini Beach,* ☎ *(808) 828-1285,* open daily from 6 a.m.–10 p.m. How about some freshwater fishing? Hook some smallmouth and largemouth bass, but remember, you'll have to toss the critters back. **Cast and Catch,** ☎ *(808) 332-9707,* will show you where these guys are bitin' (usually in reservoirs along sugarcane roads). You must have a freshwater fishing license, available from the Kokee Lodge. Guides have at least 10 years experience. The 17-foot aluminum boats are fully equipped, and all rods, tackle, live bait, and beverages are supplied. Full-day and half-day charters available. Airport and hotel pickup can be arranged. General admission: $90–$1900.

Kauai Athletic Club ★★
4370 Kukui Grove Street, Lihue, ☎ *(808) 245-5381.*
Special hours: Saturdays, 8 a.m.–6 p.m.; Sundays, 9 a.m.–4 p.m.
A REASONABLY PRICED WAY TO ASSUAGE GUILT AFTER TOO MUCH LUAU FOOD, Kauai Athletic Club offers a weight room, aerobics classes (more than 30 a week), cardio room, racquetball, squash, handball, an outdoor pool, and jacuzzi—all for a $20 day-use fee. There's even a "Fitness after Sixty" program. Just stay away from the Burger King and Taco Bell just across the street. General admission.

Kauai Lagoons Resort Golf Club ★★★
Kalapaki Beach, P.O. Box 3330, Lihue, 96766,
☎ *(808) 241-6000.*
http://www.kauailagoonsgolf.com
Located at the Kauai Marriott near the airport, the Kauai Lagoons Golf Course consists of the Kiele and Lagoons Courses, both 18-holers designed by Jack Nicklaus. The former, overlooking Kalapaki Beach and Nawiliwili Harbor, is RANKED THIRD-BEST IN THE STATE, and was the site of the 1991 PGA Grand Slam of Golf. THIS COURSE IS A MUST FOR EXPERIENCED GOLFERS—the 13th hole tees off over a bay, so it's pretty unforgiving. THE LAGOONS COURSE IS KINDER AND GENTLER, AND IS SUITABLE FOR GOLFERS OF ALL LEVELS. Reward yourself later with an excellent buffet lunch at the club's Terrace Restaurant, ☎ *(808) 241-6080.* General admission: $100–$145.

Wailua Municipal Golf Course ★★
3-5351 Kuhio Highway, Lihue, 96766, ☎ *(808) 241-6666.*
RATED IN THE TOP 75 OF ALL MUNICIPAL COURSES IN THE COUNTRY, Wailua Muni was the first course constructed on Kauai in 1937, initially built as a nine-holer. It's certainly one of the prettiest, with three oceanside holes and plenty of lush landscaping. Good for beginners as well as those who like a challenge. **PROBABLY THE BEST VALUE FOR YOUR DOLLAR,** and lots of locals play here, so reservations are a must—up to a week in advance. Greens fees are $30 on weekends; carts $20. Driving range, pro shop, putting green. General admission.

Wailua

Esprit de Corps Riding Academy
Olohena Road, Wailua, ☎ *(808) 822-4688.*
http://www.kauaihorses.com/
Guided-trail tours ranging from three hours to an all-day adventure. No more than four guests per tour. The only company on the island that lets you trot and canter your horse. **FOR RIDERS WITH SOME EXPERIENCE, ALTHOUGH BEGINNERS ARE WELCOME.** Unspoiled areas, waterfalls, edible plants, and flowers. Also offers stock-seat or western riding and hunt-seat (jumping) for advanced riders. A philanthropic concern, EDC turns over some profits to the academy's apprenticeship program for underprivileged and physically challenged local children. Weight restrictions apply. Reservations required. **HINT: BRING A BAG OF CARROT STICKS OR APPLE CHUNKS FOR YOUR HORSE.**

Kauai Water Ski and Surf Co. ★★★
4-356 Kuhio Highway, Wailua, ☎ *(808) 822-3574.*
http://www.kauai-waterski-kayak-surf.com/
Water ski the Wailua River (**THE ONLY FRESH-WATER SKIING AREA IN THE WHOLE STATE**), where conditions are ideal about 95 percent of the year. Kauai Water Ski, located in the Kinipopo Shopping Village, will provide a MasterCraft ski boat with a personal driver, equipment (including wakeboards and kneeboards), as well as instruction. Passengers can hitch a ride for free. Kayaks, surfboards, body boards, fins, and snorkel sets for rent. Also recommended is **Ski Enthusiast,** ☎ *(808) 822-2796,* open 8 a.m.–10 p.m. Expert instruction from beginner to advanced. General admission: $30–$100.

North Shore
Hanalei

Kayak Kauai Outfitters ★★★
P.O. Box 508, Hanalei, 96714, ☎ (808) 826-9844.
http://www.outfitterskauai.com/
Located one mile past the Hanalei Bridge, Kayak Kauai Outfitters specializes in guided river and ocean-kayak tours—some safe and relaxing, and others quite rigorous. **GOOD FOR FIRST-TIMERS IN REASONABLE SHAPE (AND CONFIDENT IN THE WATER!) IS THE THREE-HOUR GUIDED TOUR OF THE HANALEI RIVER AND NATIONAL WILDLIFE REFUGE, WHICH INCLUDES SNORKELING.** Also in the same category is the five-hour Wailua River and Waterfall Adventure (some hiking involved). More rad types will enjoy the Na Pali Sea Kayak Voyage along the Na Pali Coast, where participants explore a volcanic sea cave. This is quite a workout, and involves about five to six hours of intermittent paddling—just in case, the company's van picks you up at the other end! General admission: $65–$150.

Kayak Kauai Outfitters Bicycle Beach Cruise ★★★
P.O. Box 508, Hanalei, 96714, ☎ (808) 826-9844.
Two guided bicycle tours offer two perspectives of the island. The Hanalei Cruise takes in Waioli Mission and Church, taro fields, and lovely island homes before winding up in Hanalei Bay for a refreshing swim. The Kapaa Cruise involves pedaling along a level bikeway along the beach and reef; **PERHAPS YOU'LL SPY A SPOUTING HUMPBACK WHALE (IN SEASON), GREEN SEA TURTLES, OR SPINNER DOLPHINS.** This cruise also includes a swim in either a saltwater pool or freshwater stream, and/or a reef hike. Both are three hours in length, and include bicycle, helmet, and refreshments. **GREAT FOR ALL FAMILY MEMBERS.** Two cruises per day in the morning and afternoon. Call for rates.

Windsurf Kauai ★★★
P.O. Box 323, Hanalei, 96714, ☎ (808) 828-6838.
Special hours: call for appointment.
ANINI BEACH IS THE BEST PLACE TO LEARN TO WINDSURF, according to the experts, who claim that anyone can learn, regardless of age, as long as you pay attention to instructions.

Ideal conditions include a shallow, reef-protected lagoon and a steady, gentle breeze. All you have to do is bring your suit and lots of sunscreen—Windsurf Kauai will supply the rest. Also recommended is Anini Beach Windsurfing, *Box 1602, Hanalei, 96714,* ☎ *(808) 826-9463.* Also equipment rentals and sales. General admission.

Princeville

Princeville Health Club and Spa ★★★
5-3900 Kuhio Highway, Princeville, 96722, ☎ *(808) 826-5030. Special hours: Saturdays from 8 a.m., Sundays to 6 p.m.*
http://www.princeville.com/play/pvspa.html

Work out, flake out, or have someone labor over you for the day, week, or month. THESE TEMPORARY MEMBERSHIPS INCLUDE ADMISSION, PRIVATE LOCKER, UNLIMITED EXERCISE CLASSES, WEIGHT ROOM, LAP POOL, WHIRLPOOL, DRY SAUNA, AND STEAM ROOM. Spa treatments and towels extra, of course. Aerobicize or do a routine on a Lifecycle or Stairmaster (that is, if the views of Bali Hai from the floor-to-ceiling windows don't distract you). Several massage therapies, from Swedish to deep tissue to aromatherapy to Hawaiian lomi-lomi, are available. Pamper your pores with a facial using the Aveda natural-skin care line or a vaporizer, or wrap that bod in seaweed or Hawaiian sea salt. Prices for massage or facial and body treatments per hour are reasonable and include the use of the steam, sauna, Jacuzzi, and locker rooms. General admission: $12–$90.

Princeville Resort Golf Courses ★★★★
P.O. Box 3040, Princeville, 96722, ☎ *(808) 826-5000.*
http://www.princeville.com/play/pvgolf.html

A golfer's nirvana, the Princeville Resort's courses include the 18-hole Prince Course, designed by Robert Trent Jones, Jr., which has been ranked numero uno in the state by *Golf Digest*. The Makai Course, also designed by Jones, is divided into three nine-hole segments; you can choose to face the ocean, lakes, or woods, or combine the three. It was the home of the Women's Kemper Open for five years. Both the Prince and Makai courses have fantastic views—the Prince meanders through 390 acres of rolling terrain, interspersed with junglelike foliage, waterfalls, streams, and ravines. Even the jaded Jones, after designing more than 160 courses in 33 countries over a 27-year career, was moved to say: "In all the world, I never expect to find a more spectacularly beautiful place to build a golf course than Princeville, overlooking Hanalei Bay." Wow. If you opt to play the Makai Course's 27 holes all at once, you'll need to repair to the adjoining Princeville Health Club and Spa for a "Golfer's Massage," a half-hour treatment concentrating specifically on the neck, back, legs, and feet. You'll need it. General admission: $100–$200.

Princeville Tennis Club ★★★
P.O. Box 3040, Princeville, 96722, ☎ (808) 826-3620.
Centrally located next to the Princeville Resorts' Makai Clubhouse, this is one of **THE BEST CHOICES ON THE ISLAND FOR TENNIS.** There are six courts available (lower price is for resort guests), professional instruction by appointment, programs, and tournaments. Memberships are available by the week, month, quarter, or year. Full-service pro shop ($8 racquet rental, $20 ball machine rental). General admission.

South Shore
Koloa

CJM Country Stables ★★★
1731 Kelaukia Street, Koloa, 96736, ☎ (808) 742-6096.
http://www.cjmstables.com/
Offering three coast and mountain-trail rides from its headquarters in the Poipu area, CJM, which stands for "come join me," is run by Jim Miranda, a real Hawaiian paniolo (cowboy). While moseying along the bluffs overlooking Mahaulepu Beach, Miranda relates colorful stories about the area and Kauai ranching in general. The early-morning ride from 8:30–11:30 a.m. includes a breakfast picnic. Groups are purposely kept small (so they can keep track of you), with only eight riders or so per outing. General admission.

Poipu Bay Resort Golf Course ★★★
2250 Ainako Street, Koloa, 96756, ☎ (808) 742-8711.
Situated next to the Hyatt Regency Kauai on Kauai's south shore, the Poipu Bay Resort Golf Course is a 210-acre, 18-hole, par-72 Scottish-links-style course designed by Robert Trent Jones, Jr. **NICKNAMED THE "PEBBLE BEACH OF THE PACIFIC,"** this 6845-yard-long course played host to the PGA Grand Slam of Golf shortly after it opened in 1994. Among the

hazards are stunning ocean views, 86 bunkers, several lakes, and trade winds. Oh, and parts of the course stop just shy of intimidating sea cliffs. Facilities include a pro shop, clubhouse/restaurant, driving range, putting and chipping green, practice sand bunkers, and locker/shower rooms. A few minutes west, the Kiahuna Golf Club, 2545 Kiahuna Plantation Drive, ☎ *(808) 742-9595*, also designed by Jones, is a par-70, 18-hole course with 27 well-preserved archaeological sites. Look out for the 14th hole. **GREAT FUN FOR EXPERIENCED GOLFERS ON A BUDGET:** it's $55 per round, including cart. Facilities include a driving range, pro shop, snack bar, and putting green. General admission.

Poipu

Sea Sport Divers ★★★
2827 Poipu Road, Poipu, ☎ *(808) 742-9303.*
Hours: 8 a.m.–5 p.m.

Located in the Poipu area, Sea Sport Divers is Kauai's only full-service PADI and NAUI Scuba Training facility. It offers half-day, two-tank boat excursions to some of Kauai's best cave dives. One is Sheraton Caverns, just offshore from the Sheraton Kauai. These underwater grottos range from 35 to 60 feet in depth. The so-called General Store is a 65- to 80-foot deep reef with a wide variety of marine life (eels, turtles, sharks, manta rays) and a submerged 19th-century steamship to explore. For those just getting started, Sea Sport Divers will help you get certified, with free pool lessons and introductory dives (no experience necessary). Ask about private charters to Niihau, the "Forbidden Isle," with 130-foot-deep reef walls and night dives. Top-quality equipment, rentals, and repairs are available 24 hours a day. Also recommended is Fathom Five Adventures (love the name), *3450 Poipu Road, Koloa,* ☎ *(808) 742-6991*, also a five-star outfit offering certification courses and two-tank dives. It's open Monday-Saturday from 7:30 a.m.–6 p.m.; Sundays until 4:30 p.m. If you're staying on the eastern shore, there are several companies in the Kapaa area, including Aquatic Adventures, *4-1380 Kuhio Highway, 96746,* ☎ *(808) 822-1434*, a service-oriented PADI five-star dive center, and Dive Kauai Scuba Center, *976 Kuhio Highway, #C,* ☎ *(808) 822-0452*. Both offer certification and specialty dives, including wreck dives to the *Luckenbach* (no, you won't see Waylon and Willie and the boys—that's in Texas), a German freighter that

Poipu Beach

Margo Oberg's Surfing School ★★
Kiahuna Plantation Resort, Poipu Beach, ☎ *(808) 742-6411.*
Lessons by a seven-time world champion. Special beginner classes. Prices below are per person, per hour. For a complete line of surfing equipment and clothing, sales, and rentals, try Progressive Expressions, ☎ *(808) 742-6041.* General admission: $40.

The Anara Spa ★★★
Hyatt Regency Kauai, Poipu Beach, ☎ *(808) 742-1234.*
This 25,000-square-foot spa features outdoor lava-rock showers and colorful flowers. Within the facility are 10 indoor/outdoor treatment rooms, a 25-yard heated lap pool in an open courtyard, a Turkish steam bath, and Finnish saunas. La'ao Ma Anara, or day at the Spa, offers a complete Hawaiian-flavored spa treatment—after a 10-minute steam bath, you'll be coated with red clay found at the base of Waialeale (native healers find it to be extremely medicinal) mixed with sea salt. Afterwards have a lomi-lomi massage and seaweed facial, followed by lunch at Kupono Café and a complimentary hand-painted *pareo* for your pains. Not bad. General admission: $20–$130.

Kalaheo
Sports/Recreation

Kukuiolono Golf Course ★★
Kukuiolono Park, Kalaheo, 96741, ☎ *(808) 335-9940.*
Hours: 6:30 a.m.–4:30 p.m.
This nine-hole course is cheap at $5 a round. No reservations taken; first-come, first-served basis only. Facilities include a golf club/restaurant, driving range, pro shop, putting green. General admission: $5.

Makaweli

Niihau Safaris ★★
Box 370, Makaweli, HI 96769, Makaweli, 96769,

☎ *(808) 335-3500.*

The Robinson family of Niihau is (very) slowly opening the island to outsiders, including avid (and wealthy) hunters who can pay $1400 per person per day to go on wild boar (there are about 8000 on the island) and ram-stalking trips. You can hunt all by yourself or bring a party of seven (maximum). Choose your weapons—bow and arrow, shotgun, or rifle. Arrival is by helicopter, a 20-minute flight over the Kaulahiki Channel. Reservations required; for information, see Keamano Beach listing. General admission: $1400.

Waimea

Na Pali Explorer I

9633 Kaumalii Highway, Waimea, 96796, ☎ *(808) 335-9909.*
Leaves from Kikiaola Harbor between Kekaha and Waimea. Unforgettable rafting trek along Kauai's pristine coastline on the *Explorer I*, the latest in Zodiac technology. A hard-hull Hurricane Zodiac is a custom-designed craft with twin Volvo engines; a deep-V fiberglass hull for speed, maneuverability and shallow draft can glide to more remote coastal areas than most other vessels. Na Pali Coast Day Trek, beach landing at Nualolo Kai sea caves, depending on the weather. Narrated hike of ancient Hawaiian fishing village, snorkeling, continental breakfast, and catered picnic lunch.

Where to Stay

You'll find a lot of choices on the island, from budget rooms to swanky resorts with B&Bs, condos, and campsites well-represented. If you have deep pockets, like to be surrounded by other well-heeled guests, and want access to a couple of top golf courses, **Princeville Resort,** on the north shore, will probably satiate you. Visitors who like to be close to Kauai's ancestral heritage and ancient culture usually opt for east-coast accommodations—such as the famous **Coco Palms Resort**—so as to be close to the sacred **Wailua River.** The majority of visitors head straight for the south shore and **Poipu Beach** where the sun is plentiful, the surf is calm year-round, and there's is an abundance of condos, as well as hotels. For more economical hotels, motels, and apartment hotels, **Lihue** or **Kapaa** are the best places to bed down.

East Shore
Kapaa
Bed-and-Breakfasts

Alohilani Bed & Breakfast　　　$99–$109　　★★★
1470 Wanaao Road, Kapaa, 96746, ☎ *(800) 533-9316,*
☎ *(808) 823-0128.*
http://www.hawaiian.net/~alohila/
The Alohilani ("Bright Sky") Bed and Breakfast Inn has an Upcountry location above Kapaa Town, approximately 20 minutes from the airport. Accommodations consist of three units, all with cable TV, microwaves, and private baths. The most interesting is the Malulani Guest Cottage, which is detached from the main house and is filled with antiques, dolls, and other reminders of the island's past. The deck that surrounds the cottage on all sides affords views of the ocean, mountains, and valley. Breakfast is served on the deck or in the gazebo in the garden. You can expect Hawaiian coffee, fresh juices, tropical fruits, breads and muffins, and homemade jams and jellies. Amenities: balcony or patio. Three rooms. Credit cards: not accepted.

Hale 'O Wailele　　　$120–$175　　★★★★
7084-A Kahuna Road, Kapaa, 96746, ☎ *(800) 77K-AUAI,*
(808) 822-7911, FAX (808) 823-8883.
http://www.lauhala.com/kahuna/requestinfo.html
A **TERRIFIC VALUE** nestled at the base of the Makaleha Forest Reserve, Hale 'O Wailele (House of Leaping Waterfalls) is a modern plantation home turned B&B that's part of an eight-acre native Hawaiian family estate and tropical-flower farm. The three suites within the Hale all feature Hawaiian collectibles and art, imported hardwood floors, and Persian rugs, Italian marble baths, refrigerators, private sunning decks, and Jacuzzis. Large color TVs have built-in VCRs. The largest of the three suites, the Canoe, affords views of the namesake waterfalls while you lie in bed, resting on imported Egyptian cotton sheets. The suite also has a separate dining area. Activities on the estate include flower-lei making, barbecuing in the coconut grove, working out in the gym, or swimming in the new lava-rock-terraced waterfall swimming pool. If you must leave the estate, **YOU'LL BE PROVIDED WITH HIKING AND BEACH GEAR FREE OF CHARGE**; snorkeling gear, golf carts, and

mountain bikes are available for a nominal fee. Amenities: exercise room, Jacuzzi, balcony or patio. Six rooms. Credit cards: MC, V.

Kakalina's Bed & Breakfast $90–$175   ★★★
6781 Kawaihai Road, Kapaa, 96746, ☎ *(808) 822-2328.*
http://www.kakalina.com/accommodations.html
Kakalina's Bed & Breakfast is located on a working tropical flower farm. Guests are welcome to visit the gardens and enjoy the variety of exotic flora they contain. The B&B is located 10 miles from the airport, and offers easy access to either mountain or beach activities. Of the two units, the semicircular Hale Akahi suite is the most intriguing—it's the handiwork of host Bob Offley, who's a master carpenter. Both have private entrances and private baths, color TVs and VCRs, coffee makers, microwaves, refrigerators, and laundry facilities. Naturally, tropical plants and flowers are used extensively inside the house. Breakfast is usually fresh juice, fresh fruit, pastries, and Kauai (not Kona) coffee. Two rooms. Credit cards: not accepted.

Wailua Country Vacation Rentals $75–$160   ★★
505 Kamalu Road, Kapaa, 96746, ☎ *(808) 822-0166,*
FAX (808) 822-2708.
With its two-acre front yard, the Wailua Country B&B Rentals property at Kapaa well deserves the adjective "spacious." Located behind Sleeping Giant Mountain, the 5000-square-foot main residence has been recently remodeled, but retains the pre-Iniki arched Spanish facade which looks out onto numerous tropical fruit trees and a rushing brook that cuts through the lawn. Hawaiian and European antiques have been used to furnish the units and give them an exceptionally homelike feel. The beautiful oak floors are scattered with Persian and Oriental rugs. The rental units are located on the second floor. One suite has a large bath with Jacuzzi. Neither has kitchen facilities, but a breakfast of fresh-baked bread, homemade jam, fresh fruits, coffee, and tea is included in the rates. On the same property, but away from the main house, are three new cottages, with neat white paint and pink-tile roofs. Interiors have a feminine touch, with lacy curtains, plenty of white wicker, and wooden furniture. We especially like the two-bedroom cottage with its French doors opening out onto its private lawn with a strategically placed hammock under exotic fruit trees. (If you

lie very still, you'll see an astounding number of tropical birds using the birdbath or sipping nectar from the native flowers that grow with uninhibited exuberance in the shadow of Sleeping Giant Mountain). The cottages have either kitchenettes or full kitchens. Cottage guests add an extra $5 for breakfast. All units have color TVs and ceiling fans. Washer and dryer available for a fee. Amenities: Jacuzzi, balcony or patio. Six rooms. Credit cards: not accepted.

Hotels

Hotel Coral Reef $79–$99 ★★
1516 Kuhio Highway, Kapaa, 96746, ☎ *(808) 822-4481.*
http://www.bestplaceshawaii.com/vacplanner/kvp/clients/coral/

NOWHERE ELSE IN HAWAII WILL YOU FIND AN OCEANFRONT ROOM FOR THE RATES OFFERED AT THIS GEM. A haven for the budget traveler, the Coral Reef is situated in a coconut grove 50 feet from a sandy beach. The main building offers cheaper and less-desirable accommodations with no view of the ocean. The Oceanfront Building has well-proportioned rooms with ocean views, louvered windows, and private lanais. The units have been recently redecorated and the color scheme tends to run to tones of dusty rose and blue. Actually, it blends very well with the blue ocean outside and the effect is quite pleasing. No phones in rooms, but there's a pay phone in the lobby, as well as complimentary coffee service. Amenities: balcony or patio.

Kauai Coconut Beach Resort $95–$170 ★★★
P.O. Box 830, Kapaa, 96746, ☎ *(800) 22A-LOHA,*
☎ *(808) 822-3455, FAX (808) 822-1830.*
http://www.hawaiianhotels.com/Web/Main/Kcb/KCB Main.cfm?Orig=KCB

As its name implies, the Kauai Coconut Beach Resort sits gracefully within a 10-acre coconut grove along Waipouli Beach. The room rate includes a complimentary breakfast buffet and complimentary cocktails and pupus. ALONG WITH AN AWARD-WINNING FRIDAY-EVENING LUAU, there's a nightly torch-lighting ceremony and a Hawaiian immersion program ranging from storytelling to crafts demonstrations. Restaurants include the Flying Lobster, which serves up this choice crustacean at a reasonable price, and throws in a salad bar and lobster bisque to boot. Cocktails and entertainment at Cook's Landing

Lodge. Shopping opportunities nearby at Coconut Plantation and Kapaa Town. Amenities: tennis, Jacuzzi, balcony or patio, family plan. 311 rooms. Credit cards: A, CB, DC, D, MC, V.

Lihue
Condos

Aston Kauai Beach Villas $170–$295   ★★★
4330 Kauai Beach Drive, Lihue, 96766, ☎ (800) 922-7866, ☎ (808) 245-7711.
http://www.bolack.com/lodging/hawaii/13akbv.htm
These nicely priced luxury condominiums fronting a white-sand beach are surrounded by coconut palms, lush gardens, and a reflecting lagoon (with swans!). The spacious one- and two-bedroom units are fairly self-sufficient, with complete kitchens and washer/dryers. One distinct advantage the property has, though, is that it shares the facilities of the neighboring Outrigger Kauai Beach Hotel. Signing privileges are available at any of the Outrigger's restaurants. THE WAILUA GOLF COURSE IS NEXT DOOR. Amenities: tennis, balcony or patio, family plan. 150 rooms. Credit cards: A, MC, V.

Resorts

Kauai Marriott Resort and Beach Club $229–$2000   ★★★★
Kalapaki Beach, Lihue, 96766, ☎ (808) 245-5050. Rated restaurant: Kukui's
http://www.marriotthotels.com/marriott/LIHHI/home.htm
Formerly the Westin (until Iniki turned it to kindling), this stunning resort boasts an enviable location on gorgeous Kalapaki Beach, near Lihue. The pool, in particular, is spectacular and meanders over 26,000 square feet replete with bridges and fantastic animals spouting water. The gardens are meticulously cared for by an attentive staff and deserve more attention than they get from most guests. BECAUSE OF THE PROXIMITY TO THE BEACH, EXTENSIVE WATERSPORTS ARE AVAILABLE, FROM SWIMMING TO KAYAKING TO FISHING. There's horseback riding and hiking nearby, and it's adjacent to a 36-hole golf course. There are six restaurants, including the '40s Waikiki-themed Duke's Canoe Club, and two cocktail lounges. Accommodations feature mini-bars, free cable TV, and in-room movies; some rooms have ocean views. Amenities: health club,

North Shore

Anahola
Bed-and-Breakfasts

Mahina Kai $125–$200 ★★
*Box 699, Anahola, 96703, ☎ (800) 337-1134,
☎ (808) 822-9451.*
http://www.mahinakai.com/

Mahina Kai is the guest wing of a distinctive Asian-Pacific country home. We would add that the emphasis is overwhelmingly on the Asian, with wide, sloping, blue-tile roofs, water gardens, and shoji screens. **SEVERAL OF THE ROOMS HAVE SLIDING PANELS THAT OPEN ONTO PRIVATE LANAIS AND GARDENS FILLED WITH EXOTIC TROPICAL PLANTS. MAHINA KAI IS A POPULAR SETTING FOR CORPORATE MEETINGS.** There is a 1000-square-foot meeting room available in the garden Tea House and four private meeting rooms available in the main house. Continental breakfast is available for occupants of the bedrooms; the apartment has its own kitchen. Extras include bicycles, snorkeling, and beach gear. Amenities: Jacuzzi, business services. Four rooms.

Hanalei

Historic B&B $80 ★★
P.O. Box 1662, Hanalei, 96714, ☎ (808) 826-4622.
http://www.historicbnb.com/

The eclectic traveler will insist on spending at least one night at the Historic B&B when visiting Hanalei. Right in the center of town across the street from the Wishing Well Shave Ice truck, it was constructed in 1901 as a place of worship for the Japanese Buddhist workers on the local plantations. It served as a focal point for the Japanese community for more than 80 years. Today it has been meticulously restored and is listed on the National and State Historic Registries of Buildings. Co-owner Jeff Shepherd is an artist and professional chef. His artwork is displayed on the walls and he is responsible for the gourmet breakfasts that appear every morning in the breakfast room. No small children or pets. Three rooms. Credit cards: not accepted.

Condos

Hanalei Colony Resort $160–$320 ★★★
P.O. Box 206, Hanalei, 96714, ☎ *(800) 628-3004,*
☎ *(808) 826-6235, FAX (808) 826-9893.*
http://www.hcr.com/

Hanalei Colony Resort bills itself as the "last" resort before the road ends at Na Pali. It should actually say the "only" resort, as the only accommodations in the immediate area are a few vacation-home rentals. However, **NOTHING WILL EVER BE ABLE TO DETRACT FROM THE RESORT'S UNEQUALED LOCATION ON THE BEACH ON KAUAI'S NORTH SHORE.** The resort takes full advantage of a narrow strip of land between the beach and the volcanic cliffs behind it. The corner beachfront units are especially popular because of their 180-degree view of the ocean. A mai tai on one of these lanais is a real experience. All of the breezy, light-filled units have two bedrooms, separate living and dining areas, and kitchens. **A PLUS FOR WEEK-LONG VISITORS: THE SEVENTH DAY IS FREE. ASK ABOUT CONDO/CAR PACKAGES.** Note: there are no TVs, stereos, or dishwashers. This is one place you really can get away from it all. Amenities: Jacuzzi, balcony or patio, family plan. 52 rooms. Credit cards: A, DC, D, MC, V.

Hotels

Hanalei Bay Resort $185–$390 ★★★
P.O. Box 220, Hanalei, 96714, ☎ *(800) 367-5004,*
☎ *(808) 591-2235, FAX (808) 596-0158.*
http://www.hanaleibayresort.com/

Now owned by the Quintus Resorts Group, The Hanalei Bay Resort is one of the world's top "ownership" resorts, but you can rent rooms on a nightly basis. Many local residents think it has the same view of the fabled bay and the cliffs of "Bali Hai" as the tony Princeville Hotel, but at half the price. The Hanalei Bay contains 140 spacious rooms with a refrigerator and coffee maker, and studios with kitchenettes. Upper-floor units have lofts. The Bali Hai Restaurant has incredible sunset views, Pacific Rim cuisine, and **THE BEST JAZZ ON THE ISLAND** Sundays in the adjoining lounge. **SPECIAL PACKAGES AND RATES ARE ALWAYS AVAILABLE; CONTACT THEM DIRECTLY.** Amenities: tennis, Jacuzzi, balcony or patio, family plan. 215 rooms. Credit cards: A, CB, DC, D, MC, V.

Kilauea
Bed-and-Breakfasts

Hale Ho'o Maha $65–$90 ★★★

*P.O. Box 422, Kilauea, 96754, ☎ (800) 851-0291,
☎ (808) 828-1341.*
http://www.aloha.net/~hoomaha/

A TERRIFIC BUY, Hale Ho'o Maha (House of Rest) is a split-level home on five acres of landscaped grounds. Among other things, IT HAS GREAT BEACH ACCESS (the fantastic Kalihiwai Bay is a 10-minute stroll down the road, and Secret Beach is a 15-minute hike from the front door). The four guest rooms are named after tropical fruits. One of them, the Pineapple Room, features a seven-foot circular bed with a custom-quilted, pineapple-motif bedspread. All have color cable TV, phones, and ceiling fans. Two have private baths. The hosts, Toby and Kirby Searles, love the great outdoors; Toby will even take you scuba diving. If you want to explore the other side of the island, ask them about their cabin in Kokee State Park. Four rooms.
Credit cards: MC, V.

Makai Farms $90 ★★

P.O. Box 93, Kilauea, 96754, ☎ (808) 828-1874.

Accommodations at Makai Farms consist of a private, detached apartment away from the main residence on a family-owned farm devoted to the cultivation of orchids. FROM THE UPSTAIRS BEDROOM THERE ARE GORGEOUS MOUNTAIN AND OCEAN VIEWS. It has a king-size bed and sleeper sofa. Downstairs is a kitchen (light meals and snacks only, please) and bathroom with shower. There's another shower outside for washing off sandy feet. MAKAI FARMS IS IN A GREAT LOCATION JUST OUTSIDE KILAUEA, MIDWAY BETWEEN THE GOLF COURSES OF PRINCEVILLE AND ONLY MINUTES FROM THE FABLED BEACHES ON THE NA PALI COAST. Children welcome. Two-night minimum preferred. Amenities: family plan. One room.
Credit cards: not accepted.

Princeville

Hale 'Aha $115–$210 ★★★

*3875 Kamehameha Road, Princeville, 96722,
☎ (800) 826-6733, ☎ (808) 826-6733.*
http://www.pixi.com/~kauai/

A SUPER FIND FOR GOLF LOVERS, Hale'Aha overlooks the sixth green of the Princeville's Makai Golf course on one side and the ocean on the other. The three-story house is furnished in tropical pastels with touches of rattan and native wood. Bountiful continental breakfasts include fresh-fruit smoothies and Kona coffee. Ruth and Herb Bockelman, the hosts, are some of the warmest people around (although no children are permitted) and like to call their establishment "a friendly alternative to a fine hotel." We agree. Amenities: balcony or patio. Four rooms. Credit cards: MC, V.

Condos

Sealodge at Princeville $105–$130   ★★
P.O. Box 3400, Princeville, 96722, ☎ *(808) 826-7168.*
http://www.hestara.com/
Sealodge at Princeville, a cedar-shake complex on a bluff overlooking the ocean, was totally rebuilt after Hurricane Iniki, and OFFERS SPECTACULAR OCEAN VIEWS FOR A REASONABLE PRICE IN A MILLION-DOLLAR LOCATION. The secluded beach is reached via a steep path (marked "use at own risk"), but other great North Shore strands are only five minutes away. Lazier types can use the pool, which is right next door. Two-night minimum. Credit cards: not accepted.

The Cliffs at Princeville $180–$250   ★★
P.O. Box 1005, Princeville, 96714, ☎ *(808) -.*
http://www.cliffs-princeville.com/Oceanside_Resorts/ The_Cliffs/
Adjacent to the famed 45-hole Princeville Golf complex designed by Robert Trent Jones, Jr., the sprawling Cliffs at Princeville provides GOOD VALUE FOR GOLFERS WHO CAN'T AFFORD THE PRINCEVILLE HOTEL. Accommodations are either one-bedroom, a one-bedroom with loft, or four-bedroom units. Each features a fully equipped kitchen, two full baths, maid service, wet bar, color TV, guest sofabed, and two private lanais with ocean or mountain views. Some have VCRs and extra TVs. Amenities: tennis, Jacuzzi, sauna, balcony or patio, family plan. Credit cards: A, DC, D, MC, V.

Resorts

Princeville Hotel $299–$4500 ★★★★★

5520 Kahaku Road, Princeville, 96722, ☎ (800) 826-4400, ☎ (808) 826-9644, FAX (808) 826-1166.

Whatever one thinks of the Princeville Hotel and its Versailles-size lobby, with acres of obsidian and green marble, gilt-topped columns, richly embroidered Renaissance tapestries, and Greek sea-god statues, nobody disputes the fact that the hotel sits on one of the most stunning pieces of real estate on Kauai. The trio of buildings that makes up the property terraces down a ridge, directly fronting Hanalei Bay and the mysterious, saw-tooth cliffs better known in Hollywoodland as "Bali Hai." **VIEWS OF THE SUNSET FROM THE FLOOR-TO-CEILING WINDOWS OF THE LIVING ROOM, THE HOTEL'S MODESTLY NAMED LOUNGE, ARE LEGENDARY.** Besides the glorious setting, people continue to come for the **WORLD-CLASS GOLF, EXCELLENT FOOD, AND THE WARMTH OF THE STAFF (FOR ALL ITS TRAPPINGS, THE ATMOSPHERE IS COMPLETELY UNPRETENTIOUS).** Guest rooms are all nicely sized and amenity-filled, and decorated in beige or green color schemes. Try to book a Prince Junior suite, on floors 8–11; these have especially gorgeous views, which extend to the sumptuous marble baths with spa tubs and gold fixtures. One unique feature to all rooms is the "magic" window in the bathroom that becomes opaque at will by electronic means (why you'd not want to look at THAT view is a mystery). Among the hotel's entertainments is an in-house movie theater, where you can watch *South Pacific* until you gag (first-run pictures are also shown, for variety). To immerse yourself in the real thing, take a lauhala-weaving class or watch a poi-pounding demonstration. When hunger strikes, there's room service, the beach bar, or afternoon tea and snacks in the aforementioned Living Room, which also features first-class Hawaiian entertainment. There's also a large pool with a swim-up bar, three Roman-style Jacuzzis, and a wading pool for the kids. All manner of watersports, from kayaking to scuba diving, can be arranged. Amenities: tennis, health club, exercise room, Jacuzzi, sauna, balcony or patio, family plan, business services. 252 rooms. Credit cards: A, DC, D, MC, V.

South Shore
Koloa
Bed-and-Breakfasts

Island Home $80–$90 ★★
1707 Kelaukia Street, Koloa, 96765, ☎ *(808) 742-2839.*
http://www.islandhomebandb.com/
A GREAT PLACE TO STAY FOR BUDGET-MINDED TRAVELERS who want to be near the beach, a stay at Island Home ensures that the beach is never far away. A walking path near the B&B extends from Shipwreck Beach to Brennecke's Beach. You'll also get plenty of privacy at a good price. The two units in the large residence have their own entrances, tasteful interior decor, private baths, TVs and VCRs, a microwave, and refrigerator. Laundry facilities are available. Breakfasts consist of tropical fruits, beverages, and homemade breads. Coolers, beach mats, and towels are provided. Two rooms. Credit cards: not accepted.

Resorts

Hyatt Regency Kauai $280–$1800 ★★★★★
1571 Poipu Road, Koloa, 96756, ☎ *(800) 233-1234,*
☎ *(808) 742-1234, FAX (808) 742-1557.*
http://kauai.hyatt.com/property/index.jhtml
The Hyatt Regency Kauai's facilities are interesting in that their builders have deliberately eschewed the modern high-tech school of architecture and were determined to re-create traditional plantation-style dwellings of the '20s and '30s. The building that houses the main entrance and lobby is impressive. Situated above an artificial lagoon and with sturdy pillars supporting a green-tiled, hipped roof, the building is firmly anchored to its surroundings. Reminiscent of an Oriental temple, the hotel is mysterious and invites exploration. The interior of the Hyatt Regency Kauai is everything we had been led to expect. The lavish use of native woods gives a sense of stability and harks back to earlier, less-harried times. Equally evocative of another era are the cast-bronze lighting fixtures and gates used throughout the public areas. Some are authentic pieces, salvaged from demolished buildings, and others are reproductions, but we challenge you to determine which is which. We can only applaud the builder's decision to minimize the use of air conditioning in favor of wide verandas, high ceilings, and sliding doors that encourage a natural flow of air. As

a result, there is no need for artificial cooling in the public areas. GUESTS ROOMS ARE EXCEPTIONALLY LARGE WITH SEPARATE SITTING AREAS AND LARGE LANAIS. Furniture is either rattan or more substantial wooden pieces designed to complement the '20s and '30s style. The Hyatt Regency has 6 restaurants to choose from, more than 10 acres of lagoons all linked by streams, waterfalls, and waterslides, one of which is a stomach-lurching 140 feet tall. Guests can swim, float or otherwise propel themselves from lagoon to lagoon past a carefully composed tropical landscape that includes the artfully placed wreckage of an interisland schooner. IN CERTAIN CIRCLES, GOLF ON THE PAR-72, 6956-YARD COURSE DESIGNED BY ROBERT TRENT JONES, JR. IS THE MAIN REASON TO COME TO HAWAII. Others can proceed to the Anara Spa, where the preferred treatment is Hawaiian lomi-lomi massage, in which a mixture of red clay from the base of Mount Waialeale and sea salt is applied to the entire body, after which one is wrapped in ti leaves. IT'S POSSIBLE TO SPEND YOUR WHOLE VACATION WITHOUT LEAVING THE HYATT'S GROUNDS—THERE'S THAT MUCH TO DO. CALL FOR SPECIAL PACKAGE RATES. Amenities: tennis, health club, Jacuzzi, sauna, balcony or patio, family plan, club floor, business services. 600 rooms. Credit cards: A, DC, D, MC, V.

Lawai
Bed-and-Breakfasts

Marjorie's Kauai Inn $88–$96 ★★★

P.O. Box 866, Lawai, 96765, ☎ *(800) 717-8838,*
☎ *(808) 332-8838.*
http://www.marjorieskauaiinn.com/

MARJORIE'S LOVELY ROOMS ARE PERCHED OVERLOOKING THE SPECTACULAR LAWAI VALLEY. From private lanais, guests can look down on the tree tops or across at the mountains on the other side of the valley. The Valley View and Tradewind rooms have been constructed recently. Both have queen-size beds, private baths, and a mini-kitchen with microwave and coffeemaker, plus laundry facilities. THE PUKA IS AIMED AT THE SINGLE TRAVELER ON A BUDGET. It has its own private entrance, too, and a comfortable futon serves as seating as well as the bed. All rooms have cable TV and phones. Nearby activities for Marjorie's guests include ocean kayaking and sugarcane-road bike riding. Amenities: Jacuzzi, balcony or patio. Three rooms. Credit cards: not accepted.

Poipu
Bed-and-Breakfasts

Gloria's Spouting Horn Bed & Breakfast $250-$300 ★★★

4464 Lawai Beach Road, Poipu, 96756, ☎ (808) 742-6995.
http://www.gloriasbedandbreakfast.com/

Gloria's Bed & Breakfast was a fixture on the Kauai scene before Hurricane Iniki quite literally blew it out to sea. Fortunately, owners Gloria and Bob Merkle rebuilt their establishment, and the **RESULT IS WHAT MAY BE THE PLUPERFECT BED-AND-BREAKFAST ESTABLISHMENT IN HAWAII—OR ANYWHERE, FOR THAT MATTER. ALL ROOMS ARE OCEANFRONT ROOMS, AND NONE ARE MORE THAN 30 FEET FROM THE WAVES.** In the yard there's a lava-rock shower under a mango tree to wash off the saltwater off before you go inside. Each room is furnished individually with antiques. Probably the most famous room is the Puana Aloha, with a sensual canopy of intertwined willow branches. All have private Japanese-style soaking tubs. Guests get off to a good start each morning with a Hawaiian breakfast served on the lanai (or you can serve yourself and take your breakfast back to your room on a tray). Homemade pastries are served with fresh juice. Gloria uses her best English china and linens for this. She will be happy to share her recipes with guests, but they must promise to send her a recipe from the mainland (or wherever) when they get back. **GLORIA'S IS ALSO A FAVORITE VENUE FOR WEDDINGS AND GROUPS; UP TO 25 CAN BE ACCOMMODATED.** No children under 14, no pets. Amenities: balcony or patio, business services. Five rooms. Credit cards: not accepted.

Condos

Poipu Kapili $210–$575 ★★★

2221 Kapili Road, Poipu, 96756, ☎ (800) 443-7714, ☎ (808) 742-6449, FAX (808) 742-9162.
http://www.poipukapili.com/

The Poipu Kapili will more than satisfy travelers with discriminating tastes. Set on five acres, these plantation-style buildings with bright-green hipped roofs are newly rebuilt after the infamous Hurricane Iniki. **ALL OF THE APARTMENTS ARE UNUSUALLY SPACIOUS**—the one-bedroom units are at least 1150 square feet, and the two-bedroom apartments are 1820 square feet and have three bathrooms. Decor depends on the individual owner, but all feature beautiful, louvered, mahogany sliding doors and high ceilings with revolving fans. All have separate living areas, gourmet kitchens, and tons of closet space. There are extra TVs in the bedrooms; the master bedroom has a second VCR. This beach is rocky, but surfers like it for the great breaks. **SANDY POIPU BEACH PARK IS JUST A SHORT WALK AWAY.** Two-story units have patios on the ground floor and balconies (no lanais) on the second floor. **SOME THOUGHTFUL TOUCHES HELP MAKE A VISIT HERE MEMORABLE: A FRESH HERB GARDEN IS AVAILABLE FOR GUESTS TO LIVEN UP THEIR MEALS, BANANAS FROM AN EMPLOYEE'S YARD ARE SOMETIMES LEFT ON DOORSTEPS, AND THERE'S A WEEKLY POOLSIDE CONTINENTAL BREAKFAST.** There are videos ($3 per day) and paperbacks to check out in the office, but you'll have to rent them before closing time at 5 p.m. Amenities: tennis, balcony or patio. 60 rooms. Credit cards: MC, V.

Whaler's Cove $349–$619 ★★★

2640 Puuholo Road, Poipu, 96756, ☎ *(800) 367-7052,* ☎ *(808) -.*
http://www.whalers-cove.com/Oceanside_Resorts/Whalers_Cove/rates.shtml

Whaler's Cove makes the most of its beachfront location, and the buildings are laid out to the natural curve of the ocean. **UNFORTUNATELY, THERE'S NO SANDY BEACH,** but there is the sound of the waves and the wind blowing thorough the coconut palms. The reception areas and all of the individually owned units feature thousands of dollars' worth of koa wood. Each apartment has two bedrooms and two baths, a dining area, gourmet kitchens, and washer/dryer, and some have Jacuzzi tubs in the master baths. Decor varies from apartment to apartment, but they are all uniformly luxe. Some are furnished with Asian antiques, whitewashed wicker and wood, and extra-high platform beds topped with plump cushions. Facilities include a video library. **INQUIRE ABOUT THE MANY PACKAGES THE RESORT OFFERS.** An enthusiastic staff provides concierge service. Amenities: balcony or patio. 39 rooms.

Inns

Poipu Plantation $95–$168 ★★★

1792 Pe'e Road, Poipu, 96756, ☎ *(800) 733-1632,* ☎ *(808) 742-6757.*
http://www.bestinns.net/usa/hi/poipuplantation.html

Although this property, which is **WITHIN WALKING DISTANCE TO POIPU'S BEST BEACHES**, bills itself as a B&B, it really isn't. If any breakfast is served, you've got to make it yourself in the fully equipped kitchen provided in the unit. Affordable, secluded, and quiet, the seven units have one or two bedrooms. Wicker furniture and flowered chintz cushions combine nicely with hardwood floors for a feeling of tropical sophistication. Shoji screens separate the living room from the bedrooms. All have ceiling fans and air conditioning (unusual for these parts). Services include coin-op washer/dryers and an outdoor barbecue/spa area. Amenities: Jacuzzi, balcony or patio. Seven rooms. Credit cards: MC, V.

Resorts

Sheraton Kauai Beach Resort $320-$1100   ★★★

2440 Hoonani Road, Poipu, 96756, ☎ *(800) 325-3535,* ☎ *(808) 742-1661, FAX (808) 742-9777.*

http://www.sheraton-kauai.com/

A wonderful resort experience for everyone at any age, the Sheraton Kauai Beach Resort is located on a stunning, crescent-shaped, white-sand Poipu Beach. Home to **FOUR ENTICING RESTAURANTS**, the resort boasts a beach activities center, a Hawaiian Cultural Center, a spa, and nightly live entertainment. Other features will include a freshwater pool, three tennis courts, and access to five major golf courses. 413 rooms. Credit Cards: MC, V.

Poipu Beach
Bed-and-Breakfasts

Poipu Bed & Breakfast Inn $110-$250   ★★★

2720 Hoonani Road, Poipu Beach, 96756, ☎ *(800) 827-6478,* ☎ *(808) 742-1146, FAX (808) 742-6843.*

http://www.poipu-inn.com/

The Poipu Bed & Breakfast Inn is an imaginative and successful re-creation of Old Hawaii as it should have been. The main building is a 1933 plantation house, renovated and brought up to 1990s specifications. It's close enough to the beach that you can hear the waves pound outside. Guests enter the Great Room through original French doors. They are greeted by white wicker furniture, country pine, an abundance of tropical flowers, and the inn's signature antique carousel horses. Guest rooms are individually decorated with local art and tropical print fabrics. Native woods have been used lavishly on floors, ceilings, and the sliding doors, and louvered windows that let in the trade winds. Bathrooms are state-of-the-art and most have whirlpool tubs. All rooms have color TVs and VCRs, and there's a video library, but no in-room phones. Guests are welcome to have afternoon tea in the Great Room, and a continental breakfast is served a few doors down the street at the Ocean Front Inn, a sister establishment. Four rooms. Credit cards: MC, V.

Condos

Kiahuna Plantation $115–$700 ★★★
2253 Poipu Road, Poipu Beach, 96756, ☎ (800) 688-7444, ☎ (808) 742-6411, FAX (808) 742-7233.
http://www.castleresorts.com/KIA/

THIS DELIGHTFUL PROPERTY, consisting of a number of trim, low-slung white buildings spread out on a coconut grove, faces its own stretch of golden-sand beach. The former home of a sugar plantation manager, it was recently placed under the aegis of Castle Resorts, which hasn't changed anything. The individually owned units are spacious one- and two-bedroom apartments with louvered shutters and classy wood and rattan furnishings. Each has a living and dining area, fully equipped kitchen, color TV and videotape player, and ceiling fans. UNUSUAL FOR A CONDOMINIUM, THE KIAHUNA PLANTATION ALSO OFFERS A MYRIAD OF ENTERTAINMENT OPTIONS. A *"Keiki Klub"* takes kids (ages five–12) in hand for a round of daily activities, from storytelling to Hawaiian games. There's a beach-activities center, concierge, gas barbecues, and picnic tables. Across the street is the resort's own five-star tennis facility (free to guests), pro shop, and swimming pool. TWO 18-HOLE CHAMPIONSHIP GOLF COURSES, THE KIAHUNA GOLF CLUB AND POIPU BAY RESORT COURSE, ARE LOCATED NEARBY, AS IS SHOPPING AND DINING IN POIPU SHOPPING VILLAGE AND KOLOA TOWN. An added attraction on the property is Moir Gardens, featuring a world-class cactus garden. Daily maid service, laundry, beach towels. CHECK THEIR WEBSITE REGULARLY FOR INTERNET SPECIALS AND PACKAGE RATES. Amenities: tennis, balcony or patio, family plan. 330 rooms. Credit cards: A, CB, DC, D, MC, V.

West Shore

Waimea
Camping Grounds

Kokee Lodge Cabins $35–$45   ★★

P.O. Box 819, Waimea, 96796, ☎ *(808) 335-6061.*
http://www.wildernet.com/pages/activity.cfm?actid=HISPKOKIO*53168ldg&areaid=HISPKOK&rectype=Lodging&startrecord=1&fromPage=summary&CU_ID=1

A GREAT PLACE TO STAY FOR HIKERS AND NATURE LOVERS. The Kokee Lodge Cabins are in bucolic, 4345-acre Kokee State Park, which is more than 3000 feet above sea level. These rustic, mail-order-kit-style, cedar-log dwellings sleep up to seven persons. Some have just one large room, others have up to two bedrooms, with a queen-size bed in the living/kitchen/dining area. The kitchen has a working stove and refrigerator and a number of utensils. Another nice touch are the bathrooms with hot showers. Towels and bedding are supplied, but at these prices, there's no cleanup service. Because of the altitude, it tends to get cold at night, so an efficient Franklin stove is provided, and Presto logs are sold, plus there's plenty of wood to be found (but don't cut down any trees!). The Kokee Lodge within the park serves breakfast and lunch, but closes at 3:30 p.m. It's advisable to bring a supply of food and water, and perhaps your own portable barbecue grill, as none are available. 12 rooms. Credit cards: not accepted.

Resorts

Waimea Plantation Cottages $123–$650   ★★★★

9400 Kaumualii Highway, Waimea, 96796, ☎ *(800) -,*
☎ *(808) 338-1625, FAX (808) 338-1625.*
http://www.waimea-plantation.com/

Located on a spiritual plane somewhere between the ethnic chic of the Kona Village on the Big Island and the RETRO OPULENCE of the Princeville Hotel, the Waimea Plantation Cottages offer the kind of Hawaiian vacation that gets written about in *Travel & Leisure*—a VACATION IN THE SEDUCTIVE HAWAII BETWEEN THE WARS, WHEN CEILING FANS WERE HIGH-TECH AND PEOPLE TRAVELED BY INTERISLAND STEAMER. The Waimea Plantation Cottages are exactly what they say they are—plantation cottages that at one time housed employees of the Kekaha Sugar Company and Waimea Sugar Mill.

Most were built in the '20s and '30s, but one of them dates back to the 1880s. The cottages are randomly placed in a grove of 765 coconut palms that were planted in the early years of this century. The cottages have been painstakingly restored down to their corrugated iron roofs and now contain many period furnishings of mahogany, wicker, and native koa. Floors are painted wood or hardwood and covered with woven grass mats. Numerous windows covered with café curtains let in air and light. A few concessions have been made to progress and the kitchens and bathrooms (with tubs big enough for two) are completely modern. There really isn't much to do here, and that is a great part of the appeal. The black-sand beach is great for walking, but the water is muddy and the surf is usually too rough for swimming. There's a pool and a clay tennis court, which was reputedly a gift from the plantation's founder, H.P. Faye, to his wife around 1910. Horseshoe and croquet sets are available from the main office. Drinks are usually prepared by guests who enjoy them while seated in Adirondack chairs on their lanais. Waimea Plantation Cottages are usually booked well in advance. Amenities: tennis, balcony or patio. 48 rooms. Credit cards: MC, V.

Where to Eat

Your stomach will be happy on Kauai. Freshly caught fish and freshly picked produce lead off many menus, along with traditional Hawaiian flavors and an impressive assortment of ethnic cuisines. You can dine ritzy, cheap, or in between, often with a picture-postcard ocean view tossed into the deal. Lihue, in particular, has a wonderful selection of budget eateries and, yes, you'll find an all-too-ample supply of fast-food chains sprinkled about. For picnics and snacks, take advantage of local food vendors, produce stands, and farmer's markets. **DRESS IS CASUAL AT ALL BUT THE SWANKIEST RESTAURANTS.**

East Shore
Hanamaulu

Hanamaulu Restaurant & Tea House $$$ ★★★★
3-4291 Kuhio Highway, Hanamaulu, ☎ *(808) 245-2511.*
Asian cuisine.
A FIND, IF EVER THERE WAS ONE. The Hanamaulu Restaurant offers a hefty menu of Japanese and Chinese specialties at skin-

ny prices in a variety of settings—an ordinary dining room, a delightful tea house (advance reservations required) or, if you like to banter with the chef or rub elbows with fellow patrons, the sushi bar or teppanyaki counter. The ginger-fried chicken, tempura items, and sushi handrolls are all recommended. Features: private dining rooms. Reservations recommended. Credit cards: MC, V.

> **ITRAVELBOOKS TIP:** FOR A TRUE DINING EXPERIENCE, MAKE SURE TO RESERVE THE TEA HOUSE; YOU'LL NEVER FORGET IT.

Kapaa

A Pacific Café $$$ ★★★★
Kauai Village, Kuhio Highway, Kapaa, ☎ *(808) 822-0013.*
Pacific Rim cuisine.

The original. THE FIRST OF JEAN MARIE JOSSELIN'S ACCLAIMED PACIFIC RIM RESTAURANTS SITS HIDDEN AWAY IN AN OBSCURE SHOPPING CENTER LOCATION NEAR A SAFEWAY (WE MISSED IT ON OUR FIRST WALK-THROUGH). Tantalizing things await within, though. The sleek interior is designed in a sleek '40s Hawaiian-Japanese motif, with a changing exhibit of original art and a viewing kitchen for show-off chefs. This inventive cuisine features fresh, quality ingredients, including greens, veggies, and herbs grown on the restaurant's own certified farm. All dinners (menus change nightly) are accompanied by an assortment of foccacia breads and muffins, but don't neglect to order one of the appetizers called "first tastes." These are sometimes better than the entrées. A signature dish is deep-fried tiger-eye sushi with wasabi beurre blanc. Stunning. Features: own baking, rated wine cellar. Reservations required. Credit cards: A, CB, DC, D, MC.

Aloha Diner $ ★★
971-F Kuhio Highway, Kapaa, ☎ *(808) 822-3851.*
Hawaiian cuisine. Specialties: Hawaiian plate lunches, kalua pig, laulau, pipikaula.

This restaurant's name gives you a clue to what's inside: LOCAL-STYLE FOOD IN A DOWN-TO-EARTH ENVIRONMENT. Set in a small, unobtrusive shopping center, the Aloha Diner offers plate lunch combos of kalua pig or laulau with lomi salmon with a choice of rice or poi; dinners are similar, but with more choices and at a higher price. Everything is available à la carte. Friends recommend the *pipikaula*—homemade, dried sirloin fried in oil, similar to beef jerky.

Mema Thai-Chinese Cuisine $$
Wailua Shopping Plaza, Kapaa, ☎ *(808) 823-0899.*
Specialties: Crispy shrimp rolls, lemon grass soup, sweet basil seafood, vegetarian dishes.
http://www.hanaleihaven.com/mema.htm
Behind a Sizzler in a Kapaa shopping center, this LONG-TIME ETHNIC FAVE IS ELEGANTLY DECKED OUT WITH FINE LINENS, GLASSWARE, ARTWORK, AND ORCHID SPRAYS. Billed as half a Chinese restaurant, Mema's features that old standby, cashew chicken, in a mild melange of roasted nuts, garlic, and onions, stir-fried together. Vegetarians will be pleased with a huge list of choices from spring rolls to sticky rice. The various concoctions ranging from fresh basil with mixed vegetables, red chili with coconut milk, and red, green, yellow and house curries can be mixed with any meat, chicken, or seafood (even calamari and scallops with some orders) you desire. No lunch served on weekends. Owner Me Choy's siblings own **The King and I**, not far away at 901 Kuhio Highway, in the Waipouli Plaza, ☎ *(808) 822-1642.* A bit plainer in appearance, there's sometimes a friendly rivalry as to which is better. Specialties include beef, pork, or chicken sautéed in a fresh basil sauce (they grow their own herbs here) with chili, garlic, mushrooms, and oyster sauce. The King and I is open for dinner only, from 4:30–9:30 p.m. daily; until 10 p.m. Fridays and Saturdays. Credit cards: A, CB, DC, D, MC, V.

Papaya's Garden Café $ ★★★
Kauai Village, Kapaa, ☎ *(808) 742-9122.*
American cuisine. Specialties: Baked goods, espresso, vegetarian entrées and burgers.
A health-food store/café/deli/espresso bar situated in a tropical garden setting, Papaya's radiates a fine sense of well-being. Bakery goods include chocolate tofu pie and tahini maple cookies. If you're hungry for more than sweets, the kitchen issues out garden and tempeh burgers, grilled fish, chicken teriyaki, avocado sandwiches, Thai curries, stuffed baked potatoes, homemade soups, and more. To-go specials are popular, and are priced by the pound. One day they may have spanako-

pita, shepherd's pie, or marinated baked tofu. There's counter seating plus a few outside tables. Features: outside dining, own baking. Reservations not accepted. Credit cards: MC, V.

The Bull Shed $$ ★★★
796 Kuhio Highway, Kapaa, ☎ *(808) 822-3791.*
American cuisine. Specialties: Prime rib, pork baby back ribs, garlic tenderloin, Australian lamb rack, salad bar.
http://www.kauaimenu.com/htmlfolder/thebullshed.html
(Don't try saying the name of this establishment too fast if you'd been imbibing.) This old favorite, opened in 1973, is a bit hard to find for first-timers (just look for McDonalds across the street). **THE OCEAN VIEW AND BEACHSIDE LOCATION ARE MAGNIFICENT.** Long waits are guaranteed for BIG portions of the trademark dish, prime rib, garlic tenderloin (a pungent filet steeped in fresh garlic and herb marinade and broiled) ribs, chicken, and seafood. The rack of lamb is a full rack. One problem is that it can get a little stuffy, even with a non-smoking section. **WALLET-FRIENDLY PRICES.** Entrées include a trip to the salad bar. Children's menu, cocktails from 4:30 p.m. Reservations for six or more only. Features: outside dining. Credit cards: A, CB, DC, D, MC, V.

Lihue

Barbecue Inn $$ ★★
2982 Kress Street, Lihue, ☎ *(808) 245-2921.*
American cuisine. Specialties: Japanese dishes, prime rib, sandwiches on homemade bread. Closed: Sundays.
Comfortably air-conditioned, the venerable Barbecue Inn is favored by local residents and politicos. The small room is decked out with vinyl booths and a bar with a TV set constantly buzzing with sports events. Many newcomers walk in and ask, where's the barbecue? Nowhere, really; menu items are simple, unfancy things residents like (teriyaki chicken, pork chops, tempura, steak, prime rib), but are made with the finest ingredients. All sandwiches are prepared on thick-sliced, home-baked bread. Loaves are available for takeout. Produce is locally grown, and only fresh fruit is served. Features: own baking. Reservations not accepted.

Café Portofino $$ ★★★

3501 Rice Street, Pacific Ocean Plaza, Lihue,
☎ *(808) 245-2121.*
Italian cuisine. Specialties: Rabbit in wine sauce, veal shanks, calves liver, sweetbreads in cream sauce.
http://www.cafeportofino.com/body_index.html
You'd swear you were on the Riviera. Homemade pastas, sauces, breads, sorbets, and gelati are made daily in this classy, polished, authentic Italian café with a lanai offering a glimpse of lovely Kalapaki Bay. Stylish owner Guiseppe Avocadi, a native of the Italian Riviera (blue eyes, gleaming teeth, and open-neck silk shirts) presides over the festivities. Residents like it for business lunches and special occasions. Local rabbit is featured in one of the signature dishes, coniglio in a white wine, black olive, and herb sauce. Also fresh daily fish, osso bucco in an orange sauce, several veal preparations and bistecca di vitellone. Live music (usually jazz) plays Thursday–Saturday. **NO LUNCH ON WEEKENDS.** Features: outside dining, own baking, private dining rooms. Reservations recommended. Credit cards: A, CB, DC, D, MC, V.

Duke's Canoe Club $$ ★★★

On Kalapaki Beach, Lihue, ☎ *(808) 246-9599.*
American cuisine. Specialties: Fresh daily fish, tossed Caesar salad, prime rib, Koloa pork ribs, Kimo's Hula Pie. Closed Sunday.
http://hulapie.com/dukeskauai/index.html
Fresh fish brought in directly from the boats is a specialty of this restaurant and bar **(THE BAREFOOT BAR IS A HAPPENING LOCAL WATERING HOLE)** on beautiful Kalapaki Beach. This '40s Hawaiian-style eatery is dedicated in memory of the father of surfing, Duke Kahanamoku (there's another Duke's on Waikiki Beach), who surfed and canoed in this area. The hostess station is made of bamboo and covered by a thatched roof. The polished koa wood-paneled walls are hung with photos, memorabilia, and some of the Duke's surfboards. A 30-foot lava-rock waterfall, koi pond, and a 40-foot outrigger canoe complete the picture. For those who don't like fish, there's burly prime rib with the bone still in, pork ribs glazed in plum sauce (thankfully served small or regular size), shrimp scampi, even a plate of pasta with fresh veggies. Everything comes with an "all you care to eat" salad bar, which includes Caesar salad,

muffins, sourdough rolls, and steamed rice. Features: outside dining. Reservations recommended.

Hamura's Saimin $

2956 Kress Street, Lihue, ☎ *(808) 245-3271.*
Japanese cuisine. Specialties: Saimin, won ton soup, ribs, barbecue chicken and beef teriyaki sticks, lilikoi chiffon pie.

Small, medium, large, or even extra-large bowls of steaming saimin (the best in the state) are slurped day and night at this old Lihue standby. Counter seating only, and there's inevitably a wait. Soup is made to order and topped with everything from fish cake to shrimp tempura. Takeout available. Reservations not accepted.

Kauai Kitchens $ ★★

4303 Rice Street, Lihue, ☎ *(808) 245-4513.*
Specialties: Sushi, bentos, homemade fried chicken, teriyaki beef.

A small local chain (with locations in Koloa and Waimea) specializing in "quick and tasty island style" cooking to eat in or take out. Dishes range from Japanese (somen salad, teriyaki beef) to Filipino (pork adobo) to American (burgers, hamburger steak).

Ma's $ ★★

4277 Halenani Street (off Rice Street), Lihue,
☎ *(808) 245-3142.*
American cuisine. Specialties: Hawaiian and American breakfasts, sandwiches, stews, fresh fish.

A cheerful hodgepodge and a great bargain, Ma's "decor" features bright fluorescent lighting, year-round Christmas ornaments, assorted knickknacks, and stuffed animals, including a tiger and Kermit the Frog. Most of the tables are "family style," meant for at least four people. A few old red booths are placed against the wall, covered with what looks like automobile floor rugs. One woman toils behind the counter doing everything, and even comes over with a cheerful "thanks for waiting" greeting. **A WHOLE POT OF FREE COFFEE OR TEA COMES WITH BREAKFAST, WHICH IS ALMOST UNHEARD OF TODAY.** It's best for breakfast; for a few greenbacks, you get a Hawaiian breakfast of laulau, kalua pig, or *pipikaula* (jerky) with two eggs and rice. Open until 11:30 a.m. Saturday–Sunday. For a similar menu, try **Dani's,** owned by Ma's nephew, at *4201 Rice Street,* ☎ *(808) 245-4991,* open from 5 a.m.–1:30 p.m.; it's bigger and brighter, but more impersonal. **THE KALUA PIG WITH EGGS IS RECOMMENDED.** Dani's is closed on Sunday. Reservations not accepted.

Nawiliwili

JJ's Broiler $$$ ★★
Anchor Cove Shopping Center, Nawiliwili, ☎ *(808) 246-4422. American cuisine. Specialties: Black-bean prawns with spicy noodle salad, "world famous" Slavonic steak.*

JJ's Broiler has occupied this prime beachfront space for 25 years—in the beginning there was the trademark Slavonic steak (the restaurant calls it "world famous"), filets of beef steeped in garlic, wine, and butter, and a tableside salad bar. Both items, plus prime rib and barbecue chicken, are menu stalwarts, but chef Mark Sassone is trying to inch the restaurant into the regional Pacific cuisine market with such offerings as Peking chicken tacos with garlic oyster sauce, spicy wasabi rib-eye, and black-bean prawns with spicy noodle salad. **LUNCH IS A FUN AND LESS-EXPENSIVE ISLAND MELTING POT OF LIGHT BITES,** including JJ's Saimin, won ton soup, Oriental chicken salad, fish and chips, and even a pastrami-and-Swiss-cheese sandwich. Features: outside dining. Reservations recommended. Credit cards: DC, MC, V.

Kalapaki Beach Hut $ ★★
Next to Anchor Cove, Nawiliwili, ☎ *(808) 246-6330. American cuisine. Specialties: Breakfasts, Steve's famous burgers, fish and chicken sandwiches, vegetarian selections.*

Burgers have meant big business for Steve and Sharon Gerald, who own this grill (not quite a hut) with a second story that's open to Kalapaki Bay views and breezes. Many people don't know that the Geralds started the legendary Ono Char Burger stand (original in Anahola, second branch in Kapaa) before there was a "Duane" connected to it. Steve and Sharon still feature the juicy beef patties piled high with fixin's, but the new specialty item at the Hut are burgers ground fresh from Hanalei-raised buffalo. Sunday hours are 11 a.m.–3 p.m. Features: outside dining.

Puhi

Fisherman's Galley $ ★★
Highway 50, three minutes from Lihue, Puhi,
☎ *(808) 246-4700.*
Seafood cuisine. Specialties: Fresh off-the-boat seafood, lobster, burgers. Closed: Sun.

The only thing missing at the Fisherman's Galley is the ocean view (its location is in the countryside across from Kauai Community College). But the fish (usually ono, never cod, like Mrs. Paul's) in the fish and chips, fish tacos, broiled fish sandwiches, seafood melts, and homemade creamy seafood chowder were all just recently hooked and cooked by the folks who own Gent-Lee Sportfishing Charters. Many people just stop with the fish and chips, but be adventurous and order from the daily blackboard menu. Reservations recommended. Credit cards: A, MC, V.

Wailua

Dragon Inn $$ ★★
4-901 Kuhio Highway, in Waipouli Plaza, Wailua,
☎ *(808) 822-3788.*
Chinese cuisine. Specialties: Sizzling platters, Hong Kong-style roast duck.

You can come for the fairly tasty all-you-can-eat buffets that are popular with regular customers, but don't neglect to order from the Cantonese and Szechuan menu, which is peppered with unusual specialties. It's fun to eat family-style (this place caters to them) in a pleasant-but-nondescript room, served by waiters in bow ties. You might try sizzling shrimp balls with black-bean sauce, pot roast chicken, or perhaps order the Peking duck for two (a day in advance, please). Lighter appetites will delight in Chinese chicken salad. Old standbys such as sweet and sour spareribs, mu shu pork, and egg fu yung are here, too. The kitchen does not stint on portions—there'll be equal amounts of starch as well as meat on your plate. Credit cards: A, CB, DC, D, MC, V.

North Shore
Hanalei

Bali Hai Restaurant $$$ ★★★
5380 Honoiki Road, Hanalei, ☎ (808) 826-6522.
International cuisine. Specialties: Salmon Bali Hai, coconut breaded shrimp, Pacific cioppino.
http://www.hanaleibayresort.com/abouthanalei/dining.html
A romantic and quiet restaurant, with high ceilings and bilevel seating, Bali Hai is where the greatest jazz musicians on the island come to jam in the cocktail lounge on Saturdays and Sundays. Views from the open-air dining room are outstanding, so when it's raining, you might want to eat elsewhere. Service is unfailingly gracious and polite, but it can be slow. The cuisine features inventive twists on old favorites, especially at breakfast (poi pancakes). There are quite a few eclectic Pacific Rim selections, but most are familiar items that the meat and 'taters crowd will like. Among the former is the blackened ahi sashimi appetizer with sweetened wasabi soy sauce (ubiquitous with this cuisine), baked boursin cheese lightly crusted with macadamia nuts and blackened sesame seeds served with papaya coulis, and pork medallions grilled and served with a raspberry shiitake sauce. Some folks think it all sounds better on paper than it tastes on the plate. Features: outside dining, own baking. Reservations recommended. Credit cards: A, CB, DC, D, MC, V.

Hanalei Wake Up Café $$ ★★
Aku Road, Hanalei, ☎ (808) 826-5551.
American cuisine. Specialties: Omelettes, French toast, salads, fish tacos, mesquite-smoked Huli-Huli chicken.
THIS ULTRA-CASUAL, SURF-THEMED CAFÉ IS A TRIP. Decor features photos, trophies, and constantly running videos glorifying the sport. The family that runs it is a mom and three sons who go by their first names only—Kainoa is a hunky, blond godlet who's also a champion surfer and canoer. OPEN SURFER-HOURS FOR BREAKFAST; THE THING TO ORDER IS THE DESSERT-LIKE CUSTARD FRENCH TOAST, A HIGH-INTENSITY ALTERNATIVE TO EGGS FOR BREAKFAST. You'll need to paddle faster to work off the calories. A lunch and dinner (same menu) highlight is the mesquite smoked "huli-huli" chicken. Features: own baking. Reservations not accepted.

Tahiti Nui $$$ ★★
Kuhio Highway, Hanalei, ☎ *(808) 826-6277.*
American cuisine. Specialties: Fresh fish, steaks, prime rib, chicken, scampi, plate lunches, sandwiches.

This North Shore legend and party place in the heart of Hanalei just celebrated its 35th anniversary. Actually a glorified shack with six tables, it's crammed with nautical and South Pacific style artifacts. The bar/lounge is almost as popular (maybe more) than the restaurant. The cheerful proceedings are supervised by owner "Auntie" Louise Marston. **REGULAR HAPPENINGS INCLUDE IMPROMPTU MUSIC SESSIONS, HULA DANCES OR POTLUCKS.** The menu is awfully big for the size of the place, and the food better than it has to be. **TAHITI NUI TOUTS ITS BREAKFASTS, AN ECLECTIC MIX OF THINGS SUCH AS BANANA PANCAKES, EGGS FLORENTINE, LOCO MOCOS AND A THREE-EGG "INIKI CONSTRUCTION OMELET," WHICH YOU CAN FILL WITH ANYTHING FROM BACON TO SURIMI KRAB.** At lunch, the daily soups are often flavorful and good, and the hamburgers are recommended. Also, plate lunches such as hamburger steak, or fried chicken with rice and potato salad. A nice dinner appetizer is Tahitian poisson cru, fresh fish cooked in lime juice seasoned with coconut milk and spices. Follow that with the trademark dish, calamari stuffed and sautéed in a garlic butter sauce with diced tomatoes. Many folks think that the generous portions of prime rib and steaks are the only thing to order. Desserts are on the order of homemade cream pie, hula pie, or rainbow sherbet. **NO DINNER ON FRIDAY WHEN THE LUAU MOVES IN.** Children's menu. Features: outside dining, own baking, private dining rooms. Reservations required. Credit cards: DC, D, MC, V.

Kilauea

Casa di Amici $$$ ★★★
2484 Keneke Street & Lighthouse Road, Kilauea,
☎ *(808) 828-1555.*
Italian cuisine. Specialties: Boursin cheese wrapped in phyllo, zuppe of mussels with fresh tomatoes, capers, and white wine.

One of Kauai's most popular Italian restaurants, Casa di Amici is situated in the Kong Lung Center in quiet Kilauea. Surprisingly casual in appearance, the plain latticed-wood building is sort of al fresco, protected from the elements by a plastic drop. Cuisine is traditional Italian, featuring tasty, choice ingredients at reasonable prices. Many regulars start with bacio, which is boursin cheese baked in phyllo, served with tomato sauce. There's also antipasto for two, gorgonzola mushroom polenta, caesar salad with fresh Kilauea romaine, or *zuppa di cozze* (New Zealand green-lipped mussels with fresh tomatoes, capers, three kinds of bell peppers, and leeks in rich fish fumet). It's lots of fun to play with your food here, especially the mix-and-match pasta selection (bowtie, fettuccine, penne, angel hair, etc.) in light and regular portions. If you like lasagne, the Casa's version features chopped sirloin and homemade sausage melded together with grilled zucchini, eggplant, and five cheeses. Non-meat-eaters will like the vegetarian linguine. Other entrées include veal prepared three ways, chicken cacciatore, tournedos rossini, scampi, and filet mignon. These dishes are also served in light or regular portions. **REASONABLY PRICED, WELL-CHOSEN WINE LIST.** Seating is limited, so be sure to reserve. Features: own baking, rated wine cellar. Reservations required. Credit cards: A, MC, V.

Roadrunner Bakery and Café $ ★★★
2430 Oka Street, off Kilauea Road, Kilauea,
☎ *(808) 828-8226.*
Specialties: Mexican and vegan dishes, fresh-baked breads and desserts.

This Mexican café and bakery started life as an electricity transfer station for the North Shore. The large, two-story building has a unique sand floor, and mural block walls painted by two local artists. At breakfast, flour tortillas are stuffed with scrambled eggs, onions, cheese, salsa fresca, and cilantro. Burras appear for lunch and dinner too, including the unfortunately named "Black Dog" (ugh), which is roast pork, grilled Hanalei taro and black beans, covered with garlic anchoa sauce. Other items include tostadas, torta sandwiches on their crusty bread, plus special low-fat eggplant enchiladas, or grilled veggie salad with Kilauea mixed greens, jicama, white beans, and lime vinaigrette. Roadrunners makes a concession to local tastes by serving an ahi salad and ahi burrito. There's a vegan menu too. Celebrity watchers might want to know that Bette Midler and Harrison Ford are regulars. Open until 8:30 p.m. Saturdays; Sundays from 8 a.m.–1:30 p.m. Features: own baking.

Princeville

Café Hanalei $$$ ★★★★

5520 Ka Haku Road, Princeville, ☎ *(808) 826-2760. Pacific Rim cuisine. Specialties: Grilled sirloin steak with grilled Kauai onions and shiitake mushrooms.*

Situated well below the lobby of the tiered, cliffside Princeville Hotel, the Café Hanalei is cleverly designed to make you feel like you're dining over water. A series of black-marble reflecting pools gurgle quietly below your feet. The terrace of this indoor-outdoor restaurant has the feel of a villa on the Italian Riviera, with its oversize Roman urns bursting with flowers. It almost comes as a shock that the sweeping seascape ahead is of Hanalei Bay and "Bali Hai" instead of the Amalfi Coast. **THE HOTEL CLAIMS THAT THE VIEWS FROM HERE ARE SOME OF THE MOST SPECTACULAR IN HAWAII—THE ANSWER TO THAT IS A RESOUNDING YES!** Oh, and the food? Executive Chef Daniel Delbrel has conceived a people-pleasing blend of Pacific Rim cuisine, a number of Japanese dishes, and tropical-French sweets and concoctions that include a tangy/creamy rainbow-striped circlet of mousse cake flavored with fresh lilikoi and almond paste, or ginger mango creme brulee. Specialty buffets are a big feature at Café Hanalei. A breakfast spread is available daily until 10:30 a.m. (regular menu until 11 a.m.). For Sunday brunch, you might head straight for the made-to-order crepes and omelettes so you can save the heavy decisions for the elaborate dessert bar. The seafood buffet on Friday evenings may start with sashimi, tako poki salad, or crab or shrimp on a bed of ice, and end with fresh fish grilled, sautéed, or barbecued before your eyes. On the regular menu, the corn and clam chowder with Thai curry and coconut milk is a fine starter, while the stir-fried chicken salad with mixed greens, papaya, and orange-ginger dressing is one of their most popular items for lunch. Features: outside dining, own baking, Sunday brunch. Reservations recommended. Credit cards: A, CB, DC, D, MC, V.

La Cascata $$$ ★★★

5520 Ka Haku Road, Princeville, ☎ *(808) 826-2761. Associated hotel: Princeville Hotel.*
Mediterranean cuisine. Specialties: Homemade pastas, grilled fish and meat.

Situated below the Princeville Hotel's Living Room lounge, La

Cascata beckons you through a lacy iron doorway. Interior temptations are its terra-cotta floors and walls and trompe l'oeil murals. Dining here is a dressy affair, with candlelit tables, flowers, and all the accoutrements. **SUNSET VIEWS ARE HEARTBREAKING IN SUMMER.** Servers bring you addictive home-baked foccacia and breads served with olive oil instead of butter and garlic dip or tomatoes and basil. If you need a starter course after that, choose from crisp calamari cakes with tomato compote and toasted pinenut vinaigrette, Tuscany-style white-bean soup with sliced Asiago cheese, or a daily pasta special. You might enjoy spicy penne amatriciana (with pancetta, dried tomatoes, fresh rosemary, and crushed red pepper flakes) or cioppino with kona lobster over spaghettini. Desserts are the fruity (chilled lemon souffle with Kauai fruit garnish) and chocolate (tiramisu or chocolate bourbon pecan tart) kind. Children's menu. Features: own baking, non-smoking area. Reservations recommended. Credit cards: A, DC, MC, V.

South Shore
Koloa

Beach House $$$ ★★★★
5022 Lawai Road, Koloa, ☎ *(808) 742-1424.*
Specialties: Incredible appetizers and inventive desserts.
http://www.the-beach-house.com/

No wet bathing suits at this beach house, please. Not as close to the sea as it once was, the sunsets are still spectacular (arrive half an hour before). Rebuilt after Hurricane Iniki, the Beach House is now under the wing of Jean Marie Josselin of A Pacific Café fame, and is **ONLY OPEN FOR DINNER.** That's the only regret, as the old place served forgettable food and rested on the laurels of its setting. Entrées are great, but the appetizers and desserts really shine. Graze on them if you like. How about sizzling mussels with cashew lemon butter and balsamic vinegar syrup, deep-fried sashimi with wasabi soy beurre blanc, or ono firecracker (ono wrapped in a rice-paper wrapper and deep-fried) with hot-and-sour vinaigrette and cucumber kim chee? Then you'll have room for such elaborate constructions as misu misu, a lavish take on tiramisu with espresso creme anglaise and chocolate sauce, or warm chocolate bread pudding topped with a banana crisp—that is-if you can pass up the Toasted Hawaiian, a white-chocolate cake layered with haupia, and white-chocolate-toasted-nut mousse, finished with caramel sauce. Wash it down with Kona coffee or Maui tea. Features: own baking, rated wine cellar. Reservations required. Credit cards: A, CB, DC, D, MC, V.

Sueoka's Market   **$**
Koloa Road, Koloa, ☎ *(808) 742-1611.*
American cuisine. Specialties: Hamburgers, plate lunches. Closed: Sundays.
Primarily a takeout window adjacent to Sueoka Market in Old Koloa Town (no seating, unless you want to squat in the parking lot or eat in your car), Sueoka's makes great mahi-mahi sandwiches and laulau. **GREAT FOR A PICNIC ON POIPU BEACH PARK, WHICH IS JUST A SHORT DRIVE AWAY.** Reservations not accepted.

Poipu Beach

Brennecke's   **$$$**   BBB
2100 Hoone Road, Poipu Beach, ☎ *(808) 742-7588.*
American cuisine. Specialties: Scampi, Hawaiian spiny lobster, prime rib.
Totally rebuilt after Hurricane Iniki, Brennecke's is back in a two-story building across from Poipu Beach Park. Former patrons will be glad to learn that it looks just the same as it did. The menu hasn't changed much, either. The place specializes in meat and fish that's usually served broiled on kiawe wood. At lunch and dinner, start with that island stalwart, fresh sashimi, or a "local"—an Oriental-style pupu platter. Follow up with one of the three cuts of prime rib (from seven to 20 ounces), or try a sandwich on sourdough. Brennecke's also has veggie burgers and fresh island fish selections that change daily. All entrées come with a trip to the salad bar, chef Luigi's sourdough bread, steamed rice or herbed pasta, and veggies. Features: outside dining, Sunday brunch. Reservations recommended. Credit cards: A, D, MC, V.

Keoki's Paradise   **$$$**   ★★
Poipu Shopping Village, Poipu Beach, ☎ *(808) 742-7534.*
Seafood cuisine. Specialties: Fresh island fish, Koloa pork ribs, pesto shrimp macadamia, prime rib.
Lushly landscaped with hanging tropical plants and flowers, flowing waterfalls, rushing streams, and tropical fishponds, all

Keoki's Paradise needs is an ocean view. For that, you can visit its brother restaurant, Duke's Canoe Club (see listing). Keoki's has a coterie of regular patrons (both residents and travelers) who appreciate the convenient parking in its shopping center location. The nightly menu offers the fresh catch of the day prepared at least five different ways, koloa pork ribs glazed with plum sauce, and pesto shrimp macadamia with white wine. Keoki's is generous with side dishes; Caesar salad, a basket of fresh-baked bread and carrot muffins, and steamed herb rice should keep you carbo-loaded for the evening. Oh, and don't forget hula pie (like mud pie) for dessert. Enjoy the same romantic atmosphere for even less money in the bar from 4:30–11:30 p.m., where lighter fare is served daily. Live local entertainment on Thursday and Friday nights. Reservations recommended. Credit cards: A, MC, V.

Roy's Poipu Bar and Grill $$$ ★★★★
2360 Kiahuna Plantation Drive, Poipu Beach,
☎ *(808) 742-5000.*
Asian cuisine. Specialties: Fresh fish in sauces, chocolate soufflé.

Roy's Poipu Bar and Grill, located in the undistinguished Poipu Beach Shopping Center, is entertaining, loud, lively, and serves simply incredible food. Actually, the din is not so bad in the front room, and because it faces the open windows, it's quite breezy, and you get an oceanfront effect from the flaming tiki torches out front. There's a glassed-in exhibition kitchen that you can go into and talk to chefs and watch pizzas and such being made. Servers receive a daily orientation on the changing specials and can give you the skinny on every ingredient in the complex sauces. The array of appetizers are expensive, and the skimpy portions keep you wanting more. Nori-seared shrimp sticks with wasabi aioli are nose-clearingly good. Seafood pot-stickers with mango lemongrass sauce are milder, but no less delicious. The trademark chocolate soufflé with liquid chocolate center really lives up to its name. **ROY'S CLIENTELE IS YOUNG, PROSPEROUS, SHOWY, AND EXCESSIVELY TRIM—THIS IS THE PLACE TO BRING YOUR TROPHY MATE.** A trip to the rest room may be hazardous to your health, as you've got to dodge a lot of tiny tables crammed together, as well as servers, schmoozing clients, etc. If you can stand the noise and possess a bottomless wallet and a hollow leg, you may want to eat at Roy's every night. Note: there's always a wait,

even with reservations. Features: own baking, rated wine cellar.
Credit cards: A, MC, V.

The House of Seafood $$$ ★★★
1941 Poipu Kai Road, Poipu Beach, ☎ *(808) 742-6433.*
Associated hotel: Poipu Kai Resort.
Seafood cuisine. Specialties: Fresh fish in parchment paper, shrimp luau, Hawaiian spiny lobster tail.
More than a dozen varieties of island fish are available on a single night at this high-ceilinged, plant-festooned restaurant that overlooks the tennis courts of the Poipu Kai Resort. Preparations change depending on the chef's whim and whatever's fresh, and are likely to include onaga baked in parchment paper, or papio sautéed with macadamia nut sauce. Abalone appears on the regular menu, this and the Hawaiian spiny lobster are the most expensive items you'll find. Enticing starters run hot and cold, from oysters on the half-shell to sashimi and crab-stuffed mushrooms to Wailua taro clam chowder. Meat-eating friends can tag along, too (surf-and-turf combos are available), for broiled center-cut pork chops or New York steak. The dessert menu is a trip: since when have you had baked Alaska? Also, on advance notice, you can order one or more items from the kitchen's repertoire of *en flambe* concoctions, including crepes suzette, cherries jubilee, and bananas Foster. Features: own baking. Reservations recommended.

West Shore
Kalaheo

Kalaheo Steak House $$$ BB
4444 Papalina Road, Kalaheo, ☎ *(808) 332-9780.*
American cuisine. Specialties: Steaks, prime rib, Kalaheo shrimp, combination platters.
http://www.kauaimenu.com/htmlfolder/kalaheo.html
Generous steaks (Midwestern-grain fed, aged, and shipped) and monstrous, heart-stopping cuts of prime rib (the 24-ounce slab is the priciest item on the menu) and other choice meats are the specialty of this casual, Upcountry restaurant. Fish dishes are offered, too, and are mostly fresh—except for the imported ono. Lemon butter is the usual sauce with this fare, but there are other choices. Can't decide? Combo platters give you a choice of half meat and half seafood. Sides include fresh tossed salad, steamed rolls from the Bread Box Bakery, Maui

sweet wheat bread, plus baked potato and rice. Desserts are the steak-house variety: cheesecake, rum cake, and ice cream. Features: non-smoking area. Reservations not accepted. Credit cards: D, MC, V.

Kokee State Park

Kokee Lodge Restaurant $ ★★
3600 Kokee Road, Kokee State Park, ☎ *(808) 333-6061.*
American cuisine. Specialties: Homemade cornbread, sandwiches, salads, desserts.
A small, homey café with white-painted chairs and rust-red walls decorated with old photos, Kokee Lodge PROVIDES COMFORT FOOD AND SUSTENANCE TO HIKERS, CAMPERS, AND PASSERS-BY EXPLORING KOKEE STATE PARK. Light breakfasts are served, as well as sandwiches on 12-grain bread; try the homemade pineapple mustard. For a quick energy boost, there's nothing better than a slice of lilikoi pie, Alakai swamp pie (Kona coffee ice cream with an oreo crust, ice cream, macadamia nuts, and whipped cream), or "killer" fudge cake. The lodge's blend coffee comes with a special mug to take home. There's also a gift shop attached. Credit cards: D, MC, V.

Nightlife

Traditional Hawaiian entertainment is the main focus on Kauai, with luaus, island music, and the like—though you'll be able to find some discos, karaoke clubs, taverns, sports bars, and one or two comedy clubs. Most of the action takes place at resort and hotel lounges, with the more "neighborhood" venues centered around Lihue, Kapaa, and other island towns. **Kauai Community Players** presents theatrical productions several times yearly at venues in Lihue and, occasionally, the **Honolulu Symphony Orchestra** comes to town.

East Shore
Kalapaki Beach

Duke's Canoe Club Barefoot Bar ★★★
Kauai Marriott, Kalapaki Beach, ☎ *(808) 822-7447.*
Hours: 11:30 a.m.–midnight.
Live music accompanies pupus, cocktails, sandwiches, and light meals Friday through Sunday.

Lihue

Gilligan's ★★
4331 Kauai Beach Drive, Outrigger Kauai Beach, Lihue,
☎ *(808) 245-1955.*
Hours: 8 p.m.–2 a.m.

There's dancing nightly at this popular hotel hot-spot to the left of the main lobby. On Thursday night, Gilligan's turns into the Kauai Comedy Club (there's one on almost every island) with guest comics. General admission.

Hap's Hideaway ★★
4347 Rice Street, Lihue, ☎ *(808) 245-3473.*
Hours: 11 a.m.–2 a.m.

Sporting events on satellite TV, dart boards, and a CD jukebox playin' primarily country western tunes are featured at this Lihue hangout, where "every hour is happy hour."

North Shore
Hanalei

Tahiti Nui ★★★
Kuhio Highway, Hanalei, 96714, ☎ *(808) 826-6277.*
Hours: 7 a.m.–10 p.m.

Live and surprisingly varied entertainment emanate from two lounges in this long-established restaurant and bar. On Sunday afternoons from 2–5 p.m., there's a regular jazz jam session; Mondays, it's country-western night with line dancing; rock and roll rears its shaggy head after the famous luau is over every Friday from 9:30 p.m. to 1:30 a.m. Saturday, special guest entertainers (Hawaiian, blues, pop, whatever) perform, followed by dancing until closing.

Tahiti Nui Luau ★★★
Kuhio Highway, Hanalei, ☎ *(808) 826-6277.*
Hours: 6–8:30 p.m.
Closed: Fridays only.

HELD ONCE A WEEK at the wonderfully funky Tahiti Nui restaurant/lounge/showroom. Arguably Kauai's best luau (inarguably the best priced), with Tahitian-themed entertainment. The ample feast includes one drink, coffee, and punch, and features an all-you-can-eat buffet of Kalua pig, baked fish,

Hawaiian chicken, poi and other starches, salads, garlic bread, and several desserts, including chocolate cake. The show is great for the kids, since everyone is outta there early. Also on Friday and Saturday nights, join in with regulars who come by to play ukuleles and other instruments, for an informal jam session. It won't be long before you, too, will be dancing on the bar. General admission.

> **ITRAVELBOOKS TIP:** IF YOU HAVE THE OPPORTUNITY, DON'T PASS UP A CHANCE TO HEAR LIVE HAWAIIAN SLACK-KEY GUITAR; A CROSS BETWEEN THE WHINING STEEL GUITAR GENERALLY ASSOCIATED WITH HAWAIIAN MUSIC, AND TRADITIONAL ACOUSTIC FOLK MUSIC, THE SOUND IS WITHOUT COMPARE.

Princeville

The Living Room Lounge ★★★★
5520 Ka Haku Road, in the Princeville Hotel, Princeville, 96756, ☎ *(808) 826-9644.*
Hours: 7–11 p.m.
The rosy sunset at this sublime locale is entertainment enough, but if you need more, Hawaiian music is provided by a duo nightly.

Poipu Beach

Keoki's Paradise ★★★
Poipu Shopping Village, Poipu Beach, ☎ *(808) 742-7534.*
Hours: 4:30 p.m.–midnight.
Live local entertainment on Thursday and Friday nights in an open-air setting; other nights waterfalls, lush foliage, and streams will have to do.

Kuhio's ★★★
1571 Poipu Road, at the Hyatt Regency Kauai, Poipu Beach, 96756, ☎ *(808) 742-1234.*
Hours: 9 p.m.–1 a.m. Closed: Mondays.
Plush seating, lighting and camera tricks, and a sunken dance floor make for classy surroundings at this disco with a DJ (Thursday–Saturday) and karaoke on Wednesdays from 7:30 p.m. In the same hotel is Stevenson's Library, a cocktail lounge designed like a real library, with tons of gleaming koa wood,

old books, comfy couches and wing chairs, chess and backgammon boards, and a couple of billiard tables. Delicious pupus (fondue, guacamole seafood cocktail) are served with drinks. Try the tai chi, a combination mai tai and chi chi—after a few you'll be t'ai chiing all the way to your room. A cozy place to snuggle up and listen to jazz on Friday and Saturday nights. Musicians can play almost any obscure standard you can think of—but please don't ask for "Cat Scratch Fever" or "Stairway to Heaven."

West Shore
Hanapepe

Hanapepe Espresso Bar Café ★★★
3830 Hanapepe Road, Hanapepe, ☎ *(808) 335-5011.*
Hours: 6:30–9:30 p.m.
Closed: Mondays, Tuesdays, Wednesdays, Sundays.
Hawaiian slack key/contemporary and classical guitar music accompanies the vegetarian offerings at this bookstore/gift shop/espresso bar/restaurant.

Shopping

The **Kukui Grove Center,** four miles from the Lihue airport, is a huge new mall that sells just about everything you could want. Kauai is loaded with small specialty shops and family-owned retail outlets—much more fun than hitting the mall you just left back home—where you'll find scads of both high-quality and schlock souvenirs, aloha fashions, beachwear, T-shirts, fruit, flowers, etc. Outdoor markets and resort concessions are other shopping options. Book-lovers will enjoy the Hawaiiana selection at **Hanapepe Bookstore** in Hanapepe.

East Shore
Kapaa

Kela's A Glass Gallery ★★★
4-1354 Kuhio Highway, Kapaa, ☎ *(808) 822-4527.*
Hours: 10 a.m.–6 p.m.
Special hours: Saturdays. to 7 p.m. Closed: Sundays.
You won't find anything kitschy here—Larry and Sandi Barton feature beautiful and unique glassware that would grace any home, and they ship worldwide. Choose among a wide assort-

ment of handblown sculpture, vases, bowls, wine and champagne glasses, paperweights, perfume bottles, and more. More than 50 glass artists are represented here. Prices range from $10 to $2000. The selection of hand-painted and hand-carved flowers are a standout.

M. Miura Store ★★
4-1419 Kuhio Highway, Kapaa, ☎ (808) 822-4401.
Hours: 9 a.m.–5 p.m.
This fourth-generation, family-owned shop started life 90 years ago selling Chinese crack seed from big glass jars. Now you can purchase all your surf- and beach-related attire, plus surfboards and bodyboards.

Sunny Side Farmers Market ★★★
4-1345 Kuhio Highway, Kapaa, ☎ (808) 822-0494.
Hours: 8 a.m.–8 p.m.
Special hours: Sundays, 9 a.m.–8 p.m.
Unlike a lot of farmers' markets, Sunny Side is open daily. This open-air affair features fresh local fruits, flowers, and veggies (pineapple and watermelon are especially choice), crafts, clothing, and jewelry (even Niihau shell leis).

Tin Can Mailman ★★★
1353 Kuhio Highway, Kapaa, ☎ (808) 822-3009.
Well-regarded bookseller. Features new and used books, Hawaiiana, South Pacific literature, stamps, coins, tapa cloth, botanical prints, maps.

William & Zimmer Furniture ★★★
1383 Kuhio Highway, Kapaa, ☎ (808) 822-2850.
Hours: 10 a.m.–6 p.m.
A showroom for handcrafted solid koa furniture (rockers from $1300) and gift items from $5 and up. The workshop is located at 951 Kipuni Way, Kapaa.

Lihuel.

Kukui Grove Center ★★★
3-2600 Kaumualii Highway, Lihue, ☎ (808) 245-7784.
Hours: 9:30 a.m.–5:30 p.m.

Special hours: Fridays to 9 p.m., Sundays, 10 a.m.–5 p.m.

Where residents go to shop, Kukui Grove is home to all the familiar chains such as Kmart, Woolworth, Sears, Longs, Liberty House, a plethora of fashion and specialty stores, 11 restaurants, a four-plex cinema, and a free Polynesian entertainment on Fridays. A free shuttle takes guests of nearby hotels to and from the center.

Puhi

Kilohana Plantation Shops ★★★

Highway 50, 1.7 miles south of Lihue, Puhi, ☎ *(808) 245-5608.*
Hours: 9:30 a.m.–9:30 p.m.
Special hours: Sundays to 5 p.m.

A number of galleries, craft shops, and a restaurant (Gaylord's) fill the courtyard, various rooms, and bedchambers (even a cloak room!) in the main house and guest cottages of this restored 1930s-era estate. Among them are: Kilohana Galleries' The Artisan's Room, with handcrafted ceramics, wood carvings, glass, jewelry, and cards. Don't miss the hand-cast paper designs (also engraved glassware) inspired by Hawaiian quilts created by Molokai's Jule Patten, one of Hawaii's unique artists; The Hawaiian Collection Room for Niihau-shell leis, coins, stamps, and Monarchy documents, Kauai scrimshaw, and antique ivory; The Country Store in the old library, featuring mostly made-in-Kauai gifts and collectibles; Dolls & Furrie Critters live in the Sun Room and study, and although there's an emphasis on bears, this shop specializes in antique dolls in elegant, made-to-order costumes. Within the old camphouse is Kilohana Clayworks, where you can glaze and fire your own Raku ceramic bowl or vase in just 30 minutes. Note: It might take several visits (and a map) just to find your way around the complex.

Waipouli

The Coconut Marketplace ★★

4-484 Kuhio Highway, Waipouli.
Hours: 9 a.m.–9 p.m.

Gift shops, restaurants, cinemas, and hokum galore in this large resort shopping center set amid a coconut grove and conveniently located next to hotels and condos. Fun for an evening stroll. The best shop in the complex is Collector's Corner, ☎

(808) 822-3333, featuring vintage Hawaiiana, ukuleles, fabric, dinnerware, collectibles, even insects (!). Free hula show Mondays, Wednesdays, Fridays, and Saturdays at 4:30 p.m.

North Shore
Hanalei

Yellowfish Trading Company ★★★
Hanalei Center, across from Ching Young Village, Hanalei, ☎ *(808) 826-1227.*
Hours: 10 a.m.–7 p.m.
Plenty of '40s and '50s Hawaiiana, furniture, clothing, collectibles, antiques, and locally produced arts and crafts (koa paddles for your wall by artist Ray Nitta).

Kilauea

Kong Lung Center ★★★
Lighthouse Road, Kilauea, ☎ *(808) 828-1822.*
Hours: 9 a.m.–6 p.m.
Special hours: Sundays, 10 a.m.–5 p.m.
Small-but-stylish shopping center out in the sticks is clustered around a historic building that was once a (you guessed it) plantation store. It was recently placed on the list of the National Register of Historic Places. The center consists of two clothing stores, a gift shop, an excellent bakery/pizza restaurant and one of Kauai's finest Italian eateries, Casa di Amici. Within the Kong Lung Building is the **Kong Lung Co.,** ☎ *(808) 828-1822*. It has a talented buyer—here you'll find whimsical gifts, furnishings, accessories and clothing. Ascend the stairs to **Reinventions,** ☎ *(808) 828-0126,* where "gently used" fashions await. I found the selection lovely, but a tad overpriced, except for the costume jewelry (good stuff for under $10). Gifts and photographs created by local artists, plus an exhibition of flora and fauna indigenous to the region, are on offer at **The Booby Trap,** ☎ *(808) 828-1822*.

West Shore
Hanapepe

Hanapepe Bookstore and Espresso Bar Café ★★★
3830 Hanapepe Road, Hanapepe, ☎ *(808) 335-5011.*
Hours: 8 a.m.–2 p.m.
Also a highly regarded vegetarian restaurant and popular

espresso bar. We didn't see many books here, but you can pick up locally made jewelry, candles, cards, and even a Hawaiian Sovereignty Movement T-shirt.

Kauai Fine Arts
Hanapepe Road, Hanapepe, ☎ *(808) 335-3778.*
Special hours: by appointment only.
Fine collection of original antique maps and prints relating to exploration and travel from the 16th–19th century.

The Kauai Coffee and Gift Centre ★★
3734 Hanapepe Road, Hanapepe, 96716, ☎ *(808) 639-8629.*
Hours: 9:30 a.m.–6 p.m.
Situated in the old Ueoka Store in Hanapepe, the center was opened shortly after Hurricane Iniki struck in 1992 to support and promote local businesses (they also have a mail-order concern). Its specialty, of course, is island-grown coffee; free samples are given when you walk in. New flavors include Chocolate and Vanilla Macadamia Nut. Other interesting cottage industries touted here are several yummy fudge creations from the Kauai Tropical Fudge Company. Or forget chocolate—how about Pina Colada, Ginger Banana Macadamia, or Kona Coffee and Cream? There are also bags of Taro Ko chips made at the factory down the street. Non-food items include polished coconut jewelry, soaps, lovely lauhala baskets and hats, quilted pillows, flowers, plants, and Hawaiian music.

Uncle Eddie's Aloha Angels ★★
3905 Hanapepe Road, Hanapepe, ☎ *(808) 335-0713.*
Hours: 9:30 a.m.–4:30 p.m.
Angels in grass skirts, Christmas angels, angel suncatchers, angel T-shirts, angel books, angel pins—need we say more? Mail-order catalog available.

Village Gallery ★★
3890 Hanapepe Road, Hanapepe, 96716, ☎ *(808) 335-0343.*
Hours: 9:30 a.m.–4:30 p.m.
Special hours: Sundays, 11 a.m.–4:30 p.m. Closed: Mondays.
Open since November 1995, the Village Gallery, owned by artist Lew Shortridge, is the only gallery in Kauai dedicated to modern and experimental works by mostly local painters, sculptors, and photographers. Another notable gallery in Hanapepe

is Lele Aka Studio-Gallery, 3876 Hanapepe Road, ☎ *(808) 335-5267,* featuring ethereal images of Hawaiian women on oversize canvases, plus African and Hawaiian handcrafted drums and local and exotic woods. Open Monday–Saturday from 10 a.m.–6 p.m.

Kalaheo

Cane Field Clothing ★★★
2488 Kaumuali'i Highway (Highway 50), Kalaheo,
☎ *(808) 332-0267.*
Hours: 10 a.m.–5 p.m.
Special hours: Saturdays to 3 p.m. Closed: Sundays.
Recently moved from historic Hanapepe to elegant new digs in Kalaheo, this distinctive store features fashionable (but not outré) clothing, accessories, '40s and '50s English jewelry, picture frames, potpourri-filled bath oils, and aromatherapy candles.

Lawai

Old Hawaiian Trading Post ★★★
Highway 50 and Koloa Road, Lawai, ☎ *(808) 332-7404.*
Hours: 10:30 a.m.–5:30 p.m.
Special hours: Sundays, 2–5:30 p.m.
One of the best sources for the rare (and expensive) Niihau-shell leis and jewelry. Owner Akiko Coleman has been selling these painstakingly hand-gathered and hand-strung pieces for 25 years, directly from families on the "Forbidden Isle." Once made as a form of barter and sold for as low as $10, some are now worth thousands of dollars. A dying art form, each one takes as much as six months to make. There are more than 100 varieties of shells, ranging in color from pink, green, black, and chocolate brown; the fuschia-toned, minuscule kahelelani shells are the rarest and priciest. In ancient times, royalty were buried with them—*kahelelani*, loosely translated, means "pathway to heaven."

MOLOKAI

Lovely Molokai—congenial offspring of Wakea and his goddess Hina—is probably best known as home to both the now-defunct Dole Plantation and a nearly defunct leper colony. "The Friendly Isle" (once known as "The Lonely Isle," then "The Forgotten Isle") is—aside from that "forbidden" Niihau—the "most Hawaiian" isle with the highest amount of pure- or part-Hawaiian blood flowing through the veins of its approximately 6700 inhabitants. This is the spot where other Hawaii residents come to escape the rat race on *their* islands. It's a place where time—the commodity that seems to continually fly for everyone else—barely seems to budge. The "No Pressure" isle.

In the 1800s, Molokai apparently seemed like the ideal location in which to get rid of those "untouchable"—and definitely unwanted—leprosy (or Hansen's disease) victims. The place was hardly very "friendly" then—it was a harsh, isolated wilderness that turned its diseased inhabitants into a bunch of crazed animals with no food, no scruples, and no hope. At first the victims were dumped in the remote bay at Kalawao, then later were "upgraded" to the village of Kalaupapa. Their lives were a virtual hell until in came the Good Samaritan of Good Samaritans, Father Damien, a Catholic priest from Belgium who devoted his life to caring for the lepers and bringing them a modicum of dignity. Damien himself died from the disease and was beatified for his efforts (*much* later, in 1994). After Damien (now known as Blessed Damien) came and passed, various other nuns, priests, and missionaries carried on with his work. In the 1940s, sulfonate drugs were introduced and given a much bigger welcome than any God-worker or overseer, for the miraculous chemicals finally put a halt to the disease. Two decades later, the disease had been rendered noncontagious, and today only about 60 patients remain, some of them acting as tour guides for visitors.

Meanwhile, the Hawaiian Homes Act had been passed by Congress in 1921. This effectively freed up 43,000 acres of Molokai's land (not the best land, of course), to be doled out in 40-acre parcels to state residents with at least 50 percent pure Hawaiian blood coursing through their veins. Many natives grabbed the ring and went to settle on Molokai, thereby rendering it "the most Hawaiian" of the islands.

Developers would no doubt like to see more resorts, condos, restaurants, at least one good mall, requisite fast-food joints and the

482 HAWAII

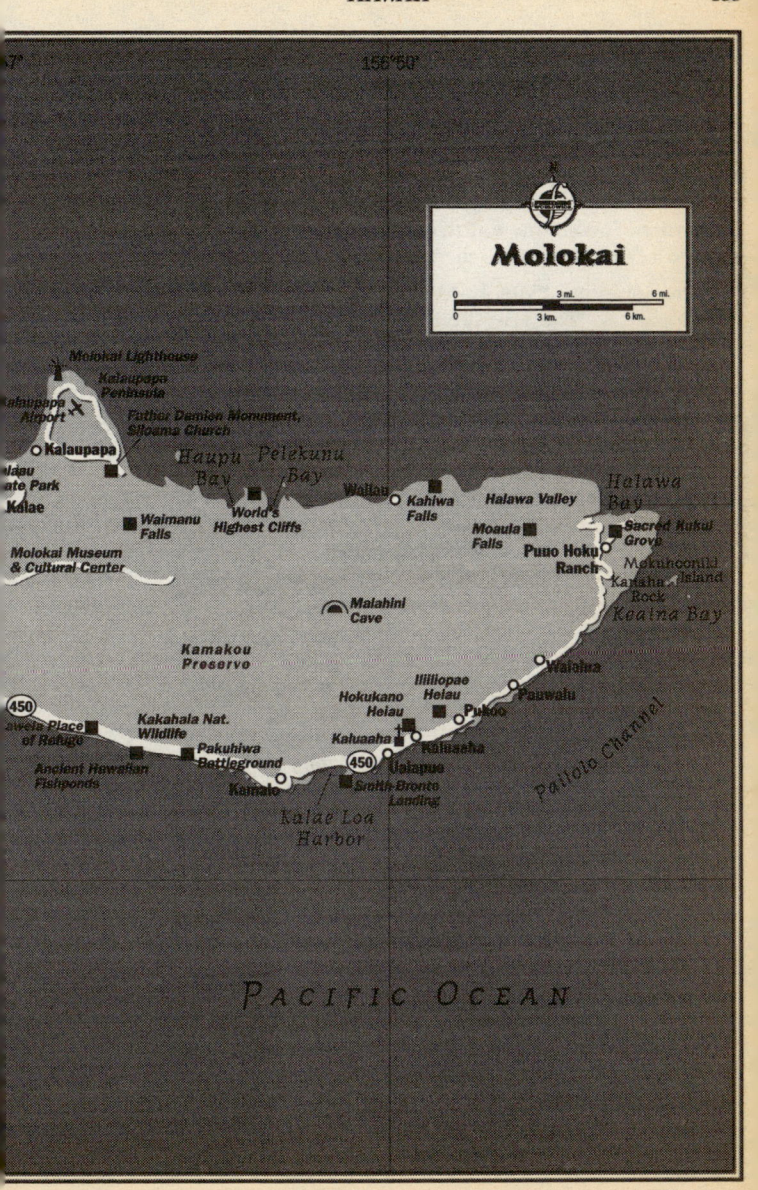

HAWAII

Molokai

- Molokai Lighthouse
- Kalaupapa Airport
- Kalaupapa Peninsula
- Father Damien Monument, Siloama Church
- Kalaupapa
- Haupu Bay
- Pelekunu Bay
- Wailau
- Kahiwa Falls
- Halawa Valley
- Halawa Bay
- Sacred Kukui Grove
- ate Park
- Kalae
- Waimanu Falls
- World's Highest Cliffs
- Moaula Falls
- Puuo Hoku Ranch
- Mokuhooniki Island
- Kanaha Rock
- Keaina Bay
- Molokai Museum & Cultural Center
- Malahini Cave
- Kamakou Preserve
- Waialna
- Pauwalu
- (450)
- Kakahala Nat. Wildlife
- Hokukano Heiau
- Iliiliopae Heiau
- Pukoo
- awela Place of Refuge
- Pakuhiwa Battleground
- Kaluaaha
- Kaluaaha
- Ancient Hawaiian Fishponds
- Kamalo
- Ualapue (450)
- Smith-Bronte Landing
- Pailolo Channel
- Kalae Loa Harbor

PACIFIC OCEAN

like. "Bring in the tourists!" they cry. They're butting heads with various "Save Molokai" groups, including the OHA (Office of Hawaiian Affairs), as well as cloutless, poverty-struck locals who don't want their island turned into a tourist mecca *nor* do they want the jobs associated with serving and cleaning up after them. Aside from other interested parties, the Molokai Ranch Development Corporation—controlled by Cooke & Castle, one of the Big Five and owner of about one-fourth of the island—is hot to see the place become a "destination." Is there any doubt as to who will win?

In the meantime, Molokai continues to maintain its public relations image as "The Friendly Isle." It's the place to come (come quickly!) for a glimpse of "real" Hawaii," coupled with absolutely nothing to do and no one to answer to except the call of sweet nature. Don't come for the shopping (there isn't much), the planned activities (ditto) or the restaurant and nightlife scene (ditto ditto). And *definitely* don't come with an attitude. You don't own the place—yet.

Molokai Facts

A.k.a.	The Friendly Island
Main city	Kaunakakai
Flower	White kuku blossom
Color	Green
Area	260 square miles
Length	38 miles
Width	10 miles
Population	7000
Highest point	Kamakou Peak (4961 feet)

Molokai Survival Guide

Getting There

You'll most likely fly into Hoolehua Airport, a one-terminal operation about eight miles west of Kaunakakai. You won't find much except a lounge, souvenir shop, lunch counter, information booth and a couple of car rental desks. Airlines are

HAWAIIAN	**(808) 553-3644**
ISLAND AIR	**(808) 567-6115**
MAHALO AIR	**(808) 567-6515**
AIR MOLOKAI	**(808) 553-3636**

Air Molokai's low-flying commuter craft provides an especially exhilarating ride.

If you're coming from Maui, you can **ferry** over on the **Maui Princess** *((808) 553-5736)*—a once-daily shuttle between Lahaina and Kaunakakai; cost is about $50 round trip.

Getting Around

There is no public transport on Molokai, so you'll either have to rent a car from

BUDGET	**(808) 567-6877**
DOLLAR	**(808) 567-6156**

or take a taxi. Most of the roads are paved and parking is as-you-please.

Taxis are usually on hand to meet flights, and can be also be hired for tours. Contact

KUKUI TOURS AND LIMOUSINES	**(808) 553-5133**
MOLOKAI STYLE SERVICES OR MOLOKAI OFF-ROAD TOURS AND TAXI	**(808) 553-9090, (808) 553-9046**

or—for tours of Kalaupapa (the leper colony)—

DAMIEN TOURS	**(808) 567-6171**

Visitor Information

Contact the **Molokai Visitors Association** *((808) 533-3876 or 800-553-0404)* for helpful information. Call ahead and they'll send you a brochure with lists of accommodations, car rentals, restaurants, airlines and other island services.

HAWAII

Bird's-Eye View

Hawaii's fifth-largest island lies just 22 miles from Oahu, yet—for now—it may as well be light years away. Measuring 260 square miles (38 miles long and 10 miles wide), most of Molokai's usable agricultural land is part and parcel of the 70,000-acre Molokai Ranch on the western edge and the comparatively minuscule 14,000-acre Puu O Hoku Ranch on the eastern edge. The hilly, pastoral west side of the island is where you'll find the luxe Kaluakoi Resort, Hawaii's largest sand beach, prairie lands, Molokai Ranch Wildlife Park, and the old pineapple plantation town of Maunaloa. The east, green and lush, harbors Halawa Valley (thought to be Hawaii's oldest settlement, dating from the 7th century) and its 300-foot waterfalls, the world's highest sea cliffs (up to 3000 feet), Molokai Forest Reserve, and Mount Kamakou (4961 high), Molokai's highest peak. The main town, Kaunakakai, situated about mid-island on the south side, has been likened to a circa-1930s, Hollywood-style, Old West movie set—easy to see why, with its hitching posts, wooden facades, and a three-block-long main street. North of Kaunakakai, you'll hit Kualapuu Reservoir (the world's largest), Palaau State Park, with its Kalaupapa Lookout and enticing Phallic Rock, and—on the northern coast—the old leper colony at Kalaupapa.

Nature Guide

Birders will be able to find a number of introduced game birds, as well as species such as the pueo (Hawaiian owl), *alae ke'oke'o* (Hawaiian coot), and *ae'o* (Hawaiian stilt). The *kukui* (candlenut tree)—prevalent around the mountainsides at lower elevations—is Hawaii's state tree, while its blossom holds reign as Molokai's official flower. Kapuaiwa Coconut Grove, west of Kaunakakai, still shelters several hundred of the palms planted back in the 1860s by King Kamehameha V when he was but a prince.

As for animals, all were imported over centuries. Goats came in from the Mediterranean, axis deer were sent over from India, pigs arrived from wherever. Around the 1960s, Molokai Ranch imported hundreds of animals from Africa, and today, about a thousand of them—from antelopes and giraffes to ostriches and zebras—roam the grounds at Molokai Ranch Wildlife Park.

Beach Finder

Molokai has a distinctive range of beaches. Some have soft white sand and wade-in-me water, others are narrow with treacherous waves and rip currents. Ask locals or the **Department of Parks, Land and Natural Resources** *(808) 567-6083* before you hit the surf.

Onealii Beach Park
Several miles east of Kaunakakai.
This centrally located beach will appeal to most families. The swimming is relatively safe, plus there's a run-around meadow, pavilion, picnic facilities, outdoor showers, and rest rooms (no lifeguards, though). Expect crowds, especially on weekends.

On the western side of the island

Papohaku Beach
Below the Kaluakoi Resort.
THIS IS HAWAII'S LONGEST BEACH—three miles long and 100-feet wide—with lots of white sand and mean rip currents. Winter months see huge swells (and surfers) but, come summer, the beach is generally safe for swimming. Outdoor showers, rest rooms, picnic facilities, and no lifeguards.

Kepuhi Beach
Also in front of Kaluakoi Resort.
Another white-sand beauty. It comes with the same warnings as Papohaku, plus year-round winds that hamper swimming (and hair-dos). Outdoor showers, no lifeguards.

Kawakiu Beach
North of Kapuhi Bay.
OFFERS EXCELLENT SWIMMING (when the water is calm) and is also a designated archeological site. Free weekend camping, no facilities, no lifeguards.

Moomomi Beach
At the northwest shore.
A favorite with residents for swimming (best in front of the community recreation center) and snorkeling. Visitors must get permission from the **Hawaiian Home Lands** *(808) 567-6104.*

Halawa Bay

Over on the east side at the far end.
Features waterfalls, a freshwater pool, snorkeling, fishing, and excellent summer swimming and winter surfing.

Adventure Guide

With no shopping or nightlife, face it—you either came to Molokai to do absolutely nothing and forget everything, *or* to have a memorable adventure.

One of the island's best **treks** is into the lush **Halawa Valley,** on the eastern side. The well-marked (albeit occasionally muddy) trail presses through fruit-tree groves, fern grottos, and ancient archeological sites until it reaches the magnificent 250-foot **Moaula Falls.** The icy mountain pool, at the bottom of the falls, is an excellent place to wash off your mud and sweat, though you should beware of the mythical lizard, *mo'o,* that supposedly resides in the pool.

Follow in the footsteps of the Molokai Mule Ride on the **trail to Kalaupapa.** The recently restored trail is fit for mules or hikers who are in good condition. You must have a permit from the **National Park Service** *(808) 567-6102* as well as a confirmed reservation with Damien Tours for the leper-colony extravaganza.

If you have a four-wheel-drive vehicle and are a somewhat stalwart hiker, you can access trails at Molokai Forest Reserve (where you'll be rewarded with glorious views and valleys) and Pepeopae Bog in the Kamakou Preserve, an almost-unbelievable isolated ecosystem protected by the **Nature Conservancy of Hawaii** *((808) 553-5236,* **http://ice.ucdavis.edu/~robyn/tnch.html***).*

Camping is allowed at **Palauu State Park,** where you'll get a view of Kalaupapa Peninsula and be close to the shameless Phallic Rock. It's a free rest, but permits are required from the **Department of Land and Natural Resources** in Hoolehua *(808) 567-6618.* Another free site is at **Moomomi Beach,** over on the northwest coast. More **beach camping** can be found at **Papohaku Beach Park** and **Onealii Beach Park,** both near Kaunakakai and both with all the necessary facilities (and both with all the expected noise and crowds). Permits cost a few bucks a day and are issued by the **Kaunakakai Office of County Parks and Recreation** *(808) 553-3204.* If you don't mind the risk of having your brains bonked by falling coconuts, you might try the royal coconut grove at **Kioea Park,** also near Kaunakakai. Get a permit from the **Hawaiian Home**

Lands Department in Hoolehua *(808) 567-6104*. **Molokai Ranch** *(808) 552-2767* offers camping at various sites on the property for around $10 per night.

For more information on **hiking, trails** and **camping** on Molokai, contact **Hawaii State Department of Land and Natural Resources** *(Palaau Park Office, Kalae 96757; (808) 567-6083)*, **Hawaiian Home Lands Department** *(P.O. Box 198, Hoolehua, 96729; (808) 567-6104)*, **Maui County Department of Parks and Recreation** *(P.O. Box 526, Kaunakakai, 96748; (808) 553-5141)* and the **Nature Conservancy of Hawaii** *(1116 Smith Street, Suite 201, Honolulu 96817; (808) 553-5136)*.

Diving and snorkeling are easy—when the water is calm, that is—and YOU'LL BE ABLE TO VIEW EVERYTHING FROM MANTA RAYS TO ANGEL FISH. Diving at **Makuhooniki Rock,** an old bombing target on the eastern side of the island, is apt to turn up World War II artifacts as well as black coral, gray reef sharks, and barracuda. Best **snorkeling spots** are, on the eastern side, **Fagans, Murphy, Honouli Wai, Honouli Maloo,** and **Sandy.** And out west: **Kaupoa, Kapukahehu, Moomomi, Poolau,** and **Kaunala.** A variety of operators will take you out or just rent you some equipment and point out the way (see "Sports" below). **Ocean kayaking** on the island during the summer months is truly superb. Experienced kayakers will be able to explore isolated valleys and remote hideaways. Kayaks can be rented, or tours arranged, through **Fun Hogs at Kaluakoi Resort** *(808) 567-9292*. **Surfers** will find good waves at **Halawa Beach, Kawaaloa Bay, Kepuhi Beach, Kanalukaha Beach, Kaunakakai Wharf,** and **Hale O Lono Beach,** but bring your own board (rentals aren't available on the island).

What Else to See

You'll get a good idea of what Molokai is all about when you explore **Kaunakakai,** the main town. The atmosphere is decidedly "laid-back," and you can load up on provisions, shop for some local crafts and souvenirs, and soak up the local ambiance. Everything is slow as proverbial molasses—even the local teens as they cruise up and down the nearby wharf (by Los Angeles standards, anyway). West of Kaunakakai is the **Kapualwa Coconut Grove,** planted back in the mid-1800s for King Kamehameha V. Thankfully, hundreds of the trees are still standing and you can parade around the grove like royalty—just watch out for falling coconuts. **Church Row,** across the way, is an exercise in side-by-side religion-with just about all the major denominations represented in churches built under a Hawaiian Home Lands' grant (you're welcome to join islanders for Sunday services). North is **Kualapuu Reservoir** (the world's largest), the mini-town of **Hoolehua** (renowned for cockfights, and site of Hawaiian Homes allotments), and **Purdy's All Natural Macadamia Nut Farm** (learn everything you never wanted to know about macadamias, then buy a sack and eat them all). **Palaau State Park** is where you'll find knockout views from **Kalaupapa Lookout** and *at* **Phallic Rock.** Re-live the horrors of leprosy (Hansen's disease in kinder, gentler language) at **Kalaupapa,** but sign up in advance for a tour with **Damien Tours.** A resident of the colony will lead you around his home turf and sit you down for a picnic lunch.

On the western side of the island, **Maunaloa** affords a good view of a plantation town, albeit without the plantation. Stop in at **Maunaloa General Store, Big Wind Kite Factory, The Plantation Gallery,** and a variety of other crafts/gallery/gift shops in the area. You have to sign up in advance for a tour of **Molokai Ranch Wildlife Park,** one of the country's most esteemed game preserves, where you can check out imported exotic beasts in some of their glory. (Tours leave from Kaluakoi Resort several times daily.) **Hale o Lono Harbor,** one mile west of Halena, is especially interesting in October, when the annual outrigger canoe competition sets off for Oahu.

Venturing eastward, you'll come to **St. Joseph Church** and then **Our Lady of Sorrows Church,** both built by Father Damien in the 1870s. Get a dose of Hawaiian-style entertainment, a barbecue, and a wagon tour at **Molokai Horse & Wagon Ride,** then make your way to the lush **Halawa Valley,** site of a 7th-century settlement—thought to be Hawaii's oldest. Ooh and aah over the views, then take a swim in the (safe) bay or cool stream and pretend you have time-traveled back to the really good old days.

Central Molokai

Hoolehua
!TRAVELBOOKS FREEBIE

Purdy's Natural Macadamia Nut Farm ★★

P.O. Box 84, Hoolehua, From Highway 470, turn left to Farrington Avenue; one mile to Lihi Pali Avenue, turn right, 96729, ☎ *(808) 567-6601.*
Hours: 9:30 a.m.–3:30 p.m.
http://molokai-aloha.com/macnuts/

A family enterprise since 1980, this 70-year-old, one-acre grove of 50 mac-nut trees is located in Hoolehua, an agricultural community in Central Molokai. The Purdy family acquired the grove through the Hawaiian Homestead Act. This law has provided opportunity for some people of Hawaiian ancestry to return to the land. The entire family helps maintain the trees and gather and prepare the nuts. A visit here is a must, ESPECIALLY FOR KIDS who love to crack open the nuts. Best of all, it's free, and Tuddie Purdy is a marvelous raconteur who is nutty about nuts. His partner Kammy might give you her recipe for macadamia nut cookies. Preservative- and pesticide-free macs and mac-nut honey are available for purchase.

Tours

Molokai Air Shuttle ★★

Hoolehua, ☎ *(808) 567-6847.*

If a long, fairly strenuous hike or the popular-but-expensive Mule Ride doesn't turn your crank, you can wing it to the Kalaupapa Peninsula on the Molokai Air Shuttle—and AT A REASONABLE PRICE. This company offers daily round-trip airfare from the Molokai Airport to the peninsula, coupled with a ground tour of the settlement by Damien Tours. Weather permitting, Molokai Air Shuttle will also throw in a free aerial tour of Molokai's North Shore. General admission: $25-$75.

Kalae
City Celebrations

Molokai Music Festival ★★

Molokai Museum and Cultural Center, Highway 470, Kalae, Four miles north of Highway 460, two miles past Kualupuu, 96748, ☎ *(808) 567-6436.*

The créme de la créme of the Hawaiian music world appears at this outdoor music festival held annually on the third Sunday in August. For more information, write: PO Box 84, Kaunakakai, HI 96748.

Tours

Molokai Museum at R.W. Meyer Sugar Mill ★★★
Four miles north of Highway 460, Kalae, two miles past Kualupuu, ☎ (808) 567-6436.
Hours: 10 a.m.–2 p.m.

Even if you think you're not interested in sugarcane processing, A VISIT TO THIS MUSEUM AND CULTURAL CENTER ADJACENT TO A LOVINGLY RESTORED SUGAR MILL IS A MUST. The mill, which is on the National Register of Historic Places, was built in the 1870s by German immigrant Rudolph W. Meyer. The simple wooden building with a metal roof houses a boiler and a fully operative, stationary steam engine, with copper evaporators for the separation of the molasses, and a flat belt-driven centrifuge for the separation of the sugar from the molasses. Outside is the original stone-lined, mule-driven, cane-crushing pit. The accessory building and research center, which is only the first phase of an ambitious project (two more buildings are expected to be added), is located about 50 yards from the mill. It was built by Honolulu architect Paul Morgan, and contains a gift shop and the mill archives. It's used for an amazing number of special community events, including the annual Moloka'i Music Festival, a taro and sweet potato festival, and monthly talks by archeologists who have worked on Molokai sites. Classes held here include loom-weaving, coconut-frond-weaving, making ukuleles from scratch (also how to play them), Hawaiian quilt-making, and much more. IT'S RUN BY BARBARA SCHONLEY, FORMERLY WITH THE MOLOKAI VISITORS ASSOCIATION; SHE'S ONE OF THE MOST KNOWLEDGEABLE PEOPLE ON THE ISLAND. General admission: Call for rates.

Kalaupapa
Historical Sites

Kalaupapa Peninsula ★★★★
Damien Tours, c/o Richard Marks, P.O. Box 1, Kalaupapa, 96742, ☎ (808) 567-6171.

Designated a National Historic Park in 1980, Kalaupapa, located on the Kalaupapa/Makanalua Peninsula on Molokai's northern coast, was the home to sufferers of leprosy, now called Hansen's Disease. After the first instances of the disease appeared in Hawaii in 1835, it became a raging epidemic. Victims were forcibly "quarantined" here in 1866, arriving on the eastern end, at Kalawao, with little food, no materials for shelter, and almost no hope of escape, except through a merciful death. Newcomers had to face treacherous seas and the peninsula's formidable 3300-foot cliffs. Already weakened by the journey and the spiritual pain of being separated from loved ones forever, they had to fight off physical attacks by the afflicted who had come before them. This hardscrabble existence continued until Father Damien de Veuster, a Belgian priest, arrived for a short visit in 1873. Almost a one-man army, Father Damien stayed on to nurse the sick, help build their homes, and dig their graves. He died of leprosy himself in 1889. Ironically, we now know that leprosy is one of the least-communicable diseases. At its height, the colony counted some 8000 people. Today, there are fewer than 100, all 50 years or older. They choose to remain, as it is the only life they've ever known. Visitors can enter the peninsula by mule, or choose to hike or fly in. Permission is required to visit the settlement itself.

Tours

Hike Kalaupapa Trail ★★★★
Damien Tours, (see above) c/o Richard Marks, P.O. Box 1, Kalaupapa, On the right side of Highway 470 between the stables and Kalaupapa Overlook, 96742, ☎ (808) 567-6171.
http://www.molokai.com/muleride/hike.html
Participants should be on the trail by 8:15 a.m. before the mules leave the Kalae stables; although you set your own pace, you should time yourself to get to the mule tie-up spot by 10:15 a.m. YOU MIGHT MEET MULES ON THE TRAIL, BUT DO NOT ATTEMPT TO PASS OR WEAVE THROUGH THEM. JUST STAY ON THE SIDE AT A SAFE PLACE AND ALLOW THE MULES TO PASS YOU. The tour bus will pick you up with the mule riders at the same time. You must have a reservation; wandering around the beach or the settlement on your own is strictly *kapu* (forbidden). The trail has been upgraded recently, but locals say the new steps on the trail make it hard on your legs going both ways. IT HELPS TO HAVE A RELIABLE PAIR OF STURDY SHOES AND TO BE IN GOOD PHYSICAL CONDITION. Minimum age is 16 years. Includes: set-

tlement tour. Bring your own lunch (and cold water), as there is no food available for sale in Kalaupapa. Cameras OK. Damien Tours' office hours are 7–9 a.m. and 5–7 p.m.

Kualupu'u
Hiking

Nature Conservancy of Hawaii Hikes ★★★
P.O. Box 220, Kualupu'u, About 1/3 of a mile before Highway 470 west from Kaunakakai, 96757, ☎ (808) 553-5236.
Conservancy guides lead hikes to Molokai's Mo'omomi and Kamakou preserves one day every month. Guides are experienced naturalists. Mo'omomi (means "Jeweled Reptile") Preserve, is near a small beach on Hawaiian Home Lands popular with islanders on the northwest coast of Molokai and was created to protect five endangered-plant species. The Keonelele coastal dunes west of Mo'omomi are of great cultural and scientific significance to geologists and experts in Hawaiian history and paleontology; it was once a native Hawaiian burial site. Kamakou Preserve, near the Waikolou Lookout, is a remote and spectacular 2774-acre native rainforest. After a ride to the entrance of the reserve via four-wheel-drive vehicle, Conservancy guides lead hikes from the Pepeopae Trail (a raised wooden boardwalk) through the forest to an untrammeled Hawaiian montane bog, and onto a dizzying point overlooking the preserve in Pelekunu Valley. The valley's 4000-foot seacliffs are reportedly the tallest in the world. To reserve a spot way in advance (there is always a two-month waiting list) and to confirm dates, call the number above. (On Oahu, *(808) 524-0779.)* Donations made to help defray costs are appreciated.

Tours

Coffees of Hawaii Wagon Tour ★★★
P.O. Box 160, Kualupu'u, 96757, ☎ (808) 567-9241.
Hours: 10 a.m.–3 p.m
http://www.coffeehawaii.com/visitus.html
The hilly area of Kualupu'u is a perfect environment for the locally grown coffee—called Muleskinner, after the hardy guys who led their animals down the switchbacks of the 3300-foot North Shore seacliffs to the Kalaupapa peninsula below on a daily basis. This is strong joe—a natural dry dark roast, which

may be richer than the brands you're used to. Another aromatic blend is Malulani Estate Coffee (Malulani means "heavenly aroma"), which is premium Arabica coffee made from select beans. In this interesting tour, you can sample the coffee for yourself and learn the history of the island's only working coffee plantation while riding in a mule-drawn wagon. Reservations required. General admission.

East Molokai

Halawa Valley
Beaches

Halawa Beach Park ★★★
Highway 450 (Kamehameha V Highway), Halawa Valley, At the eastern end of Highway 450.
PROBABLY THE MOST LUSH AND BEAUTIFUL SETTING ON THE ISLAND, THIS BLACK-SAND BEACH IS A PRIME SURFING SPOT. The downside is the usual nasty currents in winter, but the swimming is fine in summer, and many use the beach as a kick-off point for north-shore kayaking trips. Bring a picnic and bottled water (water here is not potable). Outdoor showers, pavilion, barbecue grills, parking.

Kaluaaha
Historical Sites

Iliiliopae Heiau ★★
Highway 450, 1/2 mile past the 15-mile marker, Kaluaaha.
Listed on the National Register of Historic Places, this is one of the largest *heiaus* in Hawaii–320 feet long and 120 feet wide (longer than a football field)—and was the site of human sacrifice. What remains today is the foundation, and it is believed to have been three times that size in its heyday. Legends relate that the stones to build the temple were hauled to Molokai over the mountains by *Menehune,* a mystical race of "little people" (somewhat akin to Ireland's leprechauns). Why such a large temple in Molokai? Long ago, the island was a center of religious learning and mysticism where the highest priests trained acolytes to follow in their footsteps. The *heiau* is on private property, but if you take the Molokai Horse and Wagon Tour (see "Tours"), the *heiau* is included in the itinerary.

Kamalo

St. Joseph's Church ★
Highway 450, Kamalo, 10 miles east of Kaunakakai.
Built in 1876 by Kalaupapa's Father Damien and restored in 1971, this is the second-oldest church on the island, although it is no longer used for services. Father Damien, who counted carpentry among his many other skills and gifts, built four churches outside of the Peninsula.

Mapulehu
Tours

Molokai Horse and Wagon Ride ★
At the Mapulehu Mango Grove, Mapulehu, just past mile marker 15 on Route 450 (east end), ☎ *(808) 558-8380.*
Hours: 10:30 a.m.–12:30 p.m.
http://www.hawaiiweb.com/molokai/html/sites/molokai_horse_and_wagon_ride.html
These friendly folks invite you to experience "old Hawai'i... Molokai style." This informal and informative two-hour tour in a real wagon drawn by two horses combines Hawaiian music, stories, legends, hula lessons, coconut husking, net throwing, and more. Places you'll see include the huge Mapulehu Mango Grove (the meeting point) and the sacred Iliiliopae *Heiau* (temple). General admission: $35–$60.

Twenty Mile Beach
Beaches

No Name Beach at 20 Mile Marker ★★
Highway 450, Twenty Mile Beach; go east on Highway 450 for about seven miles to 20-mile marker.
This intimate circlet of white-sand beach is number one on the East side of the island, locals say, especially in winter, when other beaches are dangerous to swim in. Bring your snorkeling gear. Rest rooms, roadside parking. Rocky Point, at the 21-mile marker, is the best surfing spot in the summer; you'll see a lot of young people there.

Kaunakakai
City Celebrations

Aloha Festivals ★★★
Downtown Kaunakakai ☎ *(808) 944-8857.*
http://www.alohafestivals.com/
The statewide Aloha Festival is a two-month-long cultural fete featuring traditional music and dance, historical ceremonies, contests, and ho'olaule'a, or block parties. It was begun in 1946 (then called Aloha Week) to honor the Makahiki, a period of time in the ancient Hawaiian calendar where war was not permitted. Special events in Molokai include the Molokai Parade and Mule Drag. Usually held in late September-early October.

Bankoh Moloka'i Hoe/Outrigger Canoe Race ★★★
Hale O Lono Harbor, Kaunakakai.
The 41-mile Molokai-to-Oahu world championship outrigger canoe race has been a big deal for 45 years running (rowing?). Starting from the Hale O Lono Harbor on Molokai Ranch property, the race crosses Kaiwi channel to a finish at Fort DeRussy Beach, in Waikiki. Participants usually include world-class teams from the United States, Australia, Canada, Tahiti, and Europe. Women's race: September; men's race: October.

Moloka'i Makahiki ★★
Kaunakakai Park and Manae Canoe Club, Kaunakakai,
☎ *(808) 553-3876.*
Long after the stale champagne memories and unkept resolutions have faded on the mainland, Molokaians are just celebrating their own New Year's festival—the Molokai Makahiki, observed annually in mid-January. Actually a festival of peace, it's a sunrise-to-sunset party in Kaunakakai, where everyone chows down on *ono grinds* (good eats) while listening to traditional music and watching dancers from various hula schools. Other activities include canoe races and arts and crafts. Makahiki is also a chance to play native games such as 'o'oihe (spear throwing), 'ulu maika, and konane (ancient forms of bowling and checkers, respectively).

Tours

ITRAVELBOOK FREEBIE:

Mapulehu Glass House ★★
P.O. Box 500, Kaunakakai, east of the 15-mile marker on Highway 450, 15 miles East of Kaunakakai, 96748,
☎ *(808) 558-8160.*
Closed: Saturdays, Sundays.
http://www.molokai.com/tropicals/
Sorry, this isn't your local Waterford crystal outlet, but a historic greenhouse built in the 1920s that specializes in exotic tropical blooms. What may be the state's largest glass house is attached to a working nine-acre certified cut-flower farm that offers free tours. After the tour, you may purchase pink and white ginger, heliconia, and more to perfume your condo or hotel room; the Glass House also ships flowers by Federal Express to your friends languishing on the mainland. Sigh. A nice stop while touring the Halawa Valley area.

Molokai Off-Road Tours & Taxi ★★
P.O. Box 747, Kaunakakai, 96748, ☎ (808) 553-3369.
As long as it isn't raining, this company's guides will take you to the entrance of the Molokai Forest Preserve (also known as Kamakou) west of Kaunakakai by four-wheel-drive vehicle, usually an air-conditioned Jeep Cherokee. From here, you do the hike yourself, and arrange a pickup time with your driver. Here you'll find a primeval, dense wonderland of giant ferns, eucalyptus, and pine, and some 500 native plant species. THE DAY-LONG HIKE (ABOUT SEVEN HOURS) ends at the Waikolou Overlook, where you can picnic (bring your own bag) while gazing at waterfalls and plunge pools in the valley below and offshore islands in the distance. Dress in layers as the climate changes quickly from hot to mighty nippy, dry to humid in a heartbeat; discuss the particulars when you make a reservation. This tour requires a minimum of three people and a max of 10.

ITRAVELBOOK TIP: EVEN IF IT'S BALMY AND WARM, PACK ADDITIONAL LAYERS IF YOU'RE PLANNING ON DOING MOUNTAIN HIKING. THE WEATHER CAN (AND USUALLY DOES) CHANGE DRASTICALLY.

The Maui Princess ★★
Kaunakakai, (808) 661-8397.
http://www.mauiprincess.com/
Used both as an excursion yacht and DAILY MODE OF TRANSPORTATION FOR MOLOKAI COMMUTERS WORKING IN MAUI, the *Maui Princess* sails daily from Lahaina Harbor Maui's Pier 3 to Kaunakakai Harbor in Molokai. The comfortable yacht has an air-conditioned main cabin, but for those wishing to travel alfresco, it provides a capacious upper-level observation deck. The sailing schedule is as follows: depart Lahaina Pier 3 at 7 a.m.; arrive Kaunakakai at 8:45 a.m.; depart Kaunakakai at 3:55 p.m.; arrive Lahaina at 5:45 p.m. The fare is $50 for adults, $25 for children. The company also offers tour packages to Molokai, including four cruise/drive deals ranging from $74 to $109; a Molokai Grand Tour, which includes a local guide; a golf package; hotel overnighters; and three Kalaupapa Tours. The Trail Hike and Settlement Tour is $139; Fly-in and Settlement Tour, $189; and Guided Mule Tour, $225 (available Monday-Friday only). Passengers must be at least 16 years of age to tour Kalaupapa. General admission: Call for rates..

West Molokai

Maunaloa
Beaches

Kepuhi Beach ★★★
Kaluakoi Road, Maunaloa, 96770.
Unless you're an experienced bodysurfer, this lovely white-sand beach in front of Colony's Kaluakoi Resort's golf course is better for long strolls, beachcombing, and sun worshiping. DANGEROUS SWIMMING CONDITIONS, even on calm days, due to strong currents. A favorite winter surfing spot (experienced only!). Facilities at the resort, parking.

Children's Activities

Kite Making/Kite Flying Classes ★★
120 Maunaloa Highway, Maunaloa, 96770,
☎ *(808) 552-2364.*
For more than 15 years, the Big Wind Kite Factory, purveyor of colorful handmade kites and windsocks, has been giving kite-making classes to the children on Molokai. Proprietor "Uncle Jonathan" Socher calls his surefire technique "20 Kids,

20 Kites, 20 Minutes." What this means is, if he can get 20 kids, he can have them each finish a kite in 20 minutes! The materials list includes brightly colored typing paper and barbecue sticks. Child impersonators (that's you and me) can also drop by and take one of Socher's daily kite-flying lessons; no strings attached (his pun, not ours). Factory tours daily. Call the store for lesson times.

City Celebrations

Moloka'i Ka Hula Piko ★★★★
Papohaku Beach Park, Maunaloa, in the Kaluakoi Resort, ☎ *(808) 553-3876.*

Contrary to the image presented by corny old Hollywood movies, hula is a highly refined form of artistic expression. It's an ancient dance, a language, that speaks of the history and aspirations of a people. MOLOKAI IS THE BIRTHPLACE OF THE HULA. At Ka'ana on the slopes of Maunaloa in west Molokai, there was once a famous hula school. Here, tradition holds, the goddess Laka first danced the hula, then traveled throughout the islands teaching others the graceful movements and chants that have been passed on through generations to today's *kumu hula*. Each year, on the third Saturday in May, Molokai celebrates the birth of hula, attracting visitors from all over the world; festivities include music, food, arts and crafts, and of course, demonstrations by hula *halaus*, or schools. The day-long program is preceded by a week of lectures on hula and Hawaiian history, as well as guided tours to historic sites celebrated in hula chants. Rooms sell out for this event; contact the Molokai Visitors Association, ☎ *(808) 553-3876,* for special travel packages.

Theme/Amusement Parks

Molokai Ranch Wildlife Conservation Park ★★★
P.O. Box 259, Maunaloa, 96770, ☎ *(808) 552-2773.*
Closed: Mondays, Sundays.
http://www.molokai.com/ranch/

Open-air safari vans allow visitors to observe and photograph more than 800 rare (and not so rare) animals from Africa and Asia such as Barbary sheep, kudu, Indian black buck, giraffe, zebras, eland, and oryx, who seem to thrive in West Molokai's pleasing, arid climate. The park encompasses 350 acres of the

53,000-acre Molokai Ranch, which many participants compare with Africa's Serengeti plain. Afterward, the kids can take turns feeding the graceful (and grateful) giraffes in the popular "giraffe picnic." Reservations required. May be cancelled in event of rain. General admission: $35-$60.

Sports

Choose from two golf courses: the flashy par-72 with all accoutrements at **Kaluakoi Golf Course,** or the relatively spartan, nine-hole course at **Ironwood Hills Golf Club.** Guests play **tennis** for free at Kaluakoi Resort (with the best facilities), Wavecrest Condos, and Ke Nani Kai Condos. Nonguests can play at Kaluakoi for a fee, or try the public courts at Molokai High School or the Kaunakakai Community Center.

Fishermen usually luck out in Molokai's fish-filled waters, reeling in big favorites such as marlin, ahi, mahi-mahi, ono, onaga, and uku. Cast your line from the shore for ulua and ama ama, or head for the south shore's fishpond sites for squid. Charter excursions will take you to the best sportfishing locations. Sailing, snorkeling, kayaking, and scuba-diving excursions are all available. If you'd rather stay on land, Molokai Ranch Outfitters Center offers a variety of **horseback rides.** One tour—the Saturday Lunch Adventure—includes swimming, kayaking, snorkeling, lunch, *and* the horse.

Central Molokai
Kalae

Ironwood Hills Golf Course ★
P.O. Box 182, Kalae, just south of Molokai Museum/Meyer Sugar Mill, 96757, ☎ *(808) 567-6000.*
This is the "people's" golf course—no membership required. Only nine holes, but you can pay a little extra to play the course all over again. No frills or facilities other than cart rental. IRONWOOD ALSO HAS SUPERIOR OCEAN VIEWS (IT HAS A 1200-FOOT ELEVATION) AND A FEW CHALLENGING HOLES. General admission: Call for greens fees.

Palaau

Palaau State Park ★★

Highway 470, Palaau, Highway 460 south to Kaunakakai, left (North) to Highway 470 to the park, ☎ (808) 567-6083.
http://www.hiohwy.com/p/palaausp.htm

This 223-acre, refreshingly cool (and somewhat damp) North Shore park is abundant with eucalyptus, pine, and plenty of green stuff. About 2000 feet above sea level, it rains a lot here—at least an inch or more per month. QUIET AND UNCROWDED, THIS IS THE LEAST-USED STATE CAMPGROUND IN THE DISTRICT. Rest rooms, but no showers, no electricity. Water, picnic tables, tentsites. Kaunakakai is 10 miles away. BEST FOR HIKING, THERE'S A TRAIL LEADING TO PHALLIC ROCK, WHICH LEGENDS CREDIT WITH GRANTING CHILDLESS WOMEN FERTILITY. *Camping is free; seven-day limit. Permits from the Division of Parks, PO Box 153, Kaunakakai, HI 96748.*

East Molokai
Halawa Valley

Chris' Adventures Bike or Hike ★★★

P.O. Box 869, Kula, HI 96790, Halawa Valley, ☎ (800) 224-5344.
Closed: Sundays.
http://www.islandsource.com/adventure/adventure8.htm

Chris and his associates offer hiking or cycling (on- and off-road) tours of Molokai's lush Halawa Valley every Thursday from 6:30 a.m.–6 p.m. You can bike along ancient Hawaiian fish ponds to the valley. Tour includes breakfast and island-style picnic lunch, 21-speed TREK bicycles, helmets, gloves, weather gear, day packs, maps, safety briefings. THIS TOUR IS RECOMMENDED FOR ALL LEVELS OF EXPERIENCE. Also offered are Maui-Lanai-Molokai "inn-to-inn vacations," (three to eight days) which combine hiking/biking with a kayak or raft adventure. Most tours are tailored to accommodate occasional practitioners of these sports, but can be geared to more-advanced levels. Price is $200–$275 per day; includes meals, transportation, equipment, lodging, extras. Call Chris' Adventures tour planner for details, dates, and trip itineraries. General admission: varies.

Halawa Valley/Moaula Falls ★★★
Halawa Valley, after the 21-mile marker on Highway 450.
This popular trail to Moaula Falls begins near Jerusalema Hou Church. The wet, slippery, two-mile trail (two hours both ways), punctuated by tropical fruit trees and lava-rock terraces, is a hardy climb through primeval jungle up to the 250-foot waterfall and pool, where the traveler is rewarded by a freezing dip in the crystal-clear water. Before doing so, people followed local legend by throwing a ti leaf into the pool; only if it floated to the surface was it safe to swim. Unfortunately, the trail to the falls is closed to hikers for the foreseeable future due to a lawsuit.

Waikolou Valley

Waikolu Valley ★★★
Highway 460 south towards Kaunakakai, Waikolu Valley, From Highway 460, turn left at Maunahui Road 10 miles to Waikolu Valley Lookout, ☎ *(808) 553-5019.*
Access to the valley is difficult; after a relatively smooth beginning, the last seven miles are extremely rough; recommendation is to park your vehicle and hike. It has the best views on the island (maybe the world) from a 4000-foot lookout to Waikolu Valley and numerous waterfalls. The downside is a persistent cloud cover; 50 percent chance of overcast, especially in winter. No water, picnic tables, or grills. Pit toilet (one). Pretty cold camping, but gorgeous and wild, and close to the Kamakou Forest Preserve trails. Better bring all supplies in, there are no facilities for miles. Permit required; five-day limit. Contact State Department of Forestry (located in Maui) at the phone number above. There's also a ranger station, where you might be able to obtain permits in person, on Oloolo Street, one mile west of Kaunakakai off Highway 460. Call ☎ *(808) 553-5019.*

Kaunakakai

Alyce C. ★
P.O. Box 825, Kaunakakai, 96748, ☎ *(808) 558-8377.*
http://www.worldwidefishing.com/hawaii/b225/
Alyce C. is Joe "Captain" Reich's baby, a 31-foot diesel-powered fishing vessel available for a full- or half-day charter; Reich provides the equipment and bait; all you have to do is show up. He'll take you and your party off the coast of Molokai to catch

plenty of ahi, mahi-mahi, ono ulua, kawakawa, and perhaps a Pacific blue marlin, if you're lucky. Reich has 20 years' experience. Whale-watching in season.

Bill Kapuni's Snorkel and Dive Adventure ★
Kaunakakai, 96748, ☎ *(808) 553-9867.*
Let Bill, a native Hawaiian and professional PADI instructor, take you on a snorkeling adventure to a secluded, unspoiled barrier reef, with warm tropical waters teeming with colorful marine life. It also has one of the most dense populations of turtles and eagle rays in Hawaii. Includes gear, soda, and chips. Air fills and tank rentals, scuba instruction. Morning tour: 7:30 and 10:30 a.m.; afternoon tour: 1 p.m. General admission: $100.

Kioea Park ★
Highway 460, one mile west of Kaunakakai ☎ *(808) 567-6296.*
This beach park is adjacent to Kamehameha V's royal Kapuaiwa Coconut Grove, where you risk being dive-bombed by errant nuts (a sign says, "Beware of Falling Coconut"). Administered by the Department of Hawaiian Homelands, it is available to visitors only if it isn't in use by native Hawaiians. Entrance is through a locked gate—you have to obtain a key from the Department to get in. Facilities include ample tentsites, a beach pavilion with electricity, picnic tables, barbecue grills, toilets, and showers. The beach is too silty for swimming or snorkeling. For permits call the number above, or write to the *Department of Hawaiian Homelands, Box 198, Hoolehua, HI 96729*. General admission: $10.

Molokai Bicycle
P.O. Box 379, Kaunakakai, 96748, ☎ *(808) 553-3931.*
Closed: Tuesdays, Thursdays, Sundays.
PHILIP KIKUKAWA'S SHOP IS THE ONLY BICYCLE-REPAIR SHOP ON THE ISLAND; he also rents mountain bikes for $25 a day; if you rent two bikes, the price drops. He also conducts informal bike tours of the island (including one to the forest reserve) when he's not busy. If you fall in love with your bike, he'll sell it to you, as well as accessories. Other cycling adventures: **Molokai Ranch Outfitters Center**, ☎ (800) 254-8871 or ☎ (808) 552-2681, offers mountain bike trail riding on the 53,000-acre

ranch (unguided). Full day is $115, including drop-off service, gourmet picnic lunch, and shuttle back to the Center.

Molokai Charters ★★
P.O. Box 1207, Kaunakakai, 96748, ☎ *(808) 553-5852.*
Billing itself as Molokai's original charter service since 1975, Richard and Doris Reed's Molokai Charters is practically the only charter service on the island. After piloting *Satan's Doll*, a rakishly named 42-foot sloop, around the world for the past four years, the couple has returned to roost once more at Kaunakakai Harbor. Packages include a two-hour sunset sail at $40 per person; a half-day sail and whale-watching (in season) excursion for $50 per person that includes soft drinks and *haole pupus;* a full-day sail to Lanai for $115 with swimming, snorkeling, and whale-watching; they promise to anchor at an isolated spot. The full-day sail includes a picnic lunch and soft drinks; snorkeling gear is available for rental. All trips are based on a minimum party of four.

Shon-A-Lei II
Kaunakakai, ☎ *(808) 553-5242.*
Skipper Steve Schonley (the "Shon" in Shon-A-Lei) takes groups on half-day, full-day, or overnight sport fishing trips; the 35-foot twin-diesel Bertrum is fully equipped. Whale-watching (December-March) and bottom fishing... who knows, you might find a school of lawyers down there. From mainland United States and Canada, call ☎ *(800) 998-FISH.*

West Molokai
Maunaloa.

Molokai Ranch Outfitters Center ★★★
P.O. Box 259, Maunaloa, 96770, ☎ *(808) 552-2681.*
Closed: Mondays, Sundays.
http://www.molokai.com/ranch/
Accompanied by a Molokai paniolo (cowboy) guide well versed in the history and culture of the island, these popular trail rides (about two hours) meander through ancient Hawaiian cultural sites and probably the world's highest sea cliffs for views of the neighbor island of Lanai. Two rides, 9 a.m. and 12:30 p.m. Age limit: 12 years. General admission: varies.

Molokai Ranch Outfitters Center/Malihini Rodeo ★★★
P.O. Box 259, Maunaloa, 96770, ☎ (808) 552-2681.
Closed: Mondays, Tuesdays, Thursdays, Saturdays, Sundays.
Molokai is big on horses and rodeos—it has its own Junior Roping Club, and now with the newly completed, state-of-the art rodeo arena, the folks at Molokai Ranch (a 53,000-acre working cattle ranch for more than 100 years) Outfitters Center offer visitors an exciting, one-of-a-kind experience—anyone (as long as they're 16 and over) can be a "Cowboy for a Day." THE FUN INCLUDES TRADITIONAL RODEO GAMES SUCH AS BARREL-RACING AND POLE-BENDING, ROPING CATTLE (AT YOUR OWN PACE, OF COURSE) WITH RANCH PANIOLOS (THE REAL THING, PODNER) TO GUIDE YOUR EVERY SHAKY MOVE. Go for it! The Malihini Rodeo takes place every Wednesday and Friday; reservations required. General admission: varies.

Where to Stay

You won't find a lot of choices and, if locals have anything to say about it, things will stay that way. Don't come expecting a lot of flash and fanfare, though the trade-off is a lot of peace and good Hawaiian hospitality. For those who can't live without the vestiges of posh, you'd best aim for the luxurious condos nearby at **Kaluakoi Villas** or **Ke Nani Kai Resort.** A smattering of other inns and condos are sprinkled about, with a couple of B&Bs tossed in. **Hotel Molokai,** a couple of miles from Kaunakakai, is a Polynesian-style favorite for the good-value-for-money set, while budget travelers (who aren't camping) usually hide out at **Pau Hana Inn,** Molokai's oldest hotel.

East Molokai
Kamalo
Bed-and-Breakfasts

Kamalo Plantation $85–$140 ★★
HC1, Box 300, Kamalo, 96748, Highway 460 to Highway 450 (past Kaunakakai), go east 10.5 miles, ☎ (808) 558-8236, FAX (808) 558-8236.
http://www.molokai.com/kamalo/
Glenn and Akiko Foster's five-acre, tropical, park-like property is at the foot of Mount Kamakou on the island's east side, just in front of Father Damien's St. Joseph's Church. Archaeology

and history buffs may be interested to know that the foundations of an ancient *heiau* (temple) are on the plantation. Your choice of accommodations include a self-contained cottage set far enough away from the main house to ensure total privacy. It sleeps two to four with a king-size bed, queen-size sleeper couch, shower, and a fully equipped kitchen (including oils and spices). Home-baked bread and fruit from the plantation's orchard, which is just steps away from the cottage, are supplied for "do it yourself" breakfasts. Lounging chairs are provided for relaxing on the outside lanai; nearby is a hammock strung between two lauhala trees. When you bestir yourself from all this languor, beach towels, mats, a cooler, and ice are on hand for your use. More sociable types may opt to lodge in the two rooms in the main house; here guests are served an "Aloha" breakfast in the dining room. The Kukui Room features a king or twin beds, microwave, refrigerator, and outside lanai; it shares a bath with the Hibiscus Room (twin waterbeds, hot pot, refrigerator, outside lanai). The Kukui Room has a private entrance, and guests staying here have the option of requesting a private bath for $10 extra per night. (The Fosters will then not rent out the Hibiscus Room.) All accommodations have tape decks and radios, but no television or telephones. No smoking indoors. Children allowed in the cottage only; no pets. Amenities: balcony or patio. Three rooms. Credit cards: not accepted.

Kawela

Ka Hale Mala $70–$80 ★★★

In the Kawela area, about five miles from Kaunakakai, Kawela, ☎ *(808) 553-9009, FAX (808) 553-9009.*
http://molokai-bnb.com/

A GREAT CHOICE FOR BARGAIN HUNTERS, Ka Hale Mala ("The Garden House") is a two-story Polynesian pole house on a 12,000-square-foot lot across from the ocean and about a five-mile walk to the beach. But you're also in the country—deer often use a trail behind the property. THE FOUR-ROOM GUEST SUITE IS 840 SQUARE FEET, WITH A FOUR-SIDED LANAI PROVIDING VIEWS OF THE TROPICAL GARDEN AND ORCHARD, WHERE YOU'RE FREE TO PICK AND EAT YOUR FILL OF POMELOS, TANGERINES, TANGELOS, OR WHATEVER EXOTIC FRUIT MAY BE GROWING AT THE TIME. The four-room guest suite features a bedroom with two single beds (two more on request), combination bath, living room with entertainment center (television, stereo, VCR on request), and two twin day beds. The fully equipped kitchen features a microwave, stove/oven, refrigerator, coffee maker, and more. Washer/dryer. Included in the rate are two mountain bikes and snorkel gear. All this for $80 per day! Your hosts will respect your privacy if you wish, but will also arrange guided tours, suggest outdoor activities, snorkel trips, visits to artists' studios, and more. Amenities: balcony or patio. One rooms. Credit cards: not accepted.

Uluapue
Cottage

Beach Cottage at Ualupue Pond   **$100**   ★★

Past the 13-mile marker in Ualapue, Uluapue, 13.5 miles east of Kaunakakai in front of Ualapue Fishpond, ☎ *(808) 576-9146.*
Located in peaceful, low-key East Molokai, this private, solar-heated cottage overlooks the historic Ualupue Fishpond, which was constructed around the 13th century; it has recently been restored. The Polynesian-style, one-bedroom dwelling (with two queen beds) was built to look old (although it was actually completed in 1993) and is surrounded by a rock wall and has its own lush garden. Amenities include a color TV and fully equipped kitchen with granite counter-tops. IF YOU'RE LOOKING FOR A PRIVATE RETREAT, THIS IS A GOOD VALUE; it can also be rented for $500 per week or $1500 per month ($10 each additional person). Supplies? Try the nearby Wavecrest Resort's general store. One room. Credit cards: not accepted.

Kaunakakai
Condos

Molokai Shores Suites   **$93–$199**   ★★★

Kamehameha Highway, P.O. Box 1037, Kaunakakai, 96748, One mile from Kaunakakai between the Pau Hana and Hotel Molokai, ☎ *(800) 535-0085,* ☎ *(808) 553-5954.*
http://www.marcresorts.com/molokaishores.html
The pleasant but unprepossessing chocolate-brown structure houses units that are like the equivalent of a pasta dinner—comfort food for the tired body. The Molokai Shores Suites offer one- and two-bedroom suites with separate living areas, fully equipped kitchens, ceiling fans, and color cable TV. Wooden louvers let as much sunshine in as you like. If you like

that top-of-the-world feel, ask for a loft suite with airy, cathedral ceilings. All have lanais where you can dine álfresco, each overlooking the pretty grounds lit with tiki torches come nightfall. Diversions on the premises include a beachfront swimming pool, barber/beauty shop, guest laundry, shuffleboard, and barbecue area. Amenities: balcony or patio. 102 rooms. Credit cards: A, DC, MC, V.

Wavecrest Resort   **$109–$169**   ★
HC01, Box 541, Kaunakakai, 96748, At the 13-mile marker in Ualupue, ☎ *(800) 367-2980,* ☎ *(808) 558-8101, FAX (808) 553-8206.*
http://www.discoveringhawaii.com/Is_Molokai/MOHotelWavecrest.html
A breezy, five-acre oceanfront property in East Molokai with a lot of swaying palms and bright tropical blooms in the well-tended yard. Recently renovated one- and two-bedroom suites are pleasantly but not spectacularly furnished and have a separate bedroom, fully equipped kitchen, sofa bed, color TV, and spacious lanai, but no telephones. Swimming pool, shuffleboard, laundry facility, barbecue grills, free parking. A small but decently stocked "general store" (how quaint!) on the premises comes in handy, since this secluded property is miles from anything. Three-night minimum stay, substantial discounts for two-week stays. Amenities: tennis, balcony or patio, family plan. Credit cards: MC, V.

Hotels

Hotel Molokai   **$82–$137**   ★
P.O. Box 546, Kamehameha Highway, Kaunakakai, 96748, Two miles east of Kaunakakai on Highway 450, ☎ *(800) 423-6656,* ☎ *(808) 553-5347, FAX (808) 553-5047.*
http://hotelmolokai.com/
The Hotel Molokai is what people used to come to Hawaii for before the days of self-contained mega-resorts where attendants spray you with Evian water at poolside every five minutes. Many travelers might consider the brown-shingled, two-story, A-frame cottage buildings a little rustic and funky, but for old-timers, the place just cries out "nostalgia." Lower-level rooms are small, dark, and gloomy, and soundproofing isn't the greatest, but the deluxe upstairs rooms and studios are quite nice and spacious, with cathedral ceilings and, best of all, a breezy

lanai with a rattan porch swing where you can cozy up to your honey (or read a good book). All rooms with portable fan, refrigerator. Some with air conditioning. TVs on request. Facilities include a gift shop, swimming pool, and poolside bar. Amenities: balcony or patio. 55 rooms. Credit cards: CB, DC, MC, V.

West Molokai
Maunaloa
Condos.

Kaluakoi Villas   **$81–$168**   ★★
1131 Kaluakoi Road, Maunaloa, 96770, ☎ *(800) 525-1470,* ☎ *(808) 552-2721, FAX (808) 552-2201.*
http://www.castleresorts.com/KKV/tour.html
A secluded oceanfront condominium retreat on the grounds of Colony's Kaluakoi Hotel and Golf Club (but under separate management). Guests here are free to use the resort's pool, 18-hole golf course, four lighted tennis courts, restaurants, and other facilities at no extra charge. The units consist of studios and one-bedroom suites with kitchenettes (refrigerator, counter-top range, microwave, cooking utensils) or the more-deluxe cottages with full kitchens. Price depends on where you're situated—you pay more for a golf course or full ocean view. All have a private lanai and color TV. Living and sleeping areas have generic tropical art, teal carpets in good repair, and attractive light-rattan furniture with floral upholstery. Amenities: balcony or patio, family plan. 95 rooms. Credit cards: A, MC, V.

Ke Nani Kai   **$95–$135**   ★★★
P.O. Box 289, Maunaloa, 96770, at the entrance to Colony's Kaluakoi Resort, ☎ *(800) 888-2791,* ☎ *(808) 552-2761.*
http://www.marcresorts.com/kenanikai.html
POPULAR WITH FAMILIES (a one-bedroom unit sleeps up to four persons) AND GOLFERS (it's set between Kaluakoi resort's eighth and 17th fairways), these two-story, one- and two-bedroom condos boast all the comforts of home (if your home is a tropical island). Bright white walls and carpeting set off handsome, high-quality, open-work rattan furniture, including glass-topped oval dining tables and ecru-and-taupe upholstered seating areas opening onto spacious lanais draped with berry-colored bougainvillea. The modern kitchens are fully equipped

with dishwasher, coffee maker-and refrigerator with automatic ice maker. Units also come with washer and dryer. Maid service every three days. Fax facilities. Although it's on Kaluakoi resort property, Ke Nani Kai has its own free-form pool and spa, and two tennis courts. Book early, as only a few condos (these are privately owned) are available at a time. Amenities: tennis, Jacuzzi, balcony or patio, business services. 120 rooms.
Credit cards: A, DC, MC, V.

Paniolo Hale $95–$265 ★★★
Lio Place, P.O. Box 190, Maunaloa, 96770, ☎ *(800) 367-2984,* ☎ *(808) 552-2731, FAX (808) 552-2288.*
http://www.paniolohaleresort.com/
Although individually decorated (mostly in wicker and rattan and chic floral fabrics), all the studio and one- or two-bedroom units in this fairly luxurious condo resort are built in true Hawaiian style, with large and spacious living areas, screened lanais, open-beam ceilings, hardwood floors with area rugs, and ceiling fans. Practicalities include color TV and washer-dryer. Kitchens are equipped with refrigerator with ice maker; one- and two-bedroom units have microwaves. Most two-bedroom units have private Jacuzzi tubs on lanais. Facilities on the property include a pool, paddle tennis, picnic tables, and barbecues. Kepuhi Beach is behind the property; as the hotel puts it, "a mere fairway away." Management provides an airport shuttle, but as with all properties on the west side, a rental car is a must for exploring. Amenities: Jacuzzi, balcony or patio. 77 rooms.
Credit cards: A, MC, V.

Where to Eat

We can't mince words (no pun intended): Foodies will be miserable on Molokai—this is just not the spot for the big wine-and-dine. You *will* find a gaggle of "fun" places—little diners and cafés that have been around for ages, serve good unpretentious food, and give you a chance to hobnob with the locals. Pizza, natural foods, fresh-baked breads, spicy Filipino dishes, fresh fish, American favorites, and plate lunches are the norm. **Ohia Lodge,** on the western side, is probably as good as you're going to get, with the dining room at **Hotel Molokai.** If you're super fussy, you'd better rent a room or condo with kitchen facilities and cook your own.

Central Molokai
Kualupu'u

Kualupuu Cookhouse $$ ★★

P.O. Box 174, Kualupu'u, 96757, From Kalae Road, turn left to Farrington Road, across from Kualupuu Market,
☎ (808) 567-6185.
American cuisine. Specialties: Burgers, plate lunches, chicken stir-fry, mahi-mahi, homemade pies and cakes.
Closed: Sundays.

TERRIFIC THINGS ARE ISSUING OUT OF THIS VINTAGE WOODEN PLANTATION COTTAGE WITH LACE VALANCES AND HAND-CARVED BOOTHS THAT SERVED AS THE COOKHOUSE OF THE DEL MONTE PLANTATION. This spiffy restaurant, with one chef working non-stop in the open kitchen, is obviously giving people what they want; A LOT OF GOOD FOOD, AT VERY FAIR PRICES. Meat is hand-ground for the delectable hamburgers, which many folks say wins hands down for the best on the island; try the Mexi-Chicken burger. Breakfast items include steak and eggs, a mahi-mahi omelette, and loco moco. Plate lunches are accompanied with a choice of green salad as well as the usual potato-mac salad or rice. Teriyaki steak and fresh seafood and the specialty, chicken stir-fry, are recommended for dinner. Service is on Hawaii time: slow. The restaurant closes at 4 p.m. on Saturdays. Features: outside dining, own baking.

Kaunakakai

Banyan Tree Terrace Restaurant $$ ★

Seaside Place, P.O. Box 546, Kaunakakai, 96748,
☎ (808) 553-5342. *Associated hotel: Pau Hana Inn.*
American cuisine. Specialties: Prime rib, short ribs, fresh fish, Boston cream pie.

Hearty breakfasts, including French toast made from Kanemitsu Bakery bread, and prime rib dinners for under $25 are the best bets at this atmospheric, local-style restaurant in the Pau Hana Inn. The fireplace in the open-to-the-breezes dining room looks big enough to roast a whole wild boar in, but it's rarely used these days. The height of the action is under the spreading banyan tree outside (it has easily passed the century mark) facing the beach. Features: outside dining. Reservations recommended. Credit cards: A, DC, MC, V.

Kamoi Snack-n-Go $ ★
P.O. Box 558, Kaunakakai, 96748, in the Kamoi Professional Center, ☎ *(808) 553-3742.*
American cuisine. Specialties: Dave's ice cream.

Basically a snack bar where you get it and go, Kamoi's is notable for featuring at least a dozen sorbets and ice creams from Dave's of Oahu every day. Exotic flavors include lilikoi, lychee, and the top-seller, green tea. Many consider these frozen treats the best in the state. Kamoi's also has frozen yogurt, candy, ices, and other evil things to make your fillings sizzle. A favored local hot spot, there are wooden benches outside in the shade to eat your cone and talk story. Features: outside dining. Reservations not accepted.

Kanemitsu Bakery & Coffee Shop $
Ala Malama Street, Kaunakakai, 96748, ☎ *(808) 553-5855.*
American cuisine. Specialties: Specialty breads, hamburgers, plate lunches.
Closed: Tuesdays.

Fresh bread from this old-fashioned bakery conjures up memories of Molokai many years after one has left the islands. The fresh, round loaves are truly special, especially the onion cheese and the long-standing favorite, Molokai French. Tropical fruit-and-nut varieties include pineapple, papaya, coconut, and passion fruit (yum!). Although you can buy packaged bread (in plastic bags) to go, the fresh-from-the-oven varieties usually sell out early in the morning. To prevent this from happening, you can buy hot loaves from the eatery's back alley from 9:30 p.m. every day except Monday (baking takes place until 3 a.m.); just knock at the double door and place your order. New additions to the baking slate include bread-making kits and Molokai Lavosh (an Armenian flatbread). Lavosh is available in three varieties: Original Sesame, Macadamia, and Brown Wheat. The coffee shop area serves hearty breakfasts, hamburgers for under $2, and plate lunches. The bread is also sold at the airport—great for gift-giving ideas. The bakery closes at 11 a.m. on Sundays. Features: own baking. Reservations not accepted.

Molokai Drive Inn $
Highway 450, Kaunakakai, 96748, Just out of downtown near the Visitor's Association, ☎ *(808) 553-5655.*
American cuisine. Specialties: Plate lunches, breakfasts.

More of a "dive inn," this down-home eatery has been a center of Molokai life since 1960. IT'S WORTH A LOOK FOR PEOPLE-WATCHING; EVERYONE STOPS IN HERE AFTER BALL GAMES, SUNDAY SERVICES, AND ALL KINDS OF SOCIAL OCCASIONS. You have a choice of air-conditioned indoor dining, picnic-style tables under an awning, or takeout. Inexpensive breakfasts, served all day, rely heavily on Spam (which we happen to like), but there are decent daily specials and plate lunches. Open until 10:30 p.m. on Fridays; 6:30 a.m.–10:30 p.m. on Saturdays and Sundays. Features: outside dining.

Molokai Pizza Café $$ ★
15 Kaunakakai Place, Kaunakakai, 96748, behind the tourist office, ☎ (808) 553-3288.
American cuisine. Specialties: Pizza, salads, fresh fish, pasta, ribs.
For about $22 you can pig out on a monstrous creation called the "Big Island Pizza" loaded with three kinds of meat, including bacon. But come here even if you don't like pizza; there's crisp salads, pasta, and even frozen yogurt. Local kids love the place; pizzas here are offered as prizes in school contests. Delivery and takeout available. Open until 11 p.m. on Fridays and Saturdays. Features: own baking.

Outpost Natural Foods $ ★
70 Makaena Place, Kaunakakai, 96748, near Kalama's Service Station, next to the Civic Center, ☎ (808) 553-3377.
American cuisine. Specialties: Vegetarian lunch bar, low-fat specials, organic produce.
Closed: Saturdays.
Actually a health food store and juice bar, OUTPOST IS AN OUTLET FOR THE BEST HOME-GROWN PRODUCE IN TOWN, AND YOU CAN BE SURE THAT THE GREENS IN YOUR PITA SANDWICH OR SALAD BOWL ARE OF THE HIGHEST QUALITY. Not only are the vegetarian dishes served here low-fat, they are also low-priced. You can eat here, but there's only one picnic table outside. A good place to recover from a Spam overdose. Closes at 3:30 p.m. on Fridays. Features: outside dining.

Oviedo's $ ★
Ala Malama Street, Kaunakakai, 96748, ☎ (808) 553-5014.
Asian cuisine. Specialties: Chicken and green papaya, pigs feet.

Oviedo's is just a counter-type operation in an old and funky location with a surfeit of plastic, but the Filipino food is tasty and sticks to the ol' ribs. The mongo bean soup is comforting, and Oviedo's makes a great chicken with green papaya. Reservations not accepted.

Rabang's Restaurant $ ★

Ala Malama Street, Kaunakakai, next door to Molokai Fish and Dive, ☎ (808) 553-5014.
Asian cuisine. Specialties: Chicken or pork adobo, halohalo, plate lunch.

Mrs. Rabang cooks up quite a diverse ethnic stew for such a small restaurant (there are only five tables)—Hawaiian plate lunches on Fridays, Chinese dishes, Filipino adobo, *halohalo* (sort of an ice cream sundae with purple yam, preserved coconut, garbanzo beans, and more) and burgers and sandwiches for the timid palate. Takeout available. The Rabangs also own the deli/grocery next door. Reservations not accepted.

West Molokai
Maunaloa

Jojo's Café $$ ★★

P.O. Box 44, Maunaloa, 96770, highway 460, past the 10-mile marker, go to the end of the road, ☎ (808) 552-2803.
Seafood cuisine. Specialties: Indian-style curries, fresh fish, desserts.
Closed: Wednesdays, Sundays.

The ONLY place to eat in Maunaloa town besides the resort, Jojo's gets many local (and visitor) votes for A ROMANTIC RESTAURANT, mostly because of the Old West-style saloon doors, vintage photographs, cozy tables, and the long, dark, antique wooden bar. Jojo is actually Girish Patel, who cooks up a mean Indian curry along with the fresh fish the restaurant is known for. Most of the menu is a potpourri of international dishes such as Korean kalbi ribs, Southern fried chicken, and Portuguese bean soup. Sandwiches are good at lunch, especially the mahi burgers. Desserts are remarkably original for a small restaurant, including the passion-fruit ice cream. Features: own baking. Reservations not accepted. Credit cards: MC, V.

Nightlife

Huh? *What nightlife?* The "scene," by most standards, is nonexistent on Molokai. On Friday and Saturday nights you can do the dance-to-Top-40s routine and hear the local band FIBRE (Friendly Isle Band Rhythmic Experience) on the **Banyan Tree Terrace** at the Pau hana Inn near Kaunakakai. **Hotel Molokai** usually hosts live entertainment on the weekends. Other than that, the choices are nil unless you happen to fall into some impromptu local entertainment.

Kaunakakai

Banyan Tree Terrace ★

P.O. Box 546, Kaunakakai, a short walk from town, 96748, ☎ *(808) 553-5342.*
Fridays and Saturdays only.
A local tradition for umpteen years is to dance and party to the Top 40 and Hawaiian band FIBRE, who have been playing under the 100-year-old banyan tree for as long as some Broadway shows have been running. Check status upon arrival. General admission: call for prices.

Shopping

The good news is that you won't ever see a mall during your stay on Molokai. The bad news is there's not much shopping of *any* sort. The big shopping "center" is along **Ala Malama Street** in Kaunakakai, where you'll find a smattering of craft and souvenir shops, as well as natural and other foods. Some of the hotels and condos have tiny shops on site, and over at **Maunaloa** (the old plantation town on the western end), there are some interesting crafts outlets and galleries.

Kaunakakai

Carol Klein-Jewelry Designer ★★★

P.O. Box 1018, Kaunakakai, 96748, ☎ *(808) 558-8569.*
Special hours: by appointment.
From her studio, Carol Klein creates such fascinating work as petroglyph-inspired jewelry in gold and silver. She also does custom work.

Designs Pacifica/Jule Patten ★★★★
P.O. Box 1365, Kaunakakai, 96748, ☎ *(808) 553-5725.*
Special hours: by appointment only.
Primarily a watercolorist, artist Jule Patten creates hand-painted paper castings that incorporate traditional Hawaiian *kapa* (quilt) designs. The complex patterns resemble a large snowflake, and frequent themes include native flowers, fruit, waterfalls, crowns, and the royal feather *kahili* (a tall pole used by *ali'i* to announce their presence). The designs appear on T-shirts and clothing and are a wonderful gift or souvenir of your trip. A favorite T-shirt with kids incorporates a Molokai spider with a marking that looks like a happy face, whether you look at it right-side-up or upside-down. She also features cloissone painting, hand-etched glassware, embossed art cards, bookbags, aprons, and pot holders. Patten, originally from Michigan, has a studio in Molokai and has exhibited in galleries all over the islands. She's sold more than 75 *kapa* paintings to the Hyatt Regency Kauai resort, where they're on display. Although her work is featured in several local boutiques, you must visit her studio, as prices are better there (call for appointment). She loves to explain the meaning of her designs; she studied for many years with traditional *kapa* artists.

Haunani's Flowers ★
P.O. Box 2038, Kaunakakai, 96748, ☎ *(808) 553-9019.*
Hours: 8:30 a.m.–5:30 p.m.
Special hours: Saturday, 9 a.m.– 1 p.m. Closed: Sundays.
Haunani's will ship and wire flower orders, including a lovely selection of cut anthuriums, worldwide. (for more flowers, see "Mapulehu Glass House").

He Ki'i Kapa (The Picture Quilt) ★★★
P.O. Box 102, Kaunakakai, 96748, ☎ *(808) 553-5408.*
Special hours: by appointment only.
Sadly, Molokai has lost two of its best-loved practitioners of the art of kapa lau (traditional Hawaiian quilt-making)—Mrs. Kewano, who passed away, and Ginger LaVoie, who taught popular quilt-making classes at Colony's Kaluakoi Resort, has since moved to Oregon. On the up side, Yvonne Friel, Mrs. Kewano's protegee and a fine artist in her own right, is teach-

Imports Gift Shop

P.O. Box 828, Kaunakakai, across from the post office, 96748,
☎ *(808) 553-5734.*
Hours: 9 a.m.–6 p.m.

Where locals go for a varied selection of casual and what passes for dressy clothing on Molokai, as well as jewelry and accessories.

Imports Gift Shop ★★

125-C Puali Place, Kaunakakai, east of the Credit Union, across Ala Malama Street from the post office, 96748,
☎ *(808) 553-5734.*
Hours: 9 a.m.–6 p.m.

This gift shop is easy to find—it always has a bright orange "Sale" sign in the window. Among the quilts, jewelry, and Hawaiiana is a witty souvenir, a "Molokai Night Life" T-shirt, featuring a quarter moon set in a black box.

Molokai Craft Fairs ★

Various locations, Kaunakakai.

Starting in November and running right up to Christmas, there are dozens of local crafts fairs—the biggest ones are at the high school and various locations in town, but many large, extended families hold them at their homes. You'll find handmade Christmas ornaments and *ono* festive foods. Watch the local paper and bulletin boards downtown for announcements—this is also a good source for news on the Saturday-morning yard sales year-round, where you can purchase one-of-a-kind antiques and memorabilia. (There are no antique shops or thrift stores in Molokai.)

Molokai Farmer's Market ★

Ala Malama Street, Kaunakakai, in front of American Savings Bank, across from the library.
Saturdays only.

Fresh produce and crafts by local artists are featured at this lively farmer's market. If you haven't had enough, meander over to a similar market in the Credit Union parking lot (also on Ala

Malama Street, across from the Post Office), which has an extensive selection of veggies and fruits.

Molokai Fish and Dive ★

Ala Malama Street, P.O. Box 567, Kaunakakai, 96748,
☎ *(808) 553-5926.*
Hours: 9 a.m.–6 p.m.
Special hours: Saturday from 8 a.m., Sunday until 2 p.m.
Jim Brocker carries what might be the largest selection of Molokai T-shirts and souvenirs in town, as well as fishing, snorkeling, and outdoor paraphernalia. He'll also rent you underwater equipment, in case you forgot yours. VERY INEXPENSIVE RENTALS.

Take's Variety Store

P.O. Box 1890, Kaunakakai, 96748, ☎ *(808) 553-5442.*
Hours: 9 a.m.–6 p.m.
Special hours: Friday 8:30 a.m.–5:30 p.m.; Saturday 7–9 p.m.
This general variety store is Molokai's best source for practical, everyday stuff. If no one else has what you want, Take's will. Also open on Sunday from 8:30 a.m. to 5:30 p.m.

West Molokai
Maunaloa

Big Wind Kite Factory ★★

120 Maunaloa Highway, Maunaloa, 96770,
☎ *(808) 552-2364.*
Hours: 8:30 a.m.–5 p.m.
Special hours: Sunday, 10 a.m.–2 p.m.
This world-famous kite store features handmade kites and windsocks made in the shop incorporating owner Jonathan Socher's and his son Zachariah's designs. Also factory tours, kite-making, and kite-flying lessons (see Children's Activities). Next door is the Plantation Gallery (same ownership), with a wide variety of items from all over the Pacific, including batik, (I still have a pareo I bought there five years ago) fabrics, T-shirts, wood carvings, quilt patterns, a good selection of Hawaiian music, and Pacific Rim arts and crafts. It also has one of the best selection of books on the island.

LANAI

This pineapple paradise has not yet been hammered to death by developers or the tourist crunch (which seem to go hand-in-hand), so hurry over for the chance to see everything. Hardly anyone comes to this isle of 2426 occupants, but the ones who *do* are formidable—celebrities, high hogs, the exuberantly rich and famous (Bill Gates chose this island for his wedding site)—those seeking luxury along with privacy. Good choice, because "The Private Island" is Lanai's current title. (Lanai, in past years, was known as "The Forbidden Island," and not too many natives even wanted to set foot there, let alone the likes of Master Gates.)

Lanai's history is hardly filled with images of peace and luxury. According to legend the place was a feeding frenzy for evil spirits and other-worlders with a penchant for human flesh and blood. Sound like the perfect getaway? Somehow along the way these spirits met their match when courageous and crafty Prince Kaululaau (who'd been banished from Maui by his father, who was sick of his son's spoiled behavior) outwitted them and drove them away (but *where?*). Anyway, Lanai was suddenly on the map for those who wanted to come over and settle down.

Fiendish spirits or not, settlement took awhile. By and by, a few thousand people cruised over to fish and farm, setting up camp mostly along the shore facing Maui. During the 1700s, Lanai was fraught with the ravages of war, taking a particularly nasty hit from Big Island warriors. Sea captains steered their vessels clear of the island, passing on tales of dangerous waters ("Shipwreck Beach" was not bequeathed that name for nothing). Lanai received only a short-lived boost when Hawaii-unifier King Kamehameha the Great began to summer over on the south shore. However, the population began to dwindle yet again though there were a few (failed) attempts to establish commercial sugar enterprises, a valiant (and scandalous) effort by Mormon missionaries to set up a colony and work the land, and a stint at cattle raising. But, all in all, the island languished until 1922, when pineapple king James D. Dole bought the entire shebang.

Dole paid $1.1 million for Lanai, planted the "golden fruit" on about 18,000 of his 89,000 acres, and turned the place into "The Pineapple Island." Lanai Plantation became the world's largest pineapple plantation, and the Dole Food Company held reign on every worker and resident—all whom were in some way connected to the pineapple business. Lanai City sprung up as the plantation town and community center, and life went on. When pineapple production in the Philippines and Malaysia took off in the 1990s, the Lanai industry was no longer profitable. But something else *was*—almighty tourism.

Dole's corporate heirs, the Big Five members Castle & Cooke, fairly jumped on the tourist bandwagon, building two luxury resorts on the island with which to lure the rich and famous. Workers who once toiled in the fields now work in the hotel industry, catering to well-heeled visitors (for the workers, their only other choice was to leave the island). Recognizing that the resorts are not going to run themselves, Castle & Cooke is trying to keep the employees content by building housing projects and refurbishing the downtown area (particularly some of the family-owned shops). It remains to be seen whether Castle & Cooke will play fair with the locals, and whether the locals can adhere to all these "improvements." Most tourists, no doubt, will welcome the "upscale" change.

Most of Lanai's residents are Filipinos—originally recruited for the pineapple fields—followed by lesser numbers of Japanese, Hawaiians, Caucasians, and a smattering of Chinese. The community is basically tight and supportive, going all-out to help one another, and visitors will be impressed by how relaxed everyone is. Lanai City, the hub of the island, is an exercise in civility and laid-back living.

Don't be put off if you're not a wealthy corporate type (or just not wealthy)—there *are* a few other options for overnighters (but just a few), and a day-trip from one of the other islands is another possibility. However, if you're rolling in big bucks and searching for a hideaway that could please even a billionaire, Lanai is waiting for you.

Lanai Facts

A.k.a.	The Private Island
Main city	Lanai City
Flower	Kaunaoa
Color	Orange
Area	140 square miles
Length	18 miles
Width	13 miles
Population	2426
Highest point	Lanaihale (3366 feet)

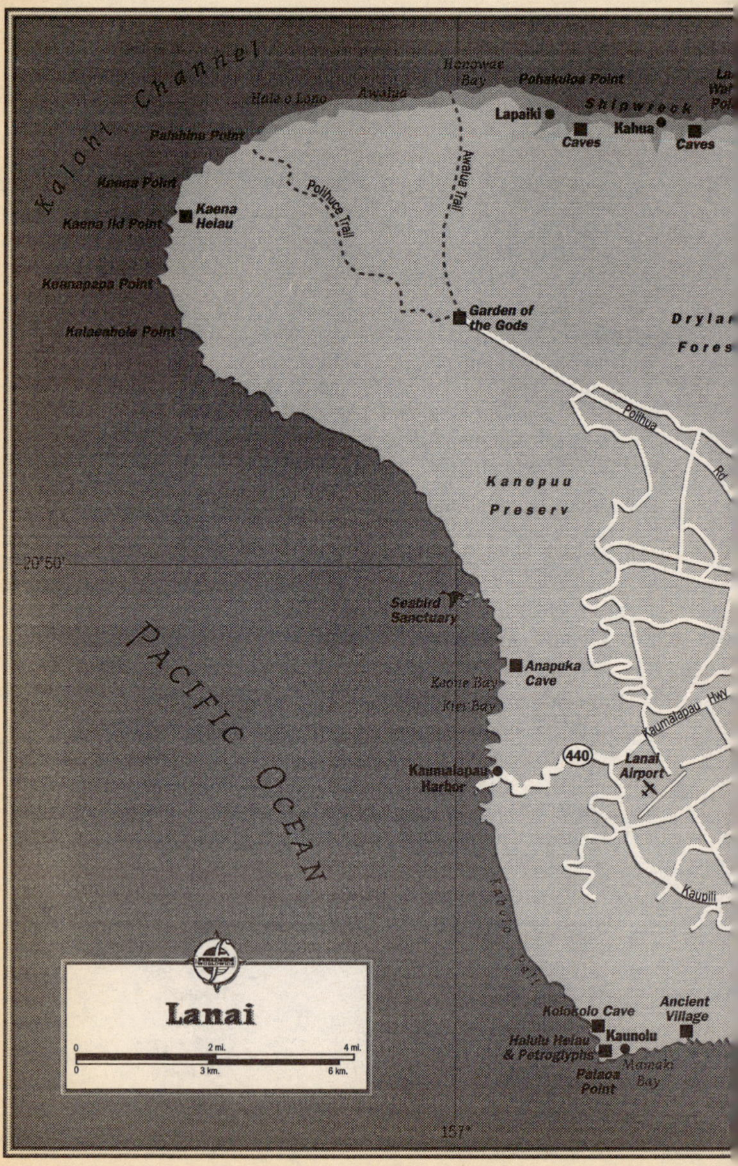
Kalohi Channel
Honowae Bay
Pohakuloa Point
Hale o Lono
Awalua
Lapaiki
Shipwreck
Kahua
Caves
Caves
Paliahina Point
Kaena Point
Kaena Iki Point
Kaena Heiau
Polihuce Trail
Awalua Trail
Keanapapa Point
Kalaeahole Point
Garden of the Gods
Polihua Rd
Kanepuu Preserv
20°50'
Seabird Sanctuary
Anapuka Cave
Kaone Bay
Kiei Bay
PACIFIC OCEAN
440
Kaumalapau Hwy
Kaumalapau Harbor
Lanai Airport
Kaupili
Kolokolo Cave
Ancient Village
Kaunolu
Halulu Heiau & Petroglyphs
Palaoa Point
Manele Bay
157°
Lanai
0 2 mi. 4 mi.
0 3 km. 6 km.

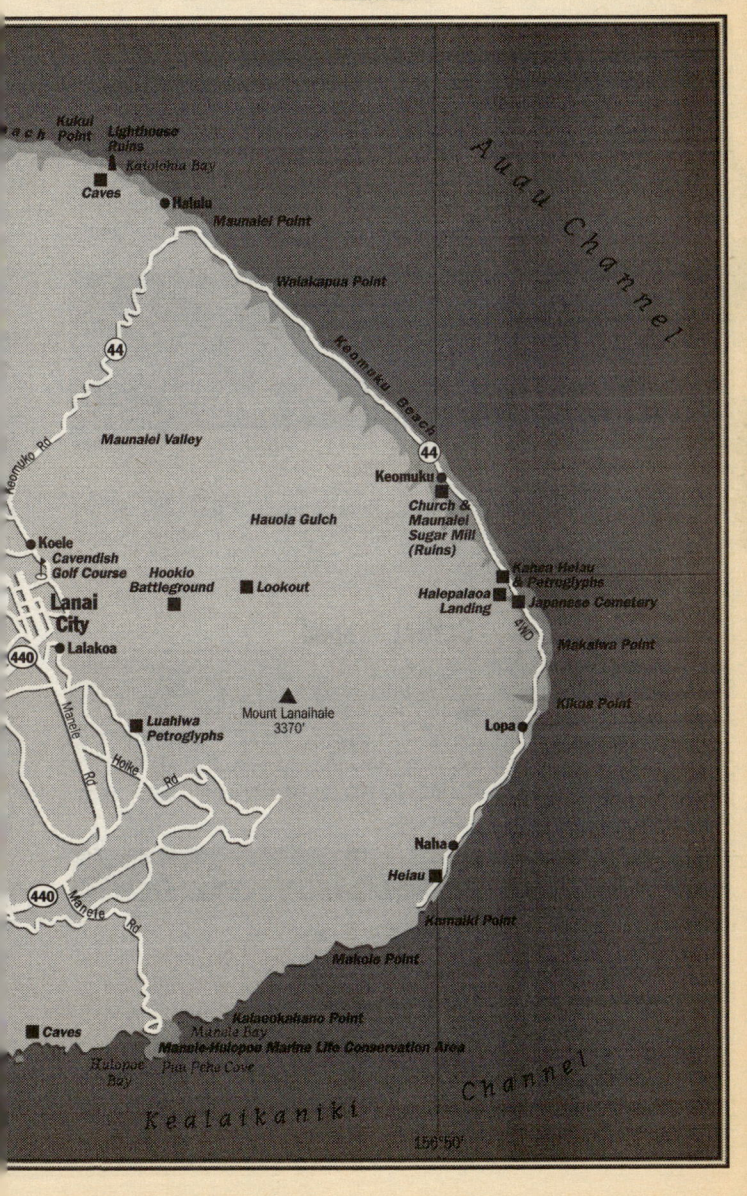

HAWAII

Lanai Survival Guide

Getting There

Lanai Airport, about four miles southwest of Lanai City, now has a new passenger terminal with a few food concessions and shops. Everything you need to know is posted on a bulletin board. (Don't go looking for the first-class lounge.) Airlines are:

HAWAIIAN	(808) 565-6977
ISLAND AIR	(800) 323-3345
MAHALO AIR	(800) 277-8333

Hawaiian Air flies DC-9 jets, the others use small commuter planes such as Twin Otters and Dornier 228s.

Expeditions (**http://www.go-lanai.com/** *(808) 661-3756)* operates ferry service five times daily from Lahaina, Maui; cost is about $75-$100 round trip.

Getting Around

ITRAVELBOOK TIP: THERE IS NO PUBLIC TRANSPORTATION ON LANAI.

Hotel Lanai provides guests with **shuttle service** to most of the major spots. The island has only 30 miles of paved road, **SO IT'S BEST TO RENT A FOUR-WHEEL-DRIVE VEHICLE FOR SOME REAL EXPLORATION.** **Lanai City Service,**

DOLLAR RENT A CAR	(808) 565-7227

—one and the same company—rents a variety of vehicles and provides airport pickup. You can call for an airport shuttle even if you don't rent from them; cost is about $10 from the terminal into Lanai City. Hotel Lanai and both resorts provide complimentary shuttle service for guests. Lanai City Service also operates a **taxi service** to paved parts of the island.

Guests staying at The Lodge at Koele or Manele Bay Hotel are provided with free mountain bikes—a great way to hit the back country.

Visitor Information

For maps, brochures, and other information, contact **Destination Lanai**, *P.O. Box 700, Lanai City, HI 96763* (<http://www.visit-lanai.net/> *(808) 565-7600*). If possible, call or write ahead of your visit.

Bird's-Eye View

THE LEAST-VISITED OF THE SIX MAJOR ISLANDS, 140-square-mile Lanai also measures in as the smallest (18 miles long and 13 miles wide). Shaped like a fat gourd, the island's eastern coast is just eight miles from Maui, and its northern shore is a mere nine miles south of Molokai (at one time the three were most likely connected). If you think of Lanai as one gigantic pineapple plantation, you're right *and* wrong. True, the island harbors the world's largest pineapple fields; however, the golden fruit actually accounts for less than one-fifth of the land. The rest of the space is serene, remote, and yours to hike, swim, or adventure upon. ONLY THREE MAIN ROADS TRAVERSE THE ISLAND, THOUGH UNPAVED ROADS (AND A FOUR-WHEEL-DRIVE VEHICLE) WILL PUT YOU ALL OVER THE PLACE. Mountain ridges run north to south along the eastern side, which is cut by the Munroe Trail which OFFERS EXQUISITE VIEWS OF NEIGHBORING ISLANDS. Assorted beaches curve from the northern shore at Polihua, around the east coast, and down to Hulope and Manele bays in the south. Mount Lanaihale—also on the eastern side—is the island's highest point (3366 feet). Most of the western region is open, rugged land—sunbaked, barren, and covered in a sort of rust-colored dirt (which turns to dust on your skin and clothing), and just perfect for growing those pineapples (around Palawi). Dramatic sea cliffs—some climbing to 1500 feet— protect the western coast, an area that can be reached only by boat. Lanai City—located about dead center in the island, at an altitude of 1700 feet with Mount Lanaihale in the distance—is home to most of the island's residents. Lined with the breezy Norfolk pines planted by New Zealander George Munro (former manager of the failed cattle ranch), the old plantation town is characterized by its colorful tin-roof houses and cheerful, laid-back locals.

Nature Guide

Lanai, au natural, was pretty barren. Consequently, much of the island's flora and fauna has been introduced over the years, either as deliberate imports or as gifts from visiting dignitaries and others.

The native bird population is dwindling. You'll have to really search to find the *apapane, amakahi,* and Hawaiian petrel. You'll have a lot better luck locating pheasants, quails, turkeys, chukar, and doves.

It won't be difficult to spot the perfectly conical Norfolk pines—they're all over Lanai City and up along the Munro Trail, along with silver oaks, eucalyptus, ironwoods, and koa. Fragrant gardenias also waft along the ridges. The *kaunaoa* (Lanai's official flower) and *pohuehue* are easy finds around the beaches.

Axis deer from India, Moulton sheep from Corsica and Sardinia, pronghorn (sort of) antelopes from North America, and feral goats are common to see.

Beach Finder

Lanai's western coast is fortressed by enormous sea cliffs, but a few good beaches curve from the north shore, around the eastern side, down to the southern bays at Hulopoe and Manele. For more information, ask at your hotel (if you're staying at one) or contact **Destination Lanai (http://www.visitlanai.net/** *(808) 565-7600).*

Hulopoe Beach

About eight miles away from Lanai City, at the southern end of Highway 440.
The island's only easy-to-get-to white-sand beach. **THE PROTECTED BEACH IS EXCELLENT FOR SWIMMING, BODYSURFING, SURFING, AND BOOGIE-BOARDING, AS WELL AS SNORKELING AND DIVING.** Locals favor this spot for swims and picnics. Facilities include barbecue pits, showers, rest rooms, picnic areas, and permit-only camping.

Polihua Beach

On the northwest shore some 11 miles from Lanai City.
If you have a four-wheel-drive, you might try this isolated white-sand beach. Although you'll find plenty of privacy (and good fishing) here, strong currents and trade winds put it on the danger list for swimming. Experienced—and fearless—surfers and bodysurfers often head in anyway. No facilities (bring your own water).

Shipwreck Beach

At the end of Keomuku Highway on the north shore (about 10 miles north of Lanai City).

You can view **petroglyphs** as well as the carnage of offshore wrecks on this eight-mile stretch of sand. This is yet another no-swim beach, but it's an excellent spot for wading, beach combing, shoreline fishing, and hunting out relics that keep washing onto shore.

Adventure Guide

You can either do nothing on Lanai, or head to the great outdoors for some action.

The **Munro Trail** is a must for **hikers**. Follow in the footsteps of New Zealander George Munro who, around the turn of the century, imported and planted Lanai's trademark Norfolk pines, believing (correctly!) they would collect moisture from the passing mist-filled trade winds. The trail runs from about a mile beyond the Lodge at Koele and ends at Manele Road. It's not an easy trek, but you'll see exquisite scenery—particularly from the lookout at **Mount Lanaihale,** the island's highest spot.

Other good hikes are into the magical **Garden of the Gods** and out to **Polihua Beach** or **Kaena Point,** up in the northern area. Adventurers will find plenty of interesting trails, or trail-blazing opportunities, on Lanai. Make sure you have good maps and directions, and take plenty of water when you venture out. Contact **Destination Lanai,** or ask at your hotel, before heading into uncharted territory.

Camping on Lanai *could* be fantastic—if it were allowed. There are plenty of gorgeous possibilities, particularly on the remote beaches, but, unfortunately, use of them is allocated only to island residents. The only official campground is a six-space site at **Hulopoe Bay,** where reservations and permits must be issued in advance by Castle & Cooke's sibling, the Lanai Land Company. Cost is about $5 per person per night, with a seven-day maximum stay. Contact **Hulopoe Bay,** Lanai Land Company, *Box L, Lanai City, HI 96763 (808) 565-7400.*

Divers love Lanai's south shore **Cathedrals,** so-named because of the cathedral-like effect of the sunlight as it bounces around the deep pinnacles, through vast caverns and delicate sheets of coral. Lobster, ghost shrimp, and spotted moray eels are some of the parishioners to be encountered. Other fine dives on the south shore are at **Sergeant Major Reef** (with a cave, archway, lava ridges, and sergeant major fish), **Menpachi Cave, Lobster Rock,** and **Monolith.**

The most popular area for both diving and snorkeling is near **Hulopole** and **Manele bays.** Clear-and-calm Hulopoe Bay—a protected Marine Life Conservation Area—affords close-ups of lava formations, coral, and an abundance of colorful tropical fish. Bring your own equipment, rent it on another island, buy it in town (expensive!), or sign on for one of the organized excursions that tosses gear into the deal. Guests of either The Lodge at Koele or Manele Bay Hotel are bestowed with complimentary snorkeling equipment. **Sailing excursions** and **private boat charters** can also be arranged through local operators, or your hotel. **Hulopoe Beach** is also a good **surfing and bodysurfing** site, though experienced surfers often hit the rough waters up at **Polihua Beach.**

What Else to See

Lanai is delightfully devoid of common stuff to do. There are no malls, traffic lights, no theme parks (thank God!), and absolutely no glitz or glitter. Pretty much all there is to see is sweet, beautiful nature (both on the land and in its people).

Lanai City is not exactly what most people think of when the word "city" pops up. The 1920s plantation town is more like a "mountain village gone troppo." Tall Norfolk pines shelter multi-colored, boxy houses with corrugated tin roofs, assorted business offices, and rustic shops and buildings, the air breezy with the scent of blossoms and the relaxed chatter of "talk stories." Most of the stores hover around **Dole Park,** a sort of town square where locals pass the time. **Kaumalapau Harbor,** Lanai's major seaport—constructed in 1926 by the Hawaiian Pineapple Company—is at the western end of Kaumalapau Highway.

Venturing north, you'll hit the **Lodge at Koele** and, a couple of miles later, the beginning of the **Munro Trail** and the "road" to **Mount Lanaihale.** Head up the Kanepuu Highway to visit **Garden of the Gods,** a magical canyon with other-worldly rocks and boulders in a variety of shapes and sizes, all changing colors and shades as the sun rises and sets. Various turnoffs near Garden of the Gods will lead you to **Shipwreck Beach, Polihua Beach, Kaena Point,** and **Kaenaiki,** the island's largest (and very remote) *heiau*.

From Lanai City, go south along Manele Road (Highway 440) and a couple of unmarked dirt roads for a look at the ancient **Luahiwa Petroglyphs.** Back on the highway, keep going to the coastal fishing village at **Kaunolu** and the former retreat of King Kamehameha the Great. You can explore the village site as well as the sacred **Halulu Heiau** ruins and **Kahekili's Leap** (a bluff where Kamehameha's warriors once jumped into the sea below, purportedly as a test of courage). Back on Manele Road, travel downhill to **Manele Bay** (location of the small boat and "tourist" harbor). Nearby are the **Manele Bay Hotel** and **Hulopoe Beach.**

Take Keomuku Road, again from Lanai City, to reach the eastern shore. Sightsee your way through **Keomuku Village** (which really has only the Hawaiian church), **Halepaloa Landing** (where sugar cane was shipped from in other days), **Lopa,** and **Naha.**

East Lanai

Keomuku
Historical Sites

Keomuku Village ★★

At the end of Keomuku Road, 8 miles from Lanai City, Keomuku, Turn right at the end of road; site is 6 miles ahead.

There was once a lot of commercial activity in this old ghost town on the northeast coast; in the 1890s, it was the site of the Maunalei Sugar Company. Unfortunately, what was once sweet turned sour, including subsequent efforts to make a go of cotton and alfalfa farming; there just wasn't enough water. You can still see the Ka Lanakila O Ka Malamala Church, built in 1903 to serve workers, and its adjacent cemetery. As early as the 1950s, the area was the coastal headquarters for the Gay family's cattle and sheep ranch. In 1956, the company folded operations, and workers looked to the greener (and rust-red) pastures of Jim Dole's pineapple plantation. Continue about two miles to Kahalepalaoa, an old wharf used to ship sugarcane to Maui. Nearby is Lopa, a picnic site and beach good for sunbathing (used by Club Lanai).

Lanai City
Children's Activities

Children's Ride ★★
Stables at Koele, P.O. Box L, Lanai City, 96763,
☎ *(808) 565-4424.*
This is a gentle way to instill a love of things equine in your youngster—an experienced instructor will slowly lead him or her around the stable at Koele's protected corral for 15 minutes on a "child-friendly" mount.

City Celebrations

Aloha Festivals ★★★
Lanai City and various locations, Lanai City,
☎ *(808) 944-8857.*
Annual statewide cultural festival (begun in 1946), featuring traditional music and dance, contests, parades, and *ho'olaule'a*, or block parties. Special events in Lanai include Aloha Beach Day and an Aloha Street Dance. Usually held in mid-October.

ITRAVELBOOKS FREEBIE

Lanai Visiting Artist Program ★★★★
Lodge at Koele, Lanai City, At the Lodge at Koele, past Cavendish Golf Course, just above Lanai City, 96763,
☎ *(808) 565-7300.*
The idea of the grand salon has come to Lanai—and it's open to all at no charge. These special events include cooking demonstrations by some of the country's most innovative chefs (Bradley Ogden of Lark Creek Inn in Marin County was a recent guest), musical concerts, lectures, and author readings (Peter Schickele, the musical satirist, who is also known as the expert on the works of "P.D.Q. Bach;" movie mogul David Wolper; and Brazilian pianist Ciao Pagano were all featured early this year within one week of each other). Hours and locations vary; call for schedule.

Historical Sites

Munro Trail ★★★
Off Keomoku Road, Lanai City, take Keomoku Road toward the Lodge, after about 1 mile turn right.
The dirt road to George Munro's famous Norfolk pine-lined ridge trail begins just past the colorful cemetery above the

Lodge at Koele. The former ranch manager of the Lanai Ranch Company, Munro, a native of New Zealand and sort of the Johnny Appleseed of Lanai, planted the trees by hand as part of a reforestation project. Although many travelers like to make the bumpy trip via four-wheel-drive vehicle, it's equally popular with hikers and off-road cyclists. The high point (literally) of the journey is standing atop the 3370-foot elevation of Mt. Lanaihale (also called the Hale), which affords a five-island view (all but Kauai) on a clear day.

Museums and Exhibits

Kaupe Cultural and Heritage Museum ★★
7th Street, Lanai City, across from Dole Park,
☎ *(808) 565-4545.*
Special hours: call for hours.
http://www.museumsusa.org/data/museums/HI/116220.htm
Lanai's first historical museum, opened in the summer of 1995, is proudly installed within the old Dole plantation administration building, which was renovated to the tune of $50,000. The 1300-square-foot museum houses photographs and memorabilia from pre- to post-pineapple days. The Bishop Museum has donated a substantial collection of rare Hawaiian artifacts to the collection.

The Shows

Lanai Playhouse ★
465 7th Street, Lanai City, ☎ *(808) 565-7500.*
Catch a current feature film for a reasonable price at this new, 150-seat theatrical venue/movie house in Lanai City; from time to time you can see Lanai City denizens take to the boards and strut their stuff. General admission: varies.

Tours

Carriage Rides ★★★
Stables at Koele, P.O. Box L, Lanai City, 96763,
☎ *(808) 565-4424.*
Along with a plethora of horseback-riding adventures, the Stables at the Lodge at Koele offers a one- or two-hour ride on a Cheyenne carriage, an intricately crafted rig pulled by a Belgian Draft horse, guided by an local driver who knows

where all the great sights are. This is the first horse-drawn carriage to be licensed in Maui County. Blankets and snacks provided; participants can plan their own itineraries.

Lanai City Service ★★
P.O. Box N, Lanai Avenue between 10th-11th Streets, Lanai City, 96763, ☎ (808) 565-7227.
Hours: 7 a.m.–7 p.m.
LANAI CITY SERVICE, WHICH IS ALSO THE DOLLAR RENT-A-CAR FRANCHISE, offers the only guided, half-day four-wheel-drive van tour (four passengers minimum, 12 passengers maximum) of some of Lanai's hard-to-get-to sites, including the Munro Trail (conditions permitting) and Shipwreck Beach. The tour leaves from two locations: at 6:45 a.m. from the Lodge at Koele (return at 1 p.m.) and 7:15 a.m. at the Manele Bay Hotel (return at 1:30 p.m.). Included are a lei greeting, coffee, breakfast rolls, mineral water, juices and sodas, and a box lunch on the beach (choice of tuna, egg salad, corned beef, turkey or veggie sandwich with potato salad). The company recommends stain-resistant clothing (but nothing can resist that rich red dirt) and a good pair of broken-in footwear. Chartered tours are available, minimum 10 passengers. Reserve at least 12 hours in advance; however, if seats are available, last-minute bookings are possible on a "first-come, first-served" basis. Tours must be paid for at the company's office in Lanai City on Lanai Avenue, but reservations can be made from the concierge desks at either of the above hotels. American Express, Visa, MasterCard and Diner's Club accepted. General admission: $60 and up.

Spinning Dolphin Charters ★★
P.O. Box 491, Lanai City, 96763, ☎ (808) 565-6613.
http://www.lanaionline.com/Merchants/spinning_dolphin.htm
In addition to private deep-sea fishing and light-tackle fishing charters, Captain Jeff Menze, a commercial fisherman and master diver, takes parties of three to six on exciting three-hour whale-watching excursions from late December through April. Captain Jeff's 28-foot, diesel-powered Omega sportfisher (called, appropriately, the *Spinning Dolphin*) is equipped with an underwater microphone that amplifies the whales' songs. Soda, juice, water, and ice are provided. All sailing times are

flexible, and can be arranged at time of booking. Menze also offers a three-hour sightseeing charter tour of Lanai from the water. You'll cruise to Nanahoa, an islet off west Lanai, one of the island's most impressive landmarks. Snorkeling can be included in the trip; this requires an additional hour, plus an additional $100. Soda, juice, and water are provided. Hours are open; arrangements made at time of booking. General admission: $300 and up.

Northeast Lanai

Shipwreck Beach
Beaches

Shipwreck Beach (Kaiolohia Bay) ★★
On the northeast shore of Lanai, Shipwreck Beach, north on Lanai Avenue, right to Keomuku Road to its end, turn left.
Although the highway to this sometimes incredibly windy beach (watch out for stinging sands—ouch) is paved, YOU'LL NEED A FOUR-WHEEL-DRIVE VEHICLE (or your own two feet) to get here. Sights along the eight-mile sands include "Federation Camp," a moniker given to describe the rustic structures used by Filipino immigrants in the 1930s (they hung out here to fish and socialize), primitive rock carvings, or petroglyphs (look for the "Do Not Deface" sign), and the rusted-out hulk of a Liberty ship towed to these shores after World War II. If you want to decorate your own beach shack with pieces of driftwood (plentiful) or glass fishing floats, this is the place to come. Otherwise, forget about watersports—conditions are too rocky and the Kalohi channel (between Lanai and Molokai) is treacherous. Hikers in good condition can follow the coastline 10 miles north to Polihua Beach.

Northwest Lanai

Kanepu'u
Historical Sites

Kanepu'u Preserve and Garden of the Gods ★★
Fraser Avenue north to Polihua Road, turn right, Kanepu'u.
http://www.hawaiiweb.com/lanai/html/sites/kanepuu_trail.html
The remnants of what was once a vast native dryland forest are located in the northwest section of Lanai, six miles out of town

on a dirt road (four-wheel-drive vehicle only). More than 400 acres have been fenced in by the Nature Conservancy of Hawaii, which manages the dryland forest, to keep feral axis deer out. Native dryland forests are one of the fastest disappearing ecosystems in the world. Kanepu'u encloses some extremely rare species of plants including *iliahi,* or Hawaiian sandalwood, native versions of olive and persimmon, and a kind of dryland gardenia tree, called *nau*. To take a monthly Nature Conservancy Hike (two hours), call the Oahu office at ☎ *(808) 537-4508,* or contact Gaylien Kaho'ohalahala, the Kanepuu field technician, at ☎ *(808) 565-7430.* Donations of $25 are requested; nonmembers receive a one-year membership in the Conservancy, including all benefits.

Palawai Basin

Luahiwa Petroglyphs ★★
Manele Road south to Hoike Road, left to water tank, Palawai Basin.
http://www.hawaiiweb.com/lanai/html/sites/Luahiwa petroglyphs.html
Lanai's largest concentration of ancient rock drawings—crude but distinctive figures of animals, canoes, and humans—are found on 34 boulders on a steep slope overlooking the Palawai Basin (agricultural and grazing land that was a Mormon colony in 1854).

South Lanai
Hulopoe Beach
Beaches

Hulopoe Beach ★★★★
Manele Road, Hulopoe Beach.
LANAI'S MOST USER-FRIENDLY AND ALL-AROUND BEST BEACH, Hulopoe Bay (and nearby Manele Bay) was once an ancient Hawaiian village dating from A.D. 900. A marine life conservation district, Hulopoe is home to cavorting spinner dolphins in season. Swimming, boogie-boarding, and snorkeling are usually all very good here, but high surf conditions exist, so use caution. A minor quibble: Although the beach is for the most part uncrowded, the passenger ferry from Maui brings in day-trippers and weekenders, so sometimes things can

get a little crazy. Top-of-the-line facilities include rest rooms, showers (outdoor), picnic areas, and barbecue pits.

City Celebrations

Pineapple Festival ★★
End of Manele Road, Hulopoe Beach, ☎ *(808) 565-7600.*
Held in early May. Annual event honoring the late (un)lamented crop. Live entertainment, food, craft booths, tastings. Times vary.

Historical Sites

Sweetheart Rock (Pu'upehe) ★★
South Lanai, Hulopoe Beach, 15 minutes walk from Hulopoe Beach.
A rock islet off the southwest point of Manele Bay, Sweetheart Rock actually has a bittersweet story. Its Hawaiian name—*Pu'upehe*—means Pehe's Hill. Pehe was the beautiful-but-unfortunate wife of a jealous cad who hid her in a cave so no other man could set eyes on her. Inevitably, she was drowned during a storm while her husband was away. After burying Pehe atop Sweetheart Rock, he later fell to his death.

Tours

Expeditions ★★
P.O. Box 10, Lahaina, HI 96767-0010, Hulopoe Beach,
☎ *(808) 661-3756.*
http://www.go-lanai.com/
Expeditions is the Lahaina- (Maui) Lanai Passenger ferry departing daily from either Manele Harbor or Lahaina Harbor at the public loading dock in front of the Pioneer Inn. Trips each way take approximately one hour. Special tour packages include snorkeling tours (round trip to Manele Harbor included, bring your own gear and lunch), Jeep expeditions, shoreline cruises (two hours round-trip, whale watching in season). For $199 and up per person, with round-trip transportation from Lahaina, you can play golf at the Experience at Koele or Challenge at Manele championship courses, or stay overnight at one of the two luxury hotels. The company will also help you tailor your own expedition. General admission: varies.

Sports

Golfers can play the Greg Norman-designed 18-hole, par-72 championship course at **Experience at Koele** (at the Lodge at Koele), or the Jack Nicklaus-designed 18-hole, par-72 course at Manele Bay Hotel (called **Challenge at Manele**). Both guests and non-guests can play, though high greens fees get even higher for nonguests. Or play nine holes in the Norfolk pines, for free, at the public **Cavendish Golf Course**. Each of the "Big Two" resorts offers three **tennis courts** apiece.

Shipwreck Beach offers good **fishing** for *papio, ulua,* and other types. Kamehameha the Great used to hit Kaunolu on the south shore when he had the fishing urge. **Kaumalapau Harbor** is a top choice for shore fishing. For the best advice on fishing holes, try befriending one of the locals. Only one charter fishing operation runs on the island, with a few more choices for **scuba diving** and **snorkeling**. Contact the Lodge at Koele if you're interested in **horseback riding**—a variety of excursions are offered for all riding levels, plus you can take lessons or arrange for a private ride.

East Lanai
Kahalepalaoa Landing

Club Lanai ★★
355 Hukilike Street, Suite 211, Kahului, Maui 96732, Kahalepalaoa Landing, ☎ *(808) 871-1144.*
http://www.hiohwy.com/c/clublana.htm
This company takes day-trippers from Maui to its own isolated and pretty beach in east Lanai (by Kahalepalaoa Harbor) for a day of snorkeling, kayaking over a turtle reef, and bicycling to remote beaches. Other choices include volleyball, croquet, or visiting a sea turtle sanctuary or a whale research center. You can also opt to swing in a hammock and do nothing at all. The fare includes an all-you-can-eat buffet lunch and open bar, plus massage therapy (extra). Club Lanai also offers scuba diving; all levels welcome. The boat leaves Lahaina Harbor daily at Slip 4 at 7:30 a.m., returning at 3:30 p.m. Reservations required. General admission: $100 and up.

Lanai City
ITRAVELBOOK FREEBIE:

Cavendish Golf Course ★

On the north side of Lanai City, Lanai City, ☎ *(808) 565-6979.*
http://www.gvhawaii.com/caven/caven.htm
For those of you who can't see paying $99 and up to play at the Manele Bay Hotel and the Lodge at Koele's five-star courses, HOW ABOUT THIS FREEBIE? (Cavendish Golf Course is a pleasant local 9-hole, par-36 course, which has the distinction of being the only free golf course in the state visitors are asked to leave a $5 donation for upkeep). No dress code, carts, club rental, or club house.

Chris' Adventures ★★★
P.O. Box 869, Kula, HI 96790, Lanai City, ☎ *(800) 224-5344.*
Special hours: Saturdays, 8-10 a.m. Closed: Sundays.
http://www.islandsource.com/adventure/adventure8.htm
Chris and his associates offer cycling on- and off-road and hiking day tours of Lanai's picturesque (and rugged) Munro Trail every Wednesday. Travelers leave by boat from Maui—or meet your guide at an arranged location if you're already on the island. These are for experienced cyclists only. Cost includes breakfast and "island-style" picnic lunch. Also available are "Inn-to-Inn Vacations," three- to eight-day biking and/or hiking trips for all levels, with options for the more advanced (or masochistic) participants. Maui-Molokai-Lanai combo trips last eight days, and include a kayak or raft adventure. Included are all meals, transportation, equipment, lodging, and all extras; price ranges from $200–$350 per day. Call Chris' Adventures tour planner for details, dates, and trip itineraries. General admission: $110 and up.

Spinning Dolphin Charters ★★
P.O. Box 491, Lanai City, 96763, ☎ *(808) 565-6613.*
http://www.lanaionline.com/Merchants/spinning_dolphin.htm
Captain Jeff Menze offers sport-fishing (deep-sea fishing and light tackle) charter trips aboard the *Spinning Dolphin II*, his 28-foot diesel-powered Omega sportfisher. On these four-hour trips (three-person minimum, six maximum), fish for marlin,

ahi, mahi-mahi, barracuda, and ono, and "fight" Hawaii's best-loved game fish, the papio. There's also a share-boat option offered, also for four hours, for $300. Soda, juice, water, and ice are provided. Hours are flexible; arrangements can be made at time of booking. General admission: $400 and up.

Stables at Koele ★★★

P.O. Box L, Lanai City, 96763, ☎ *(808) 565-4424.*

The Lodge at Koele offers a wide range of different horseback riding trips, from a 15-minute children's ride to a four-hour "private adventure" for the experienced rider. (Unfortunately, no high jinks—these are sedate "walking" rides only.) The Plantation Trail Ride is perfect for beginners or those wishing to polish old skills. For the experienced equestrian, there are several private rides for one or two guests; larger groups are accommodated by arrangement. These are tailored to the individuals' needs: itineraries may include trips to Kanepu'u, the island's rare dryland forest ecosystem. Many rides offer sweeping views of the neighbor islands with glimpses of axis deer, quail, and other wildlife. Lessons available, both Western and English. Dress code, limited boot rental. Maximum weight is 250 pounds, children must be nine years old and at least four feet high. Safety helmets provided. All riders must be able to mount and dismount on their own. Backpack lunch rides available. General admission: varies.

The Experience at Koele ★★★★★

Lodge at Koele, P.O. Box L, Lanai City, 96763,
☎ *(808) 565-4653.*
Special hours: tee times from 8 a.m.
http://www.lanairesorts.com/golf_popup.htm

This championship 18-hole, par-72 golf course, is a collaboration between designer and Australian golf pro Greg Norman and architect Ted Robinson. Almost immediately, it was lauded by *Fortune* magazine, *Andrew Harper's Hideaway Report,* and *Golf Magazine* as the best new golf course. Built on 163 acres of natural island terrain, it features the challenging Number 8 hole, where players contend with a 250-foot drop from tee to fairway, battling some formidable headwinds blowing in daily from a wooded ravine in the process. Higher greens fee is for nonguests; includes cart. General admission: $99–$200.

South Lanai
Hulopoe Beach

Challenge at Manele ★★★★
Manele Road, Hulopoe Beach, 96763, ☎ *(808) 565-2222.*
Special hours: Tuesday-Friday from 8 a.m.
http://www.golfersweb.com/challeng.htm
A relative newcomer to the golfing world, the seaside, 18-hole, par-72 Challenge at Manele course opened at the Manele Bay Hotel on Christmas Day, 1993. Designed by Jack Nicklaus, it's built on natural lava outcroppings overlooking the hotel, the bay, and the Pacific Ocean. The course features three holes constructed on the cliffs of Hulopoe Bay that use the Pacific Ocean as a water hazard. The par-3, Number 12 "signature hole" plays from a cliff 150 feet above the surf below, requiring a demanding 200-yard tee shot across the ocean. Higher prices are for nonguests. Full-service clubhouse with a good restaurant, driving range, putting green. General admission: $99–$200.

Manele Bay Hotel Tennis Center ★★★
P.O. Box 310, Manele Road, Hulopoe Beach, 96763,
☎ *(808) 565-7700.*
Tennis with ocean views is the ticket here at Manele Bay Hotel's Tennis Center, with six lighted Plexipaved courts, a fully equipped pro shop, and tournament facilities. Free to guests, fee above is for nonguests. Private instruction available. General admission: call for information.

Trilogy Ocean Sports Lanai ★★★
P.O. Box 1119, Lahaina, Maui, 96767-1119, Hulopoe Beach, Leaves from the Manele Bay Hotel, ☎ *(800) 874-2666.*
http://www.scubalanai.com/
Whether you're a seasoned scuba diver or a neophyte, Trilogy Excursions of Maui will do the right thing by you, with a group of experienced instructors intimately familiar with Lanai's famous and spectacular southern coast (rated by *Skin Diver* magazine as one of the top 10 diving sites in the world). Explore underwater coral grottos and lava caves, and have a close encounter of the safe kind with moray eels and white tip sharks. Two-tank dives: Wednesdays, Saturdays, Sundays; One-tank dives: daily. Newbies will start with a complimentary les-

son at the Manele Bay Hotel pool (given daily at 2:30 p.m.); learn the basics before venturing off to one of the southern coast's numerous protected coves and bays with the sharks. The company also offers PADI open-water certification.

Manele Bay

Hulopoe Beach Campsites ★★
Manele Road, Manele Bay, ☎ *(808) 565-6661.*
Lanai offers six overnight camping sites (about 200 yards inland from Hulopoe Beach) which must be the cheapest accommodations in town at $8 per person per night (plus a small registration fee). **LENGTH OF STAY IS ONE WEEK MAXIMUM.** Facilities include picnic tables and barbecue grills, rest rooms, outdoor shower. Permits must be obtained from the Koele Company, P.O. Box L, Lanai City, HI 96763 or by calling the number above. General admission: $8 and up.

Where to Stay

The handful of choices consists of the two ritzy (and very expensive) resorts (**Lodge at Koele** and **Manele Bay Hotel**), the vintage-1920s **Hotel Lanai,** a couple of B&Bs and the half-dozen campsites (reservations and permit required) at Hulopoe Bay.

Lanai City
Bed-and-Breakfasts

Dreams Come True $98.50 ★★
P.O. Box 525, Lanai City, 96763, a five-minute walk from the center of town, ☎ *(800) 566-6961,* ☎ *(808) 565-6961, FAX (808) 565-7056.*
http://www.circumvista.com/dreamscometrue.html
Susan and Michael Hunter have remodeled a spacious plantation-manager's house into a bed-and-breakfast about five minutes' walk from the center of town. The property, surrounded by tropical fruit gardens, is quietly tucked away within high lava-stone walls. The Hunters, who have an adjacent jewelry studio, rent out three rooms (there are a total of six bedrooms), two of which have private baths. They are furnished quite attractively with polished, antique four-poster beds. The house is decorated throughout with hand-carved screens, rare and colorful textiles, and one-of-a-kind treasures collected by the

couple on various Asian travels. Amenities include cable TV in the living room. Breakfast consists of homemade bread and fresh fruits from the garden. Children are welcome ($10 for each additional child); the Hunters have two of their own. **ALSO OFFERED ARE FOUR-WHEEL-DRIVE RENTALS AND MASSAGE SERVICES, AND BOTH IN-HOUSE AND OUT CALLS.** If you are traveling with a large party, the Hunters will rent out an additional two-bedroom house with an attached cottage with one large bedroom. Called the Jasmine Garden House, it can accommodate up to eight people. Amenities include linens, washer-dryer, cable TV, fan, full kitchen, outside shower, and beach gear. Credit cards: not accepted.

Hotels

Hotel Lanai $95–$140 ★★
828 Lanai Avenue, Lanai City, 96763, ☎ *(800) 321-4666,* ☎ *(808) 565-7211.*
http://www.hotellanai.com/
Built in 1923 as a guesthouse for Dole executives and VIPs, the Hotel Lanai was once the only lodging on the island. After a thorough refurbishment in the early 1990s, the 10 units in the main building are much the same size, but the new country decor features light, knotty-pine furniture, natural wood floors, and patchwork quilts in rose, cream, and blue shades. There's also a self-contained, plantation-style cottage with a four-poster canopy bed and period furnishings that can be had for an attractive $140 per night. Perfect for families, the suite has a separate entrance and sitting room with sofa bed. Facilities include a private garden with picnic and barbecue areas. Amenities: balcony or patio. 11 rooms. Credit cards: A, MC, V.

Resorts

The Lodge at Koele $350–$1100 ★★★★★
P.O. Box 310, Lanai City, 96763, ☎ *(800) 321-4666,* ☎ *(808) 565-7300, FAX (808) 565-4561.*
http://www.lanairesorts.com/golf_popup.htm
RATED THE #1 HAWAIIAN RESORT BY *GOLF* **MAGAZINE,** The Lodge is spectacular in a quiet, unobtrusive sort of manner. Two guest wings are connected by large porches with wicker furniture to the high-beamed Great Hall, with its 30-foot ceilings and enormous stone fireplaces. Guests can meet and greet

in a series of unique chambers, including the Music Room, a modern-day version of a Paris salon where visiting artists, writers, and musicians of world-renown perform, lecture, and read their works to the public free of charge. Special outdoor features include an ornamental glass house filled with exotic orchids, a Japanese and Hawaiian fruit garden (feel free to indulge), and an executive putting green. Guest rooms, decorated in shades of carnelian and pale blue, feature huge four-poster beds crowned with carved pineapples (lest you forget where you are), loveseats, and dark-stained wicker armchairs. Pillowed bay window seats overlook the lawns and surrounding countryside. The marble-floored baths have deep, hand-tiled tubs, and pampering products include thick robes, plenty of towels, custom toiletries, hair dryer, slippers, and makeup mirror. When you get hunger pangs, you have a choice of two dining rooms plus, an English tea room and bar, and The Experience at Koele clubhouse. Other activities include lawn bowling, horseback riding, tennis, croquet, game room, pool, hiking trails, The Experience at Koele 18-hole golf course, and access to all facilities of the beachfront Manele Bay Hotel; a shuttle between the two properties runs regularly. Amenities: tennis, horseback riding, Jacuzzi. 102 rooms. Credit cards: A, DC, MC, V.

South Lanai
Hulopoe Beach

The Manele Bay Hotel   **$250–$2000**   ★★★★

Box 310, Hulopoe Beach, 96763, Manele Road, 20 minutes from Lanai City, ☎ *(800) 321-4666,* ☎ *(808) 565-7700, FAX (808) 565-2483.*
http://www.manelebayhotel.com/manele/acc.htm

The Manele Bay Hotel offers luxurious rooms and suites, ALL WITH VERANDAS AND OCEAN AND COASTLINE VIEWS. The resort is situated on a promontory above the island's most beautiful white-sand beach, Hulopoe Bay. Its exterior is a blend of Mediterranean and traditional Hawaiian design. The interior, however, is crammed with Oriental statuary, porcelains, art and antiques; walls are painted with Chinese court scenes. Sometimes it's hard to decide where to look—the vistas of the beach from the lobby are literally jaw-dropping from any angle. Landscape schemes include five theme gardens, waterfalls, koi ponds, and lush tropical flowers. All rooms have sliding louvered doors opening to lanais. Amenities include wet bars and entertainment center with color TV and video player. Luxurious marble baths you can live in contain deep-soaking tubs, double sinks, vanity, shower for two, custom toiletries, hair dryer, slippers, and terry robes. Other facilities include a health spa, tennis complex, pool, gift shop, pool table, game room, The Challenge at Manele golf course, three dining rooms, lounge, and clubhouse. In addition, the resort shares the facilities at the Lodge at Koele; a regular shuttle service is provided between the properties. Amenities: tennis, health club, exercise room, Jacuzzi, sauna, balcony or patio. 250 rooms. Credit cards: A, CB, DC, MC, V.

Where to Eat

Again, the choices are limited. Try the two resorts for upmarket, gourmet dining, but keep in mind that the dining room at the Lodge at Koele requires men to wear a jacket and tie. Locals head for the dining room at **Hotel Lanai** for simple preparations of such favorites as omelettes, pancakes, sandwiches, steak, and chicken. For your funky, local diner/café experience, don't miss either **Blue Ginger Café** or **S & T Properties**.

Lanai City

Blue Ginger Café $ ★
407 7th Street, Lanai City, 96763, ☎ *(808) 565-6363*
Healthy, Island cuisine. Specialties: Fresh fish, saimin, mahimahi.
A down-home café and local hangout that does double duty as a bakery; the bento (Japanese box lunches) are recommended, as are the breakfast waffles. HINT: TOURISTS SHOULD KEEP A LOW PROFILE AND DRESS DOWN, AS SOME OF THE REGULARS RESENT OUTSIDERS. Features: outside dining, own baking. Reservations not accepted. Credit cards: not accepted.

Hotel Lanai Dining Room $$$ ★★
828 Lanai Avenue, Lanai City, 96763, ☎ *(808) 565-7211.*
Associated hotel: Hotel Lanai.
American cuisine. Specialties: Steaks, fresh fish, sashimi.
For a long time the only place open after 1 p.m. for meals on the island, the Hotel Lanai is still a welcome respite for eyes dazzled by the new resorts and their high prices. Sink into a

comfortable seat at a white cloth-covered table by the fire in the cozy, pine-paneled dining room, and chow down on well-prepared steaks, local fish, and chicken dishes. Afterward, an after-dinner drink and a chat with other guests on the veranda is de rigueur. For lunch, we think the cheeseburgers here are mighty fine and a great alternative to the $6 hot dogs at the Manele Bay Hotel. Reservations not accepted. Credit cards: A, MC, V.

Koele Terrace Restaurant $$ ★★★★

Box 774, Lanai City, 96763, Just outside Lanai City,
☎ *(808) 565-7300. Associated hotel: Lodge at Koele.*
International cuisine. Specialties: Roast Lanai venison with Molokai sweet pepper puree.

Extra-wide and comfy-cushioned Craftsman-style chairs invite lingering in this lovely, sun-filled dining room with floor-to-ceiling windows overlooking the Lodge at Koele's picture-postcard hillside gardens. Your breakfast omelette may be garnished with fresh basil grown on the hotel grounds: in the tradition of fine English country-house hotels (which the Lodge is clearly trying to emulate), the Lodge at Koele maintains an organic vegetable and herb farm. Venison plays a decided role on the menus: in a robust chili with black beans and spicy Jack cheese, or carpaccio with shaved reggiano, or a signature roast loin partnered with either a fried-and-mashed puree of sweet Molokai potatoes or sage polenta. For dessert, try an exotic red banana soufflé or raspberry sorbet with blueberries and fresh-baked macaroons. The Lodge's fireplace-warmed Formal Dining Room (yes, that is its name) offers a similar menu, but requires a jacket for gentlemen in the evening. Features: own baking. Jacket requested. Reservations recommended. Credit cards: A, MC, V.

S & T Property, Inc. $ ★

419 7th Street, Lanai City, 96763, Next to the Blue Ginger Café,
☎ *(808) 565-6537.*
American cuisine. Specialties: Breakfast, burgers, and sandwiches.
Closed: Wednesdays.

Sounding more like a real-estate office than the soda fountain/general store it is, **S & T PROPERTIES IS A MUST FOR VISITORS SEEKING A GLIMPSE OF THE LANAI OF YORE.** Hormel is king here, and the cholesterol-packed menu features eggs with

Spam or Vienna sausages. We like the big, juicy hamburgers and Filipino-style plate lunches. Reservations not accepted.

South Lanai
Hulopoe Beach

Hulopoe Court $$ ★★★

P.O. Box 310, Hulopoe Beach, 96763, Manele Road, 20 minutes from Lanai City, ☎ *(808) 565-7700. Associated hotel: Manele Bay Hotel.*
cuisine. Specialties: *Seared ahi with green papaya salad, Hunan-style lamb chops.*

The Mediterranean-themed Hulopoe Court offers gorgeous ocean views and Hawaiian-Regional cuisine with a distinct Asian flavor for breakfast, lunch, and dinner. Dishes are on the light and healthful side, with a focus on fresh seafood and "Lanai grown" produce. Chances are you've never had taro hashbrowns for breakfast—this is a good place to try them. If the great outdoors calls you, repair to the Pool Grill, located adjacent to the... (three guesses). Specialty sandwiches, grilled dishes, and local favorites are featured. The grill is open from 11 a.m.–5 p.m. daily. Features: own baking. Reservations recommended. Credit cards: A, DC, MC, V.

Ihilani $$$ ★★★★

P.O. Box 310, Hulopoe Beach, 96763, Manele Road, 20 minutes from Lanai City, ☎ *(808) 565-7700. Associated hotel: Manele Bay Hotel.*
Mediterranean cuisine. Specialties: *Broiled onaga in a seaweed/seafood sauce, salmon confit in virgin olive oil.*

Open only for dinner, the Mediterranean-style menu strives to accentuate the rich bounty of the state's oceans, forests, and farms. Entrées may include broiled onaga (deepwater snapper) in an elemental seaweed sauce, and the exquisite chocolate desserts are made exclusively with cocoa beans grown on the black lava slopes of Kilauea volcano in Kona; the taste is likened to that of great vintage wines. But the chef's reach also extends to Hawaii's Pacific Rim neighbors; witness an appetizer of fresh ravioli with Manila clams. Excellent selection of wines, both French and domestic, available by the glass. Features: own baking, rated wine cellar. Jacket requested. Reservations recommended. Credit cards: A, CB, D, MC, V.

Nightlife

It's slim pickings. The **Lodge at Koele** offers occasional live entertainment and performances by local residents. The landmark 1930s **Lanai Theater and Playhouse** is a 153-seat venue featuring films, theatrical performances, and other events. Or, hang with the locals at **Hotel Lanai** and swap "talk-stories" (gossip).

Shopping

The shopping scene is pretty basic and is centered in **Lanai City**. You'll find a few old-fashioned, general-type stores with everything from food to clothing, plus a sprinkling of specialty outlets and arts-and-crafts galleries. The two **resorts** house swankier shops and boutiques.

Lanai City

Akamai Trading & Gifts ★

408 8th Street, Lanai City, near the post office, 96763,
☎ *(808) 565-6587.*
Hours: 9 a.m.–5:30 p.m.
Special hours: Sundays until noon.

Pick up a Lanai logo T-shirt here as well as handmade Hawaiian flower-dyed gourds, koa wood boxes, Norfolk pine tree bowls, and Lanai potpourri.

Island Collections Gallery ★★

7th Street, Lanai City, north side of Dole Park, 96763,
☎ *(808) 565-6405.*
Hours: 9 a.m.–7 p.m.
Special hours: sometimes open at 10 a.m.

Local artisans, woodworkers, jewelers, painters, and more showcase and sell their work here. Also offered are classes for both residents and guests.

R ing Center ★

Lanai City, next to the post office, 96763,

and food market, Richard's was

HAWAII

established in 1946. Locals shop here for groceries, fresh meats, liquor, and snacks, as well as clothing, athletic shoes, and distinctive Lanai T-shirts. Also Hawaiian jewelry and souvenirs.

HAWAIIAN ITINERARIES
One-Day Itinerary

You're only in Hawaii for *one* day. One day?! Okay, maybe it's a stopover between the mainland and Australia or Indonesia or somewhere.

You'll definitely want to stay on **Oahu**. Explore **downtown Honolulu**. Check out the beautiful Eastern and Western collections at the **Honolulu Academy of Arts** and then pay a visit to **Iolani Palace**, the United States' only royal residence (this is where Queen Liliuokalani lived out her house arrest after the coup forced her out of power). The **Hawaii State Capitol**, nearby, is an interesting bit of architecture with palm-tree-shaped columns and other kitschy-and dramatic features.

Zoom in on early Hawaiian culture at the **Bishop Museum**, where you can get a close look at magnificent featherwork capes, an outrigger canoe, petroglyphs, weapons, carvings, rare jewelry, and other artifacts and exhibitions. Eat lunch in **Chinatown**, then work it off on a walk through the **historic district**, where you'll pass the venerable **Oahu Market**, the **Chinese Cultural Plaza**, the art-deco **Hawaii Theatre**, and the **Kuan Yin Buddhist Temple**. If you weren't bestowed with a lei at the airport, pick one up on Maunakea Street.

Hit **Waikiki Beach** and work on your tan with the multitudes or, for something a bit more active, take a walk over to **Kapiolani Park**—maybe check out the rose garden, or just keep ogling the view of **Diamond Head**. Dinner? Why a luau, of course! Sign up for one of the commercial feasts, for which you'll be bused to a beach with a crowd of others to pig your way into oblivion.

Back at the airport, pick up a boxed take-home **pineapple** or a package of **macadamia nuts** and get on the plane. There, you've done Hawaii.

Three-Day Itinerary

...hole days.

...Honolulu's attractions. If you're interested in ...missionaries operated, you can voyeur your ...on Houses Museum. The Hawaii ...non-boring exhibits related to

Hawaii's long maritime history—dioramas, canoes, and displays galore highlighting the various groups who arrived in the islands, from the first Polynesian settlers to the tourists like you.

Time for lunch? Backtrack over to **Restaurant Row** (bounded by Ala Moana Boulevard and Punchbowl, Pohukaina, and South streets) and pick out one of Honolulu's trendy spots. Since you won't get to see all of the islands' exotic flowers, trees, and plants, get a mini-view at the **Foster Botanical Garden,** with 14 acres of some of the most superb specimens in the South Pacific.

You *know* the **USS *Arizona* Memorial** is calling, so head over to **Pearl Harbor** for a sobering, but well-worthwhile experience. The **USS *Bowfin*,** a World War II submarine, and its related museum are conveniently located next to the *Arizona* Memorial.

Drive up the **Pali Highway** to see **Queen Emma's Summer Palace,** grand former hideaway for Queen Emma and King Kamehameha IV and, since 1915, a museum. Farther up the road, the **Nuuanu Pali Lookout** will give you a knockout view the entire length of the windward coast. Back down toward Honolulu, round out your memorial day at **Punchbowl Crater** (or **National Memorial Cemetery of the Pacific**), burial place for 37,000 American troops—marked by row upon row of white gravestones—who died in the Pacific during conflicts this century.

Ready for something cheerier? **The Contemporary Museum** offers five galleries of paintings, sculpture, and other works by top international artists. The posh café serves gourmet sandwiches, salads, and desserts. Then take windy **Tantalus Drive** up nearly to the top of 2013-foot Mount Tantalus for a thrill—and a great view. Up at the top, you'll find a variety of trails—good for that island hike you won't get in otherwise. **Round Top Drive** will lead you back into Honolulu. Do some shopping at **Ward Warehouse,** on Ala Moana Boulevard, where you'll find better-quality souvenirs, clothing, and arts and crafts than the usual tourist schlock. For a real island fashion statement, go directly to **Bailey's Antique Clothes** outlet and choose from thousands of vintage aloha shirts (lots of celebrities buy here).

Time to watch the sunset. **House Without A Key,** at the Halekulani Hotel, serves great pupu platters and exotic drinks and affords a postcard view of the Pacific and Diamond Head. Most evenings there's live entertainment. For dinner, how about **Thai Cuisine**, another celebrity favorite? Try " has expanded to three locations. The one on Kapahulu Avenue is the original, with photos of famous Keo-aficionados adorning the walls. After dinner, take in some **nightlife: Scruples,** in the Waikiki Marketplace, for the dance-your-socks-off-crowd; **Studebaker's,** on Ala Moana Boulevard (in Restaurant Row), for'50s retro; the Majaraja, in the Waikiki Trade Center, for dress-code disco; **Anna Bannana's,** on King Street, for live reggae, blues, and experimental music (and darts); **Sand Island Restaurant and Bar,** on Sand Island Access Road, for great blues jams; **Java Café,** for coffeehouse culture; or one of the large-hotel lounges for quiet island sounds and a couple of drinks—make it the **Paradise Lounge,** at the Hilton Hawaiian Village.

On **Day Three,** do the leisurely **Circle-Island tour.** Heading to **Diamond Head** to the windward side, you can breeze right past the 'burbs of Hawaii Kai around to **Koko Head** and **Hanauma Bay.** Stop for a look at the **Blow Hole,** then do a quick explore of **Sandy** and **Makapuu beach parks** (yes, those *are* daredevil surfers out there).

Visit **Sea Life Park Hawaii** (especially if you've got kids with you), for all the fishy theme-park activities plus a good look at some endangered creatures. You'll pass plenty of good beaches before reaching the **Byodo-In Temple in the Valley of the Temples Memorial Park.** Anyone who is in the least sparked by Eastern religion or culture should kick off their shoes and check out this replica of a 900-year-old Japanese temple. The gardens and grounds are pretty inspiring as well. Do lunch at **Paniolo Café,** a laid-back burger and mason-jar-margarita joint (you've come for the atmosphere, not the food).

Continuing north, it's one fantastic drive along the Pacific Ocean. The **Polynesian Cultural Center** is another sprawling theme-type attraction that provides a good bead on the lifestyles of the ancient ones (and it's another good stop for the kids). Just beyond the Turtle Bay Hilton and Country Club are famous **Sunset Beach** and **Waimea Bay.** If you've come in winter, you'll catch top surfers thumb— their toes at monster waves. Drive up **Pupukea Road** to see temple *(heiau)* as well as a spectacular North Shore vi pen-air minibus (or do the self-guided walk) at ith its 1800 lush acres, 30-plus botanical gar- h cliff divers). **Haleiwa** is your old hippie- with the associated galleries, shops, is organic). Slurp the ultimate shave ice at **Matsumoto's Grocery** and—if you're running short on time—head back to Honolulu via Kamehameha Road and H2 (and through the **pineapple plantations** and **military installations**), which will put you back near Pearl Harbor. Otherwise, continue around the island to more beaches, view points, and small communities.

Back in Honolulu, pick a restaurant for your goodbye-Hawaii splurge. We recommend **Orchids** at the Halekulani Hotel for Pacific Rim cuisine in absolutely stunning surroundings (yes, it has wonderful ocean views).

Five-Day Itinerary

For those extra two days, hop over to one of the other islands. How about a visit to old **Lahaina**, on Maui, and maybe a hair-raising drive on the **Hana Highway**? Then on to **Molokai**, for a look at some 300-foot waterfalls and the world's highest sea cliffs? Or **Kauai**, for a romantic interlude and eye-pop at **Waimea Canyon**? **The Big Island**, to ski down a volcano and take in a rodeo? Or **Lanai**, for a couple of days of absolutely nothing....

ITRAVELBOOKS FAVORITE HIDEAWAYS

Halawa Valley (Molokai)	Waterfalls, jungle, a lagoon, and beach, all hidden away in a lush (mosquito-filled) valley.
Waikamoi Ridge Trail (Maui)	Pools, waterfalls, bamboo forests, and a superbly isolated picnic setting for those willing to hike up the (mosquito-filled) ridge.
Swinging Bridges (Maui)	Man-made waterfall, swimming hole, fruit trees, bamboo forests, and a couple of swinging bridges, tucked away on the windward side of the West Maui Mountains. Beware of flash floods!
Green Sand Beach (the Big Island)	Grab a four-wheel-drive vehicle to frolic in the secluded (green) sand on Mahana Bay.
Waikiki Beach (Oahu)	For those who believe that hiding away is only a state of mind.

ITRAVELBOOKS FAVORITE VIEWS

Wailuku River State Park (the Big Island)	Head for the path adjacent to the parking lot to look out over **Rainbow Falls**. Come at sunrise to watch the rainbows form.
Onomea Bay Scenic Route (the Big Island)	A four-mile drive (off Mamalahoa Highway Scenic Drive) above the bay. The scenic valley below is filled with taro farms.
Pololu Valley Lookout (the Big Island)	Ooh and aah at the canyon's often mist-shrouded colors—red, green, amber, and purple.
Keanae Lookout (Maui)	Hana Highway twists and turns, bridges, fruit trees, pools, and forests.

ITRAVELBOOKS FAVORITE VIEWS

Kalaupapa Lookout (Molokai)	View the settlement of Kalaupapa from 1500 feet above.
Phallic Rock (Molokai)	Look *at* it, not *from* it!
Nuuanu Pali Lookout (Oahu)	The view is really supposed to be of windward Oahu, but it's just as much fun to watch the tourists battle with the gusty winds.
Diamond Head (Oahu)	Climb to the top for a great gander at Honolulu.
Waikiki Beach (Oahu)	A rare opportunity to see mounds of (pale) jiggling flesh, cavorting as one.

ITRAVELBOOKS FAVORITE PLACES FOR KIDS

Sea Life Park (Oahu)	Kids will be fascinated by the dolphins, penguins, tropical fish, and other displays, plus the Touch Pool, will wow them with starfish, giant worms, and other sea creatures.

Diamond Head (Oahu)	The hike to the top is kid-friendly—though the tunnel might be a little freaky for delicate types.
Aloha Tower Marketplace (Oahu)	Of course, they'll love the mall. This one has stage entertainers, plus a roving troupe of magicians and clowns.
Whale-watching (Maui)	Between November and April, humpback whales can be spotted off the coast.
Astronaut Ellison S. Onizuka Space Center (the Big Island)	Everyone will want to play with the computer interactive exhibits, launch a mini-space shuttle, and watch space-related films.
Molokai Ranch Wildlife Park (Molokai)	Lots of wild animals to irritate.
Searching for seashells (Maui)	Free, and it will keep them (and you) busy for *hours*.
Waikiki Beach (Oahu)	Sign them (and you?) up for surfing lessons. One day they may be riding the 30-footers on the North Shore.

ITRAVELBOOKS HAWAII APPENDIX

HAWAIIAN DELICACIES

No, Wahoo is not an exclamation of delight in the Hawaiian language. (Although perhaps it might be.) It's a fish. Unfamiliar names abound on menus across the Hawaiian islands, as do strange shapes, slimy textures, and too-vibrant–to-be-anything-but-non-FDA-approved colors. What does it all mean?

A'u	expensive and delicious broadbill swordfish or marlin
Adobo	Filipino specialty made with chicken or pork
Ahi	yellowfin tuna, one of Hawaii's best
Aku	skipjack tuna, or bonita
Bento	Japanese box lunch
Breadfruit	high-carbohydrate (and somewhat bland) Hawaiian staple served baked, roasted, fried, or boiled
Chicken luau	stew-like dish cooked with taro or spinach leaves and coconut milk
Crackseed	candy-like preserved, spiced seeds and fruits that originate in China
Dim Sum	Chinese dumplings, steamed and filled with a variety of meats and veggies
Guava	thirst-quenching, tangy tree fruit often made into juice and jellies
Hapu	Hawaiian sea bass
Haupia	a coconut pudding-like dessert, popular at luaus
Imu	the underground oven used at luaus, especially to prepare the kalua pig
Kalua pig	the star of every luau—a pig steamed in the imu, or underground oven
Kaukau	general term for "food"
Kimchee	Korean dragon-hot slaw made from pickled cabbage and hot peppers

Laulau	steamed ti leaves that have been stuffed with bananas, sweet potatoes, pork, taro shoots, and other delicacies
Lilikoi	passion fruit – yellow and seedy, with a tart flavor—often made into juice, jellies, or desserts
Limu	a seaweed garnish used in the islands since Polynesian settlement
Lomilomi salmon	raw salmon chunks mixed with onions, tomatoes, and salt—a luau dish
Macadamia nuts	small, round, buttery-rich nuts found throughout the islands in many varieties—roasted, dry-roasted, chocolate-covered, salted—all irresistible and teeming with fat
Mahimahi	common island fish often served grilled as a fish burger, also called "dolphin fish"
Manapua	steamed dough wrapped around black beans or pork
Malasadas	hole-less Portuguese donuts, deep-fried and doused with sugar
Maui onions	also known as Kula onions, sweet and mild
Moi	big-eyed, shark-headed, superior eating fish
Ono	delicious, flaky game fish, also known as "wahoo"
Pipikaula	beef jerky
Poi	superbly nutritious, pasty, and purplish Hawaiian staple made from pounded taro root
Pupus	appetizers, hors d'oeuvres, finger foods, usually served on a "pupu platter"
Saimin	also known as ramen—those big bowls of long noodles in thin broth served with veggies, meat, or fish
Sashimi	Japanese favorite consisting of thinly-sliced fish dipped in soy sauce

Spam		SPAM? Yes, Spam. A huge favorite among Hawaiians, who have a virtual love affair with this spiced luncheon meat. They stick it in everything.
Taro root		the starchy root, planted as a staple by the ancient Polynesians—roasted, baked, used for poi, or made into potato-like chips.
Ti leaves		from the Ti plant, used to wrap food; thought by the early Hawaiians to keep evil spirits away
Uku		gray snapper, a local favorite

COMMON HAWAIIAN AND PIDGIN WORDS AND EXPRESSIONS

Term	Pronunciation	Meaning
aa	(ah-ah)	the rough kind of lava
ae	(eye)	yes
aikane	(eye-kah-nay)	friend
alii	(ah-lee-ee)	Hawaiian chief, royalty, person of high rank
aloha	(ah-low-ha)	welcome, hello, goodbye, love, friendship
aole	(ah-oh-lay)	no
brah	(bra)	bro', brother, friend
cockroach		to steal or take something in an under-handed manner
da kine	(dah kyne)	thingamajig
diamondhead		east (towards Diamond Head on Oahu)
ewa	(ay-vah)	west (toward Oahu's Ewa Plantation)

HAWAII

hale	(hah-lay)	house
haole	(how-lee)	Caucasian, mainlander
hapa	(hah-pah)	half
hapa-haole	(hah-pah how-lee)	not authentically Hawaiian
hauoli la hanau	(how-oh-lee-la-hah-now)	Happy Birthday
hauoli makahiki hou	(how-oh-lee-mahkah hee-key ho-oo)	Happy New Year
heiau	(hey-ee-ow)	ancient temple
holo holo	(hoe-low hoe-low)	to bar-hop or cruise
hono	(hoe-know)	bay
hoolaulea	(ho-oh-lau-lay-ah)	gathering, celebration
kahuna	(kah-who-nah)	Hawaiian priest
kai	(kye)	ocean
kamaaina	(kah-may-eye-nah)	longtime resident
kane	(kane)	man
kapu	(kah-poo)	taboo, forbidden
kau kau	(cow cow)	food
keiki	(kay-kee)	child
kiawe	(key-ah-vay)	mesquite wood or tree
koa	(ko-ah)	an increasingly scarce tree prized for its wood
kokua	(ko-koo-ah)	help
lua	(loo-ah)	toilet
mahalo	(mah-hah-low)	thank you
makai	(mah-kye)	in the direction of the sea
malihini	(mah-lee-hee-nee)	newcomer
ohana	(oh-hah-nah)	family
pakalolo	(pah-kah-low-low)	marijuana

pau hana time	(pow hah-nah-time)	when the work day is over
shaka	(shah-kah)	Excellent!
Tutu or tutu wahine	(too-too wah hee-nee)	grandmother
Whaine	(wah-hee-nee)	woman
Wikiwiki	(wee-kee-wee-kee)	fast, quick